A Sociological Reader on Complex Organizations

A Sociological Reader on Complex Organizations

THIRD EDITION

Amitai Etzioni
Columbia University

Edward W. Lehman
New York University

HOLT, RINEHART AND WINSTON
New York   Chicago   San Francisco   Dallas
Montreal   Toronto   London   Sydney

Library of Congress Cataloging in Publication Data

Etzioni, Amitai, comp.
   A sociological reader on complex organizations.

   Includes bibliographical references and index.
   1. Organization—Addresses, essays, lectures.
I. Lehman, Edward W., joint comp. II. Title.
HM131.E8   1980   302.3'5   79-27722
ISBN 0-03-047461-2

The Library of Congress cataloged the first printing of this title as follows:
Complex organizations: A sociological reader.

Preface
to the Third Edition

More than a decade has now passed since the publication of the second edition of this volume. Comparison of the tables of contents of the previous editions (the first edition was issued under the title, *Complex Organizations: A Sociological Reader*) with this one illuminates the changing foci of modern organizational analysis. The present volume's format represents our vision of the key directions for the sociology of organizations as we enter the 1980s. Examination of the selections that have been retained and those being added, as well as of the headings under which both are placed, yields the themes that are at the "cutting-edge" of this specialty. Although important themes abound, four play particularly pivotal roles: a concern with societal guidance, a growing focus on *inter*organizational analysis, an expanding commitment to comparative analysis, and an intensified concern with sophisticated quantification.

Complex organizations are perhaps the principal vehicles for societal guidance. That is, such units—especially those that are part of or linked to the state—are major instruments for setting, pursuing, and implementing collective goals for a nation. Goods, services, and capital—society's "wealth"—are created and dispersed mainly by organizations. Health, education, and social services are now largely the responsibility of organizations. Whether we can overcome the pressing problems of our time (inequality, pollution, energy crises, alienation, and so on) depends heavily on our society's "organizational potential." Good ideas and good intentions alone cannot eliminate human miseries. Thus, organizational analysis provides a key to the understanding of modern society and its prospects for transformation. Indeed, disentangling organizational analysis from societal analysis is becoming more and more difficult. This volume extends the space devoted to the societal implications of organizations.

The focus on guidance has increased awareness that many strategic societal "products" cannot be produced or delivered by a single organization operating alone. This fact has provided the major impetus for the expansion of interorganizational analysis. The present edition has a new section (itself divided into two parts) devoted to this domain. Moreover, many of the new readings in other sections touch on this vital topic.

The growth of comparative analysis represents another response to the weaknesses of studying individual organizations in isolation. A separate section deals with the major theoretical models in the comparative analysis of organizations. In addition, the volume contains several selections dealing with empirical facets of comparative analysis. Since sociology is a generalizing discipline, a one-organization-at-a-time approach has obvious drawbacks. Researchers thus are trying to study many organizations at once in order to ascertain uniformities and differences within and among them.

The fourth trend, heightened quantitative sophistication, has been accelerated by empirical comparative analyses. The study of "populations" of organizations requires the development and use of ever more complex multivariate techniques. Therefore, more space than in earlier editions is devoted to "hard" data and the attendant tables, charts, and equations. While this reflects the growing "hardness" of the field, we have nevertheless tried to maintain a balance between theoretical and methodological selections. A mature specialty such as the sociology of organizations needs tools from both in order to continue to make progress. It is our hope that this third edition strikes such a balance while also affording the reader a fair sample of what is going on in organizational analysis.

We are grateful for the comments of Wolf Heydebrand and the editorial assistance of Mary Pockman.

E. W. L. and A. E.

New York
August 1979

Preface
to the First Edition

Complex organizations constitute one of the most important elements that make up the social web of modern societies. Most citizens of modern societies are born in a hospital, educated in a school, work in one organization or another; and to the degree that they participate in religious and political activities, these too, frequently, take place in complex organizations. In short, members of modern societies obtain a large part of their material, social, and cultural satisfactions from large-scale organizations. The way to the understanding of modern man and the society in which he lives leads, therefore, to the study of complex organizations. This volume is devoted to a review of some of the ideas, theories, and research findings concerning organizations, and concludes with a brief examination of some of the methods used in studying these social units.

By "organizations" we mean, following Parsons, social units which are predominantly oriented to the attainment of specific goals. The major types of organizations to be discussed are those which have bureaucratic characteristics, as specified by Weber. Thus, although our journey will lead us to the study of both formal and informal aspects of organizations, we shall not embark on the much longer voyage of presenting studies of "social organizations" in which all forms of patterned, regulated, or "organized" social behavior are explored.*

Some of our contributors, especially Howard S. Becker and Erving Goffman, refer to "institutions" when discussing the same category of social units designated here as organizations. Morris Janowitz sees the military as an "establishment." Whatever the term, the denotation seems to be similar. All the contributors discuss organizations—factories, prisons, offices, hospitals, churches, schools, military organizations, newspapers, voluntary associations, ships, trade-unions, governmental agencies, and universities—each of which is examined in detail by at least one contributor.

These readings were taken, as is customary, from a considerably larger body of literature. One obvious criterion of selection was that of finding writings of high quality which were brief enough to be included or could be excerpted without becoming incomprehensible or distorting the author's thesis.** More specifically,

* For a recent discussion of this concept, see Scott A. Greer, *Social Organization* (New York: Doubleday, 1955), especially pp. 5–10.
** The more important omissions are marked in the text by ellipsis dots (. . .).

an attempt was made to select material which could serve as a substitute for, or supplement to, a textbook for courses in organizational analysis. At the same time, efforts were made to refrain as much as possible from reprinting once more articles or parts of books which could be found on nearly everyone's desk. It is for this reason that some of the "classics" were not included. Omitting some of the standard selections left more room for newer contributions. Of 39 selections collected here, seven have not been published before or have been revised for this volume. Many of the other excerpts are not easily available. A number of works have been reprinted from journals and publications which have only a limited circulation or do not regularly come to the attention of students of organizations.

These readings draw considerably on recent material because in the last decade organizational analysis has rapidly developed and expanded. For the same reason, young and somewhat less well-known authors are highly represented.

This collection, like others before it, does not lay claim to completeness. Quite a few aspects of organizational study are not represented, and many approaches could not be illuminated. An effort has been made to bring into the limelight new tendencies and recent developments. Considerable space has been devoted to the study or organizational *goals* and to the application of *research techniques* to organization research. Care has been taken to call attention to three dimensions of organizational analysis which still seem to be relatively neglected. These are the study of interaction between *organization and society*; intracultural *comparative* study of organizations; and analysis of *organizational change*.

The editor benefited from extensive comments offered by his colleagues at Columbia University and at the University of California at Berkeley. Their knowledge, generous advice, and encouragement—which are herewith gratefully acknowledged—made these readings possible. I am especially indebted to Robert K. Merton, Philip Selznick, and Erving Goffman for their valuable comments on earlier outlines of this volume. The advice of John W. Riley, Jr., was most helpful, as well as the suggestions made by Renate Mayntz. Eva Etzioni served concomitantly as consultant, assistant, and companion.

A. E.

New York
December 1960

Contents

SECTION FIVE Organizational Change 381

SECTION SIX Problems of the Organizational Society 459

SECTION SEVEN Methods for the Study of Organizations 505

A Sociological
Reader on Complex
Organizations

SECTION ONE
Theories of
Organizations:
Classical and Modern

As we enter the final decades of this century the close intertwining of general theory and organizational theory becomes ever more explicit. Both types of theory focus on the interaction of rational and nonrational elements of human behavior and thought. A cardinal question for both is how best to coordinate human activities in order to make social life more effective, while at the same time coming to grips with the nonrational needs of groups and individuals. All the scholars in this section make this issue their starting point in one way or another. Several make clear that the resolution of the dilemma transcends organizational theory and has macrosociological import.

Max Weber's concerns were obviously of a more general nature. Nevertheless, he has made a significant contribution to the sociological study of organizations. Weber sees three modes of authority, and hence, three ideal types of organizational forms: traditional and charismatic authority which represent the nonrational elements and rational-legal or bureaucratic authority which, of course, represents the rational element. Each one of these modes is "connected with a fundamentally different sociological structure of executive staff and means of administration."

While Weber emphasizes the rational aspects of bureaucratic organization, Barnard places greater stress on the psychological and social aspects. He regards organizations as primarily *cooperative* systems. Barnard's interest in conscious coordination of activity parallels Weber's interest in the systematic division of task and authority and the rational control of performance. At the same time, however, Barnard focuses on the motivational and nonrational aspects of behavior.

March and Simon strive to extend the "Barnard-Simon theory of organization equilibrium." They regard it as "essentially a theory of motivation." As such, it deals with the conditions under which participation is assured, including willingness to be recruited and trained, to perform adequately in terms of quality and quantity, and to obey. The organization is seen as an exchange system in which *inducements* are handed out in exchange for *contributions* supplied. The present selection examines mainly the participation criterion of employees. The extension of this analysis to other groups of participants is suggested by the authors. These groups include buyers, suppliers, agents, and investors.

Merton's classic essay attempts to compensate for the hyperrationalistic elements in Weber's model of bureaucracy. Merton does this by focussing on the articulation between the personality and the organization as a social unit. An examination of the *bureaucrat* leads Merton to modify the rationalistic model of bureaucracies by pointing out its inherent dysfunctions. The specialized knowledge of the bureaucrat spells "trained incapacity" when the situation changes; discipline leads to devotion to means rather than devotion to ends; and personal treatment of clients and cases is carried out by interacting persons who develop primary relations. These relations in turn may have dysfunctional effects. The study of organizations, it follows, is incomplete without a study of the participants as persons rather than as simply incumbents of organizational roles.

Richard H. Hall is concerned with the interaction of organizations and the larger social structure. He reviews recent developments that see organizations either as closed systems or as open systems. The former perspective portrays organizations as shaped mainly by internal dynamics; the latter view regards organizations as highly influenced by environmental factors. Hall suggests that a contingency-choice perspective retains the best features of the closed-system and open-system models. This third perspective assumes "that organizations try to behave rationally in the face of multiple conflicting pressures, and thus attempt to control those aspects of their existence, both internal and external, that pose threats to rational actions."

The human relations school, which is now more than a half-century old, developed partly as a reaction to the extreme emphasis on rationality in other organizational theories. The most important names in this tradition are Elton Mayo and Kurt Lewin. The best known human relations studies were the first in the tradition; these were conducted at the Western Electric Company's Hawthorne works in Chicago from 1927–1932, and were labeled as the Hawthorne Studies. The findings were summarized in 1939 by Roethlisberger and Dickson in *Management and the Worker*. The human relations tradition has been subject to considerable derision and scholarly attack. Nevertheless, it survived as a viable perspective in organizational analysis. Kaplan and Tausky offer a detailed critique of current manifestations of this perspective.

One of the most important recent developments in American sociological theory is the resurgence of Marxian thought. Marxian theory tends to gravitate to the societal or intersocietal levels.

However, Wolf Heydebrand suggests that Marxism has something to offer to organizational analysis as well. In essence, Heydebrand concludes that organizational analyses are inevitably truncated if they do not consider the larger political economy in which organizations are nested.

The final selection in this section makes the impact of organizational analysis on general sociological theory most explicit. Kenneth Westhues argues that there are only two prevailing paradigms in modern social science: a class paradigm and an organization paradigm. Adoption of one or the other leads to radically different assessments of modern society. While one may question the need to *choose one paradigm or the other*, Westhues' essay illuminates how pivotal the study of organizations is for a sociological understanding of the modern world.

The Three Types of Legitimate Rule

Translated by Hans Gerth

Max Weber

Authority means the probability that a specific command will be obeyed. Such obedience may feed on diverse motives. It may be determined by sheer interest situation, hence by the compliant actor's calculation of expediency; by mere custom, that is, the actor's inarticulate habituation to routine behavior; or by mere affect, that is, purely personal devotion of the governed. A structure of power, however, if it were to rest on such foundations alone, would be relatively unstable. As a rule both rulers and rules uphold the internalized power structure as "legitimate" by right, and usually the shattering of this belief in legitimacy has far-reaching ramifications.

There are but three clear-cut grounds on which to base the belief in legitimate authority. Given pure types each is connected with a fundamentally different sociological structure of executive staff and means of administration.

I

Legal authority rests on enactment; its pure type is best represented by bureaucracy. The basic idea is that laws can be enacted and changed at pleasure by formally correct procedure. The governing body is either elected or appointed and constitutes as a whole and in all its sections rational organizations. A heteronomous and heterocephalous sub-unit we shall call "public authorities" (Behörde). The administrative staff consists of officials appointed by the ruler; the law-abiding people are members of the body politic ("fellow citizens").

Obedience is not owed to anybody personally but to enacted rules and regulations which specify to whom and to what rule people owe obedience. The person in authority, too, obeys a rule when giving an order, namely, "the law," or "rules and regulations" which represent abstract norms. The person in command typically is the "superior" within a functionally defined "competency" or "jurisdiction," and his right to govern is legitimized by enactment. Specialization sets limits with regard to functional purpose and required skill of the office incumbent.

The typical official is a trained specialist whose terms of employment are contractual and provide a fixed salary scaled by rank of office, not by amount of work, and the right to a pension according to fixed rules of advancement. His administration represents vocational work by virtue of impersonal duties of office;

ideally the administrator proceeds *sine ira et studio,* not allowing personal motive or temper to influence conduct, free of arbitrariness and unpredictability; especially he proceeds "without regard to person," following rational rules with strict formality. And where rules fail he adheres to "functional" considerations of expediency. Dutiful obedience is channeled through a hierarchy of offices which subordinates lower to higher offices and provides a regular procedure for lodging complaints. Technically, operation rests on organizational discipline.

1. Naturally this type of "legal" rule comprises not only the modern structure of state and city government but likewise the power relations in private capitalist enterprise, in public corporations and voluntary associations of all sorts, provided that an extensive and hierarchically organized staff of functionaries exists. Modern political bodies merely represent the type pre-eminently. Authority of private capitalist organization is partially heteronomous, its order is partly prescribed by the state, and it is completely heterocephalous as regards the machinery of coercion. Normally the courts and police take care of these functions. Private enterprise, however, is autonomous in its increasingly bureaucratic organization of management. The fact that, formally speaking, people enter into the power relationship (*Herrschaftsverband*) voluntarily and are likewise "free" to give notice does not affect the nature of private enterprise as a power structure since conditions of the labor market normally subject the employees to the code of the organization. Its sociological affinity to modern state authority will be clarified further in the discussion of the economic bases of power and authority. The "contract" as constitutive for the relations of authority in capitalist enterprise makes this a pre-eminent type of "legal authority."

2. Technically, bureaucracy represents the purest type of legal authority. No structure of authority, however, is exclusively bureaucratic, to wit, is managed by contractually hired and appointed officials alone. That is quite impossible. The top positions of the body politic may be held by "monarchs" (hereditary charismatic rulers), or by popularly elected "presidents" (hence plebiscitarian charismatic rulers), or by parliamentary elected presidents. In the latter case the actual rulers are members of parliament or rather the leaders of the prevailing parliamentary parties. These leaders in turn may stand close to the type of charismatic leadership or to that of notabilities. More of this below.

Likewise the administrative staff is almost never exclusively bureaucratic but usually notables and agents of interest groups participate in administration in manifold ways. This holds most of all for the so-called self-government. It is decisive that regular administrative work is predominantly and increasingly performed by bureaucratic forces. The historical development of the modern state is identical indeed with that of modern officialdom and bureaucratic organization (cf. below), just as the development of modern capitalism is identical with the increasing bureaucratization of economic enterprise. The part played by bureaucracy becomes bigger in all structures of power.

3. Bureaucracy does not represent the only type of legal authority. Other types comprise rotating office holders or office holders chosen by lot or popularly elected officers. Parliamentary and committee administration and all sorts of collegiate and administrative bodies are included under the type if and when their competency rests on enacted rules and if the use they make of their prerogative follows the type of legal administration. During the rise of the modern state collegiate bodies have made essential contributions to the development of legal

authority, especially the concept of "public authorities" (Behörde) originated with them. On the other hand, elected officialdom has played an important role in the prehistory of the modern civil service and still does so today in the democracies.

II

Traditional authority rests on the belief in the sacredness of the social order and its prerogatives as existing of yore. Patriarchal authority represents its pure type. The body politic is based on communal relationships, the man in command is the "lord" ruling over obedient "subjects." People obey the lord personally since his dignity is hallowed by tradition; obedience rests on piety. Commands are substantively bound by tradition, and the lord's inconsiderate violation of tradition would endanger the legitimacy of his personal rule, which rests merely upon the sacredness of tradition. The creation of new law opposite traditional norms is deemed impossible in principle. Actually this is done by way of "recognizing" a sentence as "valid of yore" (the *Weistum* of ancient Germanic law). Outside the norms of tradition, however, the lord's sway in a given case is restricted only by sentiments of equity, hence by quite elastic bonds. Consequently the rule of the lord divides into a strictly tradition-bound sphere and one of free favor and arbitrariness where he rules at pleasure as sympathy or antipathy move him, following purely personal considerations subject especially to the influence of "good turns."

So far as principles are followed in administration and settlement of disputes, they rest on substantive considerations of ethical equity, justice, or utilitarian expediency, not on formal considerations characteristic of the rule of law. The lord's administrative staff proceeds in the same way. It consists of personally dependent men (members of the household or domestic officials), of relatives, of personal friends (favorites), or associates bound by personal allegiance (vassals, tributory princes). The bureaucratic concept of "competency" as a functionally delimited jurisdictional sphere is absent. The scope of the "legitimate" prerogatives of the individual servant is defined from case to case at the pleasure of the lord on whom the individual servant is completely dependent as regards his employment in more important or high ranking roles. Actually this depends largely on what the servant may dare do opposite the more or less docile subjects. Personal loyalty of the faithful servant, not functional duty of office and office discipline, control the interrelationship of the administrative staff.

One may, however, observe two characteristically different forms of positional relationships, the patriarchal structure and that of estates.

1. In the purely patriarchal structure of administration the servants are completely and personally dependent on the lord; they are either purely patrimonially recruited as slaves, bondsmen-serfs, eunuchs, or extra patrimonially as favorites and plebeians from among strata lacking all rights. Their administration is entirely heteronomous and heterocephalous, the administrators have no personal right to their office, there is neither merit selection nor status honor; the material means of administration are managed under, and on account of, the lord. Given the complete dependency of the administrative staff on the lord, there is no guarantee against the lord's arbitrariness, which in this set-up can therefore have its greatest possible sway. Sultanistic rule represents the pure type. All genuine "despotism" was of this nature. Prerogatives are considered . . . ordinary property rights of the lord.

2. In the estate system the servants are not personal servants of the lord but independent men whose social position makes them presumably socially prominent. The lord, actually or according to the legitimacy fiction, bestows office on them by privilege or concession; or they have contractually, by purchase, tenancy or lease, acquired a title to their office which cannot be arbitrarily taken away from them; hence within limits, their administration is autocephalous and autonomous. Not the lord but they dispose over the material means of administration. This represents estate rule.

The competition of the officeholders for larger bailiwicks (and income) then determines the mutual delimitation of their actual bailiwicks and takes the place of "competency." Privilege often breaks through the hierarchic structure (*de non evocando, non apellando*). The category of "discipline" is absent. Tradition, privilege, feudal or patrimonial bonds of allegiance, status honor and "good will" regulate the web of inter-relations. The power prerogatives of the lord hence are divided between the lord and the privileged administrative staff, and this division of powers among the estates brings about a high degree of stereotypy in the nature of administration.

Patriarchal rule (of the family father, sib chief, father of his people [*Landesvater*]) represents but the purest type of traditionalist rule. Any "authorities" who claim legitimacy successfully by virtue of mere habituation represent the most typical contrast, on the one hand, to the position of a contractually employed worker in business enterprise; on the other, to the way a faithful member of a religious community emotionally relates to a prophet. Actually the domestic group [*Hausverband*] is the nucleus of traditionalist power structures. The typical "officials" of the patrimonial and feudal state are domestic officers with originally purely domestic tasks (dapifer, chamberlain, marshal, cupbearer, seneschal, major domo).

The co-existence of the strictly tradition-bound and the free sphere of conduct is a common feature of all traditionalistic forms of authority. Within the free sphere, action of the lord or of his administrative staff must be bought or earned by personal relations. (This is one of the origins of the institution of fees.) It is decisive that formal law is absent and that substantive principles of administration and arbitration take its place. This likewise is a common feature of all traditionalist power structures and has far-reaching ramifications, especially for economic life.

The patriarch, like the patrimonial ruler, governs and decides according to the principles of "cadi justice": on the one hand, decisions are strictly bound by tradition; however, where these fetters give leeway, decisions follow juristically informal and irrational considerations of equity and justice from case to case, also taking individual differences into account. All codifications and laws of patrimonial rulers embody the spirit of the so-called "welfare state." A combination of social ethical with social utilitarian principles prevails, breaking through all rigor of formal law.

The sociological distinction between the patriarchal power structure and that of the estates in traditionalist rule is fundamental for all states of the pre-bureaucratic epoch. (The contrast will become fully clear only in connection with its economic aspect, that is, with the separation of the administrative staff from the material means of administration or with their appropriation by the staff.) This has been historically decisive for the question whether and what status groups existed as champions of ideas and culture values.

Patrimonial dependents (slaves, bondsmen) as administrators are to be found throughout the Mideastern orient and in Egypt down to the time of the Mamelukes; they represent the most extreme and what would seem to be the most consistent type of the purely patriarchal rule devoid of estates. Plebeian freemen as administrators stand relatively close to rational officialdom. The administration by literati can vary greatly in accordance with their nature: typical is the contrast between Brahmins and Mandarins, and both in turn stand opposite Buddhist and Christian clerics—yet their administration always approximates the estate type of power structure.

The rule of estates is most clearly represented by aristocracy, in purest form by feudalism, which puts in the place of the functional and rational duty of office the personal allegiance and the appeal to status honor of the enfeoffed.

In comparison to patriarchalism, all estate rule, based upon more or less stable appropriation of administrative power, stands closer to legal authority as the guarantees surrounding the prerogatives of the privileged assume the form of special "rights" (a result of the "division of power" among the estates). This rationale is absent in patriarchal structures, with their administration completely dependent on the lord's arbitrary sway. On the other hand, the strict discipline and the lack of rights of the administrative staff within patriarchalism is more closely related to the discipline of legal authority than is the administration of estates, which is fragmented and stereotyped through the appropriation of the means of administration by the staff. Plebeians (used as jurists) in Europe's princely service have been pacemarkers of the modern state.

III

Charismatic authority rests on the affectual and personal devotion of the follower to the lord and his gifts of grace (charisma). They comprise especially magical abilities, revelations of heroism, power of the mind and of speech. The eternally new, the non-routine, the unheard of and the emotional rapture from it are sources of personal devotion. The purest types are the rule of the prophet, the warrior hero, the great demagogue. The body politic consists in the communal relationship of a religious group or following. The person in command is typically the "leader"; he is obeyed by the "disciple." Obedience is given exclusively to the leader as a person, for the sake of his non-routine qualities, not because of enacted position or traditional dignity. Therefore obedience is forthcoming only so long as people ascribe these qualities to him, that is, so long as his charisma is proven by evidence. His rule falls if he is "forsaken" by his god* or deprived of his heroic strength, or if the masses lose faith in his leadership capacity. The administrative staff is selected according to charisma and personal devotion, hence selection does not consider special qualification (as in the case of the civil servant) nor rank and station (as in the case of administration by estates) nor domestic or other forms of personal dependency (as, in contrast to the above, holds for the patriarchal administrative staff). The rational concept of "competency" is lacking as is the

*Translator's note: This allusion to Jesus' death and its interpretation as a downfall of his charismatic authority comes out more strongly in Weber's "Sociology of Charismatic Authority" ("Charismatismus," *Wirtschaft und Gesellschaft*, in *From Max Weber: Essays in Sociology*, H. H. Gerth and C. Wright Mills, trans. (New York: Oxford, 1946), p. 248. In his later work, *Ancient Judaism*, Hans H. Gerth and Don Martindale, trans. (New York: Free Press, 1952), p. 376, Weber reversed his position.

status idea of "privilege." Decisive for the legitimation of the commissioned follower or disciple is alone the mission of the lord and his followers' personal charismatic qualification. The administration—so far as this word is adequate— lacks all orientation to rules and regulations whether enacted or traditional. Spontaneous revelation or creation, deed and example, decision from case to case, that is—at least measured against enacted orders—irrational decisions are characteristic of charismatic authority. It is not bound to tradition: "It is written but I say unto you" holds for the prophet. For the warrior hero the legitimate orders vanish opposite new creations by power of the sword, for the demagogue by virtue of his annunciation or suggestion of revolutionary "natural law." In the genuine form of charismatic justice and arbitration the lord or "sage" speaks the law and the (military or religious) following gives it recognition, which is obligatory, unless somebody raises a counter claim to charismatic validity. This case presents a struggle of leaders which in the last analysis can solely be decided by the confidence of the community; only one side can be right; the other side must be wrong and be obliged to make amends.

A. The type of charismatic authority has first been developed brilliantly by R. Sohm in his *Kirchenrecht* for the early Christian community without his recognizing that it represents a type of authority. The term has since been used repeatedly without recognition of its bearing.

Early history shows alongside a few beginnings of "enacted" authority, which are by no means entirely absent, the division of all power relationships under tradition and charisma. Besides the "economic chief" (sachem) of the Indians, an essentially traditional figure, stands the charismatic warrior prince (corresponding to the Germanic "duke") with his following. Hunting and war campaigns, both demanding a leader of extraordinary personal endowments, are the secular; magic is the "sacred" place of charismatic leadership. Throughout the ages charismatic authority exercised by prophets and warrior princes has held sway over men. The charismatic politician—the "demagogue"—is the product of the occidental city state. In the city state of Jerusalem he emerged only in religious costume as a prophet. The constitution of Athens, however, was completely cut out for his existence after the innovations of Pericles and Ephialtes, since without the demagogue the state machine would not function at all.

B. Charismatic authority rests on the "faith" in the prophet, on the "recognition" which the charismatic warrior hero, the hero of the street or the demagogue, finds personally, and this authority falls with him. Yet, charismatic authority does not derive from this recognition by the subjects. Rather the reverse obtains: the charismatically legitimized leader considers faith in the acknowledgement of his charisma obligatory and punishes their violation. Charismatic authority is even one of the great revolutionary forces in history, but in pure form it is thoroughly authoritarian and lordly in nature.

C. It should be understood that the term "charisma" is used here in a completely value-neutral sense. For the sociologist the manic seizure and rage of the Nordic berserk, the miracles and revelations of any pettifogging prophecy, the demagogic talents of Cleon are just as much "charisma" as the qualities of a Napoleon, Jesus, Pericles. Decisive for us is only whether they were considered charismatics and whether they were effective, that is, gained recognition. Here, "proof" is the basic prerequisite. The charismatic lord has to prove his being sent "by the grace of god" by performing miracles and being successful in securing the good life for his following or subjects. Only as long as he can do so will he be recognized. If success fails him, his authority falters. Wherever this charismatic concept of rule by the grace of god has existed, it has had decisive ramifications. The Chinese monarch's position was threatened as soon as drought, floods, military failure or other misfortune made it appear questionable whether he stood in the grace of Heaven. Public self-impeachment and penance, in cases of stubborn misfortune, removal and possible sacrifice threatened him. Certification by miracles was demanded of every prophet (the Zwickau people demanded it still from Luther).

So far as the belief in legitimacy matters for the stability of basically legal structures of authority, this stability rests mostly on mixed foundations. Traditional habituation of "prestige" (charisma) fuses with the belief in formal legality which in the last analysis is also a matter of habit. The belief in the legitimacy of authority is shattered alike through extraordinary misfortunes whether this exacts unusual demands from the subjects in the light of tradition, or destroys the prestige or violates the usual formal legal correctness. But with all structures of authority the obedience of the governed as a stable condition depends above all on the availability of an administrative staff and especially its continuous operation to maintain order and (directly or indirectly) enforce submission to the rule. The term "organization" means to guarantee the pattern of conduct which realizes the structure of authority. The solidarity of its (ideal and material) interests with those of the lord is decisive for all important loyalty of the staff to the lord. For the relation of the lord to the executive staff it generally holds that the lord is the stronger opposite the resisting individual because of the isolation of the individual staff members and his solidarity with the lord. The lord is weak opposite the staff member as a whole when they band themselves together, as has happened occasionally in the past and present. Deliberate agreement of the staff is requisite in order to frustrate the lord's action and rule through obstruction or deliberate counter action. Likewise the opposition requires an administrative staff of its own.

D. Charismatic rule represents a specifically extraordinary and purely personal relationship. In the case of continued existence, however, at least when the personal representative of charisma is eliminated, the authority structure has the tendency to routinize. This is the case when the charisma is not extinguished at once but continues to exist in some form and the authority of the lord, hence, is transferred to successors. This routinization of charisma proceeds through

1. Traditionalization of the orders. The authority of precedents takes the place of the charismatic leader's or his staff's charismatic creativity in law and administration. These precedents either protect the successors or are attributed to them.
2. The charismatic staff of disciples or followers changes into a legal or estate-like staff by taking over internal prerogatives or those appropriated by privilege (fiefs, prebends).
3. The meaning of charisma itself may undergo a change. Decisive in this is the way in which the problem of successorship is solved, which is a burning question for ideological and indeed often material reasons. This question can be solved in various ways: the merely passive tarrying for a new charismatically certified or qualified master usually gives way to an active search for a successor, especially if none readily appears and if any strong interests are vested in the continuity of the authority structure.

Organizations as Systems of Cooperation
Chester I. Barnard

A cooperative system is a complex of physical, biological, personal, and social components which are in a specific systematic relationship by reason of the cooperation of two or more persons for at least one definite end. Such a system is evidently a subordinate unit of larger systems from one point of view; and itself embraces subsidiary systems—physical, biological, etc.—from another point of view. One of the systems comprised within a cooperative system, the one which is implicit in the phrase "cooperation of two or more persons," is called an "organization."

The number of cooperative systems having more or less definite purposes, and of sufficient duration to enlist attention and description or identification, is very large. They may be broadly classified by character of purpose or objective into a few groups which are widely different, such as churches, political parties, fraternal associations, governments, armies, industrial enterprises, schools, families. Between organizations classified in any one of these groups there are also wide differences.

The variations in concrete cooperative situations may be assigned to four preliminary classes: (a) those that relate to aspects of the physical environment; (b) those that relate to aspects of the social environment; (c) those that relate to individuals; (d) other variables.

a. An inspection of the concrete operations of any cooperative system shows at once that the physical environment is an inseparable part of it. To the extent that there are variations in the physical aspects of cooperative systems an adjustment or adaptation of other aspects of cooperation is required. Whether such variations are significant for the general study of cooperation, or whether for most purposes the physical environment may be treated as a constant, is the first question at issue. By physical environment so far as we mean geographical aspects—that is, mere location, topography, climate, etc.—it will readily be accepted that it may well be excluded from consideration for nearly all general purposes.[1] That part of the environment, however, which is regarded as the property of an organization is of different status; and that part which consists of structures, improvements, tools, machines, etc., pertains still more specifically to the organization which owns or works with them. All aspects of the physical environment are then regarded or most conveniently treated as the elements of other, physical and technical, systems between which and organizations the significant relationships may be investigated as may be required for the purpose in hand.

b. It is in most cases evident that the social elements are an important aspect likewise of a concrete cooperative situation. The social factors may be regarded as entering into the situation by several routes: (1) through being components of the individual whose activities are included in the system; (2) through their effect upon individuals, whose activities are not included, but who are hostile to the system of cooperation or whose activities potentially are factors in any way; (3) through contact of the system (either cooperative or otherwise) with other collateral cooperative systems and especially with (4) superior systems; and (5) as inherent in cooperation itself. Indirectly, social factors, of course, are also involved in the changes of the physical environment, particularly as effected by prior or other existing cooperative systems. . . .

We shall exclude all of the social environment as such from the definition of organization.

c. The exclusion of the physical and social environments from the definition of organization for general purposes will on the whole conform to ordinary usage and common sense, and will be accepted without great difficulty as a method of approach to a scientifically useful concept of organization. The question of persons, however, offers greater difficulty and doubt. Though with much vagueness and many exceptions, some of which have been already indicated, the most usual conception of an organization is that of a *group* of persons, some or all of whose activities are coordinated. The concept of the group as the dominant characteristic of cooperative systems is certainly also frequent in the literature of sociology, anthropology, and social psychology, although, as shown by Parsons,[2] systems in which at least the emphasis is upon *action* have been fundamental in the conceptual schemes of Durkheim, Pareto, and Weber.

As a working concept it may be made clear that "group" contains so many variables as to restrict the number and the firmness of any generalizations. It is unmanageable without the use of some more restricted concept. Hence, to the present writer, discussions of group cooperation often give the impression of vagueness, confusion, and implicit contradiction. The reason for this is apparent from the fact that both group and person require explicit definition. A group is evidently a number of persons plus some interrelationships or interactions to be determined. When the nature of these interrelations or interactions is described or defined, it at once appears that "person" is a highly variable thing, not merely in the sense that persons differ in many respects, but more especially because the extent and character of their participation in groups also widely varies. . . .

Now if, with reference to a particular system of cooperative action to which a person contributes, one examines all the acts of any person for even one day it will be at once evident in nearly all cases that many of these acts are outside *any* system of cooperation; and that many of the remainder are distributable among at least several such cooperative systems. The connection of any "member" with an organization is necessarily intermittent, and there is frequent substitution of persons. Again it is almost impossible to discover a person who does not "belong"—taking into account the intermittent character of his participation—at the same time to many organizations. . . .

It is evident from the foregoing that if persons are to be included within the concept "organization," its general significance will be quite limited. The bases or terms upon which persons are included will be highly variable—so much so that even within very restricted fields, such as a particular industry, "organizations" will mean a wide variety of entities. Hence, here again as when we included a part of the physical environment within the definition, the inclusion of persons may be most useful in particular instances, but of limited value for general purposes.

It nevertheless remains to consider whether it would actually be useful to adopt a definition from which persons as well as physical and social environments are excluded as components. If this is done, an organization is defined as *a system of consciously coordinated personal activities or forces.* It is apparent that all the variations found in concrete cooperative systems that are due to physical and social environments, and those that are due to persons or to the bases upon which persons contribute to such systems, are by this definition relegated to the position of external facts and factors,[3] and that the organization as then isolated is an aspect of cooperative systems which is common to all of them.

Organization will then mean a similar thing, whether applied to a military, a religious, an academic, a manufacturing, or a fraternal cooperation, though the physical environment, the social environment, the number and kinds of persons, and the bases of their relation to the organization will be widely different. These aspects of cooperation then become external to organization as defined, though components of the cooperative system as a whole. Moreover, the definition is similarly applicable to settings radically different from those now obtaining, for example, to cooperation under feudal conditions. Such a definition will be of restricted usefulness with reference to any particular cooperative situation, being only one element of such a situation, except as by its adoption we are enabled to arrive at general principles which may be usefully applied in the understanding of specific situations.

It is the central hypothesis of this book that the most useful concept for the analysis of experience of cooperative systems is embodied in the definition of a formal organization as a *system of consciously coordinated activities or forces of two or more persons.* In any concrete situation in which there is cooperation, several different systems will be components. Some of these will be physical, some biological, some psychological, etc., but the element common to all which binds all these other systems into the total concrete cooperative situation is that of organization as defined. If this hypothesis proves satisfactory it will be because (1) an organization, as defined, is a concept valid through a wide range of concrete situations with relatively few variables, which can be effectively investigated; and (2) the relations between this conceptual scheme and other systems can be effectively and usefully formulated. The final test of this conceptual scheme is whether its use will make possible a more effective conscious promotion and manipulation of cooperation among men; that is, whether in practice it can increase the predictive capacity of competent men in this field. It is the assumption upon which this essay is developed that such a concept is implicit in the behavior of leaders and administrators, explaining uniformities observed in their conduct in widely different cooperative enterprises, and that its explicit formulation and development will permit a useful translation of experience in different fields into common terms.

Notes

1. In special cases, however, this is not true; for example, where two manufacturing operations otherwise alike are conducted in two different climates. Climate may then be the most significant variable.
2. Talcott Parsons, *The Structure of Social Action* (New York: McGraw-Hill, 1937).
3. That is, external to the organization but not external to the related cooperative system. It is to be borne in mind that we are dealing with *two* systems: (1) an inclusive cooperative system, the components of which are persons, physical systems, social systems, and organizations; and (2) organizations, which are parts of cooperative systems and consist entirely of coordinated human activities.

The Theory of Organizational Equilibrium

James G. March
and Herbert A. Simon

The Barnard-Simon theory of organizational equilibrium is essentially a theory of motivation—a statement of the conditions under which an organization can induce its members to continue their participation, and hence assure, organizational survival. The central postulates of the theory are stated by Simon, Smithburg, and Thompson (1950, pp. 381–382) as follows:

1. An organization is a system of interrelated social behaviors of a number of persons whom we shall call the *participants* in the organization.
2. Each participant and each group of participants receives *from* the organization *inducements* in return for which he makes *to* the organization *contributions*.
3. Each participant will continue his participation in an organization only so long as the inducements offered him are as great or greater (measured in terms of *his* values and in terms of the alternatives open to him) than the contributions he is asked to make.
4. The contributions provided by the various groups of participants are the source from which the organization manufactures the inducements offered to participants.
5. Hence, an organization is "solvent"—and will continue in existence—only so long as the contributions are sufficient to provide inducements in large enough measure to draw forth these contributions.

The theory, like many theoretical generalizations, verges on the tautological. Specifically, to test the theory, and especially the crucial postulate 3, we need independent empirical estimates of (*a*) the behavior of participants in joining, remaining in, or withdrawing from organizations; and (*b*) the balance of inducements and contributions for each participant, measured in terms of his "utilities.".

The observation of participants joining and leaving organizations is comparatively easy. It is more difficult to find evidence of the value of variable (*b*) that does not depend on the observation of (*a*). Before we can deal with the observational problem, however, we must say a bit more about the concepts of inducements and contributions.

Inducements.   Inducements are "payments" made by (or through) the organization to its participants (e.g., wages to a worker, service to a client, income to an investor). These payments can be measured in units that are independent of their utility to the participants (e.g., wages and income can be measured in terms of dollars, service to clients in terms of hours devoted to him). Consequently, for an individual participant we can specify a set of inducements, each component of the set representing a different dimension of the inducements offered by the organization. Thus, each component of the inducements can be measured uniquely and independently of the utilities assigned to it by the participants.

Inducement utilities. For each component in the set of inducements there is a corresponding utility value. For the moment we will not be concerned with the shape of the utility function; but we do not exclude from consideration a step function. The utility function for a given individual reduces the several components of the inducements to a common dimension.

Contributions. We assume that a participant in an organization makes certain "payments" to the organization (e.g., work from the worker, fee from the client, capital from the investor). These payments, which we shall call contributions, can be measured in units that are independent of their utility to the participants. Consequently, for any individual participant we can specify a set of contributions.

Contribution utilities. A utility function transforming contributions into utilities of the individual contributor can be defined in more than one way. A reasonable definition of the utility of a contribution is the value of the alternatives that an individual foregoes in order to make the contribution. As we shall see below, this definition of contribution utilities allows us to introduce into the analysis the range of behavior alternatives open to the participant.

These definitions of inducements and contributions permit two general approaches to the observational problem. On the one hand, we can try to estimate the utility balance directly by observing the behavior (including responses to pertinent questions) of participants. On the other hand, if we are prepared to make some simple empirical assumptions about utility functions, we can make predictions from changes in the amounts of inducements and contributions, without reference to their utilities.

To estimate the inducement-contribution utility balance directly, the most logical type of measure is some variant of individual satisfaction (with the job, the service, the investment, etc.). It appears reasonable to assume that the greater the difference between inducements and contributions, the greater the individual satisfaction. However, the critical "zero points" of the satisfaction scale and the inducement-contribution utility balance are not necessarily identical. The zero point for the satisfaction scale is the point at which one begins to speak of degrees of "dissatisfaction" rather than degrees of "satisfaction." It is, therefore, closely related to the level of aspiration and . . . is the point at which we would predict a substantial increase in search behavior on the part of the organism.

The zero point on the inducement-contribution utility scale, on the other hand, is the point at which the individual is indifferent to leaving an organization. We have ample evidence that these two zero points are not identical, but, in particular, that very few of the "satisfied" participants leave an organization, whereas some, but typically not all, of the "unsatisfied" participants leave (Reynolds, 1951).

How do we explain these differences? The explanation lies primarily in the ways in which alternatives to current activity enter into the scheme (and this is one of the reasons for defining contribution utilities in terms of opportunities foregone). Dissatisfaction is a cue for search behavior. Being dissatisfied, the organism expands its program for exploring alternatives. If over the long run this search fails, the aspiration level is gradually revised downward. We assume, however, that the change in aspiration level occurs slowly, so that dissatisfaction in the short run is quite possible. On the other hand, the inducement-contribution utility balance adjusts quickly to changes in the perception of alternatives. When fewer and poorer alternatives are perceived to be available, the utility of activities foregone decreases; and this adjustment occurs rapidly.

Consequently, we can use satisfaction expressed by the individual as a measure of the inducement-contribution utility balance only if it is used in conjunction with an estimate of perceived alternatives available. Speaking roughly, only the desire to move enters into judgments of satisfaction; desire to move *plus* the perceived ease of movement enters into the inducement-contribution utility measure. Many students of mobility (particularly those concerned with the mobility of workers) have tended to ignore one or the other of these two facets of the decision to participate (Rice, Hill, and Trist, 1950; Behrend, 1953).

Direct observation of the inducement-contribution utilities, however, is not the only possible way to estimate them. Provided we make certain assumptions about the utility functions, we can infer the utility balance directly from observations of changes in the inducements or contributions measured in nonutility terms. Three major assumptions are useful and perhaps warranted. First, we assume that the utility functions change only slowly. Second, we assume that each utility function is monotonic with respect to its corresponding inducement or contribution. Although we may not know what the utility of an increase in wages will be, we are prepared to assume it will be positive. Third, we assume that the utility functions of fairly broad classes of people are very nearly the same; within a given subculture we do not expect radical differences in values. Also, we can expect that if an increase in a given inducement produces an increase in utility for one individual, it will produce an increase for other individuals.

There are other reasonable assumptions about individual utility functions; some will be indicated below when we relate individual participation to other factors. These three assumptions, however, in themselves lead to a variety of estimation procedures. Under the first assumption the short-run effect of a change in inducements or contributions will be uncontaminated by feedback effects. By the second assumption (particularly in conjunction with the third) a host of ordinal predictions can be made on the basis of knowledge of changes in the inducements and contributions. The third assumption permits us to estimate some of the cardinal properties of the inducements-contributions balance, avoiding the problem of interpersonal comparison of utilities.

Assumptions such as those listed have some a priori validity, but it is more important that much of the evidence currently available on the behavior of participants is consistent with them. Thus, predictions are frequently and often successfully made by businessmen as to the feasibility of proposed organizational plans.

Consider the analysis of a businessman exploring the feasibility of a business venture. His first step is to construct an operating plan showing what activities and facilities are required to carry on the proposed business, including estimates of the quantities of "inputs" and "outputs" of all categories. In the language of economics, he estimates the "production function." In the language of organization theory, the production function states the rates of possible conversion of contributions into inducements (Simon, 1952–53).

His second step is to estimate the monetary inducements that will be needed to obtain the inputs in the amounts required, and the monetary contributions that can be exacted for the outputs—i.e., the prices of factors of production and of product. In estimating these monetary inducements, predictions are being made as to the inducements-contributions balances of various classes of participants. Let us give some hypothetical examples:

Salaries and wages. Information is obtained on "going rates of wages" for similar classes of work in other companies in the same area. An implicit *ceteris paribus* assumption is made with respect to other inducements, or (if the work, say, is particularly unpleasant, if proposed working conditions are particularly good or bad, etc.) the monetary inducement is adjusted upward or downward to compensate for the other factors. If the problem is to attract workers from other organizations, it is assumed that a wage differential or other inducement will be required to persuade them to change.

Capital. Information is obtained on "the money market"—i.e., the kinds of alternative investment opportunities that are available, the weight attached to various elements of risk, and the levels of interest rates. It is then assumed that to induce investment, the terms (interest rates, security, etc.) must be at least equal to the inducements available in alternative investments.

The same procedure is followed for the inducements to other participants. In each case, information is required as to the alternative inducements offered by other organizations, and these establish the "zero level" of the net inducement-contribution balance. If nonmonetary factors are not comparable among alternatives, an estimated adjustment is made of the monetary inducements by way of compensation. Of course, the adjustment may just as well be made in the nonmonetary factors (e.g., in product quality).

If the planned inducements, including the monetary inducements, give a positive balance for all groups of participants, the plan is feasible. If the plan is subsequently carried out, a comparison of the actual operations with the estimates provides an empirical test of the assumptions and the estimates. If the outcomes fail to confirm the assumptions, the businessman may still choose which of the two sets of assumptions he will alter. He may interpret the result as evidence that the basic inducements-contributions hypothesis is incorrect, or he may conclude that he has estimated incorrectly the zero points of one or more of the inducements-contributions balances. The fact is, however, that such predictions are frequently made with substantial success.

The testing of the theory is not confined to predicting the survival of new enterprises. At any time in the life of an organization when a change is made—that (a) explicitly alters the inducements offered to any group of participants; (b) explicitly alters the contributions demanded from them; or (c) alters the organizational activity in any way that will affect inducements or contributions—on any of these occasions, a prediction can be made as to the effect of the change on participation. The effects may be measurable in terms of turnover rates of employees, sales, etc., as appropriate.

The Participants

The theory of organizational equilibrium, as we have formulated it here, implies a structure—an organization—underlying the equilibrium. Specifically, there must exist a social system involving the participants that exhibits both a high degree of interrelationship and substantial differentiation from other systems within the total social milieu.

Up to this point, we have not tried to be precise in defining participation. In fact, we must necessarily be somewhat arbitrary in identifying some particular individuals as participants in a given organization. A number of individuals other than those we will identify as principal participants in a business organization receive inducements from the organization and provide contributions to its existence, and under special circumstances such "participants" may assume a dominant role in determining the equilibrium of the organization. But when we describe the chief participants of most business organizations, we generally limit our attention to the following five major classes: employees, investors, suppliers, distributors, and consumers.

Most obvious in any catalogue of organizational participants are the employees, including the management. Ordinarily, when we talk of organizational participants what we mean are workers, and membership in a business organization is ordinarily treated as equivalent to employment. Employees receive wages and other gratuities and donate work (production) and other contributions to the organization. As will become obvious below, employment is the area of participation in organizations in which the most extensive research has been executed.

The role of investors as participants in the organization is explicit in the economic theory of the firm but has rarely been included in other analyses of organizational behavior. A close analogue is found in some treatises on public administration where external power groups are dealt with specifically (Simon, Smithburg, and Thompson, 1950; Truman, 1951; Freeman, 1955). Although the participation of investors in the activities of business firms is frequently less active than that of political power groups in the management of governmental units, the behavior of investing participants is not so insignificant in the general American business scene as to warrant excluding them from consideration.

The distinction between units in a production-distribution process that are "in" the organization and those that are "out" of the organization typically follows the legal definition of the boundaries of a particular firm. We find it fruitful to use a more functional criterion that includes both the suppliers and the distributors of the manufacturing core of the organization (or its analogue where the core of the organization is not manufacturing). Thus, in the automobile industry it is useful to consider the automobile dealers as component parts of an automobile manufacturing organization.

Finally, the role of consumers in an organization has, like the role of investors, been generally ignored except by economic theorists. Since consumers are clearly part of the equilibrating system, organization theory must include in its framework the major components of a theory of consumption.

Taken too literally, this conception of organizations incorporates almost any knowledge about human behavior as a part of organization theory. However, we will limit our primary attention here to the participation of employees. Labor mobility has been studied at some length by both economists and social psychologists. Consequently, we will be able to find at least some evidence for the propositions cited. In general, the areas of investment behavior, supplier behavior, and middleman behavior are less well developed; and their propositions less well documented. Consumer behavior presents a somewhat different case, being the subject of considerable research (Clark, 1958). . . .

Employee Participation: The Participation Criterion

In one respect an employee's relation to the organization is quite different from that of other participants. In joining the organization he accepts an authority relation; i.e., he agrees that within some limits (defined both explicitly and implicitly by the terms of the employment contract) he will accept as the premises of his behavior orders and instructions supplied to him by the organization. Associated with this acceptance are commonly understood procedures for "legitimating" communications and clothing them with authority for employees. Acceptance of authority by the employee gives the organization a powerful means for influencing him—more powerful than persuasion, and comparable to the evoking processes that call forth a whole program of behavior in response to a stimulus.

On the assumption that employees act in a subjectively rational manner, we can make some predictions about the scope of the authority relation from our knowledge of the inducements and contributions of the employees and other organization members (Simon, 1952–53). An employee will be willing to enter into an employment contract only if it does not matter to him "very much" what activities (within the area of acceptance agreed on in the contract) the organization will instruct him to perform, or if he is compensated in some way for the possibility that the organization will impose unpleasant activities on him. It will be advantageous for the organization to establish an authority relation when the employee activities that are optimal for the organization (i.e., maximize the inducement utility to other participants of the employee's activity) cannot be predicted accurately in advance.

These propositions can be restated in a form that permits them to be tested by looking at terms of the employment contract. A particular aspect of an employee's behavior can be (a) specified in the employment contract (e.g., as the wage rate usually is), (b) left to the employee's discretion (e.g., sometimes, but not always, whether he smokes on the job), or (c) brought within the authority of the employer (e.g., the specific tasks he performs within the range fixed by the job specification). The conditions that make it advantageous to stipulate an aspect of behavior in the contract are sharp conflict of interest (e.g., as to wage level) and some uncertainty as to what that interest is. It is advantageous to leave to the employee's discretion those aspects that are of little interest to the employer but great interest to the employee; and to subject the employee to the organization's authority in those aspects that are of relatively great interest to the employer, comparatively unimportant to the employee, and about which the employer cannot make accurate predictions much in advance of performance. . . .

To construct a series of hypotheses relating employee participation to external variables, we must first establish a criterion for "participation." Three methods of measuring participation yield substantially different results. First, we can measure the quantity of production by the individual worker. . . . Second, we can use an absence criterion. Permanent physical absence associated with leaving the company payroll represents the extreme value on the low side. Differences in on-the-job productivity are not captured by the absence criterion but employees are distinguished by their absence rates as well as their turnover rates. Third, we can use a turnover criterion: we can identify participation with the all-or-none phenomena of being on or off the organization payroll.

Although it may appear at first blush that these measures simply reflect different degrees of disassociation from the organization and, therefore, are simply different points on a common continuum, the available empirical evidence indicates no consistent relation among measures of production, absences, and voluntary turnover (Acton Society Trust, 1953; Morse, 1953; Brayfield and Crockett, 1955). The correlations are sometimes high, sometimes low; and the antecedent conditions for each result are difficult to specify. Some reasons for these findings are suggested by the available research, although substantiation is difficult.

First, under what conditions should we expect to find low absence (and/or productivity) associated with high voluntary turnover? We might expect that if extreme penalties are imposed for absence (relative to those generally expected in the group employed), absence rates will tend to be low among those who choose to stay on the job. But we should also expect to find a high rate of exit from the job. Similarly, where the ability to leave the organization is restrained (e.g., by governmental fiat), we should expect to find low voluntary turnover rates but (particularly if labor is scarce) relatively high absence rates (Mayo and Lombard, 1944).

Second, under what conditions should we expect to find a positive relation between absence and turnover? Assume (1) that motivation to avoid the demands (i.e., contributions) of the job situation stems primarily from dissatisfaction with the inducements-contributions balance, (2) that for most people motivation to seek relief through temporary absence occurs at a point related consistently to the point at which motivation to quit occurs, and (3) that the factors contributing to individual dissatisfaction are general to the population of workers rather than specific to individual workers. Under these assumptions absence and voluntary turnover will be positively related when the penalties associated with absence and withdrawal are "normal."

Although we have scarcely touched the complexity of the relation among absenteeism, sickness, and turnover, we can see that the choice of a criterion of participation will significantly affect the propositions about participation. . . .

References

The Acton Society Trust, *Size and Morale* (London: The Trust, 1953).

Behrend, J., "Absence and Labour Turnover in a Changing Economic Climate," *Occupational Psychology*, 27 (1953), pp. 69–79.

Brayfield, A. H., and W. H. Crockett, "Employee Attitudes and Employee Performance," *Psychological Bulletin*, 52 (1955), pp. 396–424.

Clark, L. H., ed., *Consumer Behavior* (New York: New York University, 1958).

Freeman, J. L., *The Political Process, Executive Bureau-Legislative Committee Relations* (New York: Random House, 1955).

Mayo, E., and G. F. Lombard, *Teamwork and Labor Turnover in the Aircraft Industry of Southern California* (Cambridge, Mass.: Division of Research, Harvard University, 1944).

Morse, N. C., *Satisfactions in the White-Collar Job* (Ann Arbor, Mich.: Survey Research Center, University of Michigan, 1953).

Reynolds, L. G., *The Structure of Labor Markets* (New York: Harper & Row, 1951).

Rice, A. K., J. M. M. Hill, and E. L. Trist, "The Representation of Labour Turnover as a Social Process," *Human Relations*, 3 (1950), pp. 349–372.

Simon, H. A., "A Comparison of Organization Theories," *The Review of Economic Studies*, 20 (1952–1953), pp. 40–48.

————, D. W. Smithburg, and V. A. Thompson, *Public Administration* (New York: Knopf, 1950), pp. 381–382.

Truman, D. B., *The Governmental Process* (New York: Knopf, 1951).

Bureaucratic Structure and Personality
Robert K. Merton

A formal, rationally organized social structure involves clearly defined patterns of activity in which, ideally, every series of actions is functionally related to the purposes of the organization.[1] In such an organization there is integrated a series of offices, of hierarchized statuses, in which inhere a number of obligations and privileges closely defined by limited and specific rules. Each of these offices contains an area of imputed competence and responsibility. Authority, the power of control which derives from an acknowledged status, inheres in the office and not in the particular person who performs the official role. Official action ordinarily occurs within the framework of pre-existing rules of the organization. The system of prescribed relations between the various offices involves a considerable degree of formality and clearly defined social distance between the occupants of these positions. Formality is manifested by means of a more or less complicated social ritual which symbolizes and supports the pecking order of the various offices. Such formality, which is integrated with the distribution of authority within the system, serves to minimize friction by largely restricting (official) contact to modes which are previously defined by the rules of the organization. Ready calculability of others' behavior and a stable set of mutual expectations is thus built up. Moreover, formality facilitates the interaction of the occupants of offices despite their (possibly hostile) private attitudes toward one another. In this way, the subordinate is protected from the arbitrary action of his superior, since the actions of both are constrained by a mutually recognized set of rules. Specific procedural devices foster objectivity and restrain the "quick passage of impulse into action."[2]

The Structure of Bureaucracy

The ideal type of such formal organization is bureaucracy and, in many respects, the classical analysis of bureaucracy is that by Max Weber.[3] As Weber indicates, bureaucracy involves a clear-cut division of integrated activities which are regarded as duties inherent in the office. A system of differentiated controls and sanctions is stated in the regulations. The assignment of roles occurs on the basis of technical qualifications which are ascertained through formalized, impersonal procedures (*e.g.*, examinations). Within the structure of hierarchically arranged authority, the activities of "trained and salaried experts" are governed by general, abstract, and clearly defined rules which preclude the necessity for the issuance of specific instructions for each specific case. The generality of the rules requires the constant use of *categorization*, whereby individual problems and cases are classified on the basis of designated criteria and are treated accordingly. The pure type of bureaucratic official is appointed, either by a superior or through the exercise of impersonal competition; he is not elected. A measure of flexibility in the bureaucracy is attained by electing higher functionaries who presumably express the will of the electorate (e.g., a body of citizens or a board of directors). The election of higher officials is designed to affect the purposes of the organization, but the technical procedures for attaining these ends are carried out by continuing bureaucratic personnel.[4]

Most bureaucratic offices involve the expectation of life-long tenure, in the absence of disturbing factors which may decrease the size of the organization. Bureaucracy maximizes vocational security.[5] The function of security of tenure, pensions, incremental salaries and regularized procedures for promotion is to ensure the devoted performance of official duties, without regard for extraneous pressures.[6] The chief merit of bureaucracy is its technical efficiency, with a premium placed on precision, speed, expert control, continuity, discretion, and optimal returns on input. The structure is one which approaches the complete elimination of personalized relationships and nonrational considerations (hostility, anxiety, affectual involvements, etc.)

With increasing bureaucratization, it becomes plain to all who would see that man is to a very important degree controlled by his social relations to the instruments of production. This can no longer seem only a tenet of Marxism, but a stubborn fact to be acknowledged by all, quite apart from their ideological persuasion. Bureaucratization makes readily visible what was previously dim and obscure. More and more people discover that to work, they must be employed. For to work, one must have tools and equipment. And the tools and equipment are increasingly available only in bureaucracies, private or public. Consequently, one must be employed by the bureaucracies in order to have access to tools in order to work in order to live. It is in this sense that bureaucratization entails separation of individuals from the instruments of production, as in modern capitalistic enterprise or in state communistic enterprise (of the midcentury variety), just as in the post-feudal army, bureaucratization entailed complete separation from the instruments of destruction. Typically, the worker no longer owns his tools nor the soldier, his weapons. And in this special sense, more and more people become workers, either blue collar or white collar or stiff shirt. So develops, for example, the new type of scientific worker, as the scientist is "separated" from his technical equipment—after all, the physicist does not ordinarily own his cyclotron. To work at his research, he must be employed by a bureaucracy with laboratory resources.

Bureaucracy is administration which almost completely avoids public discussion of its techniques, although there may occur public discussion of its policies.[7] This secrecy is confined neither to public nor to private bureaucracies. It is held to be necessary to keep valuable information from private economic competitors or from foreign and potentially hostile political groups. And though it is not often so called, espionage among competitors is perhaps as common, if not as intricately organized, in systems of private economic enterprise as in systems of national states. Cost figures, lists of clients, new technical processes, plans for production—all these are typically regarded as essential secrets of private economic bureaucracies which might be revealed if the bases of all decisions and policies had to be publicly defended.

The Dysfunctions of Bureaucracy

In these bold outlines, the positive attainments and functions of bureaucratic organization are emphasized and the internal stresses and strains of such structures are almost wholly neglected. The community at large, however, evidently emphasizes the imperfections of bureaucracy, as is suggested by the fact that the "horrid hybrid," bureaucrat, has become an epithet, a *Schimpfwort*.

The transition to a study of the negative aspects of bureaucracy is afforded by the application of Veblen's concept of "trained incapacity," Dewey's notion of "occupational psychosis" or Warnotte's view of "professional deformation." Trained incapacity refers to that state of affairs in which one's abilities function as inadequacies or blind spots. Actions based upon training and skills which have been successfully applied in the past may result in inappropriate responses *under changed conditions*. An inadequate flexibility in the application of skills, will, in a changing milieu, result in more or less serious maladjustments.[8] Thus, to adopt a barnyard illustration used in this connection by Burke, chickens may be readily conditioned to interpret the sound of a bell as a signal for food. The same bell may now be used to summon the trained chickens to their doom as they are assembled to suffer decapitation. In general, one adopts measures in keeping with one's past training and, under new conditions which are not recognized as *significantly* different, the very soundness of this training may lead to the adoption of the wrong procedures. Again, in Burke's almost echolalic phrase, "people may be unfitted by being fit in an unfit fitness"; their training may become an incapacity.

Dewey's concept of occupational psychosis rests upon much the same observations. As a result of their day to day routines, people develop special preferences, antipathies, discriminations and emphases.[9] (The term psychosis is used by Dewey to denote a "pronounced character of the mind.") These psychoses develop through demands put upon the individual by the particular organization of his occupational role.

The concepts of both Veblen and Dewey refer to a fundamental ambivalence. Any action can be considered in terms of what it attains or what it fails to attain. "A way of seeing is also a way of not seeing—a focus upon object *A* involves a neglect of object *B*."[10] In his discussion, Weber is almost exclusively concerned with what the bureaucratic structure attains: precision, reliability, efficiency. This same structure may be examined from another perspective provided by the ambivalence. What are the limitations of the organizations designed to attain these goals?

For reasons which we have already noted, the bureaucratic structure exerts a constant pressure upon the official to be "methodical, prudent, disciplined." If the bureaucracy is to operate successfully, it must attain a high degree of reliability of behavior, an unusual degree of conformity with prescribed patterns of action. Hence, the fundamental importance of discipline which may be as highly developed in a religious or economic bureaucracy as in the army. Discipline can be effective only if the ideal patterns are buttressed by strong sentiments which entail devotion to one's duties, a keen sense of the limitation of one's authority and competence, and methodical performance of routine activities. The efficacy of social structure depends ultimately upon infusing group participants with appropriate attitudes and sentiments. As we shall see, there are definite arrangements in the bureaucracy for inculcating and reinforcing these sentiments.

At the moment, it suffices to observe that in order to ensure discipline (the necessary reliability of response), these sentiments are often more intense than is technically necessary. There is a margin of safety, so to speak, in the pressure exerted by these sentiments upon the bureaucrat to conform to his patterned obligations, in much the same sense that added allowances (precautionary overestimations) are made by the engineer in designing the supports for a bridge. But this very emphasis leads to a transference of the sentiments from the *aims* of the organization onto the particular details of behavior required by the rules. Adherence to the rules, originally conceived as a means, becomes transformed into an end-in-itself; there occurs the familiar process of *displacement of goals* whereby "an instrumental value becomes a terminal value."[11] Discipline, readily interpreted as conformance with regulations, whatever the situation, is seen not as a measure designed for specific purposes but becomes an immediate value in the life-organization of the bureaucrat. This emphasis, resulting from the displacement of the original goals, develops into rigidities and an inability to adjust readily. Formalism, even ritualism, ensues with an unchallenged insistence upon punctilious adherence to formalized procedures.[12] This may be exaggerated to the point where primary concern with conformity to the rules interferes with the achievement of the purposes of the organization, in which case we have the familiar phenomenon of the technicism or red tape of the official. An extreme product of this process of displacement of goals is the bureaucratic virtuoso, who never forgets a single rule binding his action and hence is unable to assist many of his clients.[13] A case in point, where strict recognition of the limits of authority and literal adherence to rules produced this result, is the pathetic plight of Bernt Balchen, Admiral Byrd's pilot in the flight over the South Pole.

> According to a ruling of the department of labor Bernt Balchen . . . cannot receive his citizenship papers. Balchen, a native of Norway, declared his intention in 1927. It is held that he has failed to meet the condition of five years' continuous residence in the United States. The Byrd antarctic voyage took him out of the country, although he was on a ship carrying the American flag, was an invaluable member of the American expedition, and in a region to which there is an American claim because of the exploration and occupation of it by Americans, this region being Little America.
>
> The bureau of naturalization explains that it cannot proceed on the assumption that Little America is American soil. That would be *trespass on international questions* where it has no sanction. So far as the bureau is concerned, Balchen was out of the country and *technically* has not complied with the law of naturalization.[14]

Structural Sources of Overconformity

Such inadequacies in orientation which involve trained incapacity clearly derive from structural sources. The process may be briefly recapitulated. (1) An effective bureaucracy demands reliability of response and strict devotion to regulations. (2) Such devotion to the rules leads to their transformation into absolutes; they are no longer conceived as relative to a set of purposes. (3) This interferes with ready adaptation under special conditions not clearly envisaged by those who drew up the general rules. (4) Thus, the very elements which conduce toward efficiency in general produce inefficiency in specific instances. Full realization of the inadequacy is seldom attained by members of the group who have not divorced themselves from the meanings which the rules have for them. These rules in time become symbolic in cast, rather than strictly utilitarian.

Thus far, we have treated the ingrained sentiments making for rigorous discipline simply as data, as given. However, definite features of the bureaucratic structure may be seen to conduce to these sentiments. The bureaucrat's official life is planned for him in terms of a graded career, through the organizational devices of promotion by seniority, pensions, incremental salaries, *etc.*, all of which are designed to provide incentives for disciplined action and conformity to the official regulations.[15] The official is tacitly expected to and largely does adapt his thoughts, feelings and actions to the prospect of this career. But *these very devices* which increase the probability of conformance also lead to an overconcern with strict adherence to regulations which induces timidity, conservatism, and technicism. Displacement of sentiments from goals onto means is fostered by the tremendous symbolic significance of the means (rules).

Another feature of the bureaucratic structure tends to produce much the same result. Functionaries have the sense of a common destiny for all those who work together. They share the same interests, especially since there is relatively little competition in so far as promotion is in terms of seniority. In-group aggression is thus minimized and this arrangement is therefore conceived to be positively functional for the bureaucracy. However, the *esprit de corps* and informal social organization which typically develops in such situations often leads the personnel to defend their entrenched interests rather than to assist their clientele and elected higher officials. As President Lowell reports, if the bureaucrats believe that their status is not adequately recognized by an incoming elected official, detailed information will be withheld from him, leading him to errors for which he is held responsible. Or, if he seeks to dominate fully, and thus violates the sentiment of self-integrity of the bureaucrats, he may have documents brought to him in such numbers that he cannot manage to sign them all, let alone read them.[16] This illustrates the defensive informal organization which tends to arise whenever there is an apparent threat to the integrity of the group.[17]

It would be much too facile and partly erroneous to attribute such resistance by bureaucrats simply to vested interests. Vested interests oppose any new order which either eliminates or at least makes uncertain their differential advantage deriving from the current arrangements. This is undoubtedly involved in part in bureaucratic resistance to change, but another process is perhaps more significant. As we have seen, bureaucratic officials affectively identify themselves with their way of life. They have a pride of craft which leads them to resist change in established routines; at least, those changes which are felt to be imposed by others. This non-logical pride of craft is a familiar pattern found even, to judge from Sutherland's *Professional Thief*, among pickpockets who, despite the risk, delight in mastering the prestige-bearing feat of "beating a left breech" (picking the left front trousers pocket).

In a stimulating paper, Hughes has applied the concepts of "secular" and "sacred" to various types of division of labor; "the sacredness" of caste and *Stände* prerogatives contrasts sharply with the increasing secularism of occupational differentiation in our society.[18] However, as our discussion suggests, there may ensue, in particular vocations and in particular types of organization, the *process of sanctification* (viewed as the counterpart of the process of secularization). This is to say that through sentiment-formation, emotional dependence upon bureaucratic symbols and status, and affective involvement in spheres of competence and authority, there develop prerogatives involving attitudes of moral legitimacy which are established as values in their own right, and are no longer viewed as merely technical means for expediting administration. One may note a tendency for certain bureaucratic norms, originally introduced for technical reasons, to became rigidified and sacred, although, as Durkheim would say, they are *laïque en apparence*.[19] Durkheim has touched on this general process in his description of the attitudes and values which persist in the organic solidarity of a highly differentiated society.

Primary Versus Secondary Relations

Another feature of the bureaucratic structure, the stress on depersonalization of relationships, also plays its part in the bureaucrat's trained incapacity. The personality pattern of the bureaucrat is nucleated about this norm of impersonality. Both this and the categorizing tendency, which develops from the dominant role of general, abstract rules, tend to produce conflict in the bureaucrat's contacts with the public or clientele. Since functionaries minimize personal relations and resort to categorization, the peculiarities of individual cases are often ignored. But the client who, quite understandably, is convinced of the special features of *his* own problem often objects to such categorical treatment. Stereotyped behavior is not adapted to the exigencies of individual problems. The impersonal treatment of affairs which are at times of great personal significance to the client gives rise to the charge of "arrogance" and "haughtiness" of the bureaucrat. Thus, at the Greenwich Employment Exchange, the unemployed worker who is securing his insurance payment resents what he deems to be "the impersonality and, at times, the apparent abruptness and even harshness of his treatment by the clerks. . . . Some men complain of the superior attitude which the clerks have."[20]

Still another source of conflict with the public derives from the bureaucratic structure. The bureaucrat, in part irrespective of his position with*in* the hierarchy, acts as a representative of the power and prestige of the entire structure. In his official role he is vested with definite authority. This often leads to an actually or apparently domineering attitude, which may only be exaggerated by a discrepancy between his position within the hierarchy and his position with reference to the public.[21] Protest and recourse to other officials on the part of the client are often ineffective or largely precluded by the previously mentioned *esprit de corps* which joins the officials into a more or less solidary in-group. This source of conflict *may* be minimized in private enterprise since the client can register an effective protest by transferring his trade to another organization within the competitive system. But with the monopolistic nature of the public organization, no such alternative is possible. Moreover, in this case, tension is increased because of a discrepancy between ideology and fact: the governmental personnel are held to be "servants of the people," but in fact they are often superordinate, and release of tension can seldom be afforded by turning to other agencies for the necessary service.[22] This tension is in part attributable to the confusion of the status of bureaucrat and client; the client may consider himself socially superior to the official who is at the moment dominant.[23]

Thus, with respect to the relations between officials and clientele, one structural source of conflict is the pressure for formal and impersonal treatment when individual, personalized consideration is desired by the client. The conflict may be viewed, then, as deriving from the introduction of inappropriate attitudes and relationships. Conflict with*in* the bureaucratic structure arises from the converse situation, namely, when personalized relationships are substituted for the structurally required impersonal relationships. This type of conflict may be characterized as follows.

The bureaucracy, as we have seen, is organized as a secondary, formal group. The normal responses involved in this organized network of social expectations are supported by affective attitudes of members of the group. Since the group is oriented toward secondary norms of impersonality, any failure to conform to these norms will arouse antagonism from those who have identified themselves with the legitimacy of these rules. Hence, the substitution of personal for impersonal treatment within the structure is met with widespread disapproval and is characterized by such epithets as graft, favoritism, nepotism, apple-polishing, etc. These epithets are clearly manifestations of injured sentiments.[24] The function of such virtually automatic resentment can be clearly seen in terms of the requirements of bureaucratic structure.

Bureaucracy is a secondary group structure designed to carry on certain activities which cannot be satisfactorily performed on the basis of primary group criteria.[25] Hence behavior which runs counter to these formalized norms becomes the object of emotionalized disapproval. This constitutes a functionally significant defence set up against tendencies which jeopardize the performance of socially necessary activities. To be sure, these reactions are not rationally determined practices explicitly designed for the fulfillment of this function. Rather, viewed in terms of the individual's interpretation of the situation, such resentment is simply an immediate response opposing the "dishonesty" of those who violate the rules of the game. However, this subjective frame of reference notwithstanding, these reactions serve the latent function of maintaining the essential structural elements of bureaucracy by reaffirming the necessity for formalized, secondary relations and by helping to prevent the disintegration of the bureaucratic structure which would occur should these be supplanted by personalized relations. This type of conflict may be generically described as the intrusion of primary group attitudes when secondary group attitudes are institutionally demanded, just as the bureaucrat-client conflict often derives from interaction on impersonal terms when personal treatment is individually demanded.[26]

Problems for Research

The trend towards increasing bureaucratization in Western Society, which Weber had long since foreseen, is not the sole reason for sociologists to turn their attention to this field. Empirical studies of the interaction of bureaucracy and personality should especially increase our understanding of social structure. A large number of specific questions invite our attention. To what extent are particular personality types selected and modified by the various bureaucracies (private enterprise, public service, the quasi-legal political machine, religious orders)? Inasmuch as ascendancy and submission are held to be traits of personality, despite their variability in different stimulus-situations, do bureaucracies select personalities of particularly submissive or ascendant tendencies? And since various studies have shown that these traits can be modified, does participation in bureaucratic office tend to increase ascendant tendencies? Do various systems of recruitment (e.g., patronage, open competition involving specialized knowledge or general mental capacity, practical experience) select different personality types?[27] Does promotion through seniority lessen competitive anxieties and enhance administrative efficiency? A detailed examination of mechanisms for imbuing the bureaucratic codes with affect would be instructive both sociologically and psychologically. Does the general anonymity of civil service decisions tend to restrict the area of prestige-symbols to a narrowly defined inner circle? Is there a tendency for differential association to be especially marked among bureaucrats?

The range of theoretically significant and practically important questions would seem to be limited only by the accessibility of the concrete data. Studies of religious, educational, military, economic, and political bureaucracies dealing with the interdependence of social organization and personality formation should constitute an avenue for fruitful research. On that avenue, the functional analysis of concrete structures may yet build a Solomon's House for sociologists.

Notes

1. For a development of the concept of "rational organization," see Karl Mannheim, *Mensch und Gesellschaft im Zeitalter des Umbaus* (Leiden: A. W. Sijthoff, 1935), esp. 28 ff.
2. H. D. Lasswell, *Politics* (New York: McGraw-Hill, 1936), 120–121.
3. Max Weber, *Wirtschaft und Gesellschaft* (Tübingen: J. C. B. Mohr, 1922), Pt. III, chap. 6; 650–678. For a brief summary of Weber's discussion, see Talcott Parsons, *The Structure of Social Action*, esp. 506 ff. For a description, which is not a caricature, of the bureaucrat as a personality type, see C. Rabany, "Les types sociaux: le fonctionnaire," *Revue générale d'administration*, 1907, 88, 5–28.
4. Karl Mannheim, *Ideology and Utopia* (New York: Harcourt, 1936), 18n., 105 ff. See also Ramsay Muir, *Peers and Bureaucrats* (London: Constable, 1910), 12–13.
5. E. G. Cahen-Salvador suggests that the personnel of bureaucracies is largely constituted by those who value security above all else. See his "La situation matérielle et morale des fonctionnaires," *Revue politique et parlementaire* (1926), 319.
6. H. J. Laski, "Bureaucracy," *Encyclopedia of the Social Sciences*. This article is written primarily from the standpoint of the political scientist rather than that of the sociologist.
7. Weber, *op. cit.*, 671.
8. For a stimulating discussion and application of these concepts, see Kenneth Burke, *Permanence and Change* (New York: New Republic, 1935), pp. 50 ff.; Daniel Warnotte, "Bureaucratie et Fonctionnarisme," *Revue de l'Institut de Sociologie*, 1937, 17, 245.
9. *Ibid.*, 58–59.
10. *Ibid.*, 70.
11. This process has often been observed in various connections. Wundt's *heterogony of ends* is a case in point; Max Weber's *Paradoxie der Folgen* is another. See also MacIver's observations on the transformation of civilization into culture and Lasswell's remark that "the human animal distinguishes himself by his infinite capacity for making ends of his means." See Merton, "The unanticipated consequences of purposive social action," *American Sociological Review*, 1936, 1, 894–904. In terms of the psychological mechanisms involved, this process has been analyzed most fully by Gordon W. Allport, in his discussion of what he calls "the functional autonomy of motives." Allport emends the earlier formulations of Woodworth, Tolman, and William Stern, and arrives at a statement of the process from the standpoint of individual motivation. He does not consider those phases of the social structure which conduce toward the "transformation of motives." The formulation adopted in this paper is thus complementary to Allport's analysis; the one stressing the psychological mechanisms involved, the other considering the constraints of the social structure. The convergence of psychology and sociology

toward this central concept suggests that it may well constitute one of the conceptual bridges between the two disciplines. See Gordon W. Allport, *Personality* (New York: Holt, Rinehart and Winston, 1937), chap. 7.

12. See E. C. Hughes, "Institutional office and the person," *American Journal of Sociology*, 1937, 43, 404–413; E. T. Hiller, "Social structure in relation to the person," *Social Forces*, 1937, 16, 34–43.

13. Mannheim, *Ideology and Utopia*, 106.

14. Quoted from the *Chicago Tribune* (June 24, 1931, p. 10) by Thurman Arnold, *The Symbols of Government* (New Haven, Conn.: Yale University Press, 1935), 201–202. (My italics.)

15. Mannheim, *Mensch und Gesellschaft*, 32–33. Mannheim stresses the importance of the "Lebensplan" and the "Amtskarriere." See the comments by Hughes, *op. cit.*, 413.

16. A. L. Lowell, *The Government of England* (New York, 1908), I, 189 ff.

17. For an instructive description of the development of such a defensive organization in a group of workers, see F. J. Roethlisberger and W. J. Dickson, *Management and the Worker* (Boston: Harvard School of Business Administration, 1934).

18. E. C. Hughes, "Personality types and the division of labor," *American Journal of Sociology*, 1928, 33, 754–768. Much the same distinction is drawn by Leopold von Wiese and Howard Becker, *Systematic Sociology* (New York: Wiley, 1932), 222–225 *et passim*.

19. Hughes recognizes one phase of this process of sanctification when he writes that professional training "carries with it as a by-product assimilation of the candidate to a set of professional attitudes and controls, *a professional conscience and solidarity. The profession claims and aims to become a moral unit.*" Hughes, *op. cit.*, 762 (italics inserted). In this same connection, Sumner's concept of *pathos*, as the halo of sentiment which protects a social value from criticism, is particularly relevant, inasmuch as it affords a clue to the mechanism involved in the process of sanctification. See his *Folkways*, 180–181.

20. "'They treat you like a lump of dirt they do. I see a navvy reach across the counter and shake one of them by the collar the other day. The rest of us felt like cheering. Of course he lost his benefit over it. . . . But the clerk deserved it for his sassy way.'" (E. W. Bakke, *The Unemployed Man*, 79–80). Note that the domineering attitude was *imputed* by the unemployed client who is in a state of tension due to his loss of status and self-esteem in a society where the ideology is still current that an "able man" can always find a job. That the imputation of arrogance stems largely from the client's state of mind is seen from Bakke's own observation that "the clerks were rushed, and had no time for pleasantries, but there was little sign of harshness or a superiority feeling in their treatment of the men." In so far as there is an objective basis for the imputation of arrogant behavior to bureaucrats, it may possibly be explained by the following juxtaposed statements. "Auch der moderne, sei es öffentliche, sei es private, Beamte erstrebt immer und geniesst meist den Beherrschten gegenüber eine spezifisch gehobene, 'ständische' soziale Schätzung." (Weber, *op. cit.*, 652.) "In persons in whom the craving for prestige is uppermost, hostility usually takes the form of a desire to humiliate others." K. Horney, *The Neurotic Personality of Our Time*, 178–179.

21. In this connection, note the relevance of Koffka's comments on certain features of the pecking-order of birds. "If one compares the behavior of the bird at the top of the pecking list, the despot, with that of one very far down, the second or third from the last, then one finds the latter much more cruel to the few others over whom he lords it than the former in his treatment of all members. As soon as one removes from the group all members above the penultimate, his behavior becomes milder and may even become very friendly. . . . It is not difficult to find analogies to this in human societies, and therefore one side of such behavior must be primarily the effects of the social groupings, and not of individual characteristics." K. Koffka, *Principles of Gestalt Psychology* (New York: Harcourt, 1935), 668–669.

22. At this point the political machine often becomes functionally significant. As Steffens

and others have shown, highly personalized relations and the abrogation of formal rules (red tape) by the machine often satisfy the needs of individual "clients" more fully than the formalized mechanism of governmental bureaucracy.

23. As one of the unemployed men remarked about the clerks at the Greenwich Employment Exchange: "'And the bloody blokes wouldn't have their jobs if it wasn't for us men out of a job either. That's what gets me about their holding their noses up.'" Bakke, *op. cit.*, 80. See also H. D. Lasswell and G. Almond, "Aggressive behavior by clients towards public relief administrators," *American Political Science Review*, 1934, 28, 643–655.

24. The diagnostic significance of such linguistic indices as epithets has scarcely been explored by the sociologist. Sumner properly observes that epithets produce "summary criticisms" and definitions of social situations. Dollard also notes that "epithets frequently define the central issues in a society," and Sapir has rightly emphasized the importance of context of situations in appraising the significance of epithets. Of equal relevance is Linton's observation that "in case histories the way in which the community felt about a particular episode is, if anything, more important to our study than the actual behavior. . . ." A sociological study of "vocabularies of encomium and opprobrium" should lead to valuable findings.

25. *Cf.* Ellsworth Faris, *The Nature of Human Nature* (New York: McGraw-Hill, 1937), 41 ff.

26. Community disapproval of many forms of behavior may be analyzed in terms of one or the other of these patterns of substitution of culturally inappropriate types of relationship. Thus, prostitution constitutes a type-case where coitus, a form of intimacy which is institutionally defined as symbolic of the most "sacred" primary group relationship, is placed within a contractual context, symbolized by the exchange of that most impersonal of all symbols, money. See Kingsley Davis, "The sociology of prostitution," *American Sociological Review*, 1937, 2, 744–755.

27. Among recent studies of recruitment to bureaucracy are: Reinhard Bendix, *Higher Civil Servants in American Society* (Boulder, Colo.: University of Colorado Press, 1949); Dwaine Marvick, *Career Perspectives in a Bureaucratic Setting* (Ann Arbor, Mich.: University of Michigan Press, 1954); R. K. Kelsall, *Higher Civil Servants in Britain* (London: Routledge, 1955); W. L. Warner and J. C. Abegglen, *Occupational Mobility in American Business and Industry* (Minneapolis, Minn.: University of Minnesota Press, 1955).

Closed-System, Open-System, and Contingency-Choice Perspectives
Richard H. Hall

Organizations can be approached from a *closed-* or *open-*system perspective.[1] The closed-system model views organizations as instruments designed for the pursuit of clearly specified goals, and thus directing organizational arrangements and decisions toward goal achievement and toward making the organization more and more rational in the pursuit of its goals (management, structural, and aspects of economic theory). The open-system model (technology, group, individual, and some aspects of economic theory) views organizations as not only concerned with goals, but as also responding to external and internal pressures. In some cases, the open perspective virtually ignores the issue of goals.

The Organization as a Closed System

The closed-system perspective is traditionally tied to Max Weber's early writings on bureaucracy. While Weber has been overly criticized for ignoring factors that would deflect an organization from a pure closed system, much of his writing is concerned with how organizations can structure themselves for the utmost rationality.

Weber's ideal type of bureaucracy is one in which the goals and purposes are clear and explicit. Organizational rules, procedures, and regulations are derived from the goals in a manner that says in effect, "If this is the goal, then, this is the most rational procedure for achieving it." The tasks to be performed in the achievement of this goal are subdivided among the members of the organization so that each member has a limited sphere of activity that is matched to his own competence. Offices (positions) are arranged in a pyramidal hierarchy, with each office having more authority than those below it. Decision making is based upon officially established rules and criteria that are attached to the position. If a decision is required that is beyond the realm of a position at a particular level, it is passed up to the next level. Members participate in the organization on the basis of contractual (written or otherwise) agreements, and the participation is based upon remuneration, typically in the form of a wage or salary. (Voluntary organizations are obviously another matter. They have not been examined carefully from this perspective.) The person fills the office or position, so that in an important way it does not matter who the person is, since his behavior is guided by the organiza-

RichardH. Hall, *Organizations: Structure and Process*, © 1977, pp. 49–64. Reprinted by permission of Prentice-Hall, Inc., Englewood Cliffs, New Jersey. Quotations from *Organizations in Action* by James D. Thompson, © 1967, are reprinted by permission of the publisher, McGraw-Hill Book Company. Excerpts from "An Axiomatic Theory of Organizations" by Jerald Hage are used by permission of *Administrative Science Quarterly*. Excerpts from *The Social Psychology of Organizations* by Daniel Katz and Robert L. Kahn, © 1966 by John Wiley & Sons, Inc., are reprinted by permission of the publisher.

tionally established normative order. Selection for membership is based on the person's technical competence—the combination of the individual's skills and the requirements of the position determining who shall be employed and in what position. Interpersonal relationships are maintained on an impersonal basis, so that socio-emotional elements do not intrude into organizational operations.

It has been demonstrated that these elements do not appear together in reality.[2] It is also clear that this is too limited a perspective on organizations from any other bases as well. Nonetheless, this approach to organizations persists in the literature. An example is Jerald Hage's attempt to develop an "axiomatic theory of organizations."[3] The variables selected for inclusion in the theory and the indicators used to measure these variables reflect a closed-system approach, although Hage's other work does not take a closed-system view of the world.

Hage considers four organizational ends or goals.[4] The first is adaptiveness, or flexibility, and is to be measured by the number of new programs per year and the number of new techniques adopted per year. Flexibility in other contexts usually refers to adaptation to external influences or other disturbing factors, and Hage suggests that environmental influences are important. At the same time, however, new programs and new techniques can be developed on the basis of internal considerations. The second organizational end is production, or effectiveness, measured by the number of units produced per year and the rate of increase in the number of units produced per year. This is clearly an internal consideration. The third goal is efficiency, or the cost factor, and is measured by the cost per unit of output per year and the amount of idle resources per year. The final end is job satisfaction, or morale. This is measured by the employees' satisfaction with working conditions and by the turnover rate of job occupants per year. These ends involve more than just output; basically, they reflect internal organizational factors, with only minimal concern paid to external considerations. They are also part of a conceptual model that views the organization as a system in and of itself.

The "closedness" of this approach is emphasized when the means to these ends are discussed. Hage gives four organizational means.[5] The first is complexity, or specialization, which is measured by the number of occupational specialties and the level of training required for them. Complexity is necessary because "organizations must divide work into jobs in order to achieve their specific objectives." This statement is, of course, extremely close to Weber's position. The second means is centralization, or hierarchy of authority, and is measured by the proportion of occupations or jobs whose holders participate in decision making and the number of areas in which they participate. The third means is formalization, or standardization, measured as the number of jobs that are codified and the range of variation allowed within jobs. The final means is stratification, or the status system. This is measured by the differences in income and prestige among jobs and the rate of mobility between low- and high-ranking jobs or status levels. As might be expected, these means are totally internal to the organization.

From these ends and means, Hage develops a set of propositions and corollaries . . . Whether these are empirically valid is not the issue at this point. What is important is the perspective taken that organizations can be understood on the basis of these basically internal factors. As we shall demonstrate, many of the factors that Hage labels as means are in fact related. The ends part of the equation is probably too internally oriented to satisfy most organizational analysts. Nevertheless, Hage's supporting evidence is strong and provides partial substantiation for the propositions and corollaries he derives. Undoubtedly, however, factors other than the means and ends discussed have an effect on them, and thus while the theory is axiomatic, it is also incomplete.

Organizations are not closed systems for the sake of being closed systems. It is at this point that the idea of rationality within the closed system must be introduced. The closed-system perspective is a way of approaching and optimizing organizational rationality—linking means to ends. Thompson captures the essence of this point when he notes, "The rational model of an organization results in everything being functional—making a positive, indeed an optimum, contribution to the overall result. All resources are appropriate resources, and their allocation fits a master plan. All action is appropriate action, and its outcomes are predictable."[6]

A Critique of the Closed-system Perspective

Approached from a purely rational viewpoint, the organization must make a perfect link between ends and means. In the closed-system perspective, it can do so internally; it can arrange itself so that the conditions Thompson suggests can be achieved. But obviously, this is more easily said than done. In developing his critique of the rational model, Thompson says that in order to be as rational as possible, organizations must "buffer" themselves from environmental influences, anticipate those environmental changes that cannot be buffered against, and ration their resources when the environmental influences cannot be controlled.[7] This suggests strongly that *organizations are forced to move away from a purely rational model.* It also brings up the importance of environmental factors as they impinge upon the organization, a point that will be taken up shortly.

Organizations must grapple with their environment. In addition, there are two "internal" factors that cast doubt on the utility of a closed-systems perspective. The first of these internal factors is the failure of the organizational characteristics that are supposed to vary together or to characterize rational organizations to do so. Stanley H. Udy, Jr., found that "rational" and "bureaucratic" elements of organizations tended to "be mutually inconsistent in the same formal organization."[8] The presence of a hierarchy or a specialized administrative staff was not related to a performance emphasis or other indicators of an emphasis on goal attainment. Udy's data came from 150 nonindustrial societies. In a study of contemporary organizations, Hall found that the elements within organizations that were supposed to be arranged in a neat, harmonious fashion instead had weak and negative relationships with each other.[9] Both sets of findings suggest that the patterning found within organizations is based on more than conditions internal to organizations.

The second factor internal to the organization that throws doubt on the total utility of the closed-system approach is the nature of the organizational members themselves. The closed-system approach tends to assume that people will act in accordance with the organization's desires. Most of the time, this is probably the case. However, there is enough deviation from norm and role expectations to expose as extremely naive the idea that organizational members are well-oiled machines.

The James March and Herbert Simon discussion of the shortcomings of viewing humans as machines in a closed-system perspective has become a classic in the field.[10] March and Simon note that an individual must be motivated to participate and produce in the organizational setting. The individual is confronted with a series of action alternatives that he could pursue. Each of these alternatives has consequences for the individual, and the consequences in turn are valued differentially by the individual. These values are affected by the identification patterns of the individual. For instance, there can be work group identity, which may or may not have values that coincide with those of the organization. The individual is also confronted with the dynamics of the group, perhaps in a situation in which competition is required by the organization or develops on its own. In either case, individual behavior is different from what it would be under conditions of cooperation.

At the same time, the individual has external sources of identification, such as family, union, or professional organization. The literature on professionals in organizations strongly suggests that membership in a profession influences the individual employed in an organization.[11] Professional values are brought into the organization, and if the organization wants the professional to do something that is in violation of professional norms and values, the professional is apt to reject or substantially alter the organizational requirements. Professionals or trade union members are usually in the "enviable" position of being able to leave an organization for another very readily, because there are probably many other organizations ready and willing to pay for their services.

The organization member can also identify with the organization itself. This is fine, but only up to a point. If it is carried too far, or if the identification is with organizational means and not ends, it can be dysfunctional for the organization as well as for the individual. Merton's concept of the bureaucratic personality, with its rigid adherence to rules, inflexibility with clients, and unadaptability, and Victor Thompson's concept of "bureaupathology," with many of the same characteristics, are indicative of the manner in which overadherence to and identification with organizational means can deflect the individual from the behavior that is most beneficial to the organization.[12]

March and Simon also point out that there are limits to individual cognitive abilities, thus limiting the extent of rational decisions in or out of the organizational context. March and Simon propose that decisions are *satisficing* rather than optimal.[13] That is, given human limitations, even when assisted by computers, the decisions that are made in an organization are not as optimal as they would be if humans had access to, and the ability to interpret, all relevant information before making a decision. The norm of rationality itself cannot therefore be viewed as a set standard, but rather as a guideline from which deviation is expected.

The criticism of the closed-system perspective thus far has concentrated on factors that limit its utility from within the organization. As implied earlier, the major problem with this approach is that it tends to ignore external considerations. Katz and Kahn state:

> The major misconception is the failure to recognize fully that the organization is continually dependent upon inputs from the environment and that the inflow of materials and human energy is not constant. The fact that organizations have built-in protective devices to maintain stability and that they are notoriously difficult to change should not obscure the realities of the dynamic interrelationships of any social structure with its social and natural environment. The very efforts of the organization to maintain a constant external environment produce changes in organizational structure. The reactions to changed inputs to mute their possible revolutionary implications also results in changes.[14]

Katz and Kahn go on to note that there are additional misconceptions inherent in the closed-system model. They mention that there are more ways than one to produce a given outcome, and thus internal arrangements could vary rather widely to give rise to a common end. They also suggest that it is erroneous to view environmental influences as "error variances."[15] The environmental factors cannot be controlled in research or practice. Further, the closed-system approach ignores the importance of feedback for the information system of an organization.

Experience and practice in organizations indicate that the environment *does* play a major role in what happens within an organization. Since both input and output are directly related to the environment and are major components in any analysis, the closed-system perspective is, almost by definition, inadequate for a comprehensive understanding of organizations. From an empirical standpoint, too little of the variance within organizations is explained by internal factors. But despite all these shortcomings, the perspective persists in the literature and in practice, apparently for the reason that the closed-system approach does explain some of what organizations do. Organizations do try to maximize rationality, even if they are aware that they can attain only "satisficing" decisions. They do try to buffer, level, and smooth out environmental fluctuations. Since organizational actions are at least partially based on a closed-system perspective, it is a necessary component of the organizational analyst's repertoire, even though he recognizes that the technique will not be totally successful. Furthermore, the relationships found by Udy and Hall and suggested by Hage, whether positive or negative, are relationships. That is, an increase or decrease in the intensity of one internal factor is related to an increase or decrease in the intensity of another. Whether the source of the change is internal or external to the organization is thus irrelevant if the relationship is predictable. Predictable relationships are a prerequisite for theory or practice. The closed-system perspective would seem to be a similar prerequisite for the insights provided by other perspectives. With this in mind, let us examine the open-system perspective.

The Organization as an Open System

The distinction between the closed- and open-system approaches to organizations has its modern roots in the work of Alvin Gouldner. Gouldner distinguished between the "rational" and the "natural-system" models of organizations, the terms largely corresponding to our closed- and open-system perspectives, respectively. Gouldner describes the open-, or natural-, system approach as follows:

> The natural-system model regards the organization as a "natural whole," or system. The realization of the goals of the system as a whole is but one of several important needs to which the organization is oriented.[16]

One of these important needs is survival, which can lead to neglect or distortion of goal-seeking behavior. Organizational changes are seen as relatively unplanned, adaptive responses to threats to organizational equilibrium. The organization is seen as emergent, with organizational goals playing a relatively minor role in the directions in which the organization emerges. The natural-system approach also stresses the interdependence of the parts of organizations, noting that even a planned change in one part will have important, and usually unanticipated, ramifications for the rest of the system.

Gouldner's major concern is with developments within the organization that deflect it from the rational model. In a sense, this approach still views the organization as a closed system, since the emphasis is on developments and attempts to maintain homeostatic conditions within the organization. Gouldner hints at the importance of environmental factors but does not develop this consideration very far. From studies such as Michel Crozier's analysis of two French organizations, it is clear that the *general environment* surrounding an organization has a tremendous impact on how it is structured and operated, as well as on the goals it purports to seek.[17] The role of *other organizations* on the behavior of a focal organization has been clearly documented in the analyses of William Evan, J. Kenneth Benson, Howard Aldrich, Sol Levine and Paul White, and others.[18] Organizations are confronted from inside and outside with conditions that lead to the "natural" forms of development described by Gouldner. Survival is thus based on adaptation to both internal and external forces.

The open-system perspective has been more fully developed in the work of Katz and Kahn. They suggest nine common characteristics shared by all open systems:

1. *The importation of energy.* New supplies of energy are brought into the organization in the form of people and materials. This energy is supplied by other organizations or the general environment.
2. *The throughput.* This is simply the work that is done in the system (organization). The input is altered in some way as materials are processed or people are served.
3. *The output.* Whatever emerges from an organization is utilized, consumed, rejected, etc., by the environment.
4. *Systems as cycles of events.* Products sent into the environment are the basis for the source of energy for the repeating of the event. Industry uses labor and materials to produce a product that is sold. The income derived is used to buy more materials and labor. The voluntary organization can do something for its members that leads them to continue to contribute energy to the organization. In both cases the importation of new energy into the organization triggers a new cycle. Each cycle may be composed of subsystems or be a part of a larger system. At the same time, the cycles themselves are affected by changes in the total system.
5. *Negative entropy.* Organizations attempt to import more energy than they expend. Energy can be stockpiled to avoid the condition of using more energy than is imported. (The latter situation leads to organizational death.)
6. *Information input, negative feedback, and the coding process.* The information coming into an organization is coded and selected so that the organization is not inundated with more than it requires. Information provides signals from the environment, and negative feedback indicates deviations from what the environment desires. It is a control mechanism.
7. *The steady state and dynamic homeostasis.* Systems tend to maintain their basic character, attempting to control threatening external factors. As growth and expansion occur, basic system characteristics tend to remain constant. Under conditions of extreme growth or expansion, a new character may develop that will serve as a new homeostatic basis.
8. *Differentiation.* There is a tendency toward elaboration of roles and specialization of function.
9. *Equifinality.* Multiple means to the same ends exist within organizations. As knowledge increases, the number of relevant means may be reduced, but there will still be more than one way to accomplish objectives.[19]

The Katz and Kahn approach is built around the general systems model that is finding favor in many disciplines.[20] Although some of the terminology and concepts are obviously difficult to operationalize and use, the development of their system demonstrates the essence of the open-system approach. Organizations are affected by what comes into them in the form of input, by what transpires inside the organization, and by the nature of the environmental acceptance of the organization and its output. Understanding organizations involves much more than understanding goals and the arrangements that are developed for their accomplishment. . . .

A Critique of the Open-system Perspective

The open-system model is obviously much broader in its conceptual scope than is the closed-system approach. This breadth is vital for better understanding and operation of organizations. At the same time, as Etzioni suggests, the model is much more "exacting and expensive" when used for research.[21] Few researchers have the tools or the ability to take into account all the various components that must be included in even a relatively simple open-system model. The measurement of the various forms of inputs and the consequences of outputs has not been even moderately developed. For the practitioner, a full utilization of the model involves comprehending and evaluating the multiple factors that impinge upon his organization. March and Simon have stated that decision making in organizations is based on "bounded rationality." When the full implications of the open-system perspective are taken into consideration, the bounds on rationality become even more apparent.

The open-system perspective suggests that rationality within organizations is, or can be, drastically impaired and also that events occur without organizational intent—that interaction patterns, norms, and structure show tendencies to grow in number and complexity beyond what is foreseen or intended for the "official," formal system. A total acceptance of the open-system approach, especially as proposed by Gouldner, would make it appear that there is actually little need for organizations at all, since things just seem to happen. Rather obviously, this is too extreme a position. The very nature of organizations signifies that they do accomplish certain things. They do alter their inputs and produce outputs and make decisions; and these things are done on a relatively predictable and relatively stable basis. The Katz and Kahn notion of cycles of action suggests that organizational work is not composed of random actions. A basic question therefore is: Can the open-system and the closed-system perspectives be reconciled? Can the insights provided by each be combined in some way to yield more insights than does either perspective taken alone? At least partial answers to these questions are provided by James Thompson's work.

Thompson develops a set of propositions that describe how organizations act (or should act), given the fact of external and internal constraints on rationality. These propositions specify what organizations can do, in the face of threats to rationality, to stay as rational as possible. For example, "The more sectors in which the organization subject to rationality norms is constrained, the more power the organization will seek over remaining sectors of its task environment."[22] If an organization is constrained in one area, it will seek to reduce constraints in others, giving it more power in the total system than if it did not make such an attempt. For example, during an inflationary cycle, an organization with rising costs will seek power to increase its income through raising the prices for its goods and services. This is essentially a trade-off situation. The organization that is unable to gain power in other sectors and is thus totally dominated by the situation around it cannot operate in a rational manner. Most organizations have areas in which they can operate at their own discretion and therefore can subject themselves to the norm of rationality.

Thompson develops similar propositions about most areas of organizational operations. The content of these propositions is subject to empirical verification, but for our purposes, it does not really matter if the propositions are valid or not. What is important is that they form a basis for bringing the insights of the closed- and open-system approaches together. In essence, *organizations attempt to be rational, controlling their internal operations and environment to the greatest extent possible, but never achieving a totally closed, rational system.* How well the organization achieves rationality depends upon the strength of the internal and external pressures and the organization's capability of control.

In the next section, [a] perspective . . . will be presented [that] contains elements of the closed and open perspectives, but puts both within a single analytical framework.

A Contingency-choice Perspective

To derive a perspective by which the actions of organizations can be understood, three factors must be taken into account: the individuals within the organization; the environment of the organization; and the form of the organization. The basic assumption of the perspective is Thompson's, namely that organizations try to behave rationally in the face of multiple conflicting pressures, and thus attempt to control those aspects of their existence, both internal and external, that pose threats to rational actions.[23]

In this perspective the concern with individuals within the organization is limited to those of their actions that have organizational relevance; the individual is seen as the mechanism through which environmental and organizational characteristics are shaped. Karl Weick states: "Rather than talking about adapting to an external environment, it may be more correct to argue that organizing consists of adapting to an enacted environment, an environment which is *constituted* by the actions of interdependent human actors."[24] How individuals conceptualize what is happening in the environment around their organization is critical to how the organization then responds or does not respond. It is critical to note that the responses of the individuals are shaped and even determined by their position within an organization. An individual has a distinct rank and a position within the organization. Ranks and positions are not equal in their power or access to power and it is thus the perceptions of the organizational elite or key decision makers (plus the perceptions of those who are in a position to observe and interpret organizationally relevant information and pass it on to the elite) that are critical to the operations of the organization.

The perceived environment is not the same for all organizations. In some cases it is stable and highly predictable; in other cases it is fluid, changing, and almost impossible to understand. This is why "contingency" is a component of the perspective. Organizations attempt to "fit" their structure and processes to the

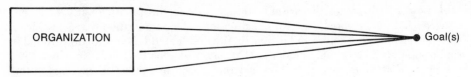

Figure 1   Deployment of organizational structure and processes under pure rationality model

perceived environment.[25] The form of the organization is thus contingent upon the environment.

. . . The forms that organizations take vary rather systematically with environmental constraints, so that the organization must be viewed as a responding entity. The organization also attempts to manipulate the environment to its own advantage, whether in such indirect ways as advertising and public relations, or through direct manipulations of political and economic events, as when attempts are made to ensure that political parties are maintained in office or supplies of raw materials are guaranteed through legal or illegal acquisitions of sources of supply.

The technique by which organizations respond to their environments depends upon the choices made within the organization; John Child calls these the "strategic choices."[26] Child argues that the internal politics of organizations determine the structural forms, the manipulation of environmental features, and the choice of relevant performance standards that are selected by the organization. The internal politics in turn depend upon the power distributions within the organization, which are themselves a structural condition subject to alteration over time.

While it is clear that such strategic choices are made as a response to the environment and to internal conditions, the number of available alternative responses by the organization is limited. Katz and Kahn suggest that organizational systems are characterized by "equifinality," or the possibility of several means available to achieve the organization's goals. The range of means available through strategic choice mechanisms is limited by the environmental constraints, the perceptual and cognitive predispositions of organizational decision makers, and the existing form of the organization, which limits the possible organizational response patterns.

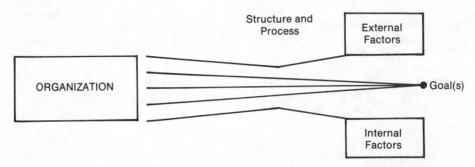

Figure 2   Deployment of organizational structure and processes under typical open-system model

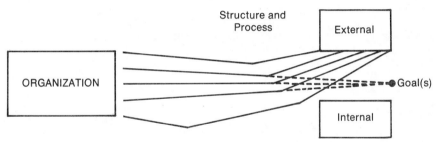

Figure 3   Deployment of organizational structure and processes under powerful threat conditions (external)

Rationality is still a key factor in the contingency-choice perspective. Organizations attempt to make their structure and operations rational by their strategic choices in regard to the environment. When the organization is threatened, the strength of the threat must be evaluated.[27] It is one thing if a few consumers are angry at an organization, but quite another when national consumer groups publish widely read attacks on an organization's product or service, and still another—and worse one—when legislation is pending that would severely regulate an organization in the private sector or eliminate an organization in the public sector. Thus, firms in the petroleum industry fight legislation that would prohibit offshore oil exploration, and government agencies fight policies that would eliminate them or absorb them into another agency. Ironically, organizations such as airlines fight the deregulation of their market. Such deregulation is seen as a severe threat to their stable environment.

The perspective that has been derived, therefore, is that organizations do operate generally under norms of rationality. Under pure rationality norms, the organization's energies would be deployed as illustrated in figure 1. Since it has been amply demonstrated in the discussion that both external and internal considerations lead to a deflection from the closed rational system, organizations under most conditions will deploy themselves in the manner indicated in figure 2. Under severe external threat, the deployment will be in the form indicated in figure 3. The power of the external and internal pressures and threats is the key variable. Unfortunately, there are no available systematic measures of the power of such threats. The perceived severity of the threat is a key to the decision making within the organization. The decision-making process itself is carried out under less than fully rational conditions.

Figure 2 indicates how organizations actually operate under most conditions. The figure is truncated, in that it ignores the transactions at the organization's input and output ends and the feedback mechanisms from these transactions, as well as the power-distribution and decision-making processes within the organization itself—all of which are important factors. Nevertheless, figures 2 and 3 do illustrate the distillation of the perspectives that have been discussed. . . .

Notes

1. This distinction and terminology follow James D. Thompson, *Organizations in Action* (New York: McGraw-Hill Book Company, 1967), pp. 4–7.

2. See Richard H. Hall, "The Concept of Bureaucracy: An Empirical Assessment," *American Journal of Sociology*, 69, No. 1 (July 1963), 32–40.

3. Jerald Hage, "An Axiomatic Theory of Organizations," *Administrative Science Quarterly*, 10, No. 3 (December 1965), 289–320.

4. *Ibid.*, p. 293.

5. *Ibid.*, pp. 293–94.

6. Thompson, *Organizations in Action*, p. 6.

7. *Ibid.*, p. 19.

8. Stanley H. Udy, Jr., "'Bureaucracy' and 'Rationality' in Weber's Organization Theory," *American Sociological Review*, 24, No. 6 (December 1959), 794.

9. Hall, "Concept of Bureaucracy."

10. James G. March and Herbert A. Simon, *Organizations* (New York: John Wiley & Sons, Inc., 1958), pp. 34–171.

11. See, for example, William Kornhauser, *Scientists in Industry* (Berkeley: University of California Press, 1963); *Administrative Science Quarterly*, 10, No. 1 (June 1965), entire issue; and Eliot Freidson, ed., *The Professions and their Prospects* (Beverly Hills, Calif.: Sage Publications, 1973).

12. Robert K. Merton, "Bureaucratic Structure and Personality," *Social Forces*, 18, No. 4 (May 1940), 560–68; and Victor Thompson, *Modern Organizations* (New York: Alfred A. Knopf, Inc., 1961), pp. 152–77.

13. March and Simon, *Organizations*, pp. 140–41.

14. Daniel Katz and Robert L. Kahn, *The Social Psychology of Organizations* (New York: John Wiley & Sons, Inc., 1966), p. 26.

15. *Ibid.*, p. 27.

16. Alvin W. Gouldner, "Organizational Analysis," in Robert K. Merton, Leonard Broom, and Leonard S. Cottrell, Jr., *Sociology Today* (New York: Basic Books, Inc., 1959), p. 405.

17. Michel Crozier, *The Bureaucratic Phenomenon* (Chicago: The University of Chicago Press, 1964).

18. William M. Evan, "The Organization-Set," in James D. Thompson, ed., *Approaches to Organizational Design* (Pittsburgh: University of Pittsburgh Press, 1966), pp. 173–91; J. Kenneth Benson, "The Interorganizational Network as a Political Economy," *Administrative Science Quarterly*, 20, No. 2 (June 1975), 229–49; Howard Aldrich, "An Organization-Environment Perspective on Cooperation and Conflict between Organizations in the Manpower Training System" in Anant Negandhi, ed., *Conflict and Power in Complex Organizations* (Kent, Ohio: Center for Business and Economic Research, Kent State University, 1972). See also Eugene Litwak and Lydia F. Hylton, "Interorganizational Analysis," *Administrative Science Quarterly*, 6, No. 4 (March 1962), 395–420; Sol Levine and Paul White, "Exchange and Interorganizational Relationships," *Administrative Science Quarterly*, 5, No. 4 (March 1961), 583–601. See also Burton R. Clark, "Interorganizational Patterns in Education," *Administrative Science Quarterly*, 10, No. 2 (September 1965), 224–37; Harold Guetzkow, "Relations Among Organizations," in Raymond V. Bowers, ed., *Studies on Behavior in Organizations: A Research Symposium* (Athens, Ga.: University of Georgia Press, 1966), pp. 13–44; and Roland L. Warren, "The Interorganizational Field as a Focus for Investigation," *Administrative Science Quarterly*, 12, No. 3 (December 1967), 369–419.

19. Katz and Kahn, *Social Psychology of Organizations*, pp. 19–26.

20. See Walter Buckley, *Sociology and Modern Systems Theory* (Englewood Cliffs, N.J.: Prentice-Hall, Inc., 1967); and Walter Buckley, ed., *Modern Systems Research for the Behavioral Scientist* (Chicago: Aldine Publishing Company, 1968).

21. Amitai Etzioni, *Modern Organizations* (Englewood Cliffs, N.J.: Prentice-Hall, Inc., 1964), p. 17.

22. J. Thompson, *Organizations in Action*, p. 32. The concept of task environment was first proposed by William R. Dill to indicate those components of the environment that are significant or potentially significant for goal setting and goal attainment. The task

environment, according to Dill, includes customers, suppliers, competitors, and regulatory groups. See Dill, "Environment as an Influence on Managerial Autonomy," *Administrative Science Quarterly*, 2, No. 4 (March 1958), 409–43.

23. James Thompson, *Organizations in Action*.

24. Karl Weick, *The Social Psychology of Organizing* (Reading, Mass.: Addison-Wesley Publishing Co., 1969), p. 27. David Silverman, *The Theory of Organizations: A Sociological Framework* (New York: Basic Books, 1971), also uses this basic framework, but emphasizes the differences among the shared definitions of the situation within organizations.

25. This approach is most closely associated with the work of Paul R. Lawrence and Jay W. Lorsch, *Organization and Environment: Managing Differentiation and Integration* (Cambridge, Mass.: Harvard Graduate School of Business Administration, 1967). The conclusions are based on their own research on business organizations and on the work of Tom Burns and G. M. Stalker, *The Management of Innovation* (London: Tavistock Publications, 1961); Joan Woodward, *Management and Technology* (London: Her Majesty's Printing Office, 1958); and others. Henry Tosi, Ramon Aldag, and Ronald Storey, "On the Measurement of the Environment: An Assessment of the Lawrence and Lorsch Environmental Subscale," *Administrative Science Quarterly*, 18, No. 1 (March 1973), 27–36, have criticized Lawrence and Lorsch's measurement of the degree of environmental uncertainty that organizations face, but the thrust of their findings continues to be replicated. See, for example, Anant R. Negandhi and Bernard C. Reimann, "A Contingency Theory of Organization Re-examined in the Context of a Developing Country," *Academy of Management Journal*, 15, No. 2 (June 1972), 137–46; Peter M. Blau and Richard A. Schoenherr, *The Structure of Organizations* (New York: Basic Books, 1971, especially Chapters 6–8); and Johannes M. Pennings, "The Relevance of the Structural Contingency Model for Organizational Effectiveness," *Administrative Science Quarterly*, 20, No. 3 (September 1975), 393–407.

26. John Child, "Organization Structure, Environment, and Performance: The Role of Strategic Choice," *Sociology*, 6, No. 1 (January 1972), 1–22.

27. When decisions between alternative goals within the organization are made, the power process is also operative. See Aaron Wildavsky, *The Politics of the Budgetary Process* (Boston: Little, Brown and Company, 1964), for a discussion of the political processes involved in determining federal budgets.

Humanism in Organizations: A Critical Appraisal*

H. Roy Kaplan and
Curt Tausky

Although the appellation human relationist is seldom used today, many contemporary organizational theorists adhere to the tradition established by Elton Mayo[1] later popularized by Douglas McGregor.[2] Contemporary human relationists are often referred to as organizational humanists, enlightened managers, or industrial democrats. Nevertheless, there remains a definite and pervasive continuity of approach to handling organizational conflict and employee motivation among the founders and their contemporary counterparts.[3] At the heart of this tradition is the belief that man is basically good, infinitely malleable, capable of perfectability, and therefore organizational goals and individual interests should be compatible.[4]

Humanist approaches stress the importance of developing meaningful work routines which afford workers an opportunity for decision making. There is no dearth of techniques developed for increasing workers' participation. While early human relationists opted for more socially skilled supervision and job enlargement, present advocates call for job enrichment.[5] Other familiar offspring of this tradition are sensitivity training and encounter groups for increasing interpersonal competence and developing the ability to handle organizational difficulties through participatory problem solving with subordinates. Even the Department of State, with the help of Argyris, has attempted this.[6]

These programs have become immensely popular and have been implemented in numerous organizations in the United States.[7] Despite this (or because of it) we think that an examination of some of the underlying assumptions of organizational humanists about employee participation and motivation is in order. This article will be devoted to such an analysis.

Models of Participation in Organization

The research of Kurt Lewin among boys' clubs and Red Cross volunteer nurses, and Lippitt and White on leadership was instrumental in supporting the hypothesis that participation in decision making increased cooperation toward attaining group goals.[8] The research was essentially a critique of unilateral power. The compatibility of participation with democratic values is obvious. Underlying both is the assumption that consensus encourages commitment to the shared decision; hence social control is more effective since it then rests, in part, on the self-control

*The authors wish to thank Richard Simpson of the Department of Sociology, University of North Carolina, for his helpful comments on an earlier draft of this article.

Reprinted from *Public Administration Review*. © 1977 by The American Society for Public Administration, 1225 Connecticut Avenue, N.W., Washington, D.C. All rights reserved.

of the participants. Organizational humanism carries this a step further by postulating a link between participation and productivity, for it is assumed that participation increases satisfaction and satisfaction is reflected in increased work effort. This is a highly tenuous assumption.

To go further than these general comments it is necessary to develop more specific models of participation in organizations. Figure 1 depicts a typology of five models of worker participation in decision making based on kinds of interaction found among superiors and subordinates. They flow in a continuum from the most structured bureaucratic type, to the least structured or delegative type.

In the bureaucratic relationship there is a definitive hierarchical pattern between leaders and followers. The leader provides detailed direction and evaluates results. Knowledge possessed by the subordinate is not reflected in his/her relationship to the superior, with the result being a highly structured job.[9]

The representative bureaucratic relationship is similar to its purer form above, but with the important difference that more than one center of power exists and these centers negotiate rules and rewards. Collective bargaining illustrates this arrangement. However, the principles embodied in the contract are binding on all parties and have the character of bureaucratic rules over the life of a contract once it is settled. Participation in decision making is not direct but through agents who represent the parties to the contract.

Especially at the administrative level of organization, the consultative bureaucratic relationship is more realistic than the pure bureaucratic type from which it differs in that superiors obtain advice or opinion from subordinates. "Talk" about the matter at hand is customary. This type also encompasses committee participation in decisions, when such participation is advisory. One reason why this model appears to more accurately reflect administrative relationships in American work organizations than in French,[10] German,[11] and to a lesser extent British,[12] is because we place less emphasis on status differences and overt deference. This is due in part to our democratic ethos and the related leveling effect of mass education. Research suggests that successful organizations in a rapidly changing environment are characterized by "organic" rather than "mechanistic" administrative forms. A rigid set of duties and unilateral command cannot cope well with change, whereas the organic systems, with more loosely defined tasks and a richer web of information exchange, are more responsive to environmental change.[13] At the interface of first-line supervision and manual work, the evidence is rather persuasive that a pure or representative bureaucratic relationship is effective in routinized situations such as mass production systems, but a form similar to consultative bureaucracy is more effective in job-shop operations on the one hand, and automated processes on the other.[14]

In the collegial relationship decision making is viewed as a process in which competence counts more than organizational rank. Interaction is of a peer nature rather than a superior-subordinate relationship. In the case of committees or task

---

Figure 1   Types of Decision Making

Most Hierarchical				Least Hierarchical
Bureaucratic	Representative Bureaucratic	Consultative Bureaucratic	Collegial	Delegative

forces the collegial relationship may include voting. At the individual level, organizational rank is viewed as an administrative mechanism to reward length of service and prior contributions. Disagreements are not solved by a superior's fiat. Rungs on the ladder of rank tend to be small in number, as in research and educational organizations. Collegial types of relationships predominate among professionals, such as the departments of a university or the R & D units of industrial firms.[15]

The extensive autonomy suggested by the delegative relationship model is unrealistic, except for isolated cases, since the conception involves autonomy of ends and means in the work setting. A senior research chemist is illustrative. Both the ends to which the research may lead, as well as the means, are at the discretion of the researcher. There are of course such instances, but the more common situation might better be described as controlled freedom. Thus, a person with extensive autonomy must periodically justify his work or forfeit the resources to continue. Empirically, then, delegation shades into a collegial relationship, i.e., the ends must be convincingly promising, and the means are discussed with, and influenced by, colleagues.

It is evident from these models that organizational humanism stresses consultative, collegial, and delegative relationships, and particularly favors the collegial type. There are, however, constraints on collegiality, the most important being the requirement that technical or professional training is recognized by colleagues as providing a foundation, a realistic basis, for taking seriously one another's judgments. Among professionals this sort of foundation may exist, but it is questionable when extended to occupational groups wherein technical training differences or on-the-job experience, reflected by rank, are important sources of know-how. Where this is the case, consultative relationships are a more realistic and viable alternative. Many superior-subordinate interactions in work settings are, we suspect, examples of this sort of consultative form.

Some Disconfirming Evidence of Organizational Humanist Assumptions about Participation

Organizational humanism holds out the tantalizing promise of increased work effort and satisfaction through participation. The preceding typology can serve as a heuristic device in an empirical analysis of the effects of participation and autonomy on employee productivity and satisfaction. In his study of the effects of worker participation in the form of codetermination and workers' management, Clegg[16] found that participation through representation did not in itself appreciably increase workers' satisfaction, and that productivity was not related to participation through representation. Tannenbaum, an advocate of participation, similarly found little relationship between participation and work satisfaction in his study of firms in capitalist and socialist countries.[17]

Tannenbaum's[18] earlier study of automobile dealerships and delivery agencies indicates that the relationship between satisfaction and work effort is tenuous. Among the 65 organizations he studied, autonomy was related to work satisfaction (correlations ranged from .03 to .55), but the correlations between job satisfaction and productivity ranged from .14 to −.18. Thus an increase in work satisfaction does not predictably yield increments in work effort. Furthermore, when workers were asked about the existing distribution of control in their organizations as compared to what they believed it ought to be, there was little difference. While a more consultative relationship was desired, workers still expected management to manage, thereby casting some doubt on the assumption that workers seek collegial relationships with their supervisors.

It does appear to be true that having a voice in the work process increases satisfaction. However, reviews of the job satisfaction literature by Brayfield and Crockett,[19] Vroom,[20] and Ronan[21] have found that there is, at best, a weak relationship between satisfaction and productivity. There is evidence indicating that absenteeism and turnover are more strongly related to satisfaction, and therefore job satisfaction remains a significant factor in the long run.[22] Neverthe-less, an interesting divergent finding emerged from Patchen's research on the TVA, where job involvement was positively correlated with absenteeism among engineers and laboratory personnel.[23]

The research by Pelz and Andrews[24] on scientists indicates that the exten-sive autonomy represented in the delegative model can be less effective in increasing scientific productivity than a collegial relationship. Mott's study of various NASA units examined a number of different leadership styles from auto-matic to participative. No relationship was found between style of leadership and the performance of NASA personnel.[25] It may be that consultative and collegial participation are deemed more important by academic theorists than by people in other, more structured forms of work organizations. Clearly, at the manual level, material rewards appear to outweigh interests in participating in decision making. There is a considerable body of literature which indicates a pronounced instru-mental orientation toward work among manual workers, their major interest being wages and security.[26] Among public sector workers, productivity bargaining is slowly increasing, and may be one way to control the costs of services such as police, fire, and sanitation.[27] The message from such bargaining is that employee acceptance of changes in work methods depends largely on their job security and pay offered. Along with a nod to Herzberg, and participation schemes, it is interesting to note, the 1972 Wingspread Symposium discussed and recom-mended material incentives for improving production in the public sector.[28]

Intertwined with the organizational humanist belief in the efficacy of partici-pation and its relation to satisfaction and productivity is the assumption that employees want jobs which afford them an opportunity for meaningful activities, e.g., intellectual challenge, responsibility, and self-actualization. For example, Likert[29] contends that every worker ". . . should see his role as difficult, important and meaningful. . . . When jobs do not meet this specification they should be reorganized so that they do." However, studies show that workers do not necessar-ily prefer larger or more interesting jobs.[30] One recent study revealed that job complexity was negatively related to powerlessness among non-mobile and down-wardly mobile men with moderate to high incomes. But among lower income, non-mobile skilled and semi-skilled workers, increased job complexity was asso-ciated with greater feelings of powerlessness.[31]

The Role of Ideology and Values in Organizational Humanist Conceptions of Worker Motivation

Organizational humanists assume that employees will strongly identify with their work if they have the opportunity for intrinsic involvement in their jobs. This assumption is largely derived from the need theory of Abraham Maslow[32] with its *sine qua non* of self-actualization through work. From this arises an admonition to management to provide workers with stimulating work that satisfies higher level needs. The following statement from Argyris illustrates this belief:

> Most jobs on the lower levels in American industry can be learned in a very short time. Most of them require some degree of mechanical aptitude and motor aptitude. . . . Almost none of the employee jobs (high and low skill) require the use of emotional or interpersonal abilities in the individual. For example, low-skill employees in plants X and Y find it very difficult to talk about their self-concept as having rich, meaningful (to them) content. . . . The high-skill employees, however, are able to discuss their self, but it is a self primarily composed of mechanical skills. It is not difficult to see why the employee eventually learns to respect himself primarily in terms of how much money he can command. Only those abilities that earn money for the company are valued by the organization.[33]

The tenor of this statement is indicative of the subjective, value-laden orientation evinced by many contemporary human relationists. As Strauss has noted, "Human relations is normative, not purely descriptive. The authors involved, each in his own way, are crusaders."[34] Warren Bennis, one of the leading advocates of organizational humanism, has stated that he and his followers are working "ambitiously to transform the basic value system of the enterprise so that humanistic and democratic values are infused and related to policy."[35] Maslow himself captured the spirit of the movement when he proclaimed "Salvation is a by-product of self-actualizing work and self-actualizing duty."[36] The thin veneer of such pronouncements barely veils the strong ideological orientation of organizational humanists.[37]

Much organizational humanist rhetoric is directed toward the hierarchical structure and extensive division of labor found in current organizations. It is believed that this is inherently dehumanizing and detrimental to the development of mature personalities. The seeming preoccupation of employees with the satisfaction of lower level needs such as money and security is blamed on work organizations which, it is contended, have nurtured this behavior by rewarding employees with the extrinsic or non-work-related incentives of salary and fringe benefits. To rectify this presumably abnormal situation, programs of job enrichment have been proposed to establish a "meaningful" motivation cycle. These programs are ostensibly designed to satisfy the higher-level needs of workers by increasing their job involvement through decentralization of authority and increased job complexity, thus developing achievement, growth, and independence among employees.[38]

Organizational humanists further contend that the dull and monotonous work prevalent in our society has led to a pervasive lack of commitment among the working population. However, data have been gathered which question the validity of this assumption. When various segments of the working population have been asked, "If by some chance you had enough money to live comfortably without working, do you think that you would work anyway, or would you not work?" the answer has been preponderantly in the affirmative. Table 1 presents a comparison of responses to this question from five studies designed to ascertain the extent of commitment work. It can be seen that there is an attachment to work not only among employed white and blue collar workers, but even among the chronically unemployed. This relationship also appears to be consistent through time as well as across social classes.

TABLE 1 *Comparative Examples of the Commitment to Work in the United States*

		Samples				
Item	Response Alternatives	National Sample of 393 Employed[1] Men	National Sample of 274 Male Blue-Collar Workers[2]	151 Middle Managers in 3 Business Firms[3]	1379 Male Vocational Technical Students[4]	275 Hard-Core Unemployed[5]
1. If by some chance you had enough money to live comfortably without working, do you think you would work anyway?	I would work anyway	80%	81%	89%	87%	84%
	I would not work	20%	19%	11%	13%	16%
2. If you were out of work, which would you rather do?	Go on welfare	—	9%	9%	16%	29%
	Take a job as a car washer that paid the same as welfare	—	91%	91%	84%	71%

1. Nancy C. Morse and Robert S. Weiss, "The Functions and Meaning of Work and the Job," *American Sociological Review*, Vol. 20 (April 1955), p. 192.
2. Curt Tausky, "Meanings of Work Among Blue Collar Men," *Pacific Sociological Review*, Vol. 12 (Spring 1969), p. 51.
3. Curt Tausky, "Occupational Mobility Interests," *Canadian Review of Sociology and Anthropology*, Vol. 4 (November 1967), p. 246.
4. Bhopinder S. Bolaria, unpublished study of vocational-technical training students, University of Maine, Orono, 1970.
5. H. Roy Kaplan and Curt Tausky, "Work and the Welfare Cadillac: The Function of and Commitment to Work Among the Hard-Core Unemployed," *Social Problems*, Vol. 19 (Spring 1972), p. 475.

Self-Actualization: Inherited or Learned?

It is not our contention that most workers are dedicated to their jobs, or that they view their work as intrinsically satisfying. However, these data indicate many persons retain strong attachments to work as a socially desirable form of activity. The aversion to welfare among the respondents that is apparent from Table 1 lends further support to this assumption. Organizational humanists overstate their argument when they proclaim that people can only achieve inner peace through intrinsically satisfying work; and it is implicit in their ideology that blocked self-actualization in the job not only leads to conflict in the workplace, but adversely affects society. These are highly tenuous assumptions, for they ignore the socio-cultural component of self-actualization, i.e., its learned character, and ascribe its existence to an innate drive in man.[39] If, however, we assume that the desire for self actualization in work is learned, then only a minority of workers through family, lengthy formal education, and peer socialization may be intrinsically dedicated to their work, such as, perhaps, academics, managers in government and private industry, scientists in basic research, and R & D engineers. However, research shows that even scientists are interested in extrinsic rewards as well as the satisfactions they derive from involvement in their work.[40]

There is evidence which indicates that most manual and lower-level salaried employees derive satisfaction off their jobs as Dubin, Champoux, and Porter found.[41] Other studies indicate that it is possible for an individual to have a strong commitment to work for the economic function it performs without having an intrinsic interest in the task.[42] This condition of "detached involvement" with respect to work may be pervasive in our society, particularly among lower class persons whose background has not prepared them for jobs which afford, nor taught them to seek, self-actualization in work.[43]

The lack of intrinsic involvement in work among large portions of the population is taken as a sign of psychological pathology by many organizational humanists. We are told by Herzberg[44] that the preoccupation of persons with "hygiene" factors, e.g., money, working conditions, and security, is abnormal; and Argyris[45] charges that such persons have been made emotionally immature by the confining structures of contemporary organizations. From the organizational humanist perspective, the organization should help its employees to mature psychologically by providing them with "meaningful" work, for which services they would work enthusiastically to achieve organizational goals.

Social Class: An Important Source of Work Motivation

When analyzing the motivations of workers, we must recognize the variability of human needs and wants. Many studies have shown that people of blue-collar origins do not seek the same things from their jobs as middle and upper class persons.[46] The desire for achievement and independence in their work is often substantially less than that exhibited by the latter groups. On both levels, but particularly among blue collar workers, we find an interest in extrinsic job factors surrounding the work situation, such as salary, fringe benefits, job security, working conditions, and, to some extent, supervision.[47] Table 2 presents data which indicate the importance of economic rewards derived from work to both white and blue collar workers, as is evidenced by their responses to items one and two. Interestingly, the middle-managers were the only group to ascribe other than economic importance to being promoted, perhaps indicating the middle-class pressure for visible occupational success.

The organizational humanist perspective on worker motivation cannot account for divergent work orientations among different levels of employees because its underlying ideological commitment and belief in the desire of all people to self-actualize through work lacks empirical justification. As noted above, the sociological literature indicates that diverse orientations toward work are in large part a function of social class membership. The socialization of persons and the opportunities available for them to obtain jobs which offer a chance for creativity and autonomy are a function of the opportunity structure in society. That many persons of blue collar origins are predominantly instrumentally oriented toward work may not be the result of stultifying organizational structures but of the type of socialization and occupational mobility they experience. Considering mobility

TABLE 2 *Economic Orientations to Work Among White and Blue Collar Workers and Students*

Items	Response Alternatives	Samples		
		National Sample 274 Male Blue Collar Workers[1]	1379 Male Vocational-Technical Students[2]	151 Middle Managers in 3 Business Firms[3]
1. Is the most important thing about getting a promotion . . .	Getting more pay	67%	62%*	78%
	Getting more respect from friends and neighbors	33%	33%	22%
2. Which job would you choose if you could be sure of keeping either job?	Better than average pay as a truck driver	73%	77%	67%
	Less than average pay as a bank clerk	27%	22%	32%
3. If you could be sure your income would go up steadily without getting a promotion, would you care about being promoted?	No	74%	60%	29%
	Yes	26%	40%	71%

* Percentages do not add to 100 due to "no answers."
1. Curt Tausky, "Meanings of Work Among Blue Collar Men," *Pacific Sociological Review*, Vol. 12 (Spring 1969), p. 51.
2. Bhopinder S. Bolaria, unpublished study of vocational-technical training students, University of Maine, Orono, 1970.
3. Curt Tausky, "Occupational Mobility Interests," *Canadian Review of Sociology and Anthropology*, Vol. 4 (November 1967), p. 246.

opportunities and socialization, it is unrealistic to argue that an instrumental orientation to work runs counter to human nature. Recent studies based upon more adequate assumptions of human motivation derived from the work of Atkinson[48] and Vroom[49] indicate people consider the attractiveness of the consequences of the outcomes of their activities and act to obtain those things which they believe they can realistically achieve.[50]

Largely based in academic surroundings which afford them opportunities for creativity and self-actualization, have organizational humanists inadvertently infused their own values into their theories and overgeneralized their perspectives to all workers?[51] We might point out that many of them have frequently fallen happily into compliance with academe's equivalent of the carrot and stick reward system which they are quick to condemn in industry, the "publish or perish" syndrome.

Conclusion

We would be naive to assume that the assumptions which are questioned here are espoused in their totality by all of the diverse writers who advocate humanism in management and the decentralization of power in organizations. However, there is an unmistakable ideological air about most of their writings which, we believe, has led to a distorted conception of employees' motivation and desire for control in organizations. Filled with exuberance to usher in a new society founded upon challenging work and participatory democracy, they consider the hierarchical structure of organizations repugnant. Clinging to a belief in the desire for men to be creative and autonomous, they label pathological the preoccupation of large segments of the contemporary labor force with material rewards. Yet, the variability and choice they claim to be basic in man and essential ingredients of a "better" society is somehow ignored in their attempts to encapsulate all workers under a single motivational scheme based upon an ideologically laden conception of man's personality.

What the data indicate to be the basis of motivation among employees differs considerably from the organizational humanist ideological perspective about this. To obtain an optimal level of effectiveness in the pursuit of organizational goals, with a minimum of conflict, individuals' differing orientations to work must be recognized; this not only makes sense, but may be healthy for pluralism when viewed within the context of people's cultural or subcultural affiliations. Generalizations aimed at neatly encapsulating the motivation of all workers regardless of occupational levels, classes, or job functions are likely to prove spurious, and decisions predicated upon them could be conducive to heightening organizational conflict, rather than its diminution.

What must ultimately be faced is the divergence between individuals' egoistic interests and organizational purposes. This appears to be an inherently intractable problem. Neither job enrichment nor participation can transmute this divergence into congruence. The functions of management in the public and private sectors are essentially similar, as Murray has argued.[52] In neither sector is management—whose members are also not immune to self-interested behavior—likely to find a panacea for the ancient problem of inducing individuals to serve collective purposes.

Notes

1. Elton Mayo, *The Human Problems of an Industrial Civilization* (New York: Macmillan, 1933), and *The Social Problems of an Industrial Civilization* (Cambridge, Mass.: Harvard University Press, 1946).
2. Douglas McGregor, *The Human Side of Enterprise* (New York: McGraw-Hill Book Company, 1960).
3. George Strauss, "Human Relations—1968 Style," *Industrial Relations*, Vol. 7 (1968), pp. 262–276.
4. See McGregor's Theory Y, *op. cit.*, and the more recent industrial humanist position of William G. Scott, *Organization Theory: A Behavioral Analysis for Management* (Homewood, Ill.: Richard D. Irwin, Inc., 1967), pp. 409–429.
5. Frederick Herzberg, "The Wise Old Turk," *Harvard Business Review* (September-October 1974), pp. 70–80. Currently, Herzberg, for example, is involved with an

extensive and expensive application of what he refers to as an "orthodox job enrichment" program at Hill Air Force Base in Ogden, Utah.

6. Chris Argyris, *Some Causes of Organizational Ineffectiveness Within the Department of State* (Washington, D.C.: Department of State Publication 8180, 1967); see also Schein and Bennis, *Personal and Organizational Change through Group Methods* (New York: John Wiley & Sons, 1965).

7. For a good review of organization design efforts see *Public Administration Review*, Vol. 34, No. 2 (March/April, 1974), pp. 97–140. Overall, some version of Theory Y is incorporated in much of OD theory and practice.

8. Kurt Lewin, "Group Decision and Social Change," pp. 197–211; and Ronald Lippitt and Ralph K. White, "An Experimental Study of Leadership and Group Life," pp. 496–511, in E. Maccoby et al. (eds.), *Reading in Social Psychology* (New York: Holt, Rinehart and Winston, 1958).

9. See the mechanistic and organic systems of organization depicted by Tom Burns and G. M. Stalker, *The Management of Innovation* (London: Tavistock Institute, 1961).

10. Desmond Graves, "Cultural Determinism and Management Behavior," *Organizational Dynamics* (Autumn 1972), pp. 46–59.

11. Robert S. Weiss, "A Structure-Function Approach to Organization," *Journal of Social Issues*, Vol. 12 (1956), pp. 61–67.

12. Graves.

13. Paul R. Lawrence and Jay W. Lorsch, *Organization and Environment: Managing Differentiation and Integration* (Boston: Graduate School of Business Administration, Harvard University Press, 1967); also Morley Segal, "Organization and Environment," *Public Administration Review*, Vol. 34, No. 3 (1974), pp. 212–220.

14. Joan Woodward, *Industrial Organization: Theory and Practice* (London: Oxford University Press, 1965); Joan Woodward, *Industrial Organization: Behavior and Control* (London: Oxford University Press, 1970); and William L. Zwerman, *New Perspectives in Organization Theory* (Westport, Conn.: Greenwood Publishing Company, 1970).

15. Joseph A. Litterer, "Research Departments Within Large Organizations," *California Management Review*, Vol. 12 (Spring 1970), pp. 77–84.

16. Hugh Clegg, *A New Approach to Industrial Democracy* (Oxford, England: Basil Blackwell, Ltd., 1963).

17. Arnold S. Tannenbaum, "Rank, Clout and Worker Satisfaction: Pecking Order, Capitalist and Communist Style," *Psychology Today*, Vol. 9 (September 1975), pp. 41–43.

18. Arnold Tannenbaum, *Control in Organizations* (New York: McGraw-Hill Book Company, Inc., 1968).

19. Arthur H. Brayfield and James H. Crockett, "Employee Attitudes and Employee Performance," *Psychological Bulletin*, Vol. 52 (1955), pp. 284–290.

20. Victor Vroom, *Work and Motivation* (New York: John Wiley & Sons, 1964).

21. W. W. Ronan, "Individual and Situational Variables Relating to Job Satisfaction," *Journal of Applied Psychology Monograph*, Vol. 54, Part 2 (February 1970), pp. 1–31.

22. Richard M. Steers and Lyman W. Porter, *Motivation and Work Behavior* (New York: McGraw-Hill, 1975), pp. 276–279.

23. Martin Patchen, *Participation, Achievement, and Involvement on the Job* (Englewood Cliffs, N.J.: Prentice-Hall, 1970), pp. 96–97.

24. Donald Pelz and Frank Andrews, *Scientists in Organizations* (New York: John Wiley & Sons, Inc., 1966).

25. Paul E. Mott, *The Characteristics of Effective Organization* (New York: Harper & Row, 1972).

26. Ely Chinoy, "The Tradition of Opportunity and the Aspirations of Automobile Workers," *American Journal of Sociology*, Vol. 57 (March 1952), pp. 453–459; William F. Whyte, *Money and Motivation: An Analysis of Incentives in Industry* (New York: Harper, 1955); Milton R. Blood and Charles L. Hulin, "Alienation, Environmental Characteristics, and Worker Responses," *Journal of Applied Psychology*, Vol. 51 (June

1967), pp. 284–290; John H. Goldthorpe, et al., *The Affluent Worker: Industrial Attitudes and Behavior* (New York: Cambridge University Press, 1968); and Rolin H. Simonds and John N. Orife, "Worker Behavior Versus Enrichment Theory" *Administrative Science Quarterly*, Vol. 20 (December 1975), pp. 606–612.

27. Sam Zagoria, "Bargaining and Productivity in The Public Sector," in Gerald Somers (ed.), *Collective Bargaining and Productivity* (Madison, Wis.: Industrial Relations Research Association, 1975), pp. 63–82.

28. Sig Gissler, "Productivity in the Public Sector: A Summary of a Wingspread Symposium," *Public Administration Review*, Vol. 32, No. 6 (November/December 1972), pp. 840–850. See also, James S. Balloun and John F. Maloney, "Beating the Cost Service Squeeze," *Public Administration Review*, Vol. 35, No. 5 (September/October 1975), pp. 531–538.

29. Rensis Likert, *New Patterns of Management* (New York: McGraw-Hill, 1961), p. 103.

30. James E. Kennedy and Harry E. O'Neill, "Job Content and Workers' Opinions," *Journal of Applied Psychology*, Vol. 47 (December 1958), pp. 372–375; M. D. Kilbridge, "Do Workers Prefer Larger Jobs?" *Personnel*, Vol. 37 (September 1960), pp. 45–48; A. C. MacKinney, P. F. Wernimont, and W. O. Galitz, "Has Specialization Reduced Job Satisfaction?" *Personnel*, Vol. 39 (January-February 1962), pp. 8–17; A. N. Turner and A. L. Michlette, "Sources of Satisfaction in Repetitive Work," *Occupational Psychology*, Vol. 36 (October 1962), pp. 215–231; Emanuel Weintraub, "The Real Cause of Workers' Discontent," *The New York Times*, Financial Section (January 21, 1973), p. 14.

31. Bill Tudor, "A Specification of Relationships Between Job Complexity and Powerlessness," *American Sociological Review*, Vol. 37 (October 1972), pp. 596–604.

32. Abraham H. Maslow, "A Theory of Human Motivation," *Psychological Review*, Vol. 5 (July 1943), pp. 370–396; and Abraham H. Maslow, *Eupsychian Management* (Homewood, Ill.: Irwin & Dorsey Press, Inc., 1965), p. 6.

33. Chris Argyris, *Interpersonal Competence & Organizational Effectiveness* (Homewood, Ill.: Irwin & Dorsey Press, 1962), pp. 32–33; also his "Some Limits of Rational Man Organization Theory," *Public Administration Review*, Vol. 33, No. 3 (May/June 1973), pp. 253–267.

34. Strauss, p. 265.

35. Warren G. Bennis, *Changing Organizations: Essays on the Development and Evolution of Human Organization* (New York: McGraw-Hill, 1966), p. 192.

36. Maslow, 1965, p. 6.

37. For further discussion of the ideological bent of industrial humanism see Herbert G. Wilcox, "Hierarchy, Human Nature, and the Participative Panacea," *Public Administration Review*, Vol. 29 (January/February 1969), pp. 58–61. Interestingly, the "new public administration" approach explicitly rejects "increased output" as a reason to adopt participation: Michael Harmon, "Social Equity and Organizational Man," *Public Administration Review*, Vol. 34, No. 1 (January/February 1974), pp. 11–18.

38. John R. Maher (ed.), *New Perspectives in Job Enrichment* (New York: Van Nostrand Reinhold Company, 1971); also, Tim McNamar, "White Collar Job Enrichment," *Public Administration Review*, Vol. 33, No. 6 (November/December 1973), pp. 563–568.

39. Abraham H. Maslow, *Motivation and Personality* (New York: Harper and Brothers, 1954), pp. 144–145; Amitai Etzioni, "A Creative Adaptation to a World of Rising Shortages," *The Annals of the American Academy of Political and Social Science*, Vol. 420 (July 1975), pp. 98–110 (on p. 101 Etzioni claims an instinctoid self-actualization drive).

40. Pelz and Andrews.

41. Robert Dubin, Joseph E. Champoux, and Lyman W. Porter, "Central Life Interests and Organizational Commitment of Blue-Collar and Clerical Workers," *Administrative Science Quarterly*, Vol. 20 (September 1975), pp. 411–421.

42. Eugene A. Friedmann and Robert J. Havighurst (eds.), *The Meaning of Work and*

Retirement (Chicago: University of Chicago Press, 1954); Nancy C. Morse and Robert S. Weiss, "The Functions and Meanings of Work and the Job," *American Sociological Review*, Vol. 20 (April 1955), pp. 191–198. Citizen-state relations may well conform to a similar kind of "detached involvement" for many people: cf., James A. Reidel, "Citizen Participation: Myths and Realities," *Public Administration Review*, Vol. 32, No. 3 (May/June 1972), pp. 211–220.

43. Furthermore, Seeman presents evidence indicating that the ramifications of alienated labor for society may be negligent or minimal. His data indicate that work alienation and other forms of alienation are negatively or only slightly correlated. Melvin Seeman, "The Urban Alienations: Some Dubious Theses from Marx to Marcuse," *Journal of Personality and Social Psychology*, Vol. 19 (August 1971), pp. 135–143; and Melvin Seeman, "The Signals of '68: Alienation in Pre-Crisis France," *American Sociological Review*, Vol. 37 (August 1972), pp. 385–402.

44. Frederick Herzberg, *Work and the Nature of Man* (New York: World Publishing Company, Inc., 1966), pp. 168–192.

45. See Argyris' evaluation and restatement of his position in "Personality and Organization Theory Revisited." *Administration Science Quarterly*, Vol. 18 (June 1973), pp. 141–167.

46. The reader is referred to footnote 26 for confirming evidence of this point.

47. Nancy C. Morse, *Satisfactions in the White-Collar Job* (Ann Arbor: University of Michigan, Institute for Social Research, 1953); Roland J. Pellegrin and Charles H. Coates, "Executives and Supervision: Contrasting Definitions of Career Success," *Administrative Science Quarterly*, Vol. 1 (1956–1957), pp. 506–517; Frank Friedlander, "Comparative Work Value Systems," *Personnel Psychology*, Vol. 18 (Spring 1965), pp. 1–20; Richard Centers and Daphne E. Bugental, "Intrinsic and Extrinsic Job Motivations Among Different Segments of the Working Population," *Journal of Applied Psychology*, Vol. 50 (June 1966), pp. 193–197; Frank Friedlander, "Importance of Work Versus Non-Work Among Socially and Occupationally Stratified Groups," *Journal of Applied Psychology*, Vol. 50 (December 1966), pp. 437–441; and H. Roy Kaplan and Curt Tausky, "Work and the Welfare Cadillac: The Function of and Commitment to Work Among the Hard-Core Unemployed," *Social Problems*, Vol. 19 (Spring 1972), pp. 469–483.

48. J. W. Atkinson (ed.), *Motives in Fantasy, Action, and Society* (Princeton, N.J.: D. Van Nostrand Company, Inc., 1958).

49. Vroom.

50. J. C. Hunt and J. W. Hill, "The New Look in Motivation Theory and Organizational Research," *Human Organization*, Vol. 28 (Summer 1969), pp. 100–109; Edward E. Lawler III, *Motivation in Work Organizations* (Monterey, Calif: Brooks/Cole 1973).

51. It is noteworthy that the recent HEW report, *Work in America* (Cambridge, Mass.: The MIT Press, 1973), indicated urban university professors were more satisfied with their jobs than various other groups of workers, p. 16.

52. Michael A. Murray, "Comparing Public and Private Management," *Public Administration Review*, Vol. 35, No. 4 (July/August 1975), pp. 364–371.

Organizational Contradictions in Public Bureaucracies: Toward a Marxian Theory of Organizations*

Wolf Heydebrand

Organizational theory, like other theories in the social sciences, has been dominated by powerful ideological forces which, taken together, have more or less successfully reproduced and legitimized the structure of capitalist society. Organizational theory is thus a historical product, reflecting and reconstructing—like all products of mental labor—more or less adequately its own practical environment. In sociology, the history of organization theory, from Taylor to Likert, from Weber to Parsons, is well documented and need not be recounted here. Economics and politics, business and public administration have their own histories of organizational theory, but substantively they differ only in academic details from that in sociology.

The purpose of this paper is to outline the beginnings of an alternative theory of organizations, based on Marxian categories and propositions. The usual procedure for developing theoretical alternatives is to begin by criticizing existing theories, to point out the issues the latter treat as marginal or non-problematic, and to emphasize the phenomena and relationships they do not or cannot explain as compared to the alternatives. In addition, one might consider spelling out the criteria for adequate theorizing, be it conceived as causal explanation, emergent interpretation, or some form of theoretical praxis. I would like to skip these important stages for purposes of this paper, partly because there is already a growing critical literature (Braverman, 1974; Cohen, 1972; Merkle, 1968; Whyte, 1973; Goldman, 1973; Karpik, 1972a; Perrow, 1972; Benson, 1973a, 1973b; Lukacs, 1968; Gintis, 1973; Lefort, 1974; Baptista, 1974; Wright, 1974). More importantly, however, there is now a need—and the possibility—of *doing* a Marxian analysis of organizations.

Needless to say, a discussion of Marxian concepts is either absent in organizational textbooks, or badly distorted, or focusing only on Marxian or neo-Marxian theories of the state (e.g., Mouzelis, 1968). Important as it is, a merely critical posture has certain limitations and pitfalls. For example, the negation of mainstream theory or orthodox methodology may serve as common ground for a variety of unorthodox, deviant, or critical positions. But negation is only one aspect of a larger process of posing, counterposing, and resolving problems—that is, transcending and superseding contradictions. In the language of dialectics, negation is but one moment within praxis. Thus, while we are negating certain

*This is a revised version of a paper presented at the Annual Meetings of the American Sociological Association, San Francisco, August 25, 1975. For helpful comments on earlier drafts of this paper, I am grateful to Isaac Balbus, Kenneth Benson, Eliot Freidson, Irwin Goffman, David Greenberg, Edward Lehman, Andrew Rollings, Sarah Rosenfield, and Carroll Seron.

rigid, reified methodological procedures, we also need to move toward transcending them *and* our own counter-position. Concretely, this means that we will not make theoretical and methodological progress if we merely counterpose new methods to old ones, hermeneutics against causal-explanatory empiricism, interpretation against the technical-rational mode of scientific method, detached analysis against evaluation, intervention, and social action. We may have a chance of developing a broader methodological praxis if we retain the interpretive mode together with the "objectifying" scientific mode as natural phases of the process of inquiry—that is, if we develop a method that becomes *practical* in the sense that it changes the object of inquiry or, at least, indicates how the object can be changed. Praxis does not replace interpretation, but includes it.

. In this paper, I will begin by presenting a few basic categories and propositions of Marxian analysis. I will then develop these ideas for increasingly concrete examples of organizations . . . In the conclusion, I will try to tie this analysis back to some more general questions of Marxian method.

Some Basic Categories and Propositions

The fundamental starting point of this analysis is the Marxian distinction between human activity as an ongoing historical process and the outcome or product of that activity (Marx, 1904, 1967, 1973). Human practical activity—or praxis—is always historically situated and can be defined in both individual and collective terms—that is, it may refer to the conscious practical activity of an individual person or to the ideologically and politically articulated organizing activities of groups, classes, or communities. This conception of praxis is to be distinguished from related meanings in philosophical pragmatism where inquiry and action are seen as part of a continuous process, but in a non-critical and ahistorical form (Bernstein, 1971; Novack, 1975).

In very general terms, the Marxian notion of praxis includes the following basic processes which can take the form of collective organizing activity: producing the means of subsistence (i.e., work and material production), producing language and the means of communication and interaction (i.e., symbolic production, consciousness as process), engaging in creative and innovative activity (material and symbolic, including artistic activity), reproducing human existence through biological, social, and ideological reproduction processes, and developing and expressing needs, including the creation of "new needs."

The sum total of outcomes or products of human practical activity—that is, the man-made material, social, and cultural world surrounding us and internalized in us—is assumed to have objective historical existence.

Two somewhat different *types of outcomes* must be distinguished: outcomes can be products, constructs, or artifacts, and they can also be activities themselves (i.e., ways of doing things, procedures, methods, techniques). The distinction becomes important when we see that activities, in the form of *established* methods or procedures, can be totally mechanical. A machine or a routine procedure thus embodies previous activity and may produce an outcome of its own, but the activity of a machine is clearly different from human practical activity.

In general, we can say that the notion of *outcomes*—whether as product or method—includes the resources and conditions of material life, the concrete historical forms of social relations, social organization, and social control, and the forms of knowledge, art, technology, consciousness as product (ideas, language), history, and ideology (the intentional, activist reproduction and construction of the world by means of language).

Marx' famous proposition that social existence *determines* consciousness can therefore be extended to read: human social life *includes* consciousness, just as the notion of 'praxis' includes conscious activity. The postulated opposition (or unity) between theory and praxis is a dualistic, non-dialectical construct.

It should also be stressed in this connection that language, as the vehicle of consciousness, plays a double role in the activity-outcome process. Language limits and guides behavior due to its crucial function in socialization and institutionalization. Language preserves and transmits traditional and established forms of social control, organization, and method, and therefore it permits specific historical actors such as church, state, commodity production to mystify reality and to conceive of things and relations as symbols, myths, and fetishes, and vice versa. But language is also one of the most creative, innovative, demystifying and liberative aspects of human practical activity. It is for this reason that language plays such an important role both in the development, communication, and diffusion of ideologies of the 'status quo' and in revolutionary imagery.

For those who have some difficulty with the concepts of dialectics, contradiction and praxis, it is of crucial importance to understand that all of these examples of activity and outcome have one element in common: they refer to *historically mediated processes* rather than formal logical categories. This means that activity and outcome are *not* synchronic or simultaneous events, *nor* that they are immediately or mechanically related, *nor* that they are simple dualistic or logical opposites. Rather, outcomes may be seen as more or less incomplete, more or less imperfect historical objectifications of conscious, practical activity.

The unity of the real-life process binding activity and outcome together in a specific social and historical context can be seen as the 'totality' within which the process occurs, within which it can be understood, and from which it can be explained. To the extent that objective historical outcomes of previous activity tend to come into contradiction with the ongoing practical activity of social groups, this unity or socio-historical totality is time and again being transformed and transcended.

There is a tendency to confuse the idea of logical contradiction (e.g., A equals non-A) or of conflict between dualistic opposites (good and evil, freedom and necessity, individual and society) with the notion of historically evolving and mediated contradictions between activity and outcome. This confusion between dualism and dialectics is probably the single most prolific source of misunderstanding and distortion of Marxian dialectics.

It is therefore crucial (and not just a matter of semantics) to maintain a theoretical distinction between the notions of *conflict* between logical, moral, or metaphysical opposites and the historical tendency toward *contradiction* between two temporally and structurally separate aspects of a unitary process: the contradiction between activity and outcome. Purely logical, positivist, moral-utopian, or ahistorical interpretations of Marxian ideas tend to miss this point. Such interpretations tend to focus, instead, either on the metaphysical "activity" of Hegelian dialectics, or on the abstract "conflict" between human nature and social order or freedom and necessity, or on the objectified historical outcomes of social and political activity (see, e.g., Popper, 1945, 1963; Tucker, 1967).

These remarks are not meant to deprecate the usefulness of the concept of conflict between two structures or interests as a descriptive or analytic category. They are merely to point to the limitations of "conflict" as an *a priori* category of social interaction and of culture (as, e.g., in Simmel's unchangeable, hence tragic conflict between "more-life" and "more-than-life", cf. Simmel, 1968; 1955), as a metaphysical principle of the human condition (Hobbes, 1962), or as a concept which is seen as essentially equivalent to the notions of historical or structural contradiction (Althusser, 1970; Godelier, 1973).

The historical character of the processes mediating between activity and outcome is particularly salient in the formation and transformation of organizations. Organizations are concrete social structures formally established for the purpose of achieving specific objectives. As such, organizations can be seen as objective historical outcomes of practical collective activity, especially activity organized around the production of material life and the reproduction of social life.

Because the concepts of *production* and *reproduction* of the human mode of life are so fundamental from the point of view of survival, mastery over nature, and the direction of human history, these concepts assume special importance in Marx' analysis of the historical development of human societies. Thus, from among the elements of the human *mode of life*, Marx singles out especially the *mode of production*, arguing that the forces of production continuously create certain objective outcomes, viz. the accumulated social *product* and the social *relations* of production. While the accumulation of the social product is a central category for the general analysis of capitalist development, it is the concepts of production and reproduction of the social relations of capitalism which are particularly important for understanding the organization of work and, hence, the structure of work organizations. From this perspective, the historical formation of the forces and relations of production is merely a special case of the fundamental process of ongoing human practical activity which, in the course of human history, is confronted not only with nature, but increasingly with its own products. The special application of this contradiction between forces and relations of production to the development of industrial capitalism is well known and constitutes the central contribution of Marxian social theory.

Since the concept of "forces of production" is still fairly abstract, let me specify it further in terms of its more concrete social and historical forms. The central core of the notion of productive forces is, of course, human labor-power— that is physical and mental labor and its extensions in terms of skills, the use of rational practices as well as science and research. In addition, productive forces refer to the use of tools, instruments and machines, and generally, the development of technical innovations and new forms of energy. Finally, the concept includes the productive self-activity of social groups and organizations, both in the sense of developing new forms of cooperation, new ways of structuring and organizing collective activity, and in the sense of creating new social needs. Historically, this may mean, for example, the development of rational forms of work organization and administration as against the control structures of traditional elites such as feudal aristocracies and crafts or professional guilds (Marx, 1967, 1973; Weber, 1968), or the development of self-management and workers' control as against current bureaucratic, oligarchic, or technocratic power structures (Gramsci, 1971; Gorz, 1964, 1970, 1973; Korsch, 1938; Adizes and Borgese, 1975; Bettelheim, 1974).

Similarly, the concept of "social relations of production" can be specified in terms of conditions and forms of ownership and control of the means of production as well as the means of administration, political control, and violence; the forms of exchange, circulation, distribution, and consumption of the social product; the forms of the division and control of labor, including especially the authority relations associated with these forms; established production and control processes, including established technologies and cybernetic control systems; and institutionalized social relations—that is, the whole spectrum of normatively and ideologically guided forms of social action and interaction, including, of course, law and state.

Given the fact that Marx developed these ideas with reference to macrosocial structures and the historical transformation of whole political economies, how relevant and useful are they for the analysis of organizations? Let me begin to respond to this not wholly rhetorical question by specifying the notion of "organizational contradiction."

Organization vs. Organizing Activity

It is not difficult to conceive of an "organization"—an established structure—as the outcome of organization as process—that is, of organizing activity. This outcome is not so much an accumulated material product or commodity as it is a social structure, a set of established social relations. As before, this distinction draws attention to "social relations" as a special type of outcome of collective activity, even though social relations, just as organizational structures, are basically dependent on the production and accumulation of material resources. Given the articulation of the activity-outcome process in terms of the two phases of organizational development, namely organizing activity vs. organizational structure as outcome, why should these phases come into contradiction with each other?

In Marxian theory it is assumed that productive forces change and grow continuously because of their roots in human practical activity, and that they can be arrested and blocked only temporarily. It is the resistance of established social relations to adaptation to the ever-changing forces of production which creates the dynamic of social and organizational contradictions. Organizing activity does not cease just because the organization has become established. However, it is possible to suspend or suppress such activity, whether in the context of self-organization of labor such as union organizing, or in the context of ongoing revolutionary activity within, or against, the revolutionary political state. The general Marxian notion of this process is that the greater the economic and political investment in the established relations of production (i.e., in the organizational apparatus) and the greater the separation of the control structure from the collectivity of producers, the greater the likelihood of a radical transformation of the established social relations. However, it is not the abstract notion of opposition or conflict between two forces, but the developing contradiction between activity and outcome which distinguishes the Marxian dialectic from the dualistic framework of "conflict theory" (Michels, 1966; Dahrendorf, 1959; Crozier, 1964; Collins, 1975). While both the forces and the relations of production can be seen as "opposite" or "conflicting" aspects of the mode of production, the crucial element in a Marxian dialectical conception is that historical activities produce historical outcomes. Specifically, the ongoing practical activity creates and establishes social relations which, as objectified and—under certain historical conditions—alienated outcomes, tend in time to come under pressure to adapt to the ever-changing forces of production. Thus, social relations and structures tend to come into contradiction with the very forces that created them as the result of specific historical processes, not as a matter of principle. In other words, the idea of a *tendency* toward the development of contradictions and their resolutions implies a more or less specifiable *probability* for such developments to occur, *not* their necessity or inevitability.

Similarly, once organizations have developed into established social structures, they tend to come into contradiction with the organizing forces of human labor and human collective self-activity. These organizing forces include all those elements that gave rise to the organization in the past and that continue to transform the organization in the present. For example, such forces include the movement-aspects of organizations (Zald and Ash, 1966) or the promise of spontaneous and liberative collective activity and yet unfulfilled goals. They also include the utopian or reactionary expectations of an ideal future society which animate the political thrust of occupational and professional status groups such as syndicates, unions and professional associations. Organizing forces are activated by groups demanding greater autonomy or insisting on some degree of reform within the established political context. Lastly, organizational forces of production that continue to develop within organizations include modernizing and rationalizing elites capable of mobilizing resources against the established technique and hegemony of traditional elites. Cases in point include: the ascendancy of modern bureaucratic administrations in growing corporate enterprises and nation-states (Weber, 1968); the dominance of monopolistic transnational corporate elites over their counterparts in the competitive sector (O'Connor, 1973); the professional and corporate resistance to certain technical innovations and their application (Stern 1959); and the controversial cost-benefit orientation of "modernizing" administrators in professional service organizations such as hospitals, schools, and universities, and in public bureaucracies such as government agencies and courts.

Organizations are not necessarily unitary entities, holistic "actors", or integrated systems, but rather sites of various developing contradictions. This means that "primary" and "secondary," "antagonistic" and "non-antagonistic" contradictions may develop between the different phases or structures of the same reality (Mao Tse-Tung, 1968; Lenin, 1915). For example, contradictions may develop between different levels of organizational hierarchies even though those "in authority", such as doctors in hospitals, judges in courts, or university faculties may find themselves on the defensive against the demands and encroachment of managers and administrators who, in turn, may reel under the impact of output and productivity quotas set at still higher levels of the system. O'Connor's (1973) analysis of the "fiscal crisis of the state" shows the capitalist state apparatus and its administrative structures to be as *necessary* for the realization of surplus-value as it is *contradictory* to the general character of private capitalist appropriation and accumulation. Yet, contradictions need not always lead to radical transformation of the established bureaucracy, but may simply appear in the form of a political "crisis" or "legitimation crisis" (Habermas, 1975; Offe, 1973). As such, these crises can be seen as surface manifestations of deeper structural contradictions. Their diagnosis as historically relatively new types of crises should, however, *not* lead contemporary observers to the too facile interpretation that state and politics are phenomena *sui generis* and autonomous, or that the class struggle has been "displaced . . . from the sphere of direct production to the sphere of administration" (O'Connor, 1970:581). Organizational contradictions may express themselves in crises where established control structures (e.g., professional authority structures) fail to respond adequately to the requirements of increased productivity, or where the autonomy of the whole organization is threatened by the crisis-triggered responses and adaptations of the larger system. Examples include the potential absorption of professionals by bureaucracies, the legislative and judicial branches of government by the executive, or the state and the "public interest" by a private economic system. Crises such as recessions, shortages or credibility gaps are probably most parsimoniously treated as surface phenomena which indicate the presence of contradictions and struggles. Frequently, the short-term solutions resulting from such crises may only deepen the more basic, underlying contradictions (Mattick, 1969).

The implications of what has been said so far are:

1. Organizations, like other social structures, must be studied in terms of the historical processes that gave rise to them so that the potential contradictions between established organization and the organizing processes become visible;

2. The viability of social structure should be measured not so much in terms of the duration, temporal stability, and growth or size of its sub-units such as organizations, but in terms of the rate at which they are generated and the rate at which new forms are emerging or old forms are disappearing (e.g., the high rate at which communes and collectives are born as compared to their relatively short duration; or new small business entries in the competitive sector vs. their bankruptcy rates);

3. Treating organizations as integral "actors" or "in action" is an abstraction which hides the specific constellation of groups and actors *within* organizations and mystifies the specific *interests* which different groups and actors have in the shape and output of organizations. The separate political, economic, and social contradictions in organizations can serve as a guide to the basic *class contradictions*—that is, the identification of actors, forces, and interests on whose behalf organizational policies are formulated and implemented and for whom the organization serves as an instrument of class struggle;

4. Organizations vary in significant ways in the extent to which structural contradictions have already developed within them, both qualitatively, and in the extent to which these contradictions have become conscious to the participants—that is, in the extent to which they are reflected in ideologies and practical political positions;

5. Organizations, while they are themselves sites of developing contradictions, are always part of a larger political economy, a macro-social and historical context, and particularly part of a socio-historical formation in which a given mode of production is tending toward dominance over others. The basic contradictions within the political economy of advanced capitalism, e.g., those between state and economy or capital and labor or—*within* capital itself—those between capital accumulation and the realization of surplus-value, will be reflected in the formation and transformation of almost all types of organizations. I will document this particular claim with respect to public bureaucracies, namely agencies of government which, in the nature of the case, play an increasingly prominent role in the confrontation between state and economy;

6. A final, but crucial point is that what appears as an abstract, purely analytical, even universal process must ultimately be described in concrete, specific, historical terms. This means that the more general, abstract, and established categories of analysis must ultimately be changed, too, if they are not to come into contradiction with the specific, concrete, historical descriptions of contemporary and future observers, a difficult epistemological problem (Marx, 1973; Rosdolsky, 1968, vol. 2).

Contradictions in Work Organizations

A prime factor in the development of the practice and ideology of organizational efficiency and cost-effectiveness is the need to increase the productivity of labor.

This observation presupposes a general analytic distinction between productive activity (labor) and the productivity of labor—that is, the relative capacity and efficiency of labor in generating surplus value. This distinction becomes especially important insofar as surplus created by increased productivity is *not* appropriated by the producers themselves, but rather by private capital or by state bureaucracies with only secondary regard to the nature, quality, or social usefulness of the product, or without regard to the social and human costs of production and its consequences for the quality of life.

Under capitalism, the growth of the productive forces of labor, skills, and technical innovations has been necessary for the creation of surplus value and the accumulation of capital, even though production and accumulation tend to come more and more into contradiction with surplus-realization and distribution (Mattick, 1969; O'Connor, 1973; Baran and Sweezy, 1966).

Under state socialism, the question of labor productivity is, of course, equally important, but perhaps more for political rather than merely economic reasons. The practice of scientific management and Taylorism was backed up by a more or less explicit system of bureaucratic-hierarchical controls *both* under capitalism (Braverman, 1974; Marglin, 1974; Stone, 1974; Wachtel, 1974; Gintis, 1973; Gorz, 1972; Hodges, 1970; Schumm-Garling, 1972) *and* under the early forms of state socialism (Bendix, 1956; Merkle, 1968; Fleron and Fleron, 1972; Gvishiani, 1972; Mallet, 1970). Thus, in organizations devoted primarily to productive activity or labor—in short, work organizations—the crucial internal contradiction arises from policies designed to rationalize work activity and the historical outcome of this process, namely a system of authority relations based on the division of labor and, most importantly, on the control of labor.

The theoretical consequences of this empirical-historical connection between the growth of bureaucratic hierarchy and the enforcement of labor productivity are flying in the face of received organizational theory. Both the functionalist and the neo-Weberian explanations of hierarchical differentiation and bureaucratic authority are based on the presumed functional-rational requirements of organizational size and complexity, and on the impersonal imperatives of task and technology. However, even the "human relations" school which developed as the result of changes in production technology, internal contradictions of scientific management, the Great Depression, and labor protest could not conceal its ultimate concern with labor productivity in the interest of private capital accumulation (Bogomolova, 1973; Perrow, 1972). The critique leveled in turn by the "human relations" school against the structural-functionalists is thus merely part of a methodological quarrel among ideological twins (Argyris, 1972).

The variations on the basic theme of how to control labor and to increase productivity depend, of course, on various distinctions to be made among organizational variables, organizational types, and organizational contexts. Notably, one may want to look at the effects of the following factors on relative surplus-value and labor productivity: (1) the nature and complexity of the work process as determined by the object of labor (e.g., manufacturing vs. service organizations); (2) the ratio of technology to labor (constant vs. variable capital) which helps to distinguish capital-intensive from labor-intensive organizations; and (3) the nature and form of organizational autonomy (e.g., the nature of control over resources and goals in such historically diverse forms as craft guilds, professional organizations, family controlled enterprises, private corporations under various conditions of stock ownership and managerial control, publicly or governmentally controlled agencies and organs of the state, and self-controlled (autonomous) organizations under various forms of economic, social, and political self-determination and self-management).

Generally, these distinctions are based on the criteria of how *labor-power* (the central force of production) is related to the *means of labor* (mainly technology), to the *object of labor* (material vs. human objects and, generally, the complexity of the task structure), to the *division of labor*, to the *control of labor* (supervision, review, budgeting, cost-accounting and auditing, and hierarchical levels and authority relations), and, finally, to the *organization of labor* (craft guilds, management or government, unions and professional associations, self-organization and self-management).

Some of these categories such as "means of labor," "object of labor," division of labor, means of production etc. are part of the conceptual core of traditional Marxist economic analysis (Lange, 1970). By contrast, the notions of control of labor and self-organization of labor have changed in their historical and political relevance and continue to be redefined from various perspectives such as Soviet sociology and systems theory (Afanasyev, 1971; Glezerman, 1971; Osipov, 1969; Gvishiani, 1972), the evolving Chinese experience (Schurman, 1968; Whyte, 1973), the "revisionist" and "humanist" critique of "statism" in Yugoslavia and Eastern Europe (Stojanovic, 1973; Markovic, 1974; Adizes and Borgese, 1975; Berger, 1969; Fromm, 1966), and the various strands of academic and critical Marxism in Europe and the United States (Fischer, 1971; Howard and Klare, 1971). Consequently, various distinctions between organizational contexts need to be made, depending on the specific historical forms of the organization and self-organization of labor as they appear, for example, under commercial or industrial capitalism, or in various stages of industrial capitalism such as competitive, oligopolistic, monopolistic, state-capitalist and trans-national (imperialist) forms, or under different forms of state socialism, (e.g., early vs. later forms, European vs. non-European forms).

Organizational contexts and environments such as monopoly capitalism or state socialism have their own internal contradictions and influence their constituent organizational structures in terms of these contradictions. For example, a crucial focus in a Marxian approach is the analysis of the relations between class structure and organizations (Goldman, 1972; Gorz, 1972; Hodges, 1971; Il Manifesto Group, 1972; Braverman, 1974), between monopoly capital and new organizational forms (Baran and Sweezy, 1966; Andreano, 1972; Karpik, 1972b, c; Touraine, 1971; O'Connor, 1973); and between technology and state bureaucracy (Mallet, 1970; Karpik, 1972d; Galbraith, 1967). Obviously, there are many other kinds of organization-environment relationships that can be analyzed in terms of the contradictions within the larger social formation. By contrast, *contradictions within work organizations*, in addition to reflecting the dynamics of the environment, may be articulated in very specific ways.

Control Structures and Contradictions: A Historical View

It may be useful at this point to delineate briefly at least three major forms of organizational control structures and their respective contradictions with developing productive forces in modern work organizations. I will not attempt to document the development of these structures in this paper except to suggest that much of the evidence is available in the corpus of Weber's work and in the history and sociology of occupations and professions.

One major historical form of organizational control structure is lodged in *occupational status groups*, with two sub-types: crafts and professions. The power of *craft guilds* is based on the monopoly over practical expertise and control over a still largely secret knowledge base. The autonomous ("free") *professions* (i.e., collegially and peer-controlled status groups) provide services to clients based on control over a theoretically and scientifically expanding as well as increasingly rationalized knowledge base. Both crafts and professions gain additional power from the use and sale of "judgment", i.e., services or decisions produced under conditions of task variability, complexity, uncertainty, or danger. Hence, successful craftsmen and professional practitioners tend to have charismatic qualities, in addition to commanding high social status, economic resources, and political power.

A second major type of organizational control structure to be distinguished here is the well-known Weberian *legal-bureaucratic* ("monocratic") organization and administration of work, with two major sub-types: *private corporate bureaucracies*, emerging within industrial capitalism, and post-feudal *public bureaucracies*, emerging with the growth of the modern nation-state and central to contemporary technocratic state apparatuses. The routinization and commodifications of tasks and technical procedures under modern capitalist and state administrations has tended to "legitimate" the rationality and near-universal functionality of bureaucratic and technocratic forms of control.

The third major form of control structure is based on the economic, social, and political *self-organization of labor* within—and against—the "social relations" of all previously developed forms of work organization and control. Examples include the formation of guilds and professional associations against the dominant interests of church, landed aristocracy, private property, and state; trade and industrial (blue-collar) unions against private capital; service and public employee (white collar) unions against the capitalist state and semi-public service organizations; workers' control and communal self-management movements against the socialist state as well as against its fore-runners in the form of union bureaucracies, the welfare state, and state capitalism.

It is important to note that the concepts of self-organization of labor and workers' control at the post-bureaucratic level are to be distinguished analytically and historically from the notion of self-government of occupational and professional status groups described. Obviously, occupational self-government is a form of self-organization of labor as, for example, in craft guilds and professional associations. But there are crucial differences.

First, occupational status groups are specialized and exclusive, whereas the category of "workers" or "labor" is inclusive and cuts across different specialities and the division of labor. Secondly, occupational and professional self-interest is by definition particularistic, whereas work-place-specific, industry-wide, or economy-wide workers' control is, in theory at least, universalistic and oriented toward acting on behalf of the "public interest." Third, occupational status groups have, as a rule, narrow economistic and work-specific interests. This is also still true of much union policy, of "co-determination", and of many current forms of self-management. However, the idea of self-organization of labor is not restricted to economistic control of the work place, but extends to social, communal, and political forms of self-organization.

Finally, occupational and professional interest groups are centrally concerned with control over the process of *production* and the jurisdiction over the provision of services, but *not* with the marketing and *distribution* of products and services. Some early syndicalist conceptions of occupational-political self-determination and industrial democracy did envisage control over both production and distribution. Insofar as they did, they can be seen as utopian forerunners of the broad workers' control model indicated here, rather than as representatives of the medieval guild structure of crafts and of early professional forms (Durkheim, 1964; Vanek, 1975; Hunnius, 1973).

Each of these three major historical forms of organizational control structures tends to come into contradiction with the previous or existing control structure, and with the new productive forces and innovative forms in which labor-power develops. Thus, the rise of scientific and professional technique is initially opposed by church and aristocracy alike and accused of the secularization and demystification of the feudal world. The rise of bureaucratic and technocratic administration, embraced by state and capital, nevertheless threatens professional autonomy, privilege, and domain and is initially opposed on grounds of subverting the quality of service, but later subordinated to professional dominance. The rise of grassroots labor protest and organization, or even of client and consumer groups, is initially suppressed by capital, union bureaucracies, the state, and the established professions. Later, however, these movement-organizations are co-opted by efforts to shift political demands for control of production into the arena of distribution and consumption (i.e., socioeconomic mobility in terms of income and prestige) or attempts are made to "turn problems of politics into problems of administration" and regulation (Mannheim, 1936; Piven and Cloward, 1971).

Needless to say, these forms of organizational development and contradiction are both historical and analytical constructs—that is, they can be situated in historical sequences like feudalism, capitalism or socialism. However, once they have developed, they may also continue to survive and therefore appear together with later forms in a given socio-historical formation. The continued dominance of the "old professions" of law and medicine in capitalist societies is a good example of the latter case, namely the somewhat anachronistic survival of occupationally generic or even regressive, but economically and politically powerful occupational status groups.

The preceding typology represents a tentative outline of a general framework for analyzing the developing contradictions between new productive forces and the respective established organizational control structures and modes of work organization. As such, the framework suggests a link between a theory of occupations and professions and a theory of work organizations (see, for example, Hirsch's 1975 insightful discussion of the need for such a link).

In this paper, I am focusing only on the first of the two types of contradictions outlined above; namely, the rise of administrative rationalization as a "productive force" . . . Professional service organizations are typical settings for this kind of contradiction insofar as professionals are still the main producers or directors ("masters") of the work process.

The fate of professions in contemporary labor markets can be described in terms of at least three complementary processes of occupational transformation. First, as employees, professionals have become bureaucratized and integrated into organizational work structures, with a corresponding delegation of formerly "professional" functions to semi-professionals and nonprofessionals (Mills, 1951).

A general correlate of this process tends to be the degradation of work (Friedmann, 1955; Braverman, 1974) and, in some cases, a proletarianization and politicization of consciousness. Second, a portion of the old professions have moved into some form of small business or self-employed entrepreneurship, with a corresponding attenuation of the "service ideal", "collectivity orientation", and professional ethic in favor of "self-orientation" and a business ethic (Alford, 1975). Third, a residual group of professionals continue to operate in terms of the classical characteristics of autonomous professional service, but do so in relatively marginal and historically unique niches protected from competition and managerial inroads.

In professional organizations such as universities and hospitals, the so-called "conflict" between professionals and bureaucrats, professional and bureaucratic authority, the "occupational" and the "administrative principle" have become a major source of professional sociological concern (Freidson, 1973; Benson, 1973b). For example, the level of development of labor power in professional work organizations, the degree of formal specialization and expertise, the nature and development of the knowledge base, the use of established technique, in short, the relative autonomy and dominance of professionals (Freidson, 1970; Crozier, 1964; Ellul, 1963) may come into contradiction with the control over resources, the control and division of labor, and the self-organization of labor. Well-organized groups of established professionals may find themselves straddling the labor-management division in organizations since their concerns with furthering productive forces as worker-producers may contradict their vested interests in established technique, past accomplishment, and the prerogatives of "professional authority" and status. Thus, the more resources and power and status interests are invested in a given system of production and authority, the more those who control it will tend to oppose further changes in technique, rationalization, and even efficiency unless the control structure is left intact. Professionals may counterpose their own innovations, skills, and meritocratic hierarchies to those of administrators and managers (Mills, 1951; Alford, 1975) as monopolistic corporations may control their markets by restricting output, undersell competitors, or temporarily suppress inventions, patents, and new techniques of production (Baran and Sweezy, 1966; Stern, 1959).

Hence, there are growing contradictions between established technologies embodying past social relations of production and new, innovative techniques representing the growth of productive forces. One important example is the contradiction between established "professional" authority whose dominance is partly the result of previous successful application of "technique", on the one hand, and further rationalization of work, usually represented by the bureaucratic-administrative forces in organizations, on the other. The professionals and, generally, the representatives of "organized labor" tend to resist further rationalization and technical innovations since these processes undercut labor autonomy as well as the social and authority relations within unions.

These contradictions are exacerbated if resources for work activity and production (i.e., the means of labor and production) are controlled not by manual or professional workers themselves, but by an outside agency (e.g., a private corporation or a government agency), since now the interest to rationalize and to introduce efficient technique is represented by a structurally separate group *within* the same organization, ostensibly representing the interest of the *whole* organization, namely, the administration. The parallel to the relations between capitalist state bureaucracy and civil class society should be obvious here since the capitalist state tends to represent the *interests of private capital* while at the same time appearing to speak for the *"public interest"* in the name of equality of opportunity, formal participatory democracy (franchise), formal equality before the law, or even classlessness (Marx, 1967).

In professional service organizations, as special cases of work organizations, the presence or absence of control over resources suggests Weber's distinction between *autonomous* organizations (where professional workers control resources, jurisdiction, mandate—a rare case under modern capitalism or state socialism) and *heteronomous* organizations (where one or more of these elements are controlled by managers, i.e., either by private capital or public authority). The locus of control over resources (e.g., external budgetary vs. internal budgetary or non-budgetary fiscal types of organizations) thus becomes a crucial variable since control over resources also implies control over labor-power.

In professional organizations, then, the system of established authority relations and the interests of the professional elites come historically more and more into contradiction with the forces of administrative innovation. Politically and ideologically, those forces, in turn, become more and more associated with the impulse to rationalize and routinize work activity, to reduce costs, and to extend control over resources and labor. Characteristically, the idea of total worker, client, and community control is even less thinkable for professionals than that of administrative modernization since self-determination of *all* producers is still below the political horizon of professional elites. Modern managers have begun to develop strategies for dealing with self-management and "co-determination," but professionals still fight their old battle against the routinization and rationalization of work and against the formidable ally of bureaucracy—technological innovation to improve efficiency and productivity. . . .

Conclusion

The view of organizations developed here aims at a dialectical-historical conception based on a critical adaptation of basic Marxian categories and propositions. Organizations, as the concrete structural manifestations of social institutions, are seen as the more or less established outcome of historically specific human practical activity. The basic dialectical process is therefore contained in the developing contradictions between activity and outcome, labor and product, forces and relations of production. Under specific historical conditions, such as the capitalist mode of production, or under state socialism, these contradictions assume a particularly problematic character since private ownership and, to a lesser extent, state control of the means of production tend to have economically and politically disastrous consequences. As Marx foresaw, the state bureaucracy itself is historically an alienated organizational form which tends to come into contradiction with the social forces that gave rise to it.

Under the political economy of state capitalism, the state tends to be co-opted, but it tends to be politically dominant under state socialism. The conscious political and practical uses of organizational contradictions for purposes of guided social transformation appear to be nowhere more developed than in contemporary China (Schurman, 1968; Bettelheim, 1974). Chinese social structures seem to embody a dialectical logic of organization such that both productive forces and the social relations of production enjoy a relatively high degree of autonomy. The practical political uses of organizational contradictions in China must therefore be clearly distinguished from those in other political economies, if only because in non-dialectical structures the contradictions result from the rigidity and resistance of the social and political control structures, whereas contradictions seem to be the conscious driving force of social change in China. In short, under advanced forms of state socialism there seems to be a historical possibility of transforming the state apparatus itself by *political means.* That possibility appears to be absent under other forms of state socialism, and certainly under monopoly and transnational capitalism and the liberal-conservative construct called "post-industrial society"

While organizations vary in the extent to which they are bureaucratized and the extent to which their resources are controlled by the self-organization of labor or by others inside or outside the organization, the basic contradiction between the established control structure and the need to rationalize the work process (i.e., the need to make labor more productive) is almost axiomatic under present historical conditions. It is clearly observable in corporations, but also in schools (Callahan, 1962; Bowles and Gintis, 1976) and universities (Newt Davidson Collective, 1974), in hospitals, in welfare agencies and—as the fiscal crisis of the public sector sharpens—in organizations under public authority and in government agencies. As a result, measures of administrative efficiency and innovation will tend to be opposed by unions and professional associations, thus introducing new rigidities and "secondary contradictions" into an already complex and reified social structure. Administrative rationalization is therefore often perceived as leading to irrationality and, ultimately, to greater inefficiency and waste. Not accidentally, the unanticipated consequences of social planning are often cited against various social reform efforts and in support of economically liberal, politically conservative, and socially anti-planning positions (Harvey, 1973).

The language of latent functions, dysfunctions, "unanticipated consequences" and of the inevitability of economic scarcity and social conflict is profoundly dualistic and non-dialectical. Throughout this paper I have stressed the importance of the distinction between dualism and dialectics by suggesting that "conflict," conceived within a logical, static, and ahistorical framework, tends to be based on antinomies—that is, on the postulated opposition between mutually irreducible principles or forces. The solution of such dualisms is necessarily external; it is based on the choice or dominance of one or the other, or on the more or less uneasy and unstable unification, "integration," or a compromise between them. This is as true for metaphysics and social theory as it is for political practice. The Aristotelian law of contradiction dictates the non-identity of A and non-A. By contrast, in a dialectical-historical framework of "totality," the historical process which binds activity and outcome, praxis and product together also *mediates* between these two moments or phases (Marx, 1973; Meszaros, 1970).

Therefore, a Marxian dialectical contradiction does not exist in and of itself, and certainly not "immediately," but it develops in the process that leads from practical activity to objective outcome. In other words a dialectical contradiction is always mediated in historical time. And typically, only when the outcome appears in its objectified form or is appropriated by someone other than the producer (alienation) does the process of reflection and self-reflection, i.e., historical consciousness of the contradiction) take on an ideological and political form. Marx' deduction of the probability of political revolution from developing historical contradictions is a well-known example of this process.

While I am claiming that the Marxian categories and propositions outlined in this paper apply to all work organizations, and probably to all known forms of social structure, the validity of these claims needs to be demonstrated further, both in terms of theoretical-historical elaboration and empirical-practical analysis . . . The theoretical tools for such an analysis are certainly available. However, if Kuhn is correct, a Marxian theory of organizations will *not* become paradigmatic in the social sciences unless there is sufficient consensus among the community of scholars—that is, until there is some degree of *ideological* consensus as to the explanatory and interpretive power of such a theory. For obvious reasons, such an ideological self-transformation of academic organization theory is highly unlikely. In the meantime, I am convinced that the praxis of organizational actors and the applied theory of scientific and technocratic management in organizations will continue to provide many more and increasingly visible examples of contradictions in organizations.

References

Adizes, Izhak and Elizabeth Mann Borgese (eds.), 1975, *Self-Management: New Dimensions to Democracy.* Santa Barbara: Clio.

Afanasyev, V. D., 1971, *The Scientific Management of Society.* Moscow: Progress Publishers.

Alford, Robert, 1975, *Health Care Politics: Ideological and Interest Group Barriers to Reform.* Chicago: University of Chicago Press.

Althusser, Louis, 1970, *For Marx.* New York: Vintage.

Andreano, R. L., (ed.), 1972, *Superconcentration/Supercorporation.* Warner Modular.

Argyris, Chris, 1972, *The Applicability of Organizational Sociology.* Cambridge: Cambridge University Press.

Baptista, Jose, 1974, "Bureaucracy, political system, and social dynamic." *Telos* 22:66–84.

Baran, Paul and Paul Sweezy, 1966, *Monopoly Capital.* New York: Monthly Review Press.

Bendix, Reinhard, 1956, *Work and Authority in Industry.* New York: Wiley.

Benson, Kenneth, 1973a, "Organizations: a dialectical view." Paper presented at the Annual Meetings of the American Sociological Association, New York City.

——— 1973b, "The analysis of bureaucratic-professional conflict: functional vs. dialectical approaches." *Sociological Quarterly* 14: 376–94.

Berger, Peter (ed)., 1969, *Marxism and Sociology.* New York: Appleton-Century-Crofts.

Bernstein, Richard, 1971, *Praxis and Action.* Philadelphia: University of Pennsylvania Press.

Bettelheim, Charles, 1974, *Cultural Revolution and Industrial Organization in China.* New York: Monthly Review Press.

Bogomolova, Nina, 1973, *"Human Relations" Doctrine: Ideological Weapon of the Monopolies.* Moscow: Progress Publishers.

Bowles, Samuel and Herbert Gintis, 1975, "Class power and alienated labor." *Monthly Review* 26(10):9–25.

——— 1976, *Schooling in Capitalist America: Educational Reform and the Contradictions of Economic Life.* New York: Basic Books.

Braverman, Harry, 1974, *Labor and Monopoly Capital.* New York: Monthly Review Press.

Callahan, Raymond, 1962, *Education and the Cult of Efficiency.* Chicago: University of Chicago Press.

Cohen, Jean, 1972, "Max Weber and the dynamics of rationalized domination." *Telos* 14:63–86.

Collins, Randall, 1975, "A Conflict Theory of Organizations." Pp. 286–347 in *Conflict Sociology.* New York: Academic Press.

Crozier, Michel, 1964, *The Bureaucratic Phenomenon*. Chicago: University of Chicago Press.

Dahrendorf, Ralf, 1959, *Class and Class Conflict in Industrial Society*. Stanford: Stanford University Press.

Durkheim, Emile, 1964, *The Division of Labor in Society*. (Preface to the 2nd edition.) New York: Free Press.

Ellul, Jacques, 1964, *The Technological Society*. New York: Vintage Books.

Fischer, George (ed)., 1971, *The Revival of American Socialism*. New York: Oxford University Press.

Fleron, Frederic and Lou Jean Fleron, 1972, "Administration theory as repressive political theory: the communist experience." *Telos* 12:63–92.

Freidson, Eliot, 1973, "Professions and the Occupational Principle." Pp. 19–38 in Eliot Freidson (ed). *The Professions and their Prospects*. Beverly Hills: Sage

———— 1970, *The Profession of Medicine*. New York: Dodd, Mead.

———— 1970, *Professional Dominance*. Chicago: Aldine-Atherton.

Friedmann, Georges, 1955, *Industrial Society*. Glencoe: Free Press.

Fromm, Erich (ed)., 1966, *Socialist Humanism*. New York: Anchor.

Galbraith, John K., 1967, *The New Industrial State*. New York: Signet.

Gintis, Herbert, 1973, "The Nature of the Labor Exchange: Toward a Radical Theory of the Firm." Harvard Institute of Economic Research, Discussion Paper #328. Cambridge, Mass: Harvard University.

Glezerman, G., 1971, *Socialist Society: Scientific Principles of Development*. Moscow: Progress Publishers.

Godelier, Maurice, 1973, "Structure and Contradiction in Capital." Pp. 334–68 in Robin Blackburn (ed.) *Ideology in Social Science*. New York: Vintage.

Goldman, Paul, 1973, "The organization caste system and the new working class." *Insurgent Sociologist* 3:41–52.

Gorz, Andre, 1973, *Socialism and Revolution*. New York: Anchor.

———— 1972, "Technical intelligence and the capitalist division of labor." *Telos*, 12:27–41

———— 1970, "Workers' control." *Socialist Revolution* 1(6):17–32.

———— 1964, *Strategy for Labor*. Boston: Beacon.

Gramsci, Antonio, 1971, *Selections from the Prison Notebooks*. New York: International Publishers.

Gvishiani, D., 1972, *Organization and Management: A Sociological Analysis of Western Theories*. Moscow: Progress Publishers.

Habermas, Juergen, 1975, *Legitimation Crisis*. Boston: Beacon.

Harvey, David, 1973, *Social Justice and the City*. Baltimore: Johns Hopkins University Press.

Hirsch, Paul, 1975, "Organizational analysis and industrial sociology: an instance of cultural lag." *The American Sociologist* 10:3–12.

Hobbes, Thomas, 1962, *Leviathan*. New York: Collier.

Hodges, Donald C., 1971, "Old and new working classes." *Radical America* 5:11–32.

———— 1970, "The relevance of 'capital' to the study of bureaucracy." *Telos*, 6:234–42.

Howard, Dick and Karl Klare (eds.), 1971, *The Unknown Dimension: European Marxism since Lenin*. New York: Basic Books.

Hunnius, Gerry, G. David Garson, and John Case (eds.), 1973, *Workers' Control: A Reader on Labor and Social Change*. New York: Vintage.

Il Manifesto Group, 1972, "Technicians and the Capitalist Division of Labor." *Socialist Revolution* 2:65–85.

Karpik, Lucien, 1972a, "Sociologie, economie politique et buts des organisations de production." *Revue Francaise de Sociologie* XIII:299–324.

———— 1972b, "Les politiques et les logiques d'action de la grande enterprise industrielle." *Sociologie du Travail* 14:82–105.

———— 1972c, "Multinational enterprises and large technological corporations." Translated from *Revue Economique* XXIII, 4:563–91.

———— 1972d, "Technological capitalism." Translated from *Sociologie du Travail* 14:2–34.

Korsch, Karl, 1938, *Karl Marx*. London: Chapman and Hall.

Lange, Oscar, 1970, "The subject matter of political economy: elementary concepts." Pp. 7–13 in David Mermelstein (ed.) *Economics*. New York: Random House.

Lefort, Claude, 1974, "What is bureaucracy?" *Telos* 22:31–65.

Lenin, V. I., 1915, *Philosophical Notebooks: Collected Works*, vol. 38, 359–63. Moscow: Foreign Language Publishing House.

Lukacs, Georg, 1968, *History and Class Consciousness*. London: Merlin.

Mallet, Serge, 1970, "Bureaucracy and technocracy in the socialist countries." *Socialist Revolution* 1:44–75.

Mannheim, Karl, 1936, *Ideology and Utopia*. New York: Harcourt Brace.

Mao Tse-Tung, 1968, *Four Essays on Philosophy*. Peking: Foreign Language Press.

Marglin, Stephen A., 1975, "What do bosses do?", Part II. *Review of Radical Political Economics* 7:20, 37.

———— 1974, "What do bosses do?" *Review of Radical Political Economics* 6:60–112.

Markovic, Mihailo, 1974, *From Affluence to Praxis*. Ann Arbor: University of Michigan.

Marx, Karl, 1973, *Grundrisse*. London: Penguin.

———— 1967, *Writings of the Young Marx on Philosophy and Society*. Lloyd D. Easton and Kurt H. Guddat (eds.) New York: Doubleday.

———— 1904, *A Contribution to the Critique of Political Economy*. Chicago: Kerr.

Mattick, Paul, 1969, *Marx and Keynes: The Limits of the Mixed Economy*. Boston: Porter Sargent.

Merkle, Judith A., 1968, "The Taylor strategy: organizational innovation and class structure." *Berkeley Journal of Sociology*. 8:59–81.

Meszaros, Istvan, 1970, *Marx's Theory of Alienation*. London: Merlin Press.

Michels, Roberto, 1966, *Political Parties*. New York: Dover.

Mills, C. Wright, 1951, *While Collar*. New York: Oxford.

Mouzelis, Nicos, 1968, *Organisation and Bureaucracy*. Chicago: Aldine.

Newt Davidson Collective, 1974, *Crisis at CUNY*.

Novack, George, 1975, *Pragmatism vs. Marxism*. New York: Pathfinder Press.

O'Connor, James, 1973, *The Fiscal Crisis of the State*. New York: St. Martin's Press.

———— 1970, "Some Contradictions of Advanced U.S. Capitalism." Pp. 577–88 in David Mermelstein (ed.) *Economics*. New York: Random House.

Offe, Claus, 1973a, *Strukturprobleme des Kapitalistischen Staates. (Structural Problems of the Capitalist State)*. Frankfurt: Suhrkamp.

———— 1973b, "The abolition of market control and the problem of legitimacy." *Working Papers on the Kapitalistate*. I:109–16; II:73–5.

Osipov, G., 1969, *Sociology: Problems of Theory and Method*. Moscow: Progress Publishers.

Perrow, Charles, 1972, *Complex Organizations: A Critical Essay*. Glenview: Scott Foresman.

Piven, Frances F. and Richard A. Cloward, 1971, *Regulating the Poor*. New York: Pantheon.

Popper, Karl, 1963, *Conjectures and Refutations*. New York: Basic Books.

———— 1945, *The Open Society and its Enemies*. London: Routledge and Kegan Paul 2 vols.

Rosdolsky, Roman, 1968, *Zur Entstehungsgeschichte des Marxschen 'Kapital'*. Frankfurt am Main: Europaeische Verlagsanstalt. 2 vols.

Schumm-Garling, Ursula, 1972, *Herrschaft in der Industriellen Arbeitsorganisation. (Domination in the Industrial Work Organization)*. Frankfurt: Suhrkamp.

Schurman, Franz, 1968, *Ideology and Organization in Communist China*. Berkeley: University of California Press.

Simmel, Georg, 1955, *Conflict*. Kurt H. Wolff (ed). Glencoe: Free Press.

———— 1968, *The Conflict in Modern Culture and Other Essays*. Peter Etzkorn (trans.). New York: Teachers College Press.

Stern, Bernhard J., 1959, "The Frustration of Technology"; "Restraints upon the Utilization of Inventions", in *Historical Sociology*. New York: Citadel.

Stojanovic, Svetozar, 1973, *Between Ideals and Reality*. New York: Oxford University Press.

Stone, Katherine, 1974, "The origins of job structures in the steel industry." *Review of Radical Political Economics* 6:113–73.

Touraine, Alain, 1971, *The Post-Industrial Society*. New York: Random House.

Tucker, Robert, 1967, *Philosophy and Myth in Karl Marx*. New York: Cambridge University Press.

Venek, Jaroslav (ed.), 1975, *Self Management: Economic Liberation of Man*. Penguin.

Wachtel, Howard, 1974, "Class consciousness and stratification in the labor process." *Review of Radical Political Economics* 6:1–31.

Weber, Max, 1968, *Economy and Society; An Outline of Interpretive Sociology*. Edited by Guenther Roth and Claus Wittich. Translators: Ephraim Fischoff and others. New York: Bedminster Press. 3 vols.

Whyte, Martin K., 1973, "Bureaucracy and modernization in China: the Maoist critique." *American Sociological Review* 38:149–63.

Wright, Erik Olin, 1974, "To control or to smash bureaucracy: Weber and Lenin on politics, the state, and bureaucracy." *Berkeley Journal of Sociology* 19:69–108.

Zald, Mayer and Roberta Ash, 1966, "Social movement organizations." *Social Forces* 44:327–40.

Class and Organization as Paradigms in Social Science*

Kenneth Westhues

Among the applications to sociology of T. S. Kuhn's (1957; 1962) studies in the history of science, the most popular has been that of R. W. Friedrichs (1970; 1974), who has defined "priestly" and "prophetic" modes of social sciences as the two dominant paradigms available to social researchers. My purpose here is to suggest that Friedrichs has applied Kuhn's work to sociology in an inappropriate way and thereby contributed to further unnecessary politicization of the discipline. In the final part of this paper, I offer an alternative application of Kuhn's work and argue for its utility through a consideration of two conflicting substantive paradigms: one based on the concept of class; the other, of organization.

Kuhn's basis for differentiating paradigms is the conceptual framework by which the scientist gives initial intelligibility to phenomena. Once a group of scientists agree on such a framework (or paradigm), they go about testing hypotheses drawn from it and trying to explain the world by means of it. A scientific revolution occurs when one such paradigm is rejected for another, as in the shift from Ptolemaic to Copernican astronomy or from Newtonian to Einsteinian physics. Friedrichs' (1970:50) basis for distinguishing paradigms, as he admits, is different from Kuhn's. Friedrichs argues that in sociology the two major paradigms are distinguished less by the incompatibility of their conceptual schema than by differences in the sociologist's self-image and in the relationship which he or she has with the phenomena studied. The priestly paradigm is defined not by a common core of concepts, axioms, and empirical assumptions, but by a common posture of "apolitical" detachment from the social world, a disinterested stance of discovering the laws which govern social reality. The prophetic paradigm, in contrast, is defined by a common posture of involvement in the subject matter of sociology and of unwillingness to accept the existing reality as absolute.

With such a characterization of sociology, Friedrichs analyzes the last fifteen years in terms of a conflict between priests and prophets. . . . In the Friedrichs model, the world of sociology is divided between those who discover reality and those who construct it, between functionalists and dialecticians, between the establishment and the radicals, or ultimately, between the bad guys and the good guys (see Collins, 1974). Such a division is not without its utility. How much of any given structure of social action one takes for granted determines to a great extent the phenomena investigated, the conceptual framework chosen, and the policy implications drawn. . . .

The trouble with an analysis of sociology in these terms is that it reduces sociologists to nothing more than political beings who take sides. . . .

*I am grateful for the comments of R. L. Henshel, J. W. Rinehart, R. D. Lambert, R. A. Gillis, P. R. Sinclair, and D. Kubat, and regret my inability to satisfy all their criticisms at once.

Reprinted in part from The American Sociologist, vol. 11 (February 1976), pp. 38–49, by permission of the author and the publisher, The American Sociological Association.

There is, however, more to sociology than mere politics. Only to the extent that there is more can we legitimately call ourselves sociologists instead of well-paid political parasites. The differentiation of paradigms within the field should rest on whatever substantive knowledge we practitioners have to offer rather than on the exaggerated political implications we like to think our work has. Scientific paradigms, as Kuhn discussed them, are made of concepts and testable hypotheses, not of personal values and attitudes. While granting that the latter greatly affect choice among the former, the stuff of which our discipline is made is the core of ideas by which we explain the social world. It may be that the single, greatest obstacle in the path of sociology is our persistent failure to distinguish, in so far as we can, the political aspects of our work from its substance. . . .

What confronts the priestly sociologist as the nature of man confronts his prophetic colleague as man's present condition; however, whether nature or condition, the present empirical phenomena beckon equally to both for analysis. . . .

The progress of sociology is better served by analyzing our differences in terms of the divergent *substantive* paradigms within which we each do our respective research. A common effort to understand the existing empirical world does not imply singularity of conceptual framework. Indeed, contemporary sociology displays a great number of such frameworks, from labeling theory to behaviorism. To say that most of these paradigms are fairly primitive does not deny that they are paradigms; the phlogiston theory in chemistry was not very sophisticated either. Moreover, considerable number of our paradigms at present embrace as many practitioners as the phlogiston ever did. There is something exhilarating as well about such variety of perspectives in sociology.

Unfortunately, the pleasure of participating in the diverse and stimulating world of contemporary sociology is marred by our too ready seizure on imputations of political bias as a tactic of discourse. When findings which appear clear and indisputable to one social scientist are rejected as meaningless by another, a reciprocal questioning of motives and doubting of integrity too often result. In many cases, issues of rancorous debate in our discipline could be resolved simply by more careful attention to what the data show. Even deeper issues of conflict, however, are not necessarily due to divergent ideological positions or the difference between prophet and priest, but rather to divergent paradigms. If this fact were understood, perhaps some unnecessary politicization of sociology could be avoided.

The following section treats class and organization perspectives as conflicting paradigms which do not necessarily rest on conflicting ideological foundations. I do not argue that these two paradigms embrace the whole of sociology, nor that other delineations of divergent substantive paradigms might not also be useful. Nonetheless, since class analysis is often regarded as a prophetic endeavor and organization study as a priestly pursuit, and since there is regular bickering between the two groups of scholars, the differentiation of class and organization as substantive paradigms may be helpful for placing the bickering on a more scholarly plane.[1]

Class Versus Organization

According to Kuhn, a paradigm is basically defined by key concepts, the labels applied to what are regarded as the most critical constellations of phenomena. In sociology, it is safe to say that paradigms are shaped to a great extent by what the sociologist regards as the most critical decision-making unit in a society. Most survey research and the study of public opinion tend to take the individual person as the decision-making unit; the resultant paradigm, one which has dominated American sociology from the beginning, is a social-psychological one (see Hinkle and Hinkle, 1954). From this point of view, what happens in a society results from the summed decisions of individuals; the unit of analysis in such a paradigm remains the individual. In contrast to this dominant paradigm in American sociology are two others, which may be called that of social class and that of organization. Neither of these regards the individual as the key decision-maker. The first defines as the basic decision-making unit a collectivity of individuals who share a common relationship to the means of production—for example, a capitalist bourgeoisie, a proletariat, or a peasantry. The second defines as the basic unit an organization—whether governmental bureaucracy, industrial corporation, social movement, elite, church, or voluntary association.

My contention here is that the choice between class and organization as key unit of decision-making is in fact a choice of paradigm, and that once this choice is made hypotheses which are crucial to sociologists of the one persuasion are not necessarily testable by or relevant to sociologists of the other persuasion. The reason is that the definition of a particular class cuts across the boundaries of classes. It is as if two people are asked to analyze a piece of paper on which are various geometric designs against a background of swirls of colors. The one, having no eye for color, talks about triangles and squares which happen to be shaded differently; the other vividly describes colors, which happen to have lines within them. There is evidence for both descriptions; a choice depends ultimately on whether the geometric designs or the colors are regarded as the dominant "fact" on the piece of paper. This is a question of paradigm, and it is a similar question which divides class theorists from organization theorists.

Marx and Weber can appropriately be regarded as the respective fathers of these two competing paradigms. Both scholars were concerned with explaining the absence of a fully human life in the social orders confronting them, and both looked to a variety of factors in the construction of their explanations. The primary source of oppression for Marx, however, was the class structure; the chief decision-making units were the capitalist bourgeoisie and its proletarian antithesis. For Weber, as Mouzelis (1967:166) has noted, "the problem is not so much class domination but bureaucratic domination—the totalitarian tendencies of large-scale organization which threaten the democratic institutions of the Western world and, on the individual level, man's potentialities for reason and free choice." Because Weber regarded organizations as the key decision-makers, he emphasized the importance of nationality, religion, ethnicity, regional identification, or other statuses as predictors of social action. Whatever might form the basis of some organized effort was worth studying (see Bendix, 1974). Because Marx saw classes as the key decision-makers, his concern was with the mechanics of class mobilization and the different outcomes of rule by one or another social class.

In the present day, class theorists have moved beyond Marx, and organization theorists beyond Weber. The paradigmatic difference, however, remains. Neo-Marxists might study corporate ownership (Zeitlin, 1974; Zeitlin et al., 1974), a national ruling class (Clement, 1975), militarism and international relations (Szymanski, 1973, 1974), or the contemporary proletariat (Rinehart, 1971, Rinehart and Okraku, 1974). Others present macro-level class analyses of particular societies, like Anderson's (1974) book on American society, or of a particular societal institution, like Milliband's (1973) excellent monograph, *The State in Capitalist Society*. Today's class theorists in sociology publish their work in mainstream journals and in journals specifically devoted to their particular paradigm, like the *Monthly Review* or the *New Left Review*. There is plenty of debate *within* this paradigm, as its adherents engage in what Kuhn calls the "puzzle-solving" of normal science (see, for instance, Poulantzas' (1969) review of Milliband's work, or Szymanski's (1974) corrections of Zeitlin's analysis of military spending. Nonetheless, what binds these scholars together is their shared commitment to the class paradigm, within which theory-building and hypotheses-testing take place.

In North America, at least, the organization paradigm can count considerably more adherents in sociology than its class counter-part. Following Mayntz (1964), I would regard as the central conceptualization in the organization paradigm the notion of the organization as a social system, which is regarded as the key decision-making unit of analysis. Major theorists within this paradigm include Robert Michels, Philip Selznick, J. G. March, Herbert Simon, R. M. Cyert, Amitai Etzioni, J. D. Thompson, and Mayer Zald. Like their class-oriented colleagues, sociologists of this persuasion have as outlets for their work both the mainstream journals and their own, most notably the *Administrative Science Quarterly*. Internal heterogeneity appears among these theorists, as in the debate over whether the organization is integrated by shared values and norms, by exchange relationship or by naked power. Divergent empirical projects nonetheless occur within the confines of a paradigm in which organization as such is the central fact.[2]

To a great extent, research done within the class paradigm is irrelevant to the concerns of sociologists of organization, and vice versa. Problems which appear interesting to one set of scholars are scarcely regarded as problems by the other set. The paradigms meet, however, at certain critical points, and the result is comparable to the grating of mismatched gears. Such friction probably occurs especially because each side offers itself as an alternative to what was suggested earlier as the dominant paradigm of American sociology. Neither class theorists nor organization theorists see the individual human being as the primary decision-maker. Each group of theorists believes that it offers a more adequate explanation of events than "nose-counters," and vies for the role of chief diagnostician of the manifest malaise of contemporary Western civilization. From within the class paradigm, Baran and Sweezy (1966) offered *Monopoly Capital*; from an organization frame of reference, Galbraith (1967) produced *The New Industrial State*. The ultimate social problem for today's class theorists is how to break the power of monopoly capitalists in an economy strangled by and starving from a surfeit of commodities. For organization theorists, the problem is how to break the power of large, mindless multinational corporations, which devour human freedom in their avoidance of entropy.

Proponents of both these paradigms regard themselves as prophetic saviors of sociology from psychologism, and of the world at large from the false consciousness of a democratic theory of "possessive individualism" (MacPherson, 1962). The two sides often seem to spend more time battling one another than battling their colleagues in the small groups laboratory, the gears of whose paradigm are perhaps so distant that they fail to grind against those of class or organization. To class analysts, students of organization tend to make what may be distinguished as four erroneous arguments: that power has been transferred from the owners of capital, is plural, shared, and inheres in organizations themselves. These four issues constitute critical points of contact between the two paradigms, and deserve to be discussed in turn.

Organization analysts challenged their class-oriented colleagues by the assertion that as capitalist societies have matured and become technologically more complex, and as capitalist enterprises have grown larger, the locus of power within the corporation has passed from owners to some group of bureaucratic functionaries (Burnham, 1941; Berle and Means, 1932). The class-paradigm response is typified by Ernst Mandel's (1970:47; see also Mills, 1963) contention that such "managerialists" confuse "the real sources of authority with the functional articulation of authority." Mandel chides such scholars for failing to distinguish between "the apparent automatism of the mechanisms and the human decisions inspired by social and economic motives" (p. 48). Galbraith (1967, 1973) threatened class theorists more recently by suggesting that corporate power now rests chiefly in the technostructure, that body of specialized experts whose collective decision-making is held as the major determinant of organizational policy. Paul Sweezy (1973:4) vehemently disagreed, accusing Galbraith of stirring up "confusion between making decisions within a given frame and deciding what goals are imposed by this frame on those operating within it."

A second issue of contention between the two paradigms concerns the notion of pluralism. From a conceptualization of class as the basic social fact, it naturally follows to question which class has the bulk of power and which others do not. Attempts to answer this question for the United States have been made by such analysts as Domhoff (1967), Kolko (1962), and Mills (1956). From a conceptualization of organizations as the basic social fact, the corresponding question is which organizations (associations, interest groups, or organized elites) have power and which do not. Answers to this question in the American context have been given by Dahl (1961) and Polsby (1963), among others. Dahrendorf's (1959) analysis of power in industrial societies represents another theory within the organization paradigm. Perhaps it is because there are thousands of organized collectivities but only a few classes that researchers of organizations tend to see power as plural while those of class see it as singular. The very concept of pluralism is a distracting non-word to class theorists, while the so-called pluralists argue that the existence of a ruling class has been too much assumed and too little demonstrated.[3]

A third issue dividing researchers of the two paradigms concerns the incentive systems by which employees are induced to give their labor to various organizations. Etzioni (1961) distinguishes coercive, utilitarian, and moral types of incentives in modern organizations. Warren (1968) proposes a typology of power, ranging from coercive forms to "expert," "reward," and "referent" types of power. Galbraith (1967:128–58) argues that the modern corporation wins the compliance of members of the technostructure less by paying them than by securing their identification with its goals. Such contemporary typologies can be regarded as variants and descendants of Weber's (1947:324–38) own distinction between traditional, charismatic, and rational-legal types of authority. Organization analysts find it interesting to compare the various means by which social systems win the commitment of their members.

Class analysts regard such studies as beside the basic point: power is not defined by the particular techniques of power-holders but by relation to the means of production. Hence, almost by definition, power in a capitalist society inheres in the ownership of property; power cannot be shared unless ownership is shared. Since ownership in Western capitalist countries is manifestly shared very little, talk of expert power, identification, higher or lower wages, or social strata defined by occupational prestige or education, only obscures the basic issue. To suggest any convergence of interests between owners and workers is absurd. Rinehart (1971:159) argues that if convergence is occurring, "it makes more sense to speak of the proletarianization of white-collar employees than of the embourgeoisment of the working class." And Sweezy (1973:6) uses the term *working class* "in a broad sense to include the great majority of those who must work for a living regardless of the color of their collars."

A fourth disagreement between researchers of the two contrasting paradigms concerns the decision-making unit itself. Organization theorists have little difficulty in regarding any social system as an actor, with its own goals, policies, strategies, and so forth. The vast literature concerning the effect of environmental variables on organizational behavior (see Thompson, 1968; Cyert and March, 1963) assumes a conception of organizations as actors. Such a conception challenges the notion of individual responsibility, and is justified on the ground that, in complex organizations, what happens is less a function of individual personalities than of organizational policy; replacement of individuals makes little difference in the actions of the organization (Haworth, 1959). The organization is often regarded as a coalition of individuals and groups with widely varying interests, but a coalition nonetheless, with its own discernible behavior, independent of its varied components. Thus, the "enemy" of the good life is a system to which members of various classes contribute and from which they receive rewards, rather than a class to which other classes have been subjugated.

The only relevant "system" which class analysts regard as an enemy is *the* capitalist system, within which class oppression necessarily occurs. These researchers accuse students of organizational behavior of reifying their subject matter and falling prey to an "ideological tendency to personify the corporation by giving it a 'soul' or 'conscience' . . ." (Clement, 1975:30). Even the critics of the so-called military-industrial complex are accused of such reification; Moskos (1974) attributes C. Wright Mills' use of this concept to "liberal" influences on an otherwise "radical" theorist.

The bureaucracy or complex organization, from the point of view of class theorists, is accorded the status of reality to a significantly lower degree than is social class. Organizations cannot be regarded as decision-makers but only as instruments of the decision-making of classes. Although class analysts might expend much effort in research on bureaucracies, particularly public administration, they insist always on relating such research to class interests. Such an orientation appears best, perhaps, in the work of Herbert Marcuse, who often appears to accept the organization paradigm (as in *One-Dimensional Man*, 1964), but who in the final analysis rejects it. Marcuse's persistent criticism of Weber is that he failed to see "that it was not 'pure,' formal, technical reason but dominative reason that was building the 'houses of bondage'—and that the *completion* of technical reason could well become the instrument of the *liberation* of man" (Marcuse, 1965:15). According to Clement (1975:9), the studies of organizations relevant to class analysts are those which "locate them clearly within the class structure of society and do not assume bureaucracies have 'a life of their own' beyond that granted by those who control them."

Organization analysts can agree with students of social class in denying any supposed apolitical or value-neutral qualities about organizations. For class analysts, however, the political values of bureaucracies are dictated by those who control them. For their colleagues in the organization paradigm, certain political values are inherent in the bureaucracy itself. Thus, these latter scholars regard class analyses as facile, simplistic and naive. A re-ordering of power relations among classes, they argue, would do little to improve the human condition unless the nature of organizations were also changed. Alvin Gouldner (1972:94), who remains within the organization paradigm notwithstanding his maverick status, made this point in response to a class-oriented critic: "Without a thoroughgoing theoretical analysis of the problem of spontaneously self-maintaining social systems, 'worker's control' could remain an inoperable ideology that serves only as a new window dressing for a familiar elitism."

Choosing Between Paradigms

If the above paragraphs have outlined the paradigmatic differences between class theorists and organization theorists, the question is what we should make of such differences. Kuhn makes some suggestions. The first is that the differences cannot be resolved through mere hypothesis-testing. Such scientists who see class as the basic fact of social life can do research until doomsday without being led to the conclusion that organization is the basic fact after all. The same point can be made of organization analysts. In terms of our earlier analogy, for one who is color-blind, all possible studies of circles and squares will not lead the person to awareness of the difference between green and blue.

Kuhn suggests, however, certain conditions under which a paradigm loses credibility and a way is opened for conversion to another. One is "the persistent failure of the puzzles of normal science to come out as they should" (Kuhn, 1962:68). An example will be helpful. Mandel (1970:47), among other class theorists, argues that the capitalistic enterprise remains under control of its board of directors. Such a board can close down the enterprise, thus "destroying the entire bureaucratic hierarchy patiently built up, without ever having previously encroached on the 'growing independence' of the research laboratories or the technological planning department." Within the class paradigm, the "puzzle" of what happens when owners want to close an enterprise should be solved by the event of closure. If repeated instances of such a desire on the part of owners did not result in closing the enterprises, but rather, for example, in their becoming publicly owned bureaucracies or cooperative ventures, the class paradigm would lose credibility. By contrast, every instance of major change in the goals or structures of modern corporations, effected by the unilateral whim of their owners, weakens the credibility of the organization paradigm. Zeitlin (1974) has reviewed a number of such instances with precisely that intent. Research problems within a particular paradigm are supposed to be soluble by its own constituent variables; when they are not, they remain unsolved puzzles tempting the researcher to cast about for new conceptual schemes.

Kuhn (1962:82) also argues that "if an anomaly is to evoke crisis, it must usually be more than just an anomaly." Every paradigm, he notes, has some unsolved puzzles, some unpredicted and inexplicable problems. This point should be some consolation to advocates of both paradigms in question here. Kuhn suggests that the really great research problem, the one watched by all practitioners and regarded as a crucial test of the worth of the paradigm, is the puzzle which, if not solved, provokes crisis. In the present context, the ongoing histories of Maoism in China, of Nyerere's *ujamaa* in Tanzania, or of class conflict in Britain are among today's major puzzles for class theorists. Should these histories not turn out as predicted, the paradigm would be vulnerable to crisis. On the other hand, the less adequate the organization variables are for explaining the behavior of the several hundred largest multinational corporations, or the policies of the increasingly large public bureaucracies in most industrialized countries, the more critical becomes the situation of the organization paradigm.

What is noteworthy in Kuhn's discussion, however, is that paradigmatic crises and shifts are precipitated by cognitive rather than emotive or political events. In the history of science, it is fundamentally a failure to predict or explain that gets a paradigm into trouble, not a failure to satisfy personal values or goals. If sociology is to be even the littlest science, our paradigms must stand or fall for these same cognitive reasons. Such a demand, I think, is an extraordinarily difficult one for sociology. The range of phenomena available to us, the myriad unsolved puzzles, the mental effort required for good research, and the diversity of research strategies all constitute a sufficiently complex and depressing situation that it is easy to lapse into the belief that choice of paradigm is nothing more than political position-taking. In the midst of such frustration it becomes easy for sociologists to commit the greatest sin open to those who pretend to be scholars, namely, the accusation that all those committed to some other paradigm have chosen it on political grounds rather than, in so far as possible, on rational, evidential grounds.

The task of distinguishing substantive paradigm from political orientation is especially difficult for organization and class analysts for two reasons. The first is that while both paradigms conflict with the liberal democratic ideology of Western capitalist nations, class analysis is notably less congruent than organization analysis. Organizations are at least recognized as legal entities (see Coleman, 1970), while classes enjoy little recognition in law. As a result, academic choice between the paradigms is easily mistaken for political choice between less and more radical postures. The progress of sociology requires, however, that its practitioners not make this mistake.

Secondly, class analysis supplements its explanation of the status quo with a political program for change, while organization analysis does not. The former displays an appealing coincidence of pure and applied sociology (see Gouldner, 1957); the key predictor of oppression on the theoretical level is the target of militant manipulation on the political level. The latter, by contrast, has far hazier applied implications. If oppression is the result not of some aggregate of people but of the very rules, impersonality, size, and authority structure of complex organizations, a political strategy for ending this oppression is more difficult to devise. As a result, the recommendations for change made by students of organization are usually few and complicated, a fact which prompts harsh criticism by students of social class.

Such a criticism is made repeatedly, of course, of Weber himself. Kolko's (1959) complaint is not that Weber "says democratic control does not exist, but that it never can and that bureaucratic domination is an imperative, inevitable outcome of history." Gouldner (1955), though an organization analyst himself, has similarly condemned not only Weber, but Selznick, Michels, and others who follow him. One is compelled to agree with Stark's (1968:388) assessment of

Weber's world-view: "It is almost impossible to look at this philosophy, this picture painted black in black, without immediately revolting against it . . ." Nonetheless, Stark immediately adds that such a hasty revolt is unbecoming the careful scholar; such a strong psychological reaction, he cautions, leads to wishful thinking. And this, I think, is the important point. The failure of a paradigm to yield clear guidelines for political action is no reason to reject it; nor is an ease or clarity of political applications any reason to accept a paradigm.

The task of the careful sociologist is to make choice of paradigm dependent, in so far as possible, neither on the degree of its congruity with prevailing ideology nor on the ease with which practical applications can be drawn from it. If we expect the world to call us scholars, choice of paradigm must be made on the basis of the adequacy of its explanations and of its ability to solve its own puzzles. Choice on these bases is difficult because it requires steadfast detachment of the scholar from current political definitions of the situation and from social problems which cry out for immediate action. Some relative detachment in the short run, however, is the necessary prerequisite for the longer-range applications a science of human behavior can be expected to produce.

Objectivity or value-freedom do not define a science; if they did, not only sociology but physics. chemistry, and all the rest would fail the test. What defines a science is the *attempt* to be objective, a commitment to try to filter out ideology from empirical knowledge, even while it is clear that the attempt ultimately fails and the commitment is basically in vain. The purpose of this article has been nothing more than to suggest that we sociologists take this definition of our field more seriously (see Von Eschen, 1974). At least some of the differences which Friedrichs would attribute to politics are due to substantive paradigms. These differences, I believe, can only be resolved by students of the class, organization, and other paradigms, as each group seeks solutions to its own puzzles and anomalies.

Notes

1. Bottomore (1975) calls broad theoretical traditions paradigms; Stehr (1974) loosely labels specialties with the same word; and Ritzer (1975) has recently attempted an all-embracing differentiation of the field into the "social facts," "social definition," and "social behavior" paradigms. It seems to me that the term *can* be legitimately applied to any substantive framework in sociology which is broader than a theory and rooted in the nonfalsifiable choice of a basic conceptual apparatus. Whether the term should be applied depends on whether the resultant analysis is helpful for understanding modern sociology.
2. It is important, however, to exclude from the organization paradigm the early schools of Frederick Taylor and Elton Mayo and the continuing research in industrial psychology. Such research, while based on data from organizations, seldom goes beyond the individual level of analysis. For the same reason, studies of stratification which use SES to predict various attitudes and behavior patterns across individuals do not properly fall within the class paradigm.
3. The difference between class-oriented and organization perspectives in the study of power at the societal level is well illustrated by two recent and major analyses of Canadian society. The first, John Porter's (1965) *Vertical Mosaic*, sought to dispel the notion that Canada is a classless, equalitarian democracy. The book suggested instead that the country is ruled by a plurality of elite groups, which "both compete and co-operate with one another" (p. 17). The decision-making units which Porter portrayed

as in control of Canada were not individuals but organizations of individuals at the top of the various institutional sectors. Wallace Clement's (1975) *Canadian Corporate Elite* is in many respects an updated sequel to Porter's book, but it goes a step further. The extent of cooperation and collective purpose among the elites appears so great to Clement that in the end he attributes the control of Canada not to a plurality of elites but to a singular upper class. Porter's reaction to Clement's book is respectful, but he adds, "The degree to which the functional separateness and institutional specialization become mitigated because of the over-all coordination and planning of a complex society should, I think, remain a problem to investigate rather than be subject to premature theoretical closure . . ." (Porter, 1975:xv). One could say that Clement's investigations were not sufficient to convert Porter to a new paradigm.

References

Anderson, C. H., 1974, *The Political Economy of Social Class*. Englewood Cliffs: Prentice-Hall.

Baran, P. A. and P. M. Sweezy, 1966, *Monopoly Capital*. New York: Monthly Review Press.

Becker, H. S., 1967, "Whose side are we on?" *Social Problems* 14 (Winter):239–247.

Bendix, R., 1974, "Inequality and social structure: A comparison of Marx and Weber." *American Sociological Review* 39 (April):149–161.

Berle, A. A. and G. Means, 1932, *The Modern Corporation and Private Property*. New York: Harcourt, Brace and World.

Bottomore, T., 1975, "Competing paradigms in macrosociology." Pp. 191–202 in A. Inkeles *et al.*, (eds.), *Annual Review of Sociology*. Palo Alto: Annual Reviews.

Burnham, J., 1941, *The Managerial Revolution*. Bloomington: Indiana University Press.

Clement, W., 1975, *The Canadian Corporate Elite*. Toronto: McClelland and Stewart.

Coleman, J. S., 1970, "Social inventions." *Social Forces* 49 (December):163–73.

Collins, R., 1974, Review of R. W. Friedrichs, *A Sociology of Sociology*, in *American Journal of Sociology* 79 (March):1364–67.

Cyert, R. M. and J. G. March, 1963, *A Behavioral Theory of the Firm*. Englewood Cliffs: Prentice-Hall.

Dahl, R. A., 1961, *Who Governs? Democracy and Power in an American City*. New Haven: Yale University.

Dahrendorf, R., 1959, *Class and Class Conflict in Industrial Society*. Stanford: Stanford University.

Domhoff, G. W., 1967, *Who Rules America?* Englewood Cliffs: Prentice-Hall.

Etzioni, A., 1961, *A Comparative Analysis of Complex Organizations*. New York: Free Press.

Friedrichs, R. W., 1970, *A Sociology of Sociology*. New York: Free Press.

———— 1974, "The potential impact of B. F. Skinner upon American sociology." *American Sociologist* 9 (February):3–8.

Galbraith, J. K., 1967, *The New Industrial State*. Boston: Houghton Mifflin.

———— 1973, *Economics and the Public Purpose*. Boston: Houghton Mifflin.

Gouldner, A. W., 1955, "Metaphysical pathos and the theory of bureaucracy." *American Political Science Review* 49 (June):496–507.

———— 1957, "Theoretical requirements of the applied social sciences." *American Sociological Review* 22 (February):92–102.

———— 1972, "A reply to Martin Shaw: Whose crisis?" *New Left Review* 71 (January-February):89–96.

Haworth, L., 1959, "Do organizations act?" *Ethics* 70 (October):59–63.

Hinkle, R. C. and G. J. Hinkle, 1954, *The Development of Modern Sociology*. New York: Random House.

Kolko, G., 1959, "A critique of Max Weber's philosophy of history." *Ethics* 70 (October):21–36.

———— 1962, *Wealth and Power in America*. New York: Praeger.

Kuhn, T. S., 1957, *The Copernican Revolution*. New York: Vintage.

———— 1962, *The Structure of Scientific Revolutions*. Chicago: University Press.

MacPherson, C. B., 1962, *The Political Theory of Possessive Individualism*. London: Oxford University.

Mandel, E., 1970, "Progressive disalienation through the building of socialist society, or the inevitable alienation in industrial society?" Pp. 31–52 in E. Mandel and G. Novack, *The Marxist Theory of Alienation*. New York: Pathfinder.

Marcuse, H., 1964, *One-Dimensional Man*. Boston: Beacon.

———— 1965, "Industrialization and capitalism." *New Left Review* 30 (March-April):3–17.

Mayntz, R., 1964, "The study of organizations." *Current Sociology* 13 (3):95–109.

Milliband, R., 1973, *The State in Capitalist Society*. London: Quartet Books.

Mills, C. W., 1956, *The Power Elite*. New York: Oxford.

———— 1963, "A Marx for the managers." Pp. 33–71 in I. L. Horowitz, (ed.), *Power, Politics and People*. New York: Ballantine. (first published with H. H. Gerth in Ethics, 1942).

Moskos, C. C., 1974, "The concept of the military-industrial complex: Radical critique or liberal bogey." *Social Problems* 21 (April):498–512.

Mouzelis, N. P., 1967, *Organization and Bureaucracy*. Chicago: Aldine.

Polsby, N. W., 1963, *Community Power and Political Theory*. New Haven: Yale University.

Porter, J., 1965, *Vertical Mosaic*. Toronto: University of Toronto.

———— 1975, "Foreword." Pp. ix–xv *in* W. Clement, *The Canadian Corporate Elite*. Toronto: McClelland and Stewart.

Poulantzas, N., 1969, "The problem of the capitalist state." *New Left Review* 58 (November-December):67–68.

Rinehart, J. W., 1971, "Affluence and the embourgeoisment of the working class: A critical look." *Social Problems* 19 (Fall):149–61.

Rinehart, J. W. and I. O. Okraku, 1974, "A study of class consciousness." *Canadian Review of Sociology and Anthropology* 11 (August):197–213.

Ritzer, G., 1975, *Sociology: A Multiple Paradigm Science*. Boston: Allyn and Bacon.

Stark, W., 1968, "The agony of righteousness: Max Weber's moral philosophy." *Thought* 43 (Autumn):380–92.

Stehr, N., 1974, "Paradigmatic crystallization: Patterns of interrelations among areas of competence in sociology." *Social Science Information* 13 (February):119–37.

Sweezy, P., 1973, "Galbraith's utopia." *New York Review of Books* 10 (15 November):3–6.

Szymanski, A., 1973, "Military spending and economic stagnation." *American Journal of Sociology* 79 (July):1–14.

———— 1974, "A reply to Friedman, Stevenson, and Zeitlin." *American Journal of Sociology* 79 (May):1462–77.

Thompson, J. D., 1968, *Organizations in Action*. New York: McGraw-Hill.

Von Eschen, D., 1974, Review of Capitalism and Imperialism, I. M. Zeitlin, in *Contemporary Sociology* 3 (September):419–21.

Warren, D. I., 1968, "Power, visibility and conformity in formal organizations." *American Sociological Review* 33 (December):915–70.

Weber, M., 1947, *Theory of Economic and Social Organization*. New York: Free Press.

Zeitlin, M., 1974, "Corporate ownership and control: The large corporation and the capitalist class." *American Journal of Sociology* 79 (March):1073–1119.

Zeitlin, M., L. A. Ewen and R. E. Ratcliff, 1974, "New princes' for old? The large corporation and the capitalist class in Chile." *American Journal of Sociology* 80 (July):87–123.

SECTION TWO
Models for Comparing Organizations

Until about two decades ago, the yield of most organizational research fell into two categories: (1) statements about an organization or organizational unit, based chiefly on case studies; and (2) statements concerning general characteristics of organizations that constituted the "upper" levels of organizational theory. Since then organizational analyses have reached the stage where it became more crucial to study systematic differences among the various social units classed as organizations. At the same time the large number of empirical studies available made comparative analysis possible. A theoretical basis for comparative analysis seemed essential because the everyday language of ordinary actors obscured essential differences among organizations which had the same ordinary language labels. For example, not all hospitals are the same; some hospitals are more like prisons, others are more like schools; some prisons are more like religious organizations while others resemble concentration camps, and so on.

Sociologists now have at their disposal several ways of classifying complex organizations. One currently popular technique is to proceed empirically using some of the newest multivariate techniques. Here organizational types are created by the empirical clusterings of several organizational traits. Other scholars, however, have proceeded theoretically. It is to the theory of comparative analysis that this section is devoted. The key works here are by Etzioni, Blau and Scott, Parsons, and Perrow. Etzioni compares complex organizations in terms of *compliance.* The study of compliance focuses on the kind of power exercised by an organization's elites to elicit involvement by lower participants. Compliance structures provide a strategic ground for comparing organizations in light of the importance of formal control within them. How participants are brought to do what the organization wants them to do provides a key basis for comparison. Moreover, differences in compliance are associated with any other kinds of organizational differences. Etzioni classifies complex organizations into three analytical types: *coercive, utilitarian,* and *normative,* depending on the main kinds of power applied to lower participants.

Blau and Scott classify organizations by the prime beneficiary of the organization's activities. Theirs is not a classification of organizational outputs. Rather it is based on who benefits or *cui bono.* The answer to that question determines the nature of an individual's participation in the organization and the pivotal kind of problem faced by each type of organization. Blau and Scott present four analytical types. In *mutual-benefit associations* the members themselves are the prime beneficiaries of the organization's activity. Owners or managers are the prime beneficiaries in *business concerns.* The *service organization* is a type in which the clients served are the prime beneficiaries. Finally, there are *commonweal organizations.* In this type the public at large receives the prime benefits.

One could suggest that Blau and Scott's typology is one based implicitly on organizational goals. The scheme offered by Talcott Parsons is explicitly a typology based on organizational goal or type of function. Parsons' typology derives from his celebrated AGIL formulation. He recognizes four types of organizations: *production organizations* which make things that are consumed by the society; *political organizations* which allocate societal resources in the pursuit of collective goals; *integrative organizations* which regulate intermember conflicts and promote working together; and *pattern-maintenance organizations* which are concerned with the creation, preservation, dissemination and application of societal beliefs, values and symbols.

Perrow divides organizations in terms of their technologies or the work done on raw materials. Two aspects of technology are critical: the number of exceptions that must be handled, and the degree to which search strategies are in terms of analyzable or unanalyzable procedures. Fundamentally, organizations, for Perrow, vary in their degree of routinization. Organizations with *routine technologies* have few exceptions and analyzable research procedures. Those with *nonroutine technologies* have many exceptions and their procedures are fundamentally unanalyzable. He suggests that organizations with more routine technologies can benefit from bureaucratic structures as that concept was conceived by Weber. The nonroutine organization pays a considerable price for long periods of personnel training, wasted materials, hit-or-miss efforts, and so forth. Bureaucratic structures are not compatible with nonroutine technologies.

All of the theoretical classifications or organizations produce valuable insights regarding the key similarities and differences among organizations. However, which is the most fruitful one is difficult to say at the moment. In the final analysis, the answer to this question depends on empirical research and not just theoretical argument.

Compliance Structures
Amitai Etzioni

A Definition of Compliance

Compliance is universal, existing in all social units. It is a major element of the relationship between those who have power and those over whom they exercise it.[1] Despite its universality, it has been chosen as a base for this comparative study because it is a central element of organizational structure. The emphasis on compliance within the organization differentiates the latter from other types of social units. Characteristics of organizations such as their specificity, size, complexity and effectiveness each enhances the need for compliance. And in turn, compliance is systematically related to many central organizational variables.

Compliance refers both to a relation in which an actor behaves in accordance with a directive supported by another actor's power, and to the orientation of the subordinated actor to the power applied.[2]

By *supported* we mean that those who have power manipulate means which they command in such a manner that certain other actors find following the directive rewarding, while not following it incurs deprivations. In this sense, compliance relations are asymmetric (or "vertical"). But it is not assumed that the subordinates have no power, only that they have less.[3]

The power-*means*, manipulated to support the directives, include physical, material, and symbolic rewards and deprivations. Organizations tend to allocate these means systematically and strive to ensure that they will be used in conformity with the organizational norms.

The *orientation of the subordinated actor* can be characterized as positive (commitment) or negative (alienation). It is determined in part by the degree to which the power applied is considered legitimate by the subordinated actor, and in part by its congruence with the line of action he would desire. We refer to this orientation, whether positive or negative, as *involvement* in the organization. In sum, there are two parties to a compliance relationship: an actor who exercises power, and an actor, subject to this power, who responds to this subjection with either more or less alienation or more or less commitment.

The next task is to use compliance as here defined to develop an analytical base for the classification of organizations. This is done in three steps. First, three kinds of *power* are differentiated; then, three kinds of *involvement* are specified; and finally, the associations of kinds of power with kinds of involvement are indicated. These associations—which constitute *compliance relationships*—then serve as the basis of our classification of organizations.

Three Kinds of Power: A Comparative Dimension

A Classification of Power

Power is an actor's ability to induce or influence another actor to carry out his directives or any other norms he supports.[4] Goldhamer and Shils state that "a person may be said to have power to the extent that he influences the behavior of others in accordance with his own intentions."[5] Of course, "his own intentions" might be to influence a person to follow others' "intentions" or those of a collectivity. In organizations, enforcing the collectivity norms is likely to be a condition determining the powerholder's access to the means of power.

Power positions are positions whose incumbents regularly have access to means of power. Statements about power positions imply a particular group (or groups) who are subject to this power. For instance, to state that prison guards have a power position implies the subordination of inmates. In the following analysis we focus on power relations in organizations between those higher and those lower in rank. We refer to those in power positions, who are higher in rank, as *elites* or as organizational *representatives*. We refer to those in subject positions, who are lower in rank, as *lower participants*.

Power differs according to the *means* employed to make the subjects comply. These means may be physical, material, or symbolic.[6]

Coercive power rests on the application, or the threat of application, of physical sanctions such as infliction of pain, deformity, or death; generation of frustration through restriction of movement; or controlling through force the satisfaction of needs such as those for food, sex, comfort, and the like.

Remunerative power is based on control over material resources and rewards through allocation of salaries and wages, commissions and contributions, "fringe benefits," services and commodities.

Normative power rests on the allocation and manipulation of symbolic rewards and deprivations through employment of leaders, manipulation of mass media, allocation of esteem and prestige symbols, administration of ritual, and influence over the distribution of "acceptance" and "positive response." (A more eloquent name for this power would be persuasive, or manipulative, or suggestive power. But all these terms have negative value connotations which we wish to avoid.)

There are two kinds of normative power. One is based on the manipulation of esteem, prestige, and ritualistic symbols (such as a flag or a benediction); the other, on allocation and manipulation of acceptance and positive response.[7] Although both powers are found both in vertical and in horizontal relationships, the first is more frequent in vertical relations, between actors who have different ranks, while the second is more common in horizontal relations, among actors equal in rank—in particular, in the power of an "informal" or primary group over its members. Lacking better terms, we refer to the first kind as *pure normative power*, and to the second as *social power*. Social power could be treated as a distinct kind of power. But since powers are here classed according to the means of control employed, and since both social and pure normative power rest on the same set of means—manipulation of symbolic rewards—we treat these two powers as belonging to the same category.

From the viewpoint of the organization, pure normative power is more useful, since it can be exercised directly down the hierarchy. Social power becomes organizational power only when the organization can influence the group's powers, as when a teacher uses the class climate to control a deviant child, or a union steward agitates the members to use their informal power to bring a deviant into line.

Organizations can be ordered according to their power structure, taking into account which power is predominant, how strongly it is stressed compared with other organizations in which the same power is predominant, and which power constitutes the secondary source of control.[8]

Neutralization of Power

Most organizations employ all three kinds of power, but the degree to which they rely on each differs from organization to organization. Most organizations tend to emphasize only one means of power, relying less on the other two. Evidence to this effect is presented below in the analysis of the compliance structures of various organizations. The major reason for power specialization seems to be that when two kinds of power are emphasized at the same time, over the same subject group, they tend to neutralize each other.

Applying force, for instance, usually creates such a high degree of alienation that it becomes impossible to apply normative power successfully. This is one of the reasons why rehabilitation is rarely achieved in traditional prisons, why custodial measures are considered as blocking therapy in mental hospitals, and why teachers in progressive schools tend to oppose corporal punishment.

Similarly, the application of remunerative powers makes appeal to "idealistic" (pure normative) motives less fruitful. In a study of the motives which lead to purchase of war bonds, Merton pointed out that in one particularly effective drive (the campaign of Kate Smith), all "secular" topics were omitted and the appeal was centered on patriotic, "sacred" themes. Merton asked a sample of 978 people: "Do you think that it is a good idea to give things to people who buy bonds?"

> Fifty per cent were definitely opposed in principle to premiums, bonuses and other such inducements, and many of the remainder thought it a good idea only for "other people" who might not buy otherwise.[9]

> By omitting this [secular] argument, the authors of her scripts were able to avoid the strain and incompatibility between the two main lines of motivation: unselfish, sacrificing love of country and economic motives of sound investment.[10]

It is possible to make an argument for the opposite position. It might be claimed that the larger the number of personal needs whose satisfaction the organization controls, the more power it has over the participants. For example, labor unions that cater to and have control over the social as well as the economic needs of their members have more power over those members than do unions that focus only on economic needs. There may be some tension between the two modes of control, some ambivalence and uneasy feeling among members about the combination, but undoubtedly the total control is larger. Similarly, it is obvious that the church has more power over the priest than over the average parishioner. The parishioner is exposed to normative power, whereas the priest is controlled by both normative and remunerative powers.

The issue is complicated by the fact that the *amount* of each kind of power applied must be taken into account. If a labor union with social powers has economic power which is much greater than that of another union, this fact may explain why the first union has greater power in sum, despite some "waste" due to neutralization. A further complication follows from the fact that neutralization may also occur through application, of the "wrong" power in terms of the cultural definition of what is appropriate to the particular organization and activity. For example, application of economic power in religious organizations may be less effective than in industries, not because two kinds of power are mixed, but because it is considered illegitimate to use economic pressures to attain religious goals. Finally, some organizations manage to apply two kinds of power abundantly and without much waste through neutralization, because they segregate the application of one power from that of the other. The examination below of combat armies and labor unions supplies an illustration of this point.

We have discussed some of the factors related to the tendency of organizations to specialize their power application. In conclusion, it seems that although there can be little doubt that such a tendency exists, its scope and a satisfactory explanation for it have yet to be established.

Three Kinds of Involvement: A Comparative Dimension

Involvement, Commitment, and Alienation

Organizations must continually recruit means if they are to realize their goals. One of the most important of these means is the positive orientation of the participants to the organizational power. *Involvement*[11] refers to the cathectic-evaluative orientation of an actor to an object, characterized in terms of intensity and direction.

The intensity of involvement ranges from high to low. The direction is either positive or negative. We refer to positive involvement as *commitment*[12] and to negative involvement as *alienation*.[13] (The advantage of having a third term, *involvement*, is that it enables us to refer to the continuum in a neutral way.) Actors can accordingly be placed on an involvement continuum which ranges from a highly intense negative zone through mild negative and mild positive zones to a highly positive zone.[14]

Three Kinds of Involvement

We have found it helpful to name three zones of the involvement continuum, as follows: *alienative*, for the high alienation zone; *moral*, for the high commitment zone; and *calculative*, for the two mild zones. This classification of involvement can be applied to the orientations of actors in all social units and to all kinds of objects. Hence the definitions and illustrations presented below are not limited to organizations, but are applicable to orientations in general.

Alienative Involvement. Alienative involvement designates an intense negative orientation; it is predominant in relations among hostile foreigners. Similar orientations exist among merchants in "adventure" capitalism, where trade is built on isolated acts of exchange, each side trying to maximize immediate profit.[15] Such an orientation seems to dominate the approach of prostitutes to transient clients.[16] Some slaves seem to have held similar attitudes to their masters and to their work.

Inmates in prisons, prisoners of war, people in concentration camps, enlisted men in basic training, all tend to be alienated from their respective organizations.[17]

Calculative Involvement. Calculative involvement designates either a negative or a positive orientation of low intensity. Calculative orientations are predominant in relationships of merchants who have continuous business contacts. Attitudes of (and toward) permanent customers are often predominantly calculative, as are relationships among entrepreneurs in modern (rational) capitalism. Inmates in prisons who have established contact with prison authorities, such as "rats" and "peddlers," often have predominantly calculative attitudes toward those in power.[18]

Moral[19] Involvement. Moral involvement designates a positive orientation of high intensity. The involvement of the parishioner in his church, the devoted member in his party, and the loyal follower in his leader are all "moral."

There are two kinds of moral involvement, pure and social. They differ in the same way pure normative power differs from social power. Both are intensive modes of commitment, but they differ in their foci of orientation and in the structural conditions under which they develop. Pure moral commitments are based on internalization of norms and identification with authority (like Riesman's inner-directed "mode of conformity"); social commitment rests on sensitivity to pressures of primary groups and their members (Riesman's "other-directed"). Pure moral involvement tends to develop in vertical relationships, such as those between teachers and students, priests and parishioners, leaders and followers. Social involvement tends to develop in horizontal relationships like those in various types of primary groups. Both pure moral and social orientations might be found in the same relationships, but, as a rule, one orientation predominates.

Actors are means to each other in alienative and in calculative relations; but they are ends to each other in "social" relationships. In pure moral relationships the means-orientation tends to predominate. Hence, for example, the willingness of devoted members of totalitarian parties or religious orders to use each other. But unlike the means-orientation of calculative relationships, the means-orientation here is expected to be geared to needs of the collectivity in serving its goals, and not to those of an individual.

As has been stated, the preceding classification of involvement can be applied to the orientations of actors in all social units and to all kinds of objects. The analysis in this book applies the scheme to orientations of lower participants in organizations to various organizational objects, in particular to the organizational power system. The latter includes (1) the directives the organization issues, (2) the sanctions by which it supports its directives, and (3) the persons who are in power positions. The choice of organizational power as the prime object of involvement to be examined here follows from a widely held conception of organization as an administrative system or control structure. To save breath, the orientation of lower participants to the organization as a power (or control) system is referred to subsequently as *involvement in the organization.* When other involvements are discussed, the object of orientation—for example, organizational goals—is specified.

Organizations are placed on the involvement continuum according to the modal involvement pattern of their lower participants. The placing of organizations in which the participants exhibit more than one mode of involvement is discussed in a later chapter.

Compliance as a Comparative Base

A Typology of Compliance

Taken together, the two elements—that is, the power applied by the organization *to* lower participants, and the involvement in the organization developed *by* lower participants—constitute the compliance relationship. Combining three kinds of power with three kinds of involvement produces nine types of compliance, as shown in the accompanying table.[20]

The nine types are not equally likely to occur empirically. *Three*—the diagonal cases, 1, 5, and 9—*are found more frequently than the other six types.* This seems to be true because these three types constitute *congruent* relationships, whereas the other six do not.

The Congruent Types. The involvement of lower participants is determined by many factors, such as their personality structure, secondary socialization, memberships in other collectivities, and so on. At the same time, organizational powers differ in the kind of involvement they tend to generate. When the kind of involvement that lower participants have because of other factors[21] and the kind of involvement that tends to be generated by the predominant form of organizational power are the same, we refer to the relationship as *congruent*. For instance, inmates are highly alienated from prisons; coercive power tends to alienate; hence this is a case of a congruent compliance relationship.

Congruent cases are more frequent than noncongruent ones primarily because congruence is more effective, and organizations are social units under external and internal pressure to be effective. The effective application of normative powers, for example, requires that lower participants be highly committed. If lower participants are only mildly committed to the organization, and particularly if they are alienated from it, the application of normative power is likely to be ineffective. Hence the association of normative power with moral commitment.

Remuneration is at least partially wasted when actors are highly alienated, and therefore inclined to disobey despite material sanctions; it is also wasted when actors are highly committed, so that they would maintain an effective level of performance for symbolic, normative rewards only. Hence the association of remuneration with calculative involvement.

Coercive power is probably the only effective power when the organization is confronted with highly alienated lower participants. If, on the other hand, it is applied to committed or only mildly alienated lower participants, it is likely to affect adversely such matters as morale, recruitment, socialization, and communication, and thus to reduce effectiveness. (It is likely, though, to create high alienation, and in this way to create a congruent state.)

A Typology of Compliance Relations

Kinds of Power	Kinds of Involvement		
	Alienative	Calculative	Moral
Coercive	1	2	3
Remunerative	4	5	6
Normative	7	8	9

The Incongruent Types.   Since organizations are under pressure to be effective, the suggestion that the six less effective incongruent types are not just theoretical possibilities but are found empirically calls for an explanation. The major reason for this occurrence is that organizations have only limited control over the powers they apply and the involvement of lower participants. The exercise of power depends on the resources the organization can recruit and the license it is allowed in utilizing them. Involvement depends in part on external factors, such as membership of the participants in other collectives (e.g., membership in labor unions[22]); basic value commitments (e.g., Catholic versus Protestant religious commitments[23]); and the personality structure of the participants (e.g., authoritarian[24]). All these factors may reduce the expected congruence of power and involvement.

A Dynamic Hypothesis.   Congruent types are more effective than incongruent types. Organizations are under pressure to be effective. Hence, to the degree that the environment of the organization allows, *organizations tend to shift their compliance structure from incongruent to congruent types* and *organizations which have congruent compliance structures tend to resist factors pushing them toward incongruent compliance structures.*

Congruence is attained by a change in either the power applied by the organization or the involvement of lower participants. Change of power takes place when, for instance, a school shifts from the use of corporal punishment to stress on the "leadership" of the teachers. The involvement of lower participants may be changed through socialization, changes in recruitment criteria, and the like.

Because the large majority of cases falls into the three categories representing congruent compliance, these three types form the basis for subsequent analysis. We refer to the coercive-alienative type as *coercive compliance;* to the remunerative-calculative type as *utilitarian compliance;* and to the normative-moral type as *normative compliance.* Students of organizational change, conflict, strain, and similar topics may find the six incongruent types more relevant to their work.

Compliance and Authority

The typology of compliance relationships presented above highlights some differences between the present approach to the study of organizational control and that of studies conducted in the tradition of Weber. These studies tend to focus on authority, or legitimate power, as this concept is defined.[25] The significance of authority has been emphasized in modern sociology in the past, in order to overcome earlier biases that overemphasized force and economic power as the sources of social order. This emphasis, in turn, has led to an overemphasis on legitimate power. True, some authority can be found in the control structure of lower participants in most organizations. True, authority plays a role in maintaining the long-run operations of the organization. But so does nonlegitimated power. Since the significance of legitimate power has been fully recognized, it is time to lay the ghost of Marx and the old controversy, and to give full status to both legitimate and nonlegitimate sources of control.

Moreover, the concept of authority does not take into account differences among powers other than their legitimacy, in particular the nature of the sanctions (physical, material, or symbolic) on which power is based. All three types of power may be regarded as legitimate by lower participants: thus there is normative,[26] remunerative, and coercive authority (differentiated by the kind of power employed, for instance, by a leader, a contractor, and a policeman.) But these powers differ in the likelihood that they will be considered legitimate by those subjected to them. Normative power is most likely to be considered legitimate; coercive, least likely; and remunerative is intermediate.

Finally, it is important to emphasize that involvement in the organization is affected both by the legitimacy of a directive and by the degree to which it frustrates the subordinate's need-dispositions. Alienation is produced not only by illegitimate exercise of power, but also by power which frustrates needs, wishes, desires. Commitment is generated not merely by directives which are considered legitimate but also by those which are in line with internalized needs of the subordinate. Involvement is positive if the line of action directed is conceived by the subordinate as both legitimate and gratifying. It is negative when the power is not granted legitimacy and when it frustrates the subordinate. Involvement is intermediate when either legitimation or gratification is lacking. Thus the study of involvement, and hence that of compliance, differs from the study of authority by taking into account the effects of the cathectic as well as the evaluative impact of directives on the orientation of lower participants.

Lower Participants and Organizational Boundaries

Before we can begin our comparisons, the following questions still remain to be answered. Why do we make compliance of lower participants the focus of the comparison? Who exactly are "lower participants"? What are the lower boundaries of an organization? In answering these questions, we employ part of the analytical scheme suggested above, and thus supply the first test of its fruitfulness.

Why Lower Participants?

Compliance of lower participants is made the focus of this analysis for several reasons. First, the control of lower participants is more problematic than that of higher participants because, as a rule, the lower an actor is in the organizational hierarchy, the fewer rewards he obtains. His position is more deprived; organizational activities are less meaningful to him because he is less "in the know," and because often, from his position, only segments of the organization and its activities are visible.[27] Second, since we are concerned with systematic differences among organizations (the similarities having been more often explored), we focus on the ranks in which the largest differences in compliance can be found. An interorganizational comparison of middle and higher ranks would show that their compliance structures differ much less than those of the lower ranks.

Who Are Lower Participants?

Organizational studies have used a large number of concrete terms to refer to lower participants: employees, rank-and-file, members, clients, customers, inmates.[28] These terms are rarely defined. They are customarily used to designate lower participants in more than one organization, but none can be used for all.

Actually, these terms can be seen as reflecting different positions on at least three analytical dimensions.[29] One is the *nature* (direction and intensity) of the actors' *involvement* in the organization. Unless some qualifying adjectives such as "cooperative" or "good" are introduced, *inmates* implies alienative involvement. *Clients* designates people with alienative or calculative involvement. *Customers* refers to people who have a relatively more alienative orientation than clients; one speaks of the clients of professionals but not ordinarily of their customers. *Member* is reserved for those who have at least some, usually quite strong, moral commitment to their organization. *Employee* is used for people with various degrees of calculative involvement.

A second dimension underlying these concrete terms is the degree to which lower participants are *subordinated* to organizational powers. Inmates, it seems, are more subordinated than employees, employees more than members, and members more than clients. A study in which subordination is a central variable would take into account that it includes at least two subvariables: the extent of control in each area (e.g., "tight" versus remote control); and the scope of control, measured by the number of areas in which the subject is subordinated. Such refinement is not required for our limited use of this dimension.

A third dimension is the amount of *performance* required from the participants by the organization: it is high for employees, low for inmates, and lowest for clients and customers.[30]

Using concrete terms to designate groups of participants without specifying the underlying dimensions creates several difficulties. First of all, the terms cannot be systematically applied. Although "members" are in general positively involved, sometimes the term is used to designate lower participants with an alienative orientation. Archibald, for instance, uses this term to refer to members of labor unions who are members only *pro forma* and who see in the union simply another environmental constraint, to which they adjust by paying dues.

> Most workers entered the yards not merely ignorant of unions, but distrustful of them. . . . They nonetheless joined the unions, as they were compelled to do, with little protest. They paid the initiation fees, averaging not more than twenty dollars, much as they would have bought a ticket to the county fair: it cost money, but maybe the show would be worth the outlay. As for dues, they paid them with resignation to the principle that all joys of life are balanced by a measure of pain.[31]

The term *customers* suggests that the actors have no moral commitments to their sources of products and services. But sometimes it is used to refer to people who buy from cooperatives, frequent only unionized barbers, and remain loyal to one newspaper—that is, to people who are willing to suffer some economic loss because they see in these sources of service something which is "good in itself"—people who, in short, have some moral commitments.

Any moral commitment on the part of mental patients, designated as *inmates*, is viewed either with surprise or as a special achievement of the particular mental hospital; on the other hand, members of labor unions are "expected" to show moral commitment and are labeled "apathetic" if they do not. The fact that some mental patients view their hospital as their home, and thus are positively involved, whereas labor union members may see their organization as a secondary group only, is hidden by the terminology employed. The same point could be made for differences in performance and in subordination.

Although the use of such concrete terms leads to overgeneralization, by implying that all lower participants of an organization have the characteristics usually associated with the label, they can also impede generalization. An illustration is supplied by studies of parishioners. Many of these studies focus on problems of participation, such as "apathy," high turnover, and declining commitment. But rarely are comparisons drawn, or insights transferred, from the study of members of voluntary associations and political organizations. Actually, all these organizations are concerned with the moral commitment of lower participants who have few performance obligations and little subordination to the organization.

Another advantage of specifying the analytical dimensions underlying these concepts is that the number of dimensions is limited, whereas the number of concrete terms grows continuously with the number of organizations studied. Thus the study of hospitals introduces patients; the analysis of churches brings up parishioners; and the examination of armies adds soldiers. Following the present procedure, we can proceed to characterize the lower participants of additional organizations by the use of the same three dimensions.

Specifying the underlying dimensions enables us not only to formulate analytical profiles of a large variety of lower participants, but also to compare them systematically with each other on these three dimensions. For instance, "soldiers" (in combat) are high on all three dimensions, whereas immates are high on subordination and alienation but low on performance; employees are medium in involvement and subordination, but high on performance obligations. The import of such comparisons will become evident later.

Finally, whereas concrete terms tend to limit analysis to participants at particular levels, analytical terms such as alienative, calculative, and moral can be applied equally well to participants at all levels of the organizational hierarchy.

Ideally, in a book such as this, we should refer to lower participants in analytical terms, those of various degrees of involvement, subordination, and performance obligations. Since this would make the discussion awkward, the concrete terms are used, but only to refer to *typical* analytical constellations. *Inmates* are lower participants with high alienation, low performance obligations, and high subordination. The term will not be used to refer to other combinations which are sometimes found among lower participants in prisons. *Members* is used to refer only to lower participants who are highly committed, medium on subordination, and low on performance obligations; it is not used to refer to alienated lower participants in voluntary associations. Similarly, other terms are used as specified below.

Lower versus Higher Participants

Higher participants have a "permanent" power advantage over lower participants because of their organizational position. Thus, by definition, higher participants as a group are less *subordinated* than lower participants. Often, though not in all organizational types, they are also more *committed*, and have more *performance obligations* (if we see decision making and other mental activities as performances). Thus the three dimensions which serve to distinguish among various types of lower participants also mark the dividing line between lower and higher participants. These very dimensions also enable us to suggest a way to delineate the organizational boundaries—that is, to distinguish between participants and nonparticipants.

*Analytical Specifications of Some Concepts Referring to Lower Participants**

Lower Participants	Nature of Involvement (Intensity and Direction)	Subordination	Performance Obligations
Inmates	High, negative	High	Low
Employees	Low, negative or positive	Medium	High
Customers	Low, negative or positive	None	Low
Parishioners	High, positive	Low	Low
Members	High, positive	Medium to Low	Low
Devoted Adherents	High, positive	High	High

* This table contains a set of definitions to be used. It is not exhaustive, either in concepts referring to lower participants or in possible combinations of "scores" on the various dimensions.

Organizational Boundaries

Students of organizations must often make decisions about the boundaries of the unit they are studying: who is a participant, who an outsider. March and Simon, for example, take a broad view of organizational boundaries: "When we describe the chief participants of most business organizations, we generally limit our attention to the following five major classes: employees, investors, suppliers, distributers, and consumers."[32]

We follow a narrower definition and see as participants all actors who are high on at least one of the three dimensions of participation: involvement, subordination, and performance. Thus, students, inmates, soldiers, workers, and many others are included. Customers and clients, on the other hand, who score low on all three criteria, are considered "outsiders."

We should like to underscore the importance of this way of delineating the organizational boundaries. It draws the line much "lower" than most studies of bureaucracies, which tend to include only persons who are part of a formal hierarchy: priests, but not parishioners; stewards, but not union members; guards, but not inmates; nurses, but not patients. We treat organizations as collectivities of which the lower participants are an important segment. To exclude them from the analysis would be like studying colonial structures without the natives, stratification without the lower classes, or a political regime without the citizens or voters.

It seems to us especially misleading to include the lower participants in organizational charts when they have a formal role, as privates in armies or workers in factories, and to exclude them when they have no such status, as is true for parishioners or members. This practice leads to such misleading comparisons as seeing the priests as the privates of the church and teachers as the lowest-ranking participants of schools, in both cases ignoring the psychological import of having "subordinates." One should not let legal or administrative characteristics stand in the way of a sociological analysis. However, the main test of the decision to delineate the organization as we have chosen follows: it lies in the scope, interest, and validity of the propositions this approach yields. . . .[33]

Notes

1. G. Simmel, "Superiority and subordination as subject matter of sociology," *Amer. J. Sociol.*, 1896, 2, 167–189, 392–415.
2. For other usages of the term see R. Bendix, "Bureaucracy: The problem and its setting," *Amer. Sociol. Rev.*, 1947, 12, 502–507, and H. L. Zetterberg, "Compliant actions," *Acta Sociologica*, 1957, 2, 179–201.
3. T. Parsons, "The distribution of power in American society," *World Politics*, 1957, 10, 139; cf. R. Dahrendorf, *Class and class conflict in industrial society* (Stanford, Calif.: Stanford University Press, 1959), p. 169.
4. See T. Parsons, *The social system* (New York: Free Press, 1951), p. 121.
5. H. Goldhamer and E. A. Shils, "Types of power and status," *Amer. J. Sociol.*, 1939, 45, 171.
6. We suggest that this typology is exhaustive, although the only way we can demonstrate this is by pointing out that every type of power we have encountered so far can be classified as belonging to one of the categories or to a combination of them.

   Boulding, Neuman, and Commons have suggested similar typologies. Boulding has developed a typology of "willingness" of persons to serve organizational ends which includes identification, economic means, and coercion. He suggests, however, that identification should be seen as an "economic" way of inducing willingness, a position which we believe is unacceptable to most sociologists. See K. E. Boulding, *The organizational revolution*, New York: Harper & Row, 1953, p. xxxi; and R. Niebuhr, "Coercion, self-interest, and love," *ibid.*, pp. 228–244.
7. T. Parsons, *The social system, op. cit.*, p. 108.
8. Two methodological problems raised by such an ordering are discussed in Chapter XII of Amitai Etzioni, *A comparative analysis of complex organizations* (New York: Free Press, 1961), pp. 297–298.
9. R. K. Merton, *Mass persuasion: The social psychology of a war bond drive* (New York: Harper & Row, 1946), p. 47.
10. *Ibid.*, p. 45.
11. *Involvement* has been used in a similar manner by Nancy C. Morse, *Satisfactions in the white-collar job* (Ann Arbor, Mich.: Survey Research Center, University of Michigan, 1953), pp. 76–96. The term is used in a somewhat different way by students of voting, who refer by it to the psychological investment in the outcome of an election rather than in the party, which would be parallel to Morse's usage and ours. See, for example, A. Campbell, G. Gurin, and W. E. Miller, *The voter decides* (Evanston, Ill.: Row, Peterson & Company, 1954), pp. 33–40.
12. Mishler defined *commitment* in a similar though more psychological way: "An individual is committed to an organization to the extent that central tensions are integrated through organizationally relevant instrumental acts." Cited by C. Argyris, *Personality and organization* (New York: Harper & Row, 1957), p. 202.
13. We draw deliberately on the associations this term has acquired from its usage by Marx and others. For a good analysis of the idea of alienation in Marxism and of its more recent development, see D. Bell, "The 'rediscovery' of alienation," *J. Phil.*, 1959, 56, 933–952, and his *The end of ideology* (New York: Free Press, 1960), pp. 335–368.
14. Several sociologists have pointed out that the relationship between intensity and direction of involvement is a curvilinear one: the more positive or negative the orientation, the more intensely it is held. L. Guttman, "The Cornell technique for scale and intensity analysis," *Educ. & Psychol. Measurement*, 1947, 7, 247–279. By the same author see "The principal components of scale analysis" in S. A. Stouffer *et al.*, *Measurement and prediction* (Princeton, N.J.: Princeton University Press, 1950), pp. 312–371, and "The principal components of scalable attitudes." In P. F. Lazarsfeld (ed.), *Mathematical thinking in the social sciences* (New York: Free Press 1954), pp. 229–230. See also E. A. Suchman, "The intensity component in attitude and opinion research," in S. A. Stouffer *et al.*, *Measurement and prediction, op. cit.*, pp. 213–276;

and E. L. A. McDill, "A comparison of three measures of attitude intensity," *Social Forces*, 1959, 38, 95–99.

15. H. H. Gerth and C. W. Mills, *From Máx Weber: Essays in sociology* (New York: Oxford, 1946), p. 67.

16. K. Davis, "The sociology of prostitution," *Amer. Sociol. Rev.*, 1937, 2, 748–749.

17. For a description of this orientation see D. Clemmer, *The prison community* (New York: Holt, Rinehart, and Winston, 1958), pp. 152 ff. Attitudes toward the police, particularly on the part of members of the lower classes, are often strictly alienative. See, for example, E. Banfield, *The moral basis of a backward society* (New York: Free Press, 1958).

18. G. M. Sykes, *The society of captives* (Princeton, N.J.: Princeton University Press, 1958), pp. 87–95.

19. The term "moral" is used here and in the rest of the article to refer to an orientation of the actor; it does not involve a value position of the observer. (See T. Parsons, E. A. Shils *et al.*, *Toward a general theory of action* (Cambridge, Mass.: Harvard University Press, 1952), pp. 170 ff.

20. A formalization of the relationship between rewards allocation (which comes close to the concept of power as used here) and participation (which, as defined, is similar to the concept of involvement) has been suggested by R. Breton, "Reward structures and participation in an organization." Paper presented to the Eastern Sociological Society, April 1960.

21. "Other factors" might include previous applications of the power.

22. On the effect of membership in labor unions on involvement in the corporation, see B. Willerman, "Overlapping group identification in an industrial setting," Paper presented to the American Psychological Association. Denver, September 1949, p. 4.

23. See W. F. Whyte *et al.*, *Money and motivation* (New York: Harper & Row, 1955), pp. 45–46. Protestants are reported to be more committed to the values of saving and productivity, whereas Catholics are more concerned with their social standing in the work group. This makes for differences in compliance: Protestants are reported to be more committed to the corporation's norms than Catholics.

24. For instance, authoritarian personality structure is associated with a "custodial" orientation to mental patients. See Doris C. Gilbert, and D. J. Levinson, "'Custodialism' and 'humanism' in staff ideology." In M. Greenblatt, D. J. Levinson, and R. H. Williams (eds.), *The patient and the mental hospital* (New York: Free Press, 1957), pp. 26–27.

25. For various definitions and usages of the concept, see C. J. Friedrich (ed.), *Authority* (Cambridge, Mass.: Harvard University Press, 1958). For a formalization of the concept in relation to power and leadership, see A. H. Barton, "Legitimacy, power, and compromise within formal authority structures—a formal model" (Bureau of Applied Social Research, Columbia University, 1958). Mimeographed.

26. The concept of "normative authority" raises the question of the difference between this kind of authority and normative power. There is clearly a high *tendency* for normative power to be considered legitimate and thus to form an authority relationship. The reason for this tendency is that the motivational significance of rewards and deprivations depends not only on the objective nature of the power applied, but also on the meaning attached to it by the subject. Coercive and remunerative means of control are considerably less dependent on such interpretations than normative ones. Most actors in most situations will see a fine as a deprivation and confinement as a punishment. On the other hand, if the subject does not accept as legitimate the power of a teacher, a priest, or a party official, he is not likely to feel their condemnation or censure as depriving. Since normative power depends on manipulation of symbols, it is much more dependent on "meanings," and, in this sense, on the subordinate, than other powers. But it is by no means necessary that the application of normative power always be regarded as legitimate.

A person may, for example, be aware that another person has influenced his behavior by manipulation of symbolic rewards, but feel that he had no right to do so, that he ought not to have such power, or that a social structure in which normative powers are concentrated (e.g., partisan control over mass media; extensive advertising) is unjustified. A Catholic worker who feels that his priest has no right to condemn him because of his vote for the "wrong" candidate may still fear the priest's condemnation and be affected by it.

27. The term "visible" is used here and throughout this article as defined by Merton: "the extent to which the norms and the role performances within a group are readily open to observation by others." *Social theory and social structure,* rev. ed. (New York: Free Press, 1957), pp. 319 ff.

28. For one of the best discussions of the concept of participation, its definition and dimensions, see J. H. Fichter, *Social relations in the urban parish* (Chicago: University of Chicago Press, 1954), Part I, *passim.*

29. The difference between concrete and analytic membership in corporations has been pointed out by A. S. Feldman, "The interpenetration of firm and society." Paper presented at the International Social Science Council Round Table on Social Implications of Technical Change. Paris, 1959.

30. Participants of a social unit might also be defined as all those who share an institutionalized set of role-expectations. We shall not employ this criterion since it blurs a major distinction, that between the organization as such and its social environment. Members of most groups share such role-expectations with outsiders.

A criterion of participation which is significant for other purposes than ours is whether lower participants have formal or actual powers, such as those reflected in the right to vote, submit grievances, or strike.

31. Katherine Archibald, *Wartime shipyards* (Berkeley and Los Angeles: University of California Press, 1947), pp. 131–132.

32. J. G. March and H. Simon, *Organizations* (New York: Wiley, 1958), p. 89.

33. A preliminary review of research conducted since the first publication of these lines by a number of scholars. See Amitai Etzioni, "Organizational Dimensions and Their Interrelations: a Theory of Compliance," in Bernard Indik and S. Kenneth Berien, eds., *People, Groups and Organizations* (New York: Teachers College Press, 1968; Columbia University Press, 1968), pp. 94–109.

Who Benefits?

Peter M. Blau and W. Richard Scott

Since formal organizations are complex social objects having diverse characteristics, any one of which may be seized upon as a basis for grouping them in one manner or another, many different classification schemes have been proposed. Some students have emphasized the distinction between private and public ownership as a basic one; some have classified organizations by size; others have concentrated attention on the specific purposes served. Another system of types focuses on the criterion of membership; thus, we may distinguish organizations manned largely by volunteers (the Red Cross), by employees (industrial firms), or by conscripts (citizen armies). Organizations have also been assigned to broad institutional areas on the basis of the function they perform for the larger society; such attempts may provide types like economic, political, religious, and educational organizations.

In contrast to these classifications which stress fairly obvious differences between organizations, there are others that use more analytical criteria of distinction.[1] Thus, Parsons differentiates four types on the basis of which one of the four fundamental problems confronting a society an organization helps to solve. Since this category system is derived from a theoretical scheme, it cuts across traditionally defined institutional areas.[2] Another analytical criterion of distinction is whether the "materials" worked on by the technical personnel of the organization are physical objects or people. The crucial difference between the two resulting types—production and service organizations—is that only the latter are confronted with problems of establishing social relations with the "objects" of their endeavors and of having to motivate them in various ways. The success of a teacher depends on doing this; that of an engineer does not.[3] It should be noted that the term "service organizations" is misleading for the general type, since not all organizations dealing with people provide a service for these same people; it is hardly correct to say that the function of a prison is to furnish services to prisoners.

Hughes provides yet another analytical classification by attempting to describe several basic models of organization found in modern society, which yields five types: (1) the voluntary association of equals, where members freely join for a specific purpose; examples include sects, clubs, and professional associations; (2) the military model, which emphasizes a fixed hierarchy of authority and status; (3) the philanthropic model, consisting of a governing lay board, an itinerant professional staff, and the clients served, as illustrated by hospitals and universities; (4) the corporation model with its stockholders, board of directors, managers, and staff; and (5) the family business in which a group of people related by kin and marriage carry on some enterprise for profit.[4]

A typology, strictly speaking, is a multidimensional classification. If organizations were, for example, divided into large public, small public, large private, and small private ones, this would be a simple typology based on the dimensions of size and ownership. A more complex typology is illustrated by Thompson and Tuden's analysis of the decision-making strategies in organizations.[5] They suggest that the type of decision made depends on two factors: (1) whether there is agreement on objectives; and (2) whether cause-effect relations are known, that is, whether there is agreement on how to bring about given objectives. The combinations of these two factors produce four types of decision-making strategies and four types of organizations considered appropriate for them. First, if there is agreement on both the objectives and on how to attain them, what Thompson and Tuden call "computational" strategies are possible; that is, decisions can be based on rational calculations. This is the situation for which the rational bureaucracy described by Weber is ideally suited. Second, if there is agreement on objectives but cause-effect relations are not fully known so that insight is needed to decide on the best course of action, a "judgmental" strategy will be used. In this case, a collegium or self-governing body of peers is preferable as an organizational form to bureaucracy. A board of directors illustrates this type, and so does a colleague group of professionals. Third, if there is agreement on how to achieve various objectives but dispute on which objectives have first priority, a "compromise" strategy is required to make collective decisions. The appropriate organization in this case is a representative body, such as the United States Congress. Finally, when there is disagreement on both the objectives and on how to achieve them, "inspirational" strategies are likely to be resorted to. These conditions are usually characterized by the absence of formal organization and by a state of anomie, and would seem to be conducive to the development of charismatic movements.

A Classification Based on Prime Beneficiary

Even though the foregoing review of classificatory schemes is only cursory, it suggests that there is no dearth of such schemes in the literature on organizations. In proposing yet another classification, we take upon ourselves the burden of demonstrating the usefulness of our scheme for increasing the understanding of formal organizations. We hope to do so by using it as a basis for discussing several of the recent empirical studies of formal organizations. First, however, we must present the typology.

Four basic categories of persons can be distinguished in relation to any given formal organization: (1) the members or rank-and-file participants; (2) the owners or managers of the organization; (3) the clients or, more generally, the "public-in-contact," which means the people who are technically "outside" the organization yet have regular, direct contact with it, under whatever label—patient, customer, law violator, prisoner, enemy soldier, student; and (4) the public-at-large, that is, the members of the society in which the organization operates.[6] We propose to classify organizations on the basis of *cui bono*—who benefits: Which of these four categories is the prime beneficiary of their operations? It must be emphasized that the prime beneficiary is not the only beneficiary, for each of the various groups who make contributions to an organization does so only in return for certain benefits received. Thus, the owners, the employees, and the customers of a business concern must each receive some recompense for their various contributions; otherwise, they would not provide the investment capital, the labor power, or the purchase price for goods, all of which are necessary for the firm's continued operation. The public-at-large also benefits from the contribution that business concerns make to the "general welfare," specifically, to the production and distribution of desired goods, and this benefit is the reason why the society permits and encourages such firms to operate. But although all parties benefit, the benefits to one party furnish the reason for the organization's existing while the benefits to others are essentially a cost. In the example cited, the prime beneficiary is the owner of the firm. He established it for the purpose of realizing a profit, and he will close it should it operate for very long showing a loss. Indeed, the public expects the owner to operate his business for his own benefit and not as a welfare institution. Contrast this situation with that of organizations whose prime beneficiary is the public. The city is not expected to close its police department or the community hospital because it fails to show a profit, but to operate it in the interest of the public even at a financial loss.[7]

Four types of organizations result from the application of our *cui bono* criterion: (1) "mutual-benefit associations," where the prime beneficiary is the membership; (2) "business concerns," where the owners are prime beneficiary; (3) "service organizations," where the client group is the prime beneficiary; and (4) "commonweal organizations," where the prime beneficiary is the public-at-large. (This classification can be combined with others to yield more refined typologies.) The following discussion of empirical studies illustrating these four types of formal organizations will clarify the distinction and show that special problems are associated with each type. Thus, the crucial problem in mutual-benefit associations is that of maintaining internal democratic processes—providing for participation and control by the membership; the central problem for business concerns is that of maximizing operating efficiency in a competitive situation; the problems associated with the conflict between professional service to clients and administrative procedures are characteristic of service organizations; and the crucial problem posed by commonweal organizations is the development of democratic mechanisms whereby they can be externally controlled by the public.

The significance of the *cui bono* criterion for defining the character of a formal organization is indicated by the fundamental changes that occur when there is a shift in prime beneficiary from one to another of the four categories. Often such changes are strongly disapproved; sometimes they are heralded as revolutionary improvements; in either case, they signify radical alterations in the basic nature of the organization. Thus, unions are mutual-benefit associations, which are expected to serve the interests of the rank and file. If union leaders usurp the role of prime beneficiary and run the union as if they owned it for their personal benefit, the organization is condemned for no longer serving the proper functions of a labor union. The same is true for a union whose membership has been displaced as prime beneficiary by its public-in-contact—the employers or their representatives—as exemplified by company unions or those whose leadership has "sold out" to management.

In the case of business concerns, the owners are expected to be prime beneficiaries. But public corporations transform owners into mere stockholders and vest controlling power in the hands of top-level employees, enabling them to govern the enterprise in their own interests.[8] Moreover, if unions become more powerful than individual employers, a situation illustrated by some segments of the garment industry, the possibility arises that instead of the owners the employees represented by the union become the prime beneficiaries. Government regulations, notably the extreme case of nationalization of industry, might succeed in making the public-at-large the prime beneficiary of a business concern. This change may, of course, be a good thing. Whether such shifts in prime beneficiary are evaluated as advantageous or disadvantageous depends on one's ideological position, but there is no doubt that they would constitute fundamental transformations of business concerns into distinctly different types of organizations.

In service organizations, if the members of the professional staff lose interest in serving clients and become primarily concerned with making their own work easier or furthering their own careers, service will suffer, since the energies and resources devoted to it will no longer be considered as contributing to the prime function of the organization but rather as a necessary cost for obtaining benefits for the staff or some segment of it.

Commonweal organizations, in sharp contrast, are not, expected to be oriented to the interests of their "clients," that is, those persons with whom they are in direct contact. A police department, for example, that enters into collusion with racketeers fails to discharge its responsibility to the public-at-large and is no longer the protective organization it is assumed to be. Likewise, if policemen solicit bribes instead of enforcing the law, or if the police commissioner runs the department primarily to further his political ambitions, the public's position as prime beneficiary of the organization suffers.

Note also that the criticism that an organization is "overbureaucratized" means quite different things in the four types of organizations.[9] In the case of mutual-benefit associations, such as unions, overbureaucratization implies centralization of power in the hands of officials. Here it does not refer to inefficiency; indeed, bureaucratized unions are often ruthlessly efficient. But in the case of business concerns overbureaucratization implies an elaboration of rules and procedures that impairs operating efficiency, and here the term is not used in reference to the power of management officials to decide on policies, since such managerial direction is expected and legitimate. Finally, service and commonweal organizations are considered overbureaucratized if in consequence of preoccupation with procedures rigidities develop which impede professional service to clients or effective service of the public interest.

Mutual-Benefit Associations

Examples of organizations in which the membership is expected to be the prime beneficiary include political parties, unions, fraternal associations, clubs, veterans' organizations, professional associations, and religious sects. There are some borderline cases. Share corporations, insofar as they can be analytically distinguished from the business concerns they own, may be considered mutual-benefit associations of shareholders. The philanthropic organization is a mixed type—part mutual-benefit, part service—because it serves its members' interests in serving the interests of others. Only "causes" that interest the members obtain their help, but such organizational activities as parties and balls must make a contribution to some outside client group.

As was suggested, the crucial issue facing this type of organization is maintaining membership control, that is, internal democracy. This involves coping with two main problems: membership apathy and oligarchical control.

Most members of mutual-benefit associations are apathetic in the sense that they are willing to leave the running of their association to an active minority.[10] This situation conflicts with the idealized conception of these associations as collectivities whose members are highly interested and actively engaged in achieving some common objective. Apparently this image of the mutual-benefit association is faithful primarily at the time of its origin and during its early struggle for existence. Evidence of widespread vigor and enthusiasm is ample in the early days of such associations as religious sects (which benefit their members by showing them the correct way to salvation). However, the very enthusiasm that marks the activities of the devoted original members leads them to attempt to persuade others of the moral superiority of their beliefs, and such proselytizing brings in new members less strongly identified with the goals of the association. Whether this infusion or other factors lead to the cooling of initial ardors, it is well established that the majority of members of mutual-benefit associations are not sufficiently interested to devote much time or energy to conducting the business of the association and are content to leave the running of the organization to a corps of active members or to a hired staff.[11] Once the organization is under the control of a minority or of hired officials, a vicious cycle begins, for in such cases business meetings are usually uninteresting and concerned with unimportant matters; members who come to these meetings obtain meager rewards for their efforts, and this condition curtails participation still further.[12]

Given a generally low level of participation in mutual-benefit associations, it is important to know what factors are related to participation—that is, what characteristics differentiate between members who participate much and those who participate little. Many studies, beginning with Komarovsky's, have shown that persons of higher socioeconomic status tend to belong to more associations and to participate more actively in them than persons of lower status.[13] Other studies show that males tend to participate more than females, those in their middle years more than those either younger or older, and those belonging to minority groups more than those in the majority.[14] The most extensive research in this area has been carried out on participation in trade unions.[15]

The measures of participation in unions utilized by different studies vary somewhat, but attendance at meetings and holding office are most frequently used. Several investigations have found that socioeconomic status exerts the same influence within the union as in the larger society: the higher the status of union members, the greater is their participation. Thus, there is usually more membership participation in craft locals, and within the same local the most active members come in disproportionate numbers from those who hold the better-paid and higher-status jobs. A somewhat contrary finding is that "union activists are disproportionately drawn from specific ethnic groups—Negroes, Mexicans, Jews, and Catholics."[16] Such underprivileged groups are, of course, the ones expected to be particularly responsive to the union's emphasis on collective effort for improvement. This expectation makes the finding that the best-paid workers are often the most active unionists particularly interesting.

Another factor that appears to exert considerable influence on participation in union activities is social contact among workers. Men who hold positions that permit them frequently to interact with fellow workers tend to be active in the union, whereas those who hold jobs that isolate them from others tend to be apathetic. In situations where an "occupational community" develops, which encourages widespread contacts between workers both on and off the job, union participation is also high.[17] The most militant unions seem to develop in industries whose workers form an "isolated mass," as Kerr and Siegel call it—that is, whose workers are segregated from the rest of the community but closely integrated with one another, as in mining and shipping.[18] Sayles and Strauss indicate that homogeneous work groups tend to participate more in union activities than heterogeneous ones, the former being groups whose members work closely together, are under the same supervisor, are engaged in the same type of work, have equal pay, belong to the same ethnic groups, or come from the same neighborhood.[19]

Surprisingly enough, studies find that workers who report high job satisfaction are more likely than dissatisfied workers to be active union members.[20] Contrary to the common stereotype, therefore, the strongest supporters of labor unions are not disgruntled workers incapable of earning an average wage but the most satisfied and highest paid ones. Workers who do not aspire to supervisory positions, and those who are highly identified with the working class are also more apt than others to participate in union activities. Putting these findings together, it becomes apparent that participation in labor unions is promoted not so much by feelings of resentment against management or more privileged groups as by a positive identification with one's work, the work group, and the working class in general.

Studies of participation and apathy deal with one aspect of the problem of internal democracy in formal associations; another facet of at least equal importance is the problem of oligarchy. A fundamental dilemma confronting mutual-benefit associations is that democratic controls are often sacrificed in the interests of promoting the effective accomplishment of objectives. To win a strike, for example, democratic procedures through which union members control their leaders may be set aside. Generally, an overriding concern with "results" easily leads to disenchantment with the often slow and tortuous democratic process—a process which sacrifices efficiency in the interests of preserving freedom of dissent—and to the development of bureaucratic mechanisms which do not depend for success on widespread membership interest or participation.[21] It was Michels who called attention to a general tendency of associations to move toward increasing centralization of control and hierarchical organization as a consequence of these processes as well as the desire of the leaders to retain and extend their power.[22] But Gouldner has pointed out that Michels' gloomy proposition of an "iron law of oligarchy" may be in part counteracted by the "iron law of democracy," which holds that no superordinate group can for very long flout the will of those it would control.[23]

What are the structural conditions that help to sustain democratic control in large-scale organizations? The writings and research of Lipset have focused on this problem.[24] Basic to the maintenance of democratic control appears to be the existence of a two-party system, resting on two strong factions that have become institutionalized and legitimated. Simply holding periodic plebiscites without the existence of a two-party or multiparty system does not produce democratic control, as the elections held in one-party nations and those held in "one-party" unions demonstrate. The chances of the existence of two or more parties or permanent factions appear to be enhanced by such conditions as the autonomy of local groups within the larger organization, the absence of severe threats to the organization's survival from its environment, a high level of skill and education among the membership, the absence of a large disparity of income and status between leaders and members, the presence of many and varied links between members, the existence of opportunities for members to acquire political skills, and the presence of channels of communication between members independent of those maintained by the officials in control. But the case study on which these conclusions are largely based does not permit a reader to tell which of these conditions are most important or what the chances are for other mutual-benefit associations to develop arrangements that sustain effective democratic control.

Business Concerns

The prime beneficiaries of business concerns are expected to be their owners. Obvious examples of this type are industrial firms, mail-order houses, wholesale and retail stores, banks, insurance companies, and similar organizations privately owned and operated for a profit. The dominant problem of business concerns is that of operating efficiency—the achievement of maximum gain at minimum cost in order to further survival and growth in competition with other organizations. To be sure, efficiency is important for other types of formal organizations as well, but only in business concerns is its significance not limited by that of other factors. All formal organizations are goal oriented, that is, established to accomplish certain objectives; hence, efficiency in the sense of effective accomplishment of objectives without undue cost is a crucial problem for all of them. Barnard uses the term efficiency differently to refer to the work satisfaction and loyalty of the organization's personnel that promote its strength beyond that needed for immediate goal attainment.[25] Efficiency in this second meaning of the term is also important for other types of formal organizations as well as business concerns. In the other three types, however, considerations of administrative efficiency in both senses of the term are expected to be subordinated to some more fundamental considerations. Thus, in mutual-benefit associations, such as unions, concern with efficiency is expected not to interfere with the membership's ability democratically to decide on the specific objectives in the organization. In service organizations, considerations of administrative efficiency must ideally not jeopardize the quality of professional service. And in respect to commonweal organizations, such as armies, maximizing of their efficiency and strength is assumed to take second place to assuring that they do not dominate the government they were created to serve but remain under its control. In business concerns, on the other hand, considerations of operating efficiency are expected to reign supreme within the limits *externally* imposed on them. Since productivity, work satisfaction, and other factors pertaining to efficiency will be discussed at length later, we shall illustrate problems of business concerns only briefly at this point with two studies of white-collar offices.

The first study, conducted by Katz and his colleagues, focused on groups of clerical workers and their supervisors in the home office of a large insurance company.[26] In a comparison of supervisors of work groups with consistently high and with consistently low productivity, it was discovered that supervisors of highly productive groups were most likely to report that they spent 50 per cent or more of their time on supervision rather than in doing the same kind of work as their subordinates. This difference seems to indicate the significance of the administrative function for productive efficiency. There was also a tendency for supervisors of the highly productive groups to describe as most important the "human relations" part of their jobs, while low-production supervisors stressed more often the production and technical aspects of their jobs. These findings suggest that, paradoxically, the more important productivity is for the supervisor the less productive is his unit. It should be noted, however, that this attitude of the supervisor might be a result of the group's low productivity as well as a determinant of it. (Cross-sectional data like these do not enable us to tell which of two related factors influences the other.) It is quite plausible that supervisors whose subordinates produce well are less concerned about productivity and accordingly less apt to mention it as the most important part of their job. The more interesting possibility, of course, is that the supervisor's anxious concern with production impedes work satisfaction and congenial informal relations—perhaps by inducing him to supervise more closely—thereby lessening productivity.

In another study of a business concern, Argyris found that superior officials in a bank were obliged to spend so much time with customers that they had little time left for supervision of subordinates.[27] This situation appeared to have some positive consequences since one of the main sources of work satisfaction reported by junior employees was that "nobody breathes down your neck all the time." However, the fact that some of these junior employees, for example the tellers, also spent most of their time interacting with customers meant that they had little opportunity to interact with one another; this focus resulted in a weak informal structure and a low degree of group solidarity. Argyris also found that the hiring procedure of the bank led to the selection of a particular type of employee— persons who possessed a strong desire for economic security and job stability, a desire to be left alone, and a dislike of aggressiveness in themselves or in others. While this type of employee was well suited for performing the routine work of the bank, promotion created problems because the very qualities that were desirable in subordinates tended to make "passive and weak" leaders, impairing the efficiency of the organization.

Service Organizations

A service organization has been defined as one whose prime beneficiary is the part of the public in direct contact with the organization, with whom and on whom its members work—in short, an organization whose basic function is to serve clients. Included in this category are social-work agencies, hospitals, schools, legal aid societies, and mental health clinics. The crucial problems of these organizations center around providing professional services. The welfare of their clients is presumed to be the chief concern of service organizations.

In the typical case, however, the client does not know what will best serve his own interest. For example, the patient is not qualified to judge whether or not it would be best for his health to undergo an operation. Hence, the client is vulnerable, subject to exploitation, and dependent on the integrity of the profes- sional to whom he has come for help. The customer in a store, on the other hand, presumably can look after his own interests.[28] Consequently, while the businessman's decisions are expected to be governed by his self-interest—as epitomized in the phrase *"caveat emptor"*—the professional's decisions are ex- pected to be governed not by his own self-interest but by his judgment of what will serve the client's interest best. The professions are institutionalized to assure, in the ideal case, that the practitioner's self-interest suffers if he seeks to promote it at the expense of optimum service to clients.[29]

Professional service also requires, however, that the practitioner maintain independence of judgment and not permit the clients' *wishes*, as distinguished from their *interests*, to influence his decisions. There are two reasons for this distinction: First, professional services are specific; the client may wish to borrow money from his lawyer, but the latter is not obligated to lend it to him; he is obligated only to serve the client's legal interests to the best of his abilities. Second, since clients are not qualified to evaluate the services they need, the professional who lets his clients decide what services he is to furnish does not provide optimum service to them.

A fundamental difference between the benefits obtained by clients of a service organization and those secured by the members of mutual-benefit associations (or by the owners of a business concern; or by the general public in the case of a commonweal organization) is the assumption that the client beneficiaries are not qualified to determine what is in their own best interest but that the member beneficiaries are so qualified. Since the members of mutual-benefit associations are the only judges of which of the many objectives the association might pursue are in their greatest interest, the problem of internal democratic control is basic. Since one group in service organizations must decide what is in the best interest of another, the basic problems here are to assure that the former serve the interest of the latter but that they do *not* let the latter determine how they are to be served.

The professionals or semiprofessionals in a service organization must steer between two dangers. On the one hand, they must not lose sight of the welfare of their clients, either through concern with their own status and career or through preoccupation with administrative problems. The latter may become manifest in rigid adherence to and enforcement of procedures or in permitting budgetary considerations to dominate all decisions (for example, considering it more important to protect the taxpayer than to serve clients adequately in a public agency). On the other hand, the professionals must not become "captives" of their clientele and surrender to them the power to determine the nature of the service furnished. To err in the first direction is to become despotic or overly rigid; to err in the second is to become subservient.[30] Both types of error are illustrated in a study of the relations between Israeli officials and new immigrants to that country.[31] Some officials became despotic and attempted to use their bureaucratic position to force clients to assume certain political and ideological roles contrary to their own predilections. By contrast, other officials sent to work as instructors in immigrant villages became subservient to the village communities and turned into their representatives for presenting the demands to the authorities, losing sight of their specific responsibility to serve the welfare of these immigrants by teaching them new skills. An illustration of an entire service organization that became subservient to its clients is provided by Clark in his study of the adult-education programs in Los Angeles.[32] Here the marginality of the entire program and the policy that only classes with a certain minimal attendance would be maintained gave the students control over the character and content of the curriculum and even the selection of instructors; clients assumed "a position of dominance over professionals in influence on program content."[33] To convert a university into a business concern that "gives the customers what they want" does not serve the best educational interests of students; rather, students are best served when professional educators determine what and how they are to be taught.

Failure to serve the welfare of clients is probably a more prevalent problem in service organizations than becoming subservient to them, and the former issue will occupy us again later. . . . Now we turn to another problem, which has received considerable attention from students of mental hospitals, namely, the sensitive nature of the professional-client relationship. Stanton and Schwartz found that when a patient in a private mental hospital was the subject of covert but basic staff disagreement he tended to become pathologically agitated; further-more, once the disagreement was brought into the open and resolved, the pa-tient's excitement terminated, often abruptly.[34] Apparently such conflicts subtly influence the interaction between staff and patient, and the disagreements among staff members are inadvertently communicated to the patient, causing his emo-tional disturbance. Caudill's study of another small hospital tends to confirm this conclusion.[35] In this case, changes in the hospital's treatment program upset hospital routines and confused staff roles; disagreements remained covert and led to less frequent encounters among the various staff groups—senior psychiatrists, residents, and nurses. Shortly thereafter, a period of rather intense collective disturbance occurred among the patients. Early attempts of each of the staff groups to deal with patient problems proved unsuccessful, partly because the endeavors of different groups were in conflict, and it was not until disagreements were brought into the open and discussed that the situation was restored to normal. Both studies suggest that conflict within an organization must become overt before it can be resolved. In many ways this situation seems analogous to individual disturbances—the mental conflict of a person must also become con-scious before he can resolve it. Another study, however, did not find disagree-ments among the staff to be associated with disturbance.[36] Wallace and Rashkis administered a paper-and-pencil test to staff members in a mental hospital over a seven-week period to obtain measures of degree of consensus on every patient; at the same time systematic observational data were collected on amount of patient disturbance. No significant relations were found between these two sets of data, although an increase in over-all consensus and a decrease in patient disturbance were noted over the period of study.[37]

Commonweal Organizations

It is not always meaningful to speak of the clients of an organization, since this term refers to both the segment of the public in direct contact with the organiza-tion and the segment that benefits from its services. In service organizations, the two are identical; hence, only when referring to these is it appropriate to speak of clients. But who would be the clients of, say, an army? Surely not the enemy it fights; neither would it be the citizens who benefit from its operations, since they are not in direct contact. An army has no clients in the above sense.

The distinctive characteristic of commonweal organizations is that the public-at-large is their prime beneficiary, often, although not necessarily, to the exclusion of the very people who are the object of the organization's endeavor. Examples of this type are the State Department, the Bureau of Internal Revenue, military services, police and fire departments, and also the research function as distinguished from the teaching function in universities. Most of these organiza-tions either perform protective services for the community or serve as its adminis-trative arm. As was pointed out earlier, the public could be considered the owners as well as the prime beneficiaries, and this type could then have been subsumed under our second category: organizations serving the interests of their owners. However, it seems preferable to separate these types since great differences in the nature and function of an organization depend on whether the community at large or a select number of owners are the prime beneficiaries.

The issue posed by commonweal organizations is that of external democratic control—the public must possess the means of controlling the ends served by these organizations. While external democratic control is essential, the internal structure of these organizations is expected to be bureaucratic, governed by the criterion of efficiency, and not democratic. The challenge facing these organizations, then, is the maintenance of efficient bureaucratic mechanisms that effectively implement the objectives of the community, which are ideally decided upon, at least in our society, by democratic methods. (*Internal* democratic control by the membership might well be at the expense of efficiency and thus lessen the organization's ability to effect the democratic will of the community.)

Three problems of commonweal organizations will be briefly discussed: the problem of power, the problem of promoting extraordinary performances, and the problem of dealing with outcasts.

The problem of power is perhaps best exemplified by the military service. In the interests of national security, most countries maintain military organizations of considerable strength. The existence of such a force creates the danger that it can be used to dominate the society that produced it, thus destroying democratic control or other forms of civilian government. This situation is illustrated by the army coups which have occurred in South American countries and the Algerian adventures of the French generals in 1961. The problem of maintaining democratic control over the military is accentuated by the background and the political orientation of its senior officers, although recent evidence reported by Janowitz indicates that changes are occurring in the composition of the officer corps.[38] Thus, in the past the officers in most countries were recruited from the aristocratic groups: half a century ago 92 percent of the military leaders of the United States originated in the upper-middle class or above it. By 1950, however, the proportion of leaders having their origin in these higher classes had decreased to about 50 percent. Similar shifts occurred in other countries; in Germany, for example, 97 percent of the military elite were recruited from the nobility in 1824, 67 percent in 1911, and by 1944 only 18 percent could claim such origins. As might be predicted from their background, military officials have been traditionally conservative in politics. This statement has been particularly true in Europe; in the United States, military leaders more often have tended to be apolitical, but most of them also have had a conservative viewpoint, and still do. The persistence of their conservatism despite the broader base of recruitment appears to result from the socialization of recruits to army traditions. For example, graduates of military academies were found to be more conservative than nonacademy men. While there are several aspects to this military conservatism, perhaps the most important and disquieting is the belief held by a considerable number of the military elite that the formation of policy on national security should be removed from civilian control and placed in the hands of the military. Janowitz concludes: "The effectiveness of civilian political control over the military is dependent only to a small extent upon the political beliefs held by the military profession."[39]

A second problem confronting some commonweal organizations is that of promoting such extraordinary performance as bravery or creativity. Military organizations must find ways of eliciting bravery from their members under combat circumstances; police and fire work also frequently call for individual heroism. Of course, bravery by itself may be insufficient for guaranteeing military success. Weber has suggested that bureaucratic discipline is more important than individual heroism for the success of an army,[40] and Janowitz indicates that the military manager has come to replace the military hero.[41] Nevertheless, it would seem to remain true that military success depends on fielding solidiers who are brave, not cowardly. And if there is less need for great heroes in today's battles, even "routine" action in combat requires much bravery. Another form of extraordinary behavior is required in research organizations, namely, scientific creativity. This elusive quality is considered by many to be inborn and thus, by definition, outside the sphere of organizational influence. Actually, however, as we will see later, organizations do influence research creativity. If extraordinary qualities are required of individuals to insure the successful operations of an organization, it is important to learn how an organization can select personnel that possess such qualities, can stimulate their further development among its staff, and can motivate and help its members to apply their relevant talents to the pursuit of organizational objectives.

A special problem is posed for organizations that are required to deal with society's outcasts, such as prisoners, against whom the public is being protected. What complicates the work of these institutions is that stamping men as outcasts not only removes them from society but also from society's control. Cloward has discussed in detail the dilemma faced by prison officials who must control inmates.[42] On the one hand, physical force is not very effective for routine control, and society has placed severe strictures on its employment in prisons. On the other hand, the attempt to offer the prisoner incentives by promising him rehabilitation and social reintegration is inhibited by society's refusal to accept prisoners after their release.

In this situation the guard finds himself in a difficult position. He is the one in continual interaction with prisoners, and he must find means to control them. It is not easy to treat a person with whom one has frequent contacts as an outcast. Moreover, the failure of the formal reward and sanctioning system forces the guard, according to Cloward, to rely on informal means of control. The guard can obligate prisoners to himself by providing them illegitimate access to desired goods and services. Such illegal alliances between guards and prisoners provide the structure by which the other prisoners are controlled—the prisoner confederates helping the guards to maintain control in the interest of retaining their own favored position.

One attempt to solve the problem of control, as well as that of rehabilitation, is to transform prisons from commonweal organizations (concerned with the protection of the public) into service organizations (oriented primarily to the needs and interests of the prisoner "clients"). An interesting problem this raises for the organization is discussed in Grusky's study of a small Midwestern prison camp.[43] He reports that the adoption of a therapeutic orientation toward prisoners resulted in enhancing their status, a circumstance likely to be disruptive for the organization, because it tended to be perceived by the guards, not without justification, as lowering their own status relative to that of the prisoners. Other consequences of the therapeutic approach were an increase in the interaction between the staff members and prisoners, a decentralization of authority (a change which may enhance the status of the middle-level staff), and a reduced dependence on bureaucratic procedures.

These studies suggest that the identity of the prime beneficiary of the organization's operations has far-reaching consequences for its structural characteristics, a conclusion which indicates the usefulness of the typology of formal organizations here proposed.

Notes

1. For examples, see Robin M. Williams, Jr., *American Society* (2d ed.), New York: Knopf, 1960, pp. 488–489.
2. Banks and credit agencies, for instance, are assigned to the political sphere rather than to the economic. Talcott Parsons, *Structure and Process in Modern Societies*, Glencoe, Ill.: Free Press, 1960, pp. 44–47.
3. See *ibid.*, pp. 20–21. Parsons mentions, as a third type, organizations that deal with cultural objects; for example, research firms which add to knowledge. For an analysis of the ways in which people are similar to as well as different from physical objects as material to be worked with by organizations, see Erving Goffman, "Characteristics of Total Institutions," Walter Reed Army Institute of Research, *Symposium on Preventive and Social Psychiatry*, Washington, D.C.: U.S. Government Printing Office, 1957, pp. 66–69.
4. Everett C. Hughes, "Memorandum on Going Concerns," unpublished paper read before the Society for Applied Anthropology, 1952.
5. James D. Thompson and Arthur Tuden, "Strategies, Structures, and Processes of Organizational Decision," James D. Thompson *et al.* (eds.), *Comparative Studies in Administration*, Pittsburgh: University of Pittsburgh Press, 1959, pp. 195–216.
6. The first three of our four types are similar to those used by Simon in his discussion of the economic firm. See Herbert A. Simon, *Administrative Behavior* (2d ed.), New York: Macmillan, 1957, pp. 16–17.
7. The reader will note that our typology is not as unequivocal on this point as it might be. In the case of a police department, is not the public also the owner, and is not therefore the owner, as in the case of the business concern, the prime beneficiary? Technically speaking, of course, the public is the owner and prime beneficiary. However, it appeared to us that there were such major differences separating the two types—public organizations and privately owned ones—that more would be lost than gained by combining them into a single type.
8. See Adolf A. Berle and Gardner C. Means, *The Modern Corporation and Private Property*, New York: Macmillan, 1932.
9. For a discussion of the conditions that lead to overbureaucratization and its opposite, see S. N. Eisenstadt, "Bureaucracy, Bureaucratization, and Debureaucratization," *Administrative Science Quarterly*, 4 (1959), pp. 302–320.
10. Bernard Barber, "Participation and Mass Apathy in Associations," Alvin W. Gouldner (ed.), *Studies in Leadership*, New York: Harper, 1950, pp. 477–504.
11. Barber suggests two reasons for membership apathy: (1) in our society, a strong cultural value defines these associations as being of less importance than family and job obligations; and (2) the existence of formal structures makes it possible for a minority to achieve the goals of the association with the majority of the members participating little or not at all. *Ibid.*, pp. 486–487.
12. See Seymour M. Lipset *et al.*, *Union Democracy*, Glencoe, Ill.: Free Press, 1956, pp. 261–262.
13. Mirra Komarovsky, "The Voluntary Associations of Urban Dwellers," Logan Wilson and William Kolb (eds.), *Sociological Analysis*, New York: Harcourt, Brace, 1949, pp. 378–392.
14. See Wendell Bell *et al.*, *Public Leadership*, San Francisco: Chandler, 1961, pp. 21–23, 44–47, 64–66, 82–84, 111–113.
15. In considerable measure the following discussion is based on a survey of this literature by Spinrad. This article provides documentation for all the statements made in our discussion of union participation for which no specific reference is provided. See William Spinrad, "Correlates of Trade Union Participation," *American Sociological Review*, 25 (1960), pp. 237–244.
16. *Ibid.*, p. 241.

17. Lipset *et al.*, *op. cit.*, pp. 71–75; 88–89.
18. Clark Kerr and Abraham Siegel, "The Interindustry Propensity to Strike," Arthur Kornhauser *et al.* (eds.), *Industrial Conflict*, New York: McGraw-Hill, 1954, pp. 189–212.
19. Leonard R. Sayles and George Strauss, *The Local Union*, New York: Harper, 1953, p. 198.
20. See, for example, Joel Seidman *et al.*, *The Worker Views His Union*, Chicago: University of Chicago Press, 1958, p. 178.
21. For a general discussion of the issue of efficiency vs. dissent in formal organizations, see Peter M. Blau, *Bureaucracy in Modern Society*, New York: Random House, 1956, pp. 105–110.
22. Robert Michels, *Political Parties*, Eden Paul and Cedar Paul (trans.), Glencoe, Ill.: Free Press, 1949 (first published, 1915), pp. 37–41.
23. Alvin W. Gouldner, "Metaphysical Pathos and the Theory of Bureaucracy," *American Political Science Review*, 49 (1955), p. 506.
24. Seymour M. Lipset, *Political Man*, Garden City, N.Y.: Doubleday, 1960, pp. 357–399; and Lipset *et al.*, *op. cit.*, pp. 3–16; 393–418.
25. Chester I. Barnard, *The Functions of the Executive*, Cambridge, Mass.: Harvard University Press, 1938, pp. 56–61, 92–94.
26. Daniel Katz *et al.*, *Productivity, Supervision and Morale in an Office Situation*, Ann Arbor: Institute for Social Research, University of Michigan, 1950.
27. Chris Argyris, *Organization of a Bank*, New Haven: Labor and Management Center, Yale University, 1954.
28. See the discussion of this point with particular reference to the medical profession in Talcott Parsons, *The Social System*, Glencoe, Ill.: Free Press, 1951, pp. 433–445, 463–465, 471–473.
29. Talcott Parsons, *Essays in Sociological Theory* (2d. ed.), Glencoe, Ill.: Free Press, 1954, pp. 34–49.
30. See Morris Janowitz *et al.*, *Public Administration and the Public*, Ann Arbor: Institute of Public Administration, University of Michigan, 1958, p. 6.
31. Elihu Katz and S. N. Eisenstadt, "Some Sociological Observations on the Response of Israeli Organizations to New Immigrants," *Administrative Science Quarterly*, 5 (1960), pp. 113–133.
32. Burton R. Clark, *Adult Education in Transition*, Berkeley: University of California Press, 1958.
33. *Ibid.*, p. 86.
34. Alfred H. Stanton and Morris S. Schwartz, *The Mental Hospital*, New York: Basic Books, 1954, pp. 342–365.
35. William A. Caudill, *The Psychiatric Hospital as a Small Society*, Cambridge, Mass.: Harvard University Press, 1958, pp. 87–127.
36. Anthony F. C. Wallace and Harold A. Rashkis, "The Relation of Staff Consensus to Patient Disturbance on Mental Hospital Wards," *American Sociological Review*, 24 (1959), pp. 829–835.
37. Two possible interpretations of these conflicting findings are: First, the relationship between consensus and disturbance may be spurious; there is more consensus about those patients who have been in the hospital for some time, and patients also tend to become less disturbed the longer they have been in the ward. Second, the important factor in promoting disturbance is not the total number of disagreements concerning a patient but rather disagreements on particularly salient issues or between particularly significant staff members.
38. See Morris Janowitz, *The Professional Soldier*, Glencoe, Ill.: Free Press, 1960, especially pp. 89–94; 236–241.
39. *Ibid.*, p. 253.
40. Weber cites Cromwell's victory over the Cavaliers as an illustration of his thesis that discipline is more significant than bravery. H. H. Gerth and C. Wright Mills (trans.

and eds.), *From Max Weber: Essays in Sociology*, New York: Oxford University Press, 1946, pp. 256–257.

41. Janowitz, *op. cit.*, p. 21.
42. Richard A. Cloward, "Social Control in the Prison," Richard A. Cloward *et al.*, *Theoretical Studies in Social Organization of the Prison*, New York: Social Science Research Council, 1960 (Pamphlet No. 15), pp. 20–48.
43. Oscar Grusky, "Role Conflict in Organization," *Administrative Science Quarterly*, 3 (1959), pp. 452–472.

Goals or Functions
Talcott Parsons

Organizations are of course always part of a larger social structure of the society in which they occur. There is necessarily a certain variability among organizations which is a function of this wider societal matrix; an American organization is never quite like a British one even though they are nearly cognate in function. Discounting this type of variability, however, organizations may in the first instance be classified in terms of the *type of goal or function* about which they are organized. The same basic classification can be used for goal types which has been used earlier in dealing with the functions of a social system. Thus we may speak of adaptive goals, implementive goals, integrative goals, and pattern-maintenance goals. The reference is always to function in the *society* as a system.

Seen in these terms the principal broad types of organization are:

1. *Organizations oriented to economic production:* The type case in this category is the business firm. Production should be understood in the full economic sense as "adding value"; it is by no means confined to physical production, e.g., manufacturing. It has been emphasized several times that every organization contributes in some way to every primary function (if it is well integrated in the society); hence we can speak only of economic *primacy*, never of an organization as being exclusively economic. This applies also to the other categories.

2. *Organizations oriented to political goals*, that is, to the attainment of valued goals and to the generation and allocation of power in the society: This category includes most organs of government, but in a society like ours, various other organizations are involved. The allocation of purchasing power through credit creation is an exercise of power in this sense; hence a good part of the banking system should be treated as residing in primarily political organizations. More generally, it seems legitimate to speak of incorporation as an allocation of power in a political sense; hence the corporate aspect of formal organizations generally is a political aspect.

3. *Integrative organizations:* These are organizations which on the societal level, contribute primarily to efficiency, not effectiveness. They concern the adjustment of conflicts and the direction of motivation to the fulfillment of institutionalized expectations. A substantial part of the functions of the courts and of the legal profession should be classed here. Political parties, whose function is the mobilization of support for those responsible for government operations, belong in this category, and, to a certain extent, "interest groups" belong here, too. Finally, those organizations that are primarily mechanisms of social control in the narrower sense, for example hospitals, are mainly integrative.

4. *Pattern-maintenance organizations:* The principal cases centering here are those with primarily "cultural," "educational," and "expressive" functions. Perhaps the most clearcut organizational examples are churches and schools. (Pattern maintenance is not here conceived to preclude creativity; hence research

is included.) The arts so far as they give rise to organization also belong here. Kinship groups are ordinarily not primarily organizations in our technical sense, but in a society so highly differentiated as our own the nuclear family approaches more closely the characteristics of an organization than in other societies. As such it clearly belongs in the pattern-maintenance category.

This primary basis of classification can be used as the point of departure for a more detailed one, by further subdividing each of the primary types into lower other subsystems. Thus in the economic case the main bases of sub-classification would include specialization in adaptive functions for the economy (financing), in goal attainment (production and marketing in a narrower sense), etc. Similar considerations will apply in the cases of the other primary types. In each of these cases a primary determinant of the type of organization is the kind of boundary-interchange operating between the societal system in which the organization is primarily anchored and the contiguous subsystem. Thus from the point of view of the economy, production and marketing are the sources of the ultimate production of goods and services to the consumer and of the input of labor services into the economy. Both consumer and worker are anchored in the first instance in the household as part of the pattern-maintenence system. Organizations oriented primarily to consumption interests are necessarily different from those oriented primarily to the financing of capital expansion.

Technology
Charles Perrow

This paper presents a perspective on organizations that hopefully will provide a basis for comparative organizational analysis, and also allow one to utilize selectively the existing theories of organizational behavior. There are four characteristics of this perspective.

First, technology, or the work done in organizations, is considered the defining characteristic of organizations. That is, organizations are seen primarily as systems for getting work done, for applying techniques to the problem of altering raw materials—whether the materials be people, symbols or things. This is in contrast to other perspectives which see organizations as, for example, cooperative systems, institutions, or decision-making systems.

Second, this perspective treats technology as an independent variable, and structure—the arrangements among people for getting work done—as a dependent variable. Goals are conceived of as being in part a dependent variable. What is held to be an independent and dependent variable when one abstracts general variables from a highly interdependent and complex social system is less of an assertion about reality than a strategy of analysis. Thus, no claim is made that for all purposes technology need be an independent variable.

Third, this perspective attempts to conceptualize the organization as a whole, rather than to deal only with specific processes or subparts. Thus, while the importance of technology has often been demonstrated within work groups or for particular organizational processes, here it will be used as a basis for dealing with the organization as an organization.

Finally, and in the long run perhaps most importantly, the perspective holds that technology is a better basis for comparing organizations than the several schemes which now exist.[1]

None of these points in itself is new, and the last section of this article discusses the uses to which the concept of technology has been put by others. However, the attempt to deal with all four points simultaneously, or, to put it differently, to pay systematic attention to the role of technology in analyzing and comparing organizations as a whole, is believed to be distinctive.

Revision of a paper read at the 1966 Annual Meeting of the American Sociological Association. This paper was prepared during the course of research on industrial corporations supported by Grant No. GS-742, National Science Foundation. Numerous colleagues criticized an earlier version unstintingly, but I would like to single out Ernest Vargas, Geoffrey Guest and Anthony Kovner, who transcended their graduate student roles at the University of Pittsburgh during the formulation of these ideas in sticky field situations.

Reprinted in part from Charles Perrow, "A Framework for the Comparative Analysis of Organizations," *American Sociological Review*, vol. 32 (April 1967), pp. 194–204, by permission of the author and the publisher, The American Sociological Association.

Technology and Raw Materials

By technology is meant the actions that an individual performs upon an object, with or without the aid of tools or mechanical devices, in order to make some change in that object. The object, or "raw material," may be a living being, human or otherwise, a symbol or an inanimate object. People are raw materials in people-changing or people-processing organizations; symbols are materials in banks, advertising agencies and some research organizations; the interactions of people are raw materials to be manipulated by administrators in organizations; boards of directors, committees and councils are usually involved with the changing or processing of symbols and human interactions, and so on.

In the course of changing this material in an organizational setting, the individual must interact with others. The form that this interaction takes we will call the structure of the organization. It involves the arrangements or relationships that permit the coordination and control of work. Some work is actually concerned with changing or maintaining the structure of an organization. Most administrators have this as a key role, and there is a variety of technologies for it. The distinction between technology and structure has its gray areas, but basically it is the difference between an individual acting directly upon a material that is to be changed and an individual interacting with other individuals in the course of trying to change that material. In some cases the material to be changed and the "other individuals" he interacts with are the same objects, but the relationships are different in each case.

There are a number of aspects of technology which are no doubt important to consider in some contexts, such as the environment of the work (noise, dirt, etc.) or the possibilities of seductive or exploitative relationships with clients, patients or customers. For our purposes, however, we are concerned with two aspects of technology that seem to be directly relevant to organizational structure. The first is the number of exceptional cases encountered in the work,[2] that is, the degree to which stimuli are perceived as familiar or unfamiliar. This varies on a scale from low to high.

The second is the nature of the search process that is undertaken by the individual when exceptions occur. We distinguish two types of search process. The first type involves a search which can be conducted on a logical, analytical basis. Search processes are always exceptional actions undertaken by the individual. They are nonroutine. No programs exist for them. If a program exists, only a very trivial search is involved in switching from one program to another program when the stimuli change.[3] But though nonroutine, one type of search may be logical, systematic and analytical. This is exemplified by the mechanical engineering unit of a firm building large machinery, or by programmers writing individual programs for slow readers in a special school. The second type of search process occurs when the problem is so vague and poorly conceptualized as to make it virtually unanalyzable. In this case, no "formal" search is undertaken, but instead one draws upon the residue of unanalyzed experience or intuition, or relies upon chance and guesswork. Examples would be work with exotic metals or nuclear fuels, psychiatric casework, and some kinds of advertising. We can conceive of a scale from analyzable to unanalyzable problems.

If we dichotomize these two continua into the presence or absence of exceptional cases and into the presence or absence of analyzable problems, we have a four-fold table as in Figure 1. The upper right-hand quadrant, cell 2, where

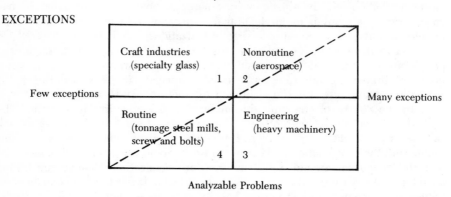

Figure 1

there are many exceptional cases and a few analytic techniques for analyzing them, is one extreme to which we will refer as nonroutine. In the lower left-hand quadrant, cell 4, we have the routine extreme, where there are few exceptions and there are analytic techniques for handling those that occur. A one-dimensional scheme would follow the dotted line from routine to nonroutine. But note that the other two quadrants may represent viable cases in themselves and they have been labeled with some industrial examples. Few cases would probably fall in the upper left-hand corner of cell 1, or lower right-hand corner of cell 3, but otherwise many organizations are expected to appear in these two cells.

Techniques are performed upon raw materials. The state of the art of analyzing the characteristics of the raw materials is likely to determine what kind of technology will be used. (Tools are also necessary, of course, but by and large, the construction of tools is a simpler problem than the analysis of the nature of the material and generally follows the analysis.) To understand the nature of the material means to be able to control it better and achieve more predictability and efficiency in transformation. We are not referring here to the "essence" of the material, only to the way the organization itself perceives it.

The other relevant characteristic of the raw material, besides the understandability of its nature, is its stability and variability; that is, whether the material can be treated in a standardized fashion or whether continual adjustment to it is necessary. Organizations uniformly seek to standardize their raw material in order to minimize exceptional situations. This is the point of de-individualizing processes found in military academies, monasteries and prisons, or the superiority of the synthetic shoe material Corfam over leather.

These two characteristics interact, of course. On the one hand, increased knowledge of the nature of the material may lead to the perception of more varieties of possible outcomes or products, which in turn increases the need for more intimate knowledge of the nature of the material. Or the organization, with increased knowledge of one type of material, may begin to work with a variety of related materials about which more needs to be known, as when a social service agency or employment agency relaxes its admission criteria as it gains confidence, but in the process sets off more search behavior, or when a manufacturing organization starts producing new but related products. On the other hand, if increased knowledge of the material is gained but no expansion of the variety of output occurs, this permits easier analysis of the sources of problems that may arise in the transformation process. It may also allow one to prevent the rise of such problems by the design of the production process.

A recent analysis of a public defender system by Sudnow highlights the twin characteristics of the material variable.[4] On the one hand, offenders are distributed into uniform categories by means of the conception of the "normal crime," and on the other hand, control over the individual offender is insured because the public defender well understands the offender's "nature"—that is, his low status, limited understanding and intellectual resources, and his impecunious condition. The technology, then, can be routine because there are few exceptions (and these are handled by a different set of personnel) and no search behavior on the public defender's part is required. The lawyer in private practice, of course, is a contrasting case.[5]

It will readily be seen that these two characteristics of the raw material are paralleled in the four-fold table of technology (Figure 2). If the technology of an organization is going to move from cell 2 to any of the other cells, it can only do so either by reducing the variability of the material and thus the number of exceptional cases that occur, or by increasing the knowledge of the material and thus allowing more analytic techniques to be used, or both. One may move from cell 2 to cell 1 with increasing production runs, clients served, accounts handled, research projects underway, agency programs administered and so forth, since this allows more experience to be gained and thus reduces the number of stimuli seen as exceptions. If technical knowledge increases, increasing the reliability of search procedures, one may move from cell 2 to cell 3. If both things happen—and this is the aim of most organizations—one may move from cell 2 to cell 4.[6]

Task and Social Structure

For our purpose, the task structure of an organization is conceived of as consisting of two dimensions, control and coordination. Control itself can be broken up into two components. They are the degree of discretion an individual or group possesses in carrying out its tasks, and the power of an individual or group to mobilize scarce resources and to control definitions of various situations, such as the definition of the nature of the raw material. Discretion here does not mean freedom from supervision or freedom simply to vary task sequences or pace of work. Both of these are compatible with routine activities, and some nonroutine tasks must be closely supervised or have precise sequences of tasks, once a program is selected, because of their critical nature. Nor does the length of time between performance reviews[7] necessarily indicate discretion. Rather, discretion involves judgments about whether close supervision is required on one task or another, about changing programs, and about the interdependence of one's task with other tasks.[8] Discretion and power may often be correlated,[9] but there is an important distinction. Power affects outcomes directly because it involves choices

Raw Material Variables
(People-Changing Examples)
PERCEIVED NATURE OF RAW MATERIAL

Not Well Understood

VARIABILITY
OF MATERIAL

Socializing instit. (e.g. some schools) 1	Elite psychiatric agency 2
Custodial institutions, vocational training 4	Programmed learning school 3

Perceived as uniform and stable

Perceived as non-uniform and unstable

Well Understood

Figure 2

regarding basic goals and strategies. Discretion relates to choices among means and judgments of the critical and interdependent nature of tasks. The consequences of decisions in the case of discretion have no direct influence on goals and strategies; these decisions are formed within the framework of accepted goals and strategies.

Coordination, on the other hand, can be achieved through planning or feedback, to use the terms proposed by March and Simon.[10] Coordination by planning refers to the programmed interaction of tasks, which interaction is clearly defined by rules or by the very tools and machinery or the logic of the transformation process. Coordination by feedback, on the other hand, refers to negotiated alterations in the nature or sequence of tasks performed by two different units.

It is now necessary to distinguish three functional or task areas within management in organizations. Area One, the design and planning function, entails such major decisions as what goods or services are to be produced, who the customers will be, the technology employed, and the source of legitimacy and capital. Area Two, the technical control and support of production and marketing, includes such functions (to use industrial terms) as accounting, product and process research, quality control, scheduling, engineering, plant management, purchasing, customer service, advertising, market research, and general sales management. (Not all are important, or even existent, of course, in all industrial organizations.) This is distinguished as a function, though not necessarily in terms of actual persons or positions, from Area Three, the supervision of production and marketing. This area involves the direct supervision of those dealing with the basic raw materials and those doing direct selling.[11] In the subsequent discussion we shall ignore marketing, and, for a time, Area One.

Figure 3 shows crudely the kinds of values that might be expected to appear in the task structure, considering only Areas Two and Three—technical control and support of production, and the supervision of production. Some global organi-

Task Structure

Task-Related Interactions

	Discre-tion	Power	Coord. w/in gp.	Interde-pendence of groups	Discre-tion	Power	Coord. w/in gp.	Interde-pendence of groups
Technical	Low	Low	Plan		High	High	Feed	
				Low				High
Superv.	High	High	Feed		High	High	Feed	
		Decentralized				Flexible, Polycentralized		
				1	**2**			
				4	**3**			
Technical	Low	High	Plan		High	High	Feed	
				Low				Low
Superv.	Low	Low	Plan		Low	Low	Plan	
		Formal, Centralized				Flexible, Centralized		

Figure 3

zational characterizations of structure are given at the bottom of each cell. Those familiar with Burns and Stalker's work will recognize cell 2 as closest to the organic structure and cell 4 as closest to the mechanistic structure.[12]

In cell 2, we have nonuniform raw materials in both areas which are not well understood, and thus present many occasions for exceptional handling. However, the search required cannot be logically conducted, but must involve a high degree of experimentation and "feel." In such a technological situation, the discretion of both those who supervise the transformation of the basic raw material, and those who provide technical help for this process, must be high. The supervisors will request help from technical personnel rather than receive orders from them, or there may not even be a clear line of distinction between the two in terms of persons. That is, the clinical psychologist or the quality control engineer will find himself "on the line" so to speak, dealing directly with patients or exotic metals and working side by side with the supervisors who are nominally of lower status. The power of both groups will be high, and not at the expense of each other. The coordination will be through feedback—that is, considerable mutual adjustment must be made. The interdependence of the two groups will be high. The development of product groups and product managers in industry provides an example, as does the somewhat premature attempt of one correctional institution to utilize a cottage system bringing both clinical and line personnel together with joint responsibility for running autonomous cottages.[13]

In the case of cell 4, uniform stable materials whose relevant nature is perceived as well understood can be handled with few exceptions occurring, and those that do occur can be taken care of with analytical search processes. In such a situation the discretion of both groups is likely to be low. This is a well-programmed production process and there is no need to allow much discretion. Indeed, there is danger in doing so. However, the power of the technical group over the supervisory group is high, for they direct the activities of the supervisors of production on the basis of routine reports generated by the supervisors. Those in Area Three are likely to see those in Area Two as hindrances to their work rather than aides. Coordination can be through planning in both groups, and the interdependence of the two groups is low; it is a directive rather than an interdependent relationship.

Cell 3 represents a variation from either of these extremes, for here, in contrast to cell 2, the existence of many exceptions which require search procedures increases both the power and the discretion of the technical group, which handles these exceptions, at the expense of the supervisory group. The supervisors of production respond to the results of these search processes rather than undertake search themselves. In the case of cell 1, the situation is reversed. Because search cannot be logical and analytical, when the infrequent exceptions occur they are handled by those in closest contact with the production process such as teachers and skilled craftsmen, and there is minimal development of administrative services. Of course, in schools that attempt to do little socialization but simply offer instruction and provide custody, technical (administrative) services grow and we move to cell 2.

Having thus related technology to task structure, let us turn to another aspect of structure—the non-task-related but organizationally relevant interactions of people. We call this the social structure.

Figure 4 follows our previous four-fold classification and indicates the variety of bases for non-task-related interactions. All are present in all organizations, but the saliency varies. In cell 2, these interactions are likely to revolve more around the mission, long-range goals, and direction of development of the organizations than around the other three bases. This is because of the task structure characteristic of a flexible, polycentric organization, or at least is related to it. The category "social identity" in cell 1 is meant to convey that the non-task-related interactions of personnel that are organizationally relevant revolve around communal or personal satisfactions born of long tenure and close working relationships. This is true especially at the supervisory level, which is a large management

(Social Structure)

The bases of non-task-related interaction

Social identity (communal)	Goal identification (mission, "character" of organization, distinctive competence, etc.)
1	2
4	3
Instrumental identity (job security, pay, protection from arbitrary power)	Work or task identification (technical satisfactions)

Figure 4

group in this type of structure. However, it is very possible, as Blauner and others have shown, for communal relations to develop in cell 4 types of organizations if the organization is located in a rural area where kinship and rural ties are strong.[14] The basis of interaction in cell 3 is instrumental identity and in cell 4, work or task identification. These would also be predicted upon the basis of the technology.

So far we have ignored Area One—design and planning. This area receives more inputs from the environment than the other areas, and thus its tasks and technologies are derived from both internal and external stimuli. If the product environment of the organization—a term meant to cover competitors, customers, suppliers, unions and regulatory agencies—were the same in all four cells of Figure 3, we would expect the design and planning areas in cell 4 to have routine tasks and techniques, and nonroutine ones in cell 2. This is because the occasions for design and long-range planning would be few in the one and many in the other. For example, at least until very recently, the decisions that executives in the primary metals industries, railroads and surface mining had to make were probably rather routine, while those executives in new industries such as electronics and aerospace were probably nonroutine.[15] One would expect that cell 1 would also be routine, and cell 3 somewhat nonroutine. But the product environment can alter all this. Organizations in cell 4 can be in a rapidly changing market situation even though the technical control and the supervision of production are fairly routine. Consumer goods industries probably deal with many decisions where the search behavior confronts unanalyzable problems such as the hemline of women's clothes, fads in the toy industry, or the length of time that tail fins or the boxy look in autos will last. Generally speaking, however, though the intrinsic characteristics of the product remain the same, rapid changes in the extrinsic characteristics will introduce nonroutine tasks in the design and planning area, even though it hardly alters the routine character of the technical control and the supervision of production.[16]

These are industrial examples, but it also seems likely that the tasks of Area One in custodial mental hospitals are quite different from those in treatment-oriented hospitals. Relations with the regulatory agencies, supplying agencies, the consumers such as courts and families, and the other agencies that compete for funds or clients, will be rather routine in the first, while they will be quite nonroutine and sensitive in the second. This would not be true, of course, if the latter have the means of isolating themselves from their environment.[17] Similarly, the market situation of vocational training institutions may change rather quickly as industrial technologies change, requiring changes in the design and planning of the institution, while the market of a public school that attempts to socialize youths will not change as often.

Goals

Finally, let us turn to the last major variable, goals. Three categories of goals can be distinguished for present purposes.[18] These are system goals, which relate to the characteristics of the system as a whole, independent of its products; product characteristic goals, which relate to the characteristics of the products the organization decides to emphasize; and derived goals, which refer to the uses to which power generated by organizational activities can be put, independent of system or product goals.

Goals

System	Product	Derived	System	Product	Derived

Stability
Few risks
Moderate to low
  profit emphasis
	Quality
	No innovations
		Conserv.
		
		1
			High growth
			High risks
			Low emphasis on
			  profit
			2
				High quality
				Innovative
					Liberal

Stability
Few risks
High profit
  emphasis
	Quantity
	No innovations
		4
		Conserv.
			3
			Moderate growth
			Some risks
			Moderate profit
			  emphasis
				Reliability
				Moderate inno-
				  vations
					Liberal

Figure 5

We would expect completely routinized organizations to stress those "system" goals of organizational stability, low risk, and perhaps high profits or economical operations rather than growth. (See Figure 5.) In terms of "product characteristic" goals, they would be more likely to emphasize quantity than quality, stable lines over unstable or diversified lines, superficial transformations (e.g., instilling discipline in deviant clients) over basic transformation (such as character restructuring), and so forth. Their "derived" goals are likely to emphasize conservative attitudes towards the government, conservative political philosophies, conservative forms of corporate giving. Also, they are perhaps more likely to have individuals who exploit, for their own benefit, relations with suppliers, and who have collusive arrangements with competitors and devious and excessive forms of management compensation. Obviously, these comments upon possible goals are open to serious question. For one thing, we lack such data on goals for a large number of organizations. Furthermore, personalities and the environment may shape goals more than the other variables of technology and structure. Finally, the link between structure and goals is an intuitive one, based upon unproven assumptions regarding attitudes generated by task relations. But the comments are meant to suggest how goals may be shaped or constrained, though hardly specified, through the influence of technology and structure.

Some Cautions

This truncated perspective ignores the role of the cultural and social environment in making available definitions of raw material, providing technologies, and restricting the range of feasible structures and goals.[19] It also ignores, for the most part, the role of the product environment—customers, competitors, suppliers, unions and regulatory agencies—and the material and human resources. These will have their independent effect upon the major variables.

In addition, it is not proposed here that there are four types of organizations. The two-dimensional scheme is conceived of as consisting of two continua. Nor are the dimensions and the specifications of the variables necessarily the best. It is argued, however, that the main variables—raw materials, technology, task and social structure, goals, and some differentiation of task areas within organizations, are critical ones. As to the assignment of independent and dependent variables, occasions can be readily cited where changes in goals, for example those brought about by changes in the market place or the personalities of top executives, have brought about changes in the technology utilized. The argument is somewhat more subtle than one of temporal priorities. Rather, it says that structure and goals must adjust to technology or the organization will be subject to strong strains. For a radical change in goals to be a successful one, it may require a change in technology, and thus in structure, or else there will be a large price paid for the lack of fit between these variables.[20] Furthermore, as one proceeds, analytically, from technology through the two kinds of structure to goals, increasingly the prior variable only sets limits upon the range of possible variations in the next variable. Thus, technology may predict task structure quite well in a large number of organizations,[21] but these two predict social structure less well, and these three only set broad limits upon the range of possible goals.

Comparative Analyses

If all this is at all persuasive, it means that we have a powerful tool for comparing organizations. The first implication of this for comparative studies is that we cannot expect a particular relationship found in one organization to be found in another unless we know these organizations are in fact similar with respect to their technology. Thus, the fact that the cosmopolitan-local relationship that worked so well in Antioch College was not found in the outpatient department of a hospital should not surprise us; the work performed by the professionals in each case was markedly different.[22] That morale was associated with bureaucracy in fairly routine public schools, but not in research organizations, is understandable.[23] Less obvious, however, is the point that types of organization—in terms of their function in society—will vary as much within each type as between types. Thus, some schools, hospitals, banks and steel companies may have more in common, because of their routine character, than routine and nonroutine schools, routine and nonroutine hospitals, and so forth. To assume that you are holding constant the major variable by comparing several schools or several steel mills is unwarranted until one looks at the technologies employed by various schools or steel mills. In fact, the variations within one type of organization may be such that some schools are like prisons, some prisons like churches, some churches like factories, some factories like universities, and so on.[24] Once this is recognized, of course, analysis of the differences between churches or whatever can be a powerful tool, as witness the familiar contrast of custodial and treatment-oriented people-changing institutions.

    Another implication is that there is little point in testing the effect of a parameter variable, such as size, age, auspices, geographical dispersion, or even national culture, unless we control for technology. For example, in the case of size, to compare the structure of a small R and D lab where the tasks of all three areas are likely to be quite nonroutine with the structure of a large bank where they are likely to be quite routine is fruitless. The nature of their tasks is so different that the structures must vary independently of their different sizes.[25] A meaningful study of the effect of size on structure can be made only if we control for technology, and compare, say, large and small banks all of which have similar services, or large and small R and D labs. Similarly, though the brilliant work of Crozier on French culture is very suggestive, many of his conclusions may stem from the fact that only very routine organizations were studied, and even those lacked many critical elements of the bureaucratic model.[26] Equally routine organizations in a protected product environment in the U.S. might have displayed the same characteristics.

Finally, to call for decentralization, representative bureaucracy, collegial authority, or employee-centered, innovative or organic organizations—to mention only a few of the highly normative prescriptions that are being offered by social scientists today—is to call for a type of structure that can be realized only with a certain type of technology, unless we are willing to pay a high cost in terms of output. Given a routine technology, the much maligned Weberian bureaucracy probably constitutes the socially optimum form of organizational structure. . . .

Notes

1. E.g., social function (schools, business firms, hospitals, etc.), as used by Talcott Parsons in *Structure and Process in Modern Society*, Glencoe, Ill.: The Free Press, 1960, pp. 44–47; who benefits, proposed by Peter M. Blau and William R. Scott in *Formal Organizations*, San Francisco: Chandler, 1962, pp. 42–45; or compliance structure, as used by Amitai Etzioni, *A Comparative Analysis of Complex Organizations*, New York: The Free Press, 1961.
2. Cf. James March and Herbert Simon, *Organizations*, New York: Wiley, 1958, pp. 141–142, where a related distinction is made on the basis of search behavior. In our view the occurrence of an exceptional case is prior to search behavior, and various types of search behavior can be distinguished.
3. *Ibid.*, p. 142.
4. David Sudnow, "Normal Crimes: Sociological Features of the Penal Code in a Public Defender Office," *Social Problems*, 12 (Winter, 1965), pp. 255–276.
5. For a more extensive treatment of raw material somewhat along these lines, see David Street, Robert Vinter and Charles Perrow, *Organization for Treatment, A Comparative Study of Institutions for Delinquents*, New York: The Free Press, 1966, Chap. 1.
6. Some organizations, such as mental hospitals, perceive that their technology is inadequate to their goals, and try to move from cell 4 to cell 2 in the search for a new technology.
7. Eliot Jaques, *The Measurement of Responsibility*, Cambridge: Harvard University Press, 1959.
8. This raises serious operationalization problems. In my own work, first-line supervisors were said to have considerable independence in some routine production situations, and to have little in some nonroutine situations, according to a questionnaire, though it was observed that the former had little discretion and the latter a good deal. Kovner found the same kind of responses with a similar question regarding control of job and pace of work among nurses in routine and nonroutine nursing units. See Anthony Kovner, "The Nursing Unit: A Technological Perspective," unpublished Ph.D. dissertation, University of Pittsburgh, 1966. See also the discrepancy between scores on a similar matter resulting from different interpretations of discretion in two studies: Rose L. Coser, "Authority and Decision-Making in a Hospital," *American Sociological Review*, 23 (February, 1958), pp. 56–64, and James L. Hawkins, and Eugene Selmanoff, "Authority Structure, Ambiguity of the Medical Task, Absence of Doctor from the Ward, and the Behavior of Nurses," Indiana University, mimeo.

9. See, for example, a developmental scheme which holds that critical tasks requiring considerable discretion are the basis for group domination in hospitals and other organizations, in Charles Perrow, "Analysis of Goals in Complex Organizations," *American Sociological Review*, 26 (April, 1961), pp. 335–341. See also the compelling illustration presented in the discussion of maintenance personnel in a thoroughly routinized cigarette factory by Michel Crozier, *The Bureaucratic Phenomenon*, Chicago: University of Chicago Press, 1964, Chap. 4.

10. *Op. cit.*, p. 160.

11. The distinction between Areas Two and Three is based upon a more limited distinction used by Joan Woodward in her brilliant study, *Industrial Organization*, London: Oxford University Press, 1965.

12. Tom Burns and G. M. Stalker, *The Management of Innovation*, London: Tavistock Publications, 1961.

13. Street *et al.*, *op. cit.*, Chaps. 5, 6. The organization is called Milton.

14. Robert Blauner, *Alienation and Freedom: The Factory Worker and His Industry*, Chicago: University of Chicago Press, 1964, Chap. 4. Blauner's theory, incidentally, is entirely consistent with the perspective proposed here, even though we do not concern ourselves explicitly in this article with the morale of hourly employees.

15. On the former see Alfred D. Chandler, Jr., *Strategy and Structure*, Cambridge, Mass.: MIT Press, 1962, pp. 329–330, and Chap. 7 in general. The discussion of social structure and time periods by Stinchcombe can be interpreted in this manner also. Those exceptions that occur in his data appear to be examples of nonroutine technologies established in periods of predominantly routine technologies, or *vice versa*. See Arthur Stinchcombe, "Social Structure and Organizations" in James March (ed.) *Handbook of Organizations*, Chicago: Rand McNally, 1965, pp. 142–169, esp. p. 158.

16. On the distinction between intrinsic and extrinsic prestige, see Charles Perrow, "Organizational Prestige, Some Functions and Dysfunctions," *American Journal of Sociology*, 66 (January, 1961), pp. 335–341.

17. Cf. Street *et al.*, *op. cit.*, Chap. 4.

18. For a full discussion of these and three others see Charles Perrow, "Organizational Goals," *International Encyclopedia of the Social Sciences*.

19. The role of the cultural and social environment is developed in somewhat more detail in a review of studies of general and mental hospitals in Charles Perrow, "Hospitals: Technology, Structure and Goals," in James March, *op. cit.*, Chap. 22.

20. This is argued in detail in Perrow, *ibid.*, pp. 926–946. Kovner finds those nursing units with the greatest divergence between technology and structure to have the lowest scores on a dimension of goal realization. *Op. cit.*, pp. 96–97.

21. Unfortunately, verification of the predicted relationships would require a large sample of organizations since there are bound to be many examples of incompatibility between the variables. However, even in a small sample, those whose structure was appropriate to their technology should have fewer "strains" than those whose structure was inappropriate. Joan Woodward, using a similar approach with 100 industrial firms found strong relationships between production systems and certain aspects of structure, though the rudimentary information and analysis on the 100 firms leaves one in doubt as to how strong. See Joan Woodward, *op. cit.*

22. Cf. Alvin Gouldner, "Cosmopolitans and Locals: Toward an Analysis of Latent Social Roles," *Administrative Science Quarterly*, 2 (December, 1957, March, 1958), pp. 281–306, 444–480, and Warren G. Bennis, N. Berkowitz, M. Affinito, and M. Malone, "Reference Groups and Loyalties in the Out-Patient Department," *Administrative Science Quarterly*, 2 (March 1958), pp. 481–500.

23. Gerald H. Moeller and W. W. Charters, "Relation of Bureaucratization to Sense of Power Among Teachers," *Administrative Science Quarterly*, 10 (December 1966), pp. 444–465. In addition, for this reason one becomes wary of propositional inventories that fail to make sufficient distinctions among organizations, but attempt to support the

propositions by illustrations that are likely to restrict the scope of the proposition to the particular type of organization used in the illustration. For the most recent example, see William A. Rushing, "Organizational Rules and Surveillance: Propositions in Comparative Organizational Analysis," *Administrative Science Quarterly*, 10 (December 1966), pp. 423–443.

24. Many of the frameworks for comparative analysis, such as those cited in footnote 1, break down because of their broad categories. The failure of some of these schemes to meaningfully order the data from a large sample of a great variety of organizations is discussed in J. Eugene Haas, Richard H. Hall and Norman J. Johnson, "Toward an Empirically Derived Taxonomy of Organizations," in Raymond V. Bowers (ed.), *Studies on Behavior in Organizations*, Atlanta: University of Georgia Press, 1966, pp. 157–180.

25. This may be a basic error in the ambitious survey conducted by Haas and his associates, *ibid*.

26. Crozier, *op. cit.*

SECTION THREE
The Structure of Organizations

Perhaps the single most important organizational feature to receive significant sociological attention concerns the matter of *organizational structure.* How the units and subunits which comprise complex organizations fit together and how well these interconnections foster the social coordination necessary for the pursuit of collective goals is perhaps the core question of organizational analysis. This is particularly true in light of the common definition of complex organizations as artificially created social units that seek specific goals. The so-called structural approach has its roots in Weber's analysis of bureaucracy and in the subsequent efforts to modify and revise that perspective. Moreover, the modern structuralists incorporate key elements from the insights of scientific management and human relations tradition while not being wedded to the exaggerated claims of either of these perspectives.

This section is divided into three main parts. The first zeroes in on the interaction of organizational structure and the goals organizations pursue. The second part is concerned with the interplay of structure and knowledge being processed within organizations. The final part of Section III concerns the relationship of organizational structure and technology or the implications of how organizations modify the raw materials they process.

If organizations can be viewed as social units oriented toward the pursuit of specific goals, their structures can be evaluated as tools which gain meaning and direction from their functions. But one of the most important lessons of the study of organizations is that the "tools" often shape the goal or the part of the goals to which they are applied. This process takes on several forms: initial goals may prove to be "utopian," and organizational personnel may adjust these goals by making them more "realistic," or the organization's original goal may be neglected without being changed officially and the organization may develop alternative or competing goals which are more in line with the interests of its staff. Or the organization may see its predominant task as maintaining or expanding itself with little care to its official or stated goals.

Thompson and McEwen examine the interaction of organizations and their environments and how this affects goals. They point out that the constantly changing environment requires organizations continuously to reappraise their goals. Reappraisal, in turn, depends upon the measurability of goals, organizational requirements, and accomplishments. The more difficult the appraisal, the more likely it is that the organization will evade societal controls. Thompson and McEwen also identify four forms of interaction within the organizational environment. Competition and three forms of cooperation—bargaining, co-optation, and coalition. The authors show how each form of interaction affects the way the environment influences the selection of organizational goals.

Cohen, March, and Olsen are concerned with decision-making or "organizational choice." Theirs is a novel view of how organizations set goals. They propose a "garbage can" model of decision-making. Fundamentally, they argue that choices occur in "garbage cans" which represent a repertoire of responses to problems. The "garbage can" contains not only proposed solutions to problems which are more or less satisfactory but also problems themselves as they have occurred and received from the past. Organizational participants and participational processes are also part of the "garbage can." Cohen, March, and Olsen regard their model as a more realistic alternative to the usual lifeless rationalistic models of goal setting and pursuit.

Baldridge and Burnham ask whether organizational or individual factors are more important for organizational innovation or the modification of goals. They compare the effects of internal structural characteristics and external structural characteristics with individual characteristics. They find that structural factors—both internal and environmental—are more important for organizational innovations than such individual factors as age, attitudes, and education. Thus, sociological rather than psychological forces seem to be more critical in the pursuit, implementation, and succession of organizational goals.

The processing of knowledge and information also occurs within organizational structures. Indeed, the articulation of structure and knowledge often plays a critical role in organization effectiveness and efficiency. The selection reproduced here from Freidson's *Profession of Medicine* analyzes the impact of physicians' officially sanctioned monopoly over technical knowledge on the structure and the functioning of the hospital. Freidson's main point is that this monopoly insures the professional dominance of physicians. The selection from Wilensky's book is concerned with the importance of knowledge with successful pursuit of organizational goals. He suggests that undue reliance on three arrangements impedes the use of what he calls "organizational intelligence." The three are hierarchy, specialization and centralization. Without some organizational routine—some hierachy, specialization and centralization—knowledge could not be converted into useful intelligence. Nevertheless, an excessive zeal for each has disruptive effects for the organization. Wilensky also notes that intelligence distortions sometimes occur because of differing "doctrines of intelligence."

The relationship between structure and how organizations process their raw materials is also central to the sociological study of complex organizations. Here we reproduce two classic pieces which take alternative views of the importance of technology in organization life. Hickson, Pugh, and Pheysey report the main findings of the Aston Group. They distinguish between three components of technology: operations technology; materials technology; and knowledge. They focus primarily on operations technology or the techniques used in the work flow activities of the organizations. They find that, although operations technology is important, it plays a secondary role in relationship to a structural trait, organizational size. Howard Aldrich disagrees. In a reanalysis of the Aston Group's data, Aldrich concludes that size is a secondary factor. Indeed he views size as a dependant variable. For Aldrich, as for Perrow, technology looms as the pivotal organizational variable. Subsequent research on the interplay of size and technology takes its lead from these two classic essays.

A. Structure and Goals

Organizational Goals and Environment

James D. Thompson
and William J. McEwen

In the analysis of complex organizations the definition of organizational goals is commonly utilized as a standard for appraising organizational performance. In many such analyses the goals of the organization are often viewed as a constant. Thus a wide variety of data, such as official documents, work activity records, organizational output, or statements by organizational spokesmen, may provide the basis for the definition of goals. Once this definition has been accomplished, interest in goals as a dynamic aspect of organizational activity frequently ends.

It is possible, however, to view the setting of goals (i.e., major organizational purposes), not as a static element but as a necessary and recurring problem facing any organization, whether it is governmental, military, business, educational, medical, religious, or other type. The goal-setting problem as discussed here is essentially determining a relationship of the organization to the larger society, which in turn becomes a question of what the society (or elements within it) wants done or can be persuaded to support.

Goals as Dynamic Variables

Because the setting of goals is essentially a problem of defining desired relationships between an organization and its environment, change in either requires review and perhaps alteration of goals. Even where the most abstract statement of goals remains constant, application requires redefinition or interpretation as changes occur in the organization, the environment, or both.

The corporation, for example, faces changing markets and develops staff specialists with responsibility for continuous study and projection of market changes and product appeal. The governmental agency, its legislative mandate notwithstanding, has need to reformulate or reinterpret its goals as other agencies are created and dissolved, as the population changes, or as non-governmental organizations appear to do the same job or to compete. The school and the university may have unchanging abstract goals, but the clientele, the needs of pupils or students, and the techniques of teaching change and bring with them redefinition and reinterpretation of those objectives. The hospital has been faced with problems requiring an expansion of goals to include consideration of preventive medicine, public health practices, and the degree to which the hospital should extend its activities out into the community. The mental hospital and the prison are changing their objectives from primary emphasis on custody to a stress on therapy. Even the church alters its pragmatic objectives as changes in the society

Reprinted in part from James D. Thompson and William J. McEwen, "Organizational Goals and Environment: Goal-Setting as an Interaction Process," *American Sociological Review*, vol. 23 (1958), pp. 23–31, by permission of the authors and the publisher, The American Sociological Association.

call for new forms of social ethics, and as government and organized philanthropy take over some of the activities formerly left to organized religion.

Reappraisal of goals thus appears to be a recurrent problem for large organization, albeit a more constant problem in an unstable environment than in a stable one. Reappraisal of goals likewise appears to be more difficult as the "product" of the enterprise becomes less tangible and more difficult to measure objectively. The manufacturing firm has a relatively ready index of the acceptability of its product in sales figures; while poor sales may indicate inferior quality rather than public distaste for the commodity itself, sales totals frequently are supplemented by trade association statistics indicating the firm's "share of the market." Thus within a matter of weeks, a manufacturing firm may be able to reappraise its decision to enter the "widget" market and may therefore begin deciding how it can get out of that market with the least cost.

The governmental enterprise may have similar indicators of the acceptability of its goals if it is involved in producing an item such as electricity, but where its activity is oriented to a less tangible purpose such as maintaining favorable relations with foreign nations, the indices of effective operation are likely to be less precise and the vagaries more numerous. The degree to which a government satisfies its clientele may be reflected periodically in elections, but despite the claims of party officials, it seldom is clear just what the mandate of the people is with reference to any particular governmental enterprise. In addition, the public is not always steadfast in its mandate.

The university perhaps has even greater difficulties in evaluating its environmental situation through response to its output. Its range of "products" is enormous, extending from astronomers to zoologists. The test of a competent specialist is not always standardized and may be changing, and the university's success in turning out "educated" people is judged by many and often conflicting standards. The university's product is in process for four or more years and when it is placed on the "market" it can be only imperfectly judged. Vocational placement statistics may give some indication of the university's success in its objectives, but initial placement is no guarantee of performance at a later date. Furthermore, performance in an occupation is only one of several abilities that the university is supposed to produce in its students. Finally, any particular department of the university may find that its reputation lags far behind its performance. A "good" department may work for years before its reputation becomes "good" and a downhill department may coast for several years before the fact is realized by the professional world.

In sum, the goals of an organization, which determine the kinds of goods or services it produces and offers to the environment, often are subject to peculiar difficulties of reappraisal. Where the purpose calls for an easily identified, readily measured product, reappraisal and readjustment of goals may be accomplished rapidly. But as goals call for increasingly intangible, difficult-to-measure products, society finds it more difficult to determine and reflect its acceptability of that product, and the signals that indicate unacceptable goals are less effective and perhaps longer in coming.

Environmental Controls over Goals

A continuing situation of necessary interaction between an organization and its environment introduces an element of environmental control into the organization. While the motives of personnel, including goal-setting officers, may be profits, prestige, votes, or the salvation of souls, their efforts must produce something useful or acceptable to at least a part of the organizational environment to win continued support.[1]

In the simpler society social control over productive activities may be exercised rather informally and directly through such means as gossip and ridicule. As a society becomes more complex and its productive activities more deliberately organized, social controls are increasingly exercised through such formal devices as contracts, legal codes, and governmental regulations. The stability of expectations provided by these devices is arrived at through interaction, and often through the exercise of power in interaction.

It is possible to conceive of a continuum of organizational power in environmental relations, ranging from the organization that dominates its environmental relations to one completely dominated by its environment. Few organizations approach either extreme. Certain gigantic industrial enterprises, such as the *Zaibatsu* in Japan or the old Standard Oil Trust in America, have approached the dominance-over-environment position at one time, but this position eventually brought about "countervailing powers."[2] Perhaps the nearest approximation to the completely powerless organization is the commuter transit system, which may be unable to cover its costs but nevertheless is regarded as a necessary utility and cannot get permission to quit business. Most complex organizations, falling somewhere between the extremes of the power continuum, must adopt strategies for coming to terms with their environments. This is not to imply that such strategies are necessarily chosen by rational or deliberate processes. An organization can survive so long as it adjusts to its situation; whether the process of adjustment is awkward or nimble becomes important in determining the organization's degree of prosperity.

However arrived at, strategies for dealing with the organizational environment may be broadly classified as either *competitive* or *cooperative*. Both appear to be important in a complex society—of the "free enterprise" type or other.[3] Both provide a measure of environmental control over organizations by providing for "outsiders" to enter into or limit organizational decision process.

The decision process may be viewed as a series of activities, conscious or not, culminating in a choice among alternatives. For purposes of this paper we view the decision-making process as consisting of the following activities:

1. Recognizing an occasion for decision, i.e., a need or an opportunity.
2. Analysis of the existing situation.
3. Identification of alternative courses of action.
4. Assessment of the probable consequences of each alternative.
5. Choice from among alternatives.[4]

The following discussion suggests that the potential power of an outsider increases the earlier he enters into the decision process,[5] and that competition and three sub-types of cooperative strategy—*bargaining, co-optation, and coalition*—differ in this respect. It is therefore possible to order these forms of interaction in terms of the degree to which they provide for environmental control over organizational goal-setting decisions.

Competition

The term "competition" implies an element of rivalry. For present purposes competition refers to that form of rivalry between two or more organizations which is mediated by a third party. In the case of the manufacturing firm the third party may be the customer, the supplier, the potential or present member of the labor force, or others. In the case of the governmental bureau, the third party through whom competition takes place may be the legislative committee, the budget bureau, or the chief executive, as well as potential clientele and potential members of the bureau.

The complexity of competition in a heterogeneous society is much greater than customary usage (with economic overtones) often suggests. Society judges the enterprise not only by the finished product but also in terms of the desirability of applying resources to that purpose. Even the organization that enjoys a product monopoly must compete for society's support. From the society it must obtain resources—personnel, finances, and materials—as well as customers or clientele. In the business sphere of a "free enterprise" economy this competition for resources and customers usually takes place in the market, but in times of crisis the society may exercise more direct controls, such as rationing or the establishment of priorities during a war. The monopoly competes with enterprises having different purposes or goals but using similar raw materials; it competes with many other enterprises, for human skills and loyalties, and it competes with many other activities for support in the money markets.

The university, customarily a non-profit organization, competes as eagerly as any business firm, although perhaps more subtly.[6] Virtually every university seeks, if not more students, better-qualified students. Publicly supported universities compete at annual budget sessions with other governmental enterprises for shares in tax revenues. Endowed universities must compete for gifts and bequests, not only with other universities but also with museums, charities, zoos, and similar non-profit enterprises. The American university is only one of many organizations competing for foundation support, and it competes with other universities and with other types of organizations for faculty.

The public school system, perhaps one of our most pervasive forms of near-monopoly, not only competes with other governmental units for funds and with different types of organizations for teachers, but current programs espoused by professional educators often compete in a very real way with a public conception of the nature of education, e.g., as the three R's, devoid of "frills."

The hospital may compete with the midwife, the faith-healer, the "quack" and the patent-medicine manufacturer, as well as with neighboring hospitals, despite the fact that general hospitals do not "advertise" and are not usually recognized as competitive.

Competition is thus a complicated network of relationships. It includes scrambling for resources as well as for customers or clients, and in a complex society it includes rivalry for potential members and their loyalties. In each case a third party makes a choice among alternatives, two or more organizations attempt to influence that choice through some type of "appeal" or offering, and choice by the third party is a "vote" of support for one of the competing organizations and a denial of support to the others involved.

Competition, then, is one process whereby the organization's choice of goals is partially controlled by the environment. It tends to prevent unilateral or arbitrary choice of organizational goals, or to correct such a choice if one is made. Competition for society's support is an important means of eliminating not only inefficient organizations but also those that seek to provide goods or services the environment is not willing to accept.

Bargaining

The term bargaining, as used here, refers to the negotiation of an agreement for the exchange of goods or services between two or more organizations. Even where fairly stable and dependable expectations have been built up with important elements of the organizational environment—with suppliers, distributors, legislators, workers and so on—the organization cannot assume that these relationships will continue. Periodic review of these relationships must be accomplished, and an important means for this is bargaining, whereby each organization, through negotiation, arrives at a decision about future behavior satisfactory to the others involved.

The need for periodic adjustment of relationships is demonstrated most dramatically in collective bargaining between labor and industrial management, in which the bases for continued support by organization members are reviewed. But bargaining occurs in other important, if less dramatic, areas of organizational endeavor. The business firm must bargain with its agents or distributors, and while this may appear at times to be one-sided and hence not much of a bargain, still even a long-standing agency agreement may be severed by competitive offers unless the agent's level of satisfaction is maintained through periodic review. Where suppliers are required to install new equipment to handle the peculiar demands of an organization, bargaining between the two is not unusual.

The university likewise must bargain. It may compete for free or unrestricted funds, but often it must compromise that ideal by bargaining away the name of a building or of a library collection, or by the conferring of an honorary degree. Graduate students and faculty members may be given financial or other concessions through bargaining, in order to prevent their loss to other institutions.

The governmental organization may also find bargaining expedient. The police department, for example, may overlook certain violations of statutes in order to gain the support of minor violators who have channels of information not otherwise open to department members. Concessions to those who "turn state's evidence" are not unusual. Similarly, a department of state may forego or postpone recognition of a foreign power in order to gain support for other aspects of its policy, and a governmental agency may relinquish certain activities in order to gain budget bureau approval of more important goals.

While bargaining may focus on resources rather than explicitly on goals, the fact remains that it is improbable that a goal can be effective unless it is at least partially implemented. To the extent that bargaining sets limits on the amount of resources available or the ways they may be employed, it effectively sets limits on choice of goals. Hence bargaining, like competition, results in environmental control over organizational goals and reduces the probability of arbitrary, unilateral goal-setting.

Unlike competition, however, bargaining involves direct interaction with other organizations in the environment, rather than with a third party. Bargaining appears, therefore, to invade the actual decision process. To the extent that the second party's support is necessary he is in a position to exercise a veto over final choice of alternative goals, and hence takes part in the decision.

Co-optation

Co-optation has been defined as the process of absorbing new elements into the leadership or policy-determining structure of an organization as a means of averting threats to its stability or existence.[7] Co-optation makes still further inroads on the process of deciding goals; not only must the final choice be acceptable to the co-opted party or organization, but to the extent that co-optation is effective it places the representative of an "outsider" in a position to determine the occasion for a goal decision, to participate in analyzing the existing situation, to suggest alternatives, and to take part in the deliberation of consequences.

The term "co-optation" has only recently been given currency in this country, but the phenomenon it describes is neither new nor unimportant. The acceptance on a corporation's board of directors of representatives of banks or other financial institutions is a time-honored custom among firms that have large financial obligations or that may in the future want access to financial resources. The state university may find it expedient (if not mandatory) to place legislators on its board of trustees, and the endowed college may find that whereas the honorary degree brings forth a token gift, membership on the board may result in a more substantial bequest. The local medical society often plays a decisive role in hospital goal-setting, since the support of professional medical practitioners is urgently necessary for the hospital.

From the standpoint of society, however, co-optation is more than an expediency. By giving a potential supporter a position of power and often of responsibility in the organization, the organization gains his awareness and understanding of the problems it faces. A business advisory council may be an effective educational device for a government, and a White House conference on education may mobilize "grass roots" support in a thousand localities, both by focussing attention on the problem area and by giving key people a sense of participation in goal deliberation.

Moreover, by providing overlapping memberships, co-optation is an important social device for increasing the likelihood that organizations related to one another in complicated ways will in fact find compatible goals. By thus reducing the possibilities of antithetical actions by two or more organizations, co-optation aids in the integration of the heterogeneous parts of a complex society. By the same token, co-optation further limits the opportunity for one organization to choose its goals arbitrarily or unilaterally.

Coalition

As used here, the term coalition refers to a combination of two or more organizations for a common purpose. Coalition appears to be the ultimate or extreme form of environmental conditioning of organizational goals.[8] A coalition may be unstable, but to the extent that it is operative, two or more organizations act as one with respect to certain goals. Coalition is a means widely used when two or more enterprises wish to pursue a goal calling for more support, especially for more resources, than any one of them is able to marshall unaided. American business firms frequently resort to coalition for purposes of research or product promotion and for the construction of such gigantic facilities as dams or atomic reactors.

Coalition is not uncommon among educational organizations. Universities have established joint operations in such areas as nuclear research, archaeological research, and even social science research. Many smaller colleges have banded together for fund-raising purposes. The consolidation of public school districts is another form of coalition (if not merger), and the fact that it does represent a sharing or "invasion" of goal-setting power is reflected in some of the bitter resistance to consolidation in tradition-oriented localities.

Coalition requires a commitment for joint decision of future activities and thus places limits on unilateral or arbitrary decisions. Furthermore, inability of an organization to find partners in a coalition venture automatically prevents pursuit of that objective, and is therefore also a form of social control. If the collective judgment is that a proposal is unworkable, a possible disaster may be escaped and unproductive allocation of resources avoided.

Development of Environmental Support

Environmental control is not a one-way process limited to consequences for the organization of action in its environment. Those subject to control are also part of the larger society and hence are also agents of social control. The enterprise that competes is not only influenced in its goal-setting by what the competitor and the third party may do, but also exerts influence over both. Bargaining likewise is a form of mutual, two-way influence; co-optation affects the co-opted as well as the co-opting party; and coalition clearly sets limits on both parties.

Goals appear to grow out of interaction, both within the organization and between the organization and its environment. While every enterprise must find sufficient support for its goals, it may wield initiative in this. The difference between effective and ineffective organizations may well lie in the initiative exercised by those in the organization who are responsible for goal-setting. . . .

Notes

1. This statement would seem to exclude anti-social organizations, such as crime syndicates. A detailed analysis of such organizations would be useful for many purposes; meanwhile it would appear necessary for them to acquire a clientele, suppliers, and others, in spite of the fact that their methods at times may be somewhat unique.

2. For the *Zaibatsu* case see Japan Council, *The Control of Industry in Japan*, Tokyo: Institute of Political and Economic Research, 1953; and Edwin O. Reischauer, *The United States and Japan*, Cambridge: Harvard University Press, 1954, pp. 87–97.

3. For evidence on Russia see David Granick, *Management of the Industrial Firm in the U.S.S.R.*, New York: Columbia University Press, 1954; and Joseph S. Berliner, "Informal Organization of the Soviet Firm," *Quarterly Journal of Economics*, 66 (August, 1952), pp. 353–365.

4. This particular breakdown is taken from Edward H. Litchfield, "Notes on a General Theory of Administration," *Administrative Science Quarterly*, 1 (June, 1956), pp. 3–29. We are also indebted to Robert Tannenbaum and Fred Massarik who, by breaking the decision-making process into three steps, show that subordinates can take part in the "manager's decision" even when the manager makes the final choice. See "Participation by Subordinates in the Managerial Decision-Making Process," *Canadian Journal of Economics and Political Science*, 16 (August, 1949), pp. 410–418.

5. Robert K. Merton makes a similar point regarding the role of the intellectual in public bureaucracy. See his *Social Theory and Social Structure*, New York: The Free Press, 1949, Chapter VI.

6. See Logan Wilson, *The Academic Man*, New York: Oxford University Press, 1942, especially Chapter IX. Also see Warren G. Bennis, "The Effect on Academic Goods of Their Market," *American Journal of Sociology*, 62 (July, 1956), pp. 28–33.

7. Philip Selznick, *TVA and the Grass Roots*, Berkeley and Los Angeles: University of California Press, 1949.
8. Coalition may involve joint action toward only limited aspects of the goals of each member. It may involve the complete commitment of each member for a specific period of time or indefinitely. In either case the ultimate power to withdraw is retained by the members. We thus distinguish coalition from merger, in which two or more organizations are fused permanently. In merger one or all of the original parts may lose their identity. Goal-setting in such a situation, of course, is no longer subject to inter-organizational constraints among the components.

A Garbage Can Model of Organizational Choice*

Michael D. Cohen, James G. March, and Johan P. Olsen

Consider organized anarchies. These are organizations—or decision situations—characterized by three general properties. The first is problematic preferences. In the organization it is difficult to impute a set of preferences to the decision situation that satisfies the standard consistency requirements for a theory of choice. The organization operates on the basis of a variety of inconsistent and ill-defined preferences. It can be described better as a loose collection of ideas than as a coherent structure; it discovers preferences through action more than it acts on the basis of preferences.

The second property is unclear technology. Although the organization manages to survive and even produce, its own processes are not understood by its members. It operates on the basis of simple trial-and-error procedures, the residue of learning from the accidents of past experience, and pragmatic inventions of necessity. The third property is fluid participation. Participants vary in the amount of time and effort they devote to different domains; involvement varies from one time to another. As a result, the boundaries of the organization are uncertain and changing; the audiences and decision makers for any particular kind of choice change capriciously.

These properties of organized anarchy have been identified often in studies of organizations. They are characteristic of any organization in part—part of the time. They are particularly conspicuous in public, educational, and illegitimate organizations. A theory of organized anarchy will describe a portion of almost any organization's activities, but will not describe all of them.

To build on current behavioral theories of organizations in order to accommodate the concept of organized anarchy, two major phenomena critical to an understanding of anarchy must be investigated. The first is the manner in which organizations make choices without consistent, shared goals. Situations of decision making under goal ambiguity are common in complex organizations. Often problems are resolved without recourse to explicit bargaining or to an explicit price system market—two common processes for decision making in the absence of consensus. The second phenomenon is the way members of an organization are activated. This entails the question of how occasional members become active and how attention is directed toward, or away from, a decision. It is important to

*We are indebted to Nancy Block, Hilary Cohen, and James Glenn for computational, editorial, and intellectual help; to the Institute of Sociology, University of Bergen, and the Institute of Organization and Industrial Sociology, Copenhagen School of Economics, for institutional hospitality and useful discussions of organizational behavior; and to the Ford Foundation for the financial support that made our collaboration feasible. We also wish to acknowledge the helpful comments and suggestions of Søren Christensen, James S. Coleman, Harald Enderud, Kåre Rommetveit, and William H. Starbuck.

Reprinted in part from *Administrative Science Quarterly*, vol. 17 (March, 1972), pp. 1–25, by permission.

understand the attention patterns within an organization, since not everyone is attending to everything all of the time.

Additional concepts are also needed in a normative theory of organizations dealing with organized anarchies. First, a normative theory of intelligent decision making under ambiguous circumstances (namely, in situations in which goals are unclear or unknown) should be developed. Can we provide some meaning for intelligence which does not depend on relating current action to known goals? Second, a normative theory of attention is needed. Participants within an organization are constrained by the amount of time they can devote to the various things demanding attention. Since variations in behavior in organized anarchies are due largely to questions of who is attending to what, decisions concerning the allocation of attention are prime ones. Third, organized anarchies require a revised theory of management. Significant parts of contemporary theories of management introduce mechanisms for control and coordination which assume the existence of well-defined goals and a well-defined technology, as well as substantial participant involvement in the affairs of the organization. Where goals and technology are hazy and participation is fluid, many of the axioms and standard procedures of management collapse.

This article is directed to a behavioral theory of organized anarchy. On the basis of several recent studies, some elaborations and modifications of existing theories of choice are proposed. A model for describing decision making within organized anarchies is developed, and the impact of some aspects of organizational structure on the process of choice within such a model is examined.

The Basic Ideas

Decision opportunities are fundamentally ambiguous stimuli. This theme runs through several recent studies of organizational choice.[1] Although organizations can often be viewed conveniently as vehicles for solving well-defined problems or structures within which conflict is resolved through bargaining, they also provide sets of procedures through which participants arrive at an interpretation of what they are doing and what they have done while in the process of doing it. From this point of view, an organization is a collection of choices looking for problems, issues and feelings looking for decision situations in which they might be aired, solutions looking for issues to which they might be the answer, and decision makers looking for work.

Such a view of organizational choice focuses attention on the way the meaning of a choice changes over time. It calls attention to the strategic effects of timing, through the introduction of choices and problems, the time pattern of available energy, and the impact of organizational structure.

To understand processes within organizations, one can view a choice opportunity as a garbage can into which various kinds of problems and solutions are dumped by participants as they are generated. The mix of garbage in a single can depends on the mix of cans available, on the labels attached to the alternative cans, on what garbage is currently being produced, and on the speed with which garbage is collected and removed from the scene.

Such a theory of organizational decision making must concern itself with a relatively complicated interplay among the generation of problems in an organization, the deployment of personnel, the production of solutions, and the oppor-

tunities for choice. Although it may be convenient to imagine that choice opportunities lead first to the generation of decision alternatives, then to an examination
of their consequences, then to an evaluation of those consequences in terms of
objectives, and finally to a decision, this type of model is often a poor description
of what actually happens. In the garbage can model, on the other hand, a decision
is an outcome or interpretation of several relatively independent streams within an
organization.

Attention is limited here to interrelations among four such streams.

Problems. Problems are the concern of people inside and outside the organization. They might arise over issues of lifestyle; family; frustrations of work;
careers; group relations within the organization; distribution of status, jobs, and
money; ideology; or current crises of mankind as interpreted by the mass media or
the nextdoor neighbor. All of these require attention.

Solutions. A solution is somebody's product. A computer is not just a
solution to a problem in payroll management, discovered when needed. It is an
answer actively looking for a question. The creation of need is not a curiosity of the
market in consumer products; it is a general phenomenon of processes of choice.
Despite the dictum that you cannot find the answer until you have formulated the
question well, you often do not know what the question is in organizational
problem solving until you know the answer.

Participants. Participants come and go. Since every entrance is an exit
somewhere else, the distribution of "entrances" depends on the attributes of the
choice being left as much as it does on the attributes of the new choice. Substantial
variation in participation stems from other demands on the participants' time
(rather than from features of the decision under study).

Choice opportunities. These are occasions when an organization is expected
to produce behavior that can be called a decision. Opportunities arise regularly
and any organization has ways of declaring an occasion for choice. Contracts must
be signed; people hired, promoted, or fired; money spent; and responsibilities
allocated.

Although not completely independent of each other, each of the streams can
be viewed as independent and exogenous to the system. Attention will be concentrated here on examining the consequences of different rates and patterns of flows
in each of the streams and different procedures for relating them.

The Garbage Can

A simple simulation model can be specified in terms of the four streams and a set
of garbage processing assumptions.

Four basic variables are considered; each is a function of time.

A *stream of choices*. Some fixed number, m, of choices is assumed. Each
choice is characterized by (a) an entry time, the calendar time at which that choice
is activated for decision, and (b) a decision structure, a list of participants eligible
to participate in making that choice.

A *stream of problems*. Some number, w, of problems is assumed. Each
problem is characterized by (a) an entry time, the calendar time at which the
problem becomes visible, (b) an energy requirement, the energy required to
resolve a choice to which the problem is attached (if the solution stream is as high
as possible), and (c) an access structure, a list of choices to which the problem has
access.

A rate of flow of solutions. The verbal theory assumes a stream of solutions and a matching of specific solutions with specific problems and choices. A simpler set of assumptions is made and focus is on the rate at which solutions are flowing into the system. It is assumed that either because of variations in the stream of solutions or because of variations in the efficiency of search procedures within the organization, different energies are required to solve the same problem at different times. It is further assumed that these variations are consistent for different problems. Thus, a solution coefficient, ranging between 0 and 1, which operates on the potential decision energies to determine the problem solving output (effective energy) actually realized during any given time period is specified.

A stream of energy from participants. It is assumed that there is some number, v, of participants. Each participant is characterized by a time series of energy available for organizational decision making. Thus, in each time period, each participant can provide some specified amount of potential energy to the organization.

Two varieties of organizational segmentation are reflected in the model. The first is the mapping of choices onto decision makers, the decision structure. The decision structure of the organization is described by D, a v-by-m array in which d_{ij} is 1 if the ith participant is eligible to participate in the making of the jth choice. Otherwise, d_{ij} is 0. The second is the mapping of problems onto choices, the access structure. The access structure of the organization is described by A, a w-by-m array in which a_{ij} is 1 if the jth choice is accessible to the ith problem. Otherwise, a_{ij} is 0.

In order to connect these variables, three key behavioral assumptions are specified. The first is an assumption about the additivity of energy requirements, the second specifies the way in which energy is allocated to choices, and the third describes the way in which problems are attached to choices.

Energy additivity assumption. In order to be made, each choice requires as much effective energy as the sum of all requirements of the several problems attached to it. The effective energy devoted to a choice is the sum of the energies of decision makers attached to that choice, deflated, in each time period, by the solution coefficient. As soon as the total effective energy that has been expended on a choice equals or exceeds the requirements at a particular point in time, a decision is made.

Energy allocation assumption. The energy of each participant is allocated to no more than one choice during each time period. Each participant allocates his energy among the choices for which he is eligible to the one closest to decision, that is the one with the smallest energy deficit at the end of the previous time period in terms of the energies contributed by other participants.

Problem allocation assumption. Each problem is attached to no more than one choice each time period, choosing from among those accessible by calculating the apparent energy deficits (in terms of the energy requirements of other problems) at the end of the previous time period and selecting the choice closest to decision. Except to the extent that priorities enter in the organizational structure, there is no priority ranking of problems.

These assumptions capture key features of the processes observed. They might be modified in a number of ways without doing violence to the empirical observations on which they are based. The consequences of these modifications, however, are not pursued here. Rather, attention is focused on the implications of the simple version described. The interaction of organizational structure and a garbage can form of choice will be examined.

Organizational Structure

Elements of organizational structure influence outcomes of a garbage can decision process (a) by affecting the time pattern of the arrival of problems, choices, solutions, or decision makers, (b) by determining the allocation of energy by potential participants in the decision, and (c) by establishing linkages among the various streams.

The organizational factors to be considered are some that have real-world interpretations and implications and are applicable to the theory of organized anarchy. They are familiar features of organizations, resulting from a mixture of deliberate managerial planning, individual and collective learning, and imitation. Organizational structure changes as a response to such factors as market demand for personnel and the heterogeneity of values, which are external to the model presented here. Attention will be limited to the comparative statics of the model, rather than to the dynamics produced by organizational learning.

To exercise the model, the following are specified: (a) a set of fixed parameters which do not change from one variation to another, (b) the entry times for choices, (c) the entry times for problems, (d) the net energy load on the organization, (e) the access structure of the organization, (f) the decision structure of the organization, and (g) the energy distribution among decision makers in the organization.

Some relatively pure structural variations will be identified in each and examples of how variations in such structures might be related systematically to key exogenous variables will be given. It will then be shown how such factors of organizational structure affect important characteristics of the decisions in a garbage can decision process.

Fixed Parameters

Within the variations reported, the following are fixed: (a) number of time periods—twenty, (b) number of choice opportunities—ten, (c) number of decision makers—ten, (d) number of problems—twenty, and (e) the solution coefficients for the 20 time periods—0.6 for each period.[2]

Entry Times

Two different randomly generated sequences of entry times for choices are considered. It is assumed that one choice enters per time period over the first ten time periods in one of the following orders: (a) 10, 7, 9, 5, 2, 3, 4, 1, 6, 8, or (b) 6, 5, 2, 10, 8, 9, 7, 4, 1, 3.

Similarly, two different randomly generated sequences of entry times for problems are considered. It is assumed that two problems enter per time period over the first ten time periods in one of the following orders: (a) 8, 20, 14, 16, 6, 7, 15, 17, 2, 13, 11, 19, 4, 9, 3, 12, 1, 10, 5, 18, or (b) 4, 14, 11, 20, 3, 5, 2, 12, 1, 6, 8, 19, 7, 15, 16, 17, 10, 18, 9, 13.

Net Energy Load

The total energy available to the organization in each time period is 5.5 units. Thus, the total energy available over twenty time periods is $20 \times 5.5 = 110$. This is reduced by the solution coefficients to 66. These figures hold across all other variations of the model. The net energy load on the organization is defined as the difference between the total energy required to solve all problems and the total effective energy available to the organization over all time periods. When this is negative, there is, in principle, enough energy available. Since the total effective energy available is fixed at 66, the net load is varied by varying the total energy requirements for problems. It is assumed that each problem has the same energy requirement under a given load. Three different energy load situations are considered.

Net energy load 0: light load. Under this condition the energy required to make a choice is 1.1 times the number of problems attached to that choice. That is, the energy required for each problem is 1.1. Thus, the minimum total effective energy required to resolve all problems is 22, and the net energy load is 22 − 66 = −44.

Net energy load 1: moderate load. Under this condition, the energy required for each problem is 2.2. Thus, the energy required to make a choice is 2.2 times the number of problems attached to that choice, and the minimum effective energy required to resolve all problems is 44. The net energy load is 44 − 66 = −22.

Net energy load 2: heavy load. Under this condition, each problem requires energy of 3.3. The energy required to make a choice is 3.3 times the number of problems attached to that choice. The minimum effective energy required to resolve all problems is 66, and the net energy load is 66 − 66 = 0.

Although it is possible from the total energy point of view for all problems to be resolved in any load condition, the difficulty of accomplishing that result where the net energy load is zero—a heavy load—is obviously substantial.

Access Structure

Three pure types of organizational arrangements are considered in the access structure (the relation between problems and choices).

Access structure 0: unsegmented access. This structure is represented by an access array in which any active problem has access to any active choice.

```
1111111111
1111111111
1111111111
1111111111
1111111111
1111111111
1111111111
1111111111
1111111111
1111111111
1111111111
1111111111
1111111111
1111111111
1111111111
1111111111
1111111111
1111111111
1111111111
1111111111
```

Access structure 1: hierarchical access. In this structure both choices and problems are arranged in a hierarchy such that important problems—those with relatively low numbers—have access to many choices, and important choices—those with relatively low numbers—are accessible only to important problems. The structure is represented by the following access array:

$$
A_1 =
\begin{array}{l}
1111111111 \\
1111111111 \\
0111111111 \\
0111111111 \\
0011111111 \\
0011111111 \\
0001111111 \\
0001111111 \\
0000111111 \\
0000111111 \\
0000011111 \\
0000011111 \\
0000001111 \\
0000001111 \\
0000000111 \\
0000000111 \\
0000000011 \\
0000000011 \\
0000000001 \\
0000000001
\end{array}
$$

Access structure 2: specialized access. In this structure each problem has access to only one choice and each choice is accessible to only two problems, that is, choices specialize in the kinds of problems that can be associated to them. The structure is represented by the following access array:

$$
A_2 =
\begin{array}{l}
1000000000 \\
1000000000 \\
0100000000 \\
0100000000 \\
0010000000 \\
0010000000 \\
0001000000 \\
0001000000 \\
0000100000 \\
0000100000 \\
0000010000 \\
0000010000 \\
0000001000 \\
0000001000 \\
0000000100 \\
0000000100 \\
0000000010 \\
0000000010 \\
0000000001 \\
0000000001
\end{array}
$$

Actual organizations will exhibit a more complex mix of access rules. Any such combination could be represented by an appropriate access array. The three pure structures considered here represent three classic alternative approaches to the problem of organizing the legitimate access of problems to decision situations.

Decision Structure

Three similar pure types are considered in the decision structure (the relation between decision makers and choices).

Decision structure 0: unsegmented decisions. In this structure any decision maker can participate in any active choice opportunity. Thus, the structure is represented by the following array:

$$
D_0 =
\begin{matrix}
1111111111 \\
1111111111 \\
1111111111 \\
1111111111 \\
1111111111 \\
1111111111 \\
1111111111 \\
1111111111 \\
1111111111 \\
1111111111
\end{matrix}
$$

Decision structure 1: hierarchical decisions. In this structure both decision makers and choices are arranged in a hierarchy such that important choices—low numbered choices—must be made by important decision makers—low numbered decision makers—and important decision makers can participate in many choices. The structure is represented by the following array:

$$
D_1 =
\begin{matrix}
1111111111 \\
0111111111 \\
0011111111 \\
0001111111 \\
0000111111 \\
0000011111 \\
0000001111 \\
0000000111 \\
0000000011 \\
0000000001
\end{matrix}
$$

Decision structure 2: specialized decisions. In this structure each decision maker is associated with a single choice and each choice has a single decision maker. Decision makers specialize in the choices to which they attend. Thus, we have the following array:

$$D_2 = \begin{matrix} 1000000000 \\ 0100000000 \\ 0010000000 \\ 0001000000 \\ 0000100000 \\ 0000010000 \\ 0000001000 \\ 0000000100 \\ 0000000010 \\ 0000000001 \end{matrix}$$

As in the case of the access structure, actual decision structures will require a more complicated array. Most organizations have a mix of rules for defining the legitimacy of participation in decisions. The three pure cases are, however, familiar models of such rules and can be used to understand some consequences of decision structure for decision processes.

Energy Distribution

The distribution of energy among decision makers reflects possible variations in the amount of time spent on organizational problems by different decision makers. The solution coefficients and variations in the energy requirement for problems affect the overall relation between energy available and energy required. Three different variations in the distribution of energy are considered.

Energy distribution 0: important people—less energy. In this distribution important people, that is people defined as important in a hierarchial decision structure, have less energy. This might reflect variations in the combination of outside demands and motivation to participate within the organization. The specific energy distribution is indicated as follows:

Decision maker	Energy	
1	0.1	
2	0.2	
3	0.3	
4	0.4	
5	0.5	$= E_0$
6	0.6	
7	0.7	
8	0.8	
9	0.9	
10	1.0	

The total energy available to the organization each time period (before deflation by the solution coefficients) is 5.5.

Energy distribution 1: equal energy. In this distribution there is no internal differentiation among decision makers with respect to energy. Each decision maker has the same energy (0.55) each time period. Thus, there is the following distribution:

Decision maker	Energy	
1	0.55	
2	0.55	
3	0.55	
4	0.55	
5	0.55	$= E_1$
6	0.55	
7	0.55	
8	0.55	
9	0.55	
10	0.55	

The total energy available to the organization each time period (before deflation by the solution coefficients) is 5.5.

Energy distribution 2: important people—more energy. In this distribution energy is distributed unequally but in a direction opposite to that in E_0. Here the people defined as important by the hierarchical decision structure have more energy. The distribution is indicated by the following:

Decision maker	Energy	
1	1.0	
2	0.9	
3	0.8	
4	0.7	
5	0.6	$= E_2$
6	0.5	
7	0.4	
8	0.3	
9	0.2	
10	0.1	

As in the previous organizations, the total energy available to the organization each time period (before deflation by the solution coefficients) is 5.5.

Where the organization has a hierarchical decision structure, the distinction between important and unimportant decision makers is clear. Where the decision structure is unsegmented or specialized, the variations in energy distribution are defined in terms of the same numbered decision makers (lower numbers are more important than higher numbers) to reflect possible status differences which are not necessarily captured by the decision structure.

Simulation Design

The simulation design is simple. . . . The $3^4 = 81$ types of organizational situations obtained by taking the possible combinations of the values of the four dimensions of an organization (access structure, decision structure, energy distribution, and net energy load) are studied here under the four combinations of choice and problem entry times. The result is 324 simulation situations.

Summary Statistics

The garbage can model operates under each of the possible organizational structures to assign problems and decision makers to choices, to determine the energy required and effective energy applied to choices, to make such choices and resolve such problems as the assignments and energies indicate are feasible. It does this for each of the twenty time periods in a twenty-period simulation of organizational decision making.

For each of the 324 situations, some set of simple summary statistics on the process is required. These are limited to five.

Decision Style

Within the kind of organization postulated, decisions are made in three different ways.

By resolution. Some choices resolve problems after some period of working on them. The length of time may vary, depending on the number of problems. This is the familiar case that is implicit in most discussions of choice within organizations.

By oversight. If a choice is activated when problems are attached to other choices and if there is energy available to make the new choice quickly, it will be made without any attention to existing problems and with a minimum of time and energy.

By flight. In some cases choices are associated with problems (unsuccessfully) for some time until a choice more attractive to the problems comes along. The problems leave the choice, and thus it is now possible to make the decision. The decision resolves no problems; they having now attached themselves to a new choice.

Some choices involve both flight and resolution—some problems leave, the remainder are solved. These have been defined as resolution, thus slightly exaggerating the importance of that style. As a result of that convention, the three styles are naturally exclusive and exhaustive with respect to any one choice. The same organization, however, may use any one of them in different choices. Thus, the decision style of any particular variation of the model can be described by specifying the proportion of completed choices which are made in each of these three ways.

Problem Activity

Any measure of the degree to which problems are active within the organization should reflect the degree of conflict within the organization or the degree of articulation of problems. Three closely related statistics of problem activity are considered. The first is the total number of problems not solved at the end of the twenty time periods; the second is the total number of times that any problem shifts from one choice to another, while the third is the total number of time periods that a problem is active and attached to some choice, summed over all problems. These measures are strongly correlated with each other. The third is used as the measure of problem activity primarily because it has a relatively large variance; essentially the same results would have been obtained with either of the other two measures.

Problem Latency

A problem may be active, but not attached to any choice. The situation is one in which a problem is recognized and accepted by some part of the organization, but is not considered germane to any available choice. Presumably, an organization with relatively high problem latency will exhibit somewhat different symptoms from one with low latency. Problem latency has been measured by the total number of periods a problem is active, but not attached to a choice, summed over all problems.

Decision Maker Activity

To measure the degree of decision maker activity in the system, some measure which reflects decision maker energy expenditure, movement, and persistence is required. Four are considered: (a) the total number of time periods a decision maker is attached to a choice, summed over all decision makers, (b) the total number of times that any decision maker shifts from one choice to another, (c) the total amount of effective energy available and used, and (d) the total effective energy used on choices in excess of that required to make them at the time they are made. These four measures are highly intercorrelated. The second was used primarily because of its relatively large variance; any of the others would have served as well.

Decision Difficulty

Because of the way in which decisions can be made in the system, decision difficulty is not the same as the level of problem activity. Two alternative measures are considered: the total number of choices not made by the end of the twenty time periods and the total number of periods that a choice is active, summed over all choices. These are highly correlated. The second is used, primarily because of its higher variance; the conclusions would be unchanged if the first were used.

Implications of the Model

An analysis of the individual histories of the simulations shows eight major properties of garbage can decision processes.

First, resolution of problems as a style for making decisions is not the most common style, except under conditions where flight is severely restricted (for instance, specialized access) or a few conditions under light load. Decision making by flight and oversight is a major feature of the process in general. In each of the simulation trials there were twenty problems and ten choices. Although the mean number of choices not made was 1.0, the mean number of problems not solved was 12.3. . . . The behavioral and normative implications of a decision process which appears to make choices in large part by flight or by oversight must be examined. A possible explanation of the behavior of organizations that seem to make decisions without apparently making progress in resolving the problems that appear to be related to the decisions may be emerging.

Second, the process is quite thoroughly and quite generally sensitive to variations in load. . . . An increase in the net energy load on the system generally increases problem activity, decision maker activity, decision difficulty, and the uses of flight and oversight. Problems are less likely to be solved, decision makers are likely to shift from one problem to another more frequently, choices are likely to take longer to make and are less likely to resolve problems. Although it is possible to specify an organization that is relatively stable with changes in load, it is not possible to have an organization that is stable in behavior and also has other desirable attributes. As load changes, an organization that has an unsegmented access structure with a specialized decision structure stays quite stable. It exhibits relatively low decision difficulty and decision maker activity, very low problem latency, and maximum problem activity. It makes virtually all decisions placed before it, uses little energy from decision makers, and solves virtually no problems.

Third, a typical feature of the model is the tendency of decision makers and problems to track each other through choices. Subject to structural restrictions on the tracking, decision makers work on active problems in connection with active choices; both decision makers and problems tend to move together from choice to choice. Thus, one would expect decision makers who have a feeling that they are always working on the same problems in somewhat different contexts, mostly without results. Problems, in a similar fashion, meet the same people wherever they go with the same result.

Fourth, there are some important interconnections among three key aspects of the efficiency of the decision processes specified. The first is problem activity, the amount of time unresolved problems are actively attached to choice situations. Problem activity is a rough measure of the potential for decision conflict in the organization. The second aspect is problem latency, the amount of time problems spend activated but not linked to choices. The third aspect is decision time, the persistence of choices. Presumably, a good organizational structure would keep both problem activity and problem latency low through rapid problem solution in its choices. In the garbage can process such a result was never observed. Segmentation of the access structure tends to reduce the number of unresolved problems active in the organization but at the cost of increasing the latency period of problems and, in most cases the time devoted to reaching decisions. On the other hand, segmentation of the decision structure tends to result in decreasing problem latency, but at the cost of increasing problem activity and decision time.

Fifth, the process is frequently sharply interactive. Although some phenomena associated with the garbage can are regular and flow through nearly all of the cases, for example, the effect of overall load, other phenomena are much more dependent on the particular combination of structures involved. Although high segmentation of access structure generally produces slow decision time, for instance, a specialized access structure, in combination with an unsegmented decision structure, produces quick decisions.

Sixth, important problems are more likely to be solved than unimportant ones. Problems which appear early are more likely to be resolved than later ones. . . . The system, in effect, produces a queue of problems in terms of their importance, to the disadvantage of late-arriving, relatively unimportant problems, and particularly so when load is heavy. This queue is the result of the operation of the model. It was not imposed as a direct assumption.

Seventh, important choices are less likely to resolve problems than unimportant choices. Important choices are made by oversight and flight. Unimportant choices are made by resolution. These differences are observed under both of the choice entry sequences but are sharpest where important choices enter relatively early. . . . This property of important choices in a garbage can decision process can be naturally and directly related to the phenomenon in complex organizations of important choices which often appear to just happen.

Eighth, although a large proportion of the choices are made, the choice failures that do occur are concentrated among the most important and least important choices. Choices of intermediate importance are virtually always made. The proportion of choice failures, under conditions of hierarchical access or decision structures is as follows:

Three most important choices	0.14
Four middle choices	0.05
Three least important choices	0.12

In a broad sense, these features of the process provide some clues to how organizations survive when they do not know what they are doing. Much of the process violates standard notions of how decisions ought to be made. But most of those notions are built on assumptions which cannot be met under the conditions specified. When objectives and technologies are unclear, organizations are charged to discover some alternative decision procedures which permit them to proceed without doing extraordinary violence to the domains of participants or to their model of what an organization should be. It is a hard charge, to which the process described is a partial response.

At the same time, the details of the outcomes clearly depend on features of the organizational structure. The same garbage can operation results in different behavioral symptoms under different levels of load on the system or different designs of the structure of the organization. Such differences raise the possibility of predicting variations in decision behavior in different organizations. One possible example of such use remains to be considered. . . .

Conclusion

A set of observations made in the study of some university organizations has been translated into a model of decision making in organized anarchies, that is, in situations which do not meet the conditions for more classical models of decision making in some or all of three important ways: preferences are problematic, technology is unclear, or participation is fluid. The garbage can process is one in which problems, solutions, and participants move from one choice opportunity to another in such a way that the nature of the choice, the time it takes, and the problems it solves all depend on a relatively complicated intermeshing of elements. These include the mix of choices available at any one time, the mix of problems that have access to the organization, the mix of solutions looking for problems, and the outside demands on the decision makers.

A major feature of the garbage can process is the partial uncoupling of problems and choices. Although decision making is thought of as a process for solving problems, that is often not what happens. Problems are worked upon in the context of some choice, but choices are made only when the shifting combinations of problems, solutions, and decision makers happen to make action possible. Quite commonly this is after problems have left a given choice arena or before they have discovered it (decisions by flight or oversight). . . .

The garbage can model is a first step toward seeing the systematic interrelatedness of organizational phenomena which are familiar, even common, but which have previously been regarded as isolated and pathological. Measured against a conventional normative model of rational choice, the garbage can process does appear pathological, but such standards are not really appropriate. The process occurs precisely when the preconditions of more normal rational models are not met.

It is clear that the garbage can process does not resolve problems well. But it does enable choices to be made and problems resolved, even when the organization is plagued with goal ambiguity and conflict, with poorly understood problems that wander in and out of the system, with a variable environment, and with decision makers who may have other things on their minds.

There is a large class of significant situations in which the preconditions of the garbage can process cannot be eliminated. In some, such as pure research, or the family, they should not be eliminated. The great advantage of trying to see garbage can phenomena together as a process is the possibility that that process can be understood, that organizational design and decision making can take account of its existence and that, to some extent, it can be managed.

Notes

1. We have based the model heavily on seven recent studies of universities: Christensen (1971), Cohen and March (1972), Enderud (1971), Mood (1971), Olsen (1970, 1971), and Rommetveit (1971). The ideas, however, have a broader parentage. In particular, they obviously owe a debt to Allison (1969), Coleman (1957), Cyert and March (1963), Lindblom (1965), Long (1958), March and Simon (1958), Schilling (1968), Thompson (1967), and Vickers (1965).
2. The model has also been exercised under conditions of a set of solution coefficients that varies over the time periods. Specifically, the following series has been used: 1, 0.9, 0.7, 0.3, 0.1, 0.1, 0.3, 0.7, 0.9, 1, 0.6, 0.6, 0.6, 0.6, 0.6, 0.6, 0.6, 0.6, 0.6, 0.6. This simulation, using only one combination of choice and problem entry times, gives results consistent with all of the conclusions reported in the present article.

References

Allison, Graham T. 1969, "Conceptual models and the Cuban missile crises." *American Political Science Review*, 63: 689–718.

Christensen, Søren, 1971, *Institut og laboratorieorganisation på Danmarks tekniske Højskole*. Copenhagen: Copenhagen School of Economics.

Cohen, Michael D., and James G. March, 1972, *The American College President*. New York: McGraw-Hill, Carnegie Commission on the Future of Higher Education.

Coleman, James S., 1957, *Community Conflict*. Glencoe: Free Press.

Cyert, Richard M., and James G. March, 1963, *Behavioral Theory of the Firm*. Englewood Cliffs: Prentice-Hall.

Enderud, Harald, 1971, *Rektoratet og den centrale administration på Danmarks tekniske Højskole*. Copenhagen: Copenhagen School of Economics.

Lindblom, Charles E., 1965, *The Intelligence of Democracy*. New York: Macmillan.

Long, Norton, 1958, "The local community as an ecology of games." *American Journal of Sociology*, 44: 251–261.

March, James G., and Herbert A. Simon, 1958, *Organizations*. New York: John Wiley.

Mood, Alexander (ed.), 1971, *More Scholars for the Dollar*. New York: McGraw-Hill, Carnegie Commission on the Future of Higher Education.

Olsen, Johan P., 1970, *A Study of Choice in an Academic Organization*. Bergen: University of Bergen.

———, 1971, *The Reorganization of Authority in an Academic Organization*. Bergen: University of Bergen.

Rommetveit, Kåre, 1971, *Framveksten av det medisinske fakultet ved Universitetet i Tromsø*. Bergen: University of Bergen.

Schilling, Warner R., 1968, "The H-bomb decision: how to decide without actually choosing." In W. R. Nelson (ed.), *The Politics of Science*. London: Oxford University Press.

Thompson, James D., 1967, *Organizations in Action*. New York: McGraw-Hill.

Vickers, Geoffrey, 1965, *The Art of Judgment*. New York: Basic Books.

Organizational Innovation: Individual, Organizational, and Environmental Impacts

J. Victor Baldridge and Robert A. Burnham

Social scientists have been increasingly interested in the diffusion processes of technological and social innovations, as indicated by the over 500 articles by Rogers in 1962 and the 1500 articles reviewed by Rogers and Shoemaker in 1971. The innovations studied cover a broad range of topics. One growing branch of the research has dealt with the diffusion of organizational innovations. The research question usually asks: What characteristics distinguish organizations that adopt many new innovations from those that adopt fewer? The Stanford Center for Research and Development in Teaching sponsored two studies that examined the adoption of organizational innovations. For this paper data from these projects have been reanalyzed (1) to test three major hypotheses about diffusion of innovation in the same research setting, and (2) to test the hypotheses in large samples since studies in diffusion of innovation in organizations have been usually small samples. The three major hypotheses are:

1. Certain *individuals* are likely to adopt innovations to innovative behavior (for example, younger, more cosmopolitan, better educated males), therefore, organizations with a high percentage of such individuals are likely to adopt more innovations (Rogers, 1962, 1971).
2. High organizational complexity and large size promote adoption of innovations because they permit specialized expertise in subunits, and because of critical masses of problems that demand solution (Wilson, 1963; Hage and Aiken, 1967; Sapolsky, 1967).
3. Heterogeneous or changing environments are likely to cause problems for organizations that promote the adoption of innovations (Evan, 1965; Terreberry, 1968; Baldridge, 1971).

Research Methodology

In 1967–1968, the first of the Stanford studies examined 20 randomly selected schools in seven districts in the San Francisco Bay Area. Extensive information about the districts and schools was collected from interviews with district superintendents and principals of individual schools, and from district records. In addition, three groups of teachers were interviewed: (1) 53 opinion leaders, who were

This paper was prepared with the assistance of Jeanette Wheeler, project writer. We wish to express our debt to several people who participated in the studies for this paper. Kenneth Knight supervised the Bay Area Project, and Thomas Gans, William Gorth, Gerald Hamrin, Olan Knight, William Penny, and William Schmick participated as coworkers. The planning and data analyses for these studies were supported in part by the Stanford Center for Research and Development in Teaching, School of Education, Stanford University.

Reprinted in part from *Administrative Science Quarterly*, vol. 20 (June 1975), pp. 165–176, by permission.

nominated by principals and department chairmen as leaders in change efforts, (2) 309 of the 428 change participants, and (3) 775 faculty members, a 50 percent random sample of all faculty members.

The second study focused on Illinois school districts in 1969–1970. Only large school districts were sampled, since small districts of one or two schools would not be considered complex organizations. The sample of 264 school districts was randomly selected from elementary school districts of over 1,000 students and secondary districts of over 500 students. Data were collected from three sources: (1) a questionnaire sent to each district superintendent; (2) punched-card records of enrollments and other characteristics of school districts for each district studied, provided by the division of finance and statistics of the Illinois Office of the Superintendent of Public Instruction; and (3) environmental and demographic data from each district drawn from the *County and City Data Book* and the *Census of Governments, 1962*. Since the available demographic and population data were based on counties and some school districts were located in more than one county, we used the information about the county in which the district offices were located; this procedure gave a reasonably accurate estimate of the population characteristics of the district. The Chicago School District was omitted from the analysis because it was assumed to be atypical. The questionnaires returned resulted in a usable sample of 184 school districts (70 percent).

The Dependent Variable: Innovations

One consistent theme in the innovation literature has been the concentration of limited kinds of technological innovations. For example, in the widely used agricultural diffusion studies, the innovation studied had several characteristics. First, it was highly technical and its effectiveness had been well proved before it was disseminated (for example, new types of seeds). Second, there was a relatively short payoff time in which the person adopting the innovation could tell whether it was working and could judge its continued use—one season's crops could usually convince a farmer to use a new seed. Third, evaluation of the innovation's technical efficiency was readily apparent and results were easily interpreted—the farmer could decide on the productivity of the new grain. Finally, the decision maker adopting the innovation was either an individual or a small group, not a complex organization—the individual farmer could choose a new seed without a complicated organizational decision.

Most major social and educational innovations are not technically narrow or easily implemented. First, the technology of such programs is complicated and depends heavily on professional judgment, creative insight, and practical experience. Second, innovations are difficult to evaluate, and the effectiveness of an innovation can rarely be evaluated in a short time. Finally, it is often a complex organization that adopts most social innovations such as, a school district, university, city government, or county welfare agency.

The complexity of the decision process and the multiple chains of command necessary to adopt an innovation make the diffusion of social innovation very complex. To examine innovations such as school integration, for example, it is critical to analyze the reward structure, the authority lines, and the decision-making processes of the organization. Although rare, research on this type of complex situation is found in the studies of community adoptions of fluoridation during the 1950s (Crain, 1962) and the adoption of innovations in complex school districts (Mort, 1947; Burnham, 1972; and Corwin, 1972).

The research reported in this paper examined organizational innovations and changes (1) with relatively unclear technologies, (2) with long-range payoffs, (3) adopted by organizations rather than individuals, and (4) difficult to evaluate. Three other conditions were imposed for this study. (1) *"Extensiveness,"* that is, the innovation had to cover a relatively large number of people and/or processes within the school. (2) *"Importance,"* that is, knowledgeable observers believed the innovation had real promise for change in a major educational area. (3) *"Longevity potential,"* that is, the innovations had to be well-established and appear able to continue for a significant period of time.

In the Bay Area study, principals, superintendents, and department chairmen specified innovations adopted that met these criteria. Of the innovations specified, one "curricular" innovation—for example, new reading program—and one "organizational" innovation—for example, new teaching approach—were selected in each school. In the Illinois study intensive interviews were held with school superintendents and a list was compiled of 20 major innovations that met the criteria. School districts were then asked to specify the ones they had adopted from the potential list.

Do Individual Characteristics and Organizational Position Determine Innovative Behavior?

In most research on the diffusion of innovation the dependent variable has usually been the characteristics of individuals adopting the innovation: what type of women will adopt birth-control pills or what kind of natives will substitute a steel ax for traditional stone ones? Sometimes the rate of adoption was the dependent variable: how fast will individuals with X characteristic adopt the innovation as compared to individuals with Y characteristic? The independent factors producing the behavior have been typically individualistic: are the adopters young or old, traditional or modern, rich or poor, opinion leaders or followers, of high social status or low? (See Rogers and Shoemaker, 1971; Rogers, 1962.) For example, Carlson (1967) studied individual characteristics as determinants of innovative behavior in educational organizations.

In spite of the individualistic tradition in the literature, we assumed that *individual* characteristics would not be particularly significant in predicting leaders in *organizational* change. The Bay Area study compared three groups: (1) opinion leaders, (2) participants, and (3) faculty. If individual characteristics were actually important for predicting change-oriented behavior, it was expected that there would be rather sharp differences with opinion leaders at one extreme and faculty at the other. The literature (Rogers, 1962; Carlson, 1967) suggested that opinion leaders would be likely to be males, older, less satisfied with their careers, of higher social origin and education, and significantly higher cosmopolitanism as measured by travel, scholarly journals read, and work experience outside their present district. However, Table 1 shows no important differences between the random sample of the faculty and the participants in change. The opinion leaders were a little older, more often males, and had slightly more education, but the differences were small and not statistically significant. Our conclusion that indi-

TABLE 1 *Comparison of Individual Characteristics*[a]

Individual Characteristics[b]	Opinion Leaders in Change (N = 53)	Participants in Change (N = 309)	All Faculty (N = 775)
Sex: Males (%)	74.1	66.6	62.4
Age	39.0	37.4	35.5
Satisfaction with career[c]	1.4	1.5	1.7
Social origins[d]	39.7	42.1	39.8
Education			
Median degree attained[e]	3.9	3.7	3.6
Units past BA	94.0	91.7	82.7
Index	8.5	8.1	7.8
Recent units	6.7	5.7	6.8
Years of work			
Inside years	7.7	7.5	6.0
Outside years	1.3	1.8	1.7
Index	6.5	6.2	5.7
Cosmopolitanism			
Median worked in other districts	2.2	1.9	1.9
Conference attended 1962	3.9	3.1	2.7
Summer institutes attended	1.2	1.1	1.1
Journals read regularly	3.4	3.3	2.9
Index	11.4	9.8	8.9

[a] Data assembled from various charts in Penny (1970: 112, 114).
[b] Median except as otherwise indicated.
[c] 5-point scale, the higher the score, the lower the satisfaction.
[d] The lower the score, the higher the social class, Hollingshead; Two-factor index of social position, range 11–77.
[e] 1 = no formal education, 3 = Bachelor's degree, 5 = Doctoral degree.

vidual characteristics are poor predictors of adoption of innovations supports the findings of Hage and Aiken (1970: 122–123):

> The results of our study [of social welfare agencies] clearly suggest that structural properties were much more highly associated with the rate of program change than attitudes toward change. This implies that the structure of an organization may be more crucial for the successful implementation of change than the particular blend of personality types of an organization.

Individual characteristics do not explain much about innovative behavior of people in the organization context. The explanation seems quite simply that when individuals are the innovation adopters, as most previous studies assumed, then individual characteristics are important. However, when organizations are the innovation adopters, then organizational characteristics probably account for differences in innovative behavior.

Organizational Positions

Factors that bridge the individual level and the organizational level are organizational *positions* and *authority roles*. The Bay Area study found a number of positional characteristics that influenced the adoption of change. The chairmen and administrators were nominated more often than teachers as (1) initiators of change, (2) evaluators of the quality of work in the change process, and (3) controlling organization sanctions such as salaries, working conditions, and class assignments (see Table 2). Department chairmen were also seen as particularly important as communication links between teachers carrying out changes and administrators supporting those changes with resources. Finally, the interviews accompanying the questionnaires indicated that the administrators were extremely important as boundary role people; that is, they served as a link between demands and ideas from the outside and the innovations being adopted within the schools. In sum, it appeared that although individual characteristics were not particularly critical in predicting who would be leaders in change efforts, organizational position and role were highly influential.

Organizational Factors: Size and Complexity

Organizational factors are rarely treated in the literature on diffusion of innovations. For example, Rogers' monumental review (1962) of the innovation literature summarized the research conclusion in 52 major propositions—*not one referred to a complex organization as the innovation adopter or to organizational features as independent variables affecting the process.* In fact, Rogers and Shoemaker, in their 1971 revision of the innovation review, explicitly state (p. 71) that "By far the most popular diffusion research topic has been variables related to individual innovativeness." Although Rogers and Shoemaker added chapters that supposedly dealt with organizational innovation, once again they actually looked at individual behavior, located this time within organizational settings.

The inattention to organizational factors persists even though most major social innovations today are adopted by complex organizations, for example, educational innovations, community-action projects, new technologies in industry, and new health-delivery programs. Thus, more attention to organizational features is needed for two reasons: (1) organizations are now the major adopters of social inventions, and (2) organizational dynamics are the major independent variables that influence the amount, the rate, and the permanence of innovations. Two characteristics affecting the capacity of an organization for innovation are its size and its administrative complexity. These factors are closely related; many studies have shown that increases in size are directly related to increases in complexity measured by hierarchical levels, the number of administrative positions, and the ratio of administrators to other employees (Blau, 1970).

Argument

In most situations increased size and complexity are expected to lead to increased innovation. With increased structural complexity there is an increase in specialists who handle specialized subtasks and initiate search procedures for more efficient techniques to accomplish their goals (March and Simon, 1958). This diversity, however, results in conflicts over resources and goals which must be resolved by integrative mechanisms, such as hierarchical decision making or joint policy making by coordinating committees. Both differentiation (in terms of structural units) and integration (in terms of coordinating mechanisms) help promote

TABLE 2 *Nominations of Leaders by Participation*

If Participants Were:	They Were Nominated as Initiators of Change			If Participants Were:	They Were Nominated as Evaluators of Change		
	Teachers	Chairmen	Administrators		Teachers	Chairmen	Administrators
Teachers (N = 279)	46% (128)	26% (72)	28% (79)	Teachers (N = 819)	48% (396)	20% (163)	32% (260)
Department chairmen (N = 87)	8% (7)	31% (27)	61% (53)	Department chairmen (N = 314)	24% (77)	26% (81)	50% (156)
Administrators (N = 106)	41% (43)	11% (12)	48% (51)	Administrators (N = 300)	40% (121)	26% (78)	34% (101)
TOTALS (N = 472)	38% (178)	23% (111)	39% (183)	TOTALS (N = 1433)	42% (594)	22% (322)	36% (517)

innovation—the former by creating specialists to seek new solutions, and the latter by providing mechanisms for overcoming conflict (see Lawrence and Lorsch, 1967). Thus, as the number of differentiated subunits increases, the quantity of alternatives and solutions also increases in response to perceived unique problems. Finally, the diversity of incentive systems and task structures resulting from differentiation helps promote innovation.

Size, too, greatly affects innovation, not only by promoting complexity (Blau, 1970), but by creating problems of coordination, control, and management which, in themselves, demand innovative practices. Moreover, increased size produces critical masses for certain problems that stimulate the adoption of innovations to handle them. For example, a small school district is unlikely to have enough handicapped students to initiate special programs for them, but a large district is apt to have many such students that dictate such programs. Finally, increased size expands the possibilities for interacting with the environment of the school district, since additional clients multiply the number of interested outsiders making their special demands.

Empirical Results

The empirical results clearly support the theoretical argument, for the increased size and complexity were positively related to innovation. The Bay Area schools and school districts showed a perfect rank order between increasing district size and increased adoption of innovations. In the individual schools the 10 largest schools had more than three times as many major innovations listed as the 10 smallest schools. In the Illinois study, when districts were separated into high adopters and low adopters of innovation, the high adopters were larger and structurally more complex than the low adopters, as indicated in Table 3. There were nearly twice as many students, 50 percent more administrative positions, twice as many full-time administrators, and about 25 percent more conflict-prevention devices. Table 4, the basic correlation matrix showing the relationship among all variables, supports these relationships: the rate of innovation is correlated with size at .46, the number of administrative components at .45, job specialization at .48, and conflict-prevention committees at .24.

Implications

The data strongly indicate that size and complexity are associated with increased adoption of educational innovation. It also seems reasonable that organizations adopting innovations will sustain those innovations to the extent that a complex organizational system is built to support them. This has important policy implications, for although we have no hard data on this judgmental issue, our analysis has led us to conclude that schools and school districts tend to be underorganized organizations; that is, compared to most complex organizations, they have less role differentiation, fewer problem-solving experts, and a smaller number of support services. Larger, more complex districts have several advantages. First, more difficult innovations can be adopted because individuals directly involved with the innovation will have support, staff help, and specialized resources available. In addition, increased complexity can provide organizational members with a career ladder that encourages adoption of innovations. A major hindrance to adoption of innovation, for example, is the essentially flat teacher

TABLE 3   *Variables in Relation to Adoptions of Innovations*

Variables and Indicators	Definition	Adoptions of Innovations[a]	
		High	Low
Size and complexity			
No. of students	District average daily attendance 1968–1969.[b]	5,335	2,561
Organizational components	Formal programs and positions in each district[c]	12.3	8.2
Specialization	No. full-time equivalent administrators assigned to programs.[c]	25.1	13.9
Conflict prevention	Frequency of use of policies defining jurisdiction and responsibilities for major depts; rules governing interdepartmental arrangements, job descriptions for administrative positions; and organizational chart.[c]	2.9	2.1
Environmental heterogeneity			
Population density	Population per square mile within each county (more density indicates more heterogeneity).[d]	2,134	1,135
Urbanization	County population classified as urban by U.S. Census Bureau (more urban indicates more heterogeneity).[d]	74.0%	58.2%
Nonwhite	Nonwhites in each county (more nonwhites indicates more heterogeneity).[d]	7.8%	4.8%
Local taxing agencies	No. public taxing agencies within the county competing with school districts for tax dollars (more agencies indicate more heterogeneity.)[e]	209.4	136.4
Government expenses for noneducation uses	Ratio of total educational expenditures to total direct general expenditures for local government (lower ratio indicates more heterogeneity).[e]	51.6%	47.2%
% Not owning home	Nonowner occupied housing in a county (less ownership indicates more heterogeneity).[d]	38.7%	34.7%
Environmental change			
Change in funds	Change in operating expenses (AV)[b]	69.4%	44.9%
Growth of county	Change in district daily attendance.[b]	17.5%	16.5%
Migration	Population in/out migration[d]	5.6%	−1.2%
Change in wealth	Change in the assessed valuation of the district (AV/ADA).[b]	1.9%	1.7%
Change in racial composition	Changes in percentage nonwhite in each district[d]	3.3%	3.1%
Wealth	Assessed valuation of district.[b]	$32,470	$31,905

[a] High adoption of innovations meant 34 percent of the possible innovations or more were adopted; low adoption meant less than 34% were adopted. These data came from superintendent's questionnaires.
[b] Data from State Education Department.
[c] Data from questionnaire completed by school superintendents.
[d] Data from U.S. Census.
[e] Data from City and County Data Book.

TABLE 4 *Basic Correlation Matrix (N = 184)*

	1	2	3	4	5	6	7	8	9	10	11	12	13	14	15	16	17
1. Students size (# students)	1.0	.68	.91	.14	.12	.35	.12	.14	-.15	-.13	.16	.12	-.04	-.16	.17	-.13	.46
2. Complexity (# of programs & positions)		1.00	.80	.18	.09	.27	.12	.12	-.13	-.13	.08	.07	-.06	-.08	.11	.05	.45
3. Specialization			1.00	.19	.09	.30	.10	.11	-.11	-.09	.13	.08	-.03	-.13	.20	-.12	.48
4. Conflict-prevention devices				1.00	.16	.20	.14	.17	-.15	-.12	-.02	.10	.10	-.05	.14	.02	.24
5. Population density					1.00	.76	.89	.99	-.88	-.88	.20	.17	-.34	-.06	.22	.18	.30
6. Urbanization (%)						1.00	.67	.80	-.72	-.59	.24	.29	-.09	-.10	.30	.12	.37
7. Nonwhite (%)							1.00	.88	-.79	-.84	.15	.13	-.38	-.02	.23	.13	.25
8. No. of local taxing agencies								1.00	-.86	-.86	.20	.21	-.29	-.07	.24	.20	.31
9. Government expenses for noneducation (%)									1.00	.80	-.16	-.09	.44	.04	-.18	-.11	-.26
10. Home ownership (%)										1.00	-.07	-.07	.64	.06	-.19	-.18	-.27
11. Funds (AV)											1.00	.64	.12	.27	-.09	-.10	.04
12. Growth of county												1.00	.25	.30	.07	-.06	.00
13. Migration													1.00	.05	-.05	-.11	-.01
14. Changes in wealth														1.00	.00	-.03	-.09
15. Changes in racial composition															1.00	.05	.17
16. Wealth																1.00	.06
17. Innovations adopted (%)																	1.00

career line with advancement usually reserved for administrators and with little incentive structure promoting adoption of innovations by teachers.

Environmental Factors

Environmental factors may also have a great influence on the diffusion of innovations. Organization theorists have given increasing attention to the environment in which an organization functions. Organizations obtain various inputs from their environments, process them, and feed back finished products. At the same time the surroundings place many demands on organizations. School districts in particular are susceptible to the influence of their various clients (Bidwell, 1965; Sieber, 1968). The educational tradition of community interest and influence continues and has been reinforced by the community-control movement of social programs such as community mental health and economic opportunity projects.

Relation of Environment to Innovation

Environmental variability provides pervasive stimuli to the organization. In a rapidly changing environment expectations increase faster than the services offered and demands for services outrun the ability to pay for them. A more heterogeneous environment with a varied clientele demands diverse services, so there is greater competition for scarce resources from the more fragmented socioeconomic and demographic forces. Increased uncertainty and diversity encourage the adoption of innovations. The character of the client population served determines the demand for services, the scope of activities, and the human resources to be utilized by an organization. Similarly, since many inputs in the exchange relationship may be resolved financially, the community's wealth is a major environmental variable.

Both the Illinois and the Bay Area studies used demographic data as indicators of the variability of the school environment. Since we assumed that heterogeneous, changing environments would pose unique problems for school districts, causing them to adopt innovations, we selected data indicative of environmental variability and heterogeneity: population density, urbanization, and percentage of nonwhites in the district, the amount of home ownership, and the number of other governmental agencies competing for resources.

Empirical Results

The environmental data came from the Illinois study, where the variables were categorized as either environmental heterogeneity or change. Table 3 shows that all six indicators of environmental heterogeneity had the predicted relationship to innovation. Four of the six were fairly strong, with districts that were high adopters having much higher population density, about 50 percent higher urbanization, and 75 percent higher rates of nonwhites, and almost twice as many other governmental agencies in their environment. The differences on expenditure rates and home ownership were not as strong, but they were in the predicted direction. The correlation matrix in Table 4 also supports our hypothesis. The relationships between indicators of environmental heterogeneity and innovation range from a low of .25 (between percentage of nonwhites and innovation) and a high of .37 (between urbanization and innovation).

The second cluster of environmental variables dealt with environmental change: changes in wealth and operating expenses, population growth of the county, in and out migration, and changes in the racial composition of the district. We hypothesized that changes in these factors would create new demands on the districts that would cause them to adopt innovations.

The results, however, did not support the hypothesis. Table 3 shows that although all the differences are in the predicted direction, districts with high adoption of innovations differed only slightly from those with low adoptions. In Table 4 the correlations between these change measures and innovation are extremely low. Therefore environmental change—at least as measured with these indicators—did not significantly influence the adoption of innovations by the school districts.

Joint Impacts of Organizational and Environmental Factors

Up to this point we have discussed the variables from the Illinois study separately, but it is important to examine the joint impact of the organizational and environmental variables.

We assumed that the various indicators of size, complexity, and environmental variability would cluster together in meaningful groups. In order to verify the clustering empirically we ran an orthogonal factor analysis using a varimax rotation. Table 5 gives the loadings for the three major factors that emerged from the

TABLE 5 *Factor Loadings for 3 Major Factors*

Factors	Factor 1 Environmental Heterogeneity	Factor 2 Size and Complexity	Factor 3 Environmental Change
Population density	.98	.01	.07
Change in funds	.96	.02	.15
% Nonwhite	.92	.04	.02
% Home ownership	−.91	−.03	.11
% Gov't expenses for noneducational agencies	−.91	−.06	.09
% Urban	.77	.27	.35
Specialization	.05	.97	.04
Size	.07	.92	.08
Components	.06	.86	.02
Conflict-Prevention devices	.23	.28	.05
Growth	.15	.04	.79
Change in wealth	−.09	−.01	−.78
Migration	−.12	.14	.76
Change in racial composition	.25	.23	.07
Wealth	.21	.19	.08
Eigenvalues	5.41	2.74	1.86
Cumulative Total Variance	.36	.54	.67

analysis. (1) *Environmental heterogeneity*, loaded highly on indicators such as population density, lack of home ownership, high percentage of nonwhite populations, and urbanization. (2) *Size and complexity*, loaded highly on indicators such as specialization of administrative positions, number of students, and the number of administrative subdivisions in the hierarchy. Although size was expected to be somewhat distinct from complexity, it actually correlated so highly with it as to be indistinguishable. (3) *Environmental change*, loaded highly on growth, change in wealth, and migration into and out of a district. It is obvious from Table 5 that the three factors account for a large amount of the variation in the independent variables, with a cumulative total variance explained of 66.8 percent, a large amount for only three major factors. We were pleased to find three independent factors that loaded so highly on intuitively meaningful indicators, and, at the same time explained such a large proportion of the variance in the set of independent variables.

Orthogonal factor analysis produces factors that are by definition independent. Since we had such clean, intuitively meaningful, and—by definition—independent factors we could use them in a multiple regression without encountering the sticky problem of multicollinearity. Table 6 shows the multiple regression of the three independent factors against innovation. In total, about 32 percent of the variance in innovation can be explained by these three factors.

For the size/complexity factor, the r with innovations was .49 and the variance explained was .24. Obviously of the three factors, size and complexity had the strongest impact on adoption of innovations. When the environmental heterogeneity factor was run against innovation, the additional amount of variance explained by this factor (after size/complexity) was 7.5 percent, indicating that this factor did affect innovation but not as much as size/complexity. Finally, the multiple regression indicated that environmental change, as we measured it, did not affect innovation very much, verifying what was indicated by earlier analyses.

Summary and Conclusions

This article has argued that research on the diffusion of innovation and organizational change has too often focused on the wrong clusters of variables. In particular, the orientation toward the early phases of the innovation cycle, the concentration on small-scale technical innovations, and the individualistic biases have hindered our understanding of major organizational innovation. In contrast, a more productive analysis of the change process should concentrate on the diffusion of complex technologies with unclear evaluations, would shift focus from individualistic variables to roles and organizational structure, and would examine closely environmental factors.

TABLE 6 *The Factors and Innovation: Correlation and Multiple Regression*

	Zero-Order r	Cumulative R	R^2	Increase in R^2	F
Size/Complexity	.49	.49	.24	.24	54.5
Environmental Heterogeneity	.27	.56	.31	.08	18.9
Environmental Change	.07	.56	.32	.01	1.1

Studies of schools in the San Francisco Bay Area and in Illinois indicate that individual characteristics—sex, age, cosmopolitanism, education—do *not* have the widely argued effect of producing more innovative behavior among individuals involved in organizational changes. This made us to look for organizational factors to explain organizational change. One type of organizational/individual combination that seemed to make some difference was organizational position and role— those who had power, sanctions, communication linkages, and boundary roles appeared as to be important in the adoption of innovations.

With respect to organizational characteristics, the results support the premise that a large, complex organization with a heterogeneous environment is more likely to adopt innovations than a small, simple organization with a relatively stable, homogeneous environment. The basic logic concerns a "demand structure." (1) Size makes a series of demands about coordination, control, and complexity to which an organization must respond. (2) Differentiation and structural complexity produce specialists searching for new solutions to the task demands within their specialized realms. (3) A heterogeneous environment surrounding an organization makes numerous demands for responsive behavior.

These structural characteristics of organizations and the relationship to the environment are powerful explainers of innovative behavior. Certainly, they cannot replace other interpretations such as the personality characteristics of administrators or the character of the innovations, but when coupled with these other explanations, they help account for much of the adoption of innovations by organizations.

References

Baldridge, J. Victor, 1971, *Power and Conflict in the University*. New York: John Wiley.

Bidwell, Charles E., 1965, "The schools as a formal organization." In James C. March (ed.), *Handbook of Organizations:* 972–1022. Chicago: Rand McNally.

Blau, Peter M., 1970, "A formal theory of differentiation in organizations." *American Sociological Review*, 35: 201–218.

Burnham, Robert, 1972, *Environmental and Structural Determinants of Innovation in School Districts*. Doctoral dissertation, Stanford University.

Carlson, R. O., 1967, *Adoption of Educational Innovations*. Eugene, Oregon: The University of Oregon.

Coleman, James Samuel, Elihu Katz, and Herbert Menzel, 1966, *Medical Innovation: A Diffusion Study*. Indianapolis: Bobbs Merrill.

Corwin, Ronald G., 1972, "Strategies for organizational innovation: an empirical comparison." *American Sociological Review*, 37:441–452.

Crain, Robert L., 1962, *Inner-city Influence in the Diffusion of Fluoridation*. Doctoral dissertation, University of Chicago.

Dal Santo, John, 1968, *School Administrators' Perception of Critical Factors of Planned Change in Selected Illinois School Districts*. Doctoral dissertation, Illinois State University.

Evan, William, 1965, "Superior-subordinate conflict in research organizations." *Administrative Science Quarterly*, 10:52–64.

Gans, T. G., 1971, *Teacher Initiative, Structural Openness, and Militant Group Conflict in Selected Secondary Schools*. Doctoral dissertation, Stanford University.

Gorth, William P., 1971, *The Loci of Authority in Schools During Change*. Doctoral dissertation, Stanford University.

Guba, Egon G., 1968, "Diffusion of innovations." *Educational Leadership*, 25:292–295.

Hage, Jerald, and Michael Aiken, 1967, "Program change and organizational properties, a comparative analysis." *American Journal of Sociology*, 72:503–519.
——— 1970, *Social Change in Complex Organizations*. New York: Random House.
Hamrin, Gerald W., 1970, *An Analysis of Factors Influencing Educational Change*. Doctoral dissertation, Stanford University.
Knight, E. E., 1967, "A descriptive model of the intra-firm innovation process." *Journal of Business*, 40:478–496.
Knight, Olan L., 1970, *Characteristics of Educators Involved in the Change Process*. Doctoral dissertation, Stanford University.
March, James G., and Herbert Simon, 1958, *Organizations*. New York: John Wiley.
Miles, M. B. (ed.), 1964, *Innovation in Education*. New York: Bureau of Publications, Teachers College, Columbia University.
Mort, Paul R., and Francis G. Cornell, 1945, *Adaptability of Public School Systems*. New York: Bureau of Publications, Teachers College, Columbia University.
Penny, William A., 1970, *Characteristics of Educators Involved in the Change Process*. Doctoral dissertation, Stanford University.
Rogers, Everett M., 1962, *Diffusion of Innovations*. New York: The Free Press.
Rogers, Everett M., and F. Floyd Shoemaker, 1971, *Communication of Innovations*. New York: The Free Press.
Sapolsky, Harvey M., 1967, "Organizational structure and innovation." *Journal of Business*, 40:497–510.
Schmick, William A., 1970, *The Influence of Organizational Positions on Change Implementation in High Schools with Elected and Appointed Department Heads*. Doctoral dissertation, Stanford University.
Sieber, Sam D., 1968, "Organizational influences on innovative roles." In Terry L. Eidell and Joanne M. Kitchel (eds.), *Knowledge Production and Utilization in Educational Administration*: 120–142. Eugene, Oregon: Center for Advanced Study of Educational Administration.
Terreberry, Shirley, 1968, "The evolution of organizational environments." *Administrative Science Quarterly*, 12:590–613.
Wilson, James O., 1963, "Innovation in organization: notes toward a theory." In J. D. Thompson (ed.), *Approaches to Organizational Design*: 193–218. Pittsburgh: University of Pittsburgh.

B. Structure and Knowledge

Patterns of Practice in the Hospital
Eliot Freidson

As varied as everyday medical practices are, . . . few can avoid taking into account the unusual but routine occasions when the patient becomes so incapacitated that he cannot walk in to see the physician, when the patient's condition is thought to require a regimen too precise or dangerous to trust to laymen at home, and when he is thought to need services requiring the coordination of a variety of special skills and machines.

Given the development of medical technology over the past fifty years, the hospital has become the place in industrial and post-industrial countries where those unusual but routine cases are treated. Thus, the hospital constitutes a major work setting for medical practice—a facility which the organization of every practice must, in one way or another, take into account. The everyday practitioner who does not or cannot personally hospitalize his patients and supervise their care in hospital must be prepared to see some of his patients transfer to practitioners who can see them through the hospital. If he is to have a stable practice he must participate in an arrangement that encourages his patients to return to him after leaving the hospital. Such arrangements are many and varied: in many European hospitals there is a rigid separation between community and hospital practice which prevents the community practitioner from caring for the patient in hospital but which also prevents the patient from seeking everyday care from hospital practitioners. While the community practitioner "loses" his patients upon hospitalization, he is assured of regaining them on discharge.

Thus, even the community practitioner without any hospital ties must incorporate arrangements into his practice that take the hospital into account. In this sense, virtually all types of medical practice in industrialized societies include within them systematic accommodations to hospitals. From this point of view, the hospital may be seen as part of medical practice as such, serving as a setting where cases inappropriate for office or home practice may be taken and treated. Historically, the hospital developed separately from conventional medical practice, being a place where the poor and the stranger, both without access to the community medical practice of the time, could find (or share) a bed and nursing care.[1] While the hospital is in reality something more than a mere creature of medical practice, nonetheless a great many of its problems can be better understood by emphasizing its status, particularly in the average community hospital in the United States, as an appendage of medical practice, struggling for greater autonomy in establishing goals and policies separate from those of the entrepreneurial community practitioner.[2]

Hospitals as Medical Practices

In examining the hospital for the degree to which it is an appendage of medical practice, we first consider the range of variation in the extent to which hospital policies and procedures are controlled by the physicians who use it as a place in which to bed and treat their patients. In the United States this range is wide, though comprehension of it is severely handicapped by a lack of systematic, empirical information about many varieties in that range. To discuss this range intelligently we must limit our definition of the word "hospital" in such a way as to exclude nursing homes, homes for the aged, "rest homes," "sanitaria," and other domiciliary institutions that may provide some nominal health care but not medical care on an intensive or daily basis. Thus, I limit myself to considering a hospital to be "an institution in which patients or injured persons are given medical or surgical care."[3]

At one extreme of the range is the *proprietary hospital*—one owned privately and run for profit. Insofar as the proprietary hospital is devoted to providing services that only physicians are licensed to give, and insofar as physicians are the gatekeepers who persuade patients to be hospitalized and decide what shall be done with them, it follows that whether or not physicians own the proprietary hospital (as is apparently common), its policies are likely to be focused on accommodating to the needs and desires of the physicians, tempered somewhat by the demands of the customer, economics, and other requisites of profit. The physician who brings in the most patients or the best-paying patients will have the greatest influence on policy. And policy in general will be dominated by the principle of laissez faire: the physician will be free to do more or less what he pleases, medically, with little or no supervision of his medical performance.[4] This kind of hospital is a literal extension of medical practice.

A somewhat similar situation was once very common in the *voluntary or community hospital* in the United States. Such hospitals are by definition not run for profit.[5] Frequently running on less than a cost basis, they receive significant amounts of support from charitable contributions and subsidies. Until recently, when hospital compensation by private and later public health insurance became the rule rather than the exception, many of the patients of the American voluntary hospital were "charity" cases, contributing little to the cost of their services. To balance the cost of the care of such "charity" cases, well-paying patients were obviously desirable to the hospital. The physicians who could bring such well-paying patients into the hospital were obviously of great importance to its survival and, as might be expected, were dominant in setting hospital policy in spite of the fact that they were neither owners of the hospital nor committed to it by employment or capital investment.[6]

More recently, however—in part because of the increased likelihood that, by private or public health insurance devices, every patient is a "paying patient," and in part because of the development of full-time, hospital-based practice— much of the control of voluntary and community hospital policies has been passing out of the hands of the community practitioner and into those of the boards that "own" and the administrators who manage the day-to-day affairs of the hospital. Policy has become divided into several spheres, medical boards controlling much of the policy specifically related to their work, and administrative staff controlling the rest, including access to the governing board. Even before such changes occurred, the voluntary hospital played an important part in shaping medical practice. Whereas in the proprietary hospital the physician could come and go at his own convenience, the physician was obliged to "donate" his services to some of the "welfare," "clinic," or "service" patients in return for the "privilege" of hospitalizing his patients in the voluntary hospital. Furthermore, because the voluntary hospital had a general aim of community service rather than the narrow one of "servicing" practitioner's needs for beds, and sometimes had nonmedical goals, it was likely to impose rules of its own on physician behavior—as for example, that the physician must conform with religious dictates in hospitals run by religious orders or run under orthodox religious auspices.

In both of the cases I have discussed so far, medical practice is distinct from the hospital as such. In other cases, medical practice becomes wholly encompassed by the hospital, not standing apart from it. The most clear-cut example of this is to be found in the *military hospital,* where physicians are full-fledged members of the organization, as committed to it and subject to discipline as other performing members. Another example is to be found in those federal, state, and municipal hospitals that are staffed by exclusively full-time medical personnel. The physician's practice lying entirely within the organization, his career is formed by his relationship to it and its personnel, like that of a civil service employee. A somewhat more complicated example of this type of relationship is to be found in the increasingly common practice of full-time medical staff members in medical schools and teaching hospitals[7]—a practice that is not as dependent upon the organization for resources as is implied by the fact of employment. Like the university professor, the full-time staff member of the medical school and the teaching hospital tends to have a national or even international "clientele": while his "practice" depends upon holding a position in an organization, his career tends to be one of high mobility, moving from one organization to another. Interestingly enough, it is the very fact that full-time practice in the hospital does not have to attract a *personal* following of clients—rather, merely serving the clients attracted by the hospital—that liberates it from the local community so as to become transferable (and marketable) to other hospitals and communities.

Finally, it is necessary to discuss a special case of hospital practice that is not "pure" but that is critical to many hospitals' supply of skilled medical work—the work of the postgraduate physicians—interns and residents, or "house staff." Much of the medical care that the house staff gives to patients in hospitals is part of what it must do in order to develop its skills for both general and specialized practice.[8] However, the work is of great value to the hospital itself, for it is medical work that no one else in the hospital can do. Whether because of their commitment to affairs outside the hospital or to research, or whether because they are in absolute short supply, the medical staff is in no position to do the work of the house staff should the latter suddenly disappear. One might expect that in hospitals without house staff—for example, proprietary hospitals and small isolated community general hospitals—most of the *medical* work that the house staff would do elsewhere must instead be performed by nurses and even aides or attendants, only the most critical being taken over by the medical staff.

A characteristic of perhaps greater sociological importance for understanding the functioning of hospitals, however, is the *transience* of house staff. Like students in a college, their orientation is toward obtaining what they feel they need from the institution (which is not necessarily the same as that needed by the staff and patients) in order that they may leave and begin their "real" life of practice. It is of course true that some interns wish to stay on to be first-year residents, some of the latter wish to be second-year residents, and so on. Furthermore, it is true that some of the house staff wish to join the medical staff of the institution in which they work. Nonetheless, their commitment to their hospital work is different from that of the commitment of others, being perhaps less intense than that of the full-time staff and more intense than that of attending staff but, in any case, of a shorter term than either. The consequences of such limited commitment may not be significant to their work in instances where episodic or short-term care is necessary. But the mere fact of their constant rotation or turnover may have serious consequences for the care they give patients who require a sustained personal relationship with a therapist. The most obvious example of this is the mental hospital, public or private: assuming that verbal psychotherapy is an efficacious method of treatment and that for its success it requires fairly close rapport between patient and therapist, turnover among individuals' therapists is patently undesirable therapeutically.

I have dwelt at length on the issue of hospital practice in order to link my discussion of medical practice in with my discussion of the hospital, but more importantly I wish to emphasize a fact that is frequently overlooked in discussions of the organization and operation of hospitals. In circumstances most commonly studied *in the United States, the physician is not so much part of the hospital as the hospital is part (and only one part) of the physician's practice.* In the most common type of American hospital—the community general hospital—the medical staff that hospitalizes patients and supervises their care is not committed to the hospital in the same way as are such full-time employees as nurses. While they are part of the hospital, as are patients, they are part of it in a very special way that is markedly variant from that of the members of such clearly bureaucratic organizations as armies, factories, and civil service bureaus.[9] By the same token, however, this hospital segment of their medical practice is markedly different in organization from the office segment. In his office practice the physician makes use of workers from other occupations but on the whole controls the initiation and maintenance of his relation with such workers. In the hospital, however, the physician is confronted with a division of labor organized and administered independently of his own individual practice and carried out by workers with occupational aspirations and perspectives which may conflict with his own. He can work alone in his office, but in the hospital he cannot fail to come into sustained contact with the larger division of labor of which he is a part. Thus, the hospital is one major proving ground for his place in that division of labor.

Ordering the Hospital Division of Labor

What groups are involved in the hospital?[10] In my definition I stressed the centrality of medical and surgical work. But while physicians and surgeons may control the performance of such work as befits a profession, they cannot do it all themselves. Furthermore, various supportive services, some domestic and some technical, are necessary for the continued operation of an institution which combines domiciliary with therapeutic services.

[In discussing] the medical division of labor it is possible to distinguish (1) physicians from (2) those workers who give direct and indirect medical services under "orders" of or supervision by physicians—medical and paramedical personnel, respectively. In the latter case we must distinguish between (a) those who serve the patient directly—primarily nursing and ward personnel but also various "therapists" and (b) those who provide technical services contributing to medical service—laboratory and other technicians. We must also mention (3) those service workers who care for the physical plant of the hospital and perform the other tasks connected with maintaining the plant and managing the food, laundry, and other services necessary for its survival, and (4) the clerical personnel who prepare, transmit, and store the written communications of the institution. We must also mention (5) those whose task is to organize, supervise, and coordinate the work of all workers in the light of the over-all objectives of the organization itself—the "administrators." In addition to these major types of everyday hospital worker, there are, of course, (6) the legal governing board of the institution, which is not a continuously working group, and (7) the patients or clients, who, while more or less passive and frequently transient, are nonetheless members of the organization. How are these relationships ordered?

In the conventional industrial organization that tends to be our commonsensical model of what an organization "really" is, the workers whose skill is used in industrial production are subordinate to the administration.[11] The plant manager or the vice-president in charge of production is naturally a key man, but the qualifications he must have to obtain and perform his job satisfactorily do not include among them the training for and capacity to be a production *worker*. Furthermore, while he does tend to be key man in the organization, his rank is shared by other vice-presidents with such other concerns as sales, finance, public relations, labor relations, and the like. In this sense, the worker who performs the primary, core task of production in the industrial organization is neither in control of the organization nor represented by an especially powerful superior. The organizational chart of the industrial organization is thus fairly logical and symmetrical, each "function," including that of production, responsible to coequal administrators who are in turn responsible to a single coordinating head or president. There is nominally, then, a single line of authority, delegated and differentiated by task—a monocratic model like that analyzed by Max Weber.

Recent discussions of organizations by such analysts of conventional corporate enterprises as Victor Thompson[12] claim that when creative and complex work is required, the monocratic model of organization is inappropriate. Those concerned with the role of the professional in the organization have suggested that something quite other than a monocratic form of organization is appropriate to the creative and complex work imputed to the professional—a company of equals, a professional organization, or, in Weber's terms, a collegial form of organization.[13] And, indeed in the hospitals discussed by Smith,[14] there is not just one line of authority but two. Essentially, Smith notes that the physician can intervene in many areas of the hospital over which he has no formal administrative jurisdiction or authority. Unlike the foreman, who is caught "in the middle" between his legitimate superiors and subordinates, the nurse is caught between two superiors, administrative and medical. The latter, however, is not her bureaucratic superior; that is to say, while the floor nurse is subject to the orders of her supervisor, who is her official superior in the hospital hierarchy, she is also subject to the orders of the physician involved in the care of her patients by virtue of his superior knowledge and responsibility. Similarly, justifying his demands by reference to the well-being of his patient, the physician can and does give "orders" to other hospital personnel even though he is not a bureaucratically defined superior. In this way the functioning of the hospital is seen to be disrupted and broken, lacking the clear, unilinear authority upon which Weber predicates efficiency and reliability in organizational performance.

However, one may ask why this situation exists so markedly in American hospitals and so much less so in industrial organizations. In the latter there are an increasing number of professionals, first as staff which plans the work performed by the line, and increasingly as research and development scientists. But if we can believe such writers as Kornhauser,[15] rather than being free to intervene in others' work as do doctors, scientists in industry are hardly free to do their own work as they please. The tribulations of staff in industry thus teach us that it is not expertise as such that grants the "authority" to intervene in others' work and immunity from retaliation by those in formal authority. Rather, we might suspect that the physician in American hospitals is in a very special position, different from that of other contemporary experts by virtue of the *content* of his expertise, the organization of his practice, and the position of his profession.

As Hall pointed out, the physician is able to intervene in many places in the hospital and justify his intervention on the basis of a "medical emergency"—a situation in which the well-being of a patient is said to be seriously in jeopardy and in which it is the physician alone who knows what is best done.[16] We all are familiar with the dominant symbolic image: the interruption of orderly routine by a violent convulsion, heart failure, a hemorrhage; the suspension of ordinary relationships and their reorganization around the masterful physician who, by his intervention, saves a life. While this no doubt happens on occasion, far more common in the hospital is the *labeling of ambiguous events as emergencies* by the doctor so as to gain the aid or resources he believes he needs. The recent creation of emergency admission committees in some hospitals—committees that review the justification of suspending ordinary procedures and priorities for admitting a doctor's patient to the hospital—suggests both that the label is not always used by individual physicians in circumstances that his colleagues would agree is "really" an emergency and that it is a powerful source of leverage in the hospital which cannot be effectively contested by any other than medical men. It is his ability to invoke life-threatening emergency and to claim exclusive capacity to evaluate and solve it that marks the physician off from many other experts in other organizations.[17]

When Does the Second Line of Authority Operate?

As I have noted in a number of contexts, "the physician" is at best a very general occupational type that can be only vaguely contrasted with "the lawyer," "the scientist," and "the engineer." There are many kinds of physicians, in the sense that systematic variations of some significance occur within the general profession. The content of the physician's work influences the kind of emergency he is likely to meet and indeed whether or not his "typical emergency" will have the rhetorical force of "a life-and-death-matter" to those he must persuade. I suggest that while all specialties (and indeed all kinds of work) have their typical emergencies, they vary in the degree to which the emergencies are generally believed by others to be critical enough to warrant suspension of everyday routine, and they vary in the degree to which such emergencies are frequent and characteristic, almost routine. In the specialty of public health, for example, the typical dramatic emergency is the outbreak of a lethal epidemic or of virulent food poisoning, a circumstance that would give the public health officer justification to breach ordinary lines of authority. However, in the United States such outbreaks are so rare and so comparatively mild that the public health officer may be expected to conform to the usual routines, bureaucratic and otherwise. And his "image" is similarly safe and bureaucratic, as the North Carolina study of specialty choice has clearly shown.[18]

In the hospital we can, holding all else equal, predict the likelihood of the intervention of this "second line of authority" (and the disordering of decision-making) by the degree to which the specialty of the physician involved permits the plausible and regular claim of "critical emergency." While the distinction may be too broad to be significant, one might suspect that the surgical specialties may be able to claim more emergency than the medical. Within medicine, obviously physical medicine is *less* likely to permit such a regular claim than is cardiology. Within surgery, ophthalmology and otolaryngology are less likely to be able to make a plausible claim of emergency than neurosurgery or orthopedic surgery. And the service specialties of pathology, roentgenology, and anesthesiology are considerably less likely to claim their own emergencies than to attach themselves to the emergencies defined by medicine and surgery.

As important as the content of work (and the claim of expertise) may be, though, I would insist that much of the problem posed by the second line of authority stems not from the substantive element of professional expertise but from the combination of his sociolegal responsibility for hospital patients with the socioeconomic independence of the physician from the hospital in the United States. As a volunteer worker, or as a guest both serving and being served by the hospital, the physician is in a position to escape many of the obligations of any member of a bureaucracy, including the exercise of bureaucratic authority: he is a relatively free agent, unrestrained by subordination to a clear organizational hierarchy. In contrast, the staff expert in the industrial organization is an employee of the organization with no necessary outside career alternatives. Furthermore, the practicing physician is recognized to be responsible for the treatment of the patient: if he were responsible but could not order about those engaged in the treatment, he would be in an intolerable position. In contrast, the staff expert in industry is responsible for his own work but not for the work of others, including those engaged in the organization's central task of production: that the expert cannot order production workers about is hardly crucial to his work. Analogous to the staff expert in industry is the pathologist in medicine: he is not responsible for the treatment of patients (production) but only for his own expert work which, while having some bearing on treatment, does not constitute treatment. It is the special responsibility of the practicing physician that inevitably involves him in the varied levels of the division of labor. Whenever the practicing physician has such personal responsibility, we will find him intervening no matter what the hierarchical and functional organization of the hospital. But the *amount, content,* and *success* of such intervention will vary with the physician's commitment to and dependence on his position in the hospital.

In brief, I would hypothesize that, all else being equal, the greater the physician's commitment to his position in the hospital, the greater his inclination to use the regular channels of authority and the more orderly the transmission of information and "orders" bearing on patient care. Empirically, the simplest example of such commitment is full-time employment with no other career alternatives, though instances do occur in which a "voluntary" staff position is so crucial to the practice of a physician as to commit him to the hospital as much if not more than employment as such. This means that we should find far more evidence of the confusion described by Smith in American hospitals than in English and European hospitals where full-time hospital practice is more common. And it means that the problem is not generic to the hospital as such, nor to those bureaucratic organizations in which professionals work. Rather, the problem stems from the special characteristics of the medical profession, from the circumstances of medical practice in general and in the United States in particular.

Conflicting Perspectives in the Hospital

We usually assume that those who are administratively responsible for an organization possess the resources to make that organization pursue the officially approved goals set for it—that is, that actual behavior in the organization will be in accord with the official view of what the organization *should* be doing. But frequently it is not. The classic study of a state mental hospital by Ivan Belknap[19] showed how an institution supposedly devoted to curing illness was instead devoted to maintaining a cruel custodial order among inmates, without making significant attempts at therapy. Furthermore, even when an official goal is more or less pursued, it is pursued in the context of interaction between the conflicting perspectives of the participants. A surgical ward, or a lying-in hospital, may be run like a tight ship by the surgical captains, but not without the friction created by the resistance of patients who may want more deference, personal service, and emotional support.[20] To understand what actually goes on in the ward, therefore, one must understand the perspectives of the participants, how they conflict with each other, and what resources each has available to allow him to assert his perspectives over the others. We may mention four perspectives here—that of the patient, of the nonprofessional aide, of the professional nurse, and of the physician in charge.

The Patient

A great deal has been written about the personal anxiety attached to being ill and about the consequent irrational character of much of the patient's behavior on the ward. The staff is less involved in the illness than is the patient. Furthermore, as a layman the patient is also less capable of arriving at the proper diagnosis of his complaint than those who take care of him and is less likely to be able to evaluate his treatment. Finally, the individual patient is concerned with his own fortunes. In contrast, the staff is concerned with the fortunes of all patients, balancing off the relative need of one patient against the need of another, in the context of the limited time and energy available. While patients may certainly vary as individuals in the degree to which they are marked by such characteristics, those characteristics distinguish patients as a group from the staff as a group.

By the nature of the situation the perspective of the patient is in conflict with that of the staff, and some of the staff effort will be devoted to controlling behavior that disrupts the ward routine. Depending on its mandate and ideology, the staff may seek to control such conflict by physical means (mechanical, electrical, chemical, or whatever), by efforts at rational explanation, pedagogy, and training, and by the techniques of psychotherapy. However, all members of the staff are not able to use all techniques of control if only by virtue of the division of labor that limits each level of the staff to the use of techniques appropriate to its "level of skill" or occupational jurisdiction. Furthermore, the resources of the patient himself can impose constraints on staff behavior.

From the accumulation of studies of interaction on the ward, a number of patient attributes seem to have important bearing on what techniques of control can be exercised by staff members seeking to order their work.[21] The grossest attribute is physical incapacity: an unconscious patient obviously poses fewer problems to the staff than a conscious one; a weak and bedridden patient fewer than an ambulatory. Another critical attribute is the patient's socio-legal identity: if he is a public charge by virtue of his "welfare" status, or a prisoner by virtue of legal commitment (in the case of drug addiction, tuberculosis, or psychosis), or something less than a responsible human being by virtue of being labeled psychotic, senile, retarded, or otherwise deficient in the qualities that grant one the right to be taken seriously, then he will have difficulty asserting his perspective in interaction on the ward. Also may be mentioned his socioeconomic resources: if he has the money (or, in Socialist countries, the political importance) to gain special care—a private-duty nurse or a hospital with a low patient-staff ratio, for example—and if he has the active support of healthy, knowledgeable, and influential friends or relatives outside the institution, he is a special problem of management. Finally, it is probable that organized and persistent problems of patient management are most likely to occur when patients are able to be in regular social interaction with each other, when they all have the same general class of ailment about which they can exchange information, and when they share a relatively long-term, chronic prognosis. Under such circumstances they are likely to form their own little society which, whether it involves "living in the cracks" or "colonizing," nonetheless becomes a source of social strength which staff must take into account.[22]

Aides, Orderlies, Attendants

Empirically, many differences may be expected among patients on wards due both to variation in patient values and knowledge and to variation in the social resources which allow the patients to assert their own perspective. Such variation exists to a much lesser degree among the staff whose function it is to get done the necessary housekeeping jobs of the ward—at least so far as values and knowledge go. It seems no accident that attendants in mental hospitals, who are lower class in the United States and the United Kingdom, and lower-class but *not* middle-class mental patients, both have a high "custodial" orientation to the management of mental illness.[23] These poorly paid, essentially untrained workers, whose job it is to handle the dirty work of the wards, cannot be expected to hold, much less to exercise, the complex conceptions of treatment espoused by professionals. However, this is not to say that they have *no* conception of treatment. Their sin is in having a lay conception that is not shared by some influential professionals. As the "Custodial Mental Illness Ideology Scale" implies, their conception of mental illness is that it is so abnormal, hopeless, irrational, and dangerous as to surpass human understanding and to require close surveillance and control in hospital. This conception is quite similar to that described by the Cummings among the citizens of a Canadian community.[24] Nonetheless, as Strauss and his associates have pointed out, the view does not imply merely punitive reactions on the part of aides: their lay orientation to the management of the mentally ill contains within it specific modes of "training" and otherwise helping patients.[25]

By definition as nonprofessional workers, then, aides, orderlies, and attendants have nonprofessional perspectives on their work. This, however, is not a terribly important practical issue for interaction on the ward unless the aide is in a position to impose his perspective on others in the ward. By virtue of being involved in work on the ward day and night, he is in a position to exercise some leverage over the patient, both by physical restraint, and by the age-old evasive tactics of the underdog everywhere—"not hearing," "forgetting," and otherwise evading the demands of the more powerful. This certainly gives him a position of some influence on any ward. What apparently consolidates and strengthens the aide's position in the state mental hospital, however, is the effective absence from the ward of other workers, combined with circumstances that effectively neutralize patient demands. It seems no accident that these "first-line" workers are powerful precisely in those settings where the patients are stripped of their identity as responsible, adult human beings, and where there is no extensive and continuous participation by professional workers in some regular, effective therapeutic process on or off the wards. The aide's role has been powerful enough to warrant extended attention only in those institutions so underfinanced as to support at best a skeleton staff of professional workers, and in those institutions filled with patients with ailments for which there is no straightforward therapy with any immediate and definite results. In the former case, there are insufficient professional staff to allow effective supervision and control of aides: they must rely on what the aide reports to them. In the latter, there is insufficient foundation of observable, unambiguous results (such as frequently follows medical or surgical treatment) to persuade attendants that there are professional techniques whose outcomes surpass lay common sense.

The Nurse

. . . The professional qualities of the nurse are, particularly in the hospital, contingent on her relation to the physician.[26] She is the agent of the supervising physician in carrying out treatment and patient care. In this sense, she represents the professional perspective on the ward. However, insofar as she represents the day-to-day administration of the ward, she is also concerned with patients as a batch—something that, in the United States, at least, the physician is less concerned with. She must, therefore, balance individual physicians' orders for the care of individual patients against the independent demands of the patients as such and against the need to manage an aggregate of cases in an administratively acceptable way. It is because, unlike the aide, the nurse serves as an adjunct of both medical and administrative authority, that she seems to be the intense focus of conflicting perspectives. Unlike the aide, the nurse is imputed professional identity, and so she is likely to be engaged in a considerably more complex system of bargaining. In bargaining with physicians, one of her prime resources lies in her first-hand knowledge and professional evaluation of what goes on in the ward through her continued presence—a strategic advantage no doubt lost in such hospitals as those in the Soviet Union, where physicians are also present in enough number on a full-time basis to make a difference. In bargaining with patients, her prime strength lies in her access to the physician, both in knowing his inside information and in being able to discuss cases with him. Thus, while she may serve as a troubled focus of conflicting perspectives, she also may very well hold the balance of power in determining the outcome of bargaining among patient and staff.

The Physician

As I have already noted, in an active treatment setting the physician largely determines what therapeutic efforts are made and, if he does not make all such efforts himself, he orders and supervises the efforts of others. Aside from preventing interaction in the ward from damaging his relation with those patients for whom he is responsible, his problem is to obtain conformity with his orders by the other staff. But while it is relatively easy to have orders followed to the letter, the spirit is more difficult. When the lay common sense of aides, orderlies, or attendants is contradicted by the physician's philosophy of treatment, there is trouble. And when the physician's philosophy of treatment threatens the routine order of the ward, his approach is even less likely to be followed. The nurse may be involved in these difficulties when her training leads her to hold a "professional" philosophy of treatment that is at variance with that of the physician. Should such conflict in philosophy exist, a considerably more delicate process of manipulation and bargaining must occur for the physician to get his way, as Strauss and his associates have shown.

When all is said and done, however, it is the physician's expertise that is his ultimate resource in his interaction with others. As the final arbiter of practice in the medical division of labor, sustained by prestige and legal mandate, he has an "authority" that is independent of administrative authority as such.[27] The "authority" of his knowledge, judgment, and responsibility being ultimately exercised in the division of labor, it follows that a "hierarchy" of expertise exists independently of the administrative hierarchy in the hospital, the physician ordering and supervising those below his superior level of skill. This leads to hierarchical behavior even in those settings where the philosophy of treatment involves attempts to set up "democratic" or "therapeutic" communities which, while nonhierarchical in intent, turn out to be hierarchical in practice. There is no court of appeal from superior training, knowledge, and judgment; technical decisions are not made by vote.

Medical Tasks and Ward Behavior

These remarks about the perspectives of participants in the ward have had to take into account such variables as the medical specialty involved and the illness being treated. Clearly, one cannot understand the regularities to be found in the hospital without bearing in mind the specialties involved, the consequences of their technical jobs, and their different demands of and from patients. One can argue that one cannot discuss the general hospital as a single organization. While we may discuss the lying-in hospital, the mental hospital, and others that specialize in particular conditions or problems of treatment as relatively homogeneous organizations, we cannot discuss the general hospital in the same way because of the varied illnesses, patients, and procedures to be found in its special wards.[28] Instead, we must break down discussion of the general hospital into the various special services and wards, each of which has its own characteristics.

There is a fair amount of evidence of significant variation in the organization of interaction and performance within the wards of the general hospital, differences apparently stemming from the presence of different specialties, which is to say different practices, different tasks, and different requirements for the performance of those tasks (or "technologies"). Perhaps the most marked difference in task that one may observe in the everyday setting of the general hospital is the difference between medicine and surgery. Burling, Lentz, and Wilson have given an excellent description of the general differences.[29] In a somewhat more analytical paper, Coser noted some of the consequences of these differences.[30] Coser pointed out that surgical tasks are more frequently of an emergency character than are medical tasks. An emergency task must be performed quickly, undelayed by debates among the participants. The responsible surgeon must make his decisions quickly, and he must be able to expect unquestioning, immediate aid. This quality of the surgical task was found to be reflected in differences in the way the exercise of authority and performance varied between the medical and surgical wards Coser studied. While the formal line of authority was much the same in both cases, in medicine there was consistent delegation of authority from the chief resident to the interns. But in surgery the chief resident did not delegate authority to his surgical subordinates. Furthermore, the social distance between the chief resident and the residents and interns under him was much greater in surgery than in medicine. Without delegated authority, the subordinate residents, interns, and even nurses on the surgical ward were all more or less "equal" in that all followed the decisions of the chief resident: the interaction among them was fairly free and informal. In contrast, on the medical ward, where the medical men but not the head nurse participated in decision-making, authority to do such was delegated down the medical hierarchy. Interaction among all participants was more formal, social distance dividing each rank from the other, rather than all from the chief resident.

Now clearly, daily routine on both medical and surgical wards can vary a great deal independently of the task, depending on the policies of the hospital administration and of the physician who serves as chief on the service. Coser's example is thus only an example, suggesting ways in which the consequences of task difference may be discerned. In another case, Seeman and Evans found surgical wards in one hospital on which the head physician tended to maximize his monopoly over decision-making, his social distance from subordinates, and his symbolic rank, and also, in the same hospital, surgical wards in which such "stratification" was low.[31] Their measure seems to refer to variations in the personal "leadership" style of the physicians in charge of the wards and does not seem addressed to the issue of task discussed by Coser and expanded on by Perrow.[32]

The "leadership style" of a superior may stem from his qualities as a person. On any ward, a physician who shares in decision-making and minimizes his social distance from subordinates may very well be a warm, accepting person. However, if he is a "warm" person he may subscribe to a "warm philosophy." And even if he is not personally "warm" he may subscribe intellectually to a treatment ideology which emphasizes the importance of social and psychological variables in influencing illness and its therapy. The ideology defines the task as something quite different than the "mere" surgical removal or repair of some troublesome condition. In this sense, the task does not stand by itself, independent of the conceptions of the participants: holding such a "routine" surgical task as an appendectomy constant, behavior on the ward may vary according to the ideology as well as to the personal qualities of the workers. It may very well be that the *outcome* of the work in the form of rates of "cure" is not much different no matter what the operative ideology or philosophy, but the organization of interaction among the workers on the ward and between workers and patients, as well as the concrete work performed, does seem to vary significantly. As sociologists, we are interested in the interaction of treatment, so that to us, the variation in *interactional outcome* by ideology as well as by task is perhaps more important than the "disease outcome."

The importance of ideology to the organization of hospital work is illustrated by another case study by Coser, which contrasts the behavior of the nursing staff on wards whose patients are held by the staff not capable of improvement with a rehabilitation center of the same hospital whose patients the staff believes can be cured.[33] In the former case, the task was defined in custodial terms—to run a neat and orderly ward. In the latter case the task was defined in therapeutic terms—to improve the patient's condition to such an extent as to allow his discharge. While the "objective" physical capacities of the patients in both instances overlap—some in the custodial wards believed improvable by hospital physicians, and some in the rehabilitation center having irreversible conditions—the ideology dominant in each seemed to govern a great deal of staff behavior.

In the "custodial" wards the nursing staff found plans to discharge a patient disruptive, for they assumed that the patient would be back after a short absence in any case. Emphasis was on orderly housekeeping and routinized records and on the mechanical side of nursing tasks. There was comparatively little staff interaction with the patients. Indeed, the high patient-staff ratio on the custodial wards seemed to lead to withdrawal from therapeutic tasks on the part of both nurses and physicians including not only withdrawal from the patients but also withdrawal from interaction with other staff members over problems of patient management. Without interaction, there was little occupational conflict on the custodial wards. In contrast, in the rehabilitation center, where an active treatment ideology prevailed (supported, we should not forget, by a very low patient-staff ratio), a great deal of patient-staff interaction took place as did a great deal of conflictful interaction among the various occupations. "Treatment philosophy" thus has clear consequences for ward interaction, consequences which can be dealt with by specifying three patterns of ward care.

Patterns of Ward Care

In my discussion thus far I have pointed, sometimes glancingly, to a number of variables which seem to have strategic relevance to understanding the performance of the staff of American hospitals. Given significant differences in the social consequences of various medical and surgical tasks, and in the consequences of various ideologies of treatment guiding how tasks are actually performed, it seems useful to distinguish among several patterns of performance to be found in hospitals or some of their wards. At one extreme may be found the *domestic-service pattern*, which is not appropriate, strictly speaking, to our definition of a hospital, but which is nonetheless found in "hospitals" which have official recognition as medical treatment institutions. This pattern involves the performance of essentially housekeeping tasks—feeding, clothing, bedding, amusing, and otherwise managing the lives of the inmates—with little effort at anything more than the routine episodic medical care that a "house doctor" resident in a hotel or on board ship may be expected to give.

The domestic-service pattern of management is founded on the assumption that nothing more can (or should) be done for the inmates than to make them comfortable or keep them out of trouble while they are residents. They are in some way inappropriate subjects for intensive therapeutic efforts—they are, for example, hopelessly retarded, crippled, or psychotic, or irreversibly helpless physically, whether by virtue of age or impairment.[34] Given this assumption, it follows that there is no need for a treatment staff. Furthermore, it follows that the quality of the staff-"patient" relationship is likely to have few of the attributes said to be characteristic of that of a professional to his client. Rather, it is likely to resemble that of a protective servant to his master or of a keeper to his charge. The former relationship seems to exist in expensive private "rest homes" and nursing homes,[35] perhaps in the Japanese mental hospital with *tsukisoi*.[36] The latter pattern, often called custodial in an invidious tone by those who feel that therapy is indicated,[37] seems to exist in the underfinanced and understaffed public mental hospitals. Whether "custodial" or otherwise, the domestic-service pattern is not one dominated or closely supervised by the medical man, whether by design or by the default of underfinancing and understaffing.

The second pattern has been called "the classical hospital care model" by Wessen,[38] though I prefer the term *"medical-intervention pattern."* Unlike the domestic-service pattern, it is dominated by the medical man. The medical man is prone to see the patient's difficulty as a transitory technical problem that can be overcome by some physical or biochemical intervention which only the physician is qualified to perform. The assumption is that the patient can be cured and discharged. But the patient is incompetent to judge what is needed and in order to be cured must put himself passively into the hands of the staff, obeying them without question and allowing them to do to him what they see fit. Similarly, the staff's work is organized by the physician's orders, initiating little itself, and primarily serving as his agent in dealing with the patient. Interaction between patient and staff thus takes on an impersonal quality, and interaction among various members becomes ordered by a professional chain of command, from the supervising physician to the registered nurse to the practical nurse and so on. This pattern is most marked on surgical floors but is also present in medicine and, in the form of the "somato-therapeutic ideology," in psychiatry.

Over the past few decades, the classical intervention pattern has been under intensive attack by many, both in and out of medicine. Quite apart from the special problem of mental illness, growing interest in psychosomatic medicine and in the theory of stress has led to seeing even superficially simple illnesses to be influenced by the feelings and motives of the patient, the illnesses no longer being considered discrete, delimited entities that can be managed independently of the patient as a person. The phrase "comprehensive care" has risen to serve as a label of the view that ailments should not be managed discretely, separately from each other by individual specialists.[39] These developments, while still more programmatic than actually realized, have come to make ambiguous the character of the classical intervention pattern, particularly in the university-affiliated hospitals where they flourish. They blur the empirical sharpness of the distinction that logic can make between the classical intervention pattern and the newer pattern of therapeutic interaction.

The pattern of *therapeutic interaction* is one that is commonly used, in its essentials, in psychotherapy. It is also, however, a pattern of organization for hospital services, much of which is referred to by psychiatric ideas of a "therapeutic" milieu, and which is implied by Wessen's discussion of the "rehabilitation model."[40] In this pattern, the patient must be persuaded to become an active participant in a process of interaction around therapy; his own motivated activity is an essential part of the pattern. Furthermore, while none but the most radical or most self-deceiving proponents of the pattern would relegate him to a subordinate or even merely equal position, the physician's position is more ambiguous than in the classical intervention pattern. He is legally and usually institutionally in charge of the case, true, but he is not held to have a monopoly over relevant treatment skills, and insofar as he recognizes that all paramedical members of the staff in interaction with the patient have access to information of value to planning therapy and that they cannot fail, in their interaction, to have influence on the patient's response to treatment, the physician must at least act like a member of a therapeutic team. He is likely to have comparatively little on-the-job social distance from his "subordinates," being less the chief and more the first among equals. Indeed, the patient himself is sometimes even held to be a member of the "team," though never to the extent of participating in all staff meetings.[41] The absolute character of the authority of expertise makes itself felt even in this pattern.

Medical Performance in the Hospital

. . . I have emphasized the influence on hospital affairs, and the division of labor embodied in the hospital, by medicine and medical practice. I have done this in spite of the fact that the physician-owned hospital is increasingly rare in modern societies, that community and state are increasingly dominant in setting general hospital policies, that hospital administrators become increasingly the strategic force in setting everyday operative policies in the hospital, and that an increasing number of nonphysician workers in the hospital lay claim to being "professionals" and attempt to behave accordingly.[42] I have adopted this emphasis in part because of my interest in medicine rather than the hospital. More importantly, I believe this emphasis is justified because of the dominant role the physician plays in determining the character of the essential activities that provide the very raison d'être of the hospital—what is done to and for the patient. Increasingly, the physician does not control the financing or the constitutional organization and administration of hospital care, but he nonetheless retains the right to determine what technical and occupational resources are needed by the patient who is under his care. This is . . . typical of a profession. Furthermore, his determinations are not subject to direct evaluation or review by any other occupation: they may be limited by purely administrative or financial decisions made by others, but they may not be directly questioned except by other physicians. This, too, is typical of a profession. His medical performance, therefore, is most likely to vary according to the role his colleagues on the medical staff play in his work and only secondarily in the special characteristics of his work, and in special circumstances of hospital practice, according to the role played by other workers in the division of labor in the hospital. Here, too, as in types of office practice, interaction with his colleagues is the critical variable in the control of his performance.

. . . I have tried to show how variations in the organization of office and hospital practice may exert systematic influence on the performance of medical work. Such variation is hypothesized on a statistical basis, predicting that the *average* performance of the total aggregate of physicians in one work-setting will conform to higher or lower medical standards, or lay standards, than the average performance of the medical population in another work-setting. I have emphasized the importance of the individual's dependence on and close interaction with his medical colleagues. While . . . I have also suggested other factors, including variation in the work itself, which seem to play a part in influencing his performance, colleague interaction is central: the more there is, the more likely medical rather than lay or individual standards will be met. . . .

Notes

1. For an excellent history, see Brian Abel-Smith, *The Hospitals, 1800–1948* (London: William Heinemann, 1964). For a brief history of the development of the hospital, see George Rosen, "The Hospital: Historical Sociology of a Community Institution," in Eliot Freidson, ed., *The Hospital in Modern Society* (New York: The Free Press of Glencoe, 1963), pp. 1–36.
2. "For the paying patient and his physicians, the hospital is primarily a service institution where the physician arranges to treat his patient," Ivan Belknap and John G. Steinle, *The Community and Its Hospitals* (Syracuse: Syracuse University Press, 1963), p. 39.
3. *Webster's New Collegiate Dictionary* (Springfield, Mass.: G. & C. Merriam Co., Publishers, 1959), p. 400.
4. See the findings on the quality of care in proprietary hospitals in New York City in "The Quantity, Quality and Costs of Medical and Hospital Care Secured by a Sample of Teamster Families in the New York Area," Columbia University School of Public Health and Administrative Medicine, n.d.
5. Such a definition is much too simple, as the discussion in Belknap and Steinle, *op. cit.*, indicates.
6. See the discussion of this period of medical domination of hospital policy in Charles Perrow, "Goals and Power Structure: A Historical Case Study," in Freidson, *op. cit.*, pp. 112–146.
7. See Patricia Kendall, "The Relationship Between Medical Educators and Medical Practitioners," *Annals of the New York Academy of Sciences*, CXXVIII (1965), 568–576, for a report of a study of the frictions between those who practice in teaching hospitals and those who practice in the community. See also the material in Raymond S. Duff and August B. Hollingshead, *Sickness and Society* (New York: Harper and Row, 1968), pp. 44–65.
8. See Cecil Sheps *et al.*, "Medical Schools and Hospitals," *Journal of Medical Education*, XL (1965), Part II, pp. 1–169, for extensive discussions of teaching hospitals and their programs.
9. For discussions of organization and function, see C. Wesley Eisele, ed., *The Medical Staff in the Modern Hospital* (New York: McGraw-Hill Book Co., 1967).
10. The most comprehensive sociological treatise on the hospital is Johann Jürgen Rohde, *Soziologie des Krankenhauses* (Stuttgart: Ferdinand Enke, 1962). A very accessible introduction to the American hospital is Temple Burling *et al.*, *The Give and Take in Hospitals* (New York: G. P. Putnam's Sons, 1956). A standard textbook on hospital administration, covering hospital operations very thoroughly, is M. T. McEachern, *Hospital Organization and Management* (Chicago: Physicians Record Co., 1957).
11. One excellent introduction to sociological approaches to the factory is Delbert C. Miller and William H. Form, *Industrial Sociology*, 2nd ed. (New York: Harper and Row, 1964).
12. Victor A. Thompson, *Modern Organization* (New York: Alfred A. Knopf, 1961).
13. See Bernard Barber, *Science and the Social Order* (New York: Collier Books, 1962), pp. 195–198. Erwin O. Smigel, *The Wall Street Lawyer* (New York: The Free Press of Glencoe, 1964), pp. 275–286; and Max Weber, *Theory of Social and Economic Organization* (New York: Oxford University Press, 1947), pp. 392–407.

14. Harvey L. Smith, "Two Lines of Authority Are One too Many," *Modern Hospitals*, LXXXIV (1955), 59–64.
15. William Kornhauser, *Scientists in Industry* (Berkeley: University of California Press, 1962).
16. Oswald Hall, "Some Problems in the Provision of Medical Services," *Canadian Journal of Economics and Political Science*, XX (1954), 456–466.
17. The invocation of "emergency" is a strategic action of some consequence in more than medical affairs. Successful claim of emergency suspends, if not destroys, the normal, the routine, the rational, and the legal. In the most obvious instance, the successful claim of emergency by a government justifies the suspension of civil liberties and due process of law. No one has yet made an extensive sociological analysis of the emergency.
18. See R. E. Coker *et al.*, "Public Health as Viewed by the Medical Student," *American Journal of Public Health*, XLIX (1959), 601–609.
19. Ivan Belknap, *Human Problems of a State Mental Hospital* (New York: McGraw-Hill Book Co., 1956).
20. Note Cartwright's finding that British maternity patients more than others are critical of the care they receive in hospital—apparently because they are often left alone during labor. Medically, maternity patients are not in so critical condition as to be believed to "need" the company of nurse or physician. Ann Cartwright, *Human Relations and Hospital Care* (London: Routledge and Kegan Paul, 1964), pp. 177–188.
21. Perhaps the most important work bearing on the patient's perspective on and resistance to staff procedures is that of Julius A. Roth. See Julius A. Roth and Elizabeth M. Eddy, *Rehabilitation for the Unwanted* (New York: Atherton Press, 1967); Julius A. Roth, "Information and the Control of Treatment in Tuberculosis Hospitals," in Freidson, *op. cit.*, pp. 293–318; and Julius A. Roth, *Timetables* (Indianapolis: Bobbs-Merrill Co., 1963).
22. The tuberculosis patients studied by Roth were of this character, which is perhaps what made them such effective antagonists. For a very useful general discussion of the organized contingencies bearing on the degree to which patients could learn from each other how to manage the ward setting (by resistance or cooperation), see Stanton Wheeler, "The Structure of Formally Organized Socialization Settings," in O. G. Brim, Jr., and Stanton Wheeler, *Socialization after Childhood, Two Essays* (New York: John Wiley & Sons, 1966), pp. 53–113.
23. See D. C. Gilbert and D. J. Levinson, "Role Performance, Ideology and Personality in Mental Hospital Aides," in M. Greenblatt *et al.*, eds., *The Patient and the Mental Hospital* (Glencoe, Illinois: The Free Press, 1957), pp. 197–208; and G. M. Carstairs and A. Heron, "The Social Environment of Mental Hospital Patients: A Measure of Staff Attitudes," in M. Greenblatt, *op. cit.*, pp. 218–230. For patients, see E. Gallagher and D. J. Levinson, *Patienthood* (Boston: Houghton Mifflin Co., 1965).
24. Elaine Cumming and John Cumming, *Closed Ranks, An Experiment in Mental Health Education* (Cambridge: Harvard University Press, 1957).
25. Anselm Strauss *et al.*, *Psychiatric Ideologies and Institutions* (New York: The Free Press of Glencoe, 1964), pp. 54–57. See also the excellent discussion in Richard F. Salisbury, *Structures of Custodial Care* (Berkeley: University of California Press, 1962), pp. 37–40.
26. There is a huge literature on the nurse and her role conflicts . . . For a recent excellent statement, see Hans O. Mauksch, "The Nurse: Coordinator of Patient Care," in James K. Skipper, Jr., and Robert C. Leonard, eds., *Social Interaction and Patient Care* (Philadelphia: J. B. Lippincott Co., 1965), pp. 251–265. And see the extensive discussion in Duff and Hollingshead, *op. cit.*
27. See my discussion of the authoritarian implications of expertise in Eliot Freidson, *Professional Dominance* (New York: Atherton Press, forthcoming), Ch. 6.
28. For discussion of classification by "technology," see Charles Perrow, "Hospitals: Technology, Structure and Goals," in James G. March, ed., *Handbook of Organizations*

(Chicago: Rand-McNally and Co., 1965), pp. 910–971. And see the comments on the noncomparability of hospitals with varying interests in the patient in Mark Lefton and William R. Rosengren, "Organizations and Clients: Lateral and Longitudinal Dimensions," *American Sociological Review*, XXXI (1966), 802–810. It is their lack of recognition of this problem that makes it difficult to evaluate the findings by Basil S. Georgopoulos and Floyd C. Mann, *The Community General Hospital* (New York: The Macmillan Co., 1962).

29. Burling *et al.*, *op. cit.*, Ch. 16.
30. Rose L. Coser, "Authority and Decision-Making in a Hospital," *American Sociological Review*, XXIII (1958), 56–64.
31. Melvin Seeman and John W. Evans, "Stratification and Hospital Care: I. The Performance of the Medical Interne; II. The Objective Criteria of Performance," *American Sociological Review*, XXVI (1961), 67–80, 193–204.
32. Perrow, "Hospitals," *op. cit.*
33. Rose L. Coser, "Alienation and the Social Structure: Case Analysis of a Hospital," in Freidson, *op. cit.*, pp. 231–265.
34. See Roth and Eddy, *op. cit.*, for a study of physically handicapped inmates.
35. See the British survey of homes for the aged—Peter Townsend, *The Last Refuge* (London: Routledge and Kegan Paul, 1962).
36. William A. Caudill, "Around the Clock Patient Care in Japanese Psychiatric Hospitals: The Role of the *Tsukisoi*," *American Sociological Review*, XXVI (1961), 204–214.
37. The value of the invidious word "custodialism," most closely identified with the work of Daniel Levinson, is unfortunately weakened by its confusion of two separate notions. The first notion is a moral one with which all must agree—that no matter how poor or deficient in ordinary human attributes, inmates should receive humane care. The second notion is an article of faith in the therapeutic results of humane management, results by no means established on a sound scientific basis. See Perrow, "Hospitals," *op. cit.*
38. Albert A. Wessen, "The Apparatus of Rehabilitation: An Organizational Analysis," in M. B. Sussman, ed., *Sociology and Rehabilitation* (Washington: American Sociological Association, 1966), pp. 170–173.
39. For a description and evaluation of a training program, see George G. Reader and Mary E. W. Goss, eds., *Comprehensive Medical Care and Teaching* (Ithaca: Cornell University Press, 1967).
40. Wessen, *op. cit.*, pp. 176–178. Obviously relevant here are some of the presently fashionable psychiatric notions of therapeutic "communities." See, for example, Maxwell Jones, *The Therapeutic Community, A New Treatment Method in Psychiatry* (New York: Basic Books, 1953).
41. This "failure" was reported in Robert Rubenstein and Harold D. Lasswell, *The Sharing of Power in a Psychiatric Hospital* (New Haven: Yale University Press, 1966).
42. For data on these and other cross-national trends, see the important essay, William A. Glaser, "American and Foreign Hospitals: Some Sociological Comparisons," in Freidson, *Hospital in Modern Society*, *op. cit.*, pp. 37–72.

Blockages to Organizational Intelligence
Harold L. Wilensky

To explain the great expansion in intelligence and major variations in the employment of experts is not to understand how their work is organized. Nor does it tell us much about variations in the quality of intelligence. And to assert the significance of slogans and preconceptions is not to discover the conditions in which sensible doctrine overcomes the less sensible.

The knowledge explosion intensifies an old problem: how to draw good intelligence from a highly compartmentalized body of knowledge and get it into the room where decisions are made. Sources of failure are legion: even if the initial message is accurate, clear, timely, and relevant, it may be translated, condensed, or completely blocked by personnel standing between the sender and the intended receiver; it may get through in distorted form. If the receiver is in a position to use the message, he may screen it out because it does not fit his preconceptions, because it has come through a suspicious or poorly regarded channel, because it is embedded in piles of inaccurate or useless messages (excessive noise in the channel), or, simply, because too many messages are transmitted to him (information overload).[1]

The disaster at Pearl Harbor is alleged to be an intelligence lesson burned into the minds of general staffs and top planners of national strategy. The failure to take the final crucial step of communicating to commanders the urgent warnings about Japan's intentions supplied by Far Eastern code analysts[2] is said to be due to "the lack of a high level joint intelligence group and the absence of a high echelon organization for national estimates and an indications center."[3] Yet, twenty-five years later, after a reorganization of the intelligence function to incorporate these structural changes, two presidents were led into disastrous military adventures based largely on miscalculation by intelligence agencies communicating at the top misleading pictures of the situation in Cuba, the Dominican Republic, and Vietnam. The vast expansion of the intelligence community has not prevented successes in the uses of intelligence—among them the excellent beach studies done for the Pacific campaign and the identification of the guided missile development center at Peenemünde in World War II, the CIA's forewarning of a Communist attempt to supply arms to the government of Guatemala in May, 1954, and the Defense Department's spotting of Soviet missiles in Cuba. Neither has it prevented a string of fateful failures.[4]

Intelligence failures are rooted in structural problems that cannot be fully solved; they express universal dilemmas of organizational life that can, however, be resolved in various ways at varying costs. In all complex social systems, hierarchy, specialization, and centralization are major sources of distortion and blockage of intelligence. The quality of intelligence is also shaped by the prevailing concepts of intelligence, the problems to be confronted, the stages of growth of

Excerpted from Chapter 3 of *Organizational Intelligence: Knowledge and Policy in Government and Industry*, by Harold L. Wilensky, © 1967 by Harold L. Wilensky, Basic Books, Inc., Publishers, New York.

the organization, and the economic, political, and cultural contexts of decision. To explore problems in the organization of the intelligence function, this chapter will employ a military analogy . . . developing propositions and using examples with wide application to government and industry.

Hierarchy

Insofar as the problem of control—coordinating specialists, getting work done, securing compliance—is solved by rewards of status, power, and promotion, the problem of obtaining accurate, critical intelligence is intensified. For information is a resource that symbolizes status, enhances authority, and shapes careers. In reporting at every level, hierarchy is conducive to concealment and misrepresentation. Subordinates are asked to transmit information that can be used to evaluate their performance. Their motive for "making it look good," for "playing it safe," is obvious. A study of 52 middle managers (mean age 37) found a correlation of +.41 ($p < .01$) between upward work-life mobility and holding back "problem" information from the boss; the men on their way up were prone to restrict information about such issues as lack of authority to meet responsibilities, fights with other units, unforeseen costs, rapid changes in production, scheduling or work flow, fruitless progress reports, constant interruptions, insufficient time or budget to train subordinates, insufficient equipment or supplies, and so on.[5] Restriction of such problem information is motivated by the desire not only to please but also to preserve comfortable routines of work: if the subordinate alerts the boss to pending trouble, the former is apt to find himself on a committee to solve the problem. The aphorism "Never volunteer for anything" is not confined to the Army; it is part of folk wisdom.

In addition to motive for holding back and distorting, there must be a corresponding opportunity. Middle-level managers, and even lower-level employees, sometimes have a near monopoly of insight into feasible alternatives. For instance, observers of man-paced factory jobs have noted the ingenuity of machinists who invent and hide cutting tools that do the work more efficiently than the prescribed ways and thereby permit more worker control of the pace. Although automation and centralization may change this, first-line supervisors still have indispensable practical knowledge of both unofficial work behavior and "bugs" in the technical system; and local plant managers in multiplant systems know the limits of their productive capacities far better than does central headquarters.[6]

Matching the motive and opportunity of the subordinate to remain silent are the superior's motive and opportunity to close his ears. The common belief that staff experts should be on tap, not on top, functions to maintain line authority and reduce the status of the staff. It acts as a self-fulfilling prophecy: the advice of low-status intelligence specialists, however good, can readily be discounted. In the Pearl Harbor case, on December 5, after weeks of being ignored as mere data collectors, subordinate officers in subordinate intelligence and research units tried to communicate their more urgent interpretations directly to the chiefs of Army and Navy war plans. "But their efforts were unsuccessful because of the poor repute associated with Intelligence, inferior rank, and the province of the specialist, or long-hair."[7]

Thus, if an organization has many ranks and if in its administrative style and symbolism it emphasizes rank, the greatest distortion and blockage will attend the upward flow of information. Organizations vary greatly in the prominence given to status display—through insignia (from the single, thin gold stripe of the cadet to the many wide stripes of the admiral); through office decor (from the gray plastic and metal desks of the stenographer to the spacious custom-made rosewood of the "top dog," from asphalt tile to one-inch pile); through forms of address (from Charlie to Mr., Sir, Your Honor, Your Excellency); and through language (from the regional dialect of the janitor to the special accent of the Oxford don). Status symbols serve to motivate performance, legitimize positions, and facilitate some kinds of communication. Without stable, comfortable, certified ways of talking and writing to one another, without observance of the rules of deference and demeanor, people of different rank or different function do not easily maintain harmony. But the harmony is achieved at the cost of lowering the quality of intelligence channeled to the top; and the symbolism tends to metastasize.[8]

Afraid that they are being deceived or kept in the dark, men at the top take action: they emphasize criteria for loyalty in recruitment and promotion, uniform indoctrination, and other efforts to create organization men. These "solutions" in turn complicate the intelligence problem: fewer fresh slants, new ideas, and critical questions will be lodged in the system or work their way to the top. A major reason for the American bank's reputation for hidebound conservatism is a hierarchical structure infused with status symbolism, which attracts and shapes conventional, bureaucratic men whose conformity limits innovation.[9] Hierarchy blocks communication; blockages lead to indoctrination; indoctrination narrows the range of communication.

Of course, information can be introduced into the system at any level; the higher it enters, the less subject it is to the processes that distort. Even the Assistant to the President, however, may have both motive and opportunity to hold back information, the more so if he has himself risen through the ranks.

The shape of the hierarchy—not merely the number of ranks but also the number of personnel at each level—conditions the upward flow of information. Where the pyramid is tall and narrows sharply at the top, providing a long promotion ladder for a few, there are many time servers at lower ranks who have neither information nor the motive for acquiring it. In the middle, among the non-mobile, there are many defensive cliques who restrict information to prevent change, many mutual aid and comfort groups who restrict information because of their resentment of their more ambitious colleagues, and many coalitions of ambitious men who share information among themselves but pass on only the portion that furthers one or more of their careers. For the purposes of intelligence, the optimal shape of the hierarchy would be relatively flat (few ranks permit a speedier diffusion of more accurate information) with a bulge in the middle (more specialists who have information and more potential managers motivated to command it).

Whatever the shape of the hierarchy, however, to extract information from those who have it typically requires the bypassing of conventional ranking systems. Efforts to resolve the dilemma of hierarchy vs. intelligence include team or project organization, devices for communicating out of channels, machinery for investigation and inspection, performance checks, and reliance on informed outsiders.

The higher in the hierarchy one goes, the less do problems correspond to the specialized structure of knowledge and the less a decision can be programmed.

Only at the lower levels of policy deliberation can the specialized expert tackle a specialized problem with a chance of solving it by the precise methods of science.[10] Further, at any level, the role of the expert is self-changing: if he is successful within his sphere of competence, if his advice is taken on matters where his specialized knowledge is relevant, he is likely to be chosen for tasks outside that sphere of competence, where his specialized knowledge may be irrelevant.[11] This is why there is so urgent a demand for generalized advisers at the top. It is also why an appropriate form of organization for industrial research and development or, more broadly, for the use of experts anywhere, is the task force—a team or project of diverse specialists who are brought together to solve a limited range of problems and then are reassigned when the task is done. Several swiftly growing corporations based on sophisticated technology, such as the IBM Corporation, have adopted this form.[12] The great advantages of the task force are flexibility, informality, the release of individual initiative, and above all the swift diffusion of information both within the team and, as team members are reassigned, throughout the organization. The disadvantage is that teams, exempt from standard rules of procedure, ambiguous in status and authority, are difficult to fit into the hierarchy or into established professional niches—prime reasons for their tendency to transform themselves into permanent specialist groups.[13] It is possible that the task force is best for higher policy deliberations and crisis situations— as in the Cuban missile crisis—and for policy-oriented research or technical development, whereas other forms of organization are appropriate for basic research.

Additional defenses against the information pathologies of hierarchy are various reporting services and statistical controls. These include the "score card" and "attention-directing" uses of accounting data in business—cost variances of individual departments, trend reports on "invisible" operations (machine performance, consumption of operating supplies), accounting statements for "profit centers"—and special "problem-solving" studies (of alternative processes, equipment, products), again done by teams, drawing on accounting information, engineering estimates, and industrial engineering standards.[14] In interpreting such data, top executives, even in very hierarchical organizations, are not entirely defenseless: they have built up a sense of reasonableness regarding performance reports; they can check submitted data for consistency. Finally, there is a universal performance check in every type of economy: the quality of performance of one organization is known by other organizations that receive its products; the metal fabricator who must work with defective steel in the Soviet Union will complain no less than his counterpart in the United States.[15]

Perhaps the most fruitful and common response to hierarchy is communication out of channels: contact men, on salary or retainer, keep in touch with outsiders who have a detached or critical view of the organization; internal communications specialists, some of whom combine close ties to local leaders and loyalties to central headquarters, report on local performance and morale. A variety of marginal men at points along the organization's boundaries supply supplementary and often crucial intelligence.

Modern military services evidence all of these responses to hierarchy. Like executives everywhere, military elites have moved from coercion and command to persuasion and manipulation: instead of a pyramidal structure, a diamond bulging in the middle; instead of ritualistic close-order drill, an accent on the training mission; instead of a mechanical assimilation of the Army way, a reduction in symbols of rank (less spit and polish, less diversity of dress); instead of standing operating procedure (SOP), group command conferences and informal briefings, bypassing normal channels.[16]

Specialization and Rivalry

As a source of information blockage and distortion, specialization may be more powerful than hierarchy. The organization of the armed forces and industry alike encourages rivalry and restriction of information. Each service, each division, indeed every subunit, becomes a guardian of its own mission, standards, and skills; lines of organization become lines of loyalty and secrecy. In industry, the personnel department defends its control over selection and training; accounting, its standards of reporting; production, its schedules of output; sales, its interests in product design and customer service—each restricting information that might advance the competing interests of the others. Top men in each are reluctant to let their subordinates "take on" rivals by asking for information for fear that their unit will betray weakness, invite counter-inquiries, or incur debt. While information can also be used to persuade potential allies and to facilitate accommodation with rivals (see discussion of the "rational-responsible" bias above), it is more commonly hoarded for selective use in less collaborative struggles for power and position.

In the armed forces, intense rivalries between services and within services—among supply and procurement, plans and operations, research and development, intelligence—lead to intelligence failures. Combined with the hierarchical distortions already mentioned, they can be fatal. In 1941, the signals of the pending attack on Pearl Harbor lay scattered in a number of rival agencies; communication lines linked them but essential messages never flowed across the lines, let alone to the top. The Army and Navy presented a picture of cordial, respectful communication, empty of solid substance.[17] In foreign affairs, the history of intelligence failures in the major capitals hints that the foreign office, the military, and the intelligence agencies seldom if ever form an effective three-way communication network. In the Bay of Pigs fiasco of 1961, for instance, the intelligence branch of the CIA was out of touch with the operations branch, which was planning the adventure; operations was only loosely in touch with the Joint Chiefs, who loosely went along; the CIA kept both President Kennedy and the Cuban exiles uninformed; the President approved a plan on the assumption of two possible outcomes, national revolt or flight to the hills—neither remotely possible; activists in the CIA and the Joint Chiefs rejected the more accurate intelligence of the Department of State (which never pressed it hard), of the British, and of alert newspaper reporters, because that intelligence contradicted the assumptions of the plan they were determined to launch.[18]. . .

The dilemma of intelligence vs. specialization is twofold: specialization is essential to the efficient command of knowledge but antithetical to the penetrating interpretation that bears on high policy; specialization and its concomitant, inter-unit rivalry, frequently block the sharing of accurate information, but if problems of upward communication can be solved, rivalry can result in great gains—the clarification of clashing alternatives and the presentation of opposing cases. The primary cost of specialization in intelligence is parochialism—the production of misleading or irrelevant information, a product of the familiar limitations of the expert.[19] The professionally biased producer of intelligence remains too distant from the intelligence user, too ignorant of policy needs, and is forced to compete with other producers for the support and guidance of the user.[20] No less obvious is the value of efficiency, that is, economy, speed, and accuracy in the performance of a task. A translator of a foreign newspaper may work better in a translation section, an economist expert in the economy of Rumania works better in the company of other social scientists concerned with Eastern Europe. The gain from constructive rivalry is another matter; it depends on administrative styles and structures that expedite the free flow of rival perspectives and solutions to the responsible executives and their general advisers.

To resolve this structural dilemma, especially in organizations dependent on technical intelligence, administrative leaders use the following devices: they recruit managers from professional or scientific staff (e.g., several top executives of the Du Pont Company have experience in their research laboratories); they bind specialists in the field closely and informally to the home staff via rotation, frequent conferences, and career lines that lead from the field to central headquarters; they expose themselves systematically to intelligence by examining multiple sources firsthand and sometimes by stimulating competition between sources.

President Franklin D. Roosevelt, despite his reputation for disorderly administration, was apparently a master of the last two techniques. "The first task of an executive, as he evidently saw it, was to guarantee himself an effective flow of information and ideas. . . . Roosevelt's persistent effort therefore was to check and balance information acquired through official channels by information acquired through a myriad of private informal and unorthodox channels and espionage networks. At times he seemed almost to pit his personal sources against his public sources."[21] He would tell his peripatetic wife, Eleanor, "'Watch the people's faces. Look at the condition of their clothes on the wash line. You can tell a lot from that. Notice their cars.'" Upon her return from a trip, the President would question her carefully.[22] As the war years approached, he worked closely with Hull and Welles but he often communicated directly with ambassadors and ministers, and in a restless search for ideas and expedients turned to a wide range of contacts outside the State Department—Ickes, Hopkins, Wallace, Cox, Baruch, the Pope, a host of friends abroad.[23]

Not only did Roosevelt rely heavily on unofficial channels, but he also fostered competition within: he would use one anonymous informant's information to challenge and check another's, putting both on their toes; he recruited strong personalities and structured their work so that clashes would be certain. "His favorite technique was to keep grants of authority incomplete, jurisdictions uncertain, charters overlapping."[24] In foreign affairs, he gave Moley and Welles tasks that overlapped those of Secretary of State Hull; in conservation and power, he gave Ickes and Wallace identical missions; in welfare, confusing both functions and initials, he assigned PWA to Ickes, WPA to Hopkins; in politics, Farley found himself competing with other political advisers for control over patronage.[25] The effect: the timely advertisement of arguments, with both the experts and the President pressured to consider the main choices as they came boiling up from below. Roosevelt was willing to suffer the cost: a drain on his subordinates' energies as well as his own, and an occasional casualty—a bitter resignation by a lieutenant who had lost the struggle once too often. . . .

The gains of calculated competition cannot be secured, however, if top decision-makers insulate themselves from the squabbles of their subordinates and force rival departments urging rival doctrines to settle differences in committee. President Eisenhower, for instance, made the National Security Council "the climax of a ponderous system of boards, staffs and interdepartmental committees through which national security policy was supposed to rise to the top."[26] As a result, the NSC was converted into a forum for intramural negotiations; what Dean Acheson called "agreement by exhaustion" blurred policy discord.[27] An ironic feature of such a system is that men of good will are moved to obfuscate their positions and overstate agreements with their rivals, on behalf of an ultimate consensus—"doves" try to impress "hawks" with their caution and toughness; hardliners sometimes try to show that they, too, are for peace.[28] The Joint Chiefs of Staff has also been more a place for courteous confusion and maneuver than a deliberative forum. When they cannot cope with issues by glittering generalities representing the lowest common denominator of agreement, such supercommittees avoid controversial issues entirely, delay decisions, refer issues to other committees, or engage in logrolling, as when the Navy trades off support for more Air Force wings in return for Air Force support for more Navy carriers.[29] Sharp questions, cogent arguments, minority positions, a clear calculation of gains and costs are lost to view.

A much discussed but little studied problem is the effect on the quality of intelligence of various bases for dividing work. We can speculate that of the typical bases—problem, project, or task (promoting employment opportunity for minorities), purpose or program (vocational rehabilitation), discipline, skill, or process (sociology, community organization, casework), industry branch or clientele (building trades, Negro youth), geography (San Francisco County)—the only one that seems generally weak for the purposes of intelligence is geographical unit. Gaps in service can be rooted in any or all of these grounds for specialization,[30] but intelligence failures are greatest if location is emphasized.

The chief limitations of specialization by territory are three. First, good intelligence cuts across arbitrary political boundaries; it is oriented toward problem, program, or discipline. One would expect an economic aid desk, a market research desk, an office of the scientific adviser, to be on the average more analytical than a State Department country desk. The success of the Council of Economic Advisers rests in part on specialization by discipline and problem. . . . Second, insofar as efficiency is at issue, territorial specialization overelaborates administrative apparatus and makes transfer of resources and information from one locality to another more difficult. It also spreads scarce technical staff too thin; attempts to duplicate staff services in every jurisdiction encounter manpower shortages.[31] Finally, in systems where the most skilled men tend to move to the top, an accent on locality will leave intelligence in the hands of the less able.

These points are evident in the recurrent subversion of attempts at regional decentralization in the Soviet Union. Whenever regional organizations have been officially made the dominant body, functional administrators in Gosplan and state committees—men concerned with supplies, innovation, investment, construction, strategic industries—were either given great power or were able to reassert their power within a short period.[32] Even in post-World War II Italy—with its highly politicized system of prefectural administration and its relatively meager level of government services—clashes between field directors of specialized state services and the regionally dominant prefects have been more and more resolved in favor of the specialists, particularly in the areas of public health and veterinary medicine.[33] . . .

The weakness of specialization by territory or locality is less apparent in contexts where program and policy are fluid and local operating conditions are highly varied and unstable—usually at a very early stage in an organization's life cycle. Here external forces may necessitate considerable decentralization of authority and with it some specialization of intelligence by territory. Typically the support of local populations must be mobilized, as in farm production control programs, or new services sold, as in adult education or the relocation of rural populations. Often the cooperation of officials in local bodies must be enlisted.[34] Above all, the regional chief must have at his command good intelligence on the pattern of local power and influence. This is important both for a sensitive interpretation of high policy in the light of local conditions and for neutralizing local interests that would subvert program goals. Furthermore, successful adaptation of high policy rests to some extent on feedback to central headquarters of information on local performance.[35]

It is paradoxical that in the early stages of organizational growth, when the need for local political intelligence is greatest, the need for centralization of authority—for the definition of goals and the indoctrination of personnel at the top[36]—is also greatest. Reinforced by the high costs of specialization by locality, the imperatives of central control understandably dominate.

In short, the merit of any basis of specialization depends on the mission to be accomplished . . . but specialization by locality is seldom effective for the purposes of intelligence.

The firmest generalization we can derive from this chapter so far is that the greater the number of ranks and the greater the number of organizational units involved in a decision process, the more the distorting influence of rank and jurisdiction and, consequently, the greater the chance of an intelligence failure. It is likely that staff experts communicate most freely with colleagues in the same specialty, second with colleagues in the same unit of the workplace, then to subordinates, and last—with greatest blockage and distortion—to superiors and rival agencies.

Centralization

Related to the information pathologies of hierarchy and specialization is the dilemma of centralization: if intelligence is lodged at the top, too few officials and experts with too little accurate and relevant information are too far out of touch and too overloaded to function effectively; on the other hand, if intelligence is scattered throughout many subordinate units, too many officials and experts with too much specialized information may engage in dysfunctional competition, may delay decisions while they warily consult each other, and may distort information as they pass it up.[37] More simply, plans are manageable only if we delegate; plans are coordinated in relation to organizational goals only if we centralize.

Central intelligence (e.g., a CIA) presents the same dangers as specialized intelligence: it keeps data collection too far from its outlet in useful policy; it encourages agreed-on estimates that conceal strong disagreement and the weights of diverse opinions (only partly offset by devices that themselves result from horsetrading and logrolling—e.g., the dissenting footnote); and it competes with its own subsidiaries for scarce personnel and documentation facilities.[38] Centralization contributes one additional danger peculiar to itself: the acquisition of unnecessary responsibility ("empire building") is always accompanied by cries of duplication and inefficiency among the units to be absorbed or eliminated. After administrative reform, a more unified, centralized intelligence agency, producing a unified consensual judgment, then fosters the illusion of security, of reliable intelligence, which, as the Bay of Pigs invasion illustrates, can conceal fantasies at the highest level.

In the minds of political, military, and industrial elites the advantages of centralized intelligence have apparently tended to outweigh these dangers. Most executives have been less concerned about preserving the independence and objectivity of their experts than about controlling them. For their part, the experts, seeing a chance for greater influence, have not been loath to secure guidance from the top. And in the organization of national strategic intelligence, the image of Pearl Harbor—the signals scattered, no central interpretive agency alert to them—has been commanding.

This debate about departmental or local vs. central or national intelligence has obscured two fundamental points. First, there is need for interpretive skills at every point where important decisions are taken; the ideal is the close integration of data collection and evaluation in every department and division, and, within the limits of budget and personnel, at every level.[39] Second, various degrees and kinds of decentralization are appropriate for various purposes and measures of effectiveness and types of intelligence. If the pathologies of hierarchy and speciali- zation can be minimized, decentralization of intelligence can be effective, but the one decisive argument against it is usually the costs. Staff experts such as scien- tists, statisticians, economists, accountants, and lawyers are expensive; the supply is limited. This typically dictates a concentration of intelligence at headquarters.

In single-purpose organizations where operating conditions at the local level are roughly uniform, and where the intelligence flow tends to involve technical communication between like-minded specialists or professionals, centralization of intelligence presents few serious problems. A study of the administrative structure of the United States Forest Service indicates an almost complete concentration of intelligence in Washington, where field-unit budgetary allocations are decided, business with other government agencies carried on, and major and minor policy changes conceived.[40] Centrifugal tendencies, reflecting somewhat varying field conditions, exist. But a tight administrative structure and smooth flow of informa- tion are maintained by recruitment, indoctrination, and rotation—the same de- vices used to cope with the costs of specialization. . . . Only men with an ardent love of the outdoors, uniform professional training in forestry, and a strong commitment to a career in the Forest Service are recruited and survive the basic training period. Nine in ten of the approximately 4,000 employees of the Service are graduates of forestry schools; when in college, many held summer jobs in the forests. They share a common lore, similar technical knowledge, and identification even before embarking on ranger training.[41] When they become rangers, they find themselves moving about from post to post, not necessarily upward; in fact, horizontal transfers, while not compulsory, are generally a prerequisite for ad- vancement.[42] Both rotation and the inculcation of the values of the Forest Service facilitate communication between headquarters and the field by keeping loyalties and career interests centrally directed.[43] Rotation and indoctrination also keep the foresters independent of private interests in the regions or communities in which they serve; the training shared at every level fosters communication of problem information up the line.[44] The classic intelligence problem of branch plant or field unit "covering up" (i.e., rigging performance figures or hiding local problems) is minimized. Infused with professionalism, imbued with *esprit de corps*, the Forest Service is able to centralize intelligence resources, yet do without close supervision and elaborate enforcement and inspection machinery. . . .

Other organizations with more diffuse or diversified goals are not so fortunate. Where field or branch products and local operating conditions vary, surveillance machinery proliferates. Such machinery is often ineffectual—especially where the local people must submit to inspection either by those outside their profession or specialty (headquarters accountants checking factory production managers) or by those of different ideological persuasion (politically appointed vocational training directors of particular states confronting educational reformers from the U.S. Office of Education). Where the social and doctrinal distance between inspectors and local operators is great, the resulting information blockage may imperil top leaders' awareness of and accommodation to local problems as well as their ability to communicate new goals to local units.

That the appropriate degree and kind of decentralization depend on the intelligence mission is best shown in a study of the controller's department in seven multi-plant companies, a study that also provides leads for solutions to the dilemmas of centralization.[45] It found that while all the controller's departments aimed to provide high-quality information services at minimum cost and, incidentally, to facilitate the training of accounting and operating executives, the effectiveness of decentralization depended on the type of information to be provided. If the primary aim is to keep score ("Are we doing well or badly?") and to direct attention ("What problems should we look into?"), then it is best to hire competent professional men who look to the controller's department for promotion, attach them to local factories and district offices, and put them under the factory manager. The formula is much geographical decentralization, some decentralization of formal authority, but very limited decentralization of loyalty. For the purpose of keeping score, the decentralization of location and authority makes it easier to gain access to resource documents and to know the reliability of source records. The accountant is close to the operating situation where the data originate. For the purpose of directing attention, such decentralization gives operating executives direct and active contact with accounting people, and thus more confidence in the operating standards and performance reports going to the boss (e.g., factory managers can negotiate standards of local performance and explain off-standard performance). For the purpose of preserving the quality of data available to central headquarters for special studies and big policy ("Shall we purchase new equipment, close this plant, develop this product?"), it is equally important to encourage loyalty to the controller's department through recruitment of professionally committed men who look there for promotion. With rare exceptions these men felt a conflict between maintaining accounting standards and getting along with factory management by not reporting unpleasant facts. But even in the most decentralized company (Eastman Kodak) they adhered to company-wide, professionally set accounting procedures. The formal organization put them close enough to the situation to be accepted by factory management and to obtain roughly accurate information; at the same time, career-line loyalty and professional identification provided enough social support for them to apply standards.

In short, there is a balance to be struck among various kinds of decentralization—of records, of location, of authority, of loyalty, and of channels of communication—an optimal or at least "workable" set of gains and losses depending upon the purposes to be pursued. This is an area where research has barely begun. . . .

Notes

1. When appropriate search procedures have been employed but the relevant message is not in the system, or when the intended receiver is not in a position to act on it (he is clearly constrained by forces beyond his control), we cannot call the instance an intelligence failure.
2. Roberta Wohlstetter, *Pearl Harbor: Warning and Decision* (Stanford: Stanford University Press, 1962), pp. 125 ff., 310 ff., 395.
3. Harry Howe Ransom, *Central Intelligence and National Security* (Cambridge: Harvard University Press, 1958), p. 58. Cf. *ibid.*, pp. 41, 54–56, *passim*.
4. For examples see Ransom, pp. 60 ff., and Richard C. Snyder and Glenn D. Paige, "The United States Decision to Resist Aggression in Korea," in *Foreign Policy Decision-Making: An Approach to the Study of International Politics*, ed. by Richard C. Snyder, H. W. Bruck, and Burton Sapin (New York: The Free Press, 1962), pp. 206–249.
5. See the unpubl. diss. (University of Michigan, 1959) by W. Read, "Factors Affecting Upward Communication at Middle Management Levels in Industrial Organizations."
6. Cf. William F. Whyte, *Money and Motivation* (New York: Harper & Brothers, 1955); Leonard R. Sayles, *Behavior of Industrial Work Groups: Prediction and Control* (New York: John Wiley & Sons, 1958); Benjamin Ward, *The Socialist Economy: A Study of Organizational Alternatives* (New York: Random House, 1967); and Melville Dalton, *Men Who Manage: Fusions of Feeling and Theory in Administration* (New York: John Wiley & Sons, 1959).
7. Wohlstetter, pp. 102, 312.
8. Cf. Chester I. Barnard, "Functions and Pathology of Status Systems in Formal Organizations," in *Industry and Society*, ed. by William Foote Whyte (New York: McGraw-Hill Book Co., 1946), pp. 46–83; Delbert C. Miller and William H. Form, *Industrial Sociology: The Sociology of Work Organizations*, 2nd edn. (New York: Harper & Row, 1964), pp. 476 ff.; and Tom Burns and G. M. Stalker, *The Management of Innovation* (London: Tavistock Publications, 1961), pp. 150–154.
9. See Chris Argyris, *Organization of a Bank* (New Haven: Labor and Management Center, Yale University, 1954), for description of the "Friendly First Bank."
10. Cf. Don K. Price, *Government and Science: Their Dynamic Relation in American Democracy* (New York: New York University Press, 1954), p. 164.
11. Harold L. Wilensky, *Intellectuals in Labor Unions: Organizational Pressures on Professional Roles* (Glencoe: The Free Press, 1956), p. 209 ff.
12. Cf. Herbert A. Shepard, "Nine Dilemmas in Industrial Research," *Administrative Science Quarterly*, I (December, 1956) 295–309; and Fred H. Goldner, "Demotion in Industrial Management," *American Sociological Review*, XXX (October, 1965), 714–724.
13. Cf. William Kornhauser, *Scientists in Industry: Conflict and Accommodation* (Berkeley and Los Angeles: University of California Press, 1962), pp. 50 ff.; and Burns and Stalker, pp. 88 ff.
14. Herbert A. Simon, Harold Guetzkow, George Kozmetsky, and Gordon Tyndall, *Centralization vs. Decentralization in Organizing the Controller's Department* (New York: American Book-Stratford Press, 1954).
15. Cf. Ward.
16. Morris Janowitz, *The Professional Soldier: A Social and Political Portrait* (Glencoe: The Free Press, 1960), pp. 38 ff. Cf. Burns and Stalker, pp. 77–96, 118–125.
17. Wohlstetter, pp. 385–395.
18. Herbert Lionel Matthews, *The Cuban Story* (New York: G. Braziller, 1961); Theodore

C. Sorensen, *Kennedy* (New York: Harper & Row, 1965); Arthur M. Schlesinger, Jr., *A Thousand Days: John F. Kennedy in the White House* (Boston: Houghton Mifflin, 1965).

19. Harold J. Laski, *The Limitations of the Expert* (London: The Fabian Society, 1931).
20. Sherman Kent, *Strategic Intelligence* (Princeton: Princeton University Press, 1949), pp. 81, 94 ff.
21. Arthur M. Schlesinger, Jr., *The Age of Roosevelt*, Vol. II: *The Coming of the New Deal* (Boston: Houghton Mifflin, 1959), pp. 522–523; cf. Robert E. Sherwood, *Roosevelt and Hopkins* (Bantam Edn., revised and enlarged. 2 vols. New York: Harper & Brothers, 1948), I, p. 62 ff.
22. James MacGregor Burns, *Roosevelt: The Lion and the Fox,* Harvest paperback edn. (New York: Harcourt, Brace and World, 1956), p. 173.
23. To what extent FDR's foreign policy failures and successes in the late 1930's can be attributed to such a casual variety of intelligence sources is a moot question.
24. Schlesinger, *The Age of Roosevelt*, p. 528.
25. Burns, pp. 173, 252, 371 ff.; Sherwood, pp. 86 ff.
26. Schlesinger, *A Thousand Days*, p. 209.
27. Schlesinger, *ibid.* Cf. Paul Y. Hammond, *Organizing For Defense: The American Military Establishment in the Twentieth Century* (Princeton: Princeton University Press, 1961), pp. 357 ff.; and Stefan T. Possony, "Organized Intelligence: The Problem of the French General Staff," *Social Research*, VIII (May 1941), pp. 226–227.
28. Cf. Theodore C. Sorensen, *Decision-making in the White House* (New York: Columbia University Press, 1963), pp. 62–63.
29. Cf. Samuel P. Huntington, *The Common Defense: Strategic Programs in National Politics* (New York and London: Columbia University Press, 1961), pp. 162 ff.; Hammond, pp. 336, 357 ff.
30. For examples from the welfare field see Harold L. Wilensky and Charles N. Lebeaux, *Industrial Society and Social Welfare* (paperbound edition with new introduction. New York: The Free Press, 1965), pp. 248 ff.
31. The "spreading-thin" argument is also used against the decentralization of intelligence. . . . The losses of locality specialization and those of decentralization, while analytically distinct, are nevertheless often closely related in concrete situations.
32. Ward; P. J. D. Wiles, *The Political Economy of Communism* (Cambridge: Harvard University Press, 1962), pp. 161 ff.; and Alec Nove, *The Soviet Economy* (New York: Frederick A. Praeger, 1961), pp. 67–96, 195–217.
33. Robert C. Fried, *The Italian Prefects: A Study in Administrative Politics* (New Haven: Yale University Press, 1963), pp. 266 ff.
34. Note, for instance, the TVA's commitment to "grassroots democracy." Philip Selznick, *TVA and the Grass Roots: A Study in the Sociology of Formal Organization* (Berkeley and Los Angeles: University of California Press, 1949).
35. Cf. James W. Fesler, "Field Organization" in *Elements of Public Administration,* ed. by Fritz Morstein Marx, 2nd edn. (Englewood Cliffs: Prentice-Hall, 1959), pp. 256–258.
36. Philip Selznick, *Leadership in Administration: A Sociological Interpretation* (Evanston: Row, Peterson & Co., 1957).
37. Cf. Wiles, pp. 141 ff.; Ward; and Kent, p. 81.
38. Cf. Ransom, pp. 81, 94, 197 ff.
39. Cf. Benno Wasserman, "The Failure of Intelligence Prediction," *Political Studies*, VIII (June 1960), pp. 156–169; and Kent, p. 81.
40. Herbert Kaufman, *The Forest Ranger: A Study in Administrative Behavior* (Baltimore: Johns Hopkins Press, 1960), pp. 68, 114, 209.
41. *Ibid.,* pp. 162 ff.
42. *Ibid.,* pp. 162 ff. The Federal Bureau of Investigation (FBI) displays similar administrative processes: for its agents it prefers lawyers and accountants; it accents strong prior commitment, heavy indoctrination, and frequent rotation.

43. *Ibid.*, pp. 165, 175, 197, 214 ff.
44. *Ibid.*, pp. 75, 176, 215–217.
45. Simon *et al.*

C. Structure and Technology

Operations Technology and Organizational Structure: An Empirical Reappraisal

David J. Hickson, D. S. Pugh, and Diana C. Pheysey

How far does technology determine the form taken by the structure of an organization?

There has been extensive research at the group and individual level of analysis, which has shown the close connection between the technology adopted, the tasks which are then performed by operatives (blue collar or white collar), and their interpersonal interaction, social norms, satisfaction, and attitudes. The seminal studies by Trist and Bamforth (1951) and by Walker and Guest (1952) have been followed by a range of work in which the studies by Blauner (1964), Herbst (1962), Lodahl (1964), Mann and Hoffman (1960), and Sayles (1958) are examples of the variety available. Outstanding contributions towards the operationalization and measurement of technological characteristics have been made by Bright (1958) and by Turner and Lawrence (1965).

But at this group and individual level, the unit of analysis has not been the organization, and formal structural features have been incidental, as they have been at the level of the societal or macro-economic approach. This goes back as far as the thinking of Marx (in Bottomore and Rubel, 1956) on the technological basis of the divorce of capital from labor, and of Durkheim (1947) on the division of labor. Latterly, comparisons have been made across nations and across industries; as for example, Gibbs and Browning (1966), and Florence (1961); and attempts have been made to indicate technological change by econometric equations combining statistics of output, capital invested, and the like, as for example, in Brown (1966) and Lave (1966).

Technology at the Level of the Organization

Few have made technology at the level of the *organization* their focus. . . . Thus the importance of technology to the structure of an organization continues as an open issue. Exponents of classical management theory such as Fayol (1949), Urwick (1947), Brech (1957), and Drucker (1955) have striven to put forward principles which would apply irrespective of task and technology. Brown (1960) who recognized that his own case for explicit formal structure was based on experience in one industry only, generalized from there. On the other hand, among the behavioral scientists, Dubin (1958) drew attention to the impact of technology on the world of work; Perrow (1967) suggested that a view of organizations as technological systems offers a better basis for comparing and comprehending them; and Walker (1962) thought that the historical movement from *line* organization to *line and staff* was due to growing technical complexity. This view

Reprinted in part from *Administrative Science Quarterly*, vol. 14 (September 1969), pp. 378–397, by permission.

was supported by Woodward's (1958, 1965) claim that only differences in technology, and not in other variables, such as size or historical background, were related to structural differences. Udy's (1959) results are in the same direction, though his data were crude and of tenuous relevance to industrialized societies.

Objective of this Study

The objective of the research reported here is to test this proposition of the "technological imperative" at the organizational level of analysis.[1] It tests the broad hypothesis that technology and structure are strongly related, utilizing data from a wider study (Pugh *et al.*, 1969a, 1969b) of the context of organization structure (context including size, ownership, dependence, operations technology, etc.).

This paper describes a classification of concepts of technology, and the operationalization of the concept used in this study. Three tests of the hypothesis are reported, first on 46 diverse organizations, then on the 31 manufacturing organizations of this larger sample, and finally again on the 31 manufacturing organizations, but with a measure of technology designed specifically for manufacturing industry. Only seven variables of structure were found to be related to technology, but from these and from the reconciliation of the overall negative results with Woodward's (1958, 1965) seemingly contradictory outcome, a revised hypothesis is developed.

Concept of Technology: A Classification

Conceptualization of an organization's technology is still at a stage where the word technology may have varying meanings. The concept has three facets, which taken together encompass the range of meanings that have been developed; *operations technology, materials technology, and knowledge technology.*

The concept of *operations technology* is used by Pugh *et al.* who define an organization's technology as "the techniques that it uses in its workflow activities" (1963:310). To Thompson and Bates it is "those sets of man-machine activities which together produce a desired good or service" (1957:325), a view represented later in the "serial interdependence" of acts in Thompson's (1967) "long-linked technology." Udy (1959), Woodward (1958, 1965), and Burack (1966, 1967) all base their operationalizations on this view. The concept may be defined as the *equipping and sequencing of activities in the workflow.* The term workflow is taken from Bakke (1959) to mean producing and distributing the output. In the wide sense it is not only factories that have workflows, but also public utilities and service organizations. A transport undertaking has equipment (buses) and a sequence of operations (bus routes). An insurance office has its pens, paper, and calculating machines, and sequences of operations in the issuing of policies, obtaining of premiums, and meeting of claims.

Materials technology, an element in the construction of Perrow's (1967) theoretical scheme, broadens the notion of technology beyond the bounds so far described. . . . This concept of technology concerns characteristics of the *materials used in the workflow.*

Knowledge technology is a concept developed in this field primarily by Perrow (1967). The generalized view of organizations as systems functioning under uncertainty, epitomized by Cyert and March's (1963) approach, is applied by

Perrow to the workflow as "the number of exceptional cases encountered in the work" (1967:195) and the degree of logical analysis achieved. . . . Knowledge technology is therefore the characteristics of the *knowledge used in the workflow*.

The overlap between concepts of technology and the meanings of such terms as charter, purpose, goal, and function presents a problem. Pugh *et al.* (1963) defined these separately and operationalized them separately, so that the number of kinds of outputs an organization creates and their variation to customer demand, for example, are treated as aspects of charter or purpose (Pugh *et al.*, 1969a); that is, what the outputs are and whether they are changed are seen as elements of charter or goals, not of technology, which has more to do with the means by which outputs are created. Taken in this sense, Harvey's (1968) operationalization of "major product changes" in terms of retooling, materials changes, and design changes is nearer the conceptualization of charter than of technology; as is also Thompson's (1967) categorization of the "primary function" of an organization as "mediating technology."

Subconcepts of Operations Technology

The project described here used only the *operations technology* concept, as already defined, which itself consists of a number of subconcepts.

First, a salient characteristic of equipment is how automated it is. As Amber and Amber put it, "The more human attributes performed by a machine, the higher is its 'order' of automaticity. Automaticity is here considered to be the self-acting capability of a device" (1962:2). This gives a constitutive subconcept of the *equipment used* in terms of *automation of equipment*.

The sequence of operations performed can be more or less rigid. This depends, according to Thompson and Bates, on "the extent to which the appropriate mechanics, knowledge, skills, and raw materials can be used for other products" (1957:329). It also depends on the extent to which operations are linked in series. There is therefore a constitutive subconcept of the *sequence of operations* in terms of *workflow rigidity*.

All work organizations have means of assessing the operations performed, whether against exact standards or merely by personal opinion. This gives a third constitutive definition, in terms of the *specificity of evaluation of operations*.

All three subconcepts of operations technology can apply to all work organizations, whether manufacturing or service.

A fourth subconcept is the continuity of the units of throughput (work in process) in the customary engineering terms of single-unit jobbing, batch, mass, or continuous-flow production. This subconcept is central to Woodward's (1958) approach on manufacturing technologies.

A similar approach to identifying subconcepts such as these is taken by Burack (1966:5).

Other possible variables that might be utilized in further work, but were eventually excluded from the project because of difficulties either in conceptualization, operationalization, data collection, or effective discrimination, were:

1. Throughput complexity (for example, number of pieces assembled, technical knowledge required); 2. Throughput cycle (time to produce a unit of output); 3. Throughput rate (outputs per time unit); 4. Operations performed (for example, extracting, assembling, disassembling, processing, fabricating, conveying, etc.); 5. Operating continuity (for example, weekdays only, 24 hours continuous); 6. Vari-

ety of sequences ("production lines"); 7. Uniformity of equipment (range of types used).

Sample and Data Collection

These concepts of technology were operationalized on data from 52 diverse work organizations with a minimum of 250 employees each, in the Birmingham area in England. (The sample and data collection have been described in earlier papers by Pugh *et al.*, 1968, 1969a). They included a variety of factories, commercial offices, public utilities, transport undertakings, retail stores, etc., both publicly owned and private, and both independent units and units owned by larger groupings.

Of these organizations, 46 were a random sample drawn from an official list of registered employers in the area, stratified by product or purpose and by size. They ranged from an insurance company with 241 employees (the number declined slightly after selection of the sample organizations) to a vehicle manufacturing concern with 25,052 employees.

Of these 46 organizations, 31 were manufacturing and 15 were service organizations. Manufacturing is defined as the creation of new physical outputs whether solid, liquid, or gaseous; therefore the manufacturing organizations included food-processing firms and a brewery, as well as engineering factories, etc., but excluded retailing, omnibus services, education, and water supply. Their size distribution was similar to that of the 46 diverse organizations (Table 1).

Data on the 52 organizations were used for scaling purposes to test the internal consistency of measures. Analyses exploring relationships between variables were performed on the sample of 46, forming a stratified representation of the region, and on the subset of 31 manufacturing organizations.

Data on both technological and structural variables were collected with the aid of standard schedules of information required, by interviews with the chief executives of the organizations (chairman, works manager, area superintendent, etc.) and with as many departmental heads as were necessary. Interviews were conducted by the authors and their colleagues, who usually carried out a tour of the site of the organization (or if several sites, of a selected representative site) to gain personal impressions to aid the scoring of technological variables.[2]

TABLE 1   *Sample of Organizations*
(Population sampled was 293 "employing units" in Birmingham, having over 250 employees: data were collected on 52 organizations.)

Size Bands Randomly Sampled (Number of Employees)	Stratified Sample of Diverse Organizations (N = 46)	Subset of Manufacturing Organizations (Excluding 15 Service Organizations) (N = 31)
251–500	16	10
501–2,000	16	13
2,001+	14	8
Size range	241[a]–25,052	284–25,052
Mean	3,370	3,411
S.D.	5,313	5,644

[a] Numbers in one organization fell below the minimum 251 after its selection.

Measurement of Operations Technology

As yet there are no adequate measures on which to score operations technology. Measurement forces a comparatively precise statement of data, so that not only the possibilities but also the defects of the research are made plain. Nearest to measurement in this field are Bright's (1958:45) "mechanization profile," which may have great potential, and Woodward's (1958:11, 1965:39) categories of production systems, although these were not necessarily conceived as, nor shown to be representing, a unitary variable. An attempt was therefore made to devise means of measuring a series of variables equivalent to the concepts of operations technology, however rudimentary such measurement might be. Earlier brief reports of scales appeared in Pugh *et al.* (1969a) and Inkson *et al.* (1967).

As a means of assessing automation of equipment, there was available the classification of automation by Amber and Amber (1962:2) in terms of the degree to which first energy and then information are provided by machines rather than by man. Organizations in the sample were scored on the five ordered categories shown in Table 2. Unfortunately, the available data were inadequate to do more than represent the automaticity scale by scoring automaticity mode (the level of automaticity of the bulk of the workflow equipment, as estimated by the research team) and the automaticity range (the score of the most automated piece of equipment used, every organization also scoring the lowest possible, zero, by using hand tools).

To measure workflow rigidity, the eight biserial items listed in Table 3 were assembled and organizations scored positively on each for rigidity; that is, for technology which is non-adaptable, limited use and invariable sequence.

The first item indicates what happens in the event of a breakdown. Does everything stop, as in some chemical or food processing? This question is also used in the seventh item; the item was dichotomized at two separate points to achieve maximum discrimination and contribution to the total scores. The second item on waiting time denoted whether the flow through the equipment is necessarily nonstop. Buffer stocks of materials or work-in-progress may permit delays at some stages of the workflow that do not affect preceding or succeeding stages. The fourth item is related to the pattern of the workflow: do materials enter at a single point and continue directly through the workflow process, or is the workflow supplied by a series of inputs at different points?

Single-purpose equipment is a judgment of the versatility of the equipment. Some machine tools may operate on a variety of substances and shapes, but the pipes and vats of a brewery would hardly be adapted to handling oil. Rerouting of

TABLE 2 *Automaticity Scale*[a]

Scale Items	Scoring
Hand tools and manual machines	0
Powered machines and tools	1
Single-cycle automatics and self-feeding machines	2
Automatic: repeats cycle	3
Self-measuring and adjusting: feedback	4

[a] From Amber and Amber (1962: Chart 1-1), who give operational definitions.

TABLE 3   *Workflow Rigidity Scale (N = 52[a])*

Scale Items	No. of Organizations Scoring Positive[b]	Item Analysis Coefficients[c]
In the event of a breakdown all workflow stops immediately	6	0.97
No waiting time possible	8	0.82
No buffer stocks and no delays possible	8	0.71
Single-source input	12	0.67
Single-purpose equipment	13	0.78
No rerouting of work possible	15	0.80
In the event of breakdown, some workflow stops immediately	35	0.95
Production or service line or lines	42	1.00

[a] For testing internal consistency and scalability, data on all available organizations were used.
[b] Scale scores compiled by scoring organizations 1 for each "rigid" item they possessed, giving a possible range of scores from 0 to 8.
[c] Mean = 0.84.

work in the sense of arranging operations in alternative orders may or may not be feasible. Finally, in the last item the term, "line," refers to whether there is a normally invariable throughput sequence.

The question that arose was whether organizations might be scored on all eight items taken together; that is, whether the items could be shown to indicate a unitary variable of workflow rigidity. This was tested by a method based on the assumptions of the Guttman (1950) scalogram (or cumulative scaling) technique as applied to binary data. The degree to which the items ran together was expressed not by the more usual "coefficient of reproducibility" but by a biserial correlation coefficient devised by Brogden (1949). In relating the distribution of organizations on each item to a hypothetical perfect pattern, it achieved a more subtle yet stronger assessment, the advantages of which are argued in detail by Levy and Pugh (1969). The mean of the coefficients for all items was 0.84 (Table 3), which justified using them to form a single scale.

A second scale indicative of the rigidity versus adaptability of the workflow was interdependence of workflow segments. This scale showed the extent to which the segments into which the workflow (or line) hierarchy divided (at the first point of division beneath the chief executive) were independent in work sequence. This simple category scale is given in Table 4. It runs from the series of mutually independent, identical workflow units of a chain of shoe shops or a municipal

TABLE 4   *Interdependence of Workflow Segments Scale*

Scale Items	Scoring
Segments duplicated in different locations, all having the same final outputs	1
Segments having different final outputs, which are not inputs of other segments	2
Outputs of segments become inputs of other segments	3

TABLE 5   *Specificity of Evaluation of Operations Scale*

Scale Items	Scoring
Personal evaluation only	1
Partial measurement (of some aspects of outputs)	2
Measurements used over virtually the whole output(s), to compare against precise specification (blueprint or equivalent)	3

swimming baths department, through the largely independent yet complementary production departments of a firm producing several different foods and beverages, to the sequential integration of vehicle assembly plants, where each department feeds its output to the next.

The concept of specificity of quality evaluation of operations was represented by a three-point classification as in Table 5. It contrasts evaluation by personal judgment (for example, by superiors), which is the only available assessment of services rendered in a retail store or a research division, with the measurement against blueprint standards achieved at some stage in most factories.

The above five scales are listed in Table 6. On 52 organizations they were highly intercorrelated, which suggested that an underlying common element might be exposed by principal components analysis. This technique extracted a large first factor accounting for 58 percent of the variance, with loadings of 0.87 on automaticity mode, 0.80 on automaticity range, 0.68 on workflow rigidity, 0.61 on interdependence of workflow segments, and 0.83 on specificity of evaluation of operations. In all, the 5 scales were comprised of 20 items. These 20 items taken together were also tested for unidimensionality by the method previously described for the workflow rigidity scale, resulting in a high mean item coefficient of 0.79.

This new overall variable was conceptualized as *workflow integration* (Table 6), the degree of automated, continuous, fixed-sequence operation in the technology. It was measured by summing the organization's scores on the five constituent scales. Table 7 shows the distribution of the sample of organizations on the scale, distinguishing service and manufacturing. It is evident that although these two categories clearly inclined towards opposite ends of the scale, the tendency was by no means so pronounced as to produce a dichotomous result. There was appreciable overlap; and there was effective discrimination within the service category and within the manufacturing category.

Several subgroups of organizations with common purposes are identified in Table 7. The prominence of vehicle manufacture in Midlands industry is noticeable, particularly since a number of the other miscellaneous engineering factories included some vehicle components in their range of outputs. The largest, most mechanized, and most integrated vehicle assembly plant in the region achieved the highest score in the sample. Measurement exposes its own weaknesses, however, and there remain ambiguities in the definition of some items which allow debatable judgments. More discriminatory scales might show less polarization of service from manufacturing. These scales are still very simple. Despite all this, a workflow integration dimension of technology potentially common to all forms of work organizations is shown to be scalable.

This workflow integration dimension might be expected to relate negatively to the use of labor as a factor of production, since high workflow integration means

TABLE 6 *Principal Variables and Main Hypothesized Relationships*

Operations Technology		Structure
Constitutive Definitions	Operationalized Variables (6 scales)	Dimensions and Main Constituent Variables (10 scales)[b]
Automation of equipment	*Workflow Integration:* summary scale including: Automaticity mode, Automaticity range	*Structuring of Activities Dimension:* including: *Overall* role specialization, Functional specialization, *Overall* standardization of procedures, *Overall* formalization (documentation)
Adaptability of workflow	Workflow rigidity, Interdependence of workflow segments	*Concentration of Authority Dimension:* including: *Overall* centralization of decisions, Autonomy of the organization, Standardization of procedures for selection and advancement, etc.
Evaluation of operations	Specificity of evaluation of operations	*Line-Control of Workflow Dimension* (vs. impersonal control): including: Subordinate-supervisor ratio (negative), Formalization of role performance recording (negative), Percentage of workflow superordinates
Unit of throughput	*Production Continuity*[a]	

[a] Woodward production system categories redefined. Applicable to manufacturing organizations only.
[b] Among 64 scales of structure used in the project as a whole.

TABLE 7 *Distribution of Sample of 46 Diverse Organizations on Scale of Workflow Integration for Operations Technology*

Score	Organization	No. of Organizations (N = 46)	Score	Organization	No. of Organizations (N = 46)
17	Vehicle manufacturer	1	—	Mechanical handling truck manufacturer	—
16	Brewery	—	—	Engineering tool manufacturer	9
—	Food manufacturer	2	10	Vehicle metal components manufacturer	—
15	Two food manufacturers	—	—	Carriage manufacturer	3
—	Packaging manufacturer	3	9	Local authority water department[a]	—
14	Local authority baths department[a]	—	—	Component manufacturer	2
—	Metal components manufacturer	3	8	Nonferrous metal processing	1
—	Metal goods manufacturer	—	7	Toy manufacturer	1
13	Metal goods manufacturer	3	—	Local authority civil engineering department[a]	—
—	Metal components manufacturer	—	6	Insurance company[a]	—
—	Vehicle tire manufacturer	—	—	Omnibus company[a]	—
—	Vehicle electrical components manufacturer	—	—	Local authority transport department[a]	4
—	Glass components manufacturer	—	5	Government repairs factory	1
—	Vehicle metal components manufacturer	—	—	Research division[a]	—
12	Commercial vehicle manufacturer	7	4	Civil engineering firm[a]	2
—	Metal components manufacturer	1	—	Savings bank[a]	—
11	Two metal components manufacturers	—	3	Cooperative chain of retail stores[a]	—
—	Printer	—	—	Chain of shoe repair stores[a]	2
—	Component manufacturer	—	2	Local authority education department[a]	—
—	Metal goods manufacturer	—	—	Department store[a]	2
—	Abrasives manufacturer	—	1	Government inspection department[a]	—
—	Domestic appliances manufacturer	—	—	Chain of retail stores[a]	2

[a] Service organizations (N = 15).

high mechanization and implies capital-intensive operation. A product-moment correlation between workflow integration and labor costs as a percentage of total costs supported the hypothesis (for $N = 46$, $r = -0.51$; for $N = 31$ manufacturing organizations, $r = -0.33$) and in doing so afforded the workflow integration scale some external validation. (It should be noted that accurate data on labor costs were difficult to obtain, and some confusion between total wage costs and costs of direct labor alone was inherent in the estimates used.)

Structural Variables

Table 6 relates workflow integration to dimensions of structure in work organizations. The isolation of these dimensions is described in a previous paper (Pugh *et al.*, 1968). Their meaning is indicated by the constituent variables from which scores on each dimension are derived. In summary, structuring of activities refers to the degree of formal regulation of the intended activities of employees (a bureaucratic dimension); concentration of authority is the degree to which authority for decisions rests in controlling units outside the organization and is centralized at the higher hierarchical levels within it; line control of workflow refers to control of operations on the throughputs being exercised directly by line management, as against impersonal control through records and procedures by staff departments.

The relationship of operations technology to structure can now be tested by multivariate correlational techniques on these dimensions and on salient constituent variables. Altogether these summarize an extensive range of the formal characteristics of structure, so they constitute the widest available test. The methodological implications of using multivariate correlational techniques with the type of scales utilized in the present analysis are examined in detail in Levy and Pugh (1969).

Table 8 shows correlations between workflow integration, column (1), size, column (2), and scales of the structural dimensions and of selected structural variables. These structural variables were selected from among the 64 available as being those most fully representing structure, or most distinctive in the sense of correlating least one with another, or correlating most with technology (Pugh *et al.*, 1968, 1969a). Among the configuration scales included are the percentages employed in each of eight specialist activities (listed from design and development to maintenance). These are from a total of 16 specializations otherwise forming the scale of functional specialization (also in Table 8), which measures the extent to which there are specialist roles for given functional activities. The configuration scales signify not the degree of specialization, but the proportion of total employees in each of the functions. The conventional titles of these scales are shown in the body of the table, but these can be restrictive and sometimes inapplicable outside manufacturing industry, and the generalized titles used are as follows:

1. Chief executive's span of control: subordinates reporting directly with no intervening level, whatever their job or status (excluding personal secretary).
2. Subordinate-supervisor ratio: the number of workflow ("production") subordinates per first line supervisor (that is, the lowest job in the hierarchy which does not include prescribed direct work on the throughputs).
3. Vertical span: number of jobs between direct worker and chief executive of the unit of organization (excluding deputies *to*, assistants *to*, and secretaries), in the longest "line."

TABLE 8 *Correlation[a] Between Scales of Operations Technology and of Size and Selected Scales of Structure*

	46 Diverse Organizations		31 Manufacturing Organizations			
	Workflow Integration	Size (Log of No. of Employees)	Workflow Integration	Size (Log of No. of Employees)	Production Continuity	Production Continuity (Size Partialled Out)
	(1)	(2)	(3)	(4)	(5)	(6)
Structural Dimensions						
Structuring of activities	0.34[b]	0.69[c]	0.17	0.78[c]	0.41	0.07
Concentration of authority	−0.30[b]	−0.10	0.00	−0.20	0.11	0.24
Line control of workflow	−0.46[c]	0.15	−0.05	0.13	−0.17	—
Structural Variables						
Overall role specialization	0.38[c]	0.75[c]	0.25	0.83[c]	0.52[c]	0.26
Functional specialization	0.44[c]	0.67[c]	0.19	0.75[c]	0.34	−0.02
Overall standardization of procedures	0.46[c]	0.56[c]	0.19	0.65[c]	0.35	0.07
Standardization of procedures for selection and advancement, etc.	−0.38[c]	0.31[b]	0.24	0.42[b]	0.43[b]	0.29
Overall formalization (documentation)	0.17	0.55[c]	0.04	0.67[c]	0.27	−0.07
Formalization of role performance recording	0.41[c]	0.42[c]	0.00	0.45[b]	−0.03	−0.30

	46 Diverse Organizations		31 Manufacturing Organizations			
	Workflow Integration	Size (Log of No. of Employees)	Workflow Integration	Size (Log of No. of Employees)	Production Continuity	Production Continuity (Size Partialled Out)
Overall centralization of decisions	-0.16	-0.39[c]	-0.05	-0.47[c]	0.00	0.28
Autonomy of the organization	0.22	0.09	0.02	0.23	-0.07	-0.19
Configuration of structure variables:						
Chief executive's span of control	0.06	0.32[b]	-0.09	0.29	0.08	-0.07
Subordinate-supervisor ratio	0.35[b]	0.05	0.02	0.04	-0.09(0.36)	—
Vertical span	0.09	0.67[c]	0.15	0.77[c]	0.51[c]	0.26
Percentages of total number of employees:						
Direct workers	-0.18	-0.26	-0.17	-0.46[c]	-0.14	0.10
Workflow superordinates	-0.53[c]	-0.13	0.02	-0.31	0.13	0.33
Nonworkflow personnel	0.34[b]	0.36[b]	0.22	0.53[c]	0.22	-0.04
Design and development	0.45[c]	-0.02	-0.08	-0.04	-0.18	—
Methods	0.38[c]	0.11	0.07	0.15	-0.03	—
Inspection	0.39[c]	0.02	0.07	-0.08	-0.15(0.62)	—
Employment	-0.03	0.05	-0.45[b]	-0.03	0.04	—
Buying and stocks	-0.05	-0.04	-0.42[b]	-0.12	-0.10	—
Workflow control	0.27	-0.19	-0.17	-0.35	-0.44[b]	-0.33
Transport and dispatch	0.19	0.06	0.32	-0.18	0.45[b]	—
Maintenance	-0.01	0.38[c]	0.05	0.13	0.20(0.46)	—
Size (log of no. of employees)	0.08	—	0.30	—	0.47[c]	—

[a] Product moment coefficients of linear correlation (r): with correlation-ratio coefficients of nonlinear correlation (η) in brackets in column 5, production continuity.
[b] Beyond 95 percent level of confidence.
[c] Beyond 99 percent level of confidence.

4. Direct workers: all employees personally providing the service or operating on the product.
5. Workflow superordinates: supervisors or managers responsible for the workflow (excluding any jobs which have prescribed direct work on the throughputs).
6. Nonworkflow personnel: all employees of whatever grade with no direct or supervisory responsibility for work on the throughputs.
7. Design and development: devising new outputs, equipment and processes.
8. Methods: assessing and devising ways of producing the output.
9. Inspection: controlling the quality of materials and equipment and outputs.
10. Employment: acquiring and allocating human resources.
11. Buying and stocks: obtaining and controlling materials and equipment.
12. Workflow control: controlling the workflow ("production control").
13. Transport and dispatch: carrying outputs and resources from place to place.
14. Maintenance: maintaining and erecting buildings and equipment.

The proportions employed in the 8 specializations not listed did not relate substantially to technology.

Relationship of Operations Technology to Structure

Test on 46 Diverse Organizations

Table 8 (column 1) shows some moderate correlations between technology and structure on 46 diverse organizations. Workflow integration appears to bear some relation to the three structural *dimensions* listed first in the table. The more the technology is integrated, the more activities tend to be formally structured, with specialist departments and formal procedures. Where the technology is *least* integrated (as in items showing negative correlations), authority tends to be concentrated at the apex in boards or with the chief executive, and workflow activities tend to be directly controlled by line management and not through staff departments and their routines. This pattern is typical of service organizations, particularly those that are publicly owned, as Pugh *et al.* (1969a) have reported previously. Equivalent correlations appear in Table 8 between workflow integration and those structural *variables* which constitute the three structural dimensions (as summarized in Table 6).

At this point it could be concluded that the broad hypothesis holds good; technology and structure are related: but the strength of multivariate research design is that it prevents premature conclusions. Pugh *et al.* (1969a: Table 8) have already demonstrated that although technology does have a diffused relationship with the structural dimensions, it always takes second place to other variables. This can be seen in Table 8 (column 2) in the correlations between structuring of activities (and the component variables in specialization, standardization, and formalization) and size. Correlations with technology are overwhelmed by those with size; and in multiple regression, Pugh *et al.* found that the combination of workflow integration with size only raised the 0.69 correlation of size alone with structuring of activities to a multiple correlation of 0.75. They found that the concentration of authority dimension was strongly and positively related to *dependence*; that the line control of workflow dimension was negatively related to *operating variability*; and that the addition of the technology scale of workflow integration added virtually nothing to the multiple correlations. (*Dependence* is a scale of the relationships that the organization has with any owning group, and with suppliers and customers, etc.; *operating variability* is a scale of organizational charter, conceptualized as "manufacturing nonstandard producer goods as against providing standard consumer service" (Pugh *et al.*, 1969a).

In short, operations technology as defined here is accounting for but a small proportion of the total variance in structural features. Other variables contribute more. *On this sample, the broad "technological imperative" hypothesis that operations technology is of primary importance to structure, is not supported.* Although this is true for all main structural features, a few specific configuration variables can be seen to be conspicuously correlated with workflow integration; and *not* with size or other contextual variables. These are subordinate-supervisor ratio, and the percentage of total personnel who are workflow superordinates or who are in design, or methods, or inspection. All are simple job-count variables; none deal with the wider administrative or hierarchical structure.

Even so, the import of these latter relationships with technology must not be overstated. They are relationships not so much with variations in technology as measured by workflow integration, but with the crude difference between service and manufacturing which is reflected in the polar tendencies of service and manufacturing organizations on that scale. Correlation coefficients obtained for subordinate-supervisor ratio (0.38) and the percentages of workflow superordinates (-0.55), design (0.58), methods (0.43), and inspection (0.43) with a service-manufacturing dichotomy, were all beyond the 99 percent level of confidence. Factories have more workers per supervisor, proportionately fewer workflow superordinates (managers and supervisors), and proportionately more designers, work-study engineers, and inspectors than do shops, local-authority services, and commercial offices.

It must therefore be recognized that this influence of service versus manufacturing will be present in relationships with other variables also. It may be obscuring a connection between technology and structure within manufacturing industry, and the "technological imperative" hypothesis applies most clearly to industry. The hypothesis would therefore be more strongly tested on manufacturing organizations alone, even through removal of the service organizations reduces the number of organizations available by one-third.

Test on 31 Manufacturing Organizations

On the 31 manufacturing organizations, there was a striking lack of association between workflow integration and all three *dimensions* of organization structure (Table 8, column 3). As in the full sample, it is size that is overwhelmingly related to structuring of activities (Table 8, column 4). The irrelevance of technology is emphasized when the effects of size are removed. The correlation of (log) size and workflow integration is 0.30 on the manufacturing subset. Then holding size constant, the partial correlation coefficient between workflow integration and structuring of activities is merely 0.10. Conversely, if the effects of workflow integration are held constant, the correlation of size with structuring is almost unchanged at 0.76.

Concentration of authority is again associated closely with dependence ($r = 0.63$) rather than with operations technology. And technology is not associated with line control.

Scores on structural dimensions, compounded of scores on several linked scales, might obscure more intricate relationships between technology and these component scales; but the correlations do not show this. Workflow integration is not substantially correlated with any of the main structural variables listed, and where some positive association is indicated, is is again overwhelmed by the correlations with size. Equally, if the five original technology scales which are the components of the workflow integration measure are examined, the outcome is very similar. Again, the only relationships that remain are with job-count variables of configuration. Within manufacturing industry, these are the proportions of personnel in the employment side of personnel work, and in buying, stock control, and storekeeping. The more integrated the technology, the fewer these are, implying decreasing problems in the acquisition and retention of both human and material resources.

This result draws attention to the risks of generalizing from single cases. The study by Scott *et al.* (1956) of greater mechanization in a steel plant describes increases in what in Table 8 are called functional specialization and overall formalization. Fensham and Hooper (1964) describe increases in vertical span and in workflow superordinates (managers) in textile mills. But the correlations in Table 8 imply that these effects of changing technology may not be true of very many cases. Indeed, they point to a much stronger positive relationship of each of functional specialization, overall formalization, and vertical span, with *size*. Thus a multiorganization multivariate approach suggests that in these case studies, the effects which were attributed primarily to technology were as likely to be due to the simultaneous growth in size of the organizations observed. Burack's (1967) analysis distinguishes "scale-of-operation effects" from "technological change," but implies that they are of equal importance. The present data suggest that operations technology has only a limited specific effect compared with size.

However, the scale of workflow integration was first devised for a sample of diverse organizations, not solely for manufacturing industry. On the subset of 31 manufacturing organizations, the intercorrelations among the component subscales of workflow integration are lower than on the sample of 46 organizations. Item analysis gives a mean item coefficient of 0.68 (for the 15 biserial items that discriminate within manufacturing organizations) compared with 0.79 on the diverse sample.

Even though the technological concepts embodied in the items of the workflow integration scale apply readily to manufacturing, and a good discrimination is achieved between such organizations, the results obtained with it could be questioned if they were not supported by criteria intended specifically for manufacturing. Woodward's (1958) classification which was included in the research design summarized in Table 6, was intended solely for manufacturing production systems. Use of this classification affords a further test of the hypothesized connection between technology and organizational structure, particularly as Woodward's (1958, 1965) own findings on a range of firms in south-east Essex are principal evidence in its favor.

Test Based on Woodward's Classification

The 10-category classification in Table 9 is that proposed by Woodward (1958:11, Figure 1). To Woodward (1958:12), this was "a scale of technical complexity. This term is used here to mean the extent to which the production process

TABLE 9 *Production Continuity: A Further Operationalization of Woodward's Classification of Production Systems*

Woodward classification Unit and small batch: I through V Large batch and mass: V through VIII Process: VIII through X	Scale of production continuity[a]	Manu-facturing organi-zations (N = 31)
I. Production of simple units to customers' orders	*Simple units:* units basically *single-piece* not assemblies; produced one by one	0
II. Production of technically complex units	*Complex units: assemblies*, produced one by one	0
III. Fabrication of large equipment in stages	*Fabrication:* one by one; workpeople come to the unit of output (which moves about very infrequently) rather than the unit moving to different workpeople	2
IV. Production of small batches	*Small batches:* equipment reset *every week* or more often, for outputs measured in *items*	11
V. Production of components in large batches subsequently assembled diversely	*Large batches:* equipment reset at intervals *longer than a week* for outputs measured in items: *but* items *assembled diversely* (i.e. variety of assembly sequences, including assembly by unit and/or small batch methods)	3
VI. Production of large batches; assembly line type	*Large batches:* as in V, but with *large-batch assembly*	5
VII. Mass production	*Mass: batch size, measured in items, is indefinite* (i.e. change of batch requires decisions on (*a*) design modification, (*b*) retooling, which are beyond the normal authority of the line production management and production planning to vary production programs)	4
VIII. Process production combined with the preparation of a product for sale by large-batch or mass-production methods	*Process:* throughputs measured by *weight or volume; but* outputs become *items at finishing stage*	0
IX. Process production of chemicals in batches	*Process:* but *ingredients* (i.e. recipes) of the throughputs *change periodically*	3
X. Continuous-flow production of liquids, gases and solid shapes	*Process:* but *constant ingredients;* (i.e. recipe change beyond the normal authority of the line production management and production planning to vary production programs)	3

[a] The predominant technology of an organization was assessed giving particular weight to its highest degree of "continuity."

is controllable and its results predictable." There is certainly a conceptual ordering in the arrangement of the categories, which suggests that they might be treated as a scale, potentially usable in correlational analysis. But the category headings are not stated primarily in terms of degrees of control and prediction, but rather in terms of the unit of throughput; unit, batch, and flow process. The conceptual ordering might therefore rather be regarded as denoting the degree of continuity of throughput units present in the production workflow, from the one-by-one of jobbing to the continuous flow of process production. This view is also taken by Starbuck (1965), who says: "It is not really accurate to call the technological variable 'complexity,' since this complexity seems to correspond to *smoothness* of production, but this was Woodward's term."

The further operationalization of these categories shown in Table 9 was therefore conceptualized as representing a production *continuity* variable. Woodward's (1958) original 10 categories were retained, rather than those used in her revised version (Woodward, 1965:39), where categories not exclusively within one or other of the three broad production groups of unit and small batch, large batch and mass, and process are removed (that is, her "mixed" categories V and VIII). Since this either destroyed the sequence, or shortened the scale, it was less useful for the analysis presented here. The main problem in further defining Woodward's categories was with the idea of "batch," particularly the question, "How small is a small batch?" Woodward's headings were in general terms and their application was not specified. The concept of time was therefore introduced, and batch size was defined by time units selected to discriminate within the particular sample. Time intervals have the advantage of being clearly definable and can be varied to suit different samples. The distinction between small batch and large batch at weekly resetting of equipment was appropriate to the data available here, but in further work can be adjusted as required.

Finally, criteria mentioned in Woodward's categories but extraneous to the continuity concept were excluded, such as, whether production was to customer's orders or consisted of liquids, gases, or solids.

Correlation coefficients between the production continuity scores (on the seven categories in Table 9 for which there were organizations), and the structural dimensions and variables appear in Table 8 (column 5). At first sight there did seem to be a relationship here between technology and structuring of activities, albeit a moderate one. It was repeated in the correlations for the variables of specialization, standardization, and formalization, from which scores on that structuring dimension were made up; and there was a 0.51 correlation with vertical span (number of levels). But again the size variable had to be reckoned with. On the present manufacturing sample, it correlated 0.47 with the technology measure (production continuity), 0.78 with structuring of activities, and 0.77 with vertical span. Again using the partial correlation technique, when (log) size was held constant, the correlation between structuring of activities and production continuity disappeared to just 0.07, and between vertical span and production continuity dropped to only 0.26. The correlations between production continuity and the structural variables with size partialled out (where the coefficient was greater than ±0.2) are given in Table 8 (column 6). Again the prima facie relationship with structure does not survive closer examination.

Even so, a few remaining relationships are found once more among the job-count variables of configuration, where the percentages of employees in workflow control (Table 8, column 6) and in transport (column 5) respectively have some negative and some positive link with production continuity over and above their connections with size.

However, in general, even the use of this different scale, approximating a classification devised specifically for manufacturing organizations, fails to show widespread significant relationships with structure. Although the scales of workflow integration and production continuity are not dissimilar, being correlated 0.46, they are far from identical. Can this be reconciled with Woodward's own study where technology was thought to be the only factor that did vary with structural features?

Comparison with Woodward's Study

The two studies are difficult to compare directly. First, the operationalization in the form of the production continuity scale might categorize slightly differently from the way Woodward may have applied her categories, although the effect on the ordering of organizations should be negligible. There are then differences in data analyses. The analysis reported here was mainly by correlation, using categories along the scale; Woodward did not herself use her proposed 9- or 10-point classifications in presenting her results, but charted and compared the distributions of firms in each of three broad production groups only.

Most critical are the differences in sample. The biases in the industrial compositions of the two regions were reflected in the distribution of organizations. In south-east Essex in 1954–55, Woodward found firms in every production category, particularly chemical and similar plants at the process end of the continuum. The Birmingham sample in 1962–1964, however, left three categories vacant (Table 9) and had a high proportion of organizations in the batch production categories in the middle of the continuum due to the prominence of engineering industry in the region. There were also variations in sample sizes: 31 throughout in the Birmingham project, and 45, 75, 78, or 80 (from among 80 firms used in comparisons) on the several variables in south-east Essex. Finally, there is an important difference in the size range of the organizations. In Birmingham, this was 284 to 25,052 employees (Table 1); in south-east Essex, Woodward (1965:41) reported 35 of the total 92 firms available being between 100 and 250 employees, and only 17 over 1,000.

Table 10 summarizes the comparison on equivalent variables of structural *configuration*. Woodward presents data only on configuration variables, not on the other aspects of structure summarized in this study by the dimensions of structuring of activities and concentration of authority.

Table 10 shows that none of the univariate *linear* relations between configuration and technology suggested in south-east Essex were repeated in the Birmingham organizations. Yet Woodward (1965:40) found relationships with "technological complexity" alone; for to her "there appeared to be no significant relations" between structure and size. It may be noted that in south-east Essex organizations technology and size appear to be unrelated.

Nor were the several *curvilinear* relationships with technology suggested in the discussion in Woodward's text (and not shown in Table 10) found in the Birmingham organizations. These were with number of specialists, definition of duties and responsibilities (Woodward, 1965:64), and amount of paperwork (1965:67), all of which in the Birmingham sample were strongly and monotonically related to size (Table 8, column 4).

TABLE 10   *Comparison with Woodward's Findings (1958, 1965)*

South-East Essex findings		Equivalent Birmingham results ($N = 31$)	
Structural Variable	Relationship[a]	Structural Variable	Relationship[b]
"Length of line of command" ($N = 80$)	Positive linear	Vertical span	0.26[c,d]
"Span of control of chief executive" ($N = 80$)	Positive linear	Span of control of chief executive	0.08
"Ratio of direct to indirect labour" ($N = 75$)	Positive linear	Not available (total hourly paid indirect labour not separated from total non-workflow personnel)	—
"Ratio of managers to total personnel" ($N = 45$)	Positive linear	Percentage of workflow super-ordinates to total employees	0.13
"Ratio of clerical and administrative staff to manual workers" ($N = 75$)	Positive linear	Percentage of nonworkflow personnel to total employees	0.04[c]
"Span of control of first-line supervisors in production departments" ($N = 78$)	∩-shaped curvilinear	Subordinate-supervisor ratio	−0.09 (0.36[e])

[a] Relationship with "technological complexity" over three production groups; unit, batch-mass, process.
[b] Product-moment (linear) correlation with production continuity scale.
[c] Partial correlation coefficient holding (log) size constant; correlations with size shown in Table 8.
[d] Not significant.
[e] Correlation-ratio coefficient of nonlinear correlation (η).

On the other hand, the ∩-shaped (concave curvilinear) relationship expected with first-line supervisor's span of control (i.e. subordinate-supervisor ratio, Table 8) *was* possible in the Birmingham results. This variable was not linearly correlated with production continuity, and reference to Table 8 (column 4) shows that it is among the few not also linked to size. Comparison as close as possible with Woodward's published data, that is, using only the broad unit production, batch-mass, process groupings, gave the confirmatory patterns shown in Table 11. The number of subordinates was greatest in the middle of the technology range, in large batch and mass. This is shown both in terms of median figures, as first published by Woodward (1958), and in the form of means calculated from her 1965 data, based on her revised 9-category classification of production systems.

A more precise indication of this relationship in the Birmingham data is given by the correlation-ratio coefficient of nonlinear correlation when η was found to be 0.36 (Table 8, column 5). This correlation might be greater were it not for the limited range of the Birmingham sample, in which the unit and process technology extremes were less well represented than in south-east Essex. Figure 1 shows the curvilinear tendency, but it is cut short at the extremes.

Relation of Operations Technology to Certain Structural Characteristics Only

This result on subordinate-supervisor ratio agrees with the assumptions in Burack's (1966) models, and with Starbuck's (1965:509) thorough and sophisticated

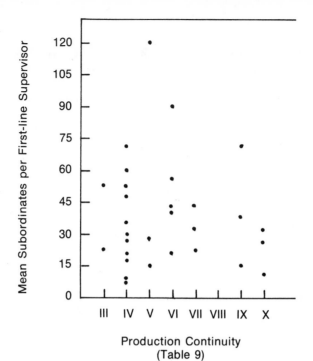

Production Continuity
(Table 9)

*Figure 1   Production Continuity vs. Mean Subordinates per First-line Supervisor for 31
Manufacturing Organizations (Table 11)*

TABLE 11   *Subordinates per First-line Supervisor in Manufacturing Organizations*

	No. of firms/ organizations	Subordinates per first-line supervisor[a]		
		Unit and small batch	Large batch and mass	Process
Medians[d] for each production category:				
South-East Essex	80	between 21 & 30	between 41 & 50	between 11 & 20
Birmingham	28[b]	30	40	27
Means[e] for each production category:				
South-East Essex	78[c]	22	46	14
Birmingham	28[b]	35	42	31

[a]First-line supervisor defined by Woodward (1965:257), as "the lowest level official who spends more than half his time on the supervision of production operations. Working charge hands are not included. The classification, "production operators," includes the total staff of all production departments including laborers and "others not necessarily on direct production work." Defined for the Birmingham study as the mean number of workflow (production) subordinates per first-line supervisor (that is, the lowest job in the hierarchy which does not include *prescribed* direct work on the throughput).

[b] Woodward's omission of firms in the "combined system" categories V and VIII of her 10-category classification and removal of the categories from her revised 9-category classification requires, for comparison, the omission of the three Birmingham organizations in these categories.

[c]Woodward's 1965 data on "averages" are on two firms fewer than her 1958 data on medians.

[d]Birmingham data calculated as from 10-category classification (Woodward, 1958: Figure 1); South-East Essex data from Woodward (1958: Figure 3).

[e]Birmingham data calculated as from revised 9-category classification (Woodward, 1965: Figure 11); South-East Essex data from Woodward (1965: Figures 19, 20).

review, where six other studies, as well as Woodward's, were found to be consistent with the assumption of a ∩-shaped function on the variable of workers per foreman. More than that it suggested that other structural variables not linearly related to technology might show a curvilinear relationship. Such variables are found only in the configuration aspect of structure; once again, they are job-counts. Table 8, column 5, shows in parentheses the nonlinear coefficients with the two further variables where curvilinear relationships with production continuity were established; that is, the percentage employed in inspection and the percentage in maintenance. The proportions engaged in both these functions increase up to the large-batch stage of production and then tend to decline, as does the subordinate-supervisor ratio. Such relationships were not found in any other configuration variables, nor with the workflow integration scale.

Therefore, although a sweeping "technological imperative" hypothesis is not supported, a residual seven variables have been identified in the tests on manufacturing industry that do have associations with technology. These are:

Structural Variables	Related to:	
	Production Continuity	Workflow Integration
Subordinate-supervisor ratio	∩-shaped curvilinear	—
Proportion in inspection	∩-shaped curvilinear	—
Proportion in maintenance	∩-shaped curvilinear	—
Proportion in workflow (production) control	Negative linear	—
Proportion in transport and dispatch	Positive linear	Positive linear
Proportion in employment (personnel) specialization	—	Negative linear
Proportion in buying and stocks specialization	—	Negative linear

What is distinctive about these variables, as compared with the large number not related to technology? Subordinate-supervisor ratio is an element of organization at the level of the operative and his immediate superior. Obviously the number of men a supervisor requires to run a row of lathes differs from the number he requires to run the more continuous integrated workflow of an automatic transfer machine. Thus, subordinate-supervisor ratio is a structural variable which reflects activities directly bound up with the operations technology itself. This is true of the next four variables also. The relative numbers engaged on inspection and maintenance are linked to the variety of equipment and operations, which tends to be greatest in batch production. Workflow (production) control tends to decline in proportion after the batch stage, for it shows a negative linear relation, but this is complicated by the intrusion of some size effects. The transport and dispatch specialization largely reflects internal transport activities related to the workflow system. Thus these four specializations are activities visibly linked to production work. By comparison, activities such as accounting or market research are not so linked, and the proportions of employees in these activities do not correlate with technology. In this light, it may be speculated that the otherwise puzzling relationships between the workflow integration scale and the proportions engaged in employment, and buying and stocks, might be due to the intermediate position of these activities. They are closer to the production work itself than is, say, accounting; but not so close as, say, inspection.

A two-part hypothesis emerges from these results. Associations with operations technology will be found only among variables of structure that are centered on the workflow. Such variables are likely to be job-counts of employees on production-linked activities, and not features of the wider administrative and hierarchical structure.

Reconciliation with Woodward's Findings

Can such a hypothesis be reconciled with Woodward's (1958, 1965) findings? Woodward found a range of structural variables, not so obviously centered on shop-floor activities as to immediately fit the hypothesis, seemingly varying with technology (Table 10). Except on the single variable of subordinate-supervisor ratio, the south-east Essex and Birmingham studies appear to be mutually inconsistent in their results; but they are not necessarily contradictory. Their differences may help to clarify the position of technology, though that clarification may be a limitation.

The inconsistency prompts another look at the differences between the two studies, notably in their samples. The sizes of the organizations in south-east Essex ranged down to 100 employees, whereas the Birmingham sample had a minimum size of 250; and there were proportionately fewer multithousand units in Essex than in Birmingham.

The study with the larger organizations showed only a limited group of distinctive variables related to technology (most aspects of structure were primarily related to variables such as size and dependence). The study with the smaller organizations linked structure widely with technology. Now in a smaller organization of 100 or so employees, all activities throughout the organization and all structural features reflecting these activities would indeed be more directly centered on the production operations and their technology. (This is corroborated by the -0.46 correlation between size (log) and percentage of direct workers (Table 8, column 4).) Thus, for example, in a smaller organization, where the production operations will be a relatively larger part of the total activities, the span of control of the chief executive may be determined by how many foremen or superintendents the operations technology requires. But in a larger organization, the number of staff department heads and coordinating managers involved in the total activities may be of more consequence for this span of control. The proportionate number of line managers (percentage of workflow superordinates), and the length of the line of command (vertical span), which also correlate negatively with size (Table 8) may similarly be less affected by technology than by growth in total activities.

Hence the two projects may not be irreconcilable if the hypothesis is construed to take account of size:

Structural variables will be associated with operations technology only where they are centered on the workflow. The smaller the organization the more its structure will be pervaded by such technological effects: the larger the organization, the more these effects will be confined to variables such as job-counts of employees on activities linked with the workflow itself, and will not be detectable in variables of the more remote administrative and hierarchical structure.

Conclusion

It would be rash to be confident with so few studies published. Although the Birmingham study used a sample representative (within its stratification) of the conurbation, and Woodward's study included about three-quarters of the firms in the area, more samples are needed in other regions and countries.[3] Indeed, the validity of the generalized representation of the overall operations technology of a unit of organization is not established. To describe the general technology of a factory as "mass," when this characterizes only some departments and other departments are engaged in small batch and process operation, is an oversimplification. The predominant technology may well have a pervasive effect, but this remains to be demonstrated. And although the workflow integration scale has high internal consistency, its external validation in terms of relating to other accepted variables is not yet adequate. Perhaps characterizations painstakingly built up machine by machine, taking each section of equipment separately, and using categories and items such as those devised by Bright (1958), Amber and Amber (1962), and Turner and Lawrence (1965), should be tried.

Given these reservations, the Birmingham results have shown that it is feasible to devise a scale of workflow integration, and to use it, together with the Woodward-derived scale of production continuity, in correlational and multivariate analyses. With these measures, the sweeping "technological imperative" hypothesis on organizational level technology and structure is not supported. Broadly speaking, operations technology did not relate to structure or did so only secondarily to other variables. This was true in successive tests on the sample of diverse organizations and on the subset of manufacturing organizations. On these results, a general "technology-causes-structure" hypothesis could only be sustained by the argument that technology also assumes size, and that to operate a given technology, an organization must be of the requisite size. This implies that size is a component of the technology concept. Such a view would not be consistent with the approach taken here, nor with Woodward's (1965: Figure 12) finding that all types of production systems appeared in every size range.

Yet further examination of the data and the use of a coefficient of nonlinear correlation reveals relationships in manufacturing organizations between technology scales and variables previously regarded as of minor interest; that is, subordinate-supervisor ratio, and the proportions of employees in inspection, maintenance, workflow (production) control, and transport and dispatch. All these are job-count variables of activities directly connected to the workflow (production) itself.

Comparison with the apparently contradictory findings by Woodward, linking technology with a wide variety of structural characteristics, leads to a final hypothesis which, concisely stated, is that *variables of operations technology will be related only to those structural variables that are centered on the workflow.* The smaller the organization, the wider the structural effects of technology; the larger the organization, the more such effects are confined to particular variables, and size and dependence and similar factors make the greater overall impact. In the smaller organizations, everyone is closer to the "shop-floor," and structural responses to the problems of size (for example) have not begun to show. In larger organizations, managers and administrators are buffered from the technology itself by the specialist departments, standard procedures, and formalized paperwork that size brings with it.

Although the hypothesis is grounded in results on manufacturing industry, it is stated in generalized terms using the word "workflow" ("production" is restricted to manufacturing) and may apply to services also, although probably not on exactly the same variables.

This interpretation breaks the stalemate between the classical management theorists and the behavioral scientists referred to at the beginning of this paper. The management theorists may well be right (up to a point): in bigger manufacturing organizations—and it is with such organizations that the better known management writers have been most associated—the basic activities of management and their structural framework are probably not much affected by the particular operations technology employed. The behavioral scientists may well be equally right (up to a point): technology makes all the difference at "shop-floor" level, and throughout smaller organizations, where nothing is far removed from the workflow itself.

Notes

1. This research was carried out at the Industrial Administration Research Unit, the University of Aston in Birmingham, England. Research conducted by the Unit is jointly supported by the Social Science Research Council and the University.
2. Data were collected by D. S. Pugh, D. J. Hickson, C. R. Hinings, C. Turner, K. M. Macdonald, W. A. T. Nichols, J. N. Fairhead.
3. Preliminary analysis of data from a partial replication on 40 diverse organizations in collaboration with J. H. K. Inkson of the Industrial Administration Research Unit appears to confirm the interpretation. A similar partial replication by J. Schwitter of Kent State University, Ohio, may disclose some variation from it in American organizations.

References

Amber, G. S., and P. S. Amber, 1962, *Anatomy of Automation*. Englewood Cliffs: Prentice-Hall.

Bakke, E. W., 1959, "Concept of the social organization." In M. Haire (ed.), *Modern Organization Theory*. New York: Wiley.

Blauner, R., 1964, *Alienation and Freedom*. Chicago: University of Chicago Press.

Bottomore, T. B., and M. Rubel (eds.), 1956, *Karl Marx: Selected Writings in Sociology and Social Philosophy*. London: Watts.

Brech, E. F. L., 1957, *Organization: The Framework of Management*. London: Longmans Green.

Bright, J. R., 1958, *Automation and Management*. Boston: Harvard Business School.

Brogden, H. E., 1949, "A new coefficient: applications to biserial correlation and to estimation of selective efficiency," *Psychometrika*, 14:169–182.

Brown, M., 1966, *On the Theory and Measurement of Technological Change*. Cambridge, England: University Press.

Brown, W., 1960, *Exploration in Management*. London: Heinemann.

Burack, E. H., 1966, "Technology and some aspects of industrial supervision: a model building approach." *Journal of Academy of Management*, 9:43–66.

—— 1967, "Industrial management in advanced production systems: some theoretical concepts and preliminary findings." *Administrative Science Quarterly*, 12:479–500.

Cyert, R. M., and J. G. March, 1963, *A Behavioral Theory of the Firm*. Englewood Cliffs: Prentice-Hall.

Drucker, P. F., 1955, *The Practice of Management*. London: Heinemann.

Dubin, R., 1958, *The World of Work*. Englewood Cliffs: Prentice-Hall.

Durkheim, E., 1947, *The Division of Labor in Society*. George Simpson trans. Glencoe: Free Press.

Fayol, H., 1949, *General and Industrial Management*. C. Storrs trans. London: Pitman.

Fensham, P. J., and D. Hooper, 1964, *The Dynamics of a Changing Technology*. London: Tavistock.

Florence, P. S., 1961, *Ownership, Control and Success of Large Companies*. London: Sweet and Maxwell.

Gibbs, J. P., and H. L. Browning, 1966, "The division of labor, technology, and the organization of production in twelve countries." *American Sociological Review*, 31:81–92.

Guttman, L., 1950, Chapters 1–4 in S. A. Stouffer *et al.*, *Measurement and Prediction*, (Vol. IV, Studies in Social Psychology in World War II series). New Jersey: Princeton University Press.

Harvey, Edward, 1968, "Technology and the structure of organizations." *American Sociological Review*, 33:247–259.

Herbst, P. G., 1962, *Autonomous Group Functioning*. London: Tavistock.

Inkson, J. H. K., R. L. Payne, and D. S. Pugh, 1967, "Extending the occupational environment: the measurement of organizations." *Occupational Psychology*, 41:33–47.

Lave, L. B., 1966, *Technological Change: Its Conception and Measurement*. Englewood Cliffs: Prentice-Hall.

Levy, P., and D. S. Pugh, 1969, "Scaling and multivariate analyses in the study of organizational variables." *Sociology*, 3, 2:193–213.

Lodahl, T. M., 1964, "Patterns of job attitudes in two assembly technologies." *Administrative Science Quarterly*, 8:483–519.

Mann, F. C., and L. R. Hoffman, 1960, *Automation and the Worker*. New York: Holt, Rinehart and Winston.

Perrow, C., 1967, "A framework for the comparative analysis of organizations." *American Sociological Review*, 32:194–208.

Pugh, D. S., D. J. Hickson, C. R. Hinings, K. M. Macdonald, C. Turner, and T. Lupton, 1963, "A conceptual scheme for organizational analysis." *Administrative Science Quarterly*, 8, 3:289–315.

Pugh, D. S., D. J. Hickson, C. R. Hinings, and C. Turner, 1968, "Dimensions of organization structure." *Administrative Science Quarterly*, 13, 1:65–105.

Pugh, D. S., D. J. Hickson, C. R. Hinings, and C. Turner, 1969a, "The context of organization structures." *Administrative Science Quarterly*, 14, 1:91.

Pugh, D. S., D. J. Hickson, and C. R. Hinings, 1969b, "An empirical taxonomy of structures of work organizations." *Administrative Science Quarterly*, 14, 1:115.

Sayles, L. R., 1958, *Behavior of Industrial Work Groups*. New York: Wiley.

Scott, W. H., J. Banks, A. H. Halsey, and T. Lupton, 1956, *Technical Change and Industrial Relations*. Liverpool: Liverpool University Press.

Starbuck, W. H., 1965, "Organizational growth and development." In J. G. March (ed.), *Handbook of Organizations*. Chicago: Rand McNally.

Thompson, J. D., 1967, *Organizations in Action*. New York: McGraw-Hill.

Thompson, J. D., and F. L. Bates, 1957, "Technology, organization, and administration." *Administrative Science Quarterly*, 2:325–343.

Trist, E. L., and K. W. Bamforth, 1951, "Some social and psychological consequences of the longwall method of coal-getting." *Human Relations*, 4:3–38.

Turner, A. N., and P. R. Lawrence, 1965, *Industrial Jobs and the Worker*. Cambridge, Mass.. Harvard University Press.

Udy, S. H., Jr., 1959, *Organization of Work*. New Haven: Human Relations Area Files Press.

——— 1961, "Technical and institutional factors in production organization." *American Journal of Sociology*, LXVII:247–260.

Urwick, L. F., 1947, *The Elements of Administration*. London: Pitman.

Walker, C. R., and R. H. Guest, 1952, *The Man on the Assembly Line*. Cambridge, Mass.: Harvard University Press.

Woodward, J., 1958, *Management and Technology*. Problems of Progress in Industry Series No. 3. London: Her Majesty's Stationery Office.

——— 1965, *Industrial Organization*. Oxford: University Press.

Technology and Organizational Structure: A Reexamination of the Findings of the Aston Group

Howard E. Aldrich

Investigators of organizational behavior have recently turned their attention to technology as an important organizational variable. While no one denies its significance, there is disagreement over whether technology is an independent or dependent variable, and over the weight to be given to technology as compared to other variables. Blauner (1964), Woodward (1965), and Perrow (1970), for instance, treat technology as an independent variable which exerts a causal influence on various aspects of organizational structure. Others, especially the Aston group of Pugh, Hickson, Hinings, MacDonald, Turner, and Lupton (1963), treat technology as a dependent variable and downgrade its importance in a theory of organization.

The purpose of this article is to investigate the importance of technology, giving special attention to whether it should be considered an independent or dependent variable in organizational theory.* This question will be examined by reanalyzing data collected by the Aston group from forty-six manufacturing and service organizations. Their research was carried out at the Industrial Administration Research Unit of the University of Aston in Birmingham, England, and has been reported in the *Administrative Science Quarterly* in a series of five articles.

Their work was chosen for two reasons. First, it represents a laudable attempt to operationalize many key organizational variables. Second, it was a long-term project, with a great deal of time devoted to data analysis and interpretation.

Reanalysis of the Pugh *et al.* data is approached from two perspectives. Their statement concerning size, technology, and structure is first examined, with an assessment made of the degree to which their interpretations are supported by a more rigorous analysis of the data. The concepts and variables they developed are then reviewed to demonstrate how they can be put together into a theory of organizational structure which makes theoretical and empirical sense. Their data is reanalyzed by means of path analysis . . . A secondary purpose of this article is to alert organization theorists to the usefulness of path analysis for studying organizational variables.

*An earlier version of this article was presented at the Conference on Technology in Organizations of the Future, held at the New York State School of Industrial and Labor Relations, November 1970. The author is grateful to the following for their comments and suggestions: Boris Allan, Peter Blau, John Child, Robert Cooper, Otis Dudley Duncan, Robert Hauser, Marshall Meyer, Neil Henry, Charles Perrow, William Starbuck, Larry Williams, and the members of the Aston group.

Reprinted in part from *Administrative Science Quarterly*, vol. 17 (March, 1972), pp. 26–40, 43, by permission.

Criticisms of the Study

The Aston group state their purpose as follows:

> The structure of an organization is closely related to the context within which it functions, and much of the variation in organization structures might be explained by contextual factors. Many such factors, including size, technology, organizational charter or social function, and interdependence with other organizations, have been suggested as being of primary importance in influencing the structure and functioning of an organization. There have been few attempts, however, to relate these factors in a comparative systematic way to the characteristic aspects of structure, for such studies would require a multivariate functional approach in both context and structure (Pugh et al., 1969: 91).

After criticizing other theorists for taking a unitary approach or assuming that any one particular organizational characteristic is the major determinant of structure, the investigators indicate their goal: a multivariate analysis of organizational variables, in an analysis treating contextual variables as independent and structural variables as dependent. (The original statement of goals, in the form of a research proposal, appeared in Pugh et al., 1963).

While their research is a part of a large-scale, long-term project, the group can be criticized for not codifying their arguments to make clear the hypothesized pattern of relations between variables. On the one hand, they argue from a causal model perspective, as seen in the following comment:

> Indeed the size of the correlations inevitably raises the question of causal implications. It is tempting to argue that these clear relationships are causal—in particular, that *size, dependence, and the charter-technology-location nexus largely determine structure* (Pugh, et al., 1969: 112).

On the other hand, they make statements denying any intent to develop a causal model:

> But a cross-sectional study such as this can only establish relationships. Causes should be inferred from a theory that generates a dynamic model about changes over time (Pugh, et al., 1969: 112).

It is clear that in spite of this disclaimer, the authors have made statements that can only be interpreted causally. For example, they repeatedly use such terms as impact, predictors, and relationships. Words such as relationship are not neutral, unless one wants to assert that he is merely interested in covariation and not causal relationships. In any case, the authors' repeated use of causal imagery and language does not allow them to fall back on a covariation argument.

The question of building a causal model is important enough to merit further attention. It is assumed that the ultimate goal of the Aston group was to develop a causal model of organizational development. Any attempt at theory construction pushes the theorist into considerations of causal relations between variables. A further assumption is that a useful place to begin such a task is with the analysis of cross-sectional data, given the lack of longitudinal data.

In response to an earlier draft of this article, Pugh stated:

> I think it is certainly possible to make some assessments and ask whether the organizational growth model is at least not contradicted by these data. It was on this basis that we suggested that our empirically tested cross-sectional typology could, in fact, be a developmental sequence (Pugh, 1971).

Pugh went on to point out that the Aston group had no longitudinal data with which to test their model directly. They did, however, follow up with a subsample of the forty-six organizations (Inkson *et al.*, 1970).

There are several reasons for the assumptions made here. First, using cross-sectional data to make inferences about organizational development makes sense if one believes that the organizations studied are at various stages in a pattern of growth which holds true across all organizations. The cross-sectional data can be assumed to have caught different organizations at different stages in a developmental sequence. This also assumes asymmetric causality, of course, which is undoubtedly a questionable assumption. Given the nature of the undertaking, however, the analysis can proceed while recognizing the tentativeness of the assumptions, rather than waiting until longitudinal data are obtained.

This article seeks to make explicit what other investigators have left implicit and taken for granted. Social scientists constantly make causal assertions based on cross-sectional data. The major advantage of using path analysis is that an investigator is forced to bring his assumptions out into the open.

A second general criticism of the Aston group is that in many cases their data analysis tends to obscure important relationships. They interpret zero-order correlations as telling something about the organizations studied, yet they also have a theory that some variables are more important than others in a causally prior sense. In the language of path analysis, many of the zero-order correlations result from the effect of an independent variable's effect on the dependent variable as mediated through an intervening variable. This can be seen not only by examining their theory, but also by considering whether it is logically and theoretically possible for twenty-six variables to be of equivalent importance, in the sense of a number of states being causally prior, in their effect on the dependent variable (Table 8 in Hickson, *et al.*, 1969: 386).

A third general criticism involves the question of the strategy of doing multivariate analysis. In discussing how to choose variables to enter into a multiple regression, they state:

> If high intercorrelations among the predictors were allowed, then, since the high correlations with the criterion would be aspects of the same relationship, the multiple correlation would not be increased to any extent. If the intercorrelations between the predictors were low, then each would make its distinct contribution to the multiple correlation (Pugh, *et al.*, 1969: 109).

The important question raised here is how to deal with the problem. Increasing the size of the multiple correlation would be of importance only insofar as it gives more confidence in the power of the variables chosen. By itself, it is of no help in determining theoretical importance. The more important pieces of information are the individual regression coefficients, standardized or unstandardized.

The investigators apparently were unaware of path analysis at the time of their data analysis, and so their solution to the problem of intercorrelated independent variables is to ask for a sample in which they are not correlated (Pugh *et al.*, 1969: 110). This requirement is unnecessary and probably impossible to fill. Path analysis allows the investigator to assess the effect of intercorrelated exogenous variables, by giving him a language for talking about such occurrences (indirect and direct effects). Path analysis does not allow the investigator to assign all of the intercorrelation effect to one of the two or more variables, of course, but its virtue lies in showing that, in the absence of more knowledge about the exogenous variables, such a procedure would be illegitimate. The fact that some of the exogenous variables are intercorrelated, moreover, should be treated as a datum. If that is the way things are, empirically, it is futile to hope for a situation in which variables are uncorrelated. (If he persists in his wish for uncorrelated exogenous variables, the investigator could take his problem into the laboratory and control them under experimental conditions.)

A fourth criticism concerns the construction of their variable called work flow integration or, in some cases, simply technology. At one point, the investigators note that many of the large correlations between technology and other variables are due to the "crude difference between service and manufacturing which is reflected in the polar tendencies of service and manufacturing organizations on [many of their scales]" (Hickson *et al.*, 1969: 388). What they do not point out is the severity of the polarity between service and manufacturing organizations. As can be demonstrated with their own data, the manner in which technology is operationalized gives an almost perfect dichotomy between the two types of organizations. There is a real question as to whether the technology measure is not simply acting as a dummy variable for manufacturing/nonmanufacturing.

Scores on the technology measure range from a low of one to a high of seventeen. The severity of the polarity can be seen when this measure is divided into two groups—one through nine and ten through seventeen, calling the first group low and the second group high on technology. Of the seventeen organizations low on technology, thirteen (76 percent) are service organizations. Of the twenty-nine organizations high on technology, twenty-seven (93 percent) are manufacturing organizations. This finding does not support the investigators' contention that "the tendency was by no means so pronounced as to produce a dichotomous result. There was appreciable overlap. . . ." (Hickson, *et al.*, 1969: 384). The technology measure differentiates between two different populations of organizations.

The effect of this dichotomy pervades their analysis. Since most of the fifteen service organizations fall in the low end of the technology scale, the effect of including them in the correlations for all forty-six organizations is artificially to enhance the correlations of technology with the other structural variables. Twenty of the twenty-six correlations between technology and other variables reported in Table 8 of Hickson *et al.* (1969) are substantially lower for the group of thirty-one manufacturing organizations than for the total group of forty-six organizations. In graphic terms, if one imagines that technology is arrayed along a horizontal axis and the structural variables along the vertical axis, the inherent dichotomy in the technology measure produces two clusters of points in space defined by the two axes: at the low end are the service firms and at the high end are the manufacturing firms.

One way of dealing with the manufacturing-service dichotomy would be to include a dummy variable in the data analysis whenever the technology measure is used. The dummy variable could take the value one for manufacturing firms and zero for service firms. Further analysis of the data, however, could indicate that the manufacturing-service dichotomy is so severe as to warrant a separate analysis for each industry type. This would be the case if it is found that the form of the relationship between variables is substantially different within the two types of firms. Only further analysis of the raw data will solve this problem. (The raw data were not available when this article was written; all analysis rely on published correlations.)

A final problem involves accepting the concepts and operational definitions of the Aston group at face value. Labels such as technology and concentration of authority may appear vague when stated in a shorthanded way. The Aston group, however, has developed and elaborated upon these concepts in a long series of articles beginning in 1963, and the present article assumes that the reader has at least some previous acquaintance with their work. No attempt will be made here to summarize all of the Aston group's research.

The problem of operational definitions is a more serious one of the extent to which the operational versions of the concepts are really valid indicators of what they purport to measure. The operationalization of such concepts as structuring of activities involves the aggregation of a multitude of indicators which are, in turn, composed of still other aggregates of multiple items. Two problems are thus posed for anyone who attempts to reanalyze or replicate the Aston group's work. First, are the indicators so complex as to defy description by a label such as structuring of activities or technology? Second, are the indicators so strongly tied to the specific empirical context of the fifty-two organizations studied that they cannot be used in other contexts?

Any empirical research involves the problem of operationalizing indicators and the ultimate test of their validity is an intersubjective one, namely, the test of whether other investigators accept and are able to replicate an investigator's findings in other contexts.

Size, Technology, and Structure

The Aston group state the importance of three variables: size, technology, and structuring of activities. Analysis of these variables reported in Hickson *et al.* (1969) will be relied on here. Their argument about the causal relationships among the three variables is summarized in their article:

> At this point it could be concluded that the broad hypothesis holds good; technology and structure are related; but the strength of multivariate research design is that it prevents premature conclusions. Pugh *et al.* (1969a: Table 8) have already demonstrated that although technology does have a diffused relationship with the structural dimensions, it always takes second place to other variables. This can be seen in Table 8 (column 2) in the correlations between structuring of activities (and the component variables in specialization, standardization, and formalization) and size. Correlations with technology are overwhelmed by those with size; and in multiple regression, Pugh *et al.* found that combination of work flow integration with size only raised the 0.69 correlation of size alone with structuring of activities to a multiple correlation of 0.75. . . . In short, operations technology . . . is accounting for but a small proportion of the total variance in structural features. . . . On this sample, the broad "technological imperative" hypothesis that operations technology is of primary importance to structure, is not supported (Hickson *et al.*, 1969: 387–388).

The authors go on to test their hypothesis by examining only the group of thirty-one manufacturing organizations. Again, they find technology to be an insignificant variable: "The irrelevance of technology is emphasized when the effects of size are removed" (Hickson *et al.*, 1969: 388).

Because they did not diagram the implications either of their conclusions or of other logical possibilities, they fail to realize the full implications of their conclusions. Many interpretations of their findings are possible, given their ambiguity about the correct causal ordering of their variables. That is, their two operations of adding technology to regression equations already containing size and of using size as a control variable in partial correlation analysis do not inevitably lead to the conclusions they draw.

The strategy of removing the effects of size can imply four different causal orderings of the three variables involved: (1) size causes technology and structure; (2) size and technology are correlated but not causally related and both are causally related to structure; (3) size causes technology and structure and, in addition, technology has an independent effect on structure; and (4) technology causes size and it, in turn, causes structure. These four possibilities are diagramed in Figure 1. We say that these four possibilities are equally implied by the Hickson *et al.* analysis because in each case, if size were controlled and the partial correlation between technology and structure examined, the partial could be smaller than the zero-order correlation between technology and structure. (The zero-order correlations are given in Table 1.)

Before proceeding with the analysis, it should be noted that with three variables and using an uncorrelated error, recursive type model, it is possible to construct eighteen different path diagrams, each with a unique causal ordering of the variables. Once it is recognized, it is easier to appreciate the amount of prior thought and selection which must go into choosing the final models one wishes to test. Selected models in Figure 1 (rather than all eighteen possible models) were chosen for the reasons given above. The models in Figure 2 were chosen because they made the most theoretical and logical sense out of the data.

While the four models in Figure 1 fit the criteria used by Hickson *et al.*, there are other grounds for evaluating their acceptability. One basis for evaluating the models is whether they fit reasonably the pattern of intercorrelations observed among the variables. Another criterion is whether the causal ordering of the variables is logically and temporally plausible. Using these criteria, Figure 1 can be considered.

Models 1b and 1c must necessarily fit the pattern of intercorrelations, since all three correlations were used to derive the path coefficients given in the diagram. These models are not true tests of the causal ordering, since both will reproduce perfectly the observed correlations. In model 1b, the theorist has left the correlation between size and technology unanalyzed, preferring simply to acknowledge the fact of their association. Both size and technology are allowed to have direct effects on structure, with size having an impact more than double that of technology. One would not infer from this model that technology was unimportant, however, but only that its impact is less than that of size. In model 1c, the theorist has gone a step further in postulating causal relations among the variables by stating that size has a direct causal impact on technology. The coefficients in 1b

TABLE 1 *Intercorrelations among Size, Technology, and Structure*

	(2) Technology	(3) Structure
(1) Size	0.08	0.69
(2) Technology		0.34

N = 46

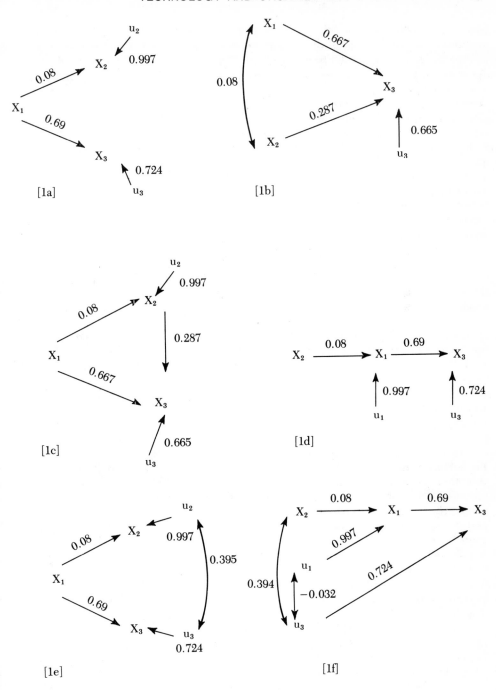

N = 46
Size = X_1
Technology = X_2
Structure = X_3

Figure 1   Six Possible Models of the Relationships Among Size, Technology, and Organizational Structure

and 1c are exactly the same; the only change is in the theorist's willingness to make a choice as to the source of the association between size and technology.

Models 1a and 1d (without the residual correlations) do not use all of the information about the pattern of intercorrelations in the derivation of their path coefficients and so a test of their adequacy is possible. The test is whether the model, as constructed, permits the theorist to reproduce correlations which were not used in the original derivation of the path coefficients. For model 1a, the basic theorem of path analysis tells us that the correlation between X_2 and X_3 should be equal to $r_{12}p_{31}$, or, since $p_{21} = r_{12}$, simply $p_{21}p_{31}$. This equivalency should hold true if X_1 is the sole cause of the association between X_2 and X_3. For model 1a, this is clearly not the case: (0.08) $(0.69) = 0.055$, whereas the actual $r_{23} = 0.34$. A correlation between the residuals of X_2 and X_3 must therefore be introduced to signify that some other unaccounted-for force is partially responsible for the association between technology and structure. In this case, the required correlation between the residuals is given by the following computation:

$$r_{23} = r_{12}p_{31} + p_{u3 \times 3} (r_{u3u2}) p_{u2 \times 2},$$
$$\text{or } 0.34 = 0.055 + 0.722 r_{u3u2}.$$

This equation is easily solved, resulting in $r_{u3u2} = 0.395$. This correlation changes model 1a to model 1e. A theorist would probably be inclined to revise his model in the light of this finding, although there is no hard and fast rule to be applied. (Some investigators suggest that it is the size of the required residual correlations as compared to the size of the path coefficients in the model that is the deciding factor.) For example, one revision of 1a would be to introduce a causal link between X_2 and X_3 as in 1c. The above procedure is the same for model 1d, and the revised model is 1f. The conclusion reached with regard to 1a would also apply to 1d. (The correlation between U_1 and U_3 in model 1f has been added for reasons that need not concern the general reader.)

On the basis of the models set forth in Figure 1, the theorist could come to several conclusions. He might accept model 1e, which states the size has a causal impact on both technology and structure and that technology and structure do not directly affect one another but are affected by some common factors other than size. These additional forces operate in a similar fashion on both and cause them to be positively correlated. Or model 1a could be revised to resemble 1c. Both 1b and 1c are necessarily compatible with the observed data. Model 1d would probably be rejected in favor of a model that allows X_2 (technology) to have a direct impact on structure, since the total effect of technology on structure is not reproduced through its indirect effect via its direct impact on size. Model 1d, however, departs radically from the conclusions reached by Hickson *et al.* in the sense that such a model was not even considered by them in their published analysis.

Reexamining the first three models in Figure 1, any one of which is congruent with the conclusions reached by Hickson *et al.*, one is struck by the implausibility of each when phrased in terms of cause and effect. All three models imply that size causes organizational structure, and two of the three imply that size causes technology.

How can size have a causal impact on organizational structure or on organizational technology? Stating that size causes structure implies that those persons in the organization responsible for its design first accumulate a body of employees of a given size and then structure the organization's activities accordingly. A more plausible position would be that such matters as the definition of appropriate employee behavior, the degree of role specialization, the degree of formalization of written procedures, and so forth are planned for and at least partially determined before there is any increase in the size of the work force.

It should be noted that many theorists who consider size an important variable have in mind things related to the magnitude of an organization's output, not the size of the labor force. For example, the use of the phrase "economies of scale" seems to indicate an important role that size plays in industrial organizations. In this case size, however, refers to the scale of an organization's operations and not necessarily to the size of the labor force. The Aston group has no measure of magnitude of output and so unfortunately many key propositions about the effects of size cannot be dealt with in this article.

The treatment of size as primarily a dependent variable is thus not as radical a departure from past practices as it would appear, since concern here is only with the number of persons a firm employs. It should be pointed out, moreover, that a truly comprehensive theory of organizational development should allow for feedback loops and reciprocal relations between size and other variables. The work reported is only a first approximation to such a theory; further data collection is needed before making a final decision as to the importance of size.

It would seem implausible that size can have a causal impact on technology. The reader will recall that the Hickson study asserts that technology "always takes second place to other variables" (Hickson *et al.*, 1969: 387). This assertion was made partially as a result of finding that correlations with technology were overwhelmed by those with size. The fallacy of dropping the analysis at this point has already been discussed. Put another way, how could one accept the statement that size is causally prior to technology in determining the structure of an organization or that size predominates over technology? The components of the technology variable used by Hickson are automation of equipment, adaptability of work flow, and evaluation of operations. While one might grant that evaluation procedures may be changed as a result of changes in the number of employees, in most cases it is clearly implausible that the level of automation or the firm's degree of work flow rigidity would be determined in response to the number of persons it employs. It is possible that in a small number of cases, anticipation of a future size causes managers to make changes in the level of automation or structure of their firm. A firm faced with rising labor costs and the need to expand production, for example, might decide to automate rather than hire more employees.

Clearly, decisions about most aspects of an organization's technology are made well in advance of hiring or changing the size of a work force. Not only can the causal ordering implied in models 1a and 1c not be accepted, but the implication of model 1b that technology and organizational size are on a level of causal priority also must be questioned. It is interesting to note that a follow-up longitudinal study by the Aston group found no association between changes in size and changes in the structuring of activities or technology of a firm (Inkson *et al.*, 1970). Technology showed almost no change, compared to changes in size.

On the basis of the above argument, one does not necessarily expect to find a high correlation between technology and size. Obviously, there are other determinants of the number of employees of an organization. The correlation of size with technology is substantially higher among the subset of manufacturing firms (0.30) than among the entire set of organizations (0.08). Before abandoning the causal sequence laid out above, the reliability and/or validity of the measures used in the Hickson study might be questioned. The small size of the observed correlations, however, is not a sufficient reason for rejecting an argument based on sound logical, temporal, and theoretical grounds. If one were to theorize in processual, dynamic terms, he would have to consider the actual developmental sequence of an organization. Size certainly does not come first. The models in Figure 2 were constructed to correspond more closely to the logical development of an organization.

The four models in Figure 2 reflect the assumption of the technological imperative rejected by the Aston group. The theory underlying all of the models treats an organization as a consciously planned, rationally designed system which develops in response to both internal and external forces, with all forces having their eventual impact through the decisions of management. In brief, the development of an organization proceeds from its initial founding and capitalization in response to perceived market opportunities, through its design based on copying and modifying an existing technology, on to the design of the organization's structure, and finally to the employment of a work force to staff the nearly completed organization. This obviously over-simplified view of the development of an organization leads to specific predictions about the causal ordering of observed organizational variables. Technology is causally prior to the size of the work force, and organizational structure is at least initially causally prior to size. Technology is also causally prior to organization structure.

Model 2a confirms the necessity of assuming that structure has a direct effect on size. When technology is assumed to be the sole cause of the association between structure and size, it is necessary to introduce a correlation of 0.707 between the residuals of the two variables. This large correlation is unacceptable, and so a direct effect of structure upon size is included in model 2b.

Model 2b is congruent with the theory of organizational development outlined above and also has a plausible substantive interpretation. The positive direct impact of technology on the structuring of activities indicates that the more automated and interdependent the operations technology, the more highly structured the activities of the organization. The negative impact of technology on size indicates that the more automated and output oriented the organization, the fewer the number of persons employed. It would be strange if the opposite were the case. In this instance, the positive zero-order correlation (0.08) masked a more plausible direct effect because the variables were not viewed in a proper theoretical context. (Hickson *et al*. apparently did not question this rather odd zero-order relationship.)

One difficulty with this interpretation is that we lack a measure of output, which is another measure of size. It is possible that more automation could lead to more persons being employed, if more automation lowered costs and allowed more output to be produced at a lower cost per unit. Thus, a more adequate test of the theory should hold output constant.

Finally, the positive direct effect of the structuring of activities variable on organizational size is probably due to the fact that firms which are highly structured, according to the way the variable was constructed by Hickson *et al*. have a highly differentiated and specialized set of work roles to fill. This type of firm requires more employees than one in which employees can be jacks of all trades. That is, as the division of labor in an organization increases, the number of employees, by definition, must necessarily increase.

To point out that model 2b was not the only way of describing how technol-

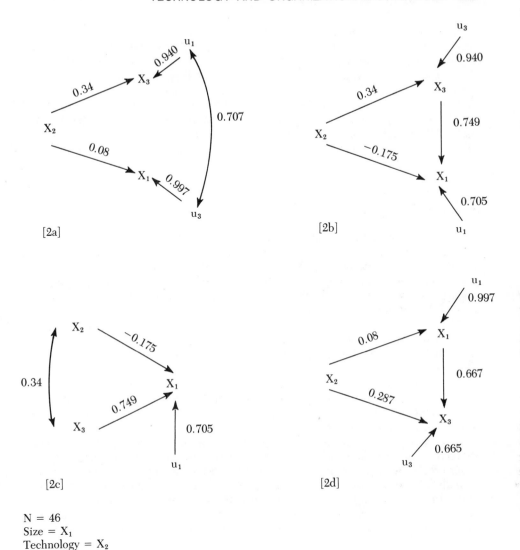

N = 46
Size = X_1
Technology = X_2
Structure = X_3

Figure 2   Additional Possible Models of the Relationships Among Size, Technology, and Structure, with Causal Importance of Technology Emphasized

ogy could plausibly play an important role in a theory of organizations involving these data, models 2c and 2d were constructed. Model 2c stops short of making a judgment about the causal priority of technology versus structure and assumes that the two have a joint impact on size. Model 2d assumes that the causal ordering of structure and size is reversed from the position hypothesized in 2b and allows size to have a positive impact on structure. In this case, technology has a positive impact on size, an outcome which was previously rejected because it runs counter to most current theories about the effect of automation on the size of a firm's work force.

More could be extracted from the models given in Figures 1 and 2. This section served simply to demonstrate the large amount of information which was lost because of the manner in which Hickson *et al.* analyzed and presented their data. Osmond's criticism of the Aston group's work also focuses on the importance assigned to size as opposed to other organizational variables. He argues that size and technology must be examined in the context of the organization's attempt to achieve its goals "within a changing and challenging environment" (Osmond, 1970: 44). In terms of a strategy for analysis, Osmond's view implies a more complex model of organizational development than is presented in Figures 1 and 2.

A Revised Model

Correlations presented in Table 2 were used in the construction of the model of organizational development given in Figure 3. The causal arrangement of the variables was determined by a reexamination of the arguments of the Aston group and on the basis of its congruence with what is known about the actual stages of organizational development. The following paragraphs set forth the causal argument in more detail.

Dependence and technology were assumed to be primary causes of organizational structure. Matters of external dependence must be settled early at the institutional level of the organization—by top management and the board of directors. Components of the dependence variable used by the Aston group are (1) dependence on the parent organization, in terms of size and degrees of autonomy; (2) representation on the policy-making body of the firm; and (3) dependence on trade unions and other organizations. Logically and temporally, dependence must have high causal priority in the model.

Technology also has high causal priority because an organization's choice of its technology is deliberate and conscious, with other aspects of organizational design following logically from the particular technology chosen. Hickson *et al.* actually have two variables measuring aspects of technology, in the sense the term is used by Thompson (1967) and Perrow (1970). One measure is operating variability, "conceptualized as being concerned with manufacturing nonstandard producer goods as against providing standard consumer service" (Pugh *et al.*, 1969:

TABLE 2 *Intercorrelations among Seven Organizational Variables*

	(2)	(3)	(4)	(5)	(6)	(7)
(1) Size	0.08	0.69	−0.10	−0.15	−0.06	−0.24
(2) Work flow integration (technology 1)		0.34	−0.30	−0.46	−0.05	0.57
(3) Structuring of activities			*	*	−0.05	0.26
(4) Concentration of authority				*	0.66	−0.22
(5) Line control of work flow					0.13	−0.57
(6) Dependence						0.05
(7) Operating variability (technology 2)						

* No information available as to the size of these correlations.

100). Organizations providing standard, low-variability services, for instance, in transport or retailing, score low as opposed to those firms producing output tailored specifically to the needs of individual consumers, for example, engineering repair firms or a packaging manufacturer. Operating variability appears, on its face, to be an important variable and the kind of dimension pointed to by Perrow in his analysis of technology. There it is described as the degree to which the organization must deal with exceptional cases and engage in nonstandardized search behavior (Perrow, 1970).

One of Osmond's major criticisms of the Aston group's concept of technology is at least partially met by including operating variability as a technology variable. Osmond contends that Pugh *et al*. "have a pretty narrow idea of what technology means, in the context of the whole organization and of all kinds of organizations" (Osmond, 1970: 43). As he points out, Woodward and her colleagues have pursued several new dimensions of manufacturing technology since the original studies were reported in 1958. The new dimensions of technology include manufacturing cycle times and product innovation frequency, with both dimensions concerned with frequency of change and flexibility. These are the dimensions emphasized by Thompson and Perrow, and operating variability seems to come very close to this new conception of technology.

A second technology variable is variously called operations technology, work flow integration, or just technology. It is defined as the "degree of automated, continuous, fixed-sequence operation in the technology" (Hickson *et al*., 1969: 384). The higher a firm's score on this measure, the lower the proportion of total costs devoted to labor costs.

Three structural variables are treated as dependent variables in the Pugh study (1969): (1) structuring of activities; (2) concentration of authority; and (3) line control of work flow. The implicitly causal argument of that study has been followed in the placement of the three variables in Figure 3, with two exceptions: size is hypothesized to be dependent on structuring of activities and to have a causal impact on line control of authority, whereas size is treated by Pugh *et al*. as an independent variable in every case. There is undoubtedly a reciprocal relationship between size and these three structural variables. An ideal test of the model would require data gathered at more than one point in time. The concern here is with an idealized developmental process and thus the causal sequence in Figure 3 is retained.

The definitions of the three structural variables given by Hickson *et al*. are:

> . . . structuring of activities refers to the degree of formal regulation of the intended activities of employees; concentration of authority is the degree to which authority for decisions rests in controlling units outside the organization and is centralized at the higher hierarchical levels within it; line control of work flow refers to control of operations on the throughputs being exercised directly by line management, as against impersonal control through records and procedures by staff departments (Hickson *et al*., 1969: 385).

The placement of size in Figure 3 follows from the arguments made in the previous section. Size is operationalized as the logarithm of the total number of employees. A more extended discussion of the causal model underlying Figure 3 will be given as specific variables are considered. Part of the following argument is taken from the work of the Aston group. Analysis will begin at the left, with exogenous variables, and continue across the diagram in the order of the postu-

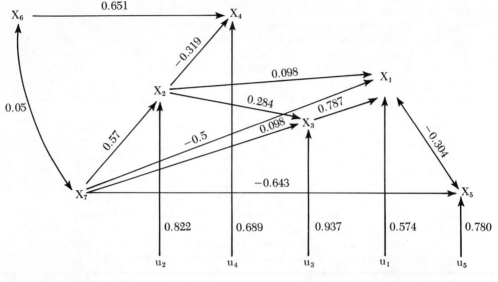

Size = X_1
Workflow integration = X_2
Structuring of activities = X_3
Concentration of authority = X_4

Line control of work flow = X_5
Dependence = X_6
Operating variability = X_7

Note: Correlations between residuals have been omitted.

Figure 3   A Revised Model of Organizational Development Based on the Findings of the Aston Group

lated causal sequence. Dependence and operating variability are exogenous variables, with their causes presumed to lie outside the system of variables in Figure 3. They are correlated with each other, but the reasons for their relationship are unclear and therefore no causal relation is postulated between them.

Pugh *et al.* hypothesize that dependence has a positive causal impact on concentration of authority "because pressure for public accountability requires the approval of central committees for many decisions" (Pugh *et al.*, 1969: 112). Work flow integration also has a causal impact on concentration of authority, with the more highly automated firms being more decentralized. An interpretation of the negative impact of work flow integration is partially obscured because of the diversity of components to the concentration of authority variable.

Operating variability has a positive impact on work flow integration, reflecting the fact that firms with a high degree of variability are highly automated manufacturing firms, while those low in variability are technologically unsophisticated service-oriented firms. Operating variability also has insignificant positive impact on structuring of activities. It has a fairly large indirect impact, however, through its effect on work flow integration, which in turn has a positive impact on structuring of activities.

Work flow integration has a direct causal impact on structuring of activities, because automation and rigidity in the work flow constrain the work force toward specialization and standardization. Work flow integration was hypothesized to have a negative impact on size; there is an inclination to dismiss the slight positive path coefficient shown in Figure 3 as insignificant, especially in view of the strong theoretical expectation that it should be negative. The insignificance of the path coefficient suggests that in this data set, given the assumptions made, work flow integration has no direct impact on size.

Two dependent variables remain to be examined. Size is treated as a function of work flow integration, structuring of activities, and operating variability. Structuring of activities is presumed to have a positive impact on size because the more highly structured firms, with their greater degree of specialization, formalization, and monitoring of role performance, simply need to employ a larger work force than less structured firms. (The path coefficient for this relationship is 0.787, the largest in Figure 3.)

The negative impact of operating variability on size is probably due to the need to remain flexible in the face of highly varying demands on the organization. Unfortunately, the true effect of operating variability is confounded by a manufacturing-service industry dichotomy in the measure.

Line control of authority, the last endogenous variable in Figure 3, is directly affected by size and operating variability. The larger the firm, the less control the line has over its work operations, with other units or levels of the firm taking over control of the line (Pugh *et al.*, 1968: 87). Finally, the greater the degree of operating variability, the less the control of work procedures by the work flow personnel themselves. Once again the break between manufacturing and service firms partially distorts the interpretation, but it is evident that firms needing to respond and adapt quickly to external demands must exercise a great deal of control over the scheduling and monitoring of activities of the line.

In summary, all but one of the path coefficients in Figure 3 is congruent with the above theory of organizational development. Furthermore, the technique of path analysis allows the application of additional tests to the model.

Further Benefits of Path Analysis

Path analysis allows the investigator to put to use information which is not directly used in the computation of path coefficients. For example, no use was made of r_{14} in the data analysis for Figure 3. The model, however, leads to a prediction of the value of r_{14}, based on the common causes of X_1 and X_4 postulated by the model. The equation giving the expected value is $r_{14} = p_{12}r_{24} + p_{13}r_{34} + p_{17}r_{47}$. The reader should note that this equation stems from the basic theorem of path analysis, and the correlations in the equation are those generated by the model and do not necessarily correspond to the observed correlations.

Elaborating upon this equation, the expected value of r_{14} is found to be 0.046, whereas the value observed in the data is -0.10. To produce the -0.10 correlation, it is necessary to introduce a correlation between the residual causes of X_1 and X_4 of -0.15. In terms of the above equation, the term $p_{u4}r_{u4u1}p_{u1}$ was added to the equation, or $(0.689)(-0.35)(0.574)$. Substantively, this residual correlation could mean that there is an additional, unknown force operating with opposite effects on X_1 and X_4 and thus tending to push them in opposing directions. A residual correlation this small, of course, could be due simply to sampling error and not to flaws in the model. (Residual correlations have not been included in Figure 3 because of space limitations.)

TABLE 3 *Predicted and Actual Correlations Between Seven Organizational Variables Based on the Model in Figure 4*

Correlation	Predicted	Actual	Required residual r
r_{14}	−0.046	−0.10	−0.135
r_{16}	−0.012	−0.06	−0.084
r_{25}	−0.370	−0.46	−0.141
r_{26}	0.028	−0.05	−0.095
r_{36}	0.013	−0.05	−0.067
r_{47}	−0.149	−0.22	−0.103
r_{56}	−0.027	0.13	0.201

Table 3 presents a comparison of predicted with actual correlations, based on Figure 3. The seven correlations predicted by the model are reasonably close to those observed in the data. Information is lacking with respect to the actual magnitude of the following correlations: r_{34}, r_{35}, and r_{45}. These are the three variables the Aston group labelled structuring of activities, concentration of authority, and line control of work flow. The Aston group asserts that these three variables are conceptually independent, and one of their articles reports that the components of the three were originally derived from a factor analysis using orthogonal factor rotation. In the actual scoring of the measures, however, no attempt was made to keep them statistically independent. Thus, the three are in fact correlated, but the size of the correlation has not been reported and so these variables are not included in Table 3.

A second major piece of information is conveyed by the data presented in Table 4 on the direct and indirect effects of four major independent variables used in Figure 3: operating variability, work flow integration, structuring of activities,

TABLE 4 *Decomposition of Zero-Order Correlations into Direct and Indirect Effects*

Dependent Variable	Direct Effect	Indirect Effect	Total Correlation
Operating variability: effects on			
work flow integration	0.570		0.57
structuring of activities	0.098	0.162	0.26
size	−0.500	0.260	−0.24
line control	−0.643	0.073	−0.57
concentration of authority		−0.149	−0.22
Work flow integration: effects on			
structuring of activities	0.284		0.34
size	0.098	0.224	0.08
line control		0.098	−0.46
concentration of authority	−0.268		−0.30
Structuring of activities: effects on			
size	0.787		0.69
Size: effects on			
line control	−0.304		−0.15

and size. Dependence is excluded because it has a direct impact only on concentration of authority and does not play a major role in the theory.

The direct effect of a variable is the unmediated effect of an independent on a dependent variable, after taking into account the effects of other independent variables. For example, the direct effect of X_2 and X_3, given by p_{32}, is 0.284. This differs from r_{23} (0.34) because part of the association between X_2 and X_3 is due to the effect of another independent variable, X_7, which has a positive causal impact on both X_2 and X_3.

The indirect effect of an independent variable given in Table 4 is that effect which is mediated through one or more intervening variables. For example, operating variability has a direct effect on line control of -0.643 and in addition has an indirect effect of 0.073 through its negative impact on size, technology, and structure, which in turn have direct and indirect effects on line control. Another example is the effect of operating variability on structure: the direct effect is 0.098, while the indirect effect through its impact on work flow integration is even larger, being $(0.57) (0.284) = 0.162$.

The direct and indirect effects do not always sum to the value of the total correlation, since part of the total correlation may be due to the effects of some other variable on both the independent and dependent variables of interest. The figures given in Table 4 convey some useful information about the causal process accounting for the correlations observed in the data. There exist several fairly large direct effects which are not evident from an inspection of zero-order relationships. Concomitantly, these large direct effects are offset by the presence of causal forces working in opposing directions. For example, the large direct negative impact of operating variability on size is partially offset by the direct positive impact of operating variability on work flow integration and structuring of activities, both of which have positive impacts on size. Thus, the causal structure underlying Figure 3 is too complex to be uncovered by a simple multiple regression analysis. Some prior theorizing about the total pattern of relationships is required.

One virtue of diagraming causal models of organizational development, apart from the advantage of making explicit the developmental sequence, lies in making apparent the complex and contradictory tendencies of organizational structure. A variable may have a positive direct impact but a negative indirect impact on another variable; or a variable may have a large indirect effect through its impact on an intervening variable but have only a small direct impact.

Conclusions

One may ask what has been learned about the importance of technology in determining other aspects of organizational structure. Hickson *et al.* dismissed technology and chose instead to emphasize the importance of size. The analysis here pointed to two problems with that approach, the first involving the logical implications of their implicit causal model and the second involving the failure of the investigators to search for alternative interpretations and arrangements of the causal relationships among the variables studied. In a follow-up study of fourteen organizations over a four- to five-year period, the Aston group found no association between changes in size and changes in the structuring of activities variable. Also, there was very little change in the technology (work flow integration) measure and so it did not vary with changes in size either (Inkson *et al.*, 1970). These findings are difficult to reconcile with the assumption that size is a key factor in organizational development.

The fact that technology emerges as a variable of major importance in a reanalysis has two implications for the study of organizations. First, with regard to the analysis of data on organizations, it demonstrates that conclusions about the significance of specific variables depend on a theory of organizational structure and development. In the absence of conscious theory building, an investigator's conclusions may come to be grounded on wholly inappropriate criteria, such as the amount of variance explained.

Second, with regard to the importance of organizational technology, the findings of this study should serve to keep alive the theorist's interest in the role of technology in organizations. If the model portrayed in Figure 3 is at all accurate, it provides a point of departure for future studies of the consequences of particular technologies upon organizational development. As developed here, the model is a dynamic one and thus cannot truly be tested by the Aston group's cross-sectional data. Given the presence of feedback loops and reciprocal causation, a true test of the model must await the gathering of longitudinal data. Nevertheless, if the assumptions of this article are accepted, then the Aston group's rejection of technology as an important variable has been shown to be ill-advised and premature.

References

Blauner, Robert, 1964, *Alienation and Freedom*. Chicago: University of Chicago Press.

Hickson, David J., Derek S. Pugh, and Diana C. Pheysey, 1969, "Operations technology and organization structure: an empirical reappraisal." *Administrative Science Quarterly*, 14:378–397.

Inkson, J., Derek S. Pugh, and David J. Hickson, 1970, "Organization context and structure: an abbreviated replication." *Administrative Science Quarterly*, 15:318–329.

Osmond, C. W., 1970, "Organization—is technology the key?" *Personnel Management*, 2:5, 43–44.

Perrow, Charles, 1970, *Organizational Analysis: A Sociological View*. Belmont, Cal.: Wadsworth Publishing Co.

Pugh, Derek S., David J. Hickson, C. R. Hinings, K. M. MacDonald, C. Turner, and T. Lupton, 1963, "A conceptual scheme for organizational analysis." *Administrative Science Quarterly*, 8:289–315.

Pugh, Derek S., David J. Hickson, C. R. Hinings, and C. Turner, 1968, "Dimensions of organization structure." *Administrative Science Quarterly*, 13:65–105.

———— 1969, "The context of organization structures." *Administrative Science Quarterly*, 14:91–114.

Pugh, Derek S., 1971, Personal communication to the author.

Thompson, James D., 1967, *Organization in Action*. New York: McGraw-Hill.

Woodward, Joan, 1965, *Industrial Organization*. London: Oxford University Press.

SECTION FOUR
Interorganizational
Relations

Complex organizations are not "islands" entire unto themselves. Appreciation of the realm of the interorganizational grew quickly with the acceptance of the notion of organizations as systems which are subjected, to varying degrees, to external forces.

Originally, the study of interorganizational relations concerned itself mainly with the ways in which other organizations impinge on the activities of a focal organization—that is, with how environmental factors (e.g., the PTA, civic groups) shape the internal structure and functioning of a single organization (e.g., a school). More recently, there has been a realization that interorganizational networks are *delivery systems* and that many strategic societal "products" cannot be allocated effectively and efficiently by single organizations acting in isolation. This second type of interorganizational analysis represents a sociology of systems composed of multiple organizations. However, this latter perspective makes clear that simply looking at how organizations orient themselves to one another is not sufficient. In addition, no interorganizational study of the second type is complete unless it recognizes that lateral bonds are encased in larger systems (what Benson calls the political economy) which may impinge on the performance of horizontal interorganizational fields.

Thus, this section is divided into two parts. The first part presents five essays which analyze how aspects of the environment shape performances by and within single organizations. The second part of Section IV presents three selections which examine the performances of systems of multiple organizations.

At the root of economic theories is a utilitarian-rationalist exchange model. Levine and White apply a sophisticated version of it to interorganizational analysis. From their perspective organizations are studied not only internally, but also in relation to one another. Levine and White focus their analysis on the relations between community health and welfare organizations where the "goods" exchanged are clients, services, and other resources. Their theory also highlights how the flow of these goods between the organizations and their environment affects the capacity of an organization to attain its particular goals.

The contribution of Litwak and Hylton lies in the extension of the analysis of the first type of interorganizational relations. They focus on the articulation of the many simultaneous efforts in which a complex society is engaged, the use of organizations to advance particular goals, and the coordination of those goals without central control. Nevertheless, their primary concern remains the adaptation of single organizations. Litwak and Hylton tell us that in many ways the relations among organizations are highly "unorganizational" but a measure of coordination is nevertheless reached.

Lieberson and O'Connor ask whether leadership or broader environmental factors are more important in accounting for organizational performance. The authors studied 167 key U.S. corporations and ask whether their sales, earnings, and profit margins over a 20-year period are influenced more by executive succession or by macroscopic factors in the industry and the economy as a whole. They conclude that "all three performance variables are affected by forces beyond their leaders' immediate control. . . ."

Meyer and Rowan examine the impact of cultural elements on organizational performances. They consider especially the role of institutional rules. Meyer and Rowan argue that institutional rules function as "myths" which organizations tend to incorporate. Successful incorporation allows an organization to achieve legitimacy, an adequate resource-base, stability, and enhanced survival prospects. Organizations whose structures become compatible with the myths of the institutional environment—in contrast with those primarily structured by the demands of technical production and exchange—decrease internal coordination and control in order to maintain legitimacy. Confidence and good faith replace more rationalistic criteria in such organizations.

Goffman presents a descriptive characterization and careful analysis of "a social hybrid which is part residential community and part formal organization." The inmates live in such social establishments; in other words, many aspects of their behavior considered "private" on the outside, are here controlled by the staff. Inmates, as a rule, do not engage in paid work; they are "taken care of." Efforts are made to limit the impact of environmental forces. For example, having a family is incompatible with the organizational structure and needs of total institutions. Entrance or exit also is usually not voluntary.

Total organizations have several important implications for today's world: They have intense effects on the moral orientation of the inmates; they constitute miniature totalitarian societies and as such may encourage research into the mentality and structure of totalitarian regimes. Total organizations tend, even more than other organizations, to divert many of their goals—such as therapy, rehabilitation, education, and religious service—toward promoting the fulfillment of the needs of the staff and the organization as a whole. Awareness of the special problems involved in these structures may lead to a reconsideration of their use in many situations. Thus, while other interorganizational analysts are interested in the balance between organizations and the society in which they operate, Goffman informs us about the balance between organizations and the "societies" which develop within them but which are shaped by external factors to some degree. This problem is common to all organizations but comes into special sharp focus in total organizations.

The remaining three essays in this section focus on the second type of interorganizational analysis. Eisenstadt examines the social context in which the bureaucratic sector of society emerges, develops, and expands. The major conditions seem to be a development of *Gesellschaft* orientations (universalistic, specific, neutral, etc.) and high differentiation of social systems from one another. Once the bureaucratic sector is fairly established, three forms of relationships between it and society may develop: first, one in which the bureaucracy maintains its distinct characteristics, so that it is the reliable servant of societal goals; second, one in which the bureaucracy penetrates into more and more spheres of life and becomes the omnipotent organ of society; and third, one in which particularistic pressures of various social groups become so intense that the conditions for effective bureaucratic activities are undermined, and the bureaucracy's value as an instrumental unit is, to a large degree, lost. The conditions are specified under which each of the three types of relationships is likely to emerge.

Benson brings some of the insights of Marxian analysis to the field of interorganizational relations. He argues that the study of particular interorganizational networks will not suffice. Rather, he believes we must focus on larger political and economic entities which impinge on and direct the performance of the network.

Lehman attempts to codify the insights of this second type of interorganizational analysis. He offers a paradigm for the analysis of interorganizational relations focussing especially on *control configurations.* He distinguishes four analytic types of interorganizational control structures. Real networks represent one or a combination of these types. The four types are *feudal, mediated, empires,* and *corporations.* They are ordered by degree of complexity, with feudal being the most elementary type.

A. Single Organizations and Their Environments

Exchange as a Conceptual Framework for the Study of Interorganizational Relationships

Sol Levine and Paul E. White

Sociologists have devoted considerable attention to the study of formal organizations, particularly in industry, government, and the trade union field. Their chief focus, however, has been on patterns within rather than between organizations. Studies or interrelationships have largely been confined to units within the same organizational structure or between a pair of complementary organizations such as management and labor. Dimock's study of jurisdictional conflict between two federal agencies is a notable exception.[1] Another is a study of a community reaction to disaster by Form and Nosow in which the authors produce revealing data on the interaction pattern of local health organizations. The authors observe that "organizational cooperation was facilitated among organizations with similar internal structures."[2] March and Simon suggest that interorganizational conflict is very similar to intergroup conflict within organizations but present no supporting data.[3] Blau has commented on the general problems involved in studying multiple organizations.[4] In pointing up the need to study the organization in relation to its environment, Etzioni specifies the area of interorganizational relationships as one of the three meriting further intensive empirical study.[5]

Health and social welfare agencies within a given community offer an excellent opportunity for exploring patterns of relationship among organizations. There are an appreciable number of such organizations in any fairly large urban American community. Most of them are small so that relatively few individuals have to be interviewed to obtain information on their interaction. Within any community setting, varying kinds of relations exist between official and voluntary organizations concerned with health and welfare. Thus welfare agencies may use public health nursing services, or information on the status of families may be shared by such voluntary organizations as the Red Cross and the Tuberculosis and Health Association.

Facilitating communication between local organizations has been a major objective of public health administrators and community organizers. Their writings contain many assertions about the desirability of improving relationships in order to reduce gaps and overlaps of medical services to the citizens, but as yet little effort has been made to appraise objectively the interrelationships that actually exist within the community.

In the following pages we should like to present our theoretical interpretation of interorganizational relationships together with a discussion of our research approach and a few preliminary findings, pointing up some of the substantive areas in organizational sociology for which our study has relevance. Our present thinking is largely based on the results of an exploratory study of twenty-two health organizations in a New England community with a population of 200,000 and

Reprinted from *Administrative Science Quarterly*, vol. 5 (March, 1961), pp. 583–601, by permission.

initial impressions of data on a more intensive study, as yet unanalyzed, of some fifty-five health organizations in another New England community of comparable size.

The site of our initial investigation was selected because we found it fairly accessible for study and relatively independent of a large metropolis; moreover, it contained a range of organizations which were of interest—a full-time health department, a welfare department, autonomous local agencies, local chapters or affiliates of major voluntary health and social welfare organizations, and major community hospitals. Of the twenty-two health organizations or agencies studied, fourteen were voluntary agencies, five were hospitals (three with out-patient clinics and two without) and three others were official agencies—health, welfare, and school. Intensive semistructured interviews were conducted with executive directors and supervisory personnel of each organization, and information was obtained from members of the boards through brief semistructured question-naires. In addition, we used an adaptation of an instrument developed by Irwin T. Sanders to locate the most influential leaders in the community for the purpose of determining their distribution on agency boards.[6] The prestige ratings that the influential leaders assigned to the organizations constituted one of the independent variables of our study.

Exchange as a Conceptual Framework

The complex of community health organizations may be seen as a system with individual organizations or system parts varying in the kinds and frequency of their relationships with one another. This system is enmeshed in ever larger systems—the community, the state, and so on.

Prevention and cure of disease constitute the ideal orientation of the health agency system, and individual agencies derive their respective goals or objectives from this larger orientation. In order to achieve its specific objectives, however, an agency must possess or control certain elements. It must have clients to serve; it must have resources in the form of equipment, specialized knowledge, or the funds with which to procure them; and it must have the services of people who can direct these resources to the clients. Few, if any, organizations have enough access to all these elements to enable them to attain their objectives fully. Under realistic conditions of element scarcity, organizations must select, on the basis of expediency or efficiency, particular functions that permit them to achieve their ends as fully as possible. By function is meant a set of interrelated services or activities that are instrumental, or believed to be instrumental, for the realization of an organization's objectives.

Although, because of scarcity, an organization limits itself to particular functions, it can seldom carry them out without establishing relationships with other organizations of the health system. The reasons for this are clear. To fulfill its functions without relating to other parts of the health system, an organization must be able to procure the necessary elements—cases, labor services, and other resources—directly from the community or outside it. Certain classes of hospitals treating a specific disease and serving an area larger than the local community probably most nearly approximate this condition. But even in this case other organizations within the system usually control some elements that are necessary or, at least, helpful to the carrying out of its functions. These may be money, equipment, or special personnel, which are conditionally lent or given. Usually agencies are unable to obtain all the elements they need from the community or through their individual efforts and, accordingly, have to turn to other agencies to obtain additional elements. The need for a sufficient number of clients, for example, is often more efficiently met through exchanges with other organizations than through independent case-finding procedures.

Theoretically, then, were all the essential elements in infinite supply there would be little need for organizational interaction and for subscription to co-operation as an ideal. Under actual conditions of scarcity, however, interorganizational exchanges are essential to goal attainment. In sum, organizational goals or objectives are derived from general health values. These goals or objectives may be viewed as defining the organization's ideal need for elements—consumers, labor services, and other resources. The scarcity of elements, however, impels the organization to restrict its activity to limited specific functions. The fulfillment of these limited functions, in turn, requires access to certain kinds of elements, which an organization seeks to obtain by entering into exchange with other organizations.

Interaction among organizations can be viewed within the framework of an exchange model like that suggested by Homans.[7] However, the few available definitions of exchange are somewhat limited for our purposes because they tend to be bound by economics and because their referents are mainly individual or psychological phenomena and are not intended to encompass interaction between organizational entities or larger systems.[8]

We suggest the following definition of organizational exchange: *Organizational exchange is any voluntary activity between two organizations which has consequences, actual or anticipated, for the realization of their respective goals or objectives.* This definition has several advantages. First, it refers to activity in general and not exclusively to reciprocal activity. The action may be unidirectional and yet involve exchange. If an organization refers a patient to another organization which then treats him, an exchange has taken place if the respective objectives of the two organizations are furthered by the action. Pivoting the definition on goals or objectives provides for an obvious but crucial component of what constitutes an organization. The co-ordination of activities of a number of individuals toward some objective or goal has been designated as a distinguishing feature of organizations by students in the field.[9] Parsons, for example, has defined an organization as a "special type of social system organized about the primacy of interest in the attainment of a particular type of system goal."[10] That its goals or objectives may be transformed by a variety of factors and that, under some circumstances, mere survival may become primary does not deny that goals or objectives are universal characteristics of organizations.

Second, the definition widens the concept of exchange beyond the transfer of material goods and beyond gratifications in the immediate present. This broad definition of exchange permits us to consider a number of dimensions of organizational interaction that would otherwise be overlooked.

Finally, while the organizations may not be bargaining or interacting on equal terms and may even employ sanctions or pressures (by granting or withholding these elements), it is important to exclude from our definition, relationships involving physical coercion or domination; hence emphasis is on the word "voluntary" in our definition.

The elements that are exchanged by health organizations fall into three main categories: (1) referrals of cases, clients, or patients; (2) the giving or receiving of labor services, including the services of volunteer, clerical, and professional personnel, and (3) the sending or receiving of resources other than labor services, including funds, equipment, and information on cases and technical matters. Organizations have varying needs of these elements depending on their particular functions. Referrals, for example, may be seen as the delivery of the consumers of services to organizations, labor services as the human means by which the resources of the organization are made available to the consumers, and resources other than labor services as the necessary capital goods.

The Determinants of Exchange

The interdependence of the parts of the exchange system is contingent upon three related factors: (1) the accessibility of each organization to necessary elements from sources outside the health system, (2) the objectives of the organization and particular functions to which it allocates the elements it controls, and (3) the degree to which domain consensus exists among the various organizations. An ideal theory of organizational exchange would describe the interrelationship and relative contribution of each of these factors. For the present, however, we will draw on some of our preliminary findings to suggest possible relationships among these factors and to indicate that each plays a part in affecting the exchange of elements among organizations.

Gouldner has emphasized the need to differentiate the various parts of a system in terms of their relative dependence upon other parts of the system.[11] In our terms, certain system parts are relatively dependent, not having access to elements outside the system, whereas others, which have access to such elements, possess a high degree of independence or functional autonomy. The voluntary organizations of our study (excluding hospitals) can be classified into what Sills calls either corporate or federated organizations.[12] Corporate organizations are those which delegate authority downward from the national or state level to the local level. They contrast with organizations of the federated type which delegate authority upward—from the local to the state or national level.

It appears that local member units of corporate organizations, because they are less dependent on the local health system and can obtain the necessary elements from the community or their parent organizations, interact less with other local agencies than federated organizations. This is supported by preliminary data presented in Table 1. It is also suggested that by carrying out their activities without entering actively into exchange relationships with other organizations, corporate organizations apparently are able to maintain their essential structure and avoid consequences resulting in the displacement of state or national goals. It may be that corporate organizations deliberately choose functions that require minimal involvement with other organizations. An examination of the four corporate organizations in our preliminary study reveals that three of them give resources to other agencies to carry out their activities, and the fourth conducts broad educational programs. Such functions are less likely to involve relationships with other organizations than the more direct service organizations, those that render services to individual recipients.

An organization's relative independence from the rest of the local health agency system and greater dependence upon a system outside the community

TABLE 1 Weighted Rankings* of Organizations Classified by Organizational Form on Four Interaction Indices

Interaction Index	Sent by	N	Sent to					Total Interaction Sent
			Voluntary		Hospitals		Official	
			Corporate	Federated	Without Clinics	With Clinics		
Referrals	Vol. corporate	4	4.5	5	3.7	4.5	5	5
	Vol. federated	10	3	4	3.7	3	4	3
	Hosps. w/o clinics	2	4.5	3	3.7	4.5	3	4
	Hosps. w. clinics	3	1	1	1.5	2	1	1
	Official	3	2	2	1.5	1	2	2
Resources	Vol. corporate	4	5	2	1	4	4	3.5
	Vol. federated	10	4	3	3	4	4	3.5
	Hosps. w/o clinics	2	2	4.5	4.5	5	3	5
	Hosps. w. clinics	3	1	1	2	1	2	1
	Official	3	3	4.5	4.5	2	1	2
Written and verbal communication	Vol. corporate	4	5	3	2	4	5	4
	Vol. federated	10	3	1	3	3	3	2.5
	Hosps. w/o clinics	2	2	5	4.5	5	4	5
	Hosps. w. clinics	3	4	4	4.5	1	1.5	2.5
	Official	3	1	2	1	2	1.5	1
Joint activities	Vol. corporate	4	4.5	4	3	5	3.5	5
	Vol. federated	10	3	3	5	3	1	3
	Hosps. w/o clinics	2	4.5	5	1	2	3.5	4
	Hosps. w. clinics	3	1	2	2	1	5	1.5
	Official	3	1	1	4	4	2	1.5

* Note: 1 indicates highest interaction; 5 indicates lowest interaction.

may, at times, produce specific types of disagreements with the other agencies within the local system. This is dramatically demonstrated in the criticisms expressed toward a local community branch of an official state rehabilitation organization. The state organization, to justify its existence, has to present a successful experience to the legislators—that a minimum number of persons have been successfully rehabilitated. This means that by virtue of the services the organization has offered, a certain percentage of its debilitated clients are again returned to self-supporting roles. The rehabilitative goal of the organization cannot be fulfilled unless it is selective in the persons it accepts as clients. Other community agencies dealing with seriously debilitated clients are unable to get the state to accept their clients for rehabilitation. In the eyes of these frustrated agencies the state organization is remiss in fulfilling its public goal. The state agency, on the other hand, cannot commit its limited personnel and resources to the time-consuming task of trying to rehabilitate what seem to be very poor risks. The state agency wants to be accepted and approved by the local community and its health agencies, but the state legislature and the governor, being the primary source of the agency's resources, constitute its significant reference group. Hence, given the existing definition of organizational goals and the state agency's relative independence of the local health system, its interaction with other community agencies is relatively low.

The marked difference in the interaction rank position of hospitals with out-patient clinics and those without suggests other differences between the two classes of hospitals. It may be that the two types of hospitals have different goals and that hospitals with clinics have a greater "community" orientation and are more committed to the concept of "comprehensive" care than are hospitals without clinics. However, whether or not the goals of the two types of hospitals do indeed differ, those with out-patient departments deal with population groups similar to those serviced by other agencies of the health system, that is, patients who are largely ambulatory and indigent; thus they serve patients whom other organizations may also be seeking to serve. Moreover, hospitals with out-patient clinics have greater control over their clinic patients than over those in-patients who are the charges of private physicians, and are thereby freer to refer patients to other agencies.

The functions of an organization not only represent the means by which it allocates its elements but, in accordance with our exchange formulation, also determine the degree of dependence on other organizations for specific kinds of elements, as well as its capacity to make certain kinds of elements available to other organizations. The exchange model leads us to explain the flow of elements between organizations largely in terms of the respective functions performed by the participating agencies. Indeed, it is doubtful whether any analysis of exchange of elements among organizations which ignores differences in organizational needs would have much theoretical or practical value.

In analyzing the data from our pilot community we classified agencies on the basis of their primary health functions: resource, education, prevention, treatment, or rehabilitation. Resource organizations attempt to achieve their objectives by providing other agencies with the means to carry out their functions. The four other agency types may be conceived as representing respective steps in the control of disease. We have suggested that the primary function determines an organization's need for exchange elements. Our preliminary data reveal, as expected, that treatment organizations rate highest on number of referrals and amount of resources received and that educational organizations, whose efforts are directed toward the general public, rate low on the number of referrals (see Table 2). This finding holds even when the larger organizations—official agencies and hospitals—are excluded and the analysis is based on the remaining voluntary agencies of our sample. As a case in point, let us consider a health organization whose function is to educate the public about a specific disease but which renders no direct service to individual clients. If it carries on an active educational program, it is possible that some people may come to it directly to obtain information and, mistakenly, in the hope of receiving treatment. If this occurs, the organization will temporarily be in possession of potential clients whom it may route or refer to other more appropriate agencies. That such referrals will be frequent is unlikely however. It is even less likely that the organization will receive many referrals from other organizations. If an organization renders a direct service to a client, however, such as giving X-ray examinations, or polio immunizations, there is greater likelihood that it will send or receive referrals.

An organization is less limited in its function in such interagency activities as discussing general community health problems, attending agency council meetings or co-operating on some aspect of fund raising. Also, with sufficient initiative even a small educational agency can maintain communication with a large treatment organization (for example, a general hospital) through exchanges of periodic reports and telephone calls to obtain various types of information. But precisely because it is an educational agency offering services to the general public and not to individuals, it will be limited in its capacity to maintain other kinds of interaction with the treatment organization. It probably will not be able to lend or give space or equipment, and it is even doubtful that it can offer the kind of instruction that the treatment organization would seek for its staff. That the organization's function establishes the range of possibilities for exchange and that other variables exert influence within the framework established by function is suggested by some other early findings presented in Table 3. Organizations were classified as direct or indirect on the basis of whether or not they provided a direct service to the public. They were also classified according to their relative prestige as rated by influential leaders in the community. Organizations high in prestige lead in the number of joint activities, and prestige seems to exert some influence on the amount of verbal and written communication. Yet it is agencies offering direct services—regardless of prestige—which lead in the number of referrals and resources received. In other words, prestige, leadership, and other organizational variables seem to affect interaction patterns within limits established by the function variable.

An obvious question is whether organizations with shared or common boards interact more with one another than do agencies with separate boards. Our preliminary data show that the interaction rate is not affected by shared board membership. We have not been able to ascertain if there is any variation in organizational interaction when the shared board positions are occupied by persons with high status or influence. In our pilot community, there was only one instance in which two organizations had the same top community leaders as board members. If boards play an active role in the activities of health organizations, they serve more to link the organization to the community and the elements it possesses than to link the organization to other health and welfare agencies. The board probably also exerts influence on internal organizational operations and on establishing or approving the primary objective of the organization. Once the objective and the implementing functions are established, these functions tend to exert their influence autonomously on organizational interaction.

TABLE 2 *Weighted Rankings* of Organizations, Classified by Function on Four Interaction Indices*

Interaction Index	Received by	N	Received from					Total Interaction Received
			Education	Resource	Prevention	Treatment	Rehabilitation	
Referrals	Education	3	4.5	5	5	5	5	5
	Resource	5	3	4	2	4	1	3
	Prevention	5	2	1	3	2	2.5	2
	Treatment	7	1	2	1	1	2.5	1
	Rehabilitation	2	4.5	3	4	3	4	4
Resources	Education	3	4.5	5	4	5	4.5	5
	Resource	5	1.5	3	3	4	3	3.5
	Prevention	5	1.5	4	2	3	4.5	3.5
	Treatment	7	3	2	1	2	2	1
	Rehabilitation	2	4.5	1	5	1	1	2
Written and verbal communication	Education	3	4	5	4.5	5	5	5
	Resource	5	3	2	2	3	2	2.5
	Prevention	5	2	4	3	4	4	3
	Treatment	7	1	1	1	2	3	1
	Rehabilitation	2	5	3	4.5	1	1	2.5
Joint activities	Education	3	4	4	1	3	4.5	4
	Resource	5	2	1	3	4	1	3
	Prevention	5	1	2	2	2	3	1
	Treatment	7	3	3	4	1	2	2
	Rehabilitation	2	5	5	5	5	4.5	5

* Note: 1 indicates highest interaction; 5 indicates lowest interaction.

TABLE 3 *Weighted Rankings* of Organizations Classified *by Prestige of Organization and by General Type of Service Offered on Four Interaction Indices*

Interaction Index	Received by	N	Received from				Total Interaction Received
			High Prestige		Low Prestige		
			Direct Service	Indirect Service	Direct Service	Indirect Service	
Referrals	High direct	9	1	1	1	1	1
	High indirect	3	3	3.5	3	3.5	3
	Low direct	6	2	2	2	2	2
	Low indirect	4	4	3.5	4	3.5	4
Resources	High direct	9	2	2	2	2	2
	High indirect	3	3	3	3	3.5	3
	Low direct	6	1	1	1	1	1
	Low indirect	4	4	4	4	3.5	4
Written and verbal communication	High direct	9	2	2	3	1	2
	High indirect	3	3	3	1	3	3
	Low direct	6	1	1	2	2	1
	Low indirect	4	4	4	4	4	4
Joint activities	High direct	9	1	1.5	2	2	2
	High indirect	3	2	1.5	1	1	1
	Low direct	6	4	3	3	4	3
	Low indirect	4	3	4	4	3	4

* Note: 1 indicates highest interaction; 5 indicates lowest interaction.

Organizational Domain

As we have seen, the elements exchanged are cases, labor services, and other resources. All organizational relationships directly or indirectly involve the flow and control of these elements. Within the local health agency system, the flow of elements is not centrally co-ordinated, but rests upon voluntary agreements or understanding. Obviously, there will be no exchange of elements between two organizations that do not know of each other's existence or that are completely unaware of each other's functions. Even more, there can be no exchange of elements without some agreement or understanding, however implicit. These exchange agreements are contingent upon the organization's domain. The domain of an organization consists of the specific goals it wishes to pursue and the functions it undertakes in order to implement its goals. In operational terms, organizational domain in the health field refers to the claims that an organization stakes out for itself in terms of (1) disease covered, (2) population served, and (3) services rendered. The goals of the organization constitute in effect the organization's claim to future functions and to the elements requisite to these functions, whereas the present or actual functions carried out by the organization constitute *de facto* claims to these elements. Exchange agreements rest upon prior consensus regarding domain. Within the health agency system, consensus regarding an organization's domain must exist to the extent that parts of the system will provide each agency with the elements necessary to attain its ends.

Once an organization's goals are accepted, domain consensus continues as long as the organization fulfills the functions adjudged appropriate to its goals and adheres to certain standards of quality. Our data show that organizations find it more difficult to legitimate themselves before other organizations in the health system than before such outside systems as the community or state. An organization can sometimes obtain sufficient elements from outside the local health system, usually in the form of funds, to continue in operation long after other organizations within the system have challenged its domain. Conversely, if the goals of a specific organization are accepted within the local agency system, other organizations of the system may encourage it to expand its functions and to realize its goals more fully by offering it elements to implement them. Should an organization not respond to this encouragement, it may be forced to forfeit its claim to the unrealized aspect of its domain.

Within the system, delineation of organizational domains is highly desired.[13] For example, intense competition may occur occasionally between two agencies offering the same services, especially when other agencies have no specific criteria for referring patients to one rather than the other. If both services are operating near capacity, competition between the two tends to be less keen, the choice being governed by the availability of service. If the services are being operated at less than capacity, competition and conflict often occur. Personnel of referring agencies in this case frequently deplore the "duplication of services" in the community. In most cases the conflict situation is eventually resolved by agreement on the part of the competing agencies to specify the criteria for referring patients to them. The agreement may take the form of consecutive handling of the same patients. For example, age may be employed as a criterion. In one case three agencies were involved in giving rehabilitation services: one took preschool children, another school children, and the third adults. In another case, where preventive services were offered, one agency took preschool children and the other took children of school age. The relative accessibility of the agencies to the respective age groups was a partial basis for these divisions. Another criterion—disease stage—also permits consecutive treatment of patients. One agency provided physical therapy to bedridden patients; another handled them when they became ambulatory.

Several other considerations, such as priorities in allocation of elements, may impel an organization to delimit its functions even when no duplication of services exists. The phenomenon of delimiting one's role and consequently of restricting one's domain is well known. It can be seen, for instance, in the resistance of certain universities of high prestige to offer "practical" or vocational courses, or courses to meet the needs of any but high-status professionals, even to the extent of foregoing readily accessible federal grants. It is evidenced in the insistence of certain psychiatric clinics on handling only cases suitable for psychoanalytic treatment, of certain business organizations on selling only to wholesalers, of some retail stores on handling only expensive merchandise.

The flow of elements in the health system is contingent upon solving the problem of "who gets what for what purpose." The clarification of organizational domains and the development of greater domain consensus contributes to the solution of this problem. In short, domain consensus is a prerequisite to exchange. Achieving domain consensus may involve negotiation, orientation, or legitimation. When the functions of the interacting organizations are diffuse, achieving domain consensus becomes a matter of constant readjustment and compromise, a process which may be called negotiation or bargaining. The more specific the functions, however, the more domain consensus is attained merely by orientation (for example, an agency may call an X-ray unit to inquire about the specific procedures for implementing services). A third, less frequent but more formalized, means of attaining domain consensus is the empowering, licensing or "legitimating" of an organization to operate within the community by some other organization. Negotiation, as a means of attaining domain consensus seems to be related to diffuseness of function, whereas orientation, at the opposite extreme, relates to specificity of function.

These processes of achieving domain consensus constitute much of the interaction between organizations. While they may not involve the immediate flow of elements, they are often necessary preconditions for the exchange of elements, because without at least minimal domain consensus there can be no exchange among organizations. Moreover, to the extent that these processes involve proffering information about the availability of elements as well as about rights and obligations regarding the elements, they constitute a form of interorganizational exchange.

Dimensions of Exchange

We have stated that all relationships among local health agencies may be conceptualized as involving exchange. There are four main dimensions to the actual exchange situation. They are:

1. *The parties to the exchange.* The characteristics we have thus far employed in classifying organizations or the parties to the exchange are: organizational form or affiliation, function, prestige, size, personnel characteristics, and numbers and types of clients served.

2. *The kinds and quantities exchanged.* These involve two main classes: the actual elements exchanged (consumers, labor services, and resources other than labor services), and information on the availability of these organizational elements and on rights and obligations regarding them.

3. *The agreement underlying the exchange.* Every exchange is contingent upon a prior agreement, which may be implicit and informal or fairly explicit and highly formalized. For example, a person may be informally routed or referred to another agency with the implicit awareness or expectation that the other organization will handle the case. On the other hand, the two agencies may enter into arrangements that stipulate the exact conditions and procedures by which patients are referred from one to another. Furthermore, both parties may be actively involved in arriving at the terms of the agreement, or these terms may be explicitly defined by one for all who may wish to conform to them. An example of the latter case is the decision of a single organization to establish a policy of a standard fee for service.

4. *The direction of the exchange.* This refers to the direction of the flow of organizational elements. We have differentiated three types:

a. Unilateral: where elements flow from one organization to another and no elements are given in return.

b. Reciprocal: where elements flow from one organization to another in return for other elements.

c. Joint: where elements flow from two organizations acting in unison toward a third party. This type, although representing a high order of agreement and co-ordination of policy among agencies, does not involve the actual transfer of elements.

As we proceed with our study of relationships among health agencies, we will undoubtedly modify and expand our theoretical model. For example, we will attempt to describe how the larger systems are intertwined with the health agency system. Also, we will give more attention to the effect of interagency competition and conflict regarding the flow of elements among organizations. In this respect we will analyze differences among organizations with respect not only to domain but to fundamental goals as well. As part of this analysis we will examine the orientations of different categories of professionals (for example, nurses and social workers) as well as groups with varying experiences and training within categories of professionals (as nurses with or without graduate education). . . .

Notes

1. Marshall E. Dimock, "Expanding Jurisdictions: A Case Study in Bureaucratic Conflict," in Robert K. Merton, Ailsa P. Gray, Barbara Hockey, Hanan C. Selvin, eds. *Reader in Bureaucracy* (New York, 1952).
2. William H. Form and Sigmund Nosow, *Community in Disaster* (New York, 1958), p. 236.
3. James G. March and H. A. Simon, *Organizations* (New York, 1958).
4. Peter M. Blau, Formal Organization: Dimensions of Analysis, *American Journal of Sociology,* 63 (1957), 58.
5. Amitai Etzioni, New Directions in the Study of Organizations and Society, *Social Research,* 27 (1960), 223–228.
6. Irwin T. Sanders, The Community Social Profile, *American Sociological Review,* 25 (1960), 75–77.

7. George C. Homans, Social Behavior as Exchange, *American Journal of Sociology*, 63 (1958), 597–606.

8. Weber states that "by 'exchange' in the broadest sense will be meant every case of a formally voluntary agreement involving the offer of any sort of present, continuing, or future utility in exchange for utilities of any sort offered in return." Weber employs the term "utility" in the economic sense. It is the "utility" of the "object of exchange" to the parties concerned that produces exchange. See Max Weber, *The Theory of Social and Economic Organization* (New York, 1947) p. 170. Homans, on the other hand, in characterizing interaction between persons as an exchange of goods, material and nonmaterial, sees the impulse to "exchange" in the psychological make-up of the parties to the exchange. He states, "the paradigm of elementary social behavior, and the problem of the elementary sociologist is to state propositions relating the variations in the values and costs of each man to his frequency distribution of behavior among alternatives, where the values (in the mathematical sense) taken by these variables for one man determine in part their values for the other." See Homans, *op. cit.*, p. 598.

9. Talcott Parsons, Suggestions for a Sociological Approach to the Theory of Organizations—I, *Administrative Science Quarterly*, 1 (1956), 63–85.

10. *Ibid.*, p. 64.

11. Alvin W. Gouldner, Reciprocity and Autonomy in Functional Theory, in Llewellyn Gross, ed., *Symposium on Sociological Theory* (Evanston, Ill., 1959); also The Norm of Reciprocity: A Preliminary Statement, *American Sociological Review*, 25 (1960), 161–178.

12. David L. Sills, *The Volunteers: Means and Ends in a National Organization* (New York, 1957).

13. In our research a large percentage of our respondents spontaneously referred to the undesirability of overlapping or duplicated services.

Interorganizational Analysis: A Hypothesis on Co-ordinating Agencies[1]

Eugene Litwak and Lydia F. Hylton

One major lacuna in current sociological study is research on interorganizational relations—studies which use organizations as their unit of analysis. There are some investigations, which bear tangentially on this problem, such as studies on community disasters and community power,[2] and the study of Gross and others on the school superintendency.[3] There are some explicit formulations of general rules of interorganizational analysis among some of the sociological classics of the past, such as Durkheim's discussion of organic society and, in a tangential way, Marx's analysis of class.[4] But little has been done in current sociological work to follow up the general problems of interorganizational analysis as compared to the problems of intraorganizational analysis, that is studies in bureaucracy.[5]

Differences Between Interorganizational and Intraorganizational Analysis

One of the major sociological functions of organizational independence is to promote autonomy. This is important when there is a conflict of values and the values in conflict are both desired. For instance, a society might stress both freedom and physical safety. These two values may conflict in many areas of life; yet the society seeks to maximize each. One way of assuring that each will be retained, despite the conflict, is to put them under separate organizational structures; i.e., have the police force guard physical safety and the newspapers guard freedom of the press. If both safety and freedom were the concern of a single organization, it is likely that when conflict arose, one of the values would be suppressed, as, for example, where the police have control over the press.

This conflict between organizations is taken as a given in interorganizational analysis, which starts out with the assumption that there is a situation of partial conflict and investigates the forms of social interaction designed for interaction under such conditions. From this point of view the elimination of conflict is a deviant instance and likely to lead to the disruption of interorganizational relations (i.e., organizational mergers and the like). By contrast, intraorganizational analysis assumes that conflicting values lead to a breakdown in organizational structure. Thus Weber's model of bureaucracy assumed that the organization had a homogeneous policy.[6] Blau's modification of Weber's analysis (i.e., the individual must internalize the policies of the organization) assumes that the organization has a single consistent system.[7] Selznick has pointed out that deficiencies in the Tennessee Valley Authority centered around the problem of conflicting values.[8]

Reprinted in part from *Administrative Science Quarterly*, vol. 11 (June 1966), pp. 31–58, by permission.

By distinguishing between interorganizational and intraorganizational analysis, the investigator is sensitized to the organizational correlates of value conflict and value consistency. Without such a distinction he might concentrate on showing that value conflicts lead to organizational breakdown without appreciating that interorganizational relations permit and encourage conflict without destruction of the over-all societal relations.

Organizational independence for autonomy is functional not only in value conflict but in most forms of social conflict. For instance, values may be theoretically consistent, but limited resources force individuals to choose between them without completely rejecting either choice. (This is one of the classic problems of economics.) Or it may be that a given task requires several specialties, i.e., a division of labor, and limited resources at times of crisis force a choice between them, although all are desirable (for example, the conflicts between the various military services). In such cases organizational independence might be given to the specialties to preserve their essential core despite competition.

A second point follows from the preceding discussion. Interorganizational analysis stresses the study of social behavior under conditions of unstructured authority. International relations between nations is the polar model for interorganizational behavior,[9] a modicum of co-ordination is necessary to preserve each nation, yet there is no formal authority which can impose co-operation. By contrast, most intraorganizational analysis is made under the assumption of a fairly well-defined authority structure. As a consequence, formal authority plays a larger role in explaining behavior within the organization than it does in interorganizational analysis with exceptions, of course, as where the society has a strong monolithic power structure and is very stable. Because of this difference, interorganizational analysis will frequently use, as explanatory variables, elements that are disregarded or minimized in intraorganizational studies.

In summary, interorganizational analyses suggest two important facets of analysis which differ somewhat from intraorganizational analysis: (1) the operation of social behavior under conditions of partial conflict and (2) the stress on factors which derive equally from all units of interaction rather than being differentially weighted by authority structure.

To point out that multiple organizations are effective in situations of partial conflict is not to suggest that they necessarily arise from such situations or that conflict is the only reason for their persistence. Multiple organizations might be the consequence of social growth. Thus in one city, there may be twenty family agencies, with no rational basis for separation except that their growth was an unplanned consequence of immediate social pressure. They might, indeed, be in the process of consolidation. Yet at any given time in a changing society, the investigator must expect to find multiple organizations because the processes of centralization and decentralization are slow. Culture values also condition the development of multiple organizations. In the field of business enterprise there is a tendency to argue that a competitive situation is a good per se; even where a monopoly is more efficient, society might reject it. Within the welfare field, family agencies may be separated by religious beliefs. In short, where there is a situation of partial conflict (which all societies must have because of limited resources for maximizing all values simultaneously), where a society is constantly changing, and where cultural values dictate it, the problem of multiple organizations will be an important one. Consequently there is a need for theories dealing with interorganizational analysis—situations involving partial conflict and interactions without a structure of formal authority.

The Problem of Co-ordination

One strategic problem in interorganizational analysis concerns co-ordination, a somewhat specialized co-ordination, since there is both conflict and co-operation and formal authority structure is lacking. If the conflict were complete, the issue could be settled by complete lack of interaction or by some analogue to war. Where the conflict overlaps with areas of support, however, the question arises: What procedures ensure the individual organizations their autonomy in areas of conflict while at the same time permitting their united effort in areas of agreement?

One such mechanism is the co-ordinating agency—formal organizations whose major purpose is to order behavior between two or more other formal organizations by communicating pertinent information (social service exchange and hospital agencies), by adjudicating areas of dispute (Federal Communications Commission), by providing standards of behavior (school accrediting organizations), by promoting areas of common interest (business associations, such as the National Association of Manufacturers, restaurant associations, grocery store associations), and so forth. What characterizes all these organizations is that they co-ordinate the behavior between two or more organizations. Furthermore, the organizations being co-ordinated are independent, because they have conflicting values or because the demands of efficiency suggest organizational specialization, yet share some common goal which demands co-operation.

From this reasoning we can advance the following hypothesis: Co-ordinating agencies will develop and continue in existence if formal organizations are partly interdependent; agencies are aware of this interdependence, and it can be defined in standardized units of action. What characterizes the three variables in this hypothesis (interdependence, awareness, and standardization of the units to be co-ordinated) is the extent to which they are tied to the organizations to be co-ordinated. By contrast, if this were an intraorganizational analysis, the development of co-ordinating mechanisms might be accounted for by authority structure with little concern for the awareness of the units to be co-ordinated, without standardization, and without significant variations in interdependence. For instance, the leadership might institute co-ordinating mechanisms because they are aware of interdependence where the units to be co-ordinated are unaware of this; or they might introduce co-ordinating mechanisms not to increase efficiency of the organization but to perpetuate their own authority structure; or they might introduce co-ordinating mechanisms despite lack of standardization because they feel this might speed up the process of standardization. In other words, authority structure is important in understanding intraorganizational behavior, while the variables suggested here for understanding interorganizational analysis may be insignificant.[10]

Study Design and Definition of Terms

In order to provide a limited test of this hypothesis, specific attention is directed to two types of co-ordinating agencies—community chests and social service exchanges. The following nine "traditional" problems of community chest and social service exchanges will be used to show how they can be accounted for by the general hypothesis about co-ordinating agencies:

1. The emergence and continuing growth of community chest programs.
2. The fluctuations in financial campaigns of community chest programs.
3. The resistance of national agencies such as the American Cancer Society to participating in the local community chest.
4. The ability of some agencies to exclude others from the chest—Catholic agencies exclude planned-parenthood agencies.
5. The development of dual campaigns—Jewish agencies and the Red Cross participate in local community chests as well as run independent national campaigns.
6. The decline of the social service exchange.
7. The fact that community chest agencies have adjudication functions while social service exchanges do not.
8. Principles of growth of new co-ordinating agencies.
9. The increasing encroachment of community chest agencies on member agencies' budget decisions.

If, in fact, it can be demonstrated that these diverse problems are all variations on a common theme (specified by our hypothesis), then we shall feel that our hypothesis has had initial confirmation. If nothing more, it has met the test of Ockham's razor.

To simplify the presentation, each element of the hypothesis will be examined separately. Although normally all are simultaneously involved, there are certain forms of co-ordination which more clearly represent the influence of one of these variables rather than another. In the concluding discussion, systematic consideration will be given to the simultaneous interaction among all three variables as well as alternative mechanisms of co-ordination (aside from the formal co-ordinating agency).

First it seems appropriate to define the three terms of the hypothesis—interdependence, awareness, and standardization. By interdependence is meant that two or more organizations must take each other into account if they are to accomplish their goals.[11] The definition of this term has been formally developed by Thomas who points out that there are several kinds of interdependency. The initial discussion here will concentrate on competitive interdependence (where one agency can maximize its goals only at the expense of another), while the later discussion will introduce and relate facilitative interdependence (where two or more agencies can simultaneously maximize their goals). By awareness we mean that the agency, as a matter of public policy, recognizes that a state of interdependency exists. By standardized actions we mean behavior which is reliably ascertained and repetitive in character, e.g., requests for funds, information on whether the client is served by another agency, price of goods, cost of living index, and the like.[12]

The Evidence on Interdependency

Historical Emergence and Continued Growth of Community Chests

If the factors accounting for the origin of community chest programs[13] are examined, one explanation which appears repeatedly is the complaints of donors and fund raisers that they were being confronted with too many requests for assistance and that fund raising was both time-consuming and economically wasteful.[14] It was at the urging of these donors and fund raisers that many of the community chest programs had their beginnings.

It is argued here that these complaints of the donors and their consequent demands for centralized fund raising were manifestations of the increasing interdependence of welfare agencies in the community, for what in effect had occurred was an increase in the number of agencies drawing on a limited local community fund. This meant that any given agency which drew from this common fund was depriving some other agency of a source of money, and that the same donor received many requests for funds. How much the donors' feelings of waste were a consequence of agencies' increasing interdependence on a limited and common pool of funds can be seen if one envisions the situation of few agencies and much money. In such cases no two agencies need go to the same donor. The donor, as a consequence, would not feel plagued by many requests and thus become aware of the inefficiency of many agencies carrying on independent fund raising activities.

Community chest programs have continued to grow partly because financial dependence has grown—agencies' demands for funds have grown at the same or a faster rate than national income.[15]

Fluctuations in Financial Campaigns of Community Chest Programs

If the development of co-ordinating agencies is a function of interdependency, then any fluctuation in interdependency should lead to a fluctuation in co-ordination. If the pool of resources in the community is suddenly decreased while the number of agencies remains the same or increases, then the agencies' competition for funds should increase and their interdependency increase accordingly. Such limitations of community funds occur during periods of crisis—natural catastrophes, depressions, or wars. In one major historical instance, in Cincinnati, the community chest program arose not as a result of donor pressures but was formed as a consequence of a disastrous flood.[16] The same point is made in the study of a modern catastrophe by Form and Nosow, who say, "Hence [inter]organizational integration is the most crucial dimension in disaster."[17]

Co-ordination should grow both in periods of prosperity (World War II) and depression, since greater interdependency can be expected in both these periods. Figure 1 indicates that the funds raised by community chest programs rose sharply during the early thirties (prior to governmental intervention in public relief) and again during the war years of the 1940's.[18] These are peak years as compared to the years immediately preceding and following. These data suggest that the co-ordinating agencies were strengthened during these periods and that interdependency, not the level of income, was an important factor. In summary, instead of three *ad hoc* explanations, i.e., war, depression, and catastrophe, we offer one which provides a general explanation for all three.[19]

Resistance of National Agencies to Local Community Chests—Fixed Markets

Interdependency should also be able to account for the fact that certain agencies are able to resist efforts to include them in the co-ordination process. The answer to such resistance should lie in part in the limited dependence of these agencies on other agencies in the community; i.e., they can raise money regard-

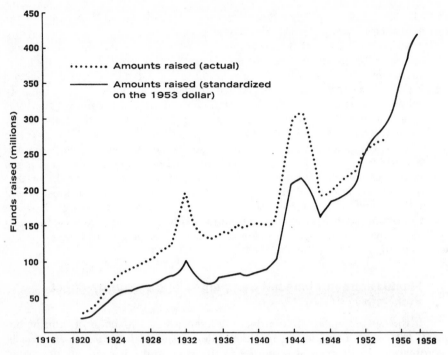

Figure 1   Federated Fund Raising

less of what other agencies in the community do. When examined, such agencies are seen to have "fixed markets" as far as fund raising is concerned. For instance, the American Cancer Society knows that in any open competition with other agencies, it will receive more funds than most other organizations, because of the public's tremendous concern with, and awareness of, the injurious effects of cancer.[20] The Red Cross is another agency which can resist, to some extent, local community chest involvement because its historic tradition has created a following among donors which amounts to a "fixed market." Fixed markets in fund raising are also enjoyed by religious agencies in cities where their members form a large element in the local community. Such agencies can generally count on receiving priority in any competition for funds. In other words, where an agency, by virtue of cultural norms (religious), historical tradition (Red Cross), or through current interest (American Cancer Society), is able to establish a "fixed money market," it is less dependent on other agencies in the community and can resist efforts at incorporation into community chest programs.

The problem of resistance to community chest programs is a variation on the same basic theme which explains the historical emergence and the fluctuation of funds raised in community chest programs.

Multiple Dependencies—Dual Campaigns and Agency Exclusions

Thus far the assumption has been that agencies are linked by one dependency relation, or if multiple dependencies exist they are consistent with each other. Where an agency has multiple relations with another and they are not consistent, i.e., some involve interdependency and some involve independence, then it will affiliate with co-ordinating agencies only on its own terms. This permits explanation of two classical problems in community chest programs—the exclusion of one agency by another and the running of dual campaigns.

For instance, Catholic agencies frequently insist that planned-parenthood agencies be excluded from community chest programs as a condition of their participation. What characterizes the Catholic agencies is mixed multiple dependencies with other agencies. Like the American Cancer Society, Catholic agencies in strong Catholic communities, have a fixed financial market. Unlike the American Cancer Society, the Catholic agencies perform services (family and recreational) that involve them in an interdependency relation with other agencies in the community. The American Cancer Society's chief service is research, which is equally valuable when done outside the confines of the community. Consequently, Catholic agencies have an incentive to join the local community chest while the Cancer Society does not. Yet, because of their financial independence, Catholic agencies can afford a policy of joining only where the situation is advantageous to them. If a Catholic agency is large, it can force the ouster of the smaller planned-parenthood organization, whose values are antithetical to theirs.

The concept of multiple and conflicting dependencies also explains why some organizations run dual campaigns. Thus Jewish agencies will frequently co-operate with the local community chest and in addition run a separate campaign. The Jewish agencies, like the Catholic agencies, may have a fixed financial market, but have local services which lead to interdependence with other agencies. In addition they have national services which are not dependent on local agencies, such as raising funds for Israel and for research on prejudice. Because of their dual service interests—local and national—their interests only partly overlap that of the local community chest. Because of their financial semi-independence they can enforce their demands for dual campaigns. Similarly, the Red Cross is also likely to run dual campaigns.

Where there are multiple dependencies, there are several possibilities which have different implications for affiliation with local co-ordination agencies. These are outlined in Table 1. Where all relations are independent of the local community, the organizations will refuse affiliation with local community chests (e.g., American Cancer Society). Where there are mixed dependencies, the organization is likely to enter the community chests only on its own terms (i.e., eliminate conflicting organizations or run dual campaigns). Where the organization has multiple dependencies and they mostly involve interdependence, there will be strong support of local co-ordinating organizations.

The Decline of Social Service Exchange

Since the 1940's there has been a steady decline in the number of social service exchanges from 320 exchanges in 1946 to 220 in 1956 to 175 in 1959.[21] If the hypothesis advanced here is correct, this decline should be a function of decreasing interdependence. To ascertain this relationship, it is necessary to know what the functions of the social service exchanges were. From the turn of the century up to the early 1930's one of the major services offered by private welfare agencies was direct material aid—money, clothing, housing, food, and the like. All agencies sought to maximize their services by providing the largest amount to the greatest number of needy. This made them interdependent, for if two agencies

TABLE 1 *Multiple Dependencies and Affiliations with Community Co-ordinating Agencies*

Services	Financially Interdependent	Financially Independent (Fixed Markets)
Interdependent (local services)	Nondenominational family services generally have no fixed financial market and have local services which are interdependent with other agencies. They will affiliate most strongly.	Catholic family agencies in strong Catholic communities have a fixed market but are dependent for services. They will affiliate with co-ordinating agencies on their own terms, i.e., elimination of planned-parenthood groups.
Independent (national services)	National health organizations whose main activity is research but which have achieved no public acceptance of their importance will affiliate with community co-ordinating agencies.	National cancer associations have a fixed market (because of the public's fear of cancer) and have independence in services because these are mostly research. They will not affiliate with local community co-ordinating agencies.
Mixed interdependent and independent (both local and national services)	Agencies such as the Red Cross have both national and local services. They are becoming less independent because their tradition is fading. Therefore they enter into local community arrangements while insisting on maintaining their identity and the right to run national mass-media campaigns.	Jewish community councils in a strong Jewish community have a fixed market. At the same time they have local services (family and recreation programs) and national services (i.e., research on antisemitism, aid to Israel, etc.). Hence they are likely to have dual campaigns.

were both providing funds to the same individual without being aware of it, neither agency was maximizing its goals. The social service exchange served an important co-ordinating function, since any client coming to an agency could be checked through the exchange to see if he was receiving aid from another agency as well.

Two developments undermined the interdependence of the agencies and led to the decline of the social service exchange. First, the government in the middle 1930's took over most of the material assistance programs. Secondly, the private agencies turned their attention to other services with a strong emphasis on psychiatric casework,[22] which did not necessitate communication between agencies. First, the client was unlikely to seek duplication of service as he might seek duplication of material benefits. Secondly, it was argued that all crucial information could be secured from the client;[23] consequently it was not necessary to have any record of prior counseling by some other agency. In addition, some theorists would argue that it would be unethical to secure information from outside sources without the client's knowledge or consent.[24] In other words, old services which were co-ordinated by the social service exchange have disappeared and the new services do not result in agency interdependence,[25] and the decline of social service exchanges can therefore be explained by the decreasing interdependence of the member agencies.

Adjudicatory Functions and Types of Interdependency

Thus far the analysis has attempted to demonstrate that a series of seemingly diverse problems might all be related to the same underlying phenomenon. A simple derivative of the interdependency hypothesis might now be taken into account. If co-ordinating agencies develop when there is agency interdependency, the type of co-ordination should vary with type of dependency. Thomas points out that there is both a competitive and a noncompetitive form of interdependency.[26] In competitive interdependency an agency seeking to maximize its goal deprives another agency of doing likewise. Thus in a community chest where there is a limited amount of social welfare funds, the more one agency receives, the less another agency will receive. By contrast, the social service exchanges dealt with a noncompetitive facilitating interdependency, where maximal goal achievement by one agency was most likely when other agencies maximized their goals as well. Interdependency explains both the rise of the community chest and the decline of the social service agencies.

However, the competitive interdependency of community chests and the facilitating interdependency of social service agencies explains one of the basic differences between these agencies—the adjudicating functions of the community chest. Where a co-ordinating agency must deal with competitive interdependence, it must have some process for adjudicating the differences which must arise. Such agencies will therefore be characterized by some judicial processes. The budget committees of community chests are frequently the core committees whose major function is to hand down judgments by approving or disapproving budget requests of competing agencies. By contrast, the social service exchanges deal with situations where member agencies have no dispute but can only increase their goal achievement by communicating through the co-ordinating agencies. This explains why social service exchanges have minor adjudicatory functions.

Growth Pattern of Co-ordinating Agencies and Some Policy Implications

Our analysis suggests that where interdependency rests on some very stable set of social relations one can anticipate the growth of the co-ordinating agencies to be constant. Since financial support is one of the most stable social conditions in a money economy such as ours, there is good reason to predict the growth and continued existence of co-ordinating agencies such as the community chest. By contrast, interdependency based on services has no such stable support, for social services frequently rest on discoveries in the social sciences. For example, psychotherapy is constantly open to the changes of scientific progress,[27] and it would be hypothesized that co-ordinating agencies dealing with such services might have a much more uncertain future. One of the policy implications which follows is that such co-ordinating agencies must be given maximum discretion to alter their functions as necessitated by new scientific developments.

Self-awareness and Co-ordinating Agencies—The Future Role of Research

Our hypothesis stated that in addition to dependency there must be self-awareness. In dealing with financial services there seems to be little problem in our moneyed economy of self-awareness. This in part explains the early emergence of the social service exchanges and the community chest. Interdependency based on services and resting on theories of social behavior might not be so easy to observe and, once observed, difficult to raise to agency self-awareness. To do this requires some publicly certified method such as scientific research. Thus it took a scientific survey such as Buell's[28] to raise to the agency policy level the fact that many agencies were treating different problems of the same families. By not being aware of this, the agencies frequently proposed programs of action to the client which were contradictory. As the social sciences develop, it is quite probable that agencies will increasingly turn to scientific research to see whether interdependence indeed exists.

Aside from the question of research, economic theorists suggest still another factor affecting public awareness of dependency. They point out that where there are many units in the field, e.g., farming, it is almost impossible to observe and communicate interdependency.[29] By contrast, where one has a few units, observability or interdependence is markedly increased. In the initial stages community welfare agencies were supported by a few wealthy individuals.[30] It was perhaps the small number of persons involved which contributed to their perception of the need for, and their ability to co-operate in, the development of community chest programs.[31] Whereas a large number of agencies will make observability of interdependence difficult, a small number reduces the need for formal co-ordinating agencies, since co-ordination can be handled informally.

Standardization of Community Chest and Encroachment on Welfare Agencies

This, in turn, points out the importance of the last term of the hypothesis—standardization of social action. In order for a co-ordinating agency to operate efficiently it must develop specialists. For such specialists to develop, however, the behavior to be co-ordinated has to be standard in character—continuing and repetitious over long periods. If, for instance, social workers in family agencies needed to consult with those in children's agencies, and each case was unique, there would be no real way of codifying this information or developing specialists in transmitting this information, and therefore no need for formal co-ordinating agencies. The most efficient way to handle this form of interdependence might be informal mechanisms of co-ordination—telephone conversations between workers, bringing in consultants, and the like.

In short, if one is to move from mechanisms of co-ordination to formal co-ordinating agencies, it is necessary to deal with standardized units of behavior. Conversely, to increase its efficiency, a co-ordinating agency must seek to standardize the behavior which makes up interagency dependency as much as possible. In this connection the growing detailed budgetary demands made by community chests on member agencies are most instructive. From the early times, where community chests asked for a rough estimate of the agencies' current budgetary needs, to the present time, where most elaborate forms are filled out for at least one year in advance, the pressure for standardization of budgetary requests has increased. The same process can be observed in social service exchanges where the drive for standardization has led to an increasingly detailed and complex categorizing of information.

However, the relationship between standardization and co-ordinating agencies is not monotonic. Thus where extreme standardization takes place, it is frequently possible to co-ordinate activities via rules or laws rather than community organization. This is ideally what the economists mean when they speak about automatic stabilizers.[32] A good illustration of how interaction between two organizations can be co-ordinated by rules are the escalator clauses in union-management contracts. It is possible to have such rules because the computation of the living cost and wage payment is standardized—rules for computing them are readily made, publicly observable, and easily checked, and if done over and over again the same results would have a high probability of occurring.

Mechanisms for Preserving Conflict

Thus far the analysis of co-ordinating mechanisms has with one exception centered on the element of co-operation or interdependence. If the interorganizational character is to be retained, there must also be some procedures for preserving autonomy and conflict. For instance, if the community chest were to concentrate just on the co-operative functions, there would be a tendency for organizational merger of member agencies or, as a minimum, the development of uniformity of services. Groups such as the community chest were originally organized around the goal of co-operation (i.e., fund raising and allocation). Group goals once set have a powerful socializing effect on members;[33] furthermore, the group tends to recruit only those who are sympathetic to its goals. Because these socialization and screening pressures for co-operation and merger have a group base, the counter-pressures for preserving organizational autonomy and conflict must have an equally pervasive influence.

One type of group mechanism designated to preserve areas of autonomy and conflict is signaled by the phrase "conflict of interest." The mechanism is a law or a professional code of ethics which says that no individual can belong to two organizations which have legitimate areas of conflict. The incipient basis for this type of mechanism can be seen in the area of welfare fund raising as well. In contrast to the community chests, community councils have in recent years more and more taken the position of defending agency autonomy (i.e., arguing that the community chest does not have the right to make the decisions about the nature and quality of services). If this incipient division of labor crystallizes, then a code of ethics might eventuate in which a person will be said to have a conflict of interest if he sits on the budget committee of the community chest and is a member of the community council committee for preserving professional control of services.

Another possible procedure for maintaining legitimate areas of conflict is to have a division of labor *within* the co-ordinating agency, with one group dealing with areas of co-operation and the other with areas of conflict and autonomy.[34] Thus the budget committee of the community chest is frequently dominated by lay people who exercise considerable control over fund raising and allocation. Problems of fund allocations frequently lead to questions about the respective merits of various services, however, and the nonprofessional members may lean heavily on their staff experts. The professional members are frequently educated to accept the legitimacy of multiple and competing forms of service and act as a barrier to demands for merger or premature resolution of conflicts.

Still another mechanism for preserving conflict is the use of the ideology of "tradition" as a decision rule. Where there has been a profusion of services in the past, such a decision rule acts to maintain existing states of conflict.[35] This mechanism is generally vulnerable, however, because it does not provide for innovation in a society where change is a cultural characteristic. Therefore, if this mechanism is to survive in our society, it is likely to be used as the courts use the concept of "precedent." The fiction of tradition is maintained, although, *de facto,* much innovation is permitted. There are a variety of other mechanisms of equal merit[36] which will not be explored here.

It must be pointed out that, while interorganizational co-ordination requires both co-operation and conflict, at any given time emphasis might be on one or the other. Thus, since the middle eighteen-hundreds, the major problem in welfare fund raising has been to develop co-operation between competing agencies. It is only recently, when community chests have become exceedingly strong, that attention has shifted to the problem of agency autonomy and preserving legitimate areas of conflict. By contrast, in the business world since the middle eighteen-hundreds primary attention has been paid to preserving areas of conflict between concerns (antitrust laws) and only recently has more attention been paid to the need to maintain co-operation (fair price laws, farmer subsidies, and so on). The researcher must therefore keep in mind that despite the exigencies of any particular situation, interorganizational co-ordination is characterized by the need to maintain areas both of conflict and of co-ordination. . . .

Notes

1. We are indebted to Henry J. Meyer for helpful comments on this paper.
2. William H. Form and Sigmund Nosow, *Community in Disaster* (New York, 1958), pp. 243–244; Floyd Hunter, *Community and Power Structure* (Chapel Hill, N. C., 1953).
3. Neal Gross, W. S. Mason, and A. W. McEachern, *Exploration in Role Analysis: Studies of the School Superintendency Role* (New York, 1958).

4. Emile Durkheim, *The Division of Labor in Society* (New York, 1947). If the concept of organization is used very broadly, it could be argued that Marx provided in his theory of class conflict a view of interorganizational analysis which, according to him, explains all social behavior.

5. The systematic study of *intra*organizational analysis has proceeded at a rapid pace since the 1940's as indicated by the many studies in bureaucracy as well as the development of industrial sociology. For a review of some of this literature, see Peter M. Blau, *Bureaucracy in Modern Society* (New York, 1956). Interorganizational analysis has received no such systematic attention. This contrasts somewhat with related social sciences, where interorganizational analysis has been a major concern. For some illustrations in economics see John K. Galbraith, *American Capitalism: The Concept of Countervailing Power* (Boston, 1952), pp. 117–157; Friedrich A. Hayek, *The Road to Serfdom* (Chicago, 1944), pp. 56–127; K. William Kapp, *The Social Costs of Private Enterprise* (Cambridge, Mass., 1950); E. F. M. Durbin, *Problems of Economic Planning* (London, 1949).

6. H. H. Gerth and C. Wright Mills, eds. and tr., *From Max Weber: Essays in Sociology* (New York, 1946), pp. 196–203.

7. *Bureaucracy in Modern Society*, pp. 57–68.

8. Philip Selznick, *TVA and the Grass Roots: A Study in the Sociology of Formal Organization* (Berkeley, Calif., 1949).

9. Current relations between the United States and Russia are a case in point. These two nations do not recognize any authority superior to them. Because of the potential destructive power of atomic warfare and the interrelated character of international relations they are interdependent, i.e., each can destroy the other or each must take the other into account in order to achieve its national goals. At the same time they have conflicting ideologies, which lead them to seek to maintain regions of legitimized conflict, i.e., national sovereignty.

10. Some of the current studies in industrial organization also suggest the need to consider localized discretion and the decentralization of authority. Seymour Melman's *Decision-Making and Productivity* (Oxford, 1958), pp. 3–23, is a case in point. It is not always easy to know when a situation fits the intraorganizational or interorganizational model. Concerns such as General Electric are nominally one organization but at times resemble a series of independent ones in coalition, while the steel industry consists of formally separated groups which for many purposes tend to act as a unit (in labor bargaining, on pricing of goods, and against political pressure groups).

11. For a more formal definition and discussion of interdependence see Edwin J. Thomas, Effects of Facilitative Role Interdependence on Group Functioning, *Human Relations*, 19 (1957), 347–366. In the definition used here the phrase "take into account" is meant in a very immediate sense for in a broad sense all organizations must take each other into account.

12. In contrast to these illustrations the diagnosis and treatment of mental illness is nonstandardized and not public in character.

13. For a detailed account of the beginnings of the federation movement see: John R. Seely *et al.*, *Community Chest* (Toronto, 1957), pp. 13–29; Frank J. Bruno, *Trends in Social Work: 1874–1956* (New York, 1957), pp. 199–206; and William J. Norton, *The Cooperative Movement in Social Work* (New York, 1927), pp. 8 ff., 112 ff.

14. Norton, *op. cit.*, pp. 50 ff., 68 ff., 113 ff.

15. An indirect measure of this is that for 1940–1955, where comparable figures were available, the amount collected by united funds (including Red Cross) increased at the same or slightly higher rate than disposable personal income. See *Trends in Giving, 1955* (New York, 1956), p. 3. The rate of increase of gross national product and united community funds is roughly similar between the period 1948 to 1958. See *Trends in Giving, 1958* (New York, 1959), p. 2.

16. Norton, *op. cit.*, pp. 96 ff., 133 ff.

17. "While in everyday affairs organizations implicitly are dependent on one another to

meet routine problems, they are rarely called out in force to function effectively *together* as one unit. Yet this is precisely what is required in a disaster—the full mobilization and cooperation of interdependent organizations, which normally operate autonomously. Hence organizational integration is the most crucial dimension in disaster" (Form and Nosow, *op. cit.*, pp. 243–244).

18. Sources of data: J. Frederic Dewhurst *et al.*, *America's Needs and Resources* (New York, 1955), p. 437; Russel H. Kurtz, *Social Work Yearbook, 1957* (New York, 1957), p. 175; *Trends in Giving, 1957, 1958, 1959* (New York, 1958, 1959, 1960). The amount of funds raised is affected by short-term crises and is therefore a more sensitive measure of organizational strength than number of organizations, which do not reflect short-term declines because of career and job commitments. Also, when the dollar value was stabilized by computing all figures on the basis of the 1953 dollar, no significant change in the character of the fluctuations occurred.

19. The reader can note from Figure 1 that there is a continued increase in funds following the Korean crisis. This period is marked by aggressive solicitations by national agencies in smaller communities leading to an increase in interdependency. In addition, smaller communities became aware of united giving because of its popularity among the larger cities. An examination of the *Annual Directory of Chests, United Funds and Councils* (UCFC) (1936 and 1956) shows that approximately one-third of the 429 community chests listed in 1936 were in towns of 25,000 or less population. In 1956, towns of this size represented better than half of the 1,182 community chests listed. Also see *United Giving in the Smaller Community* (New York, 1956).

20. For details regarding the nonparticipation of national agencies, see *Organizing a United Fund* [1953] and *United We Stand* [1958] (New York, 1954, 1959); *1958 Experience in United Funds, 1957 Experience in United Funds*, and *United Giving in the Smaller Community* (New York, 1956); and F. Emerson Andrews, *Philanthropic Giving* (New York, 1950), pp. 152 ff., 156 ff.

21. Regarding the experiences of the exchange see *Summary Report of Research on the Social Service Exchange* (New York, 1959); *Social Work Yearbook 1957*, pp. 547 ff.; Norton, *op. cit.*, pp. 22–24.

22. See note 21 and *Budget $ in a Community Chest* (New York, 1953).

23. See note 21.

24. *Ibid.*

25. More recent trends in treatment suggest that social service exchanges might be reorganized around different functions.

26. *Op. cit.*

27. In this connection the tendency among some social workers and psychoanalysts to view principles of therapy as permanently fixed displays an attitude more akin to religious movements than to the spirit of scientific progress.

28. B. Buell, *et al.*, *Community Planning for Human Services* (New York, 1952).

29. Galbraith, *op. cit.*, pp. 12–25, 33–53.

30. See note 13.

31. By contrast, current chest programs have a large mass base. However, by 1959 close to 85 per cent of the funds were collected under the aegis of business, and support for united fund drives comes from the managers of large organizations, who are relatively few in number. This estimate of 85 per cent is rough and is based on the amount given directly by corporations and the amount collected at the place of work. See *Trends in Giving, 1958*, and F. Emerson Andrews, *Corporation Giving* (New York, 1952), pp. 156–158. Like the few wealthy individuals of the past, these managers are able to see the disruptive forces in having many diverse drives.

32. E. Despres, M. Friedman, A. Hart, P. A. Samuelson, and D. H. Wallace. The Problem of Economic Instability, *American Economic Review*, 40 (1950), 505–538.

33. The socializing effect of the group on the individual has been thoroughly documented. For a recent summary see Eugene Litwak, "Some Policy Implications in Communica-

tions Theory with Emphasis on Group Factors," *Education for Social Work, Proceedings of the Seventh Annual Program Meeting* (New York, 1959), pp. 98–109.

34. For illustrations of a division of labor as a way for maintaining legitimized conflict see Blau, *Bureaucracy in Modern Society*, pp. 64–66; James D. Thompson and Arthur Tuden, "Strategies, Structures, and Processes of Organizational Decision," in James D. Thompson *et al.*, eds., *Comparative Studies in Administration* (Pittsburgh, 1959), pp. 200–202.

35. The ideology of progress rather than tradition might be used to provide for legitimate areas of conflict where the past has shown a monolithic uniformity.

36. Mechanisms might be derived by analogy from a consideration of Robert K. Merton, The Role-Set: Problems in Sociological Theory, *British Journal of Sociology*, 8 (June 1957), 106–120; and Eugene Litwak, Models of Bureaucracy Which Permit Conflict, *American Journal of Sociology*, 47 (1961), 177–184.

Leadership and Organizational Performance: A Study of Large Corporations

Stanley Lieberson and James F. O'Connor

The options of organization leaders are restricted by both the organization's internal structure and its social milieu. Therefore, a basic proposition in sociology is that a group leader's ability to implement goals reflects not only his distinctive qualities, but also social and environmental limits. When one talks about a leader's time being "right" or "wrong," he implies an interaction between leadership qualities, policy direction, and social environment. We recognize the inherent weakness of the great-man theory or any other theory that fails to consider a leader's bounds. As Freedman, *et al.* (1956:83), put it, "the influence which any *single* individual may have upon the development of groups (and especially the larger and more important groups which men have formed) is not so great as we frequently imagine . . . While no sociologist would deny the assertion that certain individuals have a disproportionate influence upon the course of development of the groups to which they belong, the evidence indicates that the influence of single individuals or handfuls of individuals is seldom as decisive as the great-man theory would lead one to believe." They cite a list of inventions and discoveries independently made by two or more people (Ogburn and Thomas, 1922) to demonstrate that the cultural base limits thought and they suggest that even major intellectual and technological advancements reflect the existing culture.

Despite its fundamental nature, this approach to leadership is not fully understood by either the public or sociologists. For many, it really matters who is elected the nation's president. Likewise, a team's success is attributed to its coach's brilliance, a corporation's performance is taken to reflect its chief executive's characteristics. In academe, gossip about the consequences of a choice for department chairmen, dean, or college president implies this perspective. The extensive sociological literature on leadership in complex organizations tends to focus on leadership qualities, mechanisms of successful administration, and nuances of interpersonal relations and feelings. Limitations on leadership effectiveness are typically seen as coming from an organization's internal structure, and involving communication blocks, factional conflicts, and underlings' abortive bureaucratic devices. (Blau and Scott, 1962:165–183; Bowers and Seashore, 1966:238–250.) Although exceptions exist, one looks harder to find studies of the impact of exogenous forces on leadership effects within organizations.

Two reasons make it difficult to determine environmental constraints on leader influence. One is the absence of controls, which applies to both popular conceptions and sociological research. One never knows what might have been

We are indebted to Lee J. Haggerty and Herbert L. Costner for helpful methodological suggestions. Raul Marin did the drafting work for Figure 1.

Reprinted in part from *American Sociological Review*, vol. 37 (April, 1972), pp. 117–130, by permission of the authors and the publisher, The American Sociological Association.

had a different man been leader. Would the Confederacy still exist, or indeed slavery, had Lincoln died at the time of Secession? An intriguing problem, but basically unanswerable. Only in an experimental situation can one directly measure variation in leadership influence. Leadership changes do not occur in identical situations in nature; hence it is hard to infer the degree to which organizational outcomes reflect a leadership effect as opposed to forces outside a leader's control. But small group experiments, while interesting and suggestive, seem not to closely approximate the complex set of forces influencing heads of large formal organizations. At the moment they offer little promise for the kind of issue raised here.

Malinowski's analysis of religion and magic suggests a second source of the popular emphasis on leadership. Malinowski argues that belief in supernatural forces provides the Trobriand Islanders with a feeling of control over important events which they are impotent to affect through natural means. Such are the rain, sun, and insects affecting crops, and the tides, gales, and unknown reefs affecting safety in an outrigger (1948:28–30). Similarly, belief in a political leader's ability to alter affairs may generate a feeling of indirect control. The ability to reward or punish incumbents through the vote implies this influence. Or consider the scapegoat function in sports: the readiness to fire coaches and managers. Whether they are *unsuccessful managers* or *managers of unsuccessful teams* is never determined. An organization in trouble is an organization whose leaders must shoulder the blame (Gamson and Scotch, 1964).

To be sure, a balanced approach recognizes that an organization's progress over time is molded by leaders' traits, as well as by constraints in the organization's character and environment. Schlesinger's description of the decision process in politics is consistent with the leadership approach taken here: "The decision is generally the result of an accommodation between his own views of what is wise and the felt pressures on him as to what is possible" (1962:769). The president of a wealthy university enjoys certain advantages over the president of an institution in constant financial crisis which are not reflections of their administrative abilities. Nevertheless, presidents may still differ in their ability to raise money, handle internal management problems, and develop successful strategies for dealing with their problems. The coach of an excellent team will have a better record than one with weaker players, but the success stories of various coaches who turn a mediocre into an exceptional team while changing few personnel suggest important differences between coaches.

A key research issue is simply to determine the relative importance of leadership and organizational environment for organizational outcomes. How much variance in organizational performance can be attributed to persons in top leadership roles? A second issue is more analytical, namely, the organizational and environmental characteristics affecting an administrator's bounds. If one assumes organizations have more than one goal and if, further, one assumes that the magnitude of restrictions on a leader's options may vary with the particular goal, then the problem becomes complex.

Leadership in Large Businesses

We compare the influence of corporate and environmental factors with the leadership effects among 167 major publicly owned corporations from 1946–1965. Using three performance variables (sales, earnings, and profit margins), we compare the influence of changes in top management (new presidents or board chairmen) with the influence of such factors as the state of the economy, the company's primary industry, and the company's position within the industry. A great advantage in using business organizations is that the dependent variables can all be quantified. One reads of President Kennedy's incredible difficulty in changing the State Department (see Schlesinger, 1965: Chapter 16), but it is hard to measure such phenomena and hence determine leadership's role in such events.

Corporate performance is not only a reflection of administrative competence. The literature in complex organizations makes clear that varied forces reduce and muffle a leader's impact (for representative examples, see Thompson, 1967:132–133; Lipset, 1968:307–329; Guest, 1962). Beyond this, an organization's formal structure plays a role. Take General Motors, for example. A recent description of the top management committee structure reveals heavy bounds on the chairman's options (Investor's Reader, 1971:22–23). He may spend no more than $250,000 on a project without others' approval. This amount is relatively small for a company of such size. The executive committee's permission is required for projects up to $2.5 million and projects beyond that figure require the finance committee's consideration. The chairman's description of his role reveals these limits. "My primary job is to reconcile different viewpoints and arrive at a consensus. Occasionally, one must make individual decisions. In those cases, it's my responsibility." (p. 23)

Aside from these well-researched controls within an organization, the environment of the organization imposes heavy limits on a leader. For business administrators, these include: competitors (both foreign and domestic); an array of government regulations and policies that affect everything from the product to interest rates; unions; consumer demands; conditions in other industries that are suppliers, consumers or transporters of the company's products; market factors affected by internal population redistribution; the state of the economy; and technological considerations. Undoubtedly, a far more extensive list could be made, but this will suffice to suggest the bounds that are, at most, only partly subject to an administrator's control.

A description of the steel industry by Demaree (1971) is a good illustration of these bounds on management in major industry. In recent years, there have been Presidential pressures against price increases, a long strike against the industry's largest single customer, a steel hauler's strike and sharply increasing costs of input materials. Contract negotiations with the United Steel Workers affect wages and, therefore, production costs. Further, because steelmaking technology has changed radically, the earlier conventional economics of the process have become obsolete. Demaree (p. 76) cites a new $1.1 billion plant started in 1961 but not completed until 1969, long after technological and market changes had totally disrupted the earlier plans. In addition, pressures from important customers like the auto and appliance industries have affected the industry's concern with product quality. Also the industry is under growing competitive pressures from both the use of substitute metals and foreign steelmakers. Finally, options are also restricted by new regulations governing pollution control.

The point of all this is not to gain sympathy for steel company leaders, but to illustrate the kinds of pressures restricting leadership. Graphically, the close correlation in sales over a twenty-year span among the nation's eight largest steel

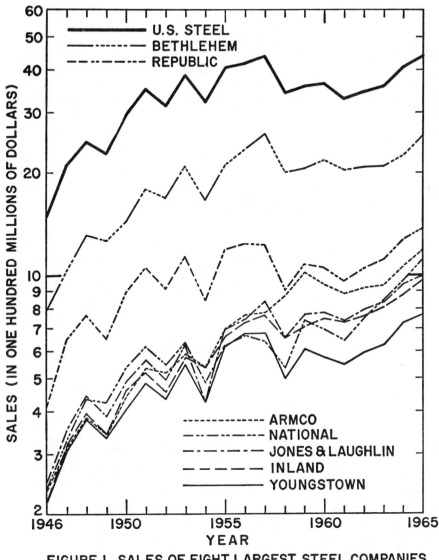

FIGURE I. SALES OF EIGHT LARGEST STEEL COMPANIES
1946-1965

Figure 1   Sales of Eight Largest Steel Companies 1946–1965

companies is striking (Figure 1). There are plenty of wiggles in the lines which are not entirely parallel for all the companies and which may possibly reflect administrative qualities, but the overall pattern suggests that a common set of forces influences sales.

Data and Methods

Because the data we use are not commonly employed by sociologists, some attention should be given to their meaning, source, and use. The three dependent variables: sales, net earnings, and profit margins, are obtained for each of 167 companies located in thirteen different industries for each year of the period 1946 to 1965. All three variables describe related, but distinct characteristics important to any profit-seeking enterprise. Sales figures tap the company's market position, earnings deal with the operation's profit (and ultimately corporate survival), and profit margin describes the net return on sales. Though the three variables are basic measures of corporate success, they are by no means exhaustive; nor are they of equal importance in each industry. The data are drawn from the *Moody's Industrial Manual* and *Moody's Transportation Manual* issued each year. These volumes contain extensive statistical information about large, publicly held corporations and appear to be primarily for the use of investors.

Technical considerations affect each measure. Excluded from sales figures are known funds listed or received by a company only in a formal sense such as excise taxes in the oil and beer industries or the sales generated in merchandising operations by departments leased to others. Earnings are the net profit (or loss) after all expenses and taxes, but exclude any "extraordinary gains or losses" not part of regular operations as may result from the sale of properties or facilities. Profit margin is merely the ratio of net earnings to sales, as defined above. Most, but not all companies, report their results on a calendar year basis. Some companies, and certain industries, do not. Department stores, for example, traditionally use a fiscal year that ends on January 31. Such minor differences between fiscal and calendar year are readily incorporated in the study, but companies that changed their fiscal year during the span covered or with greater discrepancies from a calendar year had to be excluded.

Data were gathered on all available companies in each of thirteen industries.[1] The industries were not selected randomly, but to represent varied activities with respect to: technology employed; consumer orientation of markets; government control; size; and the like. Industry selection was also restricted by the need to have a minimum number of companies with the necessary data for the time span under study. These ranged from a low of six in the ship and boat building industry and nine in the beer and soap industries to a high of eighteen in the petroleum and shoe industries. Some industries could not be considered because their companies had too diverse a total set of activities. This study generally followed the categorizing of publicly held companies by the Securities Exchange Commission (1965) into the Standard Industrial Classification (SIC).

For a variety of reasons, the number of companies included within each industry is generally far smaller than the number listed by the Securities Exchange Commission. The *Moody's* data sources are less detailed for smaller companies; companies experiencing major accounting changes had to be dropped; those starting or disappearing (usually through mergers) within the twenty years could not be included; likewise, companies engaged in major mergers during the period were omitted. Also, companies with revised fiscal years or with fiscal years too close to the middle of the calendar years could not be included.

Leadership changes were defined as the selection of a new president or chairman of the board. Although the duties of the two officials vary from company to company as well as within companies, it is safe to say that these are a company's top positions; and the chief executive officer is nearly always one or the other (Gordon, 1961:67). The yearly publication, *Poor's Register of Corporations, Directors and Executives*, was used to determine personnel changes in these positions. It is possible that for all its care, this work made errors in denoting new administrations. We could not determine when in a given year a new president or board chairman took office. It was hard to attribute performance exactly to its rightful administration during these changes.

Since a new administration takes office in different years, and for different time periods, determining the leadership effect on performance is complicated by each company's unique set of administrative patterns. Hence, we used a simple analytical method to find the proportion of total variance accounted for by each independent variable. For a given dependent variable, say sales, visualize a huge matrix in which each cell contains a specific company's sales figure for a specific year. The sum of the squared differences between each cell and the grand mean, divided by the number of cells, is the total sales variance for the matrix. The influence of any classified variable, say year, may be examined by first determining each category's mean, in this case all companies' mean sales in a given year. Each yearly mean is then subtracted from the matrix grand mean to determine the necessary adjustment for specific sales figures in that year. When the variance of these adjusted scores is determined, the difference between the initial total variance and the adjusted variance may be divided by the initial variance to determine the proportion of total variance eliminated after taking year into account. Similarly, this procedure may be used for other independent variables to determine the percent of total variance accounted for by each.

This form of analysis is also used to determine the proportion of variance explained by an added independent variable after allowing for the effect of earlier variables. For example, after adjusting each year's sales figures for the subgroup means, the influence of industry was found by subtracting each industry mean from the grand mean and using this figure to adjust the cells previously adjusted for the year effect. This procedure can be repeated for the company effect (subtracting the company mean) and for administration. Subtracting the administration mean for a given company from figures that have already incorporated the year-, industry-, and company-specific effects, will yield the administrative effect that operates independent of these others. The irregular origin and term of administrations within and between companies makes this procedure of particular advantage.

The somewhat different analytical procedure and the additional variables used in the second part of the study will be discussed later.

The Leadership Effect

In describing leadership influence on organizational performance, clearly one must consider the influence of other forces. First, the economy itself fluctuates yearly, affecting any corporation's performance. Beyond the major prosperity-depression cycles, the smaller yearly fluctuations in interest rates, inflation, labor shortages, and the like bear on a company's results. This will be measured here by considering the variance in organizational performance accounted for by subdividing the results into a yearly effect.

A second vital consideration is the company's primary industry. Granted that our categories are far from precise, nevertheless industry organizations are drawn together by a common level of demand and similarity in their technologies. Moore (1955:294) describes a number of common conditions needed to survive in the automobile industry. Thus, each industry has distinctive features which limit the options of its company's leaders. Aside from general economic fluctuations, varied factors unique to an industry may reflect specific market and supply factors, labor strikes, wage adjustments, foreign competition, market saturation, and the like. In the steel industry, for example, the demand is affected by a specific set of markets and competitors only partly like those faced by the computer industry. Hence, we consider a given company's industry before accounting for its administration's performance effect.

Finally, since companies within an industry may differ radically in size, location, facilities, suppliers, markets, and reputation, the influence of the company per se must be considered. To be sure, one may argue that the variance between an industry's companies may reflect the relative skill of earlier administrators, but the fact remains that the newly appointed leader finds himself in a situation not of his own making. One of President Kennedy's difficulties with the State Department, Schlesinger observes (1965:410–411) was its deterioration during the McCarthy era and under Franklin Roosevelt. Whether this reflects partisan bias is of no concern here, the point is clear: companies within a given industry differ in ways that will influence a new leader's impact. Were General Motors and American Motors to trade all their top executives, the two companies' positions would not likely be reversed even if the quality of management were radically different (though that is, of course, an empirical question). Such factors as the two companies' production capacity, dealership organization, financial strength, consumer acceptance, and the like would undoubtedly place enormous limits on their options. Thus, one must consider company effect in examining impact on organization performance.

Table 1 below summarizes the influence of year, industry, company, and leadership on each of the three performance variables. In all cases, the yearly effect is slight, explaining no more than three percent of the total variance in organizational performance (column 2). This surprisingly low influence may reflect the period under consideration, which was generally prosperous and included no major depression. A company's industry is considerably more important and, when combined with the year effect (column 3), accounts for from 20 to 30 percent of the variance (net income and profit margins, respectively). The impact of the company position is particularly significant for sales and net income, accounting for an additional 64.8 and 67.7 percent of the total variance even after year and industry are taken into account (subtract column 3 from column 4). The company effect on profit margins is not as great, but still accounts for 22.6 percent of the total variance.

Column 4 of Table 1 suggests that the maximum possible administration effect varies widely between tasks. The administration has small effect on sales and net income since about 90 percent of the total variance in both is accounted for by year, industry, and company effects. By contrast, since these factors account for little more than half the profit margin variance, leadership differences could influence as much as 47.1 percent (100.0–52.9) of the profit margin's total variance.

However, leader differences are quite relevant for all three performance criteria. Explained sales variance moves up 6.5 percent to 97.4 when leadership is

TABLE 1 *Variance in Performance Variables Accounted for by Selected Factors and Administration*

| Performance Variable | Total Variance (1) | Cumulative Proportion of Variance Accounted by: | | | | | Increment Due to Administration (7) | % Reduction in Unexplained Variance when Administration is Considered (8) |
		Y (2)	Y and I (3)	Y, I and C (4)	Y, I, C and A (5)	Unexplained (6)		
Sales	$1.964(10^{17})$	.031	.261	.909	.974	.026	.065	71.5
Net income	$1.654(10^{15})$	.017	.203	.880	.955	.045	.075	62.8
Profit margin	$3.634(10^{-3})$	.018	.303	.529	.674	.326	.145	30.8

Note: Y = Year; I = Industry; C = Company; A = Administration.
Column 7 = Column 5 − Column 4.
Column 8 = (Column 7/1.000 − Column 4) (100).

considered (column 5). Likewise, net income advances about as much to a total of 95.5 percent and profit margin variance leaps 15 percent to 67.4 (column 5). Thus, the leadership effect on company performance does matter. Though much sales and income variance is explained prior to considering leadership, leadership patterns account for a substantial part of the variance that remains unexplained (column 8). From 60 to 70 percent of the relatively small residuals in sales and income are accounted for by differences between top administration, and 30 percent of the more sizeable profit margin residual is explained by the 14.5 percent increment from administration.

The above research design only partly taps the leadership influence on performance variables. A substantial shift in the quality of top administration, either upward or downward, may set in motion long-term changes not immediately apparent. With such lags, a change in company position may not be properly credited to the appropriate administration. Lags in leadership effect are limited for sales or earnings since so much variance is explained by year, industry and company factors, but such is not the case with profit margins.

Accordingly, the influence of leadership changes is lagged on each performance variable for one-, two-, and three-year periods. For a one-year lag, for example, each company's performance variables in 1946 are attributed to the 1945 administration; for a two-year lag the 1944 leaders are credited with the 1946 performance, etc. This procedure has no bearing on measuring the year, industry and company effects because the lags are introduced after these factors are taken into account. However, leadership information is not available for fourteen companies as we move back to consider administration in 1943 for the three-year lag. Accordingly, column 1, Table 2, which gives the year-industry-company effects, and column 2, which gives the administrative effect without lags, differ slightly from the total sample results in columns 4 and 7 of Table 1. This is simply the effect of dropping fourteen companies.

The lag effect on sales and net income is relatively minor—differing little from the administration influence determined assuming an immediate leadership effect. This is not surprising since leadership's absolute contribution to either sales or earnings is limited by the fact that prior variables account for so much of the variance. For the leadership effect on profit margins, however, the variance accounted for increases greatly assuming either a two- or three-year lag (columns 4 and 5 of Table 2). In either case, the leadership effect explains nearly a third of the total variance. Indeed, leadership influence on profit margins exceeds that for either the industry (.273) or company (.222) effects.[2] Altogether, the four inde-

TABLE 2 *Variance Accounted for by Administration Under Assumption of a Time-lag*

Performance Variable	Variance Accounted by Year, Industry, & Company (1)	Increment Due to Administration			
		No Lag (2)	1-Year Lag (3)	2-Year Lag (4)	3-Year Lag (5)
Sales	.910	.065	.066	.065	.063
Net Income	.880	.075	.080	.070	.069
Profit Margin	.512	.152	.127	.321	.317

pendent variables account for 83 percent of the profit margin variance assuming a two-year lag in leadership effect.

In short, all three performance variables are affected by forces beyond a leader's immediate control, but the bounds on a leader's impact may vary between goals. For sales and earnings, 90 percent of total variance can be accounted for by the year-industry-company effects. Hence, though leadership accounts for much of the remaining variance, in absolute terms it is not as great an influence. By contrast, the restrictions imposed by year-industry-company effects on profit margins are less severe, though significant. Consequently, the leadership impact on this variable is much greater—indeed, it exceeds any other single influence.

If large complex organizations have more than one goal and if the leadership effect varies between these goals, then abstract debate over leadership importance is meaningless. Instead, specific research problems need study. The first problem is the degree each performance variable is influenced by non-leadership effects and, in turn, leadership influence on the remaining variance. This we have attempted with the above data. Our next step is to examine the features which determine the relative importance of both milieu and leadership effects on performance variables.

Sources of Leadership Constraint

Leadership influence can be viewed as a product of two factors: the internal and external constraints on a leader and the relative ability of leaders. If constraints are high or leadership variance low, the leaders' effect will be minimal. Our results thus far raise empirical questions about both factors. First, what characteristics determine the relative influence of non-leadership factors? These will clearly influence the maximum possible leadership effect even if leader differences were to explain all remaining variance. Second, organizations differ in their leadership's role in accounting for the remaining variance unexplained. Thus, we shall examine the characteristics of organizations whose leadership is relatively important.

Complicating the issue is the recognition that both constraints and leadership effect may differ for activities or goals within an organization. In politics, the constraints in making foreign policy are probably of a different magnitude and source than those in domestic agriculture. For some goals leaders of small nations have more room to maneuver than leaders of large nations, while the inverse holds for other issues. In other words, leaders' options within an organization may vary widely depending on the goals or activities involved.

To explore these two issues, again we used the procedure described for decomposing the variance in Table 1, but this time separately for each of the thirteen industries. Thus the relative importance of year, company and leadership on each dependent variable can be compared between industries.[3] Industries differ greatly in the percent of total variance that can be explained by the additive influences of year and company (Table 3, columns 1 through 3) as well as in percent of remaining variance accounted for by differences in top management (columns 4 through 6).

The variance explained by year and company ranges least for sales, running from 76 percent in the beer industry to 95 percent in the steel industry (column 1). However, the range is broader for net earnings, running from about 55 percent in publishing and air transportation to nearly 90 percent in petroleum refining

TABLE 3 *Variance Within Industries Accounted for by Year, Company and Administration*

Industry	% of Variance Explained by Year and Company			% of Remaining Variance Explained by Administration		
	Sales (1)	Net Earnings (2)	Profit Margin (3)	Sales (4)	Net Earnings (5)	Profit Margin (6)
Air transportation	82.0	56.5	50.1	59.2	56.2	43.1
Beer	75.8	65.5	62.7	78.2	58.5	37.5
Clay products	90.5	86.2	23.6	69.3	47.3	14.0
Cement	86.4	86.7	73.9	77.4	67.6	45.8
Chemicals	87.9	88.9	79.2	79.6	63.9	45.7
Department stores	92.5	87.5	81.5	69.0	37.9	57.8
Drugs	83.1	80.9	70.0	61.2	58.9	52.6
Petroleum refining	88.5	89.6	85.2	81.5	71.8	50.1
Publishing	84.6	54.3	38.9	67.0	57.2	60.9
Ship building	79.7	56.1	32.6	77.7	15.7	16.7
Shoes and shoe stores	78.0	75.2	64.6	66.8	58.9	41.3
Soaps and toiletries	87.1	83.9	35.9	86.1	85.0	68.7
Steel	94.8	87.6	63.0	55.1	56.9	40.2

(column 2), and widest for profit margins, with year and company accounting for only a fourth of the variance among companies producing clay products, compared to 85 percent in petroleum refining (column 3). Industries also differ greatly in the degree that year and company consistently account for each performance variable (look across the first three columns). Though the figures are fairly constant in petroleum refining, they differ greatly in both publishing and ship building. In effect, there is some support for the notion that the same environmental factors differ in strength of impact on various organizational goals and activities.

The last three columns in Table 3 also suggest that similar patterns operate for inter-industry differences in the degree that administration explains the remaining variance in organizational performance.

External Constraints and Organizational Characteristics

Since the object is to study conditions which influence organizational susceptibility to year and company constraints, we should see if inter-industry differences in the variance explained are related to other industry characteristics. Table 4's eleven variables include: size, dependency on production workers, degree of machine technology, orientation of markets, importance of scientific and engineering activities, markets, industry growth, concentration, consumer orientation and average number of company vice presidents. Unfortunately, in most instances we were only able to get summary information on all of an industry's companies. Table 4's correlations represent inferences that may not hold with data based on individual companies. Since the analysis deals with only thirteen industries, results are tentative and exploratory. To guard against overinterpretation, a fairly high zero-order correlation is required.[4] No attempt is made to consider the partial correlations, as tempting as this may be; and likewise only two dependent variables, sales

TABLE 4   *Product-Moment Correlations Between Selected Industrial Characteristics and Variance in Performance Accounted for by Year, Company and Administration*

Characteristic	Inter-industry Correlations Between Characteristics and:			
	Proportion of Total Variance Accounted for by Year and Company		Proportion of Remaining Variance Accounted for by Administration	
	Sales (1)	Profit Margins (2)	Sales (3)	Profit Margins (4)
Employees[a,d]	.568	.324	−.419	.007
Vice-presidents[a,d]	.211	.240	−.353	.630
Production worker's payroll/total payroll[c,e]	.223	.016	.057	−.764
Power costs per production worker[c,e]	.336	.569	.194	.021
Concentration ratio[c,f]	.171	.206	.551	−.086
Personal consumption/total output[b,g]	−.537	.070	.243	.492
Advertising expenditures/total output[b,g]	−.226	−.116	.295	.558
Payroll/value added[c,h]	.044	−.473	−.269	−.752
Growth in value added[c,h]	.323	.155	−.035	.612
Assets per employee[c,h]	.236	.779	.336	.182
Scientists and engineers/total employees[b,i]	.127	.374	.090	.124

[a] Data available for all 13 industries.
[b] Data available for 11 industries.
[c] Data available for 10 industries.
[d] Mean for 1955 and 1956 derived from original data.
[e] Derived from Bureau of the Census (1961 a,b).
[f] Concentration Ratio for largest 8 companies in 1963. Bureau of the Census (1970).
[g] Office of Business Economics (1969).
[h] Bureau of Domestic Commerce (1970). Payroll/Value Added based on 1958; Growth in Value Added based on: (1964 & 1965)/(1958 & 1959); Assets per Employee based on 1964.
[i] Bureau of the Census (1963).

and profit margins, are examined for pre-leadership and leadership effects. The net income variable is excluded because its inter-industry correlations are substantial with some other dependent variables.

Sales

Two key factors affect the influence of year and company on total sales variance (Table 4, column 1): the mean number of employees and the industry's market structure. The first correlation suggests that industries with large companies, at least as measured by employment, are less immune to the combined effects of the general economy and each company's position within it. Hence, relatively more total sales variance in such industries is explained by these forces. By contrast, industries having companies with smaller employment are also those offering more options and flexibility. Hence, their company sales are less influenced by combined year and company effects.

The second important variable, proportion of industry sales to consumers, is negatively associated with the influence on sales of year and company. The sales volume of industries with a high proportion of output directed to non-consumer markets is more likely to reflect the economy's influence. Industries with markets more oriented to the final consumer are less affected by general forces, presumably because each company has more room to appeal to consumer tastes, and shifts in consumer interests will have a greater impact.

Profit Margins

The influence of the year and company effects on profit margins appears to reflect industrial differences in machine technology and capital needs (Table 4, column 2). These are, of course, somewhat related factors. Industries with highly developed technologies (as measured by power consumption per employee) tend also to have great capital needs (as measured by assets per employee) and hence to be low in "labor intensity" (payroll/value added). Hence, profit margins in industries with relatively large fixed assets and greater machine technology tend to be more influenced by the year and company effects. Insofar as such industries have higher fixed overhead costs, profit margins—as contrasted with sales level—will be affected by economic demands for the industry's products and each company's position within the industry.

Leadership Effect and Organizational Characteristics

We now examine differences between industries in management's impact on performance after accounting for the influence of year and company. Table 3, columns 4 through 6, shows that the industries differ greatly in the administrative effect on variance unexplained by these prior factors. In the soap industry, leadership accounts for nearly 70 percent of the unexplained profit margin variance. By contrast, management accounts for about 15 percent in the ship building and clay products industries after these controls are applied (Table 3, column 6).[5]

Sales

The administrative effect on sales tends to vary only with the industry's degree of concentration (Table 4, column 3). Those industries whose shipment value is most concentrated in the largest eight companies are also those whose leadership effect on sales is stronger. Though the reason for this is unclear, note that the two characteristics related to the year and company effects on sales—number of employees and personal consumption—are in no way related to management impact on the remaining sales variance (compare columns 1 and 3).

This finding, along with the comparison of columns 2 and 4 below, suggests an important distinction. On the one hand are the factors affecting the remaining unexplained variance before considering management's influence, on the other, the factors affecting inter-industry differences in the leadership effect on performance after year and company are accounted for. The latter will reflect the relative uniformity of appointments as well as industry characteristics. Hence, the forces accounting for the size of an industry's year and company effect may differ from those explaining leadership effect on the remaining variance.

Profit Margins

Varied factors relate to management impact on profit margins after the year and company effects are removed. The impact tends to be greater in industries with low labor intensity and/or where production worker pay is a smaller part of total employment costs (Table 4, column 4). Presumably, here top management has more room to effect company profit. Thus, the same range of fluctuations in management skills will generate greater shifts in the profit margins of industries with lower fixed overhead.

An industry's general growth, as measured by the percent change in value added over time, also influences management impact on profit margins (column 4). Industries with rapid growth probably offered more options to managers and hence their differences will more greatly effect profit margins.

The profit margin tends to be influenced more by management in industries where advertising is important and consumers form a sizable market. Such industries contend with more ambiguous issues of taste, judgment, and customer manipulation. Hence, management's decisions about advertising styles and consumer interest will influence profit margins more than in less consumer oriented industries.

A fourth factor is surprising. Namely, the number of vice presidents in the industry's average company is directly correlated with the administrative effect on profit margins. At first we expected that industries with many vice presidents would tend to have relatively less administrative effect since the buffer between the company's operations and the top leaders would be larger. These results contradict the point we made about the duties of the chairman of General Motors. Namely, the impact of the president and chairman is increased when the policy execution is delegated to others. Hence, an increase in the number of vice presidents may give top management tighter control through better policy execution and greater feedback on company operations.

Perhaps our most important finding is that factors influencing variance in the administrative effect on profit margins generally differ from those influencing the year and company effects. Six different variables are substantially correlated with differences in administrative effect and four variables are associated with the year and company effects. Yet, only one operates, on the zero-order level at least, with both administrative and year-company influences.

Discussion

Before we suggest this study's meaning for large organizations, certain cautions should be noted. Companies may have other performance variables more greatly affected by administration and virtually unaffected by environmental constraints. Moreover, the study design may itself lead one to underestimate leadership effect on the performance variables. We excluded companies either too diversified or radically altered by mergers. We did so to infer the influence of administrative variance under relatively controlled industrial conditions. However, the quality of management may have less effect on the existing basic processes and activities in an established company. Conversely, leadership variance may have more effect on mergers, entrance into new industrial realms, radical patterns of diversification unrelated to existing company activities, and various forms of corporate financial manipulations. . . .

Finally, this study does not examine the . . . problem of [the leadership] succession process in organizations and leadership variance.

We considered two central leadership questions in this study: first, the influence of leadership on organizational performance; second, the factors associated with interorganizational differences in leadership impact. Of the first, our analysis . . . suggest[s] that in emphasizing the effect of leadership, we may be overlooking far more powerful environmental influences. Unless leadership is studied as part of a total set of forces, one cannot gauge its impact. Moreover, the leadership effect may vary greatly between goals in an organization.

The second part of the analysis . . . suggests that the leadership role must be discussed not merely in terms of general constraints on the organization and the remaining variance accounted for by the leadership effect, but in terms of the specific organizational goal. An organization's milieu may tie a leader's hands or free them depending on which goal one is assessing.

This analysis suggests that we should treat separately the forces constraining leadership and those associated with leadership influence on the remaining variance. . . .

Notes

1. See Table 3 for the industries included.
2. These figures differ slightly from the net differences shown in Table 1 (columns 3–2; 4–3) because fourteen companies are excluded in the lag analysis.
3. The industry effect is not considered in this part of the analysis because of the design used.
4. The product-moment correlations are based on thirteen, eleven or ten industries. Were these a random sample of industries, a single-tailed test of significance at the .05 level would require correlations of .476, .521 and .550, respectively, before the null hypothesis could be rejected.
5. Note that inter-industry differences in the administrative succession process are not considered. Moreover, the administrative effect on performance variables is examined here without the operation of a lag.

References

Anonymous, 1971, "Managing GM—a big responsibility." *Investor's Reader* 56 (February 3):21–28.

Blau, Peter M. and W. Richard Scott, 1962, *Formal Organizations*. San Francisco: Chandler.

Bowers, David G. and Stanley E. Seashore, 1966, "Predicting organizational effectiveness with a four-factor theory of leadership." *Administrative Science Quarterly* 11 (September):238–263.

Crecine, John P., 1967, "A computer simulation model of municipal budgeting." *Management Science* 13 (July):786–815.

——— 1970, *Defense Budgeting: Organizational Adaptation to External Constraints*. Santa Monica, California: Rand Corporation.

Demaree, Allan T., 1971, "Steel: recasting an industry under stress." *Fortune* (March):74–77, 134, 136, 141–142.

Freedman, Ronald, Amos H. Hawley, Werner S. Landecker, Gerhard E. Lenski and Horace M. Miner, 1960, *Principles of Sociology*. New York: Henry Holt.

Gamson, William A. and Norman A. Scotch, 1964, "Scapegoating in baseball." *American Journal of Sociology* 70 (July):69–72.

Gordon, Robert A., 1961, *Business Leadership in the Large Corporation*. Berkeley and Los Angeles: University of California Press.

Guest, Robert H., 1962, "Managerial succession in complex organizations." *American Journal of Sociology* 68 (July):47–54.

Lipset, Seymour Martin, 1968, *Agrarian Socialism*. Garden City, N.Y.: Anchor Books.

Malinowski, Bronislaw, 1948, *Magic, Science and Religion*. Garden City, N.Y.: Anchor Books.

Moody's Investors Service, Inc., 1946–1965, *Moody's Industrial Manual*. New York.

———— 1946–1966, *Moody's Transportation Manual*. New York.

Moore, Donald A., 1955, "The automobile industry." In Walter Adams (ed.), *The Structure of American Industry*. New York: Macmillan.

Office of Business Economics, U.S. Department of Commerce, 1969, *Input-Output Structure of the U.S. Economy: 1963*. Washington: U.S. Government Printing Office.

Ogburn, William F. and Dorothy S. Thomas, 1922, "Are inventions inevitable? A note on social evolution." *Political Science Quarterly* 37:83–98.

Schlesinger, Arthur M., Jr., 1962, "The humanist looks at empirical social research." *American Sociological Review* 27 (December):768–771.

———— 1965, *A Thousand Days: John F. Kennedy in the White House*. Boston: Houghton Mifflin.

Securities and Exchange Commission, 1966, *Directory of Companies Filing Annual Reports with the Securities and Exchange Commission*. 1965. Washington: U.S. Government Printing Office.

Standard and Poor's Corporation, 1946–1965, *Poor's Register of Corporations, Directors and Executives*. New York.

Thompson, James D., 1967, *Organizations in Action*. New York: McGraw-Hill.

U.S. Bureau of the Census, 1961a, *U.S. Census of Manufactures: 1958. Volume 2, Industry Statistics, Part 2, Major Groups 29–39*. Washington: U.S. Government Printing Office.

———— 1961b, *U.S. Census of Manufactures: 1958: Volume 2, Industry Statistics, Part 1, Major Groups 20–28*. Washington: U.S. Government Printing Office.

———— 1963, *U.S. Census of the Population: 1960*. Subject Reports. Occupation by Industry. Final Report PC(2)–7C. Washington: U.S. Government Printing Office.

———— 1970, *U.S. Census of Manufactures: 1967*. Special Report Series: Concentration Ratios in Manufacturing. MC67(S)2. 1. Washington: U.S. Government Printing Office.

U.S. Bureau of Domestic Commerce, U.S. Department of Commerce, 1970, *Industry Profiles 1958–1968*. Washington: U.S. Government Printing Office.

Institutionalized Organizations: Formal Structure as Myth and Ceremony

John W. Meyer and Brian Rowan

Formal organizations are generally understood to be systems of coordinated and controlled activities that arise when work is embedded in complex networks of technical relations and boundary-spanning exchanges. But in modern societies formal organizational structures arise in highly institutionalized contexts. Professions, policies, and programs are created along with the products and services that they are understood to produce rationally. This permits many new organizations to spring up and forces existing ones to incorporate new practices and procedures. That is, organizations are driven to incorporate the practices and procedures defined by prevailing rationalized concepts of organizational work and institutionalized in society. Organizations that do so increase their legitimacy and their survival prospects, independent of the immediate efficacy of the acquired practices and procedures.

Institutionalized products, services, techniques, policies, and programs function as powerful myths, and many organizations adopt them ceremonially. But conformity to institutionalized rules often conflicts sharply with efficiency criteria and, conversely, to coordinate and control activity in order to promote efficiency undermines an organization's ceremonial conformity and sacrifices its support and legitimacy. To maintain ceremonial conformity, organizations that reflect institutional rules tend to buffer their formal structures from the uncertainties of technical activities by becoming loosely coupled, building gaps between their formal structures and actual work activities.

This paper argues that the formal structures of many organizations in postindustrial society (Bell 1973) dramatically reflect the myths of their institutional environments instead of the demands of their work activities. The first part describes prevailing theories of the origins of formal structures and the main problem the theories confront. The second part discusses an alternative source of formal structures: myths embedded in the institutional environment. The third part develops the argument that organizations reflecting institutionalized environments maintain gaps between their formal structures and their ongoing work activities. The final part summarizes by discussing some research implications.

Throughout the paper, institutionalized rules are distinguished sharply from prevailing social behaviors. Institutionalized rules are classifications built into

Work on this paper was conducted at the Stanford Center for Research and Development in Teaching (SCRDT) and was supported by the National Institute of Education (contract no. NE-C-00-3-0062). The views expressed here do not, of course, reflect NIE positions. Many colleagues in the SCRDT, the Stanford Organizations Training Program, the American Sociological Association's work group on Organizations and Environments, and the NIE gave help and encouragement. In particular, H. Acland, A. Bergesen, J. Boli-Bennett, T. Deal, J. Freeman, P. Hirsch, J. G. March, W. R. Scott, and W. Starbuck made helpful suggestions.

Reprinted in part from the *American Journal of Sociology*, vol. 83 (September 1977), pp. 340–363, by permission of the authors and the publisher. © 1977 by The University of Chicago Press.

society as reciprocated typifications or interpretations (Berger and Luckmann 1967, p. 54). Such rules may be simply taken for granted or may be supported by public opinion or the force of law (Starbuck 1976). Institutions inevitably involve normative obligations but often enter into social life primarily as facts which must be taken into account by actors. Institutionalization involves the processes by which social processes, obligations, or actualities come to take on a rulelike status in social thought and action. So, for example, the social status of doctor is a highly institutionalized rule (both normative and cognitive) for managing illness as well as a social role made up of particular behaviors, relations, and expectations. Research and development is an institutionalized category of organizational activity which has meaning and value in many sectors of society, as well as a collection of actual research and development activities. In a smaller way, a No Smoking sign is an institution with legal status and implications, as well as an attempt to regulate smoking behavior. It is fundamental to the argument of this paper that institutional rules may have effects on organizational structures and their implementation in actual technical work which are very different from the effects generated by the networks of social behavior and relationships which compose and surround a given organization.

Prevailing Theories of Formal Structure

A sharp distinction should be made between the formal structure of an organization and its actual day-to-day work activities. Formal structure is a blueprint for activities which includes, first of all, the table of organization: a listing of offices, departments, positions, and programs. These elements are linked by explicit goals and policies that make up a rational theory of how, and to what end, activities are to be fitted together. The essence of a modern bureaucratic organization lies in the rationalized and impersonal character of these structural elements and of the goals that link them.

One of the central problems in organization theory is to describe the conditions that give rise to rationalized formal structure. In conventional theories, rational formal structure is assumed to be the most effective way to coordinate and control the complex relational networks involved in modern technical or work activities (see Scott 1975 for a review). This assumption derives from Weber's (1930, 1946, 1947) discussions of the historical emergence of bureaucracies as consequences of economic markets and centralized states. Economic markets place a premium on rationality and coordination. As markets expand, the relational networks in a given domain become more complex and differentiated, and organizations in that domain must manage more internal and boundary-spanning interdependencies. Such factors as size (Blau 1970) and technology (Woodward 1965) increase the complexity of internal relations, and the division of labor among organizations increases boundary-spanning problems (Aiken and Hage 1968; Freeman 1973; Thompson 1967). Because the need for coordination increases under these conditions, and because formally coordinated work has competitive advantages, organizations with rationalized formal structures tend to develop.

The formation of centralized states and the penetration of societies by political centers also contribute to the rise and spread of formal organization. When the relational networks involved in economic exchange and political management become extremely complex, bureaucratic structures are thought to be the most effective and rational means to standardize and control subunits. Bureaucratic control is especially useful for expanding political centers, and standardization is often demanded by both centers and peripheral units (Bendix 1964, 1968). Political centers organize layers of offices that manage to extend conformity and to displace traditional activities throughout societies.

The problem. *Prevailing theories assume that the coordination and control of activity are the critical dimensions on which formal organizations have succeeded in the modern world.* This assumption is based on the view that organizations function according to their formal blueprints: coordination is routine, rules and procedures are followed, and actual activities conform to the prescriptions of formal structure. But much of the empirical research on organizations casts doubt on this assumption. An earlier generation of researchers concluded that there was a great gap between the formal and the informal organization (e.g., Dalton 1959; Downs 1967; Homans 1950). A related observation is that formal organizations are often loosely coupled (March and Olsen 1976; Weick 1976): structural elements are only loosely linked to each other and to activities, rules are often violated, decisions are often unimplemented, or if implemented have uncertain consequences, technologies are of problematic efficiency, and evaluation and inspection systems are subverted or rendered so vague as to provide little coordination.

Formal organizations are endemic in modern societies. There is need for an explanation of their rise that is partially free from the assumption that, in practice, formal structures actually coordinate and control work. Such an explanation should account for the elaboration of purposes, positions, policies, and procedural rules that characterizes formal organizations, but must do so without supposing that these structural features are implemented in routine work activity.

Institutional Sources of Formal Structure

By focusing on the management of complex relational networks and the exercise of coordination and control, prevailing theories have neglected an alternative Weberian source of formal structure: the legitimacy of rationalized formal structures. In prevailing theories, legitimacy is a given: assertions about bureaucratization rest on the assumption of norms of rationality (Thompson 1967). When norms do play causal roles in theories of bureaucratization, it is because they are thought to be built into modern societies and personalities as very general values, which are thought to facilitate formal organization. But norms of rationality are not simply general values. They exist in much more specific and powerful ways in the rules, understandings, and meanings attached to institutionalized social structures. The causal importance of such institutions in the process of bureaucratization has been neglected.

Formal structures are not only creatures of their relational networks in the social organization. In modern societies, the elements of rationalized formal structure are deeply ingrained in, and reflect, widespread understandings of social reality. Many of the positions, policies, programs, and procedures of modern organizations are enforced by public opinion, by the views of important constituents, by knowledge legitimated through the educational system, by social prestige, by the laws, and by the definitions of negligence and prudence used by the courts. Such elements of formal structure are manifestations of powerful institutional rules which function as highly rationalized myths that are binding on particular organizations.

In modern societies, the myths generating formal organizational structure have two key properties. First, they are rationalized and impersonal prescriptions that identify various social purposes as technical ones and specify in a rulelike way the appropriate means to pursue these technical purposes rationally (Ellul 1964). Second, they are highly institutionalized and thus in some measure beyond the discretion of any individual participant or organization. They must, therefore, be taken for granted as legitimate, apart from evaluations of their impact on work outcomes.

Many elements of formal structure are highly institutionalized and function as myths. Examples include professions, programs, and technologies:

> Large numbers of rationalized professions emerge (Wilensky 1965; Bell 1973). These are occupations controlled, not only by direct inspection of work outcomes but also by social rules of licensing, certifying, and schooling. The occupations are rationalized, being understood to control impersonal techniques rather than moral mysteries. Further, they are highly institutionalized: the delegation of activities to the appropriate occupations is socially expected and often legally obligatory over and above any calculations of its efficiency.
>
> Many formalized organizational programs are also institutionalized in society. Ideologies define the functions appropriate to a business—such as sales, production, advertising, or accounting; to a university—such as instruction and research in history, engineering, and literature; and to a hospital—such as surgery, internal medicine, and obstetrics. Such classifications of organizational functions, and the specifications for conducting each function, are prefabricated formulae available for use by any given organization.
>
> Similarly, technologies are institutionalized and become myths binding on organizations. Technical procedures of production, accounting, personnel selection, or data processing become taken-for-granted means to accomplish organizational ends. Quite apart from their possible efficiency, such institutionalized techniques establish an organization as appropriate, rational, and modern. Their use displays responsibility and avoids claims of negligence.

The impact of such rationalized institutional elements on organizations and organizing situations is enormous. These rules define new organizing situations, redefine existing ones, and specify the means for coping rationally with each. They enable, and often require, participants to organize along prescribed lines. And they spread very rapidly in modern society as part of the rise of postindustrial society (Bell 1973). New and extant domains of activity are codified in institutionalized programs, professions, or techniques, and organizations incorporate the packaged codes. For example:

> The discipline of psychology creates a rationalized theory of personnel selection and certifies personnel professionals. Personnel departments and functionaries appear in all sorts of extant organizations, and new specialized personnel agencies also appear.
>
> As programs of research and development are created and professionals with expertise in these fields are trained and defined, organizations come under increasing pressure to incorporate R & D units.
>
> As the prerational profession of prostitution is rationalized along medical lines, bureaucratized organizations—sex-therapy clinics, massage parlors, and the like— spring up more easily.
>
> As the issues of safety and environmental pollution arise, and as relevant professions and programs become institutionalized in laws, union ideologies, and public opinion, organizations incorporate these programs and professions.

The growth of rationalized institutional structures in society makes formal organizations more common and more elaborate. Such institutions are myths which make formal organizations both easier to create and more necessary. After all, the building blocks for organizations come to be littered around the societal landscape; it takes only a little entrepreneurial energy to assemble them into a structure. And because these building blocks are considered proper, adequate, rational, and necessary, organizations must incorporate them to avoid illegitimacy. Thus, the myths built into rationalized institutional elements create the necessity, the opportunity, and the impulse to organize rationally, over and above pressures in this direction created by the need to manage proximate relational networks:

Proposition 1. *As rationalized institutional rules arise in given domains of work activity, formal organizations form and expand by incorporating these rules as structural elements.*

Two distinct ideas are implied here: (1A) As institutionalized myths define new domains of rationalized activity, formal organizations emerge in these domains. (1B) As rationalizing institutional myths arise in existing domains of activity, extant organizations expand their formal structures so as to become isomorphic with these new myths.

To understand the larger historical process it is useful to note that:

Proposition 2. *The more modernized the society, the more extended the rationalized institutional structure in given domains and the greater the number of domains containing rationalized institutions.*

Modern institutions, then, are thoroughly rationalized, and these rationalized elements act as myths giving rise to more formal organization. When propositions 1 and 2 are combined, two more specific ideas follow: (2A) Formal organizations are more likely to emerge in more modernized societies, even with the complexity of immediate relational networks held constant. (2B) Formal organizations in a given domain of activity are likely to have more elaborated structures in more modernized societies, even with the complexity of immediate relational networks held constant.

Combining the ideas above with prevailing organization theory, it becomes clear that modern societies are filled with rationalized bureaucracies for two reasons. First, as the prevailing theories have asserted, relational networks become increasingly complex as societies modernize. Second, modern societies are filled with institutional rules which function as myths depicting various formal structures as rational means to the attainment of desirable ends. Figure 1 sum-

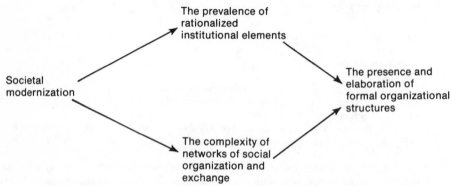

Figure 1 The Origins and Elaboration of Formal Organizational Structures

marizes these two lines of theory. Both lines suggest that the postindustrial society—the society dominated by rational organization even more than by the forces of production—arises both out of the complexity of the modern social organizational network and, more directly, as an ideological matter. Once institutionalized, rationality becomes a myth with explosive organizing potential, as both Ellul (1964) and Bell (1973)—though with rather different reactions—observe.

The Relation of Organizations to Their Institutional Environments

The observation is not new that organizations are structured by phenomena in their environments and tend to become isomorphic with them. One explanation of such isomorphism is that formal organizations become matched with their environments by technical and exchange interdependencies. This line of reasoning can be seen in the works of Aiken and Hage (1968), Hawley (1968), and Thompson (1967). This explanation asserts that structural elements diffuse because environments create boundary-spanning exigencies for organizations, and that organizations which incorporate structural elements isomorphic with the environment are able to manage such interdependencies.

A second explanation for the parallelism between organizations and their environments—and the one emphasized here—is that organizations structurally reflect socially constructed reality (Berger and Luckmann 1967). This view is suggested in the work of Parsons (1956) and Udy (1970), who see organizations as greatly conditioned by their general institutional environments and therefore as institutions themselves in part. Emery and Trist (1965) also see organizations as responding directly to environmental structures and distinguish such effects sharply from those that occur through boundary-spanning exchanges. According to the institutional conception as developed here, organizations tend to disappear as distinct and bounded units. Quite beyond the environmental interrelations suggested in open-systems theories, institutional theories in their extreme forms define organizations as dramatic enactments of the rationalized myths pervading modern societies, rather than as units involved in exchange—no matter how complex—with their environments.

The two explanations of environmental isomorphism are not entirely inconsistent. Organizations both deal with their environments at their boundaries and imitate environmental elements in their structures. However, the two lines of explanation have very different implications for internal organizational processes, as will be argued below.

The Origins of Rational Institutional Myths

Bureaucratization is caused in part by the proliferation of rationalized myths in society, and this in turn involves the evolution of the whole modern institutional system. Although the latter topic is beyond the scope of this paper, three specific processes that generate rationalized myths of organizational structure can be noted.

The elaboration of complex relational networks. As the relational networks in societies become dense and interconnected, increasing numbers of rationalized myths arise. Some of them are highly generalized: for example, the principles of universalism (Parsons 1971), contracts (Spencer 1897), restitution (Durkheim

1933), and expertise (Weber 1947) are generalized to diverse occupations, organizational programs, and organizational practices. Other myths describe specific structural elements. These myths may originate from narrow contexts and be applied in different ones. For example, in modern societies the relational contexts of business organizations in a single industry are roughly similar from place to place. Under these conditions a particularly effective practice, occupational specialty, or principle of coordination can be codified into mythlike form. The laws, the educational and credentialing systems, and public opinion then make it necessary or advantageous for organizations to incorporate the new structures.

The degree of collective organization of the environment. The myths generated by particular organizational practices and diffused through relational networks have legitimacy based on the supposition that they are rationally effective. But many myths also have official legitimacy based on legal mandates. Societies that, through nation building and state formation, have developed rational-legal orders are especially prone to give collective (legal) authority to institutions which legitimate particular organizational structures. The rise of centralized states and integrated nations means that organized agents of society assume jurisdiction over large numbers of activity domains (Swanson 1971). Legislative and judicial authorities create and interpret legal mandates; administrative agencies—such as state and federal governments, port authorities, and school districts—establish rules of practice; and licenses and credentials become necessary in order to practice occupations. The stronger the rational-legal order, the greater the extent to which rationalized rules and procedures and personnel become institutional requirements. New formal organizations emerge and extant organizations acquire new structural elements.

Leadership efforts of local organizations. The rise of the state and the expansion of collective juridiction are often thought to result in domesticated organizations (Carlson 1962) subject to high levels of goal displacement (Clark 1956; Selznick 1949; and Zald and Denton 1963). This view is misleading: organizations do often adapt to their institutional contexts, but they often play active roles in shaping those contexts (Dowling and Pfeffer 1975; Parsons 1956; Perrow 1970; Thompson 1967). Many organizations actively seek charters from collective authorities and manage to institutionalize their goals and structures in the rules of such authorities.

Efforts to mold institutional environments proceed along two dimensions. First, powerful organizations force their immediate relational networks to adapt to their structures and relations. For instance, automobile producers help create demands for particular kinds of roads, transportation systems, and fuels that make automobiles virtual necessities; competitive forms of transportation have to adapt to the existing relational context. But second, powerful organizations attempt to build their goals and procedures directly into society as institutional rules. Automobile producers, for instance, attempt to create the standards in public opinion defining desirable cars, to influence legal standards defining satisfactory cars, to affect judicial rules defining cars adequate enough to avoid manufacturer liability, and to force agents of the collectivity to purchase only their cars. Rivals must then compete both in social networks or markets and in contexts of institutional rules which are defined by extant organizations. In this fashion, given organizational forms perpetuate themselves by becoming institutionalized rules. For example:

School administrators who create new curricula or training programs attempt to validate them as legitimate innovations in educational theory and governmental requirements. If they are successful, the new procedures can be perpetuated as authoritatively required or at least satisfactory.

New departments within business enterprises, such as personnel, advertising, or research and development departments, attempt to professionalize by creating rules of practice and personnel certification that are enforced by the schools, prestige systems, and the laws.

Organizations under attack in competitive environments—small farms, passenger railways, or Rolls Royce—attempt to establish themselves as central to the cultural traditions of their societies in order to receive official protection.

The Impact of Institutional Environments on Organizations

Isomorphism with environmental institutions has some crucial consequences for organizations: (*a*) they incorporate elements which are legitimated externally, rather than in terms of efficiency; (*b*) they employ external or ceremonial assessment criteria to define the value of structural elements; and (*c*) dependence on externally fixed institutions reduces turbulence and maintains stability. As a result, it is argued here, institutional isomorphism promotes the success and survival of organizations. Incorporating externally legitimated formal structures increases the commitment of internal participants and external constituents. And the use of external assessment criteria—that is, moving toward the status in society of a subunit rather than an independent system—can enable an organization to remain successful by social definition, buffering it from failure.

Changing formal structures. By designing a formal structure that adheres to the prescriptions of myths in the institutional environment, an organization demonstrates that it is acting on collectively valued purposes in a proper and adequate manner (Dowling and Pfeffer 1975; Meyer and Rowan 1975). The incorporation of institutionalized elements provides an account (Scott and Lyman 1968) of its activities that protects the organization from having its conduct questioned. The organization becomes, in a word, legitimate, and it uses its legitimacy to strengthen its support and secure its survival.

From an institutional perspective, then, a most important aspect of isomorphism with environmental institutions is the evolution of organizational language. The labels of the organization chart as well as the vocabulary used to delineate organizational goals, procedures, and policies are analogous to the vocabularies of motive used to account for the activities of individuals (Blum and McHugh 1971; Mills 1940). Just as jealousy, anger, altruism, and love are myths that interpret and explain the actions of individuals, the myths of doctors, of accountants, or of the assembly line explain organizational activities. Thus, some can say that the engineers will solve a specific problem or that the secretaries will perform certain tasks, without knowing who these engineers or secretaries will be or exactly what they will do. Both the speaker and the listeners understand such statements to describe how certain responsibilities will be carried out.

Vocabularies of structure which are isomorphic with institutional rules provide prudent, rational, and legitimate accounts. Organizations described in legitimated vocabularies are assumed to be oriented to collectively defined, and often collectively mandated, ends. The myths of personnel services, for example, not only account for the rationality of employment practices but also indicate that personnel services are valuable to an organization. Employees, applicants, managers, trustees, and governmental agencies are predisposed to trust the hiring practices of organizations that follow legitimated procedures—such as equal opportunity programs, or personality testing—and they are more willing to participate in or to fund such organizations. On the other hand, organizations that omit environmentally legitimated elements of structure or create unique structures lack acceptable legitimated accounts of their activities. Such organizations are more vulnerable to claims that they are negligent, irrational, or unnecessary. Claims of this kind, whether made by internal participants, external constituents, or the government, can cause organizations to incur real costs. For example:

> With the rise of modern medical institutions, large organizations that do not arrange medical-care facilities for their workers come to be seen as negligent—by the workers, by management factions, by insurers, by courts which legally define negligence, and often by laws. The costs of illegitimacy in insurance premiums and legal liabilities are very real.
>
> Similarly, environmental safety institutions make it important for organizations to create formal safety rules, safety departments, and safety programs. No Smoking rules and signs, regardless of their enforcement, are necessary to avoid charges of negligence and to avoid the extreme of illegitimation: the closing of buildings by the state.
>
> The rise of professionalized economics makes it useful for organizations to incorporate groups of economists and econometric analyses. Though no one may read, understand, or believe them, econometric analyses help legitimate the organization's plans in the eyes of investors, customers (as with Defense Department contractors), and internal participants. Such analyses can also provide rational accountings after failures occur: managers whose plans have failed can demonstrate to investors, stockholders, and superiors that procedures were prudent and that decisions were made by rational means.

Thus, rationalized institutions create myths of formal structure which shape organizations. Failure to incorporate the proper elements of structure is negligent and irrational; the continued flow of support is threatened and internal dissidents are strengthened. At the same time, these myths present organizations with great opportunities for expansion. Affixing the right labels to activities can change them into valuable services and mobilize the commitments of internal participants and external constituents.

Adopting external assessment criteria. In institutionally elaborated environments organizations also become sensitive to, and employ, external criteria of worth. Such criteria include, for instance, such ceremonial awards as the Nobel Prize, endorsements by important people, the standard prices of professionals and consultants, or the prestige of programs or personnel in external social circles. For example, the conventions of modern accounting attempt to assign value to particular components of organizations on the basis of their contribution—through the organization's production function—to the goods and services the organization produces. But for many units—service departments, administrative sectors, and others—it is utterly unclear what is being produced that has clear or definable value in terms of its contribution to the organizational product. In these situations, accountants employ shadow prices: they assume that given organizational units are necessary and calculate their value from their prices in the world outside the organization. Thus modern accounting creates ceremonial production functions and maps them onto economic production functions: organizations assign externally defined worth to advertising departments, safety departments, managers, econometricians, and occasionally even sociologists, whether or not these units contribute measurably to the production of outputs. Monetary prices, in postindustrial society, reflect hosts of ceremonial influences, as do economic measures of efficiency, profitability, or net worth (Hirsch 1975).

Ceremonial criteria of worth and ceremonially derived production functions are useful to organizations: they legitimate organizations with internal participants, stockholders, the public, and the state, as with the IRS or the SEC. They demonstrate socially the fitness of an organization. The incorporation of structures with high ceremonial value, such as those reflecting the latest expert thinking or those with the most prestige, makes the credit position of an organization more favorable. Loans, donations, or investments are more easily obtained. Finally, units within the organization use ceremonial assessments as accounts of their productive service to the organization. Their internal power rises with their performance on ceremonial measures (Salancik and Pfeffer 1974).

Stabilization.   The rise of an elaborate institutional environment stabilizes both external and internal organizational relationships. Centralized states, trade associations, unions, professional associations, and coalitions among organizations standardize and stabilize (see the review by Starbuck 1976).

Market conditions, the characteristics of inputs and outputs, and technological procedures are brought under the jurisdiction of institutional meanings and controls. Stabilization also results as a given organization becomes part of the wider collective system. Support is guaranteed by agreements instead of depending entirely on performance. For example, apart from whether schools educate students, or hospitals cure patients, people and governmental agencies remain committed to these organizations, funding and using them almost automatically year after year.

Institutionally controlled environments buffer organizations from turbulence (Emery and Trist 1965; Terreberry 1968). Adaptations occur less rapidly as increased numbers of agreements are enacted. Collectively granted monopolies guarantee clienteles for organizations like schools, hospitals, or professional associations. The taken-for-granted (and legally regulated) quality of institutional rules makes dramatic instabilities in products, techniques, or policies unlikely. And legitimacy as accepted subunits of society protects organizations from immediate sanctions for variations in technical performance:

> Thus, American school districts (like other governmental units) have near monopolies and are very stable. They must conform to wider rules about proper classifications and credentials of teachers and students, and of topics of study. But they are protected by rules which make education as defined by these classifications compulsory. Alternative or private schools are possible, but must conform so closely to the required structures and classifications as to be able to generate little advantage.
>
> Some business organizations obtain very high levels of institutional stabilization. A large defense contractor may be paid for following agreed-on procedures, even if the product is ineffective. In the extreme, such organizations may be so successful as to survive bankruptcy intact—as Lockheed and Penn Central have done—by becoming partially components of the state. More commonly, such firms are guaranteed survival by state-regulated rates which secure profits regardless of costs, as with American public utility firms.
>
> Large automobile firms are a little less stabilized. They exist in an environment that contains enough structures to make automobiles, as conventionally defined,

virtual necessities. But still, customers and governments can inspect each automobile and can evaluate and even legally discredit it. Legal action cannot as easily discredit a high school graduate.

Organizational success and survival. Thus, organizational success depends on factors other than efficient coordination and control of productive activities. Independent of their productive efficiency, organizations which exist in highly elaborated institutional environments and succeed in becoming isomorphic with these environments gain the legitimacy and resources needed to survive. In part, this depends on environmental processes and on the capacity of given organizational leadership to mold these processes (Hirsch 1975). In part, it depends on the ability of given organizations to conform to, and become legitimated by, environmental institutions. In institutionally elaborated environments, sagacious conformity is required: leadership (in a university, a hospital, or a business) requires an understanding of changing fashions and governmental programs. But this kind of conformity—and the almost guaranteed survival which may accompany it—is possible only in an environment with a highly institutionalized structure. In such a context an organization can be locked into isomorphism, ceremonially reflecting the institutional environment in its structure, functionaries, and procedures. Thus, in addition to the conventionally defined sources of organizational success and survival, the following general assertion can be proposed:

Proposition 3. *Organizations that incorporate societally legitimated rationalized elements in their formal structures maximize their legitimacy and increase their resources and survival capabilities.*

This proposition asserts that the long-run survival prospects of organizations increase as state structures elaborate and as organizations respond to institutionalized rules. In the United States, for instance, schools, hospitals, and welfare organizations show considerable ability to survive, precisely because they are matched with—and almost absorbed by—their institutional environments. In the same way, organizations fail when they deviate from the prescriptions of institutionalizing myths: quite apart from technical efficiency, organizations which innovate in important structural ways bear considerable costs in legitimacy.

Figure 2 summarizes the general argument of this section, alongside the established view that organizations succeed through efficiency.

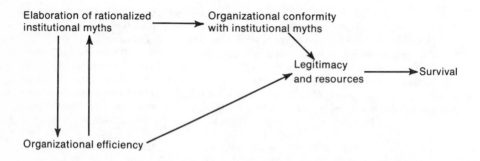

Figure 2   Organizational Survival

Institutionalized Structures and Organizational Activities

Rationalized formal structures arise in two contexts. First, the demands of local relational networks encourage the development of structures that coordinate and control activities. Such structures contribute to the efficiency of organizations and give them competitive advantages over less efficient competitors. Second, the interconnectedness of societal relations, the collective organization of society, and the leadership of organizational elites create a highly institutionalized context. In this context rationalized structures present an acceptable account of organizational activities, and organizations gain legitimacy, stability, and resources.

All organizations, to one degree or another, are embedded in both relational and institutionalized contexts and are therefore concerned both with coordinating and controlling their activities and with prudently accounting for them. Organizations in highly institutionalized environments face internal and boundary-spanning contingencies. Schools, for example, must transport students to and from school under some circumstances and must assign teachers, students, and topics to classrooms. On the other hand, organizations producing in markets that place great emphasis on efficiency build in units whose relation to production is obscure and whose efficiency is determined, not by a true production function, but by ceremonial definition.

Nevertheless, the survival of some organizations depends more on managing the demands of internal and boundary-spanning relations, while the survival of others depends more on the ceremonial demands of highly institutionalized environments. The discussion to follow shows that whether an organization's survival depends primarily on relational or on institutional demands determines the tightness of alignments between structures and activities.

Types of Organizations

Institutionalized myths differ in the completeness with which they describe cause and effect relationships, and in the clarity with which they describe standards that should be used to evaluate outputs (Thompson 1967). Some organizations use routine, clearly defined technologies to produce outputs. When output can be easily evaluated a market often develops, and consumers gain considerable rights of inspection and control. In this context, efficiency often determines success. Organizations must face exigencies of close coordination with their relational networks, and they cope with these exigencies by organizing around immediate technical problems.

But the rise of collectively organized society and the increasing interconnectedness of social relations have eroded many market contexts. Increasingly, such organizations as schools, R & D units, and governmental bureaucracies use variable, ambiguous technologies to produce outputs that are difficult to appraise, and other organizations with clearly defined technologies find themselves unable to adapt to environmental turbulence. The uncertainties of unpredictable technical contingencies or of adapting to environmental change cannot be resolved on the basis of efficiency. Internal participants and external constituents alike call for institutionalized rules that promote trust and confidence in outputs and buffer organizations from failure (Emery and Trist 1965).

Thus, one can conceive of a continuum along which organizations can be ordered. At one end are production organizations under strong output controls (Ouchi and McGuire 1975) whose success depends on the management of relational networks. At the other end are institutionalized organizations whose success depends on the confidence and stability achieved by isomorphism with institutional rules. For two reasons it is important not to assume that an organization's location on this continuum is based on the inherent technical properties of its output and therefore permanent. First, the technical properties of outputs are socially defined and do not exist in some concrete sense that allows them to be empirically discovered. Second, environments and organizations often redefine the nature of products, services, and technologies. Redefinition sometimes clarifies techniques or evaluative standards. But often organizations and environments redefine the nature of techniques and output so that ambiguity is introduced and rights of inspection and control are lowered. For example, American schools have evolved from producing rather specific training that was evaluated according to strict criteria of efficiency to producing ambiguously defined services that are evaluated according to criteria of certification (Callahan 1962; Tyack 1974; Meyer and Rowan 1975).

Structural Inconsistencies in Institutionalized Organizations

Two very general problems face an organization if its success depends primarily on isomorphism with institutionalized rules. First, technical activities and demands for efficiency create conflicts and inconsistencies in an institutionalized organization's efforts to conform to the ceremonial rules of production. Second, because these ceremonial rules are transmitted by myths that may arise from different parts of the environment, the rules may conflict with one another. These inconsistencies make a concern for efficiency and tight coordination and control problematic.

Formal structures that celebrate institutionalized myths differ from structures that act efficiently. Ceremonial activity is significant in relation to categorical rules, not in its concrete effects (Merton 1940; March and Simon 1958). A sick worker must be treated by a doctor using accepted medical procedures; whether the worker is treated effectively is less important. A bus company must service required routes whether or not there are many passengers. A university must maintain appropriate departments independently of the departments' enrollments. Activity, that is, has ritual significance: it maintains appearances and validates an organization.

Categorical rules conflict with the logic of efficiency. Organizations often face the dilemma that activities celebrating institutionalized rules, although they count as virtuous ceremonial expenditures, are pure costs from the point of view of efficiency. For example, hiring a Nobel Prize winner brings great ceremonial benefits to a university. The celebrated name can lead to research grants, brighter students, or reputational gains. But from the point of view of immediate outcomes, the expenditure lowers the instructional return per dollar expended and lowers the university's ability to solve immediate logistical problems. Also, expensive technologies, which bring prestige to hospitals and business firms, may be simply excessive costs from the point of view of immediate production. Similarly, highly professionalized consultants who bring external blessings on an organization are often difficult to justify in terms of improved productivity, yet may be very important in maintaining internal and external legitimacy.

Other conflicts between categorical rules and efficiency arise because institutional rules are couched at high levels of generalization (Durkheim 1933) whereas technical activities vary with specific, unstandardized, and possibly unique conditions. Because standardized ceremonial categories must confront technical variations and anomalies, the generalized rules of the institutional environment are often inappropriate to specific situations. A governmentally mandated curriculum may be inappropriate for the students at hand, a conventional medical treatment may make little sense given the characteristics of a patient, and federal safety inspectors may intolerably delay boundary-spanning exchanges.

Yet another source of conflict between categorical rules and efficiency is the inconsistency among institutionalized elements. Institutional environments are often pluralistic (Udy 1970), and societies promulgate sharply inconsistent myths. As a result, organizations in search of external support and stability incorporate all sorts of incompatible structural elements. Professions are incorporated although they make overlapping jurisdictional claims. Programs are adopted which contend with each other for authority over a given domain. For instance, if one inquires who decides what curricula will be taught in schools, any number of parties from the various governments down to individual teachers may say that they decide.

In institutionalized organizations, then, concern with the efficiency of day-to-day activities creates enormous uncertainties. Specific contexts highlight the inadequacies of the prescriptions of generalized myths, and inconsistent structural elements conflict over jurisdictional rights. Thus the organization must struggle to link the requirements of ceremonial elements to technical activities and to link inconsistent ceremonial elements to each other.

Resolving Inconsistencies

There are four partial solutions to these inconsistencies. First, an organization can resist ceremonial requirements. But an organization that neglects ceremonial requirements and portrays itself as efficient may be unsuccessful in documenting its efficiency. Also, rejecting ceremonial requirements neglects an important source of resources and stability. Second, an organization can maintain rigid conformity to institutionalized prescriptions by cutting off external relations. Although such isolation upholds ceremonial requirements, internal participants and external constituents may soon become disillusioned with their inability to manage boundary-spanning exchanges. Institutionalized organizations must not only conform to myths but must also maintain the appearance that the myths actually work. Third, an organization can cynically acknowledge that its structure is inconsistent with work requirements. But this strategy denies the validity of institutionalized myths and sabotages the legitimacy of the organization. Fourth, an organization can promise reform. People may picture the present as unworkable but the future as filled with promising reforms of both structure and activity. But by defining the organization's valid structure as lying in the future, this strategy makes the organization's current structure illegitimate.

Instead of relying on a partial solution, however, an organization can resolve conflicts between ceremonial rules and efficiency by employing two interrelated devices: decoupling and the logic of confidence.

Decoupling. Ideally, organizations built around efficiency attempt to maintain close alignments between structures and activities. Conformity is enforced through inspection, output quality is continually monitored, the efficiency of various units is evaluated, and the various goals are unified and coordinated. But a policy of close alignment in institutionalized organizations merely makes public a record of inefficiency and inconsistency.

Institutionalized organizations protect their formal structures from evaluation on the basis of technical performance: inspection, evaluation, and control of activities are minimized, and coordination, interdependence, and mutual adjustments among structural units are handled informally.

Proposition 4. *Because attempts to control and coordinate activities in institutionalized organizations lead to conflicts and loss of legitimacy, elements of structure are decoupled from activities and from each other.*

Some well-known properties of organizations illustrate the decoupling process:

> Activities are performed beyond the purview of managers. In particular, organizations actively encourage professionalism, and activities are delegated to professionals.
>
> Goals are made ambiguous or vacuous, and categorical ends are substituted for technical ends. Hospitals treat, not cure, patients. Schools produce students, not learning. In fact, data on technical performance are eliminated or rendered invisible. Hospitals try to ignore information on cure rates, public services avoid data about effectiveness, and schools deemphasize measures of achievement.
>
> Integration is avoided, program implementation is neglected, and inspection and evaluation are ceremonialized.
>
> Human relations are made very important. The organization cannot formally coordinate activities because its formal rules, if applied, would generate inconsistencies. Therefore individuals are left to work out technical interdependencies informally. The ability to coordinate things in violation of the rules—that is, to get along with other people—is highly valued.

The advantages of decoupling are clear. The assumption that formal structures are really working is buffered from the inconsistencies and anomalies involved in technical activities. Also, because integration is avoided disputes and conflicts are minimized, and an organization can mobilize support from a broader range of external constituents.

Thus, decoupling enables organizations to maintain standardized, legitimating, formal structures while their activities vary in response to practical considerations. The organizations in an industry tend to be similar in formal structure—reflecting their common institutional origins—but may show much diversity in actual practice.

The logic of confidence and good faith. Despite the lack of coordination and control, decoupled organizations are not anarchies. Day-to-day activities proceed in an orderly fashion. What legitimates institutionalized organizations, enabling them to appear useful in spite of the lack of technical validation, is the confidence and good faith of their internal participants and their external constituents.

Considerations of face characterize ceremonial management (Goffman 1967). Confidence in structural elements is maintained through three practices—avoidance, discretion, and overlooking (Goffman 1967, pp. 12–18). Avoidance and discretion are encouraged by decoupling autonomous subunits; overlooking anomalies is also quite common. Both internal participants and external constituents cooperate in these practices. Assuring that individual participants maintain face sustains confidence in the organization, and ultimately reinforces confidence in the myths that rationalize the organization's existence.

Delegation, professionalization, goal ambiguity, the elimination of output data, and maintenance of face are all mechanisms for absorbing uncertainty while preserving the formal structure of the organization (March and Simon 1958). They contribute to a general aura of confidence within and outside the organization. Although the literature on informal organization often treats these practices as mechanisms for the achievement of deviant and subgroup purposes (Downs 1967), such treatment ignores a critical feature of organization life: effectively absorbing uncertainty and maintaining confidence requires people to assume that everyone is acting in good faith. The assumption that things are as they seem, that employees and managers are performing their roles properly, allows an organization to perform its daily routines with a decoupled structure.

Decoupling and maintenance of face, in other words, are mechanisms that maintain the assumption that people are acting in good faith. Professionalization is not merely a way of avoiding inspection—it binds both supervisors and subordinates to act in good faith. So in a smaller way does strategic leniency (Blau 1956). And so do the public displays of morale and satisfaction which are characteristic of many organizations. Organizations employ a host of mechanisms to dramatize the ritual commitments which their participants make to basic structural elements. These mechanisms are especially common in organizations which strongly reflect their institutionalized environments.

Proposition 5. *The more an organization's structure is derived from institutionalized myths, the more it maintains elaborate displays of confidence, satisfaction, and good faith, internally and externally.*

The commitments built up by displays of morale and satisfaction are not simply vacuous affirmations of institutionalized myths. Participants not only commit themselves to supporting an organization's ceremonial facade but also commit themselves to making things work out backstage. The committed participants engage in informal coordination that, although often formally inappropriate, keeps technical activities running smoothly and avoids public embarrassments. In this sense the confidence and good faith generated by ceremonial action is in no way fraudulent. It may even be the most reasonable way to get participants to make their best efforts in situations that are made problematic by institutionalized myths that are at odds with immediate technical demands.

Ceremonial inspection and evaluation. All organizations, even those maintaining high levels of confidence and good faith, are in environments that have institutionalized the rationalized rituals of inspection and evaluation. And inspection and evaluation can uncover events and deviations that undermine legitimacy. So institutionalized organizations minimize and ceremonialize inspection and evaluation.

In institutionalized organizations, in fact, evaluation accompanies and produces illegitimacy. The interest in evaluation research by the American federal government, for instance, is partly intended to undercut the state, local, and private authorities which have managed social services in the United States. The federal authorities, of course, have usually not evaluated those programs which are completely under federal jurisdiction; they have only evaluated those over which federal controls are incomplete. Similarly, state governments have often insisted on evaluating the special fundings they create in welfare and education but ordinarily do not evaluate the programs which they fund in a routine way.

Evaluation and inspection are public assertions of societal control which violate the assumption that everyone is acting with competence and in good faith. Violating this assumption lowers morale and confidence. Thus, evaluation and inspection undermine the ceremonial aspects of organizations.

Proposition 6. *Institutionalized organizations seek to minimize inspection and evaluation by both internal managers and external constituents.*

Decoupling and the avoidance of inspection and evaluation are not merely devices used by the organization. External constituents, too, avoid inspecting and controlling institutionalized organizations (Meyer and Rowan 1975). Accrediting agencies, boards of trustees, government agencies, and individuals accept ceremonially at face value the credentials, ambiguous goals, and categorical evaluations that are characteristic of ceremonial organizations. In elaborate institutional environments these external constituents are themselves likely to be corporately organized agents of society. Maintaining categorical relationships with their organizational subunits is more stable and more certain than is relying on inspection and control.

Figure 3 summarizes the main arguments of this section of our discussion.

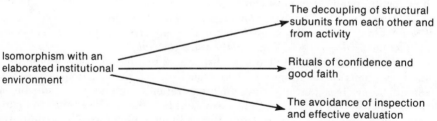

Figure 3   The Effects of Institutional Isomorphism on Organizations

Summary

Organizational structures are created and made more elaborate with the rise of institutionalized myths, and, in highly institutionalized contexts, organizational action must support these myths. But an organization must also attend to practical activity. The two requirements are at odds. A stable solution is to maintain the organization in a loosely coupled state.

No position is taken here on the overall social effectiveness of isomorphic and loosely coupled organizations. To some extent such structures buffer activity from efficiency criteria and produce ineffectiveness. On the other hand, by binding participants to act in good faith, and to adhere to the larger rationalities of the wider structure, they may maximize long-run effectiveness. It should not be assumed that the creation of microscopic rationalities in the daily activity of workers effects social ends more efficiently than commitment to larger institutional claims and purposes.

References

Aiken, Michael, and Jerald Hage. 1968. "Organizational Interdependence and Intra-organizational Structure." *American Sociological Review* 33 (December):912–30.

Bell, Daniel. 1973. *The Coming of Post-industrial Society*. New York: Basic.

Bendix, Reinhard. 1964. *Nation-Building and Citizenship*. New York: Wiley.

———. 1968. "Bureaucracy." Pp. 206–19 in *International Encyclopedia of the Social Sciences*, edited by David L. Sills. New York: Macmillan.

Berger, Peter L., and Thomas Luckmann. 1967. *The Social Construction of Reality*. New York: Doubleday.

Blau, Peter M. 1956. *Bureaucracy in Modern Society*. New York: Random House.

———. 1970. "A Formal Theory of Differentiation in Organizations." *American Sociological Review* 35 (April): 201–18.

Blum, Alan F., and Peter McHugh. 1971. "The Social Ascription of Motives." *American Sociological Review* 36 (December):98–109.

Callahan, Raymond E. 1962. *Education and the Cult of Efficiency*. Chicago: University of Chicago Press.

Carlson, Richard O. 1962. *Executive Succession and Organizational Change*. Chicago: Midwest Administration Center, University of Chicago.

Clark, Burton R. 1956. *Adult Education in Transition*. Berkeley: University of California Press.

Dalton, Melville. 1959. *Men Who Manage*. New York: Wiley.

Dowling, John, and Jeffrey Pfeffer. 1975. "Organizational Legitimacy." *Pacific Sociological Review* 18 (January):122–36.

Downs, Anthony. 1967. *Inside Bureaucracy*. Boston: Little, Brown.

Durkheim, Émile. 1933. *The Division of Labor in Society*. New York: Macmillan.

Ellul, Jacques. 1964. *The Technological Society*. New York: Knopf.

Emery, Fred L., and Eric L. Trist. 1965. "The Causal Texture of Organizational Environments." *Human Relations* 18 (February):21–32.

Freeman, John Henry. 1973. "Environment, Technology and Administrative Intensity of Manufacturing Organizations." *American Sociological Review* 38 (December):750–63.

Goffman, Erving. 1967. *Interaction Ritual*. Garden City, N.Y.: Anchor.

Hawley, Amos H. 1968. "Human Ecology." Pp. 328–37 in *International Encyclopedia of the Social Sciences*, edited by David L. Sills. New York: Macmillan.

Hirsch, Paul M. 1975. "Organizational Effectiveness and the Institutional Environment." *Administrative Science Quarterly* 20 (September):327–44.

Homans, George C. 1950. *The Human Group*. New York: Harcourt, Brace.

March, James G., and Johan P. Olsen. 1976. *Ambiguity and Choice in Organizations*. Bergen: Universitetsforlaget.

March, James G., and Herbert A. Simon. 1958. *Organizations*. New York: Wiley.

Merton, Robert K. 1940. "Bureaucratic Structure and Personality." *Social Forces* 18 (May):560–68.

Meyer, John W., and Brian Rowan. 1975. "Notes on the Structure of Educational Organizations." Paper presented at annual meeting of the American Sociological Association, San Francisco.

Mills, C. Wright. 1940. "Situated Actions and Vocabularies of Motive." *American Sociological Review* 5 (February):904–13.

Ouchi, William, and Mary Ann Maguire. 1975. "Organizational Control: Two Functions." *Administrative Science Quarterly* 20 (December):559–69.

Parsons, Talcott. 1956. "Suggestions for a Sociological Approach to the Theory of Organizations I." *Administrative Science Quarterly* 1 (June):63–85.

———. 1971. *The System of Modern Societies*. Englewood Cliffs, N.J.: Prentice-Hall.

Perrow, Charles. 1970. *Organizational Analysis: A Sociological View*. Belmont, Calif.: Wadsworth.

Salancik, Gerald R., and Jeffrey Pfeffer. 1974. "The Bases and Use of Power in Organizational Decision Making." *Administrative Science Quarterly* 19 (December):453–73.

Scott, Marvin B., and Stanford M. Lyman. 1968. "Accounts." *American Sociological Review* 33 (February):46–62.

Scott, W. Richard. 1975. "Organizational Structure." Pp. 1–20 in *Annual Review of Sociology.* Vol. 1, edited by Alex Inkeles. Palo Alto, Calif.: Annual Reviews.

Selznick, Philip. 1949. *TVA and the Grass Roots.* Berkeley: University of California Press.

Spencer, Herbert. 1897. *Principles of Sociology.* New York: Appleton.

Starbuck, William H. 1976. "Organizations and their Environments." Pp. 1069–1123 in *Handbook of Industrial and Organizational Psychology*, edited by Marvin D. Dunnette. New York: Rand McNally.

Swanson, Guy E. 1971. "An Organizational Analysis of Collectivities." *American Sociological Review* 36 (August):607–24.

Terreberry, Shirley. 1968. "The Evolution of Organizational Environments." *Administrative Science Quarterly* 12 (March):590–613.

Thompson, James D. 1967. *Organizations in Action.* New York: McGraw-Hill.

Tyack, David B. 1974. *The One Best System.* Cambridge, Mass.: Harvard University Press.

Udy, Stanley H., Jr. 1970. *Work in Traditional and Modern Society.* Englewood Cliffs, N.J.: Prentice-Hall.

Weber, Max. 1930. *The Protestant Ethic and the Spirit of Capitalism.* New York: Scribner's.

———. 1946. *Essays in Sociology.* New York: Oxford University Press.

———. 1947. *The Theory of Social and Economic Organization.* New York: Oxford University Press.

Weick, Karl E. 1976. "Educational Organizations as Loosely Coupled Systems." *Administrative Science Quarterly* 21 (March):1–19.

Wilensky, Harold L. 1965. "The Professionalization of Everyone?" *American Journal of Sociology* 70 (September):137–58.

Woodward, Joan. 1965. *Industrial Organization, Theory and Practice.* London: Oxford University Press.

Zald, Mayer N., and Patricia Denton. 1963. "From Evangelism to General Service: The Transformation of the YMCA." *Administrative Science Quarterly* 8 (September):214–34.

The Characteristics of Total Institutions
Erving Goffman

Social establishments—institutions in the everyday sense of that term—are buildings or plants in which activity of a particular kind regularly goes on. . . . Each captures something of the time and interest of its members and provides something of a world for them; in brief, every institution has encompassing tendencies. When we review the different institutions in our Western society we find a class of them which seems to be encompassing to a degree discontinuously greater than the ones next in line. Their encompassing or total character is symbolized by the barrier to social intercourse with the outside that is often built right into the physical plant: locked doors, high walls, barbed wire, cliffs and water, open terrain, and so forth. These I am calling total institutions, and it is their general characteristics I want to explore.[1] This exploration will be phrased as if securely based on findings but will in fact be speculative.

The total institutions of our society can be listed for convenience in five rough groupings. *First*, there are institutions established to care for persons thought to be both incapable and harmless; these are the homes for the blind, the aged, the orphaned, and the indigent. *Second*, there are places established to care for persons thought to be at once incapable of looking after themselves and a threat to the community, albeit an unintended one: TB sanitariums, mental hospitals, and leprosoriums. *Third*, another type of total institution is organized to protect the community against what are thought to be intentional dangers to it; here the welfare of the persons thus sequestered is not the immediate issue. Examples are: Jails, penitentiaries, POW camps, and concentration camps. *Fourth*, we find institutions purportedly established the better to pursue some technical task and justifying themselves only on these instrumental grounds: Army barracks, ships, boarding schools, work camps, colonial compounds, large mansions from the point of view of those who live in the servants' quarters, and so forth. *Finally*, there are those establishments designed as retreats from the world or as training stations for the religious: Abbeys, monasteries, convents, and other cloisters. This sublisting of total institutions is neither neat nor exhaustive, but the listing itself provides an empirical starting point for a purely denotative definition of the category. By anchoring the initial definition of total institutions in this way, I hope to be able to discuss the general characteristics of the type without becoming tautological.

Before attempting to extract a general profile from this list of establishments, one conceptual peculiarity must be mentioned. None of the elements I will extract seems entirely exclusive to total institutions, and none seems shared by every one of them. What is shared and unique about total institutions is that each exhibits many items in this family of attributes to an intense degree. In speaking of "common characteristics," then, I will be using this phrase in a weakened, but I think logically defensible, way.

Reprinted in part from Erving Goffman, "The Characteristics of Total Institutions," in *Symposium on Preventive and Social Psychiatry*, 15–17 April 1957, Walter Reed Army Institute of Research, Washington, D.C., by permission of the author and publisher.

Totalistic Features

A basic social arrangement in modern society is that we tend to sleep, play and work in different places, in each case with a different set of coparticipants, under a different authority, and without an over-all rational plan. The central feature of total institutions can be described as a breakdown of the kinds of barriers ordinarily separating these three spheres of life. *First*, all aspects of life are conducted in the same place and under the same single authority. *Second*, each phase of the member's daily activity will be carried out in the immediate company of a large batch of others, all of whom are treated alike and required to do the same thing together. *Third*, all phases of the day's activities are tightly scheduled, with one activity leading at a prearranged time into the next, the whole circle of activities being imposed from above through a system of explicit formal rulings and a body of officials. *Finally*, the contents of the various enforced activities are brought together as parts of a single over-all rational plan purportedly designed to fulfill the official aims of the institutions.

Individually, these totalistic features are found, of course, in places other than total institutions. Increasingly, for example, our large commercial, industrial and educational establishments provide cafeterias, minor services and off-hour recreation for their members. But while this is a tendency in the direction of total institutions, these extended facilities remain voluntary in many particulars of their use, and special care is taken to see that the ordinary line of authority does not extend to these situations. Similarly, housewives or farm families can find all their major spheres of life within the same fenced-in area, but these persons are not collectively regimented and do not march through the day's steps in the immediate company of a batch of similar others.

The handling of many human needs by the bureaucratic organization of whole blocks of people—whether or not this is a necessary or effective means of social organization in the circumstances—can be taken, then, as the key fact of total institutions. From this, certain important implications can be drawn.

Given the fact that blocks of people are caused to move in time, it becomes possible to use a relatively small number of supervisory personnel where the central relationship is not guidance or periodic checking, as in many employer-employee relations, but rather surveillance—a seeing to it that everyone does what he has been clearly told is required of him, and this under conditions where one person's infraction is likely to stand out in relief against the visible, constantly examined, compliance of the others. Which comes first, the large block of managed people or the small supervisory staff, is not here at issue; the point is that each is made for the other.

In total institutions, as we would then suspect, there is a basic split between a large class of individuals who live in and who have restricted contact with the world outside the walls, conveniently called *inmates*, and the small class that supervises them, conveniently called *staff*, who often operate on an 8-hour day and are socially integrated into the outside world.[2] Each grouping tends to conceive of members of the other in terms of narrow hostile stereotypes, staff often seeing inmates as bitter, secretive and untrustworthy, while inmates often see staff as condescending, highhanded and mean. Staff tends to feel superior and righteous; inmates tend, in some ways at least, to feel inferior, weak, blameworthy and guilty.[3] Social mobility between the two strata is grossly restricted; social distance is typically great and often formally prescribed; even talk across the boundaries may be conducted in a special tone of voice. These restrictions on contact presumably help to maintain the antagonistic stereotypes.[4] In any case, two different social and cultural worlds develop, tending to jog along beside each other, with points of official contact but little mutual penetration. It is important to add that the institutional plant and name come to be identified by both staff and inmates as somehow belonging to staff, so that when either grouping refers to the views or interests of "the institution," by implication they are referring (as I shall also) to the views and concerns of the staff.

The staff-inmate split is one major implication of the central features of total institutions; a second one pertains to work. In the ordinary arrangements of living in our society, the authority of the workplace stops with the worker's receipt of a money payment; the spending of this in a domestic and recreational setting is at the discretion of the worker and is the mechanism through which the authority of the workplace is kept within strict bounds. However, to say that inmates in total institutions have their full day scheduled for them is to say that some version of all basic needs will have to be planned for, too. In other words, total institutions take over "responsibility" for the inmate and must guarantee to have everything that is defined as essential "layed on." It follows, then, that whatever incentive is given for work, this will not have the structural significance it has on the outside. Different attitudes and incentives regarding this central feature of our life will have to prevail.

Here, then, is one basic adjustment required of those who work in total institutions and of those who must induce these people to work. In some cases, no work or little is required, and inmates, untrained often in leisurely ways of life, suffer extremes of boredom. In other cases, some work is required but is carried on at an extremely slow pace, being geared into a system of minor, often ceremonial payments, as in the case of weekly tobacco ration and annual Christmas presents, which cause some mental patients to stay on their job. In some total institutions, such as logging camps and merchant ships, something of the usual relation to the world that money can buy is obtained through the practice of "forced saving"; all needs are organized by the institution, and payment is given only after a work season is over and the men leave the premises. And in some total institutions, of course, more than a full day's work is required and is induced not by reward, but by threat of dire punishment. In all such cases, the work-oriented individual may tend to become somewhat demoralized by the system.

In addition to the fact that total institutions are incompatible with the basic work-payment structure of our society, it must be seen that these establishments are also incompatible with another crucial element of our society, the family. The family is sometimes contrasted to solitary living, but in fact the more pertinent contrast to family life might be with batch living. For it seems that those who eat and sleep at work, with a group of fellow workers, can hardly sustain a meaningful domestic existence. Correspondingly, the extent to which a staff retains its integration in the outside community and escapes the encompassing tendencies of total institutions is often linked up with the maintenance of a family off the grounds. . . .

Total institutions, then, are social hybrids, part residential community, part formal organization, and therein lies their special sociological interest. There are other reasons, alas, for being interested in them, too. These establishments are the forcing houses for changing persons in our society. Each is a natural experiment, typically harsh, on what can be done to the self.

Having suggested some of the key features of total institutions, we can move on now to consider them from the special perspectives of the inmate world and the staff world.

The Inmate World

Mortification Processes

It is characteristic of inmates that they come to the institution as members, already full-fledged, of a *home world*, that is, a way of life and a round of activities taken for granted up to the point of admission to the institution.[5] It is useful to look at this culture that the recruit brings with him to the institution's door—his *presenting culture*, to modify a psychiatric phrase—in terms especially designed to highlight what it is the total institution will do to him. Whatever the stability of his personal organization, we can assume it was part of a wider supporting framework lodged in his current social environment, a round of experience that somewhat confirms a conception of self that is somewhat acceptable to him and a set of defensive maneuvers exercisable at his own discretion as a means of coping with conflicts, discreditings and failures.

Now it appears that total institutions do not substitute their own unique culture for something already formed. We do not deal with acculturation or assimilation but with something more restricted than these. In a sense, total institutions do not look for cultural victory. They effectively create and sustain a particular kind of tension between the home world and the institutional world and use this persistent tension as strategic leverage in the management of men. The full meaning for the inmate of being "in" or "on the inside" does not exist apart from the special meaning to him of "getting out" or "getting on the outside."

The recruit comes into the institution with a self and with attachments to supports which had allowed this self to survive. Upon entrance, he is immediately stripped of his wonted supports, and his self is systematically, if often unintentionally, mortified. In the accurate language of some of our oldest total institutions, he is led into a series of abasements, degradations, humiliations, and profanations of self. He begins, in other words, some radical shifts in his *moral career*, a career laying out the progressive changes that occur in the beliefs that he has concerning himself and significant others.

The *stripping processes* through which *mortification of the self* occurs are fairly standard in our total institutions. Personal identity equipment is removed, as well as other possessions with which the inmate may have identified himself, there typically being a system of nonaccessible storage from which the inmate can only reobtain his effects should he leave the institution. As a substitute for what has been taken away, institutional issue is provided, but this will be the same for large categories of inmates and will be regularly repossessed by the institution. In brief, standardized defacement will occur. In addition, ego-invested separateness from fellow inmates is significantly diminished in many areas of activity, and tasks are prescribed that are *infra dignitatem*. Family, occupational, and educational career lines are chopped off, and a stigmatized status is submitted. Sources of fantasy material which had meant momentary releases from stress in the home world are denied. Areas of autonomous decision are eliminated through the process of collective scheduling of daily activity. Many channels of communication with the outside are restricted or closed off completely. Verbal discreditings occur in many forms as a matter of course. Expressive signs of respect for the staff are coercively and continuously demanded. And the effect of each of these conditions is multiplied by having to witness the mortification of one's fellow inmates.

We must expect to find different official reasons given for these assaults upon the self. In mental hospitals there is the matter of protecting the patient from himself and from other patients. In jails there is the issue of "security" and frank punishment. In religious institutions we may find sociologically sophisticated theories about the soul's need for purification and penance through disciplining of the flesh. What all of these rationales share is the extent to which they are merely rationalizations, for the underlying force in many cases is unwittingly generated by efforts to manage the daily activity of a large number of persons in a small space with a small expenditure of resources.

In the background of the sociological stripping process, we find a characteristic authority system with three distinctive elements, each basic to total institutions.

First, to a degree, authority is of the *echelon* kind. Any member of the staff class has certain rights to discipline any member of the inmate class. This arrangement, it may be noted, is similar to the one which gives any adult in some small American towns certain rights to correct and demand small services from any child not in the immediate presence of his parents. In our society, the adult himself, however, is typically under the authority of a *single* immediate superior in connection with his work or under authority of one spouse in connection with domestic duties. The only echelon authority he must face—the police—typically are neither constantly nor relevantly present, except perhaps in the case of traffic-law enforcement.

Second, the authority of corrective sanctions is directed to a great multitude of items of conduct of the kind that are constantly occurring and constantly coming up for judgment;[6] in brief, authority is directed to matters of dress, deportment, social intercourse, manners and the like. In prisons these regulations regarding situational proprieties may even extend to a point where silence during mealtime is enforced, while in some convents explicit demands may be made concerning the custody of the eyes during prayer.

The third feature of authority in total institutions is that misbehaviors in one sphere of life are held against one's standing in other spheres. Thus, an individual who fails to participate with proper enthusiasm in sports may be brought to the attention of the person who determines where he will sleep and what kind of work task will be accorded to him.

When we combine these three aspects of authority in total institutions, we see that the inmate cannot easily escape from the press of judgmental officials and from the enveloping tissue of constraint. The system of authority undermines the basis for control that adults in our society expect to exert over their interpersonal environment and may produce the terror of feeling that one is being radically demoted in the age-grading system. On the outside, rules are sufficiently lax and the individual sufficiently agreeable to required self-discipline to insure that others will rarely have cause for pouncing on him. He need not constantly look over his shoulder to see if criticism and other sanctions are coming. On the inside, however, rulings are abundant, novel, and closely enforced so that, quite characteristically, inmates live with chronic anxiety about breaking the rules and chronic worry about the consequences of breaking them. The desire to "stay out of trouble" in a total institution is likely to require persistent conscious effort and may lead the inmate to abjure certain levels of sociability with his fellows in order to avoid the incidents that may occur in these circumstances.[7]

It should be noted finally that the mortifications to be suffered by the inmate may be purposely brought home to him in an exaggerated way during the first few days after entrance, in a form of initiation that has been called *the welcome*. Both staff and fellow inmates may go out of their way to give the neophyte a clear notion of where he stands.[8] As part of this *rite de passage*, he may find himself called by a term such as "fish," "swab," etc., through which older inmates tell him that he is not only merely an inmate but that even within this lowly group he has a low status.

Privilege System

While the process of mortification is in progress, the inmate begins to receive formal and informal instruction in what will here be called the *privilege system*. Insofar as the inmate's self has been unsettled a little by the stripping action of the institution, it is largely around this framework that pressures are exerted, making for a reorganization of self. Three basic elements of the system may be mentioned.

First, there are the *house rules*, a relatively explicit and formal set of prescriptions and proscriptions which lay out the main requirements of inmate conduct. These regulations spell out the austere round of life in which the inmate will operate. Thus, the admission procedures through which the recruit is initially stripped of his self-supporting context can be seen as the institution's way of getting him in the position to start living by the house rules.

Second, against the stark background, a small number of clearly defined *rewards or privileges* are held out in exchange for obedience to staff in action and spirit. It is important to see that these potential gratifications are not unique to the institution but rather are ones carved out of the flow of support that the inmate previously had quite taken for granted. On the outside, for example, the inmate was likely to be able to unthinkingly exercise autonomy by deciding how much sugar and milk he wanted in his coffee, if any, or when to light up a cigarette; on the inside, this right may become quite problematic and a matter of a great deal of conscious concern. Held up to the inmate as possibilities, these few recapturings seem to have a reintegrative effect, re-establishing relationships with the whole lost world and assuaging withdrawal symptoms from it and from one's lost self.

The inmate's run of attention, then, especially at first, comes to be fixated on these supplies and obsessed with them. In the most fanatic way, he can spend the day in devoted thoughts concerning the possibility of acquiring these gratifications or the approach of the hour at which they are scheduled to be granted. The building of a world around these minor privileges is perhaps the most important feature of inmate culture and yet is something that cannot easily be appreciated by an outsider, even one who has lived through the experience himself. This situation sometimes leads to generous sharing and almost always to a willingness to beg for things such as cigarettes, candy and newspapers. It will be understandable, then, that a constant feature of inmate discussion is the *release binge fantasy*, namely, recitals of what one will do during leave or upon release from the institution.

House rules and privileges provide the functional requirements of the third element in the privilege system: *punishments*. These are designated as the consequence of breaking the rules. One set of these punishments consists of the temporary or permanent withdrawal of privileges or abrogation of the right to try to earn them. In general, the punishments meted out in total institutions are of an order more severe than anything encountered by the inmate in his home world. An institutional arrangement which causes a small number of easily controlled privileges to have a massive significance is the same arrangement which lends a terrible significance to their withdrawal.

There are some special features of the privilege system which should be noted.

First, punishments and privileges are themselves modes of organization peculiar to total institutions. Whatever their severity, punishments are largely known in the inmate's home world as something applied to animals and children. For adults this conditioning, behavioristic model is actually not widely applied, since failure to maintain required standards typically leads to indirect disadvantageous consequences and not to specific immediate punishment at all. And privileges, it should be emphasized, are not the same as prerequisites, indulgences or values, but merely the absence of deprivations one ordinarily expects one would not have to sustain. The very notions, then, of punishments and privileges are not ones that are cut from civilian cloth.

Second, it is important to see that the question of release from the total institution is elaborated into the privilege system. Some acts will become known as ones that mean an increase or no decrease in length of stay, while others become known as means for lessening the sentence.

Third, we should also note that punishments and privileges come to be geared into a residential work system. Places to work and places to sleep become clearly defined as places where certain kinds and levels of privilege obtain, and inmates are shifted very rapidly and visibly from one place to another as the mechanisms for giving them the punishment or privilege their cooperativeness has warranted. The inmates are moved, the system is not.

This, then, is the privilege system: a relatively few components put together with some rational intent and clearly proclaimed to the participants. The overall consequence is that cooperativeness is obtained from persons who often have cause to be uncooperative.[9]

Immediately associated with the privilege system we find some standard social processes important in the life of total institutions.

We find that an *institutional lingo* develops through which inmates express the events that are crucial in their particular world. Staff too, especially its lower levels, will know this language, using it when talking to inmates, while reverting to more standardized speech when talking to superiors and outsiders. Related to this special argot, inmates will possess knowledge of the various ranks and officials, an accumulation of lore about the establishment, and some comparative information about life in other similar total institutions.

Also found among staff and inmates will be a clear awareness of the phenomenon of *messing up*, so called in mental hospitals, prisons, and barracks. This involves a complex process of engaging in forbidden activity, getting caught doing so, and receiving something like the full punishment accorded this. An alteration in privilege status is usually implied and is categorized by a phrase such as "getting busted." Typical infractions which can eventuate in messing up are: fights, drunkenness, attempted suicide, failure at examinations, gambling, insubordination, homosexuality, improper taking of leave, and participation in collective riots.

While these punished infractions are typically ascribed to the offender's cussedness, villainy, or "sickness," they do in fact constitute a vocabulary of institutionalized actions, limited in such a way that the same messing up may occur for quite different reasons. Informally, inmates and staff may understand, for example, that a given messing up is a way for inmates to show resentment against a current situation felt to be unjust in terms of the informal agreement between staff and inmates,[10] or a way of postponing release without having to admit to one's fellow inmates that one really does not want to go.[11]

In total institutions there will also be a system of what might be called *secondary adjustments*, namely, technics which do not directly challenge staff management but which allow inmates to obtain disallowed satisfactions or allowed ones by disallowed means. These practices are variously referred to as: the angles, knowing the ropes, conniving, gimmicks, deals, ins, etc. Such adaptations apparently reach their finest flower in prisons, but of course other total institutions are overrun with them too.[12] It seems apparent that an important aspect of secondary adjustments is that they provide the inmate with some evidence that he is still, as it were, his own man and still has some protective distance, under his own control, between himself and the institution. In some cases, then, a secondary adjustment becomes almost a kind of lodgment for the self, a churinga in which the soul is felt to reside.[13]

The occurrence of secondary adjustments correctly allows us to assume that the inmate group will have some kind of a *code* and some means of informal social control evolved to prevent one inmate from informing staff about the secondary adjustments of another. On the same grounds we can expect that one dimension of social typing among inmates will turn upon this question of security, leading to persons defined as "squealers," "finks," or "stoolies" on one hand, and persons defined as "right guys" on the other.[14] It should be added that where new inmates can play a role in the system of secondary adjustments, as in providing new faction members or new sexual objects, then their "welcome" may indeed be a sequence of initial indulgences and enticements, instead of exaggerated deprivations.[15] Because of secondary adjustments we also find *kitchen strata*, namely, a kind of rudimentary, largely informal, stratification of inmates on the basis of each one's differential access to disposable illicit commodities; so also we find social typing to designate the powerful persons in the informal market system.[16]

While the privilege system provides the chief framework within which reassembly of the self takes place, other factors characteristically lead by different routes in the same general direction. Relief from economic and social responsibilities—much touted as part of the therapy in mental hospitals—is one, although in many cases it would seem that the disorganizing effect of this moratorium is more significant than its organizing effect. More important as a reorganizing influence is the *fraternalization process*, namely, the process through which socially distant persons find themselves developing mutual support and common *counter-mores* in opposition to a system that has forced them into intimacy and into a single, equalitarian community of fate.[17] It seems that the new recruit frequently starts out with something like the staff's popular misconceptions of the character of the inmates and then comes to find that most of his fellows have all the properties of ordinary decent human beings and that the stereotypes associated with their condition or offense are not a reasonable ground for judgment of inmates.[18]

If the inmates are persons who are accused by staff and society of having committed some kind of a crime against society, then the new inmate, even though sometimes in fact quite guiltless, may come to share the guilty feelings of his fellows and, thereafter, their well-elaborated defenses against these feelings. A sense of common injustice and a sense of bitterness against the outside world tends to develop, marking an important movement in the inmate's moral career.

Adaptation Alignments

The mortifying processes that have been discussed and the privilege system represent the conditions that the inmate must adapt to in some way, but however pressing, these conditions allow for different ways of meeting them. We find, in fact, that the same inmate will employ different lines of adaptation or tacks at different phases in his moral career and may even fluctuate between different tacks at the same time.

First, there is the process of *situational withdrawal*. The inmate withdraws apparent attention from everything except events immediately around his body and sees these in a perspective not employed by others present. This drastic curtailment of involvement in interactional events is best known, of course, in mental hospitals, under the title of "regression." Aspects of "prison psychosis" or "stir simpleness" represent the same adjustment, as do some forms of "acute depersonalization" described in concentration camps. I do not think it is known whether this line of adaptation forms a single continuum of varying degrees of withdrawal or whether there are standard discontinuous plateaus of disinvolvement. It does seem to be the case, however, that, given the pressures apparently required to dislodge an inmate from this status, as well as the currently limited facilities for doing so, we frequently find here, effectively speaking, an irreversible line of adaptation.

Second, there is the *rebellious line*. The inmate intentionally challenges the institution by flagrantly refusing to cooperate with staff in almost any way.[19] The result is a constantly communicated intransigency and sometimes high rebel-morale. Most large mental hospitals, for example, seem to have wards where this spirit strongly prevails. Interestingly enough, there are many circumstances in which sustained rejection of a total institution requires sustained orientation to its formal organization and hence, paradoxically, a deep kind of commitment to the establishment. Similarly, when total institutions take the line (as they sometimes do in the case of mental hospitals prescribing lobotomy[20] or army barracks pre-scribing the stockade) that the recalcitrant inmate must be broken, then, in their way, they must show as much special devotion to the rebel as he has shown to them. It should be added, finally, that while prisoners of war have been known staunchly to take a rebellious stance throughout their incarceration, this stance is typically a temporary and initial phase of reaction, emerging from this to situa-tional withdrawal or some other line of adaptation.

Third, another standard alignment in the institutional world takes the form of a kind of *colonization*. The sampling of the outside world provided by the establishment is taken by the inmate as the whole, and a stable, relatively contented existence is built up out of the maximum satisfactions procurable within the institution.[21] Experience of the outside world is used as a point of reference to demonstrate the desirability of life on the inside; and the usual tension between the two worlds collapses, thwarting the social arrangements based upon this felt discrepancy. Characteristically, the individual who too obviously takes this line may be accused by his fellow inmates of "having found a home" or of "never having had it so good." Staff itself may become vaguely embarrassed by this use that is being made of the institution, sensing that the benign possibilities in the situation are somehow being misused. Colonizers themselves may feel obliged to deny their satisfaction with the institution, if only in the interest of sustaining the counter-mores supporting inmate solidarity. They may find it necessary to mess up just prior to their slated discharge, thereby allowing themselves to present involuntary reasons for continued incarceration. It should be incidentally noted that any humanistic effort to make life in total institutions more bearable must face the possibility that doing so may increase the attractiveness and likelihood of colonization.

Fourth, one mode of adaptation to the setting of a total institution is that of *conversion*. The inmate appears to take over completely the official or staff view of himself and tries to act out the role of the perfect inmate. While the colonized inmate builds as much of a free community as possible for himself by using the limited facilities available, the convert takes a more disciplined, moralistic, monochromatic line, presenting himself as someone whose institutional enthusiasm is always at the disposal of the staff. In Chinese POW camps, we find Americans who became "pros" and fully espoused the Communist view of the world.[22] In army barracks there are enlisted men who give the impression that they are always "sucking around" and always "bucking for promotion." In prisons there are "square johns." In German concentration camps, longtime prisoners sometimes came to adopt the vocabulary, recreation, posture, expressions of aggression, and clothing style of the Gestapo, executing their role of straw-boss with military strictness.[23] Some mental hospitals have the distinction of providing two quite different conversion possibilities—one for the new admission who can see the light after an appropriate struggle and adapt the psychiatric view of himself, and another for the chronic ward patient who adopts the manner and dress of attendants while helping them to manage the other ward patients with a stringency excelling that of the attendants themselves.

Here, it should be noted, is a significant way in which total institutions differ. Many, like progressive mental hospitals, merchant ships, TB sanitariums and brain-washing camps, offer the inmate an opportunity to live up to a model of conduct that is at once ideal and staff-sponsored—a model felt by its advocates to be in the supreme interests of the very persons to whom it is applied. Other total institutions, like some concentration camps and some prisons, do not officially sponsor an ideal that the inmate is expected to incorporate as a means of judging himself.

While the alignments that have been mentioned represent coherent courses to pursue, few inmates, it seems, carry these pursuits very far. In most total institutions, what we seem to find is that most inmates take the tack of what they call *playing it cool*. This involves a somewhat opportunistic combination of secondary adjustments, conversion, colonization and loyalty to the inmate group, so that in the particular circumstances the inmate will have a maximum chance of eventually getting out physically and psychically undamaged.[24] Typically, the inmate will support the counter-mores when with fellow inmates and be silent to them on how tractably he acts when alone in the presence of staff.[25] Inmates taking this line tend to subordinate contacts with their fellows to the higher claim of "keeping out of trouble." They tend to volunteer for nothing, and they may even learn to cut their ties to the outside world sufficiently to give cultural reality to the world inside but not enough to lead to colonization.

I have suggested some of the lines of adaptation that inmates can take to the pressures that play in total institutions. Each represents a way of managing the tension between the home world and the institutional world. However, there are circumstances in which the home world of the inmate was such, in fact, as to *immunize* him against the bleak world on the inside, and for such persons no particular scheme of adaptation need be carried very far. Thus, some lower-class mental hospital patients who have lived all their previous life in orphanages, reformatories and jails, tend to see the hospital as just another total institution to which it is possible to apply the adaptive technics learned and perfected in other total institutions. "Playing it cool" represents for such persons, not a shift in their moral career, but an alignment that is already second nature.

The professional criminal element in the early periods of German concentration camps displayed something of the same immunity to their surroundings or even found new satisfactions through fraternization with middle-class political prisoners.[26] Similarly, Shetland youths recruited into the British merchant marine are not apparently threatened much by the cramped arduous life on board, because island life is even more stunted; they make uncomplaining sailors because from their point of view they have nothing much to complain about. Strong religious and political convictions may also serve perhaps to immunize the true believer against the assaults of a total institution, and even a failure to speak the language of the staff may cause the staff to give up its efforts at reformation, allowing the nonspeaker immunity to certain pressures. . . .[27]

Consequences

Total institutions frequently claim to be concerned with rehabilitation, that is, with resetting the inmate's self-regulatory mechanisms so that he will maintain the standards of the establishment of his own accord after he leaves the setting.[28] In fact, it seems this claim is seldom realized and even when permanent alteration occurs, these changes are often not of the kind intended by the staff. With the possible exception presented by the great resocialization efficiency of religious institutions, neither the stripping processes nor the reorganizing ones seem to have a lasting effect.[29] No doubt the availability of secondary adjustments helps to account for this, as do the presence of counter-mores and the tendency for inmates to combine all strategies and "play it cool." In any case, it seems that shortly after release, the ex-inmate will have forgotten a great deal of what life was like on the inside and will have once again begun to take for granted the privileges around which life in the institution was organized. The sense of injustice, bitterness and alienation, so typically engendered by the inmate's experience and so definitely marking a stage in his moral career, seems to weaken upon graduation, even in those cases where a permanent stigma has resulted.

But what the ex-inmate does retain of his institutional experience tells us important things about total institutions. Often entrance will mean for the recruit that he has taken on what might be called a *proactive status*. Not only is his relative social position within the walls radically different from what it was on the outside, but, as he comes to learn, if and when he gets out, his social position on the outside will never again be quite what it was prior to entrance. Where the proactive status is a relatively favorable one, as it is for those who graduate from officers' training schools, elite boarding schools, ranking monasteries, etc., then the permanent alteration will be favorable, and jubilant official reunions announcing pride in one's "school" can be expected. When, as seems usually the case, the proactive status is unfavorable, as it is for those in prisons or mental hospitals, we popularly employ the term "stigmatization" and expect that the ex-inmate may make an effort to conceal his past and try to "pass."[30]

The Staff World

Humane Standards

Most total institutions, most of the time, seem to function merely as storage dumps for inmates, but as previously suggested, they usually present themselves to the public as rational organizations designed consciously, through and through, as effective machines for producing a few officially avowed and officially approved ends. It was also suggested that one frequent official objective is the reformation of inmates in the direction of some ideal standard. This contradiction, then, between what the institution does and what its officials must say that it does, forms the central context of the staff's daily activity.

Within this context, perhaps the first thing to say about staff is that their work, and hence their world, has uniquely to do with people. This people-work is not quite like personnel work nor the work of those involved in service relationships. Staffs, after all, have objects and products to work upon, not relationships, but these objects and products are people.

As material upon which to work, people involve some of the considerations characteristic of inanimate objects. Just as an article being processed through an industrial plant must be followed by a paper shadow showing what has been done by whom, what is to be done, and who last had responsibility for it, so human objects moving, say, through a mental hospital system must be followed by a chain of informative receipts detailing what has been done to and by the patient and who had most recent responsibility for him. In his career from admission suite to burial plot, many different kinds of staff will add their official note to his case file as he temporarily passes under their jurisdiction, and long after he has died physically his marked remains will survive as an actionable entity in the hospital's bureaucratic system. Even the presence or absence of a particular patient at a given meal or for a given night may have to be recorded so that cost-accounting can be maintained and appropriate adjustments rendered in billing.

Other similarities between people-work and object-work are obvious. Just as tin mines or paint factories or chemical plants may involve special work hazards for employees, so (staffs believe at least) there are special dangers to some kinds of people-work. In mental hospitals, staffs believe that patients may strike out "for no reason" and injure an official. In army prisons, staff "is ever haunted by the spectre of riot, revolt or mutiny. . . ."[31] In TB sanitariums and in leprosoriums, staff feel they are being specially exposed to dangerous diseases.

While these similarities between people- and object-work exist, it is, I think, the unique aspects of people as material to work upon that we must look to for the crucial determinants of the work-world of staff.

Given the physiological characteristics of the human organism, it is obvious that certain requirements must be met if any continued use is to be made of people. But this, of course, is the case with inanimate objects, too; the temperature of any storehouse must be regulated, regardless of whether people or things are stored. However, persons are almost always considered to be ends in them-selves, as reflected in the broad moral principles of a total institution's environing society. Almost always, then, we find that some technically unnecessary standards of handling must be maintained with human materials. This maintenance of what we can call humane standards comes to be defined as one part of the "responsibil-ity" of the institution and presumably is one of the things the institution guaran-tees the inmate in exchange for his liberty. Thus, prison officials are obliged to thwart suicidal efforts of the prisoner and to give him full medical attention even though in some cases this may require postponement of his date of execution. Something similar has been reported in German concentration camps, where inmates were sometimes given medical attention to tidy them up into a healthier shape for the gas chamber.

A second special contingency in the work-world of staff is the fact that inmates typically have statuses and relationships in the outside world that must be taken into consideration. (This consideration, of course, is related to the previ-ously mentioned fact that the institution must respect some of the rights of inmates qua persons.) Even in the case of the committed mental patient whose civil rights are largely taken from him, a tremendous amount of mere paper-work will be involved. Of course, the rights that are denied a mental patient are usually transferred to a relation, to a committee, or to the superintendent of the hospital itself, who then becomes the legal person whose authorization must be obtained for many matters. Many issues originating outside the institution will arise: Social Security benefits, income taxes, upkeep of properties, insurance payments, old age pension, stock dividends, dental bills, legal obligations incurred prior to commitment, permission to release psychiatric case records to insurance com-panies or attorneys, permission for special visits from persons other than next of kin, etc. All of these issues have to be dealt with by the institution, even if only to pass the decisions on to those legally empowered to make them.

It should be noted that staff is reminded of its obligations in these matters of standards and rights, not only by its own internal superordinates, by various watchdog agencies in the wider society, and by the material itself, but also by persons on the outside who have kin ties to inmates. The latter group present a special problem because, while inmates can be educated about the price they will pay for making demands on their own behalf, relations receive less tutoring in this regard and rush in with requests for inmates that inmates would blush to make for themselves.

The multiplicity of ways in which inmates must be considered ends in themselves and the multiplicity of inmates themselves forces upon staff some of the classic dilemmas that must be faced by those who govern men. Since a total institution functions somewhat as a State, its staff must suffer somewhat from the tribulations that beset governors.

In the case of any single inmate, the assurance that certain standards will be maintained in his own interests may require sacrifice of other standards, and implied in this is a difficult weighing of ends. For example, if a suicidal inmate is to be kept alive, staff may feel it necessary to keep him under constant deprivatizing surveillance or even tied to a chair in a small locked room. If a mental patient is to be kept from tearing at grossly irritated sores and repeating time and again a cycle of curing and disorder, staff may feel it necessary to curtail the freedom of his hands. Another patient who refuses to eat may have to be humiliated by forced feeding. If inmates of TB sanitariums are to be given an opportunity to recover, it will be necessary to curtail freedom of recreation.[32]

The standards of treatment that one inmate has a right to expect may conflict, of course, with the standards desired by another, giving rise to another set of governmental problems. Thus, in mental hospitals, if the grounds gate is to be kept open out of respect for those with town parole, then some other patients who otherwise could have been trusted on the grounds may have to be kept on locked wards. And if a canteen and mailbox are to be freely available to those on the grounds, then patients on a strict diet or those who write threatening and obscene letters will have to be denied liberty on the grounds.

The obligation of staff to maintain certain humane standards of treatment for inmates represents problems in itself, as suggested above, but a further set of characteristic problems is found in the constant conflict between humane standards on one hand and institutional efficiency on the other. I will cite only one main example. The personal possessions of an individual are an important part of the materials out of which he builds a self, but as an inmate, the ease with which he can be managed by staff is likely to increase with the degree to which he is dispossessed. Thus, the remarkable efficiency with which a mental hospital ward can adjust to a daily shift in number of resident patients is related to the fact that the comers and leavers do not come or leave with any properties but themselves and do not have any right to choose where they will be located. Further, the efficiency with which the clothes of these patients can be kept clean and fresh is related to the fact that everyone's soiled clothing can be indiscriminately placed in one bundle, and laundered clothing can be redistributed not according to ownership but according to rough size. Similarly, the quickest assurance that patients going on the grounds will be warmly dressed is to march them in file past a pile of the ward's allotment of coats, requiring them for the same purposes of health to throw off these collectivized garments on returning to the ward.

Just as personal possessions may interfere with the smooth running of an institutional operation and be removed for this reason, so parts of the body itself may conflict with efficient management and the conflict resolved in favor of efficiency. If the heads of inmates are to be kept clean and the possessor easily identified, then a complete head shave is efficacious, regardless of the damage this does to appearance. On similar grounds, some mental hospitals have found it useful to extract the teeth of "biters," give hysterectomies to promiscuous female patients, and perform lobotomies on chronic fighters. Flogging on men-of-war as a form of punishment expressed the same conflict between organizational and humane interests:[33]

> One of the arguments advanced by officers of the Navy in favor of corporal punishment is this: it can be inflicted in a moment; it consumes no valuable time; and when the prisoner's shirt is put on, *that* is the last of it. Whereas, if another punishment were substituted, it would probably occasion a great waste of time and trouble, besides thereby begetting in the sailor an undue idea of his importance.

I have suggested that people-work differs from other kinds because of the tangle of statuses and relationships which each inmate brings with him to the institution and because of the humane standards that must be maintained with respect to him. Another difference occurs in cases where inmates have some rights to visit off the grounds, for then the mischief they may do in civil society becomes something for which the institution has some responsibility. Given this responsibility, it is understandable that total institutions tend not to view off-grounds leave favorably. Still another type of difference between people-work and other kinds, and perhaps the most important difference of all, is that by the exercise of threat, reward or persuasion human objects can be given instructions and relied upon to carry them out on their own. The span of time during which these objects can be trusted to carry out planned actions without supervision will vary of course a great deal, but, as the social organization of back wards in mental hospitals teaches us, even in the limiting case of catatonic schizophrenics, a considerable amount of such reliance is possible. Only the most complicated electronic equipment shares this capacity.

While human materials can never be as refractory as inanimate ones, their very capacity to perceive and to follow out the plans of staff insures that they can hinder the staff more effectively than inanimate objects can. Inanimate objects cannot purposely and intelligently thwart our plans, regardless of the fact that we may momentarily react to them as if they had this capacity. Hence, in prison and on "better" wards of mental hospitals, guards have to be ready for organized efforts at escape and must constantly deal with attempts to bait them, "frame" them, and otherwise get them into trouble. This leads to a state of anxiety in the guard that is not alleviated by knowledge that the inmate may be acting thus merely as a means of gaining self-respect or relieving boredom.[34] Even an old, weak, mental patient has tremendous power in this regard; for example, by the simple expedient of locking his thumbs in his trouser pockets he can remarkably frustrate the efforts of an attendant to undress him.

A third general way in which human materials are different from other kinds and hence present unique problems is that, however distant staff manages to stay from them, they can become objects of fellow-feeling and even affection. Always there is the danger that an inmate will appear human. If what are felt to be hardships must be inflicted on the inmate, then sympathetic staff will suffer. And on the other hand, if an inmate breaks a rule, staff's conceiving of him as a human being may increase their sense that injury has been done to their moral world. Expecting a "reasonable" response from a reasonable creature, staff may feel incensed, affronted and challenged when this does not occur. Staff thus finds it must maintain face not only before those who examine the product of work but before these very products themselves.

The capacity of inmates to become objects of staff's sympathetic concern is linked to what might be called an involvement cycle sometimes recorded in total institutions. Starting at a point of social distance from inmates, a point from which massive deprivation and institutional trouble cannot easily be seen, the staff person finds he has no reason not to build up a warm involvement in some inmates. The involvement, however, brings the staff members into a position to be hurt by what inmates do and by what they suffer, and also brings him to a position from which he is likely to threaten the distant stand from inmates taken by his fellow members of the staff. In response, the sympathizing staff member may feel he has been "burnt" and retreat into paper-work, committee-work or other staff-enclosed routine. Once removed from the dangers of inmate contact, he may gradually cease to feel he has reason to remain so, and thus the cycle of contact and withdrawal may be repeated again and again.

When we combine together the fact that staff is obliged to maintain certain standards of humane treatment for inmates and may come to view inmates as reasonable, responsible creatures who are fitting objects for emotional involvement, we have the background for some of the quite special difficulties of people-work. In mental hospitals, for example, there always seem to be some patients who dramatically act against their own obvious self-interest. They drink water they have themselves first polluted; they rush against the wall with their heads; they tear out their own sutures after a minor operation; they flush false teeth down the toilet, without which they cannot eat and which take months to obtain; or smash glasses, without which they cannot see. In an effort to frustrate these visibly self-destructive acts, staff may find itself forced to manhandle these patients. Staff then is forced to create an image of itself as harsh and coercive, just at the moment that it is attempting to prevent someone from doing to himself what no human being is expected to do to anyone. At such times it is extremely difficult for staff members to keep their own emotions in control, and understandably so.

Moral Climate

The special requirements of people-work establish the day's job for staff, but this job must be carried out in a special moral climate. For the staff is charged with meeting the hostility and demands of the inmates, and what it has to meet the inmate with, in general, is the rational perspective espoused by the institution. It is the role of the staff to defend the institution in the name of its avowed rational aims—to the inmate as well as to outsiders of various kinds. Thus, when inmates are allowed to have incidental face-to-face contact with staff, the contact will often take the form of "gripes" or requests on the part of the inmate and of justification for prevailing restrictive treatment on the part of the staff. Such, for example, is the general structure of staff-patient interaction in mental hospitals. Further, the privileges and punishments meted out by staff will often be couched in a language that reflects the legitimated objectives of the institution, even though this may require that inmates or low-level members of staff translate these responses into the verbal language of the privilege system.

Given the inmates over whom it has charge and the processing that must be done to these objects, staff tends to evolve what may be thought of as a *theory of human nature*. This verbalized perspective rationalizes the scene, provides a subtle means of maintaining social distance from inmates and a stereotyped view of them, and gives sanction to the treatment accorded them.[35] Typically, the theory covers the "good" and "bad" possibilities of inmate conduct, the forms that messing up takes and the instructional value of privileges and punishments. In army barracks, officers will have a theory about the relation between discipline and obedience under fire, about the qualities proper to men, about the "breaking point" of men, and about the difference between mental sickness and malingering. In prisons, we find currently an interesting conflict between the psychiatric and the moral-weakness theory of crime. In convents, we find theories about the way in which the spirit can be weak and strong, and the ways its defects can be combatted. Mental hospitals, it should be noted, are especially interesting in this connection because staff members pointedly establish themselves as specialists in the knowledge of human nature who must diagnose and prescribe on the basis of this philosophy. Hence, in the standard psychiatric textbooks there are chapters on "psychodynamics" and "psychopathology" which provide charmingly explicit formulations of the "nature" of human nature.

Given the fact that the management of inmates is typically rationalized in terms of the ideal aims or functions of the establishment and that certain humane standards will form part of this ideal, we can expect that professionals ostensibly hired to service these functions will likely become dissatisfied, feeling that they are being used as "captives" to add professional sanction to the privilege system and that they cannot here properly practice their calling. And this seems to be a classic cry. At the same time, the category of staff that must keep the institution going through continuous contact with inmates may feel that they too are being set a contradictory task, having to coerce inmates into obedience while at the same time giving the impression that humane standards are being maintained and that the rational goals of the institution are being realized. . . .

Institutional Differences

One important difference among total institutions is found in the spirit in which recruits enter the establishment. At one extreme we find the quite involuntary entrance of those who are sentenced to prison, committed to a mental hospital, or impressed into the crew of a ship. It is perhaps in such cases that staff's version of the ideal inmate has least chance of taking hold among the inmates. At the other extreme, we find religious institutions which deal only with those who feel they have gotten the call and, of these volunteers, take only those who seem to be the most suitable and the most serious in their intentions. In such cases, conversion seems already to have taken place, and it only remains to show the neophyte along what lines he can best discipline himself. Midway between these two extremes we find institutions like the army barracks whose inmates are required to serve, but who are given much opportunity to feel that this service is a justifiable one required in their own ultimate interests. Obviously, significant differences in tone will appear in total institutions, depending on whether recruitment is voluntary, semivoluntary or involuntary.

Another dimension of variation among total institutions is found in what might be called their *permeability*, that is, the degree to which the social standards maintained within the institution and the social standards maintained in the environing society have influenced each other sufficiently to minimize differences.[36] This issue, incidentally, gives us an opportunity to consider some of the dynamic relations between a total institution and the wider society that supports it or tolerates it.

When we examine the admission procedures of total institutions, we tend to be struck with the impermeable aspects of the establishment, since the stripping and leveling processes which occur at this time directly cut across the various social distinctions with which the recruit entered. St. Benedict's advice[37] to the abbot tends to be followed:

> Let him make no distinction of persons in the monastery. Let not one be loved more than another, unless he be found to excel in good works or in obedience. Let not one of noble birth be raised above him who was formerly a slave, unless some other reasonable cause intervene.

Thus, the new cadet in a military school finds that discussions "of wealth and family background are taboo," and that "Although the pay of the cadet is very low, he is not permitted to receive money from home."[38]

Even the age-grading system of the wider society may be stopped at the gates, as nicely suggested in a recent memoir[39] of an ex-nun:

> Gabrielle moved to the place that would ever be hers, third in line of forty postulants. She was third oldest in the group because she had been third to register

on that day less than a week ago when the Order had opened its doors to new entrants. From that moment, her chronological age had ceased and the only age she would henceforth have, her age in the religious life, had started.

It is, of course, by suppressing outside distinctions that a total institution can build up an orientation to its own system of honor. There is a sense then in which the harshest total institution is the most democratic, and in fact the inmate's assurance of being treated no worse than any other of his fellows can be a source of support as well as a deprivation.

But regardless of how radical a total institution appears to be, there will always be some limits to its reshuffling tendencies and some use made of social distinctions already established in the environing society, if only so it can conduct necessary affairs with this society and be tolerated by it. Thus, there does not seem to be a total institution in Western society which provides batch living completely independent of sex; and ones like convents that appear to be impervious to socioeconomic gradings, in fact tend to apportion domestic roles to converts of rural peasant background, just as the patient garbage crews in our prize integrated mental hospitals tend to wholly Negro.[40] More important, perhaps, than the fact that total institutions differ in overall permeability to outside standards, we find that each is permeable with respect to different social standards.

One of the most interesting differences among total institutions is to be found in the social fate of their graduates. Typically, these become geographically dispersed; the difference is found in the degree to which structural ties are maintained in spite of this distance. At one end of the scale we find the year's graduates of a particular Benedictine abbey, who not only keep in touch informally but find that for the rest of their life their occupation and location have been determined by their original membership. At the same end of the scale, we find ex-convicts whose stay in prison orients them to the calling and to the nationwide underworld community that will comprise their life thereafter. At the other end of the scale, we find enlisted men from the same barracks who melt into private life immediately upon demobilization and even refrain from congregating for regimental reunions. Here, too, are ex-mental patients who studiously avoid all persons and events that might connect them with the hospital. Midway between these extremes, we find "old-boy" systems in private schools and graduate universities, which function as optional communities for the distribution of life-chances among sets of fellow graduates.

Notes

1. The category of total institutions has been pointed out from time to time in the sociological literature under a variety of names, and some of the characteristics of the class have been suggested, most notably perhaps in Howard Roland's neglected paper, "Segregated Communities and Mental Health," in *Mental Health Publication of the American Association for the Advancement of Science*, No. 9, edited by F. R. Moulton, 1939. A preliminary statement of the present paper is reported in the *Third Group Processes Proceedings*, Josiah Macy Foundation, edited by Bertram Schaffner, 1957.

2. The binary character of total institutions was pointed out to me by Gregory Bateson, and proves to be noted in the literature. See, for example, Lloyd E. Ohlin, *Sociology and the Field of Corrections*, Russell Sage Foundation, New York; 1956, pp. 14, 20. In those special situations where staff too is required to live in, we may expect staff

members to feel they are suffering from special hardships and to have brought home to them a status-dependency on life on the inside which they did not expect. See Jane Cassels Record, "The Marine Radioman's Struggle for Status," *American Journal of Sociology*, Vol. LXII, 1957, p. 359.

3. For the prison version, see S. Kirson Weinburg, "Aspects of the Prison's Social Structure," *American Journal of Sociology*, Vol. 47, 1942, pp. 717–726.

4. Suggested in Ohlin, *op. cit.*, p. 20.

5. There is reason then to exclude orphanages and foundling homes from the list of total institutions, except insofar as the orphan comes to be socialized into the outside world by some process of cultural osmosis, even while this world is being systematically denied him.

6. The span of time over which an employee works at his own discretion without supervision can in fact be taken as a measure of his pay and status in an organization. See Elliot Jacques, *The Measurement of Responsibility: A Study of Work, Payment, and Individual Capacity*, Harvard University Press, Cambridge, 1956. And just as "time-span of responsibility" is an index of position, so a long span of freedom from inspection is a reward of position.

7. Staff sometimes encourages this tendency for inmates to stand clear of one another, perhaps in order to limit the dangers of organized inmate resistance to institutional rule. Through an interesting phrase, inmates may be officially encouraged to "do their own time."

8. For the version of this process in concentration camps, see Elie A. Cohen, *Human Behaviour in the Concentration Camp*, Jonathan Cape, n.p., 1954, p. 120. For a fictionalized treatment of the welcome in a girls' reformatory, see Sara Norris, *The Wayward Ones*, Signet Pocket Books, New York, 1952, pp. 31–34.

9. An excellent description of this model universe as found in a state mental hospital may be found in Ivan Belknap, *Human Problems of a State Mental Hospital*, McGraw-Hill, New York, 1956, p. 164.

10. For example, see Morris G. Caldwell, "Group Dynamics in the Prison Community," *Journal of Criminal Law, Criminology and Police Science*, Vol. 46, 1956, p. 656.

11. There are some interesting incidental social functions of messings up. First, they tend to limit rigidities which might occur were seniority the only means of mobility in the privilege system. Secondly, demotion through messing up brings old-time inmates in contact with new inmates in unprivileged positions, assuring a flow of information about the system and the people in it.

12. See, for example, Norma S. Hayner and Ellis Ash, "The Prisoner Community as a Social Group," *American Sociological Review*, Vol. 4, 1939, pp. 364 ff. under "Conniving Processes"; also, Caldwell, *op. cit.*, pp. 650–651.

13. See, for example, Melville's extended description of the fight his fellow seamen put up to prevent the clipping of their beards in full accordance with Navy regulations. Melville, *White Jacket* Grove Press, New York, n.d., pp. 333–347.

14. See, for example, Donald Clemmer, "Leadership Phenomenon in a Prison Community," *Journal of Criminal Law, Criminology and Police Science*, Vol. 28, 1938, p. 868.

15. See, for example, Ida Ann Harper, "The Role of the 'Fringer' in a State Prison for Women," *Social Forces*, Vol. 31, 1952, pp. 53–60.

16. For concentration camps, see the discussion of "Prominents" throughout Cohen, *op. cit.*; for mental hospitals, see Belknap, *op. cit.*, p. 189. For prisons, see the discussion of "Politicos" in Donald Clemmer, *The Prison Community*, Christopher Publishing House, Boston, 1940, pp. 277–279, 298–309; also Hayner, *op. cit.*, p. 367; and Caldwell, *op. cit.*, pp. 651–653.

17. For the version of this inmate solidarity to be found in military academies, see Sanford M. Dornbusch, "The Military Academy as an Assimilating Institution," *Social Forces*, Vol. 33, 1955, p. 318.

18. An interesting example of this re-evaluation may be found in a conscientious objector's experience with nonpolitical prisoners, see Alfred Hassler, *Diary of a Self-Made*

Convict, Regnery, Chicago, 1954, pp. 74, 117. In mental hospitals, of course, the patient's antagonism to staff obtains one of its supports from the discovery that, like himself, many other patients are more like ordinary persons than like anything else.

19. See, for example, the discussion of "The Resisters," in Edgar H. Schein, "The Chinese Indoctrination Program for Prisoners of War," *Psychiatry*, Vol. 19 (1956), pp. 160–161.

20. See, for example, Belknap, *op. cit.*, p. 192.

21. In the case of mental hospitals, those who take this line are sometimes called "institutional cures" or are said to suffer from "hospitalitis."

22. Schein, *op. cit.*, pp. 167–169.

23. See Bruno Bettelheim, "Individual and Mass Behavior in Extreme Situations," *Journal of Abnormal and Social Psychology*, Vol. 38, 1943, pp. 447–451. It should be added that in concentration camps, colonization and conversion often seemed to go together. See Cohen, *op. cit.*, pp. 200–203, where the role of the "Kapo" is discussed.

24. See the discussion in Schein, *op. cit.*, pp. 165–166 of the "Get-Alongers," and Robert J. Lifton, "Home by Ship: Reaction Patterns of American Prisoners of War Repatriated from North Korea," *American Journal of Psychiatry*, Vol. 110, 1954, p. 734.

25. This two-facedness, of course, is very commonly found in total institutions. In the state-type mental hospital studied by the writer, even the few elite patients selected for individual psychotherapy, and hence in the best position for espousal of the psychiatric approach to self, tended to present their favorable view of psychotherapy only to the members of their intimate cliques. For a report on the way in which army prisoners concealed from fellow offenders their interest in "restoration" to the army, see the comments by Richard Cloward in Session 4 of *New Perspectives for Research on Juvenile Delinquency*, ed. by Helen L. Witmer and Ruth Kotinsky, U.S. Department of Health, Education and Welfare, Children's Bureau Bulletin, 1955, especially p. 90.

26. Bettelheim, *op. cit.*, p. 425.

27. Thus, Schein, *op. cit.*, p. 165 fn., suggests that Puerto Ricans and other non-English-speaking prisoners of war in China were given up on and allowed to work out a viable routine of menial chores.

28. Interestingly enough, staff is expected to be properly self-regulating upon first coming to the total institution, sharing with members of other kinds of establishments the ideal of needing merely to learn procedure.

29. The strongest evidence for this, perhaps, comes from our knowledge of the readjustment of repatriated brain-washed prisoners of war. See, for example, Lawrence E. Hinkle, Jr., and Harold G. Wolff, "Communist Interrogation and Indoctrination of 'Enemies of the State,'" *Archives of Neurology and Psychiatry*, Vol. 76, 1956, p. 174.

30. As Cloward, *op. cit.*, pp. 80–83, implies, one important kind of leverage staff has in regard to inmates and one factor leading inmates to act convertible in presence of staff is that staff can give the kind of discharge that may appear to reduce stigmatization. Prison barracks officials can hold up the possibility of the inmate's "restoration" to active duty and, potentially, an honorable discharge; mental hospital administrators can hold up the possibility of a "clean bill of health" (discharged as cured) and personal recommendations.

31. Cloward, *op. cit.*, p. 82.

32. Extremely useful material on TB sanitariums as total institutions will be available in the forthcoming work by Julius A. Roth, Committee on Human Development, University of Chicago. Preliminary statements may be found in his articles "What Is an Activity?" *Etc.*, Vol. XIV, Autumn 1956, pp. 54–56, and "Ritual and Magic in the Control of Contagion," *American Sociological Review*, Vol. 22, June 1957, pp. 310–314.

33. Melville, *op. cit.*, p. 139.

34. For comments on the very difficult role of guard, see McCorkle and Korn, *op. cit.*, pp. 93–94, and Gresham M. Sykes, "The Corruption of Authority and Rehabilitation," *Social Forces*, Vol. 34, 1956, pp. 257–262.

35. I derive this from Everett C. Hughes' review of Leopold von Wies's *Spätlese*, in *American Journal of Sociology*, Vol. LXI, 1955, p. 182. A similar area is covered under

the current anthropological term "ethnopsychology," except that the unit to which it applies is a culture, not an institution.

36. If the analogy were to be carried out strictly, we would have to say of course that every total institution had a semipermeable membrane about it, since there will always be some standard equally maintained on the inside and outside, the impermeable effects being restricted to certain specific values and practices.

37. St. Benedict, *Holy Rule*, Ch. 2.

38. Dornbusch, *op. cit.*, p. 317. The classic case of this kind of echelon leveling is found perhaps in the fagging system in British public schools.

39. Kathryn C. Hulme, *The Nun's Story*, Little, Brown, Boston, 1956, pp. 22–23.

40. It seems to be true that within any given establishment the topmost and bottommost roles tend to be relatively permeable to wider community standards, while the impermeable tendencies seem to be focused in the middle ranges of the institution's hierarchy.

B. Interorganizational Networks and Society

Bureaucracy, Bureaucratization, and Debureaucratization

S. N. Eisenstadt

Conditions of Development of Bureaucratic Organizations

We shall start with an analysis of the conditions of development of bureaucratic organizations and see to what extent these conditions can explain the existence of different inherent tendencies in their development and their patterns of activities . . . .

The available material suggests that bureaucratic organizations tend to develop in societies when:

1. There develops extensive differentiation between major types of roles and institutional (economic, political, religious, and so forth) spheres.
2. The most important social roles are allocated not according to criteria of membership in the basic particularistic (kinship or territorial) groups, but rather according to universalistic and achievement criteria, or criteria of membership in more flexibly constituted groups such as professional, religious, vocational, or "national" groups.
3. There evolve many functionally specific groups (economic, cultural, religious, social-integrative) that are not embedded in basic particularistic groups, as, for example, economic and professional organizations, various types of voluntary associations, clubs, and so forth.
4. The definition of the total community is not identical with, and consequently is wider than, any such basic particularistic group, as can be seen, for instance, in the definition of the Hellenic culture in Byzantium or of the Confucian cultural order.
5. The major groups and strata in the society develop, uphold, and attempt to implement numerous discrete, political, economic, and social-service goals which cannot be implemented within the limited framework of the basic particularistic groups.
6. The growing differentiation in the social structure makes for complexity in many spheres of life, such as increasing interdependence between far-off groups and growing difficulty in the assurance of supply of resources and services.
7. These developments result to some extent in "free-floating" resources, i.e., manpower and economic resources as well as commitments for political support which are neither embedded in nor assured to any primary ascriptive-particularistic groups, as, for example, monetary resources, a relatively free labor force, and a free political vote. Consequently, the various institutional units in the society have to compete for resources, manpower, and support for the implementation of their goals and provision of services; and the major social units are faced with many regulative and administrative problems.

The available material suggests that bureaucratic organizations develop in relation to such differentiation in the social system. Bureaucratic organizations can help in coping with some of the problems arising out of such differentiation, and they perform important functions in the organization of adequate services and

Reprinted in part from *Administrative Science Quarterly*, vol. 4 (December, 1959), pp. 302–320, by permission.

coordination of large-scale activities, in the implementation of different goals, in the provision of resources to different groups and in the regulation of various intergroup relations and conflicts. Such bureaucratic organizations are usually created by certain elites (rulers, economic entrepreneurs, etc.) to deal with the problems outlined and to assure for these elites both the provision of such services and strategic power positions in the society.

Thus in many historical societies bureaucratic administrations were created by kings who wanted to establish their rule over feudal-aristocratic forces and who wanted, through their administration, to control the resources created by various economic and social groups and to provide these groups with political, economic, and administrative services that would make them dependent on the rulers.

In many modern societies bureaucratic organizations are created when the holders of political or economic power are faced with problems that arise because of external (war, etc.) or internal (economic development, political demands, etc.) developments. For the solution of such problems they have to mobilize adequate resources from different groups and spheres of life.

Obviously, these conclusions have to be tested and amplified. . . .

Bureaucratization and Debureaucratization

It is through continuous interaction with its environment that a bureaucratic organization may succeed in maintaining those characteristics that distinguish it from other social groups. The most important of these characteristics, common to most bureaucratic organizations and often stressed in the literature, are specialization of roles and tasks; the prevalence of autonomous, rational, nonpersonal rules in the organization; and the general orientation to rational, efficient implementation of specific goals.[1]

These structural characteristics do not, however, develop in a social vacuum but are closely related to the functions and activities of the bureaucratic organization in its environment. The extent to which they can develop and persist in any bureaucratic organization is dependent on the type of dynamic equilibrium that the organization develops in relation to its environment. Basically, three main outcomes of such interaction or types of such dynamic equilibrium can be distinguished, although probably each of them can be further subdivided and some overlapping occurs between them.

The first type of equilibrium is one in which any given bureaucratic organization maintains its autonomy and distinctiveness. The basic structural characteristics that differentiate it from other social groups and in which it implements its goal or goals (whether its initial goal or goals are added later) are retained and it is supervised by those who are legitimately entitled to do this (holders of political power, "owners," or boards of trustees).

The second main possibility is that of bureaucratization. This is the extension of the bureaucracy's spheres of activities and power either in its own interests or those of some of its elite. It tends toward growing regimentation of different areas of social life and some extent of displacement of its service goals in favor of various power interests and orientations. Examples are military organizations that tend to impose their rule on civilian life, or political parties that exert pressure on their potential supporters in an effort to monopolize their private and occupational life and make them entirely dependent on the political party.

The third main outcome is debureaucratization. Here there is subversion of the goals and activities of the bureaucracy in the interests of different groups with which it is in close interaction (clients, patrons, interested parties). In debureaucratization the specific characteristics of the bureaucracy in terms both of its autonomy and its specific rules and goals are minimized, even up to the point where its very functions and activities are taken over by other groups or organizations. Examples of this can be found in cases when some organization (i.e., a parents' association or a religious or political group) attempts to divert the rules and working of a bureaucratic organization (school, economic agency, and so forth) for its own use or according to its own values and goals. It makes demands on the members of bureaucratic organizations to perform tasks that are obviously outside the specific scope of these organizations. . . .

Many overlappings between these various tendencies and possibilities may, of course, develop. The tendencies toward bureaucratization and debureaucratization may, in fact, develop side by side. Thus, for instance, a growing use of the bureaucratic organization and the extension of its scope of activities for purposes of political control might be accompanied by deviation from its rules for the sake of political expediency. The possibility of these tendencies occurring in the same case may be explained by the fact that a stable service-oriented bureaucracy (the type of bureaucracy depicted in the Weberian ideal type of bureaucracy) is based on the existence of some equilibrium or *modus vivendi* between professional autonomy and societal (or political) control. Once this equilibrium is severely disrupted, the outcome with respect to the bureaucracy's organization and activity may be the simultaneous development of bureaucratization and debureaucratization in different spheres of its activities, although usually one of these tendencies is more pronounced. . . .

Some Variables in the Study of Bureaucracy

It is as yet very difficult to propose any definite and systematic hypothesis about this problem since very little research is available that is specifically related to it.[2]

What can be done at this stage is, first, to point out some variables that, on the basis of available material and the preceding discussion, seem central to this problem, and then to propose some preliminary hypotheses, which may suggest directions in which research work on this problem may be attempted.

On the basis of those discussions we would like to propose that (a) the major goals of the bureaucratic organization, (b) the place of these goals in the social structure of the society, and (c) the type of dependence of the bureaucracy on external forces (clients, holders of political power, or other prominent groups) are of great importance in influencing both its internal structure and its relation with its environment. These different variables, while to some extent interdependent, are not identical. Each brings into relief the interdependence of the bureaucratic organization with its social setting from a different point of view.

The bureaucracy's goals, as has been lately shown in great detail by Parsons,[3] are of strategic importance, because they constitute one of the most important connecting links between the given organization and the total social structure in which it is placed. That which from the point of view of the organization is the major goal is very often from the point of view of the total society the function of the organization. Hence the various interrelations between a bureaucratic organization, other groups, and the total society are largely mediated by the nature of its goals. This applies both to the resources needed by the organization and to the products it gives to the society.[4]

But it is not merely the contents of the goals, i.e., whether they are mainly political, economic, cultural, and so forth, that influence the relation of the organization with its environment, but the place of the goals in the institutional structure of the society as well. By the relative place of the specific goals of any given bureacratic organization within the society we mean the centrality (or marginality) of these goals with respect to the society's value and power system and the extent of legitimation it affords them. Thus there would obviously be many differences between a large corporation with critical products and a small economic organization with marginal products; between a political party close to the existing government performing the functions of a "loyal opposition" and a revolutionary group; between established churches and minority or militant sects; between fully established educational institutions and sectarian study or propaganda groups.

A third variable which seems to influence the bureaucracy's structural characteristics and activities is the extent and nature of its dependence on external resources and power. This dependence or relation may be defined in terms of

1. The chief function of the organization, i.e., whether it is a service, market, or membership recruitment agency. (This definition is closely related to, but not necessarily identical with, its goals.)
2. The extent to which its clientele is entirely dependent upon its products, or conversely, the type and extent of competition between it and parallel agencies.
3. The nature and extent of the internal (ownership) and external control.
4. The criteria used to measure the success of the organization as such and its members' performance, especially the extent of changes in the behavior and membership affiliation of its clients (as, for instance, in the case of a political party).
5. The spheres of life of its personnel that the activities of a given bureaucratic organization encompass.

It is not claimed that this list is exhaustive, but it seems to provide some preliminary clues as to the possible direction of further research on the problem.

All these variables indicate the great interdependence existing between the bureaucratic organization and its social environment. Each variable points to some ways in which a bureaucratic organization attempts to control different parts of its environment and to adapt its goals to changing environment or to different ways in which groups outside the bureaucracy control it and direct its activities. The outcome of this continuous interaction varies continuously according to the constellation of these different variables.

Conditions of Bureaucratization and Debureaucratization

On the basis of the foregoing considerations and of current research like that of Janowitz,[5] of historical research on which we have reported already, and research in progress on the relations between bureaucratic organization and new immigrants in Israel,[6] we propose several general hypotheses concerning the conditions that promote autonomy or, conversely, bureaucratization or debureaucratization

The first of these hypotheses proposes that the development of any given bureaucratic organization as a relatively autonomous service agency is contingent upon the following conditions obtaining in its social setting:

1. Relative predominance of universalistic elements in the orientations and goals of the groups most closely related to the bureaucracy.
2. Relatively wide distribution of power and values in the economic, cultural, and political spheres among many groups and the maintenance of continuous struggle and competition among them or, in other words, no monopoly of the major power positions by any one group.
3. A wide range of differentiation among different types of goals.
4. The continuous specialization and competition among different bureaucratic organizations and between them and other types of groups about their relative places with regard to implementation of different goals.
5. The existence of strongly articulated political groups and the maintenance of control over the implementation of the goals by the legitimate holders of political, communal, or economic power.

Thus a service bureaucracy, one that maintains both some measure of autonomy and of service orientation, tends to develop either in a society, such as the "classical" Chinese Empire or the Byzantine Empire from the sixth to the tenth century, in which there exist strong political rulers and some politically active groups, such as the urban groups, aristocracy, and the church in the Byzantine Empire, or the literati and gentry in China, whose aspirations are considered by the rulers.[7] It also tends to develop in a democratic society in which effective political power is vested in an efficient, strong, representative executive. In both cases it is the combination of relatively strong political leadership with some political articulation and activity of different strata and groups (an articulation which necessarily tends to be entirely different in expression in historical empires from modern democracies) that facilitates the maintenance of a service bureaucracy.

In some societies a group may establish a power monopoly over parts of its environment and over the definition and establishment of the society's goals and the appropriation of its resources. This group may use the bureaucracy as an instrument of power and manipulation, distort its autonomous function and service orientation, and subvert some of its echelons through various threats or inducements for personal gratification. Historically the most extreme example of such developments can be found in those societies in which the rulers developed political goals that were strongly opposed by various active groups that they tried to suppress, such as in Prussia in the seventeenth and eighteenth centuries, in many conquest empires such as the Ottoman, or in the periods of aristocratization of the Byzantine Empire.[8] Modern examples of this tendency can be found in totalitarian societies or movements. Less extreme illustrations can also be found in other societies, and it should be a major task of comparative research to specify the different possible combinations of the conditions enumerated above and their influence on the possible development of bureaucratic organizations.

The development of a bureaucratic organization in the direction of debureaucratization seems to be connected mainly with the growth of different types of *direct* dependence of the bureaucratic organization on parts of its clientele. At this stage we may propose the following preliminary hypotheses about the influence that the type of dependency of the bureaucracy on its clients has on some of its patterns of activity. First, the greater its dependence on its clientele in terms of their being able to go to a competing agency, the more it will have to develop techniques of communication and additional services to retain its clientele and the more it will be influenced by different types of demands by the clientele for services in spheres that are not directly relevant to its main goals. Second, insofar as its dependence on its clients is due to the fact that its criteria of successful organizational performance are based on the number and behavior pattern of the organization's members or clients (as is often the case in semipolitical movements, educational organizations, and so forth), it will have to take an interest in numerous spheres of its clients' activities and either establish its control over them or be subjected to their influence and direction. Finally, the greater its *direct* dependence on different participants in the political arena, and the smaller the basic economic facilities and political assurance given by the holders of political power—as is the case in some public organizations in the United States and to some extent also in different organizations in Israel[9]—the greater will be its tendency to succumb to the demands of different political and economic pressure groups and to develop its activities and distort its own rules accordingly.

As already indicated, in concrete cases some overlapping between the tendencies to bureaucratization and debureaucratization may occur. Thus, for instance, when a politically monopolistic group gains control over a bureaucratic organization, it may distort the rules of this organization in order to give special benefits to the holders of political power or to maintain its hold over different segments of the population. On the other hand, when a process of debureaucratization sets in because of the growing pressure of different groups on a bureaucracy, there may also develop within the bureaucratic organization, as a sort of defense against these pressures, a tendency toward formalization and bureaucratization. This shows that the distinctive characteristics of a specific bureaucratic organization and role have been impinged upon in different directions, and one may usually discern which of these tendencies is predominant in different spheres of activity of the bureaucracy. It is the task of further research to analyze these different constellations in greater detail.

Notes

1. See, for instance, P. M. Blau, *Bureaucracy in Modern Society* (New York, 1956). Blau summarizes much of the available literature on this problem.
2. Thus, for instance, in existing literature there is but little distinction between conditions which make for the growth of bureaucracy and those conducive to increasing bureaucratization. Gouldner's polemics against those who foresee the inevitability of bureaucratization are to some extent due to the lack of this distinction in the available literature. See his "Metaphysical Pathos and the Theory of Bureaucracy." *American Political Science Review*, 49 (1955), 496–507.
3. See T. Parsons, "Suggestions for a Sociological Approach to the Theory of Organization, I and II," *Administrative Science Quarterly*, 1 (June and Sept. 1956), 63–85, 225–239.
4. See "Trend Report," *Current Sociology*, Vol. 7 (1958), 99–163.
5. See M. Janowitz, D. Wright, and W. Delany, *Public Administration and the Public— Perspectives toward Government in a Metropolitan Community* (Ann Arbor, 1958), which is one of the few available works that have a bearing on this problem. We would also like to mention the work of J. A. Slesinger, who has worked with Janowitz, and who has recently proposed several hypotheses concerning some of the factors that might influence aspects of the development of bureaucracy that are of interest to us. See

Slesinger, "A Model for the Comparative Study of Public Bureaucracies," Institute of Public Administration, University of Michigan, 1957 (mimeographed).

6. See E. Katz and S. N. Eisenstadt, "Some Sociological Observations on the Response of Israeli Organizations to New Immigrants," *Administrative Science Quarterly*, Vol. 5 (1960), 113–133.

7. For a more complete discussion of some of the problems of these societies see the references in note 4.

8. Hans Rosenberg, *Bureaucracy, Aristocracy and Autocracy: The Prussian Experience, 1660–1815* (Cambridge, Mass., 1958); A. Lybyer, *The Government of the Ottoman Empire in the Time of Suleiman the Magnificent* (Cambridge, Mass., 1913); and Eisenstadt, Internal Contradictions.

9. See Janowitz *et al.*, *op. cit.*, pp. 107–114, and Katz and Eisenstadt, *op. cit.*

The Interorganizational Network as a Political Economy

J. Kenneth Benson

. . . Despite the obvious and growing prominence of interorganizational phenomena, research and theory concerning the topic offer little hope at this point of providing an adequate approach. Empirical research and empirically grounded theory in interorganizational relations currently display two deficiencies. First, there is a problem of conceptual confusion and overlap. The interorganizational relation has proven to be a complex, variegated, multilevel phenomenon. Research attention has been devoted to different elements, components, and levels. Each effort has produced a unique formulation, although a few common elements pervade much of the work—the concept of domain consensus being one (Litwak and Hylton, 1962; Levine and White, 1961; Downs, 1967; Warren, 1967; Thompson, 1967: 25–38; Aldrich, 1971; Marrett, 1971). If progress is to be made in this field, an integrative theoretical framework is needed. Such a scheme should bring order to the diverse concepts and explanatory principles previously proposed, providing analytical boundaries and linkages that would permit the accumulation of complementary findings.

Second, interorganizational research and theory have been insufficiently concerned with issues of macrostructure. The larger problems of postindustrial society have, for the most part, escaped the notice of interorganizational analysts. Attention has been directed to patterns of interagency cooperation and exchange, while problems of interorganizational and institutional dominance go unexamined. That these separate concerns are potentially connected is a possibility largely neglected. A few exceptions to this tendency may be noted, such as in the work of Crozier (1972; 1973a; 1973b) and Zald (1970), but the general pattern is clear.

This article proposes a theoretical perspective for interorganizational relations which is intended to solve these problems. The political-economy perspective is integrative in the sense that a number of diverse concerns of interorganizational research are brought together in a general framework. Beyond this, the focus upon resources and power permits a direct connection between the interorganizational field and the realm of societal organization or macrostructure.

The scheme was developed on the basis of an empirical study of relations between a series of human service agencies. The conceptions forming the theory reflect its empirical origins at several points. Thus, the scheme does not achieve generalizability to all types of interorganizational networks. Networks of business

The paper on which this article is based was presented at the Eighth World Congress of Sociology, International Sociological Association, Toronto, Canada, August 18–24, 1974. Work on the paper was supported in part by Research Grant RD-2326-G, Social and Rehabilitation Service, United States Department of Health, Education and Welfare, and in part by the Agricultural Experiment Station, University of Missouri-Columbia. Helpful comments by Michel Crozier on an earlier draft are gratefully acknowledged.

Reprinted in part from *Administrative Science Quarterly*, vol. 20 (June, 1975), pp. 229–249, by permission.

organizations, for example, appear to lie beyond the reach of the present scheme. Nevertheless, the focus on resources should provide a basis on which future extensions of the scheme will be accomplished.

The Interorganizational Network

The basic unit of analysis is the network of organizations. Such a unit consists of a number of distinguishable organizations having a significant amount of interaction with each other. Such interaction may at one extreme include extensive, reciprocal exchanges of resources or intense hostility and conflict at the other. The organizations in a network may be linked directly or indirectly. Some networks, for example, may consist of a series of organizations linked by multiple, direct ties to each other. Others may be characterized by a clustering or centering of linkages around one or a few mediating or controlling organizations. Networks may thus be quite varied and their characteristics should be objects of explanation.

The interorganizational network is treated here as an emergent phenomenon, delineating a kind of analysis with distinctive features and concerns. The network, as an emergent entity, has characteristics which are objects of investigation in their own right. This is a departure from much interorganizational literature in which analysis is concentrated on a focal organization and its environment, including its organization set (Evan, 1966). In this literature the organization-environment nexus has been the unit of analysis. Thus, the interorganizational field has developed primarily as an extension of organizational analysis. Even in studies where networks have been recognized as important, they have often been analyzed primarily for their effects upon a focal organization (Terreberry, 1968). Recently, a few studies focusing on the network as an emergent phenomenon have been produced (Turk, 1970, 1973a, 1973b; Aldrich, 1972).

Political-Economic Forces

The interorganizational network may be analyzed in terms of two related, but partially autonomous, sets of concepts. Analysis may be focused on interaction patterns concerned with the actual performance of core functions or purposes of the organizations. For example, the analysis of cooperative or competitive interaction between two public agencies in the delivery of their mandated services might be the focus of investigation. Analysis of relations of this kind has been the predominant concern of interorganizational analysts. While the importance of this mode of analysis is recognized in the present framework, phenomena on this level are ultimately dependent upon deeper and more fundamental processes. The second, deeper mode of analysis is focused on the processes of resource acquisition, that is, the activities undertaken by organization participants in pursuit of an adequate supply of organizational resources. Interactions of organizations may occur at either level—in the delivery of mandated services or in the acquisition of resources.

The fundamental argument in the present formulation is that interactions at the level of service delivery are ultimately dependent upon resource acquisition. Considerations of resource adequacy determine, within fairly restrictive limits, the nature of interactions in the performance of mandated functions. Phenomena at the level of service delivery are partially autonomous in the sense that orderly patterns of dependence linking variables at that level may be discovered. For example, common or consensual domain conceptions may be associated with cooperative work relations. Furthermore, reasonably precise and accurate theoretical models may be applied to phenomena at the level of service delivery. Nevertheless, interactions must be explained ultimately at the level of resource acquisition.

The present formulation rests upon a system resource view of organizations. Following Yuchtman and Seashore (1967), it is assumed that organization decision makers are typically oriented to the acquisition and defense of an adequate supply of resources. Such an orientation becomes, for decision makers, an operational definition of the purposes of the organization and thus of their responsibilities as decision makers. Abstract purposes, charter goals, and the like come to be translated into ongoing programs, established structures, and the training history of personnel. Once this process has reached an advanced stage, decision makers are responsible largely for maintaining or expanding this established organizational machine. Abstract goal statements then recede into the background of shared assumptions, which are taken for granted, and may be employed primarily to provide continuing ideological legitimation for ongoing activities. This perspective fits some organizations better than others. Generally, it is more appropriate for older, larger, and more complex organizations. Such an orientation is also more likely to exist in organizations with multiple goals than in those with a unitary or simple goal structure.[1]

Two basic types of resources are central to the political economy of interorganizational networks. These are money and authority. Organization decision makers are oriented to the acquisition and defense of a secure and adequate supply of these resources. Authority refers to the legitimation of activities, the right and responsibility to carry out programs of a certain kind, dealing with a broad problem area or focus. Legitimated claims of this kind are termed domains. The possession of a domain permits the organization to operate in a certain sphere, claim support for its activities, and define proper practices within its realm. Money is of obvious importance in the mounting of programs, the recruitment and retention of personnel, and the purchase of buildings and equipment. Money and authority are interrelated in that there is a generalized expectation of balance or correlation between the two. Authority to conduct activities is generally assumed to imply a claim upon money adequate to performance in the prescribed sphere.

A variety of other items, such as personnel, might have been treated as resources. Aldrich (1972: 15), working with an analytical framework similar to the present one, has identified four types of resources: funds, personnel, information, and products and services. In the present article the resources list is limited to the two which are most fundamental. Given money and authority, other needed commodities may be acquired, while the reverse is probably not possible. Money and authority may be required to recruit personnel, while personnel may not be necessary to the acquisition of money. At the current stage of knowledge, however, any listing of resources must be somewhat arbitrary.

The assertion that organizations pursue an adequate supply of money and authority leaves a number of questions unanswered. Many different actions may be compatible with this broad requirement. Thus, research must be addressed to the elaboration of operational decision criteria or decision rules governing interagency relations. Exploration of this problem in research conducted by Benson *et al.* (1973) produced basic action orientations of agency administrators in their dealings with other agencies. These are enumerated as a suggestive, but by no means definitive, list.

A. The fulfillment of program requirements. The organization is oriented to the maintenance of order and effectiveness in its established programs. . . . The organization's claim to a supply of resources (money and authority) will typically be based upon the adequacy and effectiveness of its established programs. Thus, agency officials are reluctant to undertake tasks or to tolerate practices of other agencies which interfere with the fulfillment of present programs. And, they will exert pressures upon other agencies to cease practices disruptive of program requirements.
B. The maintenance of a clear domain of high social importance. The administrators are oriented to the maintenance of a clear-cut, uncluttered claim that includes a set of important activities. Such a domain is characterized by *one or more* of the following attributes: (1) exclusiveness—a claim untrammelled, unchallenged by other organizations; (2) autonomy—a claim permitting the performance of activities independently, without supervision, direction, or shared authority by another agency; (3) dominance—a claim permitting authoritative direction of other agencies operating in a specified sphere. Allocations of funds and authority are based on the domain held by an agency. The greater the domain approximates the criteria above, the greater the hold over funds and authority assigned to the sphere of activities in question.
C. The maintenance of orderly, reliable patterns of resource flow. The organizations are oriented to see that the support network operates in a predictable, dependable way that permits the agency to anticipate an adequate and certain flow of resources.
D. The extended application and defense of the agency's paradigm. The organization participants are committed to their agency's way of doing things—to its own definitions of problems and tasks and its own techniques of intervention. This might be called a technological-ideological commitment. Organizations which use or espouse other approaches are seen as irresponsible or immoral. And, efforts are made to see that the "proper" definitions and techniques are adopted (1973: 112–113).

Organizations taking other approaches constitute an implicit threat to the security of resource flow into an agency. Thus, efforts are made to refute and discredit competing ideological claims and to establish the superiority of one's own technology.

The bases of differential power within a network may be divided into two broad categories. These are internal network structure and external linkages of network organizations. Each may be briefly elaborated. First, some organizations gain power vis-à-vis others because of other features of network organization. Some organizations may provide services vital to all or to a large number of the organizations in the network. Such organizations may then gain power from the centrality of their functions. For example, where network organizations are engaged in the delivery of multiple, differentiated services to clients, an organization at the center of referral flow, namely, one to which all or many clients must be referred, may gain power over those at the periphery. This occurs because centrality makes an organization crucial to the resource acquisition of other agencies. Power may be said to derive from the central organization's control over strategic contingencies confronted by the peripheral organizations. Continued or increased funding may depend upon the successful placement of clients and successful placement may depend upon the policies of the organization at the center of referral flow. Thus, strategic location in the referral network gives the central organization enhanced bargaining power vis-à-vis the peripheral organizations.[2]

State employment security agencies may gain power in many networks because clients must be referred for job placement. The proportion of clients referred from a community action agency to an employment security office will typically be much higher than the proportion flowing in the opposite direction. Thus, the employment agency is less dependent on the community action agency than vice versa. Much analytical work remains to be done in order to specify the intranetwork bases of interorganizational dominance.

The second source of network dominance lies in the linkage of organizations to a larger pattern of social organization. Network organization may become committed to the interests and ideologies of groups in the larger society, for example, political parties, racial or ethnic minorities, or social classes. Interorganizational dominance may be derived in part from these ties. An agency may be able to mobilize forces external to the network as a means of controlling resource flow within it. Thus, interorganizational power relations cannot be fully understood without attention to the larger pattern of societal dominance.

The degree of interorganizational power derived from these sources may be determined by three factors: (1) the size of the group or groups which may be expected to support the organization, (2) the degree of mobilization of supporting groups, and (3) their social rank. The power of an agency derives from the specific combination of these factors. Some organizations may gain power from the sheer numbers of people who can be mobilized to support their claims. For example, public welfare agencies in many states are powerful partly because of the large numbers of recipients who can be mobilized in their behalf, even though the recipients individually are low in social rank. By contrast, rehabilitation agencies serve relatively small numbers of clients but appear to draw support from small numbers of strategically placed professionals, for example, educators and psychologists in state and federal bureaus. Further, professional associations linked to rehabilitation causes, such as those in the guidance and counseling fields, provide a great deal of support. In addition, the strong affinity of rehabilitation ideology to the individualist tenets of private enterprise serves to mitigate opposition from business interests, if not to gain positive support from that quarter. Much theoretical and empirical work is needed, however, to establish and clarify the linkage of interorganizational power differentials to coalitions and interest groups in the larger society.

Interorganizational power, whatever its source, may have a variety of effects upon network relations. Administrators in powerful agencies should be able to defend their resource flow, claim new domains, resist claims advanced by less powerful agencies, and block the creation of competitive organizations Thus, the primary effects of interorganizational power lie in the control of network resources, including the flow of resources to other agencies.

This control may be exercised in diverse ways. The powerful organization may see that its domain is protected through the requirement that new agencies refer appropriate clients to it or through the provision that the powerful agency must approve or even license the activities of weaker agencies. The powerful agency may set eligibility criteria for weaker agencies that assure their failure or at least their poor performance. The powerful agency may see that the terms of interorganizational exchange are set in a way that protects its dominance. The weaker agency will therefore remain weak because the terms of exchange work to the advantage of the strong.

The secondary expression of interorganizational power is in the process of negotiation between organizations. The powerful organization can force others to accept its terms in negotiations to establish cooperative programs or to settle disputes. Power permits one organization to reach across agency boundaries and determine policies or practices in weaker organizations. Failure or refusal of the weaker organization to accede to the demands of the stronger can have serious repercussions for the resource procurement of the weaker organization.

Networks do not always manifest clear-cut dominance patterns in which one or a few organizations are all-powerful. Rather, cases in which a number of minimally powerful parties confront each other on terms approximating equality are frequently encountered. Such networks are often blocked and noncooperative because all of the agencies suffer from resource shortages and none can muster power sufficient to dictate terms to the others. Such a condition appears common, perhaps even typical, in networks composed of private philanthropic agencies delivering social services. The existence of such networks does not invalidate the theoretical perspective developed here. Rather, stalemated or blocked networks of this kind should be explicable on the basis of the sources of power of the parties. In such networks each organization has power sufficient to maintain its autonomy and none is able to dominate the others.

Superstructure of Sentiments and Interactions

Previous interorganizational research has focused to a considerable degree upon sentiments and interactions. Much research has been addressed to patterns of cooperation or coordination between agencies, for instance, the sharing of such facilities as buildings and computers, the use of common referral forms and other devices to improve the flow of clients, the exchange of personnel, and the like. In addition, a great deal of attention has been paid to attitudes and opinions shared or not shared by participants in two or more organizations. Consensus on domains and similarities of agency philosophies have been investigated. Further, there is a tendency to hypothesize causal dependencies among these phenomena, for example, arguing that consensus on operating philosophies produces cooperative relations (Miller, 1958; Hollister, 1970; Braito, Paulson, and Klonglan, 1972).

The present formulation deals with sentiments and cooperative interactions in a way that grants significance to these phenomena without losing sight of their ultimate dependence upon underlying political and economic forces. Sentiments and cooperative interactions are treated as a superstructure, analogous in a loose way to the Marxian conception. Orderly relations are assumed to exist among phenomena at the level of superstructure, for instance, between consensus and cooperation. The phenomena at this level, however, are hypothesized to be controlled in the final analysis by more fundamental considerations of resource acquisition and dominance.

Interorganizational Equilibrium

The metaphor for analyzing superstructure is provided by the concept of equilibrium. An interorganizational network is equilibrated to the extent that participant organizations are engaged in highly coordinated, cooperative interactions based on normative consensus and mutual respect. In research by Benson *et al.* four dimensions of interorganizational equilibrium have been identified.

Domain Consensus: Agreement among participants in organizations regarding the appropriate role and scope of an agency.

Ideological Consensus: Agreement among participants in organizations regarding the nature of the tasks confronted by the organizations and the appropriate approaches to those tasks.

Positive Evaluation: The judgment by workers in one organization of the value of the work of another organization.

Work Coordination: Patterns of collaboration and cooperation between organizations. Work is coordinated to the extent that programs and activities in two or more organizations are geared into each other with a maximum of effectiveness and efficiency (1973: 51).

The Hypothesis of Balance

In the present formulation a tendency toward balance of the equilibrium components is anticipated. It is argued that increases in one equilibrium component tend to be associated with increases in the others. Similarly, decreases in one component tend to be associated with decreases in the others. Thus, interaction among the components may produce circular processes of equilibration, moving the network toward equilibrium, or disequilibration, moving the network away from equilibrium. Other things being equal, the network tends to become balanced but not necessarily equilibrated. The components tend to assume similar levels, for example, high-domain consensus associated with high-work coordination or low-domain consensus association with low-work coordination. The components, however, may become balanced at varying equilibrium levels.[3]

The occurrence of imbalanced networks suggests the effects of variables not included in the equilibrium model. Various conditions under which networks function may produce imbalances. A network, for example, may have high consensus on domains and ideologies and strongly positive reciprocal evaluations and yet display a low degree of work coordination because of a lack of resources. Due to lack of resources, one or more agencies in the network may be too small to enter cooperative ventures despite high levels of consensus and reciprocal evaluation with other agencies. In a contrary example, some networks may display high levels of work coordination despite low levels on the other components because of legislation which requires coordination or formal regulations which strictly prescribe modes of interaction. The paradigm in the Table clarifies the relation between equilibrium and balance and provides examples of several types of balanced and imbalanced networks.

The Political-Economic Base

Although the four components of interorganizational equilibrium are linked in a system tending toward balance, phenomena at this level must be explained ultimately at the substructural level.

The general argument for the dependence of superstructure is that substructural events place restrictive limits upon the potential range of variation of the equilibrium components. Thus, some portion of the variation in work coordination may be attributable to domain consensus and the other equilibrium components. Potential levels of work coordination, however, that is, its limits at any given time, are fixed by the structure of political-economic forces. Each equilibrium component is integrally tied to the positions of agencies in the political economy.

Domains and ideologies are important to the acquisition and defense of an

TABLE 1 *Equilibrium Model*

Types of Systems	Domain Consensus	Ideological Consensus	Interorganizational Evaluation	Work Coordination
			Levels of	
I. Balanced systems				
A. High equilibrium	high	high	high	high
B. Moderate equilibrium	moderate	moderate	moderate	moderate
C. Low equilibrium	low	low	low	low
II. Imbalanced systems: (hypothetical examples)				
A. Forced coordination	low	low	low	high
B. Consensual inefficiency	high	high	high	low
C. Evaluative imbalance	high	high	low	high

agency's position in the marketplace. Authority and money flow to an agency on the basis of its sphere of activities—services provided, clients served, and so forth—and its technology—its approach to its tasks. On the basis of a prescribed sphere of action and an approved strategy or technique, an agency becomes the recipient of a flow of funds and authority. The agency's ideology is involved here because it essentially is a way of talking about and rationalizing its technology. The ideology asserts a connection between assigned tasks and chosen procedures. In many instances ideology becomes a substitute for technology in appeals for funds and authority. Appeals may be made and accepted on the basis of ideological assertions without any direct exposure or examination of actual procedures. Where human services are concerned, the line between ideology and technology is often hazy because treatment often consists of the transmission of attitudes and values. The domain and ideological-technological commitments of an organization, then, provide a basis for resource flow. Consensus between agencies on matters of domain and ideology can therefore occur only within limits set by their market positions. Agencies can agree on matters of domain and ideology only to the extent that such agreement does not threaten their interests.

This structure becomes particularly acute where domain claims of two agencies are in conflict, as when each claims the same or similar spheres of activity. To achieve consensus in this context requires either a carefully worked out compromise in which interests of the agencies are protected or the upholding of one set of claims at the expense of the other. Similarly, the boundaries of potential ideological agreement are highly restrictive where the agencies are engaged in advancing opposed or incompatible strategies for addressing a common problem. One agency may stress community organizing, while the other emphasizes individual counseling as a means of combatting unemployment. In such a case the affirmation of one approach undercuts the other with consequent damage to the resource acquisition capacities of one party.

One may construct eclectic ideologies providing a place for all approaches or strategies at issue, but such formulations are rendered unstable by underlying interest conflict. Thus, in this case too, the resolution of dissonance requires a careful process of negotiation to resolve fundamental interest conflicts as a prerequisite to genuine ideological consensus. Through extended contact and negotiation, ideologies providing justification for a negotiated division of labor and for a diversity of integrated approaches to common tasks may be developed. Such developments, however, are difficult to produce and precarious to maintain. Forceful intervention by third parties or insistent environmental pressures are generally necessary to sustain relations of the duration and intensity required.

Coordination of work between organizations also varies within restrictive limits set at the deeper and more fundamental level of resource acquisition. Administrators undertake or refuse to undertake cooperative ventures on the basis of reasonably careful calculations of costs and returns at the level of resource acquisition. Coordination proposals which threaten the program efficiency of an agency or its established ties to supporting publics are resisted. Proposals which strengthen the agency's position in the resource game are more likely to be adopted. Thus, even where there is substantial consensus on domains and ideologies, work coordination may be restricted because of conflicting or threatened interests. Even in the absence of consensus, calculations of mutual advantage may draw agencies into coordinated ventures. Such developments may be due to direct intervention by a third party, alterations of resource markets, or a variety of other factors. Once such coordinated activities are under way, a tendency toward domain and ideological consensus is likely to occur. Thus, movement toward or away from equilibrium may begin from the activity side—coordination—or from the normative side—domains and ideologies.

Interorganizational Evaluation

The fourth component of the equilibrium model, interorganizational evaluation, is also dependent in important ways upon substructure. Interagency judgments are affected significantly by the positions of agencies in the political economy. Competition for funds and authority is likely to encourage negative interagency judgments. This is apt to occur even where the agencies advance similar ideologies and utilize similar technologies. The development of coordinated work may also fail to mitigate negative judgments if interest conflicts are not resolved. In some instances it is likely that coordination will intensify negative evaluations if underlying interest conflicts are not resolved. For example, if coordination is forced by third-party interventions, demanded by changing environmental constraints, or accomplished by the dominance of one agency over another, interest conflicts and associated negative judgments may be intensified. Similarly, organizations may agree on their respective domains, thus displaying domain consensus, and yet register negative judgments if other sources of interest conflict have not been resolved, for example, where the relative monetary priorities attached to specific services are in dispute.

Summary

The components of interorganizational equilibrium tend to vary together or, in other words, to achieve balance. This balancing tendency may move a network toward or away from equilibrium; it may also, in some cases, stabilize the network at a given equilibrium level. The equilibrium components, however, are dependent upon the alignment of political-economic forces. These forces place restrictive limits upon the range of potential variation in equilibrium components. Within these limits, the balance hypothesis is operative.

Network Environments

The interorganizational network is significantly affected by environmental conditions. These conditions provide a social context within which network relations are negotiated.

The obvious difficulty with the idea of environment is that of sorting out those aspects of the larger social world which are most relevant to network events. Thus, one must provide conceptual structure and boundaries of the environment. Otherwise, it becomes a residual category in which diverse factors, causes, and conditions may be indiscriminately grouped.

The present analysis focuses upon those aspects of the environment which directly and significantly affect the alignment of political and economic forces in networks. Specifically, the environment is important insofar as it affects (1) the supply of the two resources, money and authority, to a network and (2) the distribution of power within a network. The environment may be analyzed in terms of its structure or organization and its change or transformation.

Organization of the Environment

The environment relevant to resource transactions and power differentials in a network is an organized, structured entity even though its structure is difficult to discern. Little significance is attached here to randomized, unorganized environments like the simpler models described by Emery and Trist (1965) and Terreberry (1968). The relevant environment consists of a number of organizations, such as lobbies, government bureaus, and foundations; officials, such as legislators; and publics, such as advocates of government reform, and recipients of agency services. These participants—organizations, officials, and publics—are linked in interaction patterns centering on the governance of a given network, that is, the distribution of resources and power within the network. The environment relevant to a given network is to some extent unique. The degree of overlap or coalescence of network environments, however, is an important focus of investigation. Organizations, publics, and officials having a significant influence upon the determination of network events, specifically the distribution of resources and power, are included in the relevant environment.

The structure of the environment refers to patterned relations among the participants and between participants on the one hand, and the network, on the other hand. The important dimensions of variation in this structure are as follows:[4]

1. Resource concentration/dispersion is the extent to which control over resource disbursements to the network resides finally in one or a few participants. Concentrated environments are those in which resources are channeled through one or a few outlets. Dispersed environments are those in which resources flow through multiple channels. Some networks may be composed of organizations all of which are dependent upon a unitary funding or domain validating channel. Other networks may be supplied by multiple channels, either with a separate and exclusive channel to each agency or with many shared channels entering the network.
2. Power concentration/dispersion is the extent to which some participants in the environment dominate others. Some environments are characterized by clear-cut patterns of dominance in which some participants control others. Other environments have power dispersed through many or all of the participants. Resource concentration is not necessarily tied to power concentration. Resources may flow through a single channel, even

though control over policies governing that channel is dispersed. Similarly, multiple resource channels may be controlled through dominance patterns among environment participants.

3. Network autonomy/dependence is the extent to which the network is controlled by environmental forces. Some networks, although receiving resources from an environment, develop a high degree of autonomy from environmental pressures and constraints. For example, arguments about the military-industrial complex generally allege that a linked set of organizations has gained the capacity to control the environment from which it draws its funds and authority. Other networks, by contrast, are clearly subordinate to and dependent upon their environments. Social service networks tend to be subservient and dependent in this way.

4. Environmental dominance patterns can be equated with the types of participants exercising power in the environment. This dimension concerns the basis of dominance in network environments. To what extent is power concentrated in bureaucracies? To what extent does power reside in such publics as racial groups, social classes, clientele groups, and others? How does a pattern of dominance in the environment affect decisions, actions, or policies related to a network?

At this point in the analytic scheme, issues of macrostructure—the relation between societal organization and network organization—are encountered. Since each network may have a unique environment, it may be possible to discover structural differences in distinct societal sectors or institutional spheres or a common pattern repeated through a series of network environments may point to societal regularities. Crozier (1972), for example, recently offered a similar suggestion.

5. Resource abundance/scarcity is the amount of resources at the disposal of the environment. Some network environments are richly endowed, others are characterized by resource scarcity. In American society the social service sector is disadvantaged in comparison with the military and industrial sectors (Galbraith, 1967, 1973). There are also important differences over time in resource levels. The vastly increased flow of funds and program authorizations for manpower development in the 1960s produced substantial changes in manpower service networks, including many new cooperative ventures, new interorganizational dominance patterns, and the like. Agencies which had previously maintained distance and detachment from problems of poverty and unemployment were drawn suddenly into competition for the mandates and funds to pursue programs in this field (Levitan and Mangum, 1969).

6. Control mechanisms, incentive versus authoritative, are the means of control by the environment over networks. Network control may be formal and authoritative, involving the delegation of authority in bureaucratic fashion to agencies in a network, or exercised through incentive structures in which agencies are drawn into the provision of certain services by the availability of resources (Turk, 1973b). Many networks may display combinations of these control mechanisms and the combinations may be varied in form. Mechanisms of control may change over time, with profound implications for network organization. Recent heated debates over block grants, revenue sharing, and other devices indicate that officials attach much importance to modes of linkage.

Social Change in Networks

The interorganizational network may be subject to change from a variety of sources. The general conditions under which the network and its environment are linked may undergo change with consequent impact upon the network. For example, such changing economic conditions as a recession may reduce the supply of resources and produce a reduction of cooperative ventures as agencies become increasingly conservative. Structural changes in the mode of societal organization, for example, toward more authoritarian rule, may push all networks toward greater accountability and restrictiveness. In the present analysis, however, attention is focused upon strategic options available to participants in a network and its environment. Otherwise stated, this discussion is concentrated upon strategies for changing network organization. Strategic options are discussed with reference to the conditions under which each is feasible.

Four basic strategies may be identified, although each may appear in varied forms. The four strategies are defined by the means employed to effect network change.

Cooperative Strategies

In cooperative strategies change is sought through agreements and joint planning in which each affected social unit participates and exercises options. Network alterations coming out of such a process are typically compromises agreed upon by the affected organizations. Such compromises usually involve a process of negotiation and exchange through which each party has voluntarily given up some valued condition in exchange for similar concessions on the part of others.

Cooperative strategies are widely used and may be the most frequently employed strategies. Included are many contractual agreements in the social services field. An example is a contract between a public rehabilitation agency and a private manpower training organization providing that the latter, in exchange for specific monetary compensation, will provide certain vocational training to clients referred by the former.

Despite the frequency of cooperative strategies, the conditions for their success are restrictive. Such strategies are limited to situations in which each party has some minimal degree of power vis-à-vis other parties. Each party must hold something of value for the other party and be capable of resisting the others' demands. Only then can cooperative strategies be effective. If a party cannot withhold something of value from another, there is no basis for the latter to make concessions. Agreements reached where the minimal conditions for cooperative exchange are absent simply express and formalize the clear-cut dominance of one party over the other.

This does not mean that equality is a precondition for cooperative strategies. On the contrary, exchange between unequals is common. The important consideration is that neither party be powerless in relation to others. Each party must be capable at a minimum of sustaining itself as an operating concern despite opposition or harassment by other parties.

Agreements may cover a wide variety of products or behavior of organizations. Exchanges of funds, personnel, facilities, and clients are among the more obvious. Of equal importance are agreements to cease disruptive or harassing activities. Thus, agencies often enter into agreements to stop interfering with each other. Such an agreement may permit each to fulfill its program requirements more effectively and assure itself a continuing or increasing flow of resources.

In some networks other strategies may be necessary prerequisities of exchange. An actor seeking change in the form of cooperative agreements may find it necessary first to alter the balance of power between target agencies. This would change the terms of exchange, the positions from which parties must negotiate. Many programs intended to produce enhanced cooperation between agencies fail because cooperation is sought without attending to underlying power relations. For example, it is widely agreed that a program designed to produce coordination among manpower programs, the Cooperative Area Manpower Planning System, failed because it relied wholly upon the voluntary cooperation of participant organizations and provided for no change in the underlying political-economic forces which had previously kept the agencies apart.

Disruptive Strategies

The second major strategy involves the purposive conduct of activities which threaten the resource-generating capacities of a target agency. Such activities are undertaken in order to force change upon the target agency, including altered relations with other participants in its network or environment. Such tactics must effectively attack vital resource-maintaining functions in order to be successful. This can be accomplished in a number of ways, including (a) domain violations— the invasion of the target agency's domain by the conduct of programs falling clearly within its domain, (b) fund diversion—the acquisition of funds which might otherwise have gone to the target agency, and (c) program circumvention— activities which interfere with the program effectiveness of the target agency and thereby diminish its capacity to compete for funds and authority. Disruptive tactics are varied, but each involves a tendency to undermine the position of the target agency in its political economy and to use this as a means of producing change. Some brief examples follow:

In domain violation a community-controlled health center may perform medical services as a means of forcing change upon a nearby medical center. This is a mode of challenge advocated by many community organizers (Etzkowitz and Schoflander, 1969). In fund diversion an antipoverty agency may draw funds for manpower training from bureau sources previously reserved for established federal-state employment agencies (Randall, 1973). With program circumvention a welfare agency may flood a rehabilitation agency with referrals, thus causing high administrative costs and low success rates in the latter (Benson *et al.*, 1973).

Two conditions of the political economy appear to favor disruptive tactics: (1) a substantial power imbalance between agencies such that the more powerful agency can largely disregard nondisruptive requests and demands from the weaker one, and (2) a substantial fragmentation in resource channels such that one agency may sustain disruptive actions despite the objections and resistance of another even though the other is more powerful. In the first instance, disruptive strategies are chosen where normatively prescribed communications and pressures are not effective. In the second, breaks in the resource system and a certain disconnectedness are necessary if disruptive tactics are not to be quickly stifled by the countermoves of a powerful target agency.

The federal antipoverty program, with its autonomy from established bureaus and initial strong support from the President, provided a power base from which disruptive strategies were sustained for a time. For a limited period, community action agencies, although weaker than established federal and state agencies, were able to launch and maintain competitive manpower programs, challenging legal aid programs, and massive referral campaigns despite resistance from established agencies. Eventually, a political coalition emerged with sufficient power to curtail these efforts, but this was after significant innovations and new interagency linkages had been forced upon the target agencies (Donovan, 1967; Benson, 1971).

Manipulative Strategies

The third major type of strategy involves the purposeful alteration of environmental constraints affecting the flow of resources. Such action is undertaken as a means of producing change in interorganizational networks and in the program priorities and technological commitments of agencies. Rather, on the basis of specific assumptions about resource-seeking orientations or agencies, the conditions affecting resource acquisitions are altered. This type of strategy is analogous to governmental regulation of the economy through the manipulation of interest rates, tax rates, and money supply.

Manipulative strategies of particular importance in interagency relations include the alteration of the total volume of resources flowing into a network. Resource flow may be increased or decreased as a means of changing the probabilities of network events. By diminishing the flow of resources, one may squeeze out marginal programs and interagency linkages, that is, those known or assumed to have low priorities in the target network. Correlatively, by increasing the flow of resources, one may assure that such marginal programs and linkages will be maintained or expanded. The process is analogous to that governing minority employment in the United States economy—the last hired, first fired principle.

Another manipulative strategy is the alteration of resource channels. Resource flow may be diverted from existing channels and into new ones as a means of changing the priorities operative within a network. Such a strategy involves changing the fundamental connections between a network of agencies and the supportive sectors in its environment. Agencies in the network then become linked to new sources of funds and authority and thus responsive to the priorities, emphases, and commitments of such sources as organizations, bureaus, and publics. An example of such a tactic in recent events is provided by federal revenue sharing. The shift of funds from federal bureaus centered in Washington to state, county, and municipal governments will probably cause agencies in the manpower field to become more responsive to pressures emanating from the new sources. This will likely produce substantive changes in the conduct of programs and in the extent and type of interagency ties.

Manipulative strategies require a certain minimal degree of network autonomy or decentralization. Specific agencies in a network must be free to initiate, maintain, or terminate certain programs and interagency linkages. The manipulating agency or other social unit either foregoes direct and authoritative control over network events or lacks power to exercise control. Such a structural pattern is characteristic of federal-state intergovernmental relations in the United States.

Although such a tactic typically belongs to an executive office—a governor's or the President's—or a legislative body—state legislatures or the United States Congress, it may be employed by other participants in network-environment events. Publics may be mobilized to demand increased or decreased resources for a specific network. Welfare rights groups have demanded increased funds for welfare programs. Taxpayers' lobbies have pushed for decreases in budgets for government agencies. This suggests that events often develop out of the nexus of convergent and divergent strategies of multiple actors. Thus, an adequate understanding of strategies must include the bases of power and influence among network-relevant organizations, publics, and offices.

Authoritative Strategies

The fourth general type of strategy involves the authoritative alignment or realignment of network relations. In this case the relations between agencies are precisely specified by an authoritative participant such as an executive office or a legislative body. Precise specification of relations includes the regulation of contacts, referrals, resource sharing, and other details. It establishes positive and negative boundaries of the interagency relations, specifying what must and must not be done.

Authoritative strategies may stem from a wide variety of participant bodies. Government bureaus, legislatures, executive offices, judicial bodies, and publics may utilize authoritative strategies. The essential criterion delineating this type of strategy is the utilization of a dominant position in the flow of resources—money and authority—to specify the nature of programs and linkages at subordinate levels. These strategies are authoritative in the sense that the directing agent uses its power to mandate precise activities and not merely to encourage or reward those activities. This implies, too, that the directing agency is sufficiently powerful in relation to a network to permit a precise specification. An actor this powerful generally will have other options, such as to manipulate resource levels and channels. Only an eminently powerful actor, however, will have the capacity to specify activities precisely. Put otherwise, the option of choosing an authoritative strategy lies only with a particularly powerful participant, while other strategies may be selected by a variety of actors. Authoritative strategies may be quite varied.

Some prominent examples include the introduction of new programs and agencies. Power may be used to create new agencies or new programs in established agencies. Such new activities may have required, mandated connections to each other or to existing activities. For example, the WIN—Work Incentives—program was initiated in the late 1960s to reduce welfare rolls by getting welfare recipients into training programs leading to job placements. Employment security agencies and welfare agencies were required to cooperate in the WIN program and reciprocal obligations were precisely spelled out in law and bureau policies.

Another example is the formalization of relations. Power may be used to tighten up relations between agencies by precisely specifying linkages which have been previously left informal or variable. Mutual obligations and boundaries may be precisely set in such a process. Such a formalization process appears often to be a response at high levels to problems generated by crescively formed relations at lower levels. For example, aggressive community action agencies may develop informal relations with local employment security offices. These informal relations may be quite varied from one locality to another, thus producing administrative problems at state, regional, and national offices. Legislation or executive orders may then be instituted to regularize the relations and introduce some order in them.

A third example is the comprehensive reorganization of relations. Power may be used to rearrange an entire system of interagency boundaries and linkages. A network or a series of networks may develop gradually in response to distinct problems or needs. Periodically, this development may produce problems which can only be solved in a thoroughgoing reorganization. Interested parties may then seek to mobilize sufficient power to carry through such a comprehensive process. For example, in recent years a number of state legislatures have initiated government reorganization programs. Such programs appear often to be stimulated by a concern for cost-saving through reduction of duplication and through regrouping agencies to permit economies of scale, as in the case of sharing computers (Bell, 1972).

Authoritative strategies are available only under limited conditions. The initiating party must have sufficient power vis-à-vis the network in question to implement the change process even though some agencies resist. Few potential actors enjoy this kind of power across a varied collection of agencies and networks. Generally, the more complex the problem in terms of number of agencies and salience of issues, the smaller is the number of potential actors. For some interagency problems only the Congress or the President can potentially provide solutions. Further, the political forces playing upon the potential actors may be so complex and contradictory that comprehensive solutions are not feasible. Therefore, in an authoritative strategy, attention must be paid to the mobilization of political forces and the formation of an effective coalition.

Sequential Strategies

Interagency relations may develop through stages or sequences in which strategies change over time. It is likely that orderly patterns may be discovered in the succession or sequencing of strategies. For example, cooperative agreements between some agencies may be possible only after a period of disruptive contact through which one has gained bargaining power in relation to the other. Similar sequential ordering may characterize other strategies as well. It is therefore important that elongated event sequences be analyzed to discover patterns of strategy succession.

Combined Strategies

Another possibility to be explored is the combining of strategic options. At a given point in time agencies may be simultaneously pursuing two or more strategies. These may be analytically distinct strategies occurring simultaneously or inextricably confounded strategies. For example, an agency may attempt to negotiate an agreement while maintaining a competitive program for its bargaining value, thus combining disruptive and cooperative strategies.

Comparability of Networks

The scheme developed here might be extended to deal with a wider variety of interorganizational networks, including business organizations, by dealing with several issues. The first concerns the comparability of action orientations. To what extent are the action orientations of administrators similar across a variety of organizations? Some (Yuchtman and Seashore, 1967) have argued that in large-scale, modern organizations a concern with resource acquisition is pervasive. Such a concern is presumably manifest in both industrial and public organizations. This problem is extremely complex, however, since it involves a large set of issues regarding the coalescence of organizational structures in advanced industrial societies.

The second issue concerns the transferability of resources between networks. Are items of value in one network comparable to those in another? Factors which count as resources in one set of organizations may not be counted as such in another. The resources of concern to a public service agency may in some ways be noncomparable to those of value in a business or industry. For example, authority, a primary resource for public agencies, may have no equivalent in industry or business networks. Thus, concern about domains in the sense of grants of authority may be restricted to public organizations where a clear connection to the polity exists. To complicate matters further, it is a formidable task at present to find a calculus whereby equivalencies between different types of resources might be established. A business executive may be able to calculate at least roughly the financial return from capturing a specific market, but an agency administrator has less certain means of calculating the dollar value of a domain. Thus, the unification of the resource concept across different types of networks is not immediately feasible. It is possible that current trends toward government regulation of and protection for large-scale industrial enterprises may bring forth an era in which domains and markets, paradigms and technologies, and the like become more nearly comparable. As the public–private and administration–market disjunctions become eroded in the advanced industrial societies, a general theory of interorganizational networks may come into view.[5]

Conclusion

The interorganizational field has been viewed as a political economy. This formulation emphasizes the distinction between substructure and superstructure. At the level of substructure, differentially powerful organizations interact in pursuit of the scarce resources of money and authority. Power in these interactions is said to derive from sources: (1) network structures or patterns of direct linkage between agencies in a specific network—for example, control by network agency over contingencies vital to resource acquisition by another network agency, and (2) extranetwork structure or patterns of linkage between network agencies and organizations, officials, and publics in the network environment—for example, ties of an agency to important interest groups in the society.

Environmental forces and conditions have important effects upon network relations. The environment is said to be organized and certain dimensions of environment structure are important to network events. These dimensions include (1) resource concentration/dispersion, (2) power concentration/dispersion, (3) network autonomy/dependence, (4) environmental dominance patterns, (5) resource abundance/scarcity, and (6) environment-network control mechanisms.

Four general strategies for changing network relations were identified on the basis of the political economy view. These are (1) cooperative strategies in which change is sought through agreements and joint planning; (2) disruptive strategies in which resource-generating capacities of agencies are threatened; (3) manipulative strategies in which the supply of and sources of the resources money and authority are tactically altered; and (4) authoritative strategies in which network relations are precisely fixed by prescriptive action of resource controlling agencies, offices, or bodies.

Preliminary suggestions were offered regarding the conditions under which a particular strategy is likely to be selected and be effective. These suggestions generally concerned attributes of the network-environment power structure.

A superstructure of interagency sentiments and interactions was identified. Four analytical dimensions were specified at this level. These are: (1) domain consensus or agreement between agencies on the role and scope of each; (2) ideological consensus, agreement between agencies on the appropriate approaches to their common or similar tasks; (3) evaluation or the judgments between agencies of the quality of work of each; and (4) work coordination, referring to the conduct of joint, cooperative, or articulated activities and programs. These four dimensions form a system of interrelated variables which vary, together. The system tends toward balance in the sense that high levels on one dimension tend to be associated with high levels on others. A strain toward balance is assumed. Imbalance of the system is said to create a tension or strain toward consistency. A network, however, may become balanced at varying levels. Thus, while an equilibrated system consisting of high levels on all four dimensions may be preferred or normatively prescribed, no tendency toward equilibrium is assumed.

Each of the four dimensions of interorganizational equilibrium is grounded in conditions of the political economy. The alignment of political-economic forces places limits upon the range of potential variation of the equilibrium components. This suggests that network relations may become stabilized in nonequilibrated conditions because of the effects of political-economic forces. It also suggests that change agents who attempt to alter the superstructure of sentiments and interactions without attending to underlying political-economic conditions can be successful only within a restricted range.

The principal strength of this perspective is that it establishes a genuinely interorganizational level of analysis. The analytical focus is upon the characteristics of interagency networks and their environments. The unitary organization appears in the scheme as an actor with variable strategic options but not as the focus of attention. The phenomena to be explained are interorganizational linkages, not intraorganizational structures or behaviors. Further, explanatory variables are sought in the structure of networks and network-environment linkages. Beyond this, the proposed perspective links the analysis of interorganizational phenomena to features of societal macrostructure.

A secondary advantage of the theoretical perspective is that it provides some order to the diverse inquiries which have come to be identified with interorganizational analysis. The scheme accords a place to those studies which have been concerned principally with sentiments and cooperative interactions. It puts those concerns in a larger theoretical context. In addition, it accords an important place to those studies which have focused on fundamental issues of power and resources. Further, it provides a way of bringing these several modes of analysis together within a single framework which suggests directions for further theoretical integration.

Notes

1. An organization has an internal polity or political economy. Decision makers are those in positions of dominance within the organization (Zald, 1970; Wamsley and Zald, 1973a, 1973b).

2. The similarity of this argument to theories of intraorganizational power emphasizing control over uncertainty should be acknowledged (Crozier, 1964, 1972, 1973a, 1973b; Woodward, 1970; Lawrence and Lorsch, 1969; Hickson *et al.*, 1971.) Wamsley and Zald (1973a, 1973b) recently applied the concept to interorganizational power.
3. The formulation of the balance hypothesis is similar to the Homans (1950), Myrdal (1944), and Buckley (1967) formulations of systems theory.
4. The analytic problem posed here is similar to that addressed by Emery and Trist (1965) and Terreberry (1968) in dealing with the emergence of turbulent and disturbed reactive environments. In formulating these dimensions, the author acknowledges the influence of Aldrich (1972), although the present formulation departs from Aldrich's in some significant ways.
5. For divergent discussions of the trend, see Crozier (1973a, 1973b), Galbraith (1967), and Habermas (1970).

References

Aldrich, Howard, 1971, "Organizational boundaries and inter-organizational conflict." *Human Relations*, 24: 279–293.

———— 1972, "An organization-environment perspective on cooperation and conflict between organizations in the manpower training system." In A. Negandhi (ed.), *Conflict and Power in Complex Organizations*: 11–37. Kent, Ohio: Center for Business and Economic Research, Kent State University.

Bell, George A., 1972, *Reorganization in the States*. Lexington, Ky.: The Council of State Government.

Benson, J. Kenneth, 1971, "Militant ideologies and organizational contexts: the war on poverty and the ideology of 'black power'." *The Sociological Quarterly* 12: 328–339.

Benson, J. Kenneth, Joseph T. Kunce, Charles A. Thompson, and David L. Allen, 1973, *Coordinating Human Services, A Sociological Study of an Interorganizational Network*. Columbia, Mo.: Regional Rehabilitation Research Institute, Monograph Series No. 6.

Braito, Rita, Steve Paulson, and Gerald Klonglan, 1972, "Domain consensus: a key variable in interorganizational analysis." In Merlin B. Brinkerhoff and Phillip R. Kunz (eds.), *Complex Organizations and Their Environments*: 176–192. Dubuque, Ia.: Brown.

Buckley, Walter, 1967, *Sociology and Modern Systems Theory*. Englewood Cliffs, N.J.: Prentice-Hall.

Crozier, Michel, 1964, *The Bureaucratic Phenomenon*. Chicago: University of Chicago Press.

———— 1972, "The relationship between micro and macrosociology, a study of organizational systems as an empirical approach to problems of macrosociology." *Human Relations*, 25: 239–251.

———— 1973a, "The problem of power." *Social Research*, 40: 211–228.

———— 1973b, *The Stalled Society*. New York: Viking Press.

Donovan, John C., 1967, *The Politics of Poverty*. New York: Pegasus.

Downs, Anthony, 1967, *Inside Bureaucracy*. Boston: Little, Brown.

Emery, F. E., and E. L. Trist, 1965, "The causal texture of organizational environments." *Human Relations*, 18: 21–31.

Etzkowitz, Henry, and Gerald M. Schoflander, 1969, *Ghetto Crisis, Riots or Reconciliation?* Boston: Little, Brown.

Evan, William, 1966, "The organization set: toward a theory of interorganizational relations." In James D. Thompson (ed.), *Approaches to Organizational Design*: 173–191. Pittsburgh: University of Pittsburgh Press.

Galbraith, John Kenneth, 1967, *The New Industrial State*. Boston: Houghton Mifflin.

———— 1973, "Power and the useful economist." *The American Economic Review*, 63: 1–11.

Habermas, Jürgen, 1970, *Toward a Rational Society: Student Protest, Science, and Politics.* Translated by Jeremy Shapiro. Boston: Beacon Press.

Hickson, D. J., C. R. Hinings, C. A. Lee, R. E. Schneck, and J. M. Pennings, 1971, "A strategic contingencies theory of intraorganizational power," *Administrative Science Quarterly,* 6: 216–229.

Hollister, C. David, 1970, "Inter-organizational conflict: the case of police and youth bureaus and the juvenile court." Paper presented at the 65th Annual Meeting of the American Sociological Association, Washington, D.C.

Homans, George C., 1950, *The Human Group.* New York: Harcourt, Brace, and World.

Lawrence, Paul R., and Jay W. Lorsch, 1969, *Organization and Environment.* Homewood, Ill.: Irwin.

Levine, Sol, and Paul E. White, 1961, "Exchange as a conceptual framework for the study of interorganizational relationships." *Administrative Science Quarterly,* 5: 583–601.

Levitan, Sar, and Garth L. Mangum, 1969, *Federal Training and Work Programs in the Sixties.* Ann Arbor, Mich.: The University of Michigan, Institute of Labor and Industrial Relations.

Litwak, Eugene, and Lydia F. Hylton, 1962, "Interorganizational analysis: a hypothesis on coordinating agencies." *Administrative Science Quarterly,* 6: 395–426.

Marrett, Cora Bagley, 1971, "On the specification of interorganizational dimensions." *Sociology and Social Research,* 56: 83–99.

Miller, Walter B., 1958, "Inter-institutional conflict as a major impediment to delinquency prevention." *Human Organization,* 17: 20–23.

Myrdal, Gunnar, 1944, *An American Dilemma.* New York: Harper and Row.

Randall, Ronald, 1973, "Influence of environmental support and policy space on organizational behavior." *Administrative Science Quarterly,* 18: 236–247.

Terreberry, Shirley, 1968, "The evolution of organizational environments." *Administrative Science Quarterly,* 12: 590–613.

Thompson, James D., 1967, *Organizations in Action.* New York: McGraw-Hill.

Turk, Herman, 1970, "Interorganizational networks in urban society: initial perspective and comparative research." *American Sociological Review,* 35: 1–19.

———— 1973a, "Comparative urban structure from an interorganizational perspective." *Administrative Science Quarterly,* 18: 37–55.

———— 1973b, *Interorganizational Activation in Urban Communities.* Washington: American Sociological Association.

Wamsley, Gary, and Mayer N. Zald, 1973a, "The political economy of public organizations." *Public Administration Review,* 33: 62–73.

———— 1973b, *The Political Economy of Public Organizations.* New York: Praeger.

Warren, Roland L., 1967, "The interorganizational field as a focus for investigation." *Administrative Science Quarterly,* 12: 397–419.

Woodward, Joan (ed.), 1970, *Industrial Organization: Behavior and Control.* London: Oxford University Press.

Yuchtman, Ephraim, and Stanley E. Seashore, 1967, "A system resource approach to organizational effectiveness." *American Sociological Review,* 32: 891–903.

Zald, Mayer N., 1970, "Political economy: a framework for comparative analysis." In Mayer N. Zald (ed.), *Power in Organizations:* 221–261. Nashville, Tenn.: Vanderbilt University Press.

A Paradigm for the Analysis of Interorganizational Relations

Edward W. Lehman

As we see it, existing interorganizational models suffer from one of two deficiencies. Some writers tend to employ an implicit utilitarian-pluralist perspective that leads them (a) to view the adaptation of organizations to one another largely in terms of the needs and self-interests of *individual* organizations; and hence, (b) mostly to be concerned with explaining the performances of the single organizations rather than of the total network of which these units are a part.[1]

Other writers have become more aware of the interorganizational field as an emergent entity. This new understanding is stimulated in part by increased interest in how interdependent units make joint policy, as well as by concern over how such decisions can be made most effectively. However, these recent efforts are somewhat oversimplified because many have offered models of interorganizational relations that are built on the degree of conformity to or departure from some intraorganizational, rationalistic prototype (either bureaucratic or management science in nature).[2] In the course of our discussion, we suggest that other models, based in part on analogies to the development of national and international political communities, at times may be more fruitful.[3] The principal advantage of these "political" analyses is that they focus on the state of a multimember field in its own right while not committing themselves to the imagery of bureaucratic control. In other words, the overall adaptation of a system (and not just of one member) is studied, but centralized, hierarchic control is viewed as just one of several modes of potentially successful coordination.

Configuration and Content of Relations

Social relationships—whether microscopic (that is, among individual actors) or macroscopic (that is, among collectivities)—can be analyzed along at least five analytically distinct dimensions which, to some degree, vary independently of each other; the first deals with the configuration of the relationship and the latter four with its content. In a sense, configuration is the form of a relationship and content refers to its substance. In the present study, the concept of configuration points to the sociometric map of interorganizational control. We use the concept of content of interorganizational relations primarily to focus on the kinds of resources involved in the transactions among health care units. However, we also talk about how germane particular transactions are for health care systems (that is, their salience), whether transactions are all in one direction or whether there is some degree of reciprocity (that is, their symmetry), and whether transactions involve one, few, or many different kinds of resources (that is, their scope).

Reprinted from *Coordinating Health Care: Explorations in Interorganizational Relations*, Sage Library of Social Research, vol. 17, by Edward W. Lehman, © 1975, pp. 24–40, by permission of the Publisher, Sage Publications, Inc. (Beverly Hills/London).

Because we focus on a multiplicity of dimensions and not just one, our efforts are more than typologic; they represent a preliminary attempt at a paradigm for interorganizational relations.

A Typology of Interorganizational Configurations

The paradigm's central elements are *control configurations* that characterize different interorganizational fields. The special focus on control seems appropriate because of our concern with how pluralities of organizations coordinate their activities. We suggest that the success of coordination is explained in large part by the efficacy of control. Hence, we first offer a value-added typology of interorganizational control configurations. It is value-added because: (1) the configurations listed first are more "simple" and reflect less conscious control of an interorganizational field, while subsequent ones are progressively more "complex" and contain more deliberate patterns of control; and (2) each succeeding pattern contains all of the elements of the preceding ones plus at least one "added" factor. Thus, the value-added approach differs radically from the "property-space" strategy more commonly employed in sociology (although neither probably is so frequently used as are ad hoc typologies). In the property-space approach, each type is analytically "air tight" and differs from every other type in terms of two or more logically distinct attributes. On the other hand, what is especially important about a value-added typology is that all the values of a preceding type are present in a subsequent one; that is, nothing from a preceding level is lost but something "new" is added on. (The most extensive use of the value-added approach has been made by Smelser, 1963.)

We suggest that, theoretically, there are three broad patterns of control configurations and that the list is logically *exhaustive*. The three categories are: (1) a field of laterally linked organizations; (2) mediated interorganizational relations; and (3) guided interorganizational relations. In turn, our typology is cross-cut by three dimensions: (1) the degree to which interorganizational contacts entail procedures simply to inform or to consult one another versus the degree to which such contacts entail arrangements for actual co-decision-making about the future state of the field; (2) the degree to which the resources necessary for the wielding of systemic power (that is, for deciding upon joint goals, for pursuing them, and for implementing them) remain in the hands of the member organizations; and (3) the extent to which the responsibility for wielding systemic power is attributed to the individual member organizations versus the extent to which it is centered in an agency acting in the name of the entire field. (On the concept of systemic power, see Lehman, 1969).

A Laterally Linked Field: Interorganizational Feudalism

We here suggest an analogy between the most simple forms of interorganizational configurations, on the one hand, and the feudal societies of medieval Europe, as well as some aspects of contemporary international relations, on the other hand. For present purposes, European feudal societies may be characterized as macroscopic social systems. In these systems, the foci of identification and integration for member units (for example, fiefs, baronies, duchies, and so on) were largely internal rather than directed toward some center of systemic power.

Furthermore, such systems lacked a strong controlling overlayer (for example, a Napoleonic state) that could exercise effective systemic power in either the market or political sector. Even where there was some collectivity-orientation, both the responsibility for wielding systemic power and the control of the requisite resources tended to be localized largely in the member units themselves. In any event, joint decision-making was only intermittent, and interaction consisted mainly of informing or consulting one another. (The classic characterization of feudalism is to be found in Bloch, 1931.)

Similarly, just because the U.S.S.R. and the United States today have become part of an interdependent international field (for example, "global system"), one cannot assume that these nation-states cooperate in regular, effective joint decision-making, or that they have surrendered significant portions of their claims to and resources for wielding systemic power to some supra-agency. To the extent to which these two nations are not in conflict, their cooperation consists mainly of sending one another sufficiently clear signals about their own interests and intentions to prevent nuclear confrontation. Even proposed programs for further cooperation appear to be mainly along these lines. These programs suggest activities such as increasing international exchange (that is, in economic trade, tourism, cultural exchanges) or "defusing" the Cold War, which also often represents a form of exchange insofar as the transactions frequently proposed are devices such as mutual deescalation of the arms race.

There is more than a superficial similarity between these two cases and configurations found in some interorganizational fields. The simplest form of interorganizational control configuration resembles medieval feudalism and U.S.–Soviet relations because: (1) the activities of the member units are more heavily oriented to mutual information and consultation than to joint decision-making; (2) the member units retain control of the field's strategic resources; and (3) the responsibility for wielding systemic power is dispersed among the administrative centers of the member organizations. Obviously, there is considerable internal variation within this category of configuration. The degree to which contacts among organizations are intermittent or sustained and the varying quality of interaction (that is, the kind of resources involved, the salience, the direction of the flow, the scope) are two possible ways to discriminate among different types of interorganizational feudalism. However, from a policy-research perspective, how often units merely inform and consult one another versus the degree to which they also co-decide is probably the most important aspect of internal variation. Nonetheless, because our model is value-added, the issue is not simply one of informing and consulting versus co-deciding, but rather, informing and consulting plus progressively more intensive modes of co-deciding; that is, units that set and pursue common goals and cooperate in this pursuit and implementation inform and consult one another by definition. On the other hand, if we accept the proposition put forward by some authors that supramembership goal-setting, pursuit, and implementation are more effective and efficient than most comparable intermember mechanisms, then we would expect the range of co-decision-making in a feudalistic field to remain quite restricted because key resources are bound to member organizations and specialized centers of systemic power are absent (see Etzioni, 1968; Gamson, 1968; and Lehman, 1969). Thus, in contrast to the subsequent rungs in the model, we anticipate that interorganizational feudalism would involve more informing and consulting and less intense co-deciding.

Mediated Interorganizational Configurations: A "Coordinated" Field

The next rung in our typology involves a situation in which formal units exist to coordinate the articulation of several organizations. A useful analogy here is between such an interorganizational field and the role played by the international inspection teams set up under the Korean armistice and the 1954 Geneva agreements on Vietnam. The proposed function of neutral on-site inspectors in the U.S.S.R.–U.S. disarmament arrangements also fits into this analogy. In all of these actual or proposed international procedures, a coordinating unit (for example, inspectors) exists to facilitate the agreements and the transfer of information between nation-states. However, such units are fundamentally of a "service" character. Insofar as co-decision-making occurs, the requisite centers of control are still localized in the participating nation-state. The service units do not guide relations; at best, they "coordinate" them.

An interorganizational field with a mediated configuration consists of a plurality of organizations, each unit of which has its own set of goals and collaborates periodically with the others. Collaboration among the organizations is facilitated by an agency that funnels resources, communications, and services. Harrison's study of the American Baptist Convention indicates that it was first organized strictly for such a mediating role; key resources and controls were initially in the hands of local congregations. Only gradually did the central administrative structure acquire a relatively independent resource-base, greater control over intracongregational activities, and a capacity to set denominationwide policy. Hence, Harrison presents us with an illuminating picture of how a mediated configuration evolved out of a more feudalistic one and how, in turn, pressures arose that transformed it into a guided configuration (see Harrison, 1959).

In sum, the mediated configuration adds two factors not found on the feudalistic level. First and foremost, it introduces a new type of unit, which is not present in the simple feudal field. However, this unit provides coordination and services to the other units in the field rather than guidance. Second, the ratio of purely informing and consulting activities to co-deciding activities is likely to be more greatly weighted toward the latter than in a feudal context. Nonetheless, in light of the aforementioned hypothesis about supramembership control and effective wielding of systemic power, we suggest that co-decision-making in a mediated field is still largely on an ad hoc basis and most of the operative goals are simply those of each participating organization.

Guided Interorganizational Configurations: Empires and Corporations

The final rung on our typology is reserved for guided configurations. These patterns are specifically concerned with co-decision-making and they presume that control is exercised by an agency acting for or on the system as a whole. We distinguish between two main subtypes of guided configurations based on whether the agency is a "member-elite", that is, one of the units participating in the interorganizational field, or a "system-elite," that is, an administrative unit to some degree external to the field. We label these patterns "empires" and "corporations" respectively.

The similarity is striking between an interorganizational field dominated by a member-elite unit and those political systems often referred to as empires. Empires tend to be characterized by at least one core "metropolitan" unit (for example, Britain) that is strongly identified with the entire system, both by itself and in the opinion of others (for example, the Roman Empire, the British Empire). Etzioni (1965: 79) characterizes such political systems in the following way:

> There was a mixture of exploitation and responsibility in the orientation of the core country of empires to those subordinated to it; the orientation of bloc "superpowers" to other bloc members tends to be governed primarily by expediency. The core countries used to view the empire as an extension of their own politics; they often attempted to assimilate the subordinate units into the core country. . . . The modern bloc superpower, on the other hand, views the bloc as a limited partnership with outsiders. (The Soviet system comes closer to an empire than a bloc from this viewpoint.) At least some local elites in the subordinate countries responded by identifying with the empire, a phenomenon less intensively reproduced in the attitudes of members of blocs to the superpowers.

While the major thrust of this quotation is to distinguish empires from mere blocs in the field of international relations, the more crucial distinction for the interorganizational analyst is between "empires," that is, systems guided by member-elites, and cases of simple feudalism. Because supramembership identifications, normative bonds, and comprehensive control tend to be weaker among organizations than among countries, what we call interorganizational "empires" in actuality probably fall somewhere between Etzioni's categories of empires and blocs. Although it may be useful to place different guided configurations along such a continuum (that is, empire versus bloc), we suggest that it is more important to distinguish member-elite guidance from ordinary lateral linkages. A close examination of many situations apparently composed merely of laterally linked, autonomous units may reveal that one of the members controls the "lion's share" of resources and frequently is attributed the right to act in the name of the system as a whole. To treat such configurations as cases of interorganizational feudalism would be as misleading as regarding the relationship of the Soviet Union and Czechoslovakia as if both had equal leverage in the system they form.

Member-elite units represent one vehicle through which guidance may be exercised over an interorganizational field. The major alternative to this arrangement occurs when guidance is offered by a superordinate administrative agency that makes policy for some set of organizations in a given field, that is, a system-elite. A good intersocietal analogue of this corporate configuration is the case of the European Economic Community (E.C.C.)—the Common Market. This enterprise began as a supranational organization intended to make policy about coal and steel output by the six Western European member-countries. Although the guidance it originally exercised was highly limited in scope, especially when viewed within the context of the totality of interaction among these states, this zone has gradually grown to encompass more and more of the shared economic life of the societies involved, and has even begun to spill over into the political sector.

Municipal health departments probably represent one interorganizational analogue of the Common Market. Thus, participating health and welfare units are all subject to policies and programs formulated within some administrative overlayer. However, this example can be misleading, because city health departments tend to make rather inclusive decisions and exercise some form of final authority over the member units. Comparison to the Common Market sensitizes us to the fact that among corporate configurations, both the scope of the joint decisions and the degree of social control that the administrative overlayer is able to exert over participating organizations may vary markedly. The previously mentioned case of the American Baptist Convention is possibly more representative of corporately guided interorganizational bonds. Here, although there is a systemic power over-layer, the latter's decision-making capabilities are far from comprehensive, and member congregations still retain considerable autonomy compared, let us say, to the Catholic Church.

The Content of Interorganizational Relations

The four other dimensions of our prospective paradigm focus on the content (as opposed to the configuration or form) of interorganizational relations. We begin here by asking about the substance of the transactions occurring in the field, that is, what are resources that provide the basis for articulation? It should be obvious that efforts to characterize resources in terms of some set of meaningful sociologi-cal categories can take a variety of alternative directions. For instance one can classify resources by what kinds of social relationships they are likely to promote (for example, whether they are normative, utilitarian, or coercive), or which of society's functional problems they most help to solve (for example, whether the resources are geared primarily toward adaptation, goal-attainment, integration, or pattern-maintenance). On the other hand, we find it particularly useful to examine resources in terms of their primary significance for the organizations that utilize them.

In all organizations, resources may be classified as being either relevant primarily for the implementation of the organization's goals, or dealing with some necessary but ancillary (that is, non-goal) problems the organization faces. It is clear that this is a *relative* classification of resources. That is, a resource that is primarily goal-relevant in one setting may have ancillary significance in another, or vice versa. For example, the presence of an x-ray machine in a hospital contributes to that unit's ability to deal successfully with its treatment goals, whereas the same machine in the New York Telephone Company's medical office is oriented toward an ancillary need of the Bell System.

In a heterogeneous interorganizational field, the goal relevance of particular resources possibly may vary markedly from organization to organization. Thus, in the articulation between a hospital and a professional linen service, sheets, pillow cases, lab coats, and so on are ancillary resources for the former and goal-relevant resources for the latter. Fortunately for us, this problem is not so acute, because our focus is primarily on the networks created among health care units as we have narrowly defined them. Therefore, because of the homogeneity of the kind of fields we are looking at, a goal-relevant resource and an ancillary one, for the most part, retain the same labels from one organization to the next throughout the study. We began our investigations with the following provisional cataloguing of major resources in the health field.

1. Goal-relevant resources:
    a. health-relevant facilities and equipment
    b. professional, semiprofessional, and technical staff
    c. "consumers," (that is, clients, patients, and so on)
    d. medical and diagnostic communications, information, advice, ideas, and so on.

2. Ancillary resources:
   a. facilities and equipment of an administrative or service sort
   b. administrative and all other nonprofessional pesonnel
   c. administrative communications, information, advice, ideas, and so on
   d. standardized procedures (that is, two or more units agree to use compatible administrative routines)

This initial classification of resources, for the most part, proved to be a useful mode of categorizing the substance of interorganizational relations. Nonetheless, without further supplementation, a simple enumeration of the kinds and frequencies of resources yields at best a highly partial picture of the content of interorganizational relations. To begin with, one also would like to know how intensive the transactions are; that is, how many *different* kinds of resources are employed in the joint activities of particular organizations. This aspect of content we label the "scope" of interorganizational relations. In fields whose scope is narrow, participating organizations transact only a limited amount of joint business, depending on one or a few types of resources. Organizations in fields whose scope is broad share or exchange several kinds of activities that involve a plurality of resource-types.

However, two different interorganizational fields may share roughly an equal number of activities and still differ considerably in the nature of their transactions. Hence, the examination of the content of interorganizational relations profits not only from an understanding of the types of resources involved and the scope of relationships, but also from a grasp of the *salience* of the transactions for the overall system. For example, health care units that share only a joint billing procedure and common laundry obviously have different interactions from those that share an E.E.G. technician as well as radiotherapy equipment but nothing else. A major difficulty is how one best judges and compares the salience of particular transactions for the state of a system. The issue would be infinitely more complicated if the participating units were highly heterogeneous and had markedly divergent goals. However, by restricting ourselves to fields made up of health care units, this problem can be largely bracketed in the present study. Because goal activities and ancillary activities are roughly the same from organization to organization in our study, we can safely assume that the exchange involving only the former is more salient than the exchange of only the latter. Thus, in the preceding example, the sharing of the E.E.G. technician and the radiotherapy equipment is presumed to be a more salient interaction, although formally no broader in scope, because it deals with goal-activities, while joint billing procedures and a common laundry have to do with ancillary tasks.

The question of salience comes close to the one about the types of resources involved. However, by treating the issues as analytically distinct, we remind ourselves that the relevance a transaction may have for some state of a multiorganizational field may be different from its significance for the goal attainment of any particular organization.

We of course recognize that there may be significant variation in salience within both goal-relevant and ancillary activities. We begin our investigations assuming that, all other things being equal: (1) the sharing or exchange of treatment facilities and equipment as well as of professional, semiprofessional, and technical personnel is more salient for a field than the referrals of patients or clients and the sharing and exchange of medical communications, and so on; and (2) the sharing or exchange of administrative equipment and personnel and all other nonprofessional personnel is more salient than the sharing or exchange of administrative communications, and so on, as well as the use of standardized routines.

Finally, a fuller appreciation of the content of interorganizational relations benefits from an understanding of what resources flow in which directions in the interactions; that is, the *symmetry* of transactions. From what sociologists know about exchange, dependence, and power, it seems important to determine not only what kinds and how many resources the units are sharing or exchanging, but also whether one organization is exclusively a supplier and another a recipient or whether there is, in fact, some authentic reciprocity inherent in the relationship; and if the latter is the case, what is the precise ratio of that reciprocity. (see Blau, 1964 and Emerson, 1962). For one thing, such knowledge would appear to be indispensable for ascertaining whether or not there was a member-elite unit in a field whose systemic power situation previously may have been obscure.

Summary: Some Ingredients of a Paradigm for the Study of Lateral Interorganizational Bonds

The purpose of this study is to explore the types of relationships that have developed among health care units in the United States. In the process of this examination, we wish to better understand what makes some interorganizational fields flourish and others founder. The foregoing discussion focused on the several dimensions that we feel illuminate such an analysis. These dimensions may be treated as a provisional paradigm for the study of interorganizational relations. The paradigm is provisional in the sense that no paradigm is ever complete because additional theoretical and empirical work inevitably offers new or revised dimensions. Also, the paradigm is partial to the degree that it concerns basically lateral bonds and is intended neither for the study of primarily hierarchical relationships among organizations nor their stratification. With these limitations in mind, let us briefly review the dimensions of our paradigm:

1. The Basic Ingredient of Interorganizational Relations
   a. Control configurations
   b. Content
      1. resource-types
      2. scope
      3. salience
      4. symmetry
2. The Fundamental Issues of a Typology of Control Configurations
   a. The topic(s) of control
      1. only informing and consulting
      2. informing and consulting plus varying degrees of co-deciding
   b. The locus of the requisite resources for wielding systemic power
      1. dispersed among the member organizations
      2. in the hands of some elite unit
   c. The locus of responsibility for exercising systemic power
      1. in the hands of the member organizations
      2. in the hands of a supramembership agency
3. A Value-Added Typology of Control Configurations
   a. A laterally linked multiorganizational field: interorganizational feudalism
   b. A mediated interorganizational field

    c. A guided interorganizational field
      1. guidance by a member-elite: "empires"
      2. guidance by a system-elite: "corporations"
4. Types of Resources
    a. Basic Query: What is the most fruitful way to classify resources involved in interorganizational processes?
    b. A Suggestion: Classification of resources on the basis of the type of organizational activities they contribute to:
      1. goal-relevant resources
      2. resources focused on ancillary activities
    c. Major Difficulty: How applicable is such a classification in studies of highly heterogeneous interorganizational fields (that is, where there is a low correlation between what is a "goal-relevant" activity from organization to organization)?
5. The Scope of Interorganizational Relations: How many different kinds of resources are involved?
    a. Narrow scope—interorganizational fields in which transactions are limited to one or a few types of resources
    b. Broad scope—interorganizational fields in which transactions entail several types of resources
6. The Salience of Interorganizational Relations: How germane is (are) the resource(s) being shared or exchanged for the state of the interorganizational field?
    a. Basic Query: What is the most fruitful way to talk about salience of resources?
    b. A Suggestion: Classify salience in the same way as resources in general:
      1. most salient—goal-relevant resources
      2. least salient—resources focused on ancillary activities
    c. Major Problems:
      1. applicability to heterogeneous interorganizational fields (as in 4c above)
      2. how can we deal in some consistent way with the fact that neither all goal activities nor all ancillary activities are equally salient?
7. The Symmetry of Interorganizational Relations: In which direction(s) do resources "flow" among organizations?
    a. The degree of symmetry in the sharing or exchange of resources may be classified by the extent to which it is either:
      1. one way, or
      2. reciprocal
    b. Basic Query: What is the relationship between symmetry, power, and dependence in a given interorganizational field?

As in all paradigms, the ultimate test of the fruitfulness of ours is in the questions it helps to raise and to order in some theoretically meaningful way. In the last analysis, of course, "fruitfulness" is not enough. A paradigm should offer alternative answers to the questions it has raised. It is only through empirical research that the validity of the alternative answers can be assessed. Hence, although a paradigm is not an hypothesis, a proposition, or a theory, it too must face the scrutiny of empirical data. There is the implicit assumption in every paradigm that questions must be answered and not just posed . . . .

Notes

1. See especially Blau and Scott (1962: chps. 3 and 8); Caplow (1964: 201–228); Clark (1956: 327–336); Cyert and March (1963: 4–6, 11); Elling and Halebsky (1961: 185–209); Emery and Trist (1965: 21–32); Evan (1966: 173–191); Levine and White (1961: 583–601); Levine, White, and Paul (1963: 1183–1195); Litwak and Hylton (1962: 395–420); March

and Simon (1958: 131–135); Perrow (1961: 335–341); Reid (1970: 84–101); Simpson and Gully (1962: 344–351); Terreberry (1968: 590–613); Thompson (1962: 309–326; 1967); Thompson and McEwen (1958: 23–31).
2. See Dill (1962: 131–161); Guetzkow (1966: 13–44); Litwak (1969); Marrett (1971: 83–99); Mott (1968; 1970: 55–69); Starkweather (1970: 4–44); Thompson (1970: 156–167); Turk (1970: 1–19); and Warren (1967: 396–419; 1970: 114–129). The works of Litwak and Warren represent the most significant advances here.
3. Our work is especially influenced by Etzioni (1965). See also Deutsch et al. (1957); Haas (1958); and Rosenau (1969: 44–63).

References

Blau, P. M. (1964) Exchange and Power in Social Life. New York: John Wiley.
————— and W. R. Scott (1962) Formal Organizations. San Francisco: Chandler.
Bloch, M. (1931) "Feudalism, European," pp; 203–210 in vol. 6 of Encyclopedia of Social Sciences. New York: Macmillan.
Caplow, T. (1964) Principles of Organization. New York: Harcourt, Brace & World.
Clark, B. R. (1956) "Organizational adaptation and precarious values." Amer. Soc. Rev. 21 (June): 327–336.
Cyert, R. M. and J. G. March (1963) A Behavioral Theory of the Firm. Englewood Cliffs, N.J.: Prentice-Hall.
Deutsch, K. et al. (1957) Political Community and the North Atlantic Area. Princeton, N.J.: Princeton Univ. Press.
Dill, W. R. (1962) "The impact of environment on organizational development," pp. 131–161 in Sydney Mailick and E. H. Ness (eds.) Concepts and Issues in Administrative Behavior. Englewood Cliffs, N.J.: Prentice-Hall.
Elling, R. H. and S. Halebsky (1961) "Organizational differentiation and support: a conceptual framework." Admin. Sc. Q. 6 (September): 185–209.
Emerson, R. M. (1962) "Power-dependence relations." Amer. Soc. Rev. 27 (February): 31–40.
Emery, F. E. and E. L. Trist (1965) "The causal texture of organizational environments." Human Relations 18 (February): 21–32.
Etzioni, A. (1965) Political Unification. New York: Holt, Rinehart and Winston.
————— (1968) The Active Society. New York: Free Press.
Evan, W. M. (1966) "Organization-set: toward a theory of interorganizational relations," pp. 173–191 in James D. Thompson (ed.) Approaches to Organizational Design. Pittsburgh: Univ. of Pittsburgh Press.
Gamson, W. A. (1968) Power and Discontent. Homewood, Ill.: Dorsey.
Guetzkow, H. (1966) "Relations among organizations," pp. 13–44 in Raymond V. Bowers (ed.) Studies on Behavior in Organizations. Athens: Univ. of Georgia Press.
Haas, E. B. (1958) The Uniting of Europe. Stanford, Calif.: Stanford Univ. Press.
Harrison, P. M. (1959) Authority and Power in the Free Church Tradition. Princeton, N.J.: Princeton Univ. Press.
Lehman, E. W. (1969) "Toward a macrosociology of power." Amer. Soc. Rev. 34 (August): 453–465.
Levine, S. and P. E. White (1961) "Exchange as a conceptual framework for the study of interorganizational relationships." Admin. Sci. Q. 5 (March): 583–601.
————— and B. D. Paul (1963) "Community interorganizational problems in providing medical care and social services." Amer. J. of Public Health 53 (August): 1183–1195.
Litwak, E. (1969) "Toward the theory of coordination between formal organizations." Unpublished paper. Ann Arbor: Univ. of Michigan School of Social Work.
————— and L. F. Hylton (1962) "Interorganizational analysis: a hypothesis on coordinating agencies." Admin. Sci. Q. 6 (March: 395–420.

March, J. G. and H. A. Simon (1958) Organizations. New York: John Wiley.

Marrett, C. B. (1971) "On the specification of interorganizational dimensions." Sociology and Social Research 56 (October): 83–99.

Mott, B. (1968) Anatomy of a Coordinating Council. Pittsburgh: Univ. of Pittsburgh Press.

——— (1970) "Coordination and inter-organizational relations in health," pp. 55–69 in U.S. Department of Health, Education and Welfare, Public Health Service, Health Services and Mental Health Administration, Inter-Organizational Research in Health: Conference Proceedings. Washington, D.C.: U.S. Government Printing Office.

Perrow, C. (1961) "Organizational prestige: some functions and dysfunctions." Amer. J. of Sociology 66 (January): 335–341.

Reid, W. J. (1970) "Inter-organizational cooperation: a review and critique of current theory," pp. 84–101 in U.S. Department of Health, Education and Welfare, Public Health Service, Health Services and Mental Health Administration, Inter-Organizational Research in Health: Conference Proceedings. Washington, D.C.: U.S. Government Printing Office.

Rosenau, J. N. (1969) "Toward the study of national-international linkages," pp. 44–63 in James N. Rosenau (ed.) Linkage Politics: Essays on the Convergence of National and International Systems. New York: Free Press.

Simpson, R. L. and W. H. Gully (1962) "Goals, environmental pressures, and organizational characteristics." Amer. Soc. Rev. 27 (June): 344–351.

Smelser, N. S. (1963) Theory of Collective Behavior. New York: Free Press.

Starkweather, D. B. (1970) "Health facility merger and integration: a typology and some hypotheses," pp. 4–44 in U.S. Department of Health, Education and Welfare, Public Health Service, Health Services and Mental Health Administration, Inter-Organizational Research in Health: Conference Proceedings. Washington, D.C.: U.S. Government Printing Office.

Terreberry, S. (1968) "The evolution of organizational environment." Admin. Sci. Q. 12 (March): 590–613.

Thompson, J. D. (1962) "Organizations and output transactions." Amer. J. of Sociology 68 (November): 309–326.

——— (1967) Organizations in Action. New York: McGraw-Hill.

——— (1970) "Thoughts on inter-organizational relations: a conclusion," pp. 156–167 in U.S. Department of Health, Education and Welfare, Public Health Service, Health Services and Mental Health Administration, Inter-Organizational Research in Health: Conference Proceedings. Washington, D.C.: U.S. Government Printing Office.

——— and W. J. McEwen (1958) "Organizational goals and environment: goal-setting as an interaction process." Amer. Soc. Rev. 23 (February): 23–31.

Turk, H. (1970) "Interorganizational networks in urban society: initial perspectives and comparative research." Amer. Soc. Rev. 35 (February): 1–19.

Warren, R. L. (1967) "The interorganizational field as a focus of investigation." Admin. Sci. Q. (December): 396–419.

——— (1970) "Alternative strategies of inter-agency planning," pp. 114–129 in U.S. Department of Health, Education and Welfare, Public Health Service, Health Services and Mental Health Administration, Inter-Organizational Research in Health: Conference Proceedings. Washington, D.C.: U.S. Government Printing Office.

SECTION FIVE
Organizational
Change

If the concept of change is interpreted loosely most studies in this volume deal with organizational change in one way or another. Since organizations are planned social units oriented to specific goals under relatively rational and self-conscious leadership, they are probably more prone to change than most other social units. Some studies discuss changes in goals; others, changes in structure; still others discuss changes in the relationship between organizations and their social environments. But if the term "change" is conceived more strictly as change in the organization as a unit rather than as change in this or that variable; if the term "study of change" means to determine the factors which further change the conditions under which a steady state is maintained, in contrast to the conditions under which it is undermined or substituted; if it means to specify the alternative courses open to changing a structure and the conditions under which this or that path is chosen, then the study of organizational change—as well as the study of change in all other social units—is still a relatively undeveloped field. The following studies contribute, each in its own way, to a more systematic analysis of organizational change.

McCleery makes a major structural change the focus of his study. He examines the change of a prison from an authoritarian structure to a liberal one. He raises such cardinal questions as the nature of organizational structure and power (McCleery emphasizes communication processes), unanticipated consequences of managerial policy (e.g., decrease in the degree of arbitrariness led to a temporary increase in inmate disorder), the role of external agencies in internal changes (e.g., the legislature had to support the liberalization of the prison), and other issues. In toto, McCleery supplies a broad portrait of a change of organization from one structure to another, including a detailed analysis of the transition period and the mechanisms of transformation, such as turnover of personnel, redefinition of authority and power positions, rechanneling of communications processes, and change in the potency of various goals.

In their study of the control of the Chinese peasantry by the Communist Party and the peasants' response to Party control, Skinner and Winckler make Etzioni's theory of compliance fully dynamic. They show how the tensions and incompatibilities of each stage lead to the initiation of the next compliance pattern. In a field in which theory and data tend to follow separate routes, the authors' ability to join the two—to their mutual benefit—is noteworthy.

Freeman and Hannan study the growth and decline patterns in 805 California school districts. They consider previous findings that the relationship of size and administrative intensity are the same during growth as during decline phases. Freeman and Hannan's findings refute this hypothesis. Their study is also noteworthy for the sophisticated multivariate procedures that were employed.

Meyer and Brown study the formalization of personnel procedures in 229 city, county, and state finance agencies. They reject the hypothesis that these changes are due largely to internal organizational processes. Rather, they suggest that the changes are a function of origins and subsequent effects of the environment. While origins and environmental factors account for the degree of formal personnel procedures, formalization itself has its impact on other organizational changes. Meyer and Brown here give special attention to the rise of multitier hierarchies and the decentralization of decision-making. Greater openness to environmental factors at the time of organization formation accounts for the effects of origins.

Policy Change in Prison Management
Richard H. McCleery

The Theoretical Context

The power of man over man is the brute fact of political experience. Much of political theory is devoted to a search for the real or ideal foundations on which power is based. Depending in large part on the time in which a philosopher writes, the basis of political power may be found in force, ownership of the means of production, natural law, or divine right. Each of these bases of power may seem dominant in a culture at some stage of its historical development. As a theory for our time, this paper will suggest the role of communication patterns as a basis for a system of authority and power.

Direct application of coercive force may be regarded as the most primitive basis of power in interpersonal relations. When social affairs approach a state of anarchy, a Thomas Hobbes may take that principle as the heart of his argument. The measure of stability or even civilization, however, is the development of alternative foundations for the social order. In stable societies, a pattern of communication appears in close connection with the power structure; and the "authoritative allocation of values" becomes a matter of definition and assignment rather than snatch and grab. While abstract political theory may find an ultimate basis of authority in force, empirical research in politics often equates interaction with influence and processes of definition with power.[1]

The immediate focus of this study is on administration and the management of men in a situation which presents power relations with naked clarity—the prison. The bulk of administrative theory notwithstanding, the administrator is strictly limited in the sanctions which he can apply to sustain authority, and even the power of summary dismissal is a relic from a more primitive economic era. These limitations do not apply to prison management where force and fear stand ready as instruments of control. The task of analysis here is to weigh the role of force in comparison to the communication patterns as the basis of power. . . .

If we assume that communication patterns serve as one functional equivalent for force in sustaining the power structure of a stable society, these propositions would seem to follow:

1. Change in a formal power structure should be reflected in the patterns of communication and contact of the group.
2. Change in the patterns of communication, however instituted, should react on the system of formal power and authority, causing either its collapse or a resort to other means for its support.
3. A failure of the communication patterns to correspond to a given system of authority should result in anarchy and produce an increased resort to force.

Excerpted from *Policy Change in Prison Management*, by permission of the author and the publisher, Governmental Research Bureau, Michigan State University, 1957.

383

The Research Context

The prison, as a distinctive system of power, provides a setting in which to examine the above propositions. The present discussion is drawn from the context of a broader study of prison management in transition which compared the processes of inmate society under authoritarian and more liberal prison administrations. . . .

The prison presents special advantages as a setting for the study of communications and power. In familiar communities, power is a complex which includes large elements of habit, tradition, loyalty and even affection. Customary deference is supported by a differentiation in status symbols and by class functions accumulated over centuries. The exercise of power in the prison, while not entirely independent of these elements, is clarified by its greater dependence on authority. The prison regime tends to suppress all class distinctions in dress and possessions and to reduce its subject to a uniform status of subordination. Hence in the relative absence of a symbolic basis of class distinction, the functional bases of those distinctions which do emerge and characterize inmate society to a marked degree become more evident. The commanding position of the "old con," his power to compel and coerce other inmates, may be traced to the process by which he creates the definitions accepted by his society.

Although the prison should not be taken uncritically as a society in microcosm, the comparative isolation of its social process from the impact of external variables provides a rare opportunity for systematic analysis. The vast majority of interaction patterns in inmate society begin and end within the walls and are subject to a measure of official control and manipulation. Finally, the identification of formal and informal systems of behavior is simplified by a sharp distinction between the ruling and subject class of the prison community.

The discussion to follow will consider the administrative and social characteristics of an authoritarian prison, certain liberal changes introduced and their consequences, and the basis of reconstruction in inmate and official societies.

The Authoritarian Prison

Organization and Communications

The formal organization and official policy of the traditional prison recognized industry as a goal and reform as a hope along with the objective of custodial control. However, one basic proposition emerging from this study is that formal organization is modified by the location and control of communication channels. Thus, while the prison had a work program, its inmates were sentenced to "hard labor," and the economic self-sufficiency of the institution was an ideal, the effective roles of industry and the industrial supervisor were institutionalized in their relations with the custodial force.

The Warden and his Deputy were the only policy-making officials of the institution. At the beginning of this study, the main divisions of the staff were the custodial force, organized in three watches under a Senior Captain, and the work line supervisors. Past attempts to vitalize a treatment program had atrophied by that time into a single position—an ex-guard supervised recreation. There were other functions performed within the walls—a kitchen, an admissions and records office, and a hospital—but these seemed to have no independent organizational status.

The entire staff accepted those implications for organizational structure which were institutionalized in the custodial force. The structure of that force was borrowed directly from military organization. The steps in its uniformed and disciplined hierarchy served as the measure by which those who performed non-custodial services determined their own status within the structure of formal organization. Hence the admissions officer insisted upon the rank of Captain which he had earned through many years of custodial service.

The nerve center for all institutional communication lay in the office of the Captain of the Yard. This location was dictated by the primary interest of custodial officials in the hour-by-hour reports on the location and movement of men. However, it was not just the report of counts and the time books of the work line supervisors but all orders, requests and reports which passed through this communications center. With the issuance of orders and the assignment of men channeled through a communication system controlled by custody, the perceived status of work line supervisors was below that of the guards from whom, in effect, they took their orders. . . .

Record items of costs, production, or the needs of the men might be ignored, but control information was never overlooked. The institutional pressures which dominated the office in which communication centered dictated its content and use. Custodial control of communications, and the interactional patterns thus established, imposed custodial attitudes, values and behaviors throughout the industrial program, negating its formal position and purpose.

Work supervisors had little contact with the Director of Industry but daily contact with the guards. Their ability to communicate their day-to-day needs depended on the influence involved in that contact. But contact normally involves effective communication only to the extent that shared attitudes and values are present.[2] As a result, supervisors came to think, act and dress like the guards. They justified labor in terms of disciplinary rather than productive or training results, maintained sharp class distinctions on the job, and repressed the rare examples of initiative which appeared among their inmate employees. Accepting that definition of labor and the status of the supervisor, inmates opposed the industrial program and gave the minimum tolerable effort to it. Supervisors, in turn, borrowed custodial attitudes which explained failures of production on the basis of the malice and incompetence of the inmates. The institutionally shared belief in the limited possibilities of prison industry further reduced its role.

The status of other functions performed in the prison was subverted in a similar way, and this may be illustrated most clearly in respect to professional services. Psychological diagnosis and medical treatment were carried on in the institution. Referral to and reports from these services were passed through custodial channels which emphasized security considerations above all else. Psychological services seemed to the inmates to be an adjunct of disciplinary control, and medical treatment appeared to be geared to the detection of malingering. Consequently, inmates believed, with some justification, that these services were subordinated to custody, and the prison community in general regarded the professional with a contempt inconsistent with his formal status and the real motive of his work.[3] The "bug doctor" was considered lower than a "screw." That contempt, in turn, reduced the actual function of professional services to insignificance.

Thus, its control of communication permitted custody to co-opt the efforts of other institutional units to the support of its own function and status. . . .

Delegating a monopoly over communication controls has different and more dictatorial power implications for a society than simply delegating a monopoly over the instruments of force. Censorship goes beyond action to control over how men think. It goes beyond overt resistance to sap the very will to resist. It removes from the universe of discourse the premises on which criticism might be based. Thus, it gains a blind and fatalistic conformity not only while the eye of authority is on the subject but even while it sleeps. Inmates regarded the traditional structures of authority in the old prison as mean, abusive and unjust; but, most important, they regarded it as inevitable. . . .

There is an anarchic tendency in the principle of backing up the subordinate which would seem to maximize discretionary authority throughout an organization. The absence of two-way communications controlled that tendency in the authoritarian prison. All communication flowed upward, leaving each superior better informed than his subordinate and limiting the information on lower levels on which discretion could be based. Official definitions alone are not enough to establish the legitimacy of senior officials and enforce discipline in a strict hierarchy of rank. The patterns of communication in the authoritarian institution established the official hierarchy as a relative intellectual elite and legitimized the assumption that the superior was correct on any question. The superior was always better informed. . . .

Decisions are influenced as much by withholding information as by injecting it into communication channels. However, subordinate officers hesitated to stop reports or deny requests where there was any possibility of being reversed later. Each superior reinforced his place in the hierarchy with a wider sphere of movement and access to personal contact than those of his subordinates. While the fundamental basis of status in both inmate and official societies was power to command others, prestige was closely related to freedom of movement. The power to exert influence was directly proportioned to one's access to communication channels and information. . . .

Procedures of Governing

The character of the prison as a system of power may be further illustrated in the procedures of decision, control and ordinary operation. The Warden was free to express the principle of having a constructive industrial policy. Given custodial control over operational decision, however, the practice of using inmate labor only in menial tasks of no value to the inmate and little use to the state contradicted formal declarations of institutional policy but illustrated a principle of wide application in this social system. Decision reflects the interests which are communicated most effectively on the administrative level at which decisions are made. The institutional autocrat is not responsible to his subordinates, but he is no less responsive than any other executive to those who define the premises of his discretion.

In the authoritarian prison, the exercise of coercive power based essentially on force constituted one foundation of social control. But this power was, perhaps, least effective when it took the form of punitive sanctions imposed on individuals.

A high degree of discipline was maintained with the minimum of direct sanctions. A vital basis of social control lay in procedures of regimentation—frequent counts and assemblies—which imposed a psychology of domination and placed the subject in a posture of silence, respect and awe. Recognition of distinctions in rank was imposed in all inmate-official contacts by the requirements of a salute and special forms of address.

More punitive forms of control rested on summary procedure and a few rules as broad in their import as the officer's sense of insubordination. Control, rather than "justice" in the familiar sense, was the object. Hence, there was no place for a body of principles or "constitutional" rights to restrain disciplinary procedure. Secret accusation was the rule, and the accused had no notice, hearing, counsel or appeal. The resulting atmosphere of "terror," produced as much by secrecy as by the actual use of informers was vital to formal control and a key to values and social structures in inmate society. . . .

The distinguishing characteristic of ordinary operations in the authoritarian prison was the absence of alternatives for behavior permitted to or provided for the inmates. Rewards went only for ritual conformity, and initiative was as suspect to the static inmate community as to the officials. This accent on conformity did not prevent—in fact, seemed to require—the emergence of a complex organization in inmate society. Silence was imposed wherever inmates congregated, but the patterns of inmate organization and communication could not be suppressed by even the most rigid silent system. They could only be controlled. . . .

The Inmate Social System

Reason would seem to indicate what official policy assumed in the old prison: that men stripped of all but the necessities of life would be equal and that they would be ready to attack the system which reduced them to that condition. However, analysis must deal with two predominant facts of the situation. Inmate society was structured in terms of striking inequalities, and, under normal circumstances, it was geared to adjustment rather than rebellion. Only under exceptional conditions, to be examined later, did violent and aggressive men emerge to a position of leadership in prison life.

Inmate society demanded and the officials asserted, as a basic premise of prison life, that all inmates be treated alike. In spite of this, the basic interpersonal relationship in inmate society was that of dominance and subordination. The highest personal value in that system was placed on the exercise of coercive power.[4] This suggests that a fundamental goal of control over men was uncritically borrowed by the inmates from the administration.[5] While there are striking parallel values expressed in dress and habit between inmate and official society, the pursuit of power was not simply an end in itself.

A goal of the inmates was to achieve integrity and independence from official sanctions—to gain deliverance from perils. To gain this type of freedom, the society enforced conformity on its members by sanctions more severe than those employed by officials. In defiance of formal premises of equality, inmate society was structured in a power hierarchy at least as sharply defined and static as that of the officials. It was defended in its independence by a basic imperative of the code: "Never talk to a screw."

The absence of published regulations or official orientation for new men, the secrecy and arbitrariness of disciplinary action, the shocking unfamiliarity of the prison world to men just arrived, and the demands imposed by regimentation—all these combined to make the new inmate dependent on the experienced prisoner.[6] The old inmate knew the uncertain limits of official tolerance in a system which, of necessity, prohibited far more than it punished. He could share on his own conditions the knowledge which made life tolerable for the new man.

Knowledge of prison operations made for physical adjustment, but knowledge of explanations was required to make life psychologically tolerable. Inmates, no less than other men, needed rationalizations to give meaning to their daily lives. This was not provided by the authoritarian prison system. In the words of an old guard, "We don't have to make excuses to inmates." Senior officials dismissed the importance of the inmate grapevine because it was inaccurate, but its importance lay in its very inaccuracy. The myths and fantasies circulated by the grapevine performed vital adjustive functions for inmate society, explaining events in satisfying ways, holding officials in contempt, and attributing a certain dignity to the inmate class. Initiation into these mysteries of the inmate tribe was as important as the process of physical adjustment, and it was sharing in these myths of solidarity, more than physical association, which gave a certain unity to the inmate group. . . .

Inmate society protected itself from the betrayal of both its power structure and its myths by ostracizing such men from communication and the benefits of membership. At the same time, it regarded isolates as fair game for abuse, exploitation and domination. Constant emphasis on the idea of the "rat" supported a maximal valuation of power in inmate society and still restricted the most obvious recourse to power—an appeal by informers to official sanctions. The demand for equality was not a demand against the administration but an assertion among inmates that power gained by contacts outside inmate society had no legitimacy there. Denial of validity to outside contacts protected the inmate culture from criticism and assured the stability of its social order. . . .

Inmate leaders were men able to explain, predict, or control to some degree a situation in which others were helpless and confused. Lesser men gained security and protection by attaching themselves to those leaders and supplying them the petty tribute which conveyed status.[7] This type of dominance depended on access to informal communication, contacts on the grapevine and, also, contacts with official sources. Because these men were expected to manipulate power and mediate between the forces of official action and their followers, they were given a license to talk with officials never permitted to men of unproven dependability. . . .

Under stable conditions, inmate culture supported custodial values. Its accent on conformity, on doing one's own time without fear or complaint, on avoiding behavior which would "bring on the heat," on never talking to a "screw," all these were ideally suited to custodial control. In a period of disorganization or challenge to inmate values, however, aggressiveness became the assertion of a moral independence and contempt for officials played a special, self-justifying role. The inmate whose rebellion was undeterred by the most violent official sanctions was elevated to the role of a Promethean hero.[8] The utter disregard of consequences, expressed by attacks on officials or repeated attempts to escape, assumed the stature of moral courage enhanced by the disproportionate weight of the punishment resulting. Under certain conditions, the ability to resist power bravely became the equivalent of an ability to manipulate power. With the collapse of a system by which adjustive definitions of the situation were applied throughout the inmate community, the hero was called on to give violent assertion to the values of the group.

Traditional inmate culture accented the values of adjustment within the walls and the rejection of outside contacts. It supported a social hierarchy, reduced new arrivals to subordination, and adjusted its own social conflicts with sanctions more severe than those available to the guards. As will be indicated by later developments in the prison, control of a disorganized mass of men was beyond the ability of the guard force. Control of a rigid social system in which the vast majority of definitions and sanctions were informally imposed was a far more simple matter. Hence the custodial goals of peace, order and adjustment dictated an alliance between senior officers and inmate leaders in the interests of stability and to the end of minimizing the role of the hero.

In some respects it could be said that the inmates ran the authoritarian prison. Senior inmates, at least, had a voice in the assignment of men and the distribution of privileges. Integrating contacts between officials and high status inmates were conducted in a responsible way. Both groups shared a sincere contempt for "rats." Their exchanges were not moved by a desire to employ sanctions against individuals or to gain immediate private advantage so much as by a wish to maintain a condition of peace and order in which each senior group enjoyed the advantage of its position. Each group held power in its own sphere by means of ability to predict events and extended that power by intercommunication which violated the norms of both systems. In order to maintain these contacts with inmates which provided warning of danger, officials were willing to tolerate a considerable amount of rule evasion, pilfering, and petty exercises of power by inmate leaders. These privileges stabilized the inmate society. While the authoritarian prison is often accused of tolerating abuse, corruption, exploitation and inequality, such things were permitted in the interests of security and adjustment—the values most firmly institutionalized in the system.

Summary

The analysis so far has identified systems of communication intimately allied with the structure of power in both inmate and official societies. The unit of the official system which administered communications as a means of control imposed its values and assumed a commanding role in the institution as a whole. At the same time, a power hierarchy emerged in the presumptively egalitarian inmate community which seemed directly related to its communication and informational environment.

The Liberal Revolution

Three phases can be distinguished in the prison's period of transition. The first runs from the death of the old Warden in 1946 to the end of 1950. In that period, a liberal group appeared in the administration, gained formal authority, and revolutionized the policies of the institution. In the next phase, from 1950 through 1953, the liberal group engaged in a contest with the guards for control over operating procedures and, in effect, for control over the population. The present section will trace these developments. A following section will outline that contest, in which control was nearly lost, to its result in the defeat of the "old guard." The final period from 1954 through 1955 was one of reconstruction, adjustment, and, as stated by the officials, "tightening up the organization."

The seeds of revolution were contained in the appointment of five men from 1946 through 1949 who had no previous penal experience and who would not or could not adjust to traditional processes by which custody had become fixed as the dominant institutional goal. While these appointments were policy acts, they did not, in themselves, indicate a policy change, and the consequences which were to follow from altered patterns of behavior were not anticipated. The extent to which these new men injected inconsistent patterns of behavior from the free community into the prison, as much as their democratic policy statements later, marks the change as a liberal or democratic revolution. . . . The tactics of their revolt were little more than the habits of open communication, concern for "justice" as well as control, and performance as well as conformity, the rejection of status differentials in social contact, and the determination to be informed of their own responsibilities—all of which they imported from free society. Yet these simple behaviors, inconsistent with the authoritarian tradition, had a direct impact on policy and organization throughout the institution.

Reformulation of Policy

The disciplined traditions of the custodial force and the attitudes toward authority held by its members blocked their access to the open door of the new Warden. Those who took advantage of that access were the new employees who were conscious of the traditional chain of command only as a device by which their functions were frustrated. Other non-custodial employees in the past had resigned in the face of these frustrations or had accepted the attitudes and goals of custody with their acceptance of its communication channels. This group was spared the custodial orientation (with its narrow definition of purposes, roles and possibilities within the prison) by a practice of turning to one another and the license it took in turning to the Warden for definitions. The new men were members of the official staff, but they were not members of the official community in the sense of sharing the goals and values which gave an integrity to that group. . . .

As the new men by-passed conventional channels and turned to the Warden for definitions, they found that officer sensitive to the limits on his discretion imposed by custodial control of communication. His efforts to inquire through the custodial force into rumors of corruption in the prison had been frustrated for a year, forcing him to employ an outside investigator. The dismissal of several guards as a result of that inquiry, based in part on testimony taken from inmates, had lowered custodial morale and strained relations with that group. In this situation, the new men were able to form themselves into a policy caucus around the Warden and participate in the making of the definitions they sought. In turn this gave the functions represented by the new men (industry, education, and treatment) a hearing in policy decisions which they had not previously enjoyed.

When other units gained a share in policy definitions, the techniques of controlling decision by controlling the information on which it was based reacted against custodial officials. The new group was able to inject a wider range of pertinent considerations for policy than had reached the Warden in the past. As officials charged with treatment responsibilities gained access to the decision-making forum, this constituted a virtual representation of the interests and welfare of the inmates. This representation was reflected in a number of minor policy changes.

One of the first projects of the liberal group was to establish a clear conception of its own functions in the institution. To that end it produced a formal diagram of the organization. In contradiction to the actualities of custodial domination and the effective goals of the agency, the organizational chart placed the functions of treatment and industry on a level with the guard force. This, in itself, was a critical redefinition of roles if not of powers. Then, discarding its advisory capacity, the next step of the liberal group was to formalize its position as a policy agency for internal affairs. The guard force, the largest numerical group of employees, had only minority representation on the policy committee, and other officials of importance in the old power hierarchy were excluded altogether.

The next project of the liberal group was a Policy and Philosophy Manual. There was little formal statement of policy in the traditional prison between the establishing statute and the descriptive "wake 'em, work 'em, etc." of the guards. An authoritarian system is necessarily weak in operational ideology because it must resolve issues by appeal to the superior official rather than by appeal to principle. Authoritarian discipline is subverted by the publication of principles to which an appeal from persons can be made. Given a constitution or a law of the twelve tables, the weakest man in the community is armed with a weapon against the strongest. However, a Manual was published for the institution, and it asserted "rehabilitation through treatment and constructive industry" as the primary institutional purpose. It stated that "the democratic approach to management is the soundest" and contained commitments to:

> The delegation to lower management levels of all possible responsibility and authority commensurate with sound management.
> A practice of constant consultation, dissemination of information, and discussion of problems up and down the management chain.

These concepts were directly inconsistent with authoritarian hierarchy and control. Custodial officers were members of the council that produced the document, but they made no effective resistance to its publication. Unable to communicate effectively in the new policy forum, suspicious and on the defensive, the guard force withdrew from the area of general policy and fell back on its control over the actual operations, procedures and communications in the prison yard. The liberal group had no impact on that area until it could translate its formalized principles into operating procedures.

The Procedural Revolution

From a legalistic point of view, it would seem that the revolution in the prison had been accomplished by 1950. The liberal group had gained formal status, drafted a "constitution" and seized control of the policy-making centers thus created. In terms of the daily operating procedures of the institution, however, the change had scarcely begun. While work supervisors continued to report and take orders through the guards, their programs and the emphasis of their work continued along essentially traditional lines. The policy-making group had gained status without gaining influence. It wrote new regulations and the guards continued to enforce the old. At this point—one not uncommon in the administration of penal or other institutions—a reformulation of general policy had exerted little visible impact on actual procedures.

While efforts of the policy group to legislate patterns of behavior and standards of action were defeated in the execution, that group was able to adjust institutional patterns of communication to the new policy. The principle that all those affected by a decision should have an understanding of the issues and a voice in their determination dictated the holding of discussion meetings in several sections of the organization. Led by the treatment director, these discussions proved most effective in the newly established and more complex units of the industrial program. There they provided a means by which the interests of the work supervisors were advanced past the custodial hierarchy, and the supervisors responded briskly to the change. As an outcome of these meetings, prison rules were revised to abandon the time-honored salute in all contacts between inmate and supervisor and to give up other elements of regimentation on the work line which had hindered productivity in the past. The abandonment of these status distinctions at work opened the way to more active communication on the job, improved production, the development of workshop communities of interest, and habits of interaction quite inconsistent with the continuing demands of life in the cell blocks. The more open contacts between supervisors and inmates provided a basis for turning later to the supervisors rather than the guards for direct reports on the men. As might be expected, efforts to conduct similar discussion sessions with the custodial force brought little response.

At the start of 1951, an inmate council was established with a right to debate any issue and advance proposals for staff consideration. This Council, with an adviser from the treatment unit, formed working committees for such areas as food, hobby and craft work, education, recreation, and public relations. It would seem especially significant in terms of the type of analysis advanced here that the Council called itself "the voice of the inmates."

Later developments began to challenge the realities of custodial control in one area after another. In times past, punishment, inmate promotions, job assignments, good-time allowances, and every type of petty privilege had been administered by custody in terms of consideration of control. Seniority and the appearance of adjustment within the walls were used as a basis for the distribution of privilege. This reinforced the dominance of conservative and con-wise old prisoners. When the administration of privileges was, in effect, delegated to senior inmates, that served the interest of control as much by strengthening the inmate social structure as by applying sanctions to individuals. The administrative processes involved in this management of incentives were mainly informal and summary. That does not mean, however, that the operating decisions were not rational on the criterion of custodial control. A basic tactic of the liberal group was to alter the method and, hence, the dominant motive by which those operating decisions were made.

The treatment office claimed a voice in decisions on privilege and punishment on the grounds that privilege should be "meaningful" and that incentives should be concentrated behind their recently defined "goals of the institution." In defense of treatment-oriented personnel, it must be admitted that they had little conception of how all operations had been geared to the goals of security. By failing to share in institutional goals as defined by the guard force, they failed to comprehend the rationale of traditional procedures. They had little understanding of the economy of scarcity which prevailed in the yard or the extent to which a privilege or a larger sphere of movement extended to the "wrong" inmate could disturb the prison's social order. The philosophy of the treatment unit accented the importance of the individual, and this is the crucial basis on which the changes introduced may be called a "democratic" revolution. The focus of treatment men on the individual—a focus permitted by their lack of custodial responsibilities—was crucial in their conflict with the authoritarian tradition.

Participation in the expanding group of activities sponsored by treatment became the basis of a record. At the same time, the more complex processes of production required work supervisors to reward inmates on the basis of productivity as well as conduct. A report of the inmate's work record was channeled directly to the treatment office. Such records were inserted as relevant to daily operating decisions, and the decisions responded to the interests which were communicated most effectively. The traditional "time off for good behavior" became a committee decision in which six factors, only one of which was conduct, were weighted equally. The interest of teaching men a trade was taken as a ground for moving the administration of transfers to the treatment unit and away from custodial administration. By that time, the terminology and ideology of "individual development" rather than "good conduct" had been imposed on the reports of supervisors.

The treatment unit, armed with an expanding record, first asserted an informed interest and then assumed the management of functions in one area after another, extending finally to recreation and entertainment. These changes in the location of effective discretion within the agency tended to leave the custodial force with nothing but its guns as a basis of control. Rising disorder in the inmate community indicated that such a basis is weak indeed. The present section has indicated that the range of discretion possessed by a unit of administration tends to be as wide and no wider than the store of information on which decision is based.

The Impact of Administrative Change

As new concepts of policy were incorporated into the procedures of daily administration, these had a direct effect on the patterns of communication and interpersonal contact within the prison. The communication patterns of both official and inmate societies were altered to the point that they no longer served to support the traditional power hierarchy or gain acceptance for its authority. This section will trace the development of a rebellion among members of the once disciplined custodial force and, with reference to the prison's disciplinary records, the rise in anarchy in the inmate population. . . .

The Revolt of the "Old Guard"

While significant changes took place elsewhere in the institution, the custodial force retained the traditional patterns of communication from an earlier day. Just as the new officials had avoided indoctrination with custodial attitudes, the bulk of the guard force remained isolated from the new concepts and principles of the policy manual. Three years after its publication, few of the guards knew of its existence. Written declaration from above proved incapable of challenging the rationalizations which emerged within the group. Men whose daily work required them to be constantly ready to shoot an inmate arrived at a conception of inmates as persons who might justifiably be shot.

The system of limited communication to subordinates, which supported an authoritarian hierarchy in both official and inmate groups, was supplemented by a grapevine which supplied each level of the hierarchy with self-justifying and conservative values. Acceptance of these values as legitimate was the price of peer group acceptance in all ranks. Thus, a limited communication pattern within the guard force protected the traditional set of custodial attitudes from challenge or criticism. At the same time, their isolation frequently left watch officers less well-informed than the inmates they guarded, reversing the conditions of the past and removing the legitimate basis of the guard's authority.

The guards tended to blame the treatment unit and its programs for the decline in their status which inevitably followed. The over-all consequences of procedural change were to flatten the status pyramid of the prison community by providing equal access to influence and information, narrowing the gaps of social distance which made up a formal hierarchy of authority.

In order to understand the resistance of the custodial force, it is necessary to see the situation as the guards viewed it. New officials violated the chain of command at every turn and dismissed the traditional prerogatives of rank. The failure of treatment officers to maintain distinctions of class threatened the psychology of domination so central to control, and led guards to see the treatment officials as on a level with the inmates themselves. Policy discussions with the Inmate Council challenged control based on secrecy and fear simply by supplying the rational basis for actions which had appeared to be arbitrary before. The inmates had more direct and effective representation in policy than the guards. Custodial accounting for the movement of men was confounded by the treatment activities. Finally, the guards felt with some reason that they knew far more about the behavior of prisoners in the authoritarian institution than did treatment officials. The guards were in the most favorable position to see inmates exploiting new activities in pursuit of the old goals of dominance and power. . . .

The old guard launched a counterattack with the only weapons remaining to it. The Inmate Council, meeting with its staff adviser in the yard, was free from harassment. However, completely literal enforcement of old regulations against movement and communication brought the follow-up activities of Council committees and treatment-sponsored clubs to a halt. Inmates who were "getting out of their place" through participation in new activities were the subject of disciplinary reports. Gaining access to the treatment office was made so complex and, for selected inmates, so humiliating that many who valued their self-respect in the yard abandoned the effort. Requests sent through the custodial channels to the treatment office were often lost. The custodial force perpetuated a distinction in the yard between "right inmates" and "politicians," who were assumed to be using contact with the treatment office for their own advantage. Guards manipulated traditional inmate values by asking men returning from the treatment office how much they had "beaten their time." In the face of those pressures, inmates employed in the Treatment Unit arranged for passes to work until lock-up and stayed out of the yard. In spite of the expanding number of privileges which could be manipulated by contacts in the treatment office, the influence of its inmate employees was neutralized.

By the beginning of 1953, the revolt of the old guard reached the height of its effectiveness. Conservative inmates had withdrawn from the Inmate Council, and the younger men who replaced them were exploiting the Council to an extent which challenged the faith of even the liberal officials. The inmate clubs and associations sponsored by the Treatment Unit had collapsed, and voluntary class attendance was in decline. Violence and escape had risen to a point at which new emphasis on custodial values of repression and control was required. The Deputy Warden, once a leader for liberal changes, sided with custody in the staff conferences and threatened a split in that group.

For all practical purposes, the guard force had regained control over the operation of the prison. However, it had lost control over formal policy statements as it lost its monopoly over communication channels. The old guard, ambitious for legitimacy as well as practical success, sought alliances outside the prison with men discharged earlier and with community groups which supported their position. Represented by a minority bloc in the legislature which was seeking an issue, the old guard took its policy contest into the field of politics.

Legislative hearings on the prison opened with a series of charges which indicated, by their nature, their source in the active custodial force. A stand was taken on those matters which seemed most like mismanagement to the old guard: promotion and discipline. However, what the guards called favoritism was proved to be a sound promotion on the basis of "merit." What the guards considered abuses of discipline in the failure to back up subordinates was defended as a policy of judicial fairness. The staff was able to meet the legislative inquiry with a convincing mass of records and documentary material while the guards, in making the charges, were limited to the information they could leak. Hence, the position of the old guard, which had a great deal of merit from the standpoint of authoritarian control or custody and a strong prospect of success in the conflict with the institution, was flatly rejected in the more democratic forum of the legislature. By pressing for a definition of policy in a forum beyond the range of their effective influence and communication, the guards gained only the endorsement of the liberal position and a final repudiation of their own.

The prison had changed in its character from a military dictatorship to an institution in which the role of armed forces was subordinated to the objective of treatment. While some guards persisted in their belief that all control over the inmates had been lost, a decline in escape, violence and disorder indicated, and the inmate community generally recognized, that the treatment unit had assumed control. . . .

Change and Social Disorganization

Discussion thus far has indicated that a shift in communication patterns and their control produced a drastic shift of power within a highly formalized organizational structure. The course of that change was delayed, modified, but seldom reversed by formal definitions of status and authority. The power of a unit to define a course of action for others was directly related to its store of information and capacity to transmit that information to the locale of decision. A change parallel to that in official society may be traced in the inmate community with even greater clarity in the absence of any official legitimacy for the power structure which existed there.

The first period of policy change was marked by little disturbance and relatively high morale in the yard. The investigation which crippled guard-inmate commerce brought no sanctions against the dominant inmate clique. While some activities by which inmate leadership supported its position were cut off, others appeared, and the inmate leaders were able to monopolize new privileges and claim credit for the sunshine. Control over the orientation of new men maintained the conservative inmate group in power as long as the guard force controlled the procedures of prison life. The early periods of low custodial morale and the revision of disciplinary procedures were followed by an outbreak of escape and some rise in disorder, but records show that these figures had returned to normal by 1949.

After that time, however, new activities and relationships in the treatment and production units began to create new communities of interest in the inmate body with a functional leadership of their own. As activities began to involve more and more cooperative supervision by officials, the "rat concept" of the old inmate culture and the sanctions against contact with officials were weakened. Old leaders often abandoned the opportunities for contact and information which appeared in connection with new work lines when accepting these opportunities involved accepting new relationships with officers and their fellows. The leaders drew into a more overt alliance with guard officials and sustained their position by traditional means in the prison yard. During the first part of the transition, the social consequences of the new work situations were isolated from the power structure and social processes of the prison yard, but the Council opened new avenues to recognition even there.

The old inmate leaders were like the custodial force in not being able to operate effectively in the context of group discussion and decision-making. In spite of a conservative majority of senior inmates on the first Council, a clique of new men seized the initiative in drafting the Council's constitution and bylaws, writing in provision for themselves. New officials thought the Council was a substantial privilege for the inmates, involving some small measures of control as well as a voice in prison affairs. To old inmate leaders it was a small boon in comparison to the position they had once enjoyed. The first months of the Council's operation provoked widespread inmate resistance and opposition, ending with the resignations of several old leaders. However, that move came too late to discredit the Council as a route to influence in the prison for a different class of men.

By the middle of 1951, the monolithic structure of inmate society had developed broad cracks. The marginally criminal first offenders, the lowest caste in the old prison, had found a focus of interest and organization in the Treatment Unit and the Council. As official frankness, publication of rules, and a formal orientation program made new men independent of the indoctrination by old cons, another group of tough, young, reform-school graduates declared their independence from old inmate leadership and embarked on a radical course of exploitation and troublemaking. In the following year, neither the traditional "code" nor old leadership commanded the respect which permitted them to define roles or adjust conflicts in the community. In the absence of controlling definitions, disputes were increasingly submitted to the arbitration of force, and the status of the physically powerful and aggressive men advanced.

Factions in the yard corresponded to those which split the administration in 1953. Conservative leaders allied with the old guard to neutralize the influence of inmates associated with the treatment program. However, the mounting disciplinary reports for that year did not reflect a direct conflict between those two elements. It was the young toughs, unwilling to accept definitions from any other group, who were out of control. In the face of these disturbances, created by an element of the inmate body that literally took orders from no one, the guard force and security measures were increased. The failure of these measures to restrain increasing disorder indicates the importance of informal social control, even in a society governed mainly by force and fear. . . .

This was the type of situation in which young men turned to follow "heroes" who dramatically asserted the ideals of toughness and resistance. Men made desperate by long sentences once had been absorbed into inmate society by the acceptance of values and definitions which made for adjustment. Now such men were encouraged by youthful followers to live up to newspaper reputations by sensational escapes and Promethean rebellion. It was the adverse publicity from such escapades which helped to establish the setting for the revolt of the old guard. At one critical point, a mass break-out was averted by posting machine guns on the roof and transferring inmate leaders of the younger group to another prison. Inmate society was close to a condition of anarchy in which the only recognized authority was that provided by physical force. This is not to say that attacks against officials were the rule. Official control over the instruments of force prevented this. What is significant to the analysis here is the complete failure of leadership and authority within the inmate community itself—the transfer of influence from the leader to the hero.

Reconstruction

A change in customary patterns of communication appeared to produce disorder and the collapse of authority in both official and inmate societies. This result occurred by way of the subversion of status attached to positions and conflict for the acceptance of inconsistent definitions. The emergence of a new order and stability in the prison seems anticlimactic by contrast. It involved little more than the development of patterns of communication by which all elements of the community gained the definitions on which stability is based.

Press reports of the legislative hearing which debated penal policy seem to have had a stabilizing influence on the inmates. Issues which had seemed, at first, to be little more than an administrative contest for power were defined for everyone on the level of principle. Inmates themselves entered into the debate on policy with an unprecedented interest. The position of the old guard was supported by testimony from one of the old leaders, but two of the major "heroes" of the inmate community submitted a letter to the legislative hearing in support of the new administrative position.

When the legislative debates were over, the Warden met with the inmates in a series of open discussions which are credited with a major role in restoring order. He took the lead in providing definitions and explanations of the situation so necessary to a sense of security but which no inmate group in the period of factionalism was able to supply. The role of the young toughs declined in the inmate community, and rates of escape and violence immediately dropped.

The central fact in the defeat of the old guard and those of their senior officers who remained was its recognition of the staff committee as an authoritative source of definitions for the prison. Prior to the legislative endorsement of a liberal position, the guards thought of themselves as custodians of the true or real institutional goals. It was this conviction which had armed them to circulate inconsistent definitions and also to remain aloof from the new policy centers. To the extent that the guards accepted the legitimacy of the new policy source, this acceptance worked to reduce tension in two ways. It reduced the circulation of contradictory definitions which had generated conflicts in the inmate body, but it also led the guards to a more active communication with and participation on policy councils. In the period of "tightening up the organization," policy has begun to incorporate more and more of the custodial point of view. Regular meetings between the Superintendent and the watches serve to bring considerations of security to bear on each decision.

With the defeat of the old guard, systematic efforts to isolate the influence of treatment-oriented inmates ceased, and a new social order began to emerge in the prison yard. Direct contacts between inmates and officials were taken as a matter of course. As a result, the idea of the "rat," with its implications for all inmate social process and structure, is almost forgotten at present. . . .

The transition involved a transfer of power from one unit of the agency to another. However, this change in the administration must be considered something more than simply a palace revolution. Inmate culture reflects certain qualitative differences in the present prison government. Wider access to officials constitutes a wider distribution of influence within the prison community which is reflected by a concern for inmate interests and welfare in policy. It protects against much of the exploitation and abuse which characterized inmate society in the past. While disciplinary rates have returned toward normal after the crisis, they will never be as low as was the case in the authoritarian prison. They reflect a greater initiative and a wider range of total activity in the inmate body. Even more significantly, they reflect a willingness of the inmates to accept official sanctions in the arbitration of inmate conflicts. The inmate community has abandoned many of the sanctions by which it imposed conformity on its own members.

Voluntary enrollment in treatment and education programs has shown a constant increase since the period of conflict. Such participation has become accepted as a means of gaining recognition in inmate society as well as official rewards. The programs sustain an atmosphere in which inmate attitudes are colored by ideas other than those generated within their own society and conditions in which a majority of the men are willing to accept officially sponsored ideas. An uncensored, inmate-edited newspaper, published in the treatment office, supplements the Warden's meetings with the men and prevents other inmate groups from gaining a monopoly on definition and interpretation.

Attempts by radical groups to capture the Inmate Council and to manipulate privileges administered through that agency have been defeated by inmates with little official intervention. The Council is not a strong and active organization, but it does insure that the inmates who speak with the most authority among their fellows are those in closest touch with the officials. The most striking distinction between the present inmate society and the past is the relative absence of powerful inmate leaders. Inmates elected to the Council by their fellows have less influence than the leadership which emerged in the authoritarian environment. Newly admitted inmates are no longer assigned to the lowest social status, social mobility is greater, and men with talent are recruited into activities in the yard by which status may be earned. A significant difference between past and present inmate society is indicated by the program of orientation carried on cooperatively by officials and the Council.

Conclusions

The three propositions advanced for analysis are supported by the evidence of this study. The unit which dominated the work of the old prison supported its position by control over the communication system. As those communication patterns were altered, a new policy emerged. Control over policy permitted the staff committee to formalize a drastic reassignment of roles and purposes in the institution, and this shift was followed by changes in the traditional patterns of contact for both official and inmate societies. The new principles and policy center did not become authoritative in practice until they gained the support of new communication patterns. During the interval in which communication patterns failed to correspond to the formal authority of the institution, anarchy and disorganization demanded an increased resort to force. On the basis of this evidence, it may be asserted that a pattern of communication serves as a functional equivalent for force in maintaining or subverting a stable system of authority. . . .

Notes

1. A review of the approach which identifies power structures in terms of patterns of contact and the communication of influence is found in Robert Agger, "Power Attributions in the Local Community: Theoretical and Research Considerations," *Social Forces*, 34 (May, 1956), pp. 322–331. For more general theoretical treatment, see Harold Lasswell and Abraham Kaplan, *Power and Society* (New Haven: Yale University Press, 1950).
2. There is no effective execution of orders in an agency except as some motive or sentiment appears in connection with and in support of the activity. In the absence of some more complex sentiment, the desire to earn wages may be enough to gain a tolerable level of activity, but the activity itself seems to produce sentiments in respect to the work among the employees. The manner in which the work is then carried on and the aspects of the work which gain emphasis in time are colored by the sentiments held about it and the manner of their communication. For a careful analysis of the relationships between activity, interaction and sentiment, note George Homans, *The Human Group* (New York: Harcourt, 1950).
3. The contrast between the formal and the effective status of professionals in penal work has been generally noted. Harvey Powelson and Reinhard Bendix discuss the conflict with custodial forces and the attitudes of inmates which negate the work of the professional in prisons. "Psychiatry in Prison," *Psychiatry*, 14 (February, 1951), pp. 73–86.
4. The apparent contradiction between the tight power hierarchy of inmate society and its constant demand for equality of treatment is discussed by Lloyd McCorkle and Richard Korn, "Resocialization Within Walls," *The Annals*, 293 (May, 1954), pp. 89 ff.
5. Erich Fromm writes, in his study of authoritarian culture, "In any society the spirit of the whole culture is determined by the spirit of those groups that are most powerful in that society." *Escape from Freedom* (New York: Holt, Rinehart and Winston, Inc., 1941), pp. 112 f. Only the most cynical approach could apply that proposition directly to the prison and claim that the spirit of the inmate population is taken directly from its rulers. This is too uncharitable to the rulers. However, a reformulation of the proposition in more behavioral terms permits its application to the prison. The effective pursuit of security by the ruling class of the prison imposes patterns of contact and social process upon the subjects which, in turn, dictate the dominant goals and values which can emerge in their society.
6. The complex processes by which the new inmate becomes oriented or "prisonized" in his unfamiliar setting are outlined by Donald Clemmer, "Observations on Imprisonment

as a Source of Criminality," *The Journal of Criminal Law and Criminology*, 41 (September–October, 1950), pp. 311–319. For those interested in intensive study of the prison as a setting for the management of men, the most substantial work on prison government is Clemmer's *The Prison Community* (Boston: The Christopher Publishing House, 1940).

7. The significance of the constant exchange of food and goods in inmate society has led to conflicting interpretation. Norman Hayner and Ellis Ash believe that "the organization of this community is primarily an economic arrangement devoted to obtaining goods and services denied by the administration." "The Prison Community as a Social Group," *American Sociological Review* 4 (June, 1949), p. 369. The present study suggests that conspicuous display of goods and privileges among inmates serves only to symbolize status which must be earned by other means. The symbols declare an ability to manipulate power, and inmate society supplies these symbols to men undergoing punishment or in death row when the only function performed by such men is to resist power bravely.

8. The elements of a hero-making situation are identified by Orrin Klapp, "The Creation of Popular Heroes," *The American Journal of Sociology*, 54 (September, 1948), pp. 135–141. In the prison setting, any collapse of the myths by which inmates justify themselves and their place in the world seems to demand some aggressive assertion of the idea that they are not defeated and helpless.

Compliance Succession in Rural Communist China: A Cyclical Theory

G. William Skinner and Edwin A. Winckler

Analysis of the structure of compliance in Communist China reveals a regular pattern in the interaction between the Chinese Communist Party and the peasantry over the last nineteen years. Repeatedly since "liberation" the Party has shifted its primary reliance from exhortation to coercion and then to remuneration. Repeatedly the peasantry has passed from a tentative enthusiasm through disillusion to a calculative indifference. In this paper, then, we posit a compliance cycle through which the goals of the regime, its prescriptions for leadership style, the actual behavior of cadremen, and the reactions of the peasantry have run. First, we summarize the elements of compliance theory and construct a model of cycles and phases in a compliance system. Second, we trace the reordering of compliance arrangements in rural Communist China since 1949 and relate these changes to the succession of compliance cycles. Third, we summarize some of the organizational correlates of compliance cycles in the Chinese countryside.

Compliance System and Compliance Cycle

A compliance *relationship* is one in which "one actor behaves in accordance with a directive supported by another actor's power."[1] A compliance *system* is an assembly of such relationships seen in relation to the goals which the actors are trying to achieve. A compliance *cycle* is a recurring sequence of compliance arrangements and performance outcomes within a compliance system. This sequence may be divided into *phases* showing characteristic phenomena at the behavioral, structural, and systemic levels. In *behavioral* terms, a compliance cycle is a characteristic sequence in which goals become salient to a superordinate, types of power are applied by the superordinate, and modes of involvement are experienced by the subordinate. In *organizational* terms, a compliance cycle is the analogous sequence in the compliance structure relating an elite and lower participants, and related sequences in such organizational correlates of compliance structure as recruitment and socialization, elite structure and charisma, communication and cohesion.[2] Finally, in *systemic* terms a compliance cycle is a sequence of relationships among the external requirements and obligations of the organization, the internal arrangements through which the organization responds to these requirements, and the performance outcome, including the criteria and procedures for evaluating performance.[3] In this brief paper we limit ourselves primarily to the behavioral level of analysis, detailing the relationships among goals, power, and involvement, with only a summary statement of organizational correlates and systemic relationships.

This essay is a thorough revision of a paper entitled "Compliance and leadership in rural Communist China: a cyclical theory," presented by the first author at the 1965 annual meeting of the American Political Science Association. Copyright © 1969 by G. William Skinner and Edwin A. Winckler.

Before presenting a detailed typology of goals, power, and involvement, it may be helpful to outline the causal relationships in the theory in general terms. The theory stipulates that certain kinds of goals are best pursued through certain types of power, because each type of power produces a given mode of involvement, and certain modes of involvement are best suited to achieving particular kinds of goals. When goals, power, and involvement are not congruent, the theory predicts that there will be a decline in performance, creating costs for the superordinates and thus a tendency for change toward congruence. There are two basic directions in which causation may flow. Moving downward, superordinates choose a set of goals, select a power mix they think will achieve those goals, and succeed in molding the involvement of the subordinates to gain compliance. Moving upward, subordinates tend uncontrollably toward a particular mode of involvement, forcing superordinates to change their power mix, and eventually also their immediate goals. Such successive changes in compliance structure are the focus of this paper.

Following the analysis of Amitai Etzioni, we distinguish among ideological goals, order goals, and economic goals. *Ideological* goals involve getting people to understand or believe the right things, or to do the right things voluntarily and for the right reasons. *Order* goals involve preventing people from doing the wrong things, more or less without regard to why they refrain from doing them, and without any expectation that they will make a positive contribution. *Economic* goals involve inducing people to produce and exchange goods and services. In similar fashion, we distinguish among normative, coercive, and remunerative power. Power is *normative* when it is based on persuasion, promises, and the manipulation of symbolic rewards. Power is *coercive* when it rests on the application or threat of physical sanctions or forceful deprivation of basic needs. Power is *remunerative* when it rests on the rationalized exchange of compliance for material rewards. To each of these kinds of power corresponds a kind of involvement. Normative power generates and is appropriate for manipulating *commitment*, or relatively intense and definitely positive involvement. Coercive power generates and is appropriate for restraining *alienation*, or relatively intense and definitely negative involvement. Remunerative power generates and is appropriate for influencing *indifference*, or involvement which is neither very positive nor very negative, and very low in intensity. Thus in this very simple typology of motivation, compliance results from either enthusiasm, fear, or acceptance of instructions within a calculatively established "zone of indifference." Each kind of goal may be pursued through the application of any kind of power, but for each kind of goal one type of power is particularly effective. Intense or prolonged application of normative power is effective in changing attitudes and is therefore fundamental to the achievement of ideological goals. Normative power will also sustain intense performance of activities for short periods of time, and is therefore useful for all kinds of goals in extraordinary campaigns or emergencies. Coercive power is relatively effective in deterring people from undesired activities, and is therefore particularly fundamental to the achievement of order goals. Coercive power will also sustain performance of activities for short periods of time, and is therefore also useful in emergencies. In the long run a steady background of coercion probably also contributes to attitude change and therefore to ideological goals. Remunerative power is particularly suited to maintaining the performance of activities over a long period of time, and is therefore particularly fundamental to the achievement of economic goals.

Quite obviously superordinates may pursue more than one kind of goal at a

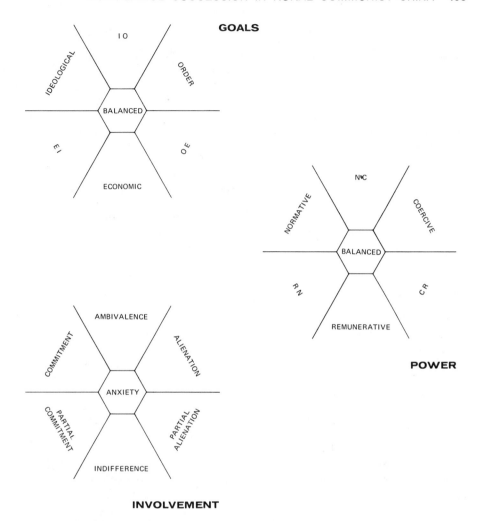

Figure 1   Typologies of Goals, Power, and Involvement Displayed on Analogous Fields

time, using more than one type of power, and producing mixed reactions on the part of subordinates. The possible mixed types for goals, power, and involvement may be diagrammed conveniently as shown in Figure 1. The many possible combinations among compound types of goals, power, and involvement which this typology opens up create complex problems and contradictory tendencies of managers of a compliance system. We argue that the "search" behavior of the Chinese Communist political system in exploring after a compliance state which offers satisfactory returns on order, economic, and ideological goals is a symptom of significant contradictions among the compliance requirements of these goals, given the structure of Chinese society and the particular form of the Communist leadership's ambitions. As Cyert and March have pointed out, such contradictions are quite normal in large organizations, and are commonly handled in at least two ways: compartmentalization in space and sequential attention over time.[4] Compartmentalization in space is particularly unfeasible in a closely knit territorial system at the local level in rural Communist China, putting particular pressure on the other mechanism of adjustment, sequential attention over time. This is, in systemic terms, the basic cause of the compliance cycling we shall describe.

Having in hand definitions of the elements of a compliance system, we are now in a position to construct a formal model of compliance cycling. This may be done conveniently by constructing separate cycles for goals, power, and involvement, and then superimposing these cycles in order to study the pattern of coincidence among them. In this paper we must limit ourselves to considering the particular goal, power, and involvement cycles which we believe apply to Communist China between 1949 and 1968, and to the phases of the compliance cycle into which they concatenate.[5] These are the patterns which, in our argument, were recurrently generated by the particular distribution of power and interests which prevailed in China during this historical period.

As regards goals, the pattern of successive salience is that generated by moving clockwise around the goal field: E, EI, I, IO, O, OE. This *goal cycle* appears to be partially intentional and partially inadvertent. The exact priorities and trade-offs among these goals from the point of view of individuals or factions within the Party leadership has been both complex and inscrutable. However, the net result of the decision-making process, whatever it has been, may be described roughly as follows: While the regime (in common with all successful rulers) could not afford to ignore completely any of the three types of goals, it has, nonetheless, behaved as though when it achieved a satisfactory level of order it tried to maximize economic and ideological goals, favoring the latter whenever minimal attainment of the former permitted. Because of intervening variables in the compliance system to be described below, this tendency to sacrifice economics to ideology has led repeatedly to a crisis in the order and economic sectors. These preferences and their consequences are reflected in the formal features of the goal cycle diagrammed upper-left in Figure 2. Here rapid change in the goal mix is indicated by a thin line, slower change by a proportionately thicker line. It will be noted that the goal mix achieves relative stability during three periods of the cycle. One is seen at the most extreme portion (i.e., that farthest from the Balanced sector) of the goal-mix trajectory, namely the tip of the "ostrich egg" in the lower portion of the I sector; it represents the goal mix which obtains during that happy portion of the upsurge when the effectiveness of the power mix and the commitment of the masses have not yet been called into question. A second temporal period during which goals change slowly comes when the trajectory is in the upper portion of the OE sector; it represents the goal mix—a relatively balanced one; it should be noted—preferred during the crisis phases. The third point of relative stability occurs during the relaxed, utilitarian phases when the goal mix settles into the left portion of the E sector.

As regards power, the pattern of successive emphasis is that generated by moving clockwise around the power field: R, RN, N, NC, C, CR. This *power cycle* appears to be generated by the alternation in power of leaders representing alternative philosophies of compliance, proponents of normative power being basically in the stronger position, but forced to accede to the proponents of remunerative power at those phases of the cycle in which economic performance and social order are dangerously impaired. Coercive power is relied upon by both sides to maintain production and order during the critical transition from the N to the R regimes. It should be stressed that the power cycle, like the goal cycle, is a matter of relative emphasis: a substantial fixed component of each kind of power is maintained throughout the cycle, with the leadership, insofar as it commands the

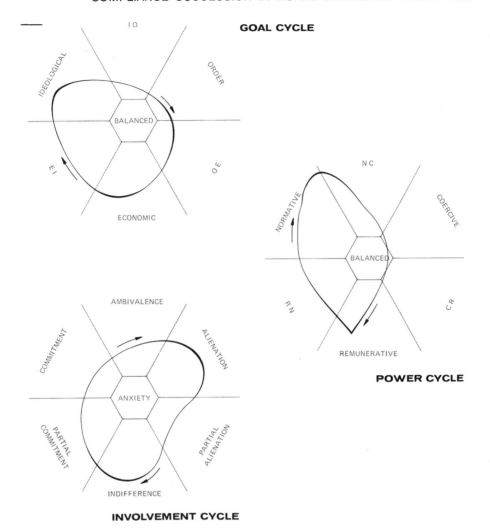

Figure 2   *Models of the Goal Cycle, Power Cycle, and Involvement Cycle*

resources, adjusting an additional variable component for particular purposes. There are two ways of looking at the power cycle, one stressing the joint effect of the three components of the power mix, the other stressing their separate movements. Stressing joint effect, the diagram at the center-right of Figure 2 shows the trajectory of the power cycle which is more or less typical for Communist China.[6] In the case of power, two periods of relative stability in the mix occur. One is seen at the most extreme (that is, the least balanced) portion of the leaf-shaped trajectory, where the tip of the leaf overlaps the N and NC sectors: this represents the power mix during the high tide of the cycle. The other period of slow change in the power mix is represented by the thickened portion of the trajectory near the stem of the leaf—the predominantly R mix, with more N than C, of the liberal phases of the cycle. Stressing movement of separate components, a generalized time-flow model of an NCR power cycle, and the particular form approximating those which have occurred in Communist China, are both shown in Figure 3. Using the former

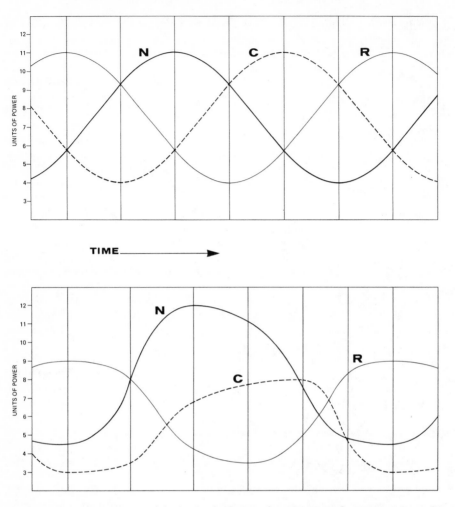

Figure 3   Top: Time-flow Model of a Perfectly Regular Power Cycle. Bottom: Time-flow Model of a Power Cycle Modified to Fit the Chinese Case.

as a foil, we may note in the latter the over-all high level of N, a relative restraint in the use of R even at its maximum, and a reluctance to employ large amounts of C (except, as we shall note below, against a small percentage of the population). Both the maximum and minimum are shown highest for N, intermediate for R, and lowest for C. The power cycle in Communist China is further defined by a "stretching out," relative to the generalized cycle, of the phases when N predominates in the mix, and a foreshortening of those in which the proportion of C is relatively high.

As regards involvement, the pattern of succession is that generated by moving clockwise around the involvement field: indifference, partial commitment, commitment, ambivalence, alienation, partial alienation, and back to indifference. This *involvement cycle* is, in the Chinese case, typically precipitated by an increase in normative power, applied in order to communicate and instill a new set of goals and to elicit performance in service of those goals. Most lower participants respond to this campaign with some increase in intensity and positiveness of involvement. Under successive applications of normative power, however, those who share the regime's goals are likely to move well into commitment, while those who do not will bend around into ambivalence and alienation. As the campaign comes to seem more and more shrill in its threats and promises and less and less substantial in its accomplishments, an increasing number of lower participants move over into alienation. Only when economic goals become salient again and normative power is replaced by remunerative power do these subordinates become mollified and drift back again to indifference, thereby completing the involvement cycle. A fairly typical involvement cycle is diagramed at the lower left in Figure 2.[7] Thickening in the kidney-shaped trajectory indicates the two phases of the cycle when involvement is relatively stable: during the latter stages of the crisis when alienation is great, and during the liberal phase when involvement is one of calculative indifference.

Having constructed separate cycles for goals, power, and involvement, we may now superimpose them to construct a compliance cycle. Figure 4 shows the superimposition of the power and involvement cycles. At the broadest level of analysis, this superimposition reveals three major interactions between power and involvement. During the first third of the cycle (on Figure 4, approximately from the beginning of segment 3 through segment 14) power "pulls" involvement to higher intensity, which is to say that changes in the power mix designed to induce commitment on the part of lower participants are successful. During the second third of the cycle (on Figure 4, approximately from the beginning of segment 15 through segment 29), involvement begins by constraining power and eventually "pulls" it to a more balanced and more nearly congruent mix. During the last third (from the beginning of segment 29 through segment 2), power "overtakes" involvement and once again leads it, this time to lower intensity; the changes in the power mix designed to reduce alienation are successful.

While these three movements of power and involvement capture in a general way the rhythm of advance and retreat of the Chinese political system, a finer division of the cycle based on somewhat different criteria will facilitate descriptive analysis. This scheme yields six phases, of which the first, third, and fifth are inaugurated when involvement enters, respectively, the Indifference, Commitment, and Alienation sectors, while the second, fourth, and sixth begin when the power mix enters, respectively, the RN, NC, and CR sectors. The designations for these phases and for the three pairings of them which reflect the broader picture are:

P6	Demobilization	} liberal phases
P1	Normalcy	
P2	Mobilization	} radical phases
P3	High Tide	
P4	Deterioration	} crisis phases
P5	Retrenchment	
P6	Demobilization	} liberal phases
P1	Normalcy	

It may be noted that the two radical phases are that portion of the cycle when the power mix is in the RN and N sectors, the crisis phases are that portion when the

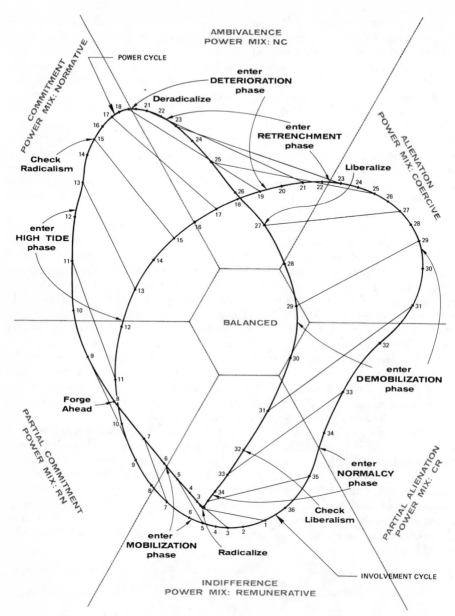

Figure 4   The Compliance Cycle: Interaction Between Power and Involvement and the Sequence of Compliance Phases

The entire span of the power cycle has been subdivided into 36 equal time segments, defined and numbered so that Segment 1 begins when the R component of the power mix is at a minimum. The 36 segments into which the involvement and goal cycles have also been subdivided are synchronized with those of the power cycle.

power mix is in NC or C, while the liberal phases are that portion when the power mix is CR or R.

If we now superimpose the goal and power cycles, as in Figure 5, we can

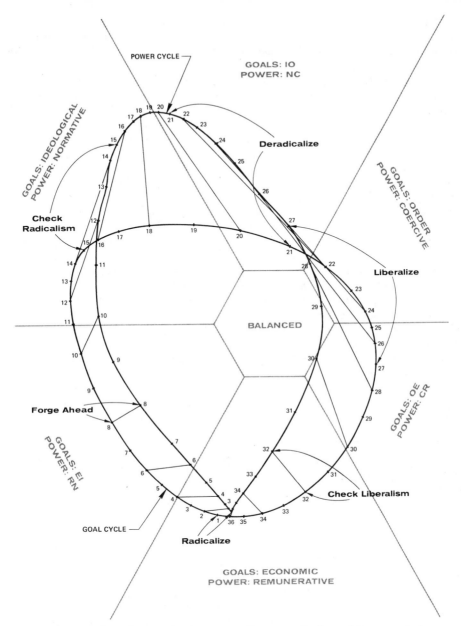

Figure 5   The Policy Cycle: Interaction Between Goals and Power and the Sequence of Policy Decisions

discern the *policy cycle* which they together define. The major point here is that for the greater part of the compliance cycle the effective power mix does not match the goals being pursued very exactly. While a moderate shift in goals during the Normalcy phase inaugurates the power cycle and goals "lead" power at an only modest distance during the first six time segments, thereafter accelerating changes in the power mix "overtake" changes in the goal mix and power remains more radical than goals until well into Demobilization. During the ascent, the power mix has a higher component of both N and C than would be appropriate for prevailing goals, while its normative component remains unsuitably high during the descent as well.

These features reflect our impression of what has occurred repeatedly in Communist China. The discrepancy between power and goals which develops during the radical phases rests on an ideological tenet of the N-proponents which holds that the proper kind of normative power properly administered is more efficacious than remunerative power in achieving economic as well as ideological ends. In affirming the power of socialist thinking to achieve production victories, the regime propagates policies and encourages procedures which are unrealistically related to goals. It would appear, furthermore, that the barrage of propaganda accompanying the radical phases colors the perceptions of lower-level cadres, who begin to see miracles and report them to superiors. Others succumb to pressure for performance by consciously over-reporting, thereby further masking the discrepancy. Readjustment in the power mix during the crisis phases is slow not only because problems of face make it difficult to enunciate or implement abrupt policy changes, not only because of the lingering belief that whatever went wrong did so because of poor implementation rather than poor theory, but also because N-proponents fail to encourage feedback for fear that the full facts will discredit them. Thus, aspects of the power struggle which typically develops during the crisis phases as R-proponents challenge the incumbents further retard the reduction of power-goal discrepancy.

A formal analysis of the NCR power cycle suggests six critical turning points, each occurring when one of the components of the power mix is at its peak or its nadir in relation to the other two. It would appear that critical political decisions mark these turning points in the changing power mix, and these are incorporated into our model as the Six Decisions:

Decision to	Occurring When the Following Ratio Is at a Maximum
Radicalize	$R / N + C$
Forge Ahead	$R + N / C$
Curb Radicalism	$N / C + R$
Deradicalize	$N + C / R$
Liberalize	$C / N + R$
Curb Liberalism	$C + R / N$

We may now gather the various strands of our analysis together through a phase-by-phase tour of our generic model of the compliance cycle in Communist China. The reader may wish to refer back to the diagrammatic representations of the relationship between power and involvement in Figure 4, between goals and power in Figure 5, and to the time-flow representation in Figure 6, which displays the Six Decisions and the six compliance phases against the rising and falling curves of the N, C, and R components of the power cycle.

Phase One, Normalcy, begins when involvement, recovering from the intensity and negative feelings generated by the previous cycle, crosses again into the Indifference sector of low intensity and neutral feelings. As total power input approaches its minimum, the system settles into equilibrium. Goals, power, and involvement are roughly congruent, with none producing any significant tenden-

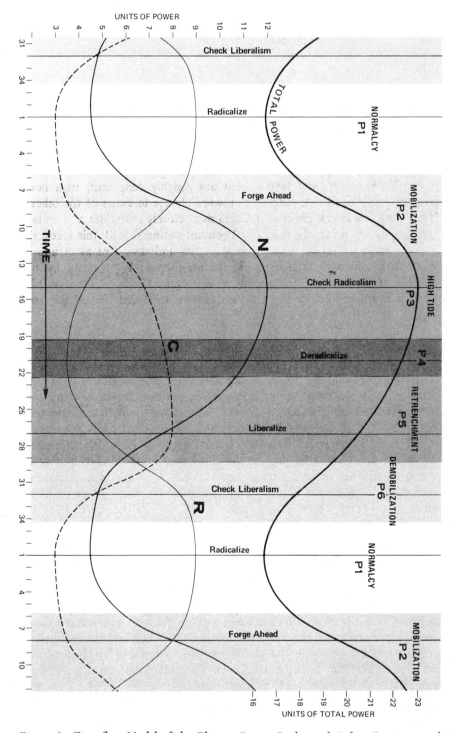

Figure 6   Time-flow Model of the Chinese Power Cycle, with Policy Decisions and Compliance Phases Superimposed

cies toward change in either of the others. It is during this liberal phase that China most closely resembles a "normal" agrarian society going about its usual peasant business. With this recovery, N proponents within the elite again seize the initiative. Just as N and C reach their minimum relative to R, the atmosphere is tightened by the Decision to Radicalize, inaugurating a new cycle. Goals, in other words, move leftward toward ideology, pulling power somewhat toward the normative, which in turn has a slight effect on involvement.

Phase Two, Mobilization, begins as power crosses into the RN sector, R proponents having definitely lost their ability to contain the N proponents. Mobilization sees rapid changes in the power mix—changes which overshoot goals and are relatively effective in raising involvement to high positive levels. Although considerable strain between power and involvement characterizes the entire phase, the moving compliance structure approximates the congruent type whereby a predominantly RN power mix elicits partial commitment. The Decision to Forge Ahead, which determines the general goals of the big push to come and enumerates the highly normative strategies for achieving them, comes when C-power is at a relative minimum and R-power is still being maintained at high levels. Policies which it inaugurates accelerate the ascent of C and the descent of R.

Phase Three, High Tide, begins as involvement, responding to the normative blandishments of the previous mobilization phase, moves into Commitment. Total power input reaches its maximum, C continuing to rise, R continuing to fall, and N reaching its peak. Power continues to be more radical than goals, while in the course of the phase involvement begins to constrain power. That is, the structure of compliance slips in the course of Phase Three from an effective one in which normative power and committed involvement are congruent, to a less effective one in which normative power must contend with the increasing disaffection and ambivalence of the peasantry. The Decision to Check Radicalism, which at midphase moderates the big push, leads to a downturn in the input of N power and deceleration in the rates at which R- and C-power are changing.

Phase Four, Deterioration, begins as power, responding to the growing recalcitrance of lower participants, moves over into the NC sector. Deterioration is a period of impending crisis: lower participants are becoming speedily more alienated, and in response the goal mix moves rapidly from I toward O. Change in the power mix is sluggish, however, for reasons already suggested; N power is reduced, but R remains low and steady, C high and steady. As a result, the discrepancy between power (NC) and involvement (ambivalence) widens throughout the phase. In these straits, N-proponents have no choice but to deradicalize, which decision is the R-proponents' entering wedge.

Phase Five, Retrenchment, begins as involvement, unmollified by the too little and too late curbing of radical excesses, moves squarely into alienation. During retrenchment the crisis comes to a head. Faced with serious alienation among the peasantry and shocked by production declines, the leadership forgets its scruples and effects a radical and rapid change in the power mix: N is phased out in favor of R, and with the Decision to Liberalize, C too is allowed to decline. Shortly after a period of fleeting congruence, when a maximally coercive power mix impinges on alienated peasants, power "overtakes" involvement and begins leading it to lower intensity. The crisis is then past.

Phase Six, Demobilization, begins as power, overtaking involvement and beginning to reduce alienation through a steeply rising component of remuneration, moves into the CR sector. C plummets and N eases into a less precipitous decline. The Decision to Check Liberalism slows the rate of change of all three components, setting in train the policies which cause them to level off in the subsequent phase of Normalcy.

This schematization, it should be emphasized, is specific to the temporal patterning of compliance arrangements at a particular level of periodicity and level of institutional significance in the compliance system of Communist China. Compliance cycles may occur at many levels, ranging from the diurnal, marketing-week, seasonal and annual schedules whereby work and leisure in agricultural China are arranged, through the cycles accompanying major campaigns to transform particular institutions, to the grand eras of new democratic revolution, socialist construction, and cultural revolution into which the Chinese Communists themselves periodize their own history. Such cycles may or may not be causally related to each other, they may or may not be similar in the nature and sequence of their phases, and they may or may not be related to secular change. We would argue that cycles of different lengths occur in the compliance arrangements surrounding components of the social system lying at different levels of generality. The more fundamental the component, the longer the cycle.[8]

System and Cycle in China

The particular level of cycling treated here is a specific consequence of the succession of campaigns through which the Chinese Communists have attempted to revolutionize Chinese society. As need hardly be said, socialism and communism are themselves prescriptive compliance theories, and these campaigns therefore have precisely to do with the alteration of compliance arrangements. As such, these campaigns and their often unanticipated compliance consequences are easy to identify, being a matter of explicit historical record. Nevertheless we feel there is something to be gained from their analysis in terms of organizational theory, in particular a more systematic analysis of the internal dynamics of each campaign, and a more complete statement of the organizational correlates of these instances of compliance cycling.

On our analysis there have been eight cycles of radicalization and deradicalization at the national level in the 19 years since the People's Republic of China was established. The dating of these cycles, which lasted two or three years each, is indicated by the following dates for the first, third, and fifth of the six decisions.

	Decision to Radicalize (Normalcy)	Decision to Check Radicalism (High Tide)	Decision to Liberalize (Retrenchment)	Decision to Radicalize (Normalcy)[9]
C1	Winter 1949–1950	Fall 1950	Spring 1951	Fall 1951
C2	Fall 1951	Summer 1952	Spring 1953	Fall 1953
C3	Fall 1953	Summer 1954	Winter 1954–1955	Spring 1955
C4	Spring 1955	Spring 1956	Fall 1956	Summer 1957
C5	Summer 1957	Winter 1958–1959	Spring 1959	Summer 1959
C6	Summer 1959	Spring 1960	Winter 1960–1961	Fall 1962
C7	Fall 1962	Winter 1963–1964	Winter 1964–1965	Fall 1965
C8	Fall 1965	Winter 1966–1967	Summer 1968	

Drastic reforms in rural society were being pushed only in cycles 1, 4, 5, and 6. Other cycles saw major developments in urban China, accompanied in the countryside by efforts to mop-up after the last major reform or prepare for the next one.

The restructuring of rural society which occurred during the first decade of Communist rule involved five stages. We shall relate these stages to cycles after briefly characterizing each stage. During the *first stage*, land reform, the entire farming population was divided into five classes: landless farmhands, "poor," "middle," and "rich" peasants, and landlords. In this stage the first four categories were mobilized to struggle against the landlords, the economic basis of whose power and prestige was destroyed through confiscation of land, livestock, and equipment. When this stage was over, some 60 million households, about half the total number of rural families, had benefited through redistribution, and the previous local elite had been eliminated as a class. The *second stage* saw the formation of mutual-aid teams, normally composed of 6–15 households. As first organized, these were usually seasonal and temporary, involving only limited reciprocity with regard to labor, draft animals and farm tools. Most teams were subsequently transformed into permanent units involving unrestricted use of these production factors. If completed everywhere, this stage would have reduced the total number of basic production units from 120 million to approximately 15 million. The *third stage* involved the formation of small agricultural producers' cooperatives, in which the peasant household invested its land, draft animals and tools, receiving dividends for their use. At the same time, the "rich-peasant economy" was brought to an end. Better-off households which prior to land reform owned more land than they tilled, the so-called "rich" peasants, were singled out as enemies of the masses and their surplus land confiscated for the new cooperative. If completed everywhere, the new cooperative production unit of 20–40 households would have numbered approximately 3.5 million. The *fourth stage* typically involved the merger of the small agricultural producers' cooperatives into larger collective farms. This stage saw massive restrictions on the family-farm economy for, in the collective, income was distributed not according to the holdings which each household had contributed but according to the labor performed by the working adults in each family. At the conclusion of this stage over 93 percent of all rural households belonged to approximately 750,000 collectives. The *fifth stage* was that of people's communes, production units so greatly enlarged that they could be merged with the basic-level units of government administration. As in the first and third stages, the topmost remaining class became the object of political and economic discrimination. At High Tide in late 1958 there were 24,000 communes.

These five stages were passed through in the course of the first five cycles. However, stage and cycle are not in perfect alignment. First, many localities and even entire regions skipped one or more stages altogether. Thus approximately two-fifths of rural households were never grouped into mutual-aid teams, while the third stage of lower-level cooperatives was skipped by a majority of both localities and households. In Szechwan and parts of other provinces, most localities went directly from cooperatives to communes, skipping the collective stage. Second, different localities passed through particular stages during different cycles. Thus, while land reform was carried out in most parts of China in C1, in many of the "old liberated areas" it had been completed in 1947–1949, while in many of the "new liberated areas" in the South and Southwest it was substantially completed only in C2. Similarly, mutual-aid teams were set up in precocious areas in C1, in most areas in C2, and in backward areas not until C3. By C5, however, most localities were on the same schedule. There remained, of course, variation in the alacrity and effectiveness with which local cadres executed directives. In general there seems to have been less variation in the timing of local policy cycles than in the extent of actual policy implementation and corresponding severity of the involvement cycle.

Let us now provide a quick review of compliance cycling in the countryside. Liberation in most parts of the country was followed by a retreat from coercion and recourse to R-power, in particular through the rent reduction program. Once the goodwill of the peasantry had been secured in this fashion (that is, as soon as their orientation to the regime had been brought around to one at least as positive as calculative involvement), mobilization for land reform (C1P2) was inaugurated. The intensity of peasant involvement was rapidly raised during P2–3, climaxing with the struggle meetings against landlords. Recourse to coercion, which began to rise with the antidespot program of P3, approached its peak when the property of landlords was confiscated in P4. Excesses in the treatment of landlords had by this time led to anxiety and revulsion on the part of many peasants (that is, their involvement had swung around to ambivalence), while fear of being stigmatized as "rich peasants" had depressed the productive zeal of many less impoverished families within the peasantry. R-power began to rise again as confiscated land was redistributed, while the concerted effort to round up "criminal and counter-revolutionary elements" was the final manifestation of C before it was allowed to plummet. With the issuance of title deeds, peasant involvement was allowed to recede to a state of low intensity, and the renewed salience of economic goals was expressed in the production drive inaugurated in P6. That the power mix had become predominantly R was apparent by July 1951, when a prominent Communist leader criticized cadres for persisting in utopianism instead of encouraging the peasants to get rich.[10]

Cycle Two, 1951–1953, was severe in the city and mild in the countryside, except of course in those areas where land reform was only then in progress. Although radicalization came in the cities in the fall of 1951, the Decision to Radicalize in rural China may be taken as the directive on formation of mutual-aid teams issued by the Central Committee of the Chinese Communist Party on 15 December 1951. A primary concern of the top leadership was the erosion of the political base built up in the villages during land reform because of the withdrawal from political involvement and preoccupation with economic gain on the part of both peasants and cadres. Mobilization was inaugurated through a transition in the emulation campaign to increase production from an emphasis on the superior moral qualities of peasant labor heroes to an emphasis on the superiority of collective organization. High Tide objectives in various areas included formation of mutual-aid teams, water conservancy projects and experiments with lower-level cooperatives. These organizational objectives were linked to such ideological campaigns as that to "aid Korea, resist America." Despite the relative modesty of these objectives and the air of caution and experiment with which they were approached, P4 saw the deterioration of cadre leadership characteristic of later, more severe cycles. Peasants were sometimes forced to join mutual-aid teams by threatening to expel them from peasant associations or by denying loans to the recalcitrant. Discrimination against individual independent farmers and violation of middle peasants' interests in teams had, as admitted by the Party in the wake of the campaign, "injured the incentive to produce." Other evidence of peasant disaffection in P5 was the "blind flow" of peasants into the cities and the rising death rate among draft animals due to overwork and neglect. P6 accordingly saw a campaign against "bureaucracy, commandism and violations of socialist laws and discipline" among cadres at the county level and above, while a milder course of education in Party principles and methods was conducted among the nascent organizations at the lowest levels. Also during C2P6, with the repudiation of coercion and renewed salience of economic goals, mutual-aid teams which had been made permanent during radicalization reverted to the seasonal type during liberalization, an early example of the two-steps-forward one-step-backward rhythm characteristic of the next three cycles as well.

The Decision to Radicalize inaugurating C3 was the introduction of state control of the purchase and sale of grain following the 1953 harvest. Mobilization began in the winter of 1953–1954, with High Tide in most areas the winter of 1954–1955. The national target for cooperatives set in the directive of December 1953 was 35,800, raised to 500,000 by September 1954, and reaching 630,000 by February 1955, when the campaign was called off. No less than a fifth of all peasant households had been organized. This effort, immense by comparison with that of C2, generated cadre "errors" and peasant disaffection on a correspondingly larger scale. As in the course of 1954 cadres felt increasingly pressed to demonstrate the superiority of cooperative organization, some forced middle peasants to join in order to appropriate their productive resources. The winter of 1954–1955 (C3P4–5) was notable for the neglect, sale, or slaughter of livestock. Other evidence of peasant alienation was reluctance during the winter slack season to improve land and maintain water-control installations, failure to collect and apply fertilizer, and a reduction in the total area sown to winter grain crops. The decision of February 1955 to liberalize was forced by a growing shortage of grain and the recognition that, in the words of the *People's Daily*, "there is nobody to take charge of spring plowing and production." Spring 1955 (C3P6) saw reintroduction of material incentives to overcome recalcitrance in spring sowing, together with a renewed emphasis on the productive significance of well-to-do peasants. Reversion to less socialist forms of organization occurred on a wide scale, Mao himself reporting that in Chekiang 15,000 out of 53,000 cooperatives had been dissolved. Normalcy extended through the autumn harvest, as provincial leaders laid plans to carry into effect Mao's dramatic Decision to Radicalize of late July.

With the lines of command to the basic levels more or less in place, in late 1955 the Party leadership was for the first time in a position to order reorganization more or less simultaneously across the entire nation. This, in the course of cycles 4 and 5, it did. Whereas only half of all peasant households had been involved in the reorganization of cycle 3, when in autumn 1955 a good harvest enabled the radicals to Forge Ahead the consequent socialist upsurge of cycle 4 carried over three-fifths of all peasant households into fully socialist collectives. By the onset of Deterioration in May 1956, less than a tenth of the peasantry remained outside either cooperatives or collectives. Given the speed, scope, and extremism of the campaign, cadres were forced to rely significantly on coercion, including arbitrary deduction of wage points, refusal to assign people jobs, increases in tax assessments, denial of access to irrigation facilities, freezing bank deposits and arbitrary increase in delivery quotas. Troops appeared to "aid agriculture," and security defense committees were established to protect from sabotage the trees, equipment, granaries, and crops now owned by the collectives. C4P4 saw indiscriminate slaughter of livestock and another mass exodus to the cities.

Despite substantial evidence of peasant disaffection, the new organizational machinery was kept in place, the Decision of Check Radicalism taking the form of a stream of directives adjusting the prices for specific crops, and instructing cadres not to neglect the breeding of animals and the cultivation of crops other than grain. The fall of 1956 saw new directives "strengthening production leadership and organization construction" in the face of obvious difficulties on the part of cadres in carrying out their new managerial responsibilities, combined with some relaxation in government control of rural markets. Further concessions to liberalism followed in the spring of 1957, peaking in the rural areas in the early summer with an expansion in the size of private plots. In urban China the political pendulum had already begun to swing leftward, however, following the alarming criticism voiced during the brief liberal "100 flowers" period. A severe antirightist campaign was launched in the late spring in the urban areas, reaching rural China in the fall in the somewhat milder form of a "socialist education campaign."

Although basic decisions about the direction which Chinese agriculture should take apparently hung in the balance from the fall of 1957 until the spring of 1958, the fall and winter of 1957 was a classic mobilization phase, combining the campaign to educate the peasants in socialism with extensive mobilization of labor for work on water conservancy projects. Following hesitancy on the part of some and daring organizational innovation on the part of others, this mobilization snow-balled into the classic cycle of them all, the Great Leap Forward and communization. Between the Decision to Forge Ahead of August and the Decision to Check Radicalism of December, the enthusiasm of local cadres for their burgeoning organizational empires, and to a significant extent the enthusiasm of poor and lower-middle peasants for free supply and instant modernization, swept rural China forward to the threshold of communism. Or at least so it seemed. A bumper harvest in the fall of 1958 and a timely retrenchment in the spring of 1959 left the issue in doubt. Opponents of the strategy of mass mobilization argued at a decisive meeting in August 1959 that despite the tidying-up they had received, communes were "a mess." They lost. With preparations for the 10th anniversary of the Chinese People's Republic, with a revived stress on the significance of class struggle and the necessity for purifying the leadership cores at the basic levels, and with a renewed drive for production in both industry and agriculture, the Great Leap Forward lumbered off into a second cycle of radicalization, crisis and retreat. What exactly the involvement cycle was doing is difficult to piece together, but it is doubtful that the peasants were greatly mollified by the aborted liberalization of the spring of 1959 or greatly enthused by the exhausting re-radicalization of fall 1959 to fall 1960. It is likely that some dip in their alienation did occur, however, as cadres were rectified in the winter of 1959–1960 for having pushed the peasants too hard and for having imposed collective institutions to which the peasants objected. In the fall of 1960 it became clear that, owing to bad weather, misallocation of resources and declining incentives, agricultural output was catastrophically low. In November Deradicalization was launched with a campaign to rectify the "five Communist styles" among overbearing cadres. As the countryside passed through a winter of hunger, alienation, and disorder, the 9th Plenum of January 1961 embarked on a program of full-scale liberalization.

The seventh cycle in rural Communist China began with the radicalizing communique of the 10th Plenum, held in September 1962. This cycle got off to a long slow start, reminiscent of the long transition between the land reform and collectivization cycles. An important issue was, once again, whether the basic-level cadres were sufficiently skilled to carry a mass movement to the people. Between 1952 and 1954 the Party had first rectified its special district and county organizations, educated its basic-level cadres to their tasks, and then proceeded with mass mobilization. Between 1962 and 1964 the regime, having been forced temporarily to abandon mass mobilization, tried to re-educate its basic-level cadres and, after disappointing results from both mild and severe approaches, turned again to rectify the county levels and above. The basic-level cadres, having only partially recovered from their alienation at the severe rectifications through which they were put in the course of the retreat from the Great Leap Forward, were subjected first to an educative mobilization (September 1962–September 1964), then to a sharp rectification at the hands of higher Party officials and the newly-formed Poor and Lower-Middle Peasant Associations (September 1964–January 1965), and then again to more lenient treatment. The major point for our purposes is that, for the peasantry itself, cycle 7 never really got off the ground. Except for tentative moves to restrict the free market and reduce the size of private plots, radicalization consisted only of exhortatory socialist education campaigns, and the attempt to repair the rural Party organization.

The latest cycle, and the one most obscure in its implications for the rural areas, is of course the Great Proletarian Cultural Revolution. Although the relationship among these events is unclear, it appears that Mao was disappointed in the result of various campaigns to get the country moving again, and turned to rectify the highest levels of the Party organization, while attempting to assemble the leadership for a new mass movement at the basic levels through an alliance of young radicals, disadvantaged workers, PLA personnel and the more radical "old" cadres. The countryside, largely insulated from the radical phases of the Cultural Revolution in the urban areas in 1966, became briefly involved in January 1967, and perhaps more substantially involved in the spring of 1968. Although the Cultural Revolution has clearly moved on to something of a retrenchment phase, it is too early to present a consecutive account of compliance policy in the countryside during this cycle.

The Six Phases: Organizational Correlates

Having reviewed the history of compliance cycling in Communist China, we must now turn to the organizational content and systemic context of each of the six phases of the cycle. All the elements of the generic account which follows do not necessarily occur in full or at all in all cycles, or in all phases of any cycle.

Phase One: Normalcy. During Normalcy the State and Party organizations bear their lightest loads. Projects to revolutionize rural society overnight are temporarily set aside. While economic objectives are pursued, many of the decisions and most of the tasks of agriculture are decentralized into private hands. The task environment of the organization is perceived as the routine technical inputs required for increased agricultural production. Viewing the problem under a long time horizon, policy makers apply a long-linked technology involving development of a chemical fertilizer industry, mechanization of farming, and long-term programs to raise the level of technical education of the peasants. The complex interdependencies among farming operations themselves, among the agricultural and other sectors of the economy, and among the economic and other aspects of modernization are appreciated, and coordination is attempted through standardization, planning, and mutual adjustment. The appropriate local leaders are therefore those with the relevant technical skills: the most able farmers and such government agents as agricultural extension workers. At the local level the scope (the number of activities in which lower participants jointly participate) of government-led organizations is at its most narrow, and their pervasiveness (the number of activities inside and outside the organization for which the organization tries to set norms) is at its lowest. Recruitment to positions of leadership is differentiated in both means and criteria by self-selection: the most able farmers again become the economic leaders of the natural farming community, while only the dedicated activists compete for Party membership. In regard to both instrumental and expressive activities, the role of the cadres is limited to that of officials who supervise and regulate activities which they do not organize and lead. Communication between cadres and peasants is slight and restricted to instrumental matters, a balance of upward flow of reports on tasks and output and downward flow of routine instructions and indirect incentives. Charisma in the organization is limited to the very top, to the idea of The Party and its Great Leader, Mao Tse-tung. There is little pressure for the recruitment of the population at large into collective economic organizations or into the Party and its mass organizations. Accordingly, socialization is largely informal and largely restricted to instrumental matters. The level of consensus demanded from the masses does not go actively beyond agreement on work assignments and output quotas. Cohesion in work groups of lower participants is entirely derived from extra-organization affiliations; the salience of membership in formal organizations is at a minimum in the lives of the populace. Locality-wide solidarity among peasants is defined in traditional terms, a by-product of the conflicts and alliances in the segmentary structure of a traditional Chinese community. The economic rationality of both the traditional farming methods employed and the few innovations being pushed result in an agricultural performance which is basically both efficient in its use of resources and effective in meeting the needs of the country.

Phase Two: Mobilization. Mobilization is a period of organizational expansion. Ideological objectives are revived, and normative means are again applied to economic ends. The task environment of the organization is perceived as one of both technical and social opportunity, a promise of increased output through investment and capital formation on the one hand, and through mass mobilization on the other. To meet this medium-run opportunity a mediating technology is applied, the government acting as entrepreneur in bringing together under-utilized labor and capital. The scope of government organizations widens as they seize the initiative in capital construction projects and drives to increase production. Pervasiveness rises as socialist norms are set for these activities and for related activities outside of organization boundaries. Recruitment to leadership positions is stepped up, while both selectivity and socialization are brought to bear through a rectification of the leaders of the basic levels of the Party and mass organizations. Credentials for leadership combine the red and the expert. Cadres increase their participation in instrumental activities, mobilizing informal instrumental leaders to greater efforts. They also increase their efforts at expressive leadership, conducting campaigns among the masses to secure attitude change and increase production. With the expansion of organizational functions, the volume of communication between cadre and peasants increases through mass meetings and study sessions, becoming expressive as well as instrumental, the downward flow of ideology and instructions outweighing the upward flow of information about local conditions. Similarly, the volume of internal communication between organizational levels increases through face-to-face and telephone conferences. With the role of the Party hierarchy and Party line in directing social action again stressed, the aura of charisma surrounding the Party chain of command intensifies. As for the masses, recruitment to membership in economic and political organizations rises, becoming less selective, excluding only those with definitely bad expressive credentials. Although there is some tendency on the part of cadres to exclude from production organizations those with poor instrumental credentials (that is, the less able farmers and those without animals or equipment), the government insists on discrimination in their favor, since by and large these are the poor and lower-middle peasants who are the vanguards of socialism. The level of consensus demanded of lower participants rises to include at first the terms of participation in collective organizations, and later the new methods and goals of these organizations. With the mandatory rise in the level of collective endeavor comes an effort to define socialist norms of cohesion within work groups; with the expansion in the size of collective units comes an effort to promote solidarity within the revolutionary ranks. The government's attempt to make the performance of agriculture more effective shows real results, owing both to the rise in investment and the increase in labor input.

Phase Three: High Tide. High Tide finds the organization at its maximal expansion. Ideological goals and ideological means are both at their peak. The task environment of the organization is perceived almost entirely in terms of the manipulation of collective motivation, the seizing of the opportunity to transform both nature and society through the collective mobilization of will-power. An intensive technology is applied to these short-run problems, with little appreciation of problems of interdependence, and little effort devoted to coordination. Scope is, in principle, unlimited: as many activities as possible should be carried out through collective action. As a result, both the salience of participation in formal organization, and the tensions generated by that participation, are at their highest. However, these tensions are successfully channeled into constructive action by defining sentiments of struggle as the driving force of revolutionary accomplishment. Pervasiveness is also, in principle, unlimitedly high: there is no aspect of life which ought to be immune from the demands of socialist morality. Cadres now wholly usurp both the instrumental and expressive functions of informal leaders, the ethos of the new socialist community denying all legitimacy to the natural community and its leaders. The credentials for cadre leadership shift toward the expressive; charisma spreads across this rank of professionals in the art of sparking revolutionary transformation. Authority is decentralized so that local leaders can give full play to their charismatic powers and reap full benefit from the particular revolutionary topography of their locality. As for the masses, recruitment now aspires to the totally inclusive: even former landlords and rich peasants are now admitted. Efforts at expressive resocialization therefore continue unabated. Organizational effectiveness requires not only consensus on organizational goals, but on general values as well: in the absence of remunerative incentives, commitment to ideology is the only basis for action. Work-group cohesion is in theory absolute: there is no distinction among the role of worker, soldier, and citizen. Solidarity within the revolutionary ranks is also theoretically absolute, not only within the greatly expanded local community, but also in the nation at large. The performance outcome of these efforts is difficult to evaluate in the short run from an economic point of view, and in any case the criteria of performance applied are neither those of efficiency nor those of effectivenes, but an extrinsic standard of the socialist correctness of the productive efforts themselves. There is, indeed, progress in attitude change, in breaking through traditional habits and inhibitions, and in widening the definition of the political community.

Phase Four: Deterioration. Deterioration is a phase of incipient contraction of organizational responsibilities and energies. The task environment has become moderately unstable and moderately threatening: there are fears of both instrumental and expressive sabotage on the part of "bad elements" who have sneaked into the organization. The remedy is, however, "more of the same": purify the leadership cores by rectifying deviations, and renew the flagging campaign. Readings on most organizational variables continue to be the same as in Phase Three. However, tension, which increases under conditions of scarcity and growing problems of managing over-large collective units, begins to break out as antagonism to leaders and among subcollectivities, instead of being channeled into socialist construction. Formal leaders continue to override informal leaders in both instrumental and expressive domains, but as the upsurge of enthusiasm ebbs they become less effective in their roles. Their charisma is diminished by their association with instrumental activities, their extensive interaction with lower participants, the intimation of failure, the demands they are forced to make on lower participants, and, in some cases, their corruption and abuse of authority. Among the masses, dissensus develops as departures from traditional norms become unsettling to many, the feasibility of attaining organization goals comes to be doubted, and the unwisdom of many of the recent social and technical innovations begins to become clear. Thus dissensus focuses on organizational means, and increasingly on the terms of participation, while demands for consensus retreat to goals and increasingly to performance obligations themselves. As scarcities develop and the elan of successful reorganization dissipates, natural cohesions and local rivalries disrupt the larger solidarity of the revolutionary ranks. In communications, gaps develop both between leaders and led and between organizational levels; a rising tide of misinformation brings on an increasing distrust of upward moving reports, and an increasing irrelevance of superordinate's directives.

Phase Five: Retrenchment. With retrenchment, a sharp contraction in the ambitions and capabilities of formal organization sets in. The task environment now appears definitely threatening on both the instrumental and expressive sides. Needed on the instrumental side is the rematching of organizational units to manageable segments of the task environment, the application of technical expertise, and a major effort to re-establish coordination of a fragmented economy. Needed on the expressive side is a tightening of party discipline, a containment of alienation both among cadres and masses, and a greater severity of control until the crisis is past. The scope of activities managed by the organization and the salience of participation to lower participants both fall, reducing both the level of tension and the complexity of managerial tasks. The collaboration of informal instrumental leaders is again sought, with cadres retreating to instrumental supervision and a vain attempt to continue to provide expressive support for instrumental activities, while quietly abandoning their intervention in expressive matters. Communication between leaders and led, and between organizational levels, is at a nadir; instead of messages circulating upward to superiors, the superiors descend in waves to see what is going on and obtain reliable production information. Cadres lose an immense amount of face in the course of rectifications designed to check both over severe and over lenient leadership styles, and to transfer to the basic-level cadre the blame for failure of the mobilization strategy; it is doubtful that anyone in the organization has much charisma left, except for Mao on the wishful assumption that "he doesn't know what's really going on." As for the masses, the level of consensus demanded declines to that of performance obligations, while dissensus focuses on the demand to participate in collective organization at all. Membership becomes more selective, in fact, through the withdrawal of the most alienated members. Subcollectivities definitely split off from the socialist community, forming cohesive groups which are antagonistic to collective organization, and often to each other. It is now clear that economic performance has been poor. The State, concerned over the poor return on its investments, retrenches in its expenditures, showing an increasing concern for efficiency and a decreasing regard for effectiveness.

Phase Six: Demobilization. In the course of demobilization, government organization contracts toward its minimal role in society. The task environment is seen as less threatening, less unstable, but as more heterogeneous in both the instrumental and expressive spheres: needed are greater decentralization of tasks and minor decisions, coupled with a centralization of major decisions and supervision. With the abandonment of hopes for short-run gains in production, the time horizon expands, and serious attention is again given to developing and coordinating a long-linked agricultural technology. Although there is no formal declaration of retreat, scope and pervasiveness contract rapidly. Supervision of expressive matters is relinquished, pretensions of expressive leadership in support of production are abandoned, and cadres retreat to positional official supervisors of instrumental activities, tolerating a high degree of initiative by natural leaders. Minimal communication is restored as the pressure to achieve and report the impossible is relaxed. The charisma of even the top Party leadership passes into eclipse. More of the less committed withdraw from formal leadership positions and from membership in collective organizations. Organizational demands for consensus are limited to task performance and output quotas, while work group cohesion is again derived largely from natural affiliations. Agricultural production recovers with the restoration of incentives and the return to economically rational performance criteria.

Notes

1. Amitai Etzioni, *A Comparative Analysis of Complex Organizations* (New York: Free Press, 1961), p. 3.
2. For an explanation of these variables, see Etzioni, Part II.
3. For the systemic analysis on which this paper draws, see James D. Thompson, *Organizations in Action* (New York: McGraw-Hill, 1967).
4. Richard M. Cyert and James G. March, *A Behavioral Theory of the Firm* (Englewood Cliffs, N.J.: Prentice-Hall, 1963), Ch. 6.
5. A completely general discussion would consider all the possible sequences in which goals and combinations of goals might become salient, all the possible sequences in which superordinates might shift their reliance among types and combinations of types of power, and all the possible sequences in which subordinates might move from one mode of involvement to another. Such a general discussion would also consider in detail all the possible combinations of each of these goal, power, and involvement cycles with one another.
6. The power-mix field, it should be noted, has three coordinate axes—N, C and R—each

radiating from the center of the field and bisecting its sector. The three axes, with 120 degrees between them, define a field the units of which are equilateral triangles instead of squares. The leaf-shaped curve shown in Figures 2, 4, and 5 is a plotting on this field of the values built into the time-flow diagrams in Figures 3 and 6.

7. The involvement field is set apart by its formal features from the goal and power fields. It has a single vertical dimension, namely intensity of involvement, increasing from low at the bottom to high at the top. The horizontal dimension is direction of involvement, neither positive nor negative at the center of the field, increasingly positive as one moves leftward from the center, increasingly negative as one moves rightward. The typology imposed on this field, which yields 7 types of involvement, omits the two logical possibilities which are theoretically anomalous and presumably empirically rare: involvement which is at once low in intensity and extremely positive, and that which is low in intensity and extremely negative.

8. Cf. Neil J. Smelser, *Theory of Collective Behavior* (New York: Free Press, 1963), Ch. 2; and Anthony Downs, *Inside Bureaucracy* (Boston: Little, Brown, 1967), Ch. 14.

9. The decision to radicalize is listed twice for the convenience of the reader, since it ends the previous cycle as well as inaugurating the one to come.

10. Po I-po. Cited in Kenneth R. Walker, "Collectivization in Retrospect," *China Quarterly*, 26 (1966), p. 11.

Growth and Decline Processes in Organizations*

John Freeman and Michael T. Hannan

Introduction

Since the original articles by Melman (1951) and Terrien and Mills (1955), researchers have most often attempted to explain variations in administrative intensity through reference to size. Administrative intensity is defined as the relative sizes of two personnel components in organizations: administrative (or "supportive") and production-worker (or "direct"). In its most recent form, the linkage between this variable and size has been asserted by Blau and a number of collaborators (Blau, 1970; Blau and Schoenherr, 1971; Blau, 1972; Blau, 1973). The essential idea is that bigger organizations have more highly elaborated structures with regard to both horizontal and vertical differentiation. Size has positive effects on administrative intensity because these elaborate structures produce coordination problems for which the organization compensates by hiring additional administrators. On the other hand, bigger organizations have previously made investments in organizational patterns required to manage a higher level of work activity. As Blau (1972:18) put it: ". . . the investment of administrative time required for organizing operations is not proportionate to their volume, increasing far less than the volume of work increases." In addition, larger size makes for a more efficient use of specialized administrative effort. Skills and abilities are not infinitely divisible. So small organizations are less able to use administrative manpower efficiently.

> If the volume of administrative work increases less than proportionately as the volume of operations increases; and if the volume of work governs the number of persons needed to accomplish it, in administration as well as in operations; it follows that the number of persons in administration increases less than that in operations; and hence that the proportion of administrative personnel decreases as the total number of employees decreases . . . (Blau, 1972:18)

Increases in size lead to increases in differentiation which in turn lead to increases in administrative intensity. But increases in size also produce economies of scale which counteract effects via differentiation. Since in most organizations the negative direct effects of size exceed the positive indirect effects, the bivariate relationship is negative.[1]

In another recent article, Hendershot and James (1972:151) found that school districts which had previously experienced more rapid growth[2] displayed

*An earlier draft of this paper was presented at the Eighth World Congress of the International Sociological Association, Toronto, Canada. We are indebted to John W. Meyer for useful criticisms.

Reprinted from *American Sociological Review*, vol. 40 (April, 1975), pp. 215–228, by permission of the authors and the publisher, The American Sociological Association.

the usual negative relationship between size and administrative intensity. But districts which had experienced slow growth did not show a consistent relationship. Furthermore, districts which experienced slow growth displayed increases in administrative intensity while those which grew rapidly showed decreases. However, their inferences are based mainly on categorized interval scale data for which subcell n's are often quite small. Although their discussion suggests a monotonic relationship between rate of growth and change in administrative intensity, their data show a curvilinear relationship.

Hendershot and James attempt to explain the differences for rapid and slow growers by positing different lags for the relations of size (enrollment) with the administrative component and with the production-worker component. We want to examine the implications of this possibility from a more general perspective.

If the numerator and denominator of the usual A/P ratio are related to size by causal lags of different lengths, two design implications follow. First, the ratios are not unitary from a theoretical perspective. Since the numerator and denominator are related to other variables in different ways, the ratio will behave erratically as the other variables vary. The implication is that one should decompose the A/P ratio into its components and study the effects of other variables on the components and on each other. The second design implication is that one should employ dynamic models to study administrative intensity. If lags in adjustment enter the process in a central way, only dynamic models estimated from longitudinal observations can clarify the nature of the relations.

It is commonplace to argue that cross-sectional analysis of the inter-relation of organization dimensions will ordinarily lead to inferences quite different from those suggested by longitudinal analysis (Tsouderos, 1955; Haire, 1959; Starbuck, 1965; Meyer, 1972). There are at least three broad reasons why the two methods ought to yield such differences. One likely possibility concerns specification error in the models estimated. It is commonly the case that omitted variables in a cross-section are different from those in a time series. This will ordinarily result in quite different empirical findings. A second reason for expecting a divergence of cross-sectional and longitudinal findings is that advanced by Hendershot and James, differences in the lag structures for certain variables in the model. It is certainly true that if one studies a cross-section of organizations which are adjusting to equilibria such that different variables adjust at different rates, one should expect to find differences from what would be seen in a longitudinal investigation of the adjustment process.

It is notoriously difficult to induce the proper lag structure from empirical analysis of a panel of observations. For this reason it is more fruitful to consider the third possibility. This is a failure of the equilibrium assumption which underlies cross-sectional analysis (Coleman, 1968). Repeated cross-sections from a panel of organizations which are out of equilibrium will ordinarily produce estimates varying considerably from cross-section to cross-section. Depending upon which of them one takes, the results will be closer or farther from those estimated from a time series.

Failures of equilibrium can arise for an enormous diversity of reasons. We find one possibility intriguing from a substantive point of view. This is the possibility that *the process relating the sizes of organizational components may differ in organizational growth as opposed to decline.* We argue below why we expect such differences. The bulk of literature on administrative intensity is cross-sectional. It should be apparent that, if the processes of study are not symmetric in growth and decline, cross-sectional analysis mixing growers and decliners will obscure the processes of interest.

In the next section we consider the effects of changes in demand for organizational services on various personnel categories. While the approach is intended to be general, the specifics of this theory are generated by characteristics at least partly peculiar to the organization under study—school districts. It is our position that the relationship between enrollment and the direct component (teachers) should be symmetrical in growth and decline, but this should not be the case with the supportive component. Increases in enrollment should have greater effects than declines. Underlying these expectations is a "featherbedding" logic which places emphasis on the assumption that cutbacks in the supportive component are more costly in the short-run for decision-makers than overstaffing. An implication of this position is that cyclical rises and falls in enrollments can lead to increases in administrative intensity.

We follow the theoretical discussion with a description of the data. A set of regression equations are used to analyze the data. These are based on representations of the processes of interest in differential equations. Weighted least squares estimates are compared for subsamples of growing and declining districts.

After discussing the empirical findings, we trace out some implications of the model for the study of administrative intensity.

Developing a Dynamic Model of Organizational Demography

The supportive and direct components of organizations may change their relative sizes either through internal processes involving job changes or through processes based on in-and-out migration (i.e., hiring and firing). Since we do not have data allowing us to distinguish between these processes, we take advantage of a characteristic of formal organizations that distinguishes them from most other units of social organization—the fact that each member of the organization's population occupies a formally designated position. We focus on expansion or contraction in the number of positions filled by members of the organization's population to model the differences between growth and decline.

A. The Direct Component

The direct component in school districts is composed of teachers. Although professional staff also provide services to pupils, we consider these supportive because they are less central to the mandates of most districts.[3] Positions for teachers, like positions for direct component members in other kinds of organizations, are added and deleted because demand for services (or products) changes.

If enrollments reflect demand for services, we can expect a positive correlation with number of teachers. We can be more precise than this, however. Limited funds and competing demands for the allocation of those funds place lower limits on class sizes in school districts. Upper limits on class size also exist. We believe that these are rooted in the community served by each district. Parents expect to find small classes in areas with highly reputed schools and larger classes in less reputed areas. They often make decisions to move partly on the basis of school reputation. We believe that the result is a *norm of maximum acceptable class size*. In affluent areas we would expect parents to object if their children find themselves with forty others in most classes. This may be acceptable to parents in less affluent areas. We combine these speculations in an *assumption of constant class size*. We assume that school districts establish an equilibrium between community-based upper limits on class size and financially-based lower limits.[4] The result is that while size of enrollment may not be proportionately related to number of teachers, *change in enrollments ought to have proportionate effects on change in number of teachers*. This norm should operate in both growth and decline situations. *So for teachers we would expect decline to be the opposite of growth.*

B. The Supportive Component

We expect the supportive component to respond to changes in enrollments too. As demand for services provided by school districts expands, more students must be enrolled. There are more records to keep. More supplies have to be purchased, controlled and disbursed. And since school districts receive part of their revenues from governmental programs in which pupil-days in class is used as the basis of funding formulas, more pupils mean more accounting. At the same time, expanded enrollment means an expanded direct component. The usual expectation is that coordination and control problems generated by larger direct components lead to expansions in the supportive component. If this is true, we can expect both the direct component and enrollment to have effects on the supportive component.

Many supportive component members perform functions which are as much linked to the *school* as to the student. As Blau (1973:68–74) and others have pointed out, differentiation often carries with it minimal levels of support for departments. This is one of the factors producing economies of scale. For example, each school has to have a principal and a secretary.[5] It must have a janitor.

Since we do not at present have data on number of schools over time, we must treat it as an unmeasured intervening variable. However, an important implication rests on the fact that schools represent a sizeable capital investment for districts and closing them causes inconvenience for students and their parents. Many people make house purchasing decisions with proximity to schools in mind, just as they consider school quality. In consequence, it is probably cheaper over a two or three year period in both monetary and social cost terms for districts to operate underused schools than to close them. If part of the supportive component is tied to schools as much as to enrollments, declining enrollments should not be matched (proportionately) by cuts in the supportive component. Administrators are responsible for such decisions. Cuts in the supportive component usually result in firing personnel and reduction of staffs. In each school, and at the district level, they are likely to resist cuts. If nothing else, they may *delay* cuts.

It seems reasonable to argue that larger supportive components will be more successful at resisting cuts than small ones. The bureaucratic apparatus is populated with supportive component members. It is better able to protect its members when it is large because outside critics will find it difficult to obtain information. School district administrators, like other bureaucrats, can defend their staffs through reference to disruption of important functions which only they are in a position to realistically assess. Further, critics are likely to accept additions to both direct and supportive components. So long as the pie is expanding, allocation decisions are relatively easy to make. In decline, critics may push for allocation of those cuts to the supportive component. We argue that they will find it difficult to buttress those arguments with facts, particularly since the "court" to whom they must appeal has a stake in maintaining an "adequate" supportive staff. The bigger that staff is, the more elaborate the bureaucratic apparatus is likely to be, and the more difficult it becomes to pierce the wall of secrecy and impersonality which contribute to its defensive capability.

Both parents, whose children may have to attend a more distant school, and administrators have a community of interest in forestalling cuts. One of the implications of this position is that a *given increment of decline in enrollment will produce a smaller decline in the supportive component than the same increment of growth in enrollment.*

C. Disaggregating the Supportive Component

One of the serious problems pervading the administrative intensity literature is the variation in definition from study to study. Rushing's (1967) suggestion that research would be improved if more specific subcategories of the administrative (supportive) component were studied seems to be a good one.

Our data include fulltime equivalent counts of *professional staff* (who provide nonteaching services directly to students), *administrators*, (who are responsible for control and finance)[6] and a residual category which we call *nonprofessional staff.* The defining criterion for this last group is that they are not required to have special educational certificates. The category is residual in the sense that it includes a segment of the organization's population which is functionally diverse. Secretaries and clerks are lumped together with janitors and school bus drivers.

Making predictions for nonprofessional and professional staff is difficult. We have data on these more specific personnel categories covering only two years. Professional staff members perform functions which are in many ways "luxuries" for school districts. Librarians, guidance counselors and the like often perform tasks which can also be performed by teachers. A district in serious financial trouble may choose to abandon some of these functions altogether. On the other hand, special programs supported by state and federal money often create positions for professional staff.

Nonprofessional staff also present problems. Some members of this component (e.g., secretaries and clerks) perform work for administrators. Cuts in this component would increase the burden on administrators. Others perform jobs which are tied more directly to schools than to enrollments. An underused school probably requires nearly the same janitorial staff as a fully used school. On the other hand, nonprofessional staff occupy a low level in the status hierarchy of the district. Because their skills are not scarce, they can be replaced later with relative ease. This should make it easier to fire them.

While we are unable to develop specific hypotheses pertaining to these components, we do expect the same general causal process to operate. Analyses based on administrators, professional and nonprofessional staff will be informative if only to show whether the difference between growth and decline is due to its operation in only one of them.

Cross-sectional studies intended to discover the effects of organizational size on structure are based on the assumption that decline is simply the opposite manifestation of the same causal process occurring with growth. To this point we have argued that there are theoretical reasons for questioning this often unrecognized assumption. In the next section we describe our data set and develop a strategy for analysis which displays striking differences in the two processes.

Data and Methods

A. The Data[7]

The California State Department of Education gathers data on school districts every year. These data are used by the Legislature in its budgetary deliberations and by other state agencies in planning for educational needs. The virtue of these data lies in the constancy of variable definition over time and across reporting organizations. These definitions are built into the State Education Code which requires districts to report. So the number of missing cases is very small. Very small districts have been omitted from the analysis. Elementary school districts with less than 101 average daily attendance, and high school districts with less than 301 average daily attendance are not reported in California data. Approximately 100 districts were omitted because they underwent unification over the period of time covered by the longitudinal analysis (1968 to 1972). This leaves 769 districts as our sample.

Following Haas et al. (1963:12), we define the "supportive component" (SUP) as "those persons engaged in activities which contribute *indirectly* to the attainment of organizational goals." The "direct component" is the number of teachers (T) in the district.[8]

The supportive component is broken down into the following exhaustive categories:

(1) Professional Staff (PROF)—a certificated employee who performs a service for pupils in direct contact with them (e.g., guidance counselors, librarians, school nurses);

(2) Administrators (A)—a certificated employee who does not provide a service directly to pupils (e.g., principals, superintendents, financial officers);

(3) Nonprofessional Staff (NPS)—employees whose jobs do not require educational certification (e.g., janitors, cafeteria workers excluding dieticians, secretaries, clerks).

(4) SUP = PROF + A + NPS.

B. Analysis of Growers and Decliners

Our procedure is to divide the sample into subsamples of continuous growers and decliners and to analyze each separately. Growers are those districts whose size has increased each year in the period (either 1968–72 or 1970–72 depending on the analysis)[9] while decliners are those whose size has decreased.

In the analysis of the size of the direct component (teacher), the natural size dimension on which to separate growers and decliners is enrollment (E). For analysis of variations in size of the supportive component, this choice is quite conservative. There are a great many school districts which lost enrollment but gained teachers over the period. This means that the E-decliners subsample includes many districts where the size of the direct component increased. This fact tends to obscure possible differences between growth and decline. For these analyses, we chose to analyze the subsamples defined in terms of continous growth or decline in number of teachers as well as those defined by enrollment.

All of our inferences concerning the symmetry or asymmetry of growth and decline depend on differences in regression estimates for the subsamples of growers and decliners. The method depends on the assumption that the two sets of subsamples differ only on the growth-decline dimension. As we will see in the empirical analysis, there are considerable size differences between growers and decliners. Those districts in which enrollment declined are half again as large as those which grew, but those in which teaching staff declined are very much larger than those in which T grew.

The size difference is troubling because the relations of interest may be nonlinear with respect to size. If the subsamples are concentrated on different segments of the size axis in such a case, we would be led to mistakenly infer that different processes characterize the growers and decliners.

We have conducted a detailed examination of possible size nonlinearities. In no case have we found any statistically significant nonlinear terms in our regression models (.05 level). These results strongly suggest that the differences we find between growers and decliners are not due to size differences between the subsamples.

The scanty data on resources and expenditures which we have gathered also show differences between subsamples. Assessed valuation per pupil is slightly higher among growers and expenditures per pupil higher among decliners. We have introduced both variables into each of the regression models reported. In no case do the coefficients of interest change substantially with the introduction of resources or expenditures.[10]

Although we cannot categorically state that these or other variables do not produce the differences reported below, we are confident on the basis of the internal consistency of our analyses that the differences reflect the processes we have hypothesized. In the future we will have the capacity to use 1970 Census data on districts to study this problem in more depth. But the present analysis proceeds on the assumption that the only important systematic difference between the growers and decliners is just that—growth vs. decline.

C. The Model

In developing a model to represent the theoretical ideas described above, we wish to distinguish between effects of *change* in independent variables over a specified period of time and other effects of that variable. In particular, we want to control for the effects of previous changes in that variable as well as scale factors, such as the norm of maximum acceptable class size.

Our empirical analysis concentrates on estimation of regression models of the following form:

$$Y_t = \alpha_0 + \alpha_1 Y_{t-k} + \alpha_2 X_{t-k} + \alpha_3 \Delta X_t + u_t \qquad (1)$$

where $\Delta X_t = X_t - X_{t-k}$, and Y_t is the size of some personnel component at time t, Y_{t-k}, the value of the same variable measured k periods earlier and X_{t-k} is a measure of either demand (enrollments) or of the size of the direct component.

The model in (1) is chosen for several reasons. It is perhaps the simplest model to estimate among the class of models which allow for the separation of the effects of initial size and change during some period. In addition, the model is consistent with a dynamic representation of the demographic processes. In particular, Coleman (1968) shows that (1) is a solution to the following differential equation:

$$\frac{dY}{dt} = q + rY + sX. \tag{2}$$

Equation (2) states that the rate of change in some component depends both on the existing size of the component, Y, and on some other factors, X. But (2) will yield stable equilibria only if $r \leq 0$ (i.e., $\alpha_1 \leq 1$). In such a case, the rate of change in the size of the component decreases with size of the component. So the term rY contributes a self-decelerating component to the process. In most instances, such a negative feedback on the rate of change arises due to unobserved causal loops. For instance, as the size of the supportive component increases it may give rise to political opposition which slows down the rate of growth (Blau, 1970). Unless the net consequence of all such unobserved loops is negative, the process will not be stable. In each case we consider, the results are consistent with stability. The translation from (2) to (1) takes the following form.[11]

$$q = \alpha_0 C/\Delta t \tag{3a}$$

$$r = \ln \alpha_1/\Delta t \tag{3b}$$

$$s = [C/2\Delta t] \quad [\alpha_2 + \alpha_3(\alpha_1 - 1)/(1 - C)] \tag{3c}$$

where

$$C = \ln \alpha_1/(\alpha_1 - 1). \tag{3d}$$

We employ the following estimators, suggested by Coleman:

$$\hat{q} = \hat{\alpha}_0 \hat{C}/\Delta t \tag{4a}$$

$$\hat{r} = \ln \hat{\alpha}_1/\Delta t \tag{4b}$$

$$\hat{s} = [\hat{C}/2\Delta t] \quad [\hat{\alpha}_2 + \hat{\alpha}_3 \hat{C}(\hat{\alpha}_1 - 1)(1 - \hat{C})] \tag{4c}$$

$$\hat{C} = \ln \hat{\alpha}_1/(\hat{\alpha}_1 - 1) \tag{4d}$$

where the α's are ordinary least squares estimates from (1).[12]

The first feature of the pair of equations (1) and (2) to notice is that they imply that for growers and decliners to follow the same process, all of the parameters of (1) must be the same for the two. It follows that the most direct test of the symmetry of growth and decline is to estimate (1) separately for growers and decliners and to test the null hypothesis that the parameters are the same for both categories. The complete estimation model is:

$$T_t = \beta_0 + \beta_1 T_{t-k} + \beta_2 E_{t-k} + \beta_3 \Delta E_t + u_t \tag{5}$$

$$SUP_t = \gamma_0 + \gamma_1 SUP_{t-k} + \gamma_2 T_{t-k} + \gamma_3 \Delta T_t + v_t, \tag{6}$$

and the differential equations are

$$\frac{dT}{dt} = a + bT + cE \tag{7}$$

$$\frac{dSUP}{dt} = d + eSUP + fT. \tag{8}$$

Equation (6) is estimated for SUP and each of its components, A, PROF and NPS. In each case our main hypothesis is that growers and decliners will be identical for (5) and differ for (6).

We are also interested in testing a more refined hypothesis, namely that administrative intensity will tend to be smaller in growth than in decline. That is, we expect a sort of supportive component "featherbedding" in decline. The next step is to develop specific hypotheses for this proposition in terms of (6).

Our expectation is that a given increment of size (of demand or of the direct component) will produce a larger increment of SUP in growth than the same change, taken as a decrement, will decrease SUP. For example, suppose an increase of one hundred teachers yields an increase of twenty SUP. We expect that a decrease of one hundred teachers will tend to produce a decrease of only ten or fifteen SUP. Such a result can arise in a number of ways.

The proposition that growth is different from decline has to this point been formulated largely in terms of the effects of changes in the size of the direct component (net of initial size) on the supportive component. This focuses attention on γ_3, the coefficient of ΔT_t in (6). Our hypothesis is that γ_3 will be positive for both growers and decliners but that it will be greater for growers. In this case both the regression model (6) and the differential equation (8) yield the same qualitative inferences, since if γ_3 is positive and greater for growers, f will be greater (net of γ_1) for growers.[13]

There is a second implication of the "featherbedding" argument that concerns γ_3 in equation (6), the "autoregression" term. Earlier we argued that large supportive components would tend to resist cuts in decline. Such resistance can be represented in terms of relative dampening of growth-decline. In the differential equation (8), e represents these effects. As long as e is negative, effects of changes in enrollments and in the direct component are dampened down over time. The larger is this negative effect, the less the long-run effects of environmental changes. In other words, high levels of resistance to cuts implies large negative values of e. In particular, the dampening effects ought to be greater in decline than in growth.

According to (4b), $\hat{e} = \ln\hat{\gamma}_1/\Delta t$. So if e is to be a larger negative quantity for decliners, γ_1 must be smaller for decliners. That is, our argument implies that the autoregression coefficient, γ_1, will be smaller in decline than growth.

In summary, we hypothesize first that (5) will be identical for growers and decliners but that (6) will be different. Second, we hypothesize that the autoregression term γ_1 will be greater for growers as will the coefficient of the change term γ_3.

D. Estimation

Two problems arise in the estimation of our regression models. Both concern the distributions of the disturbances u_t and v_t. Recall that for ordinary least squares (OLS) to be consistent (unbiased in large samples) the disturbances must be uncorrelated with regressors. For OLS to be efficient, the disturbances must have the same variance from observation to observation ("homoscedasticity"). There is reason to suspect that u_t and v_t fail on both counts.

The first problem, correlation of disturbances and regressors, follows from the suspected autocorrelation of the disturbances and the presence of lagged dependent variables in the models. If the omitted causes of, say, SUP are stable over time for districts, they will certainly be correlated with lagged SUP. In such cases OLS "gives credit" to the lagged dependent variable for the stable portion of the disturbances. As a result, $\hat{\beta}_1$ and $\hat{\gamma}_0$ will be upwardly biased. And, at least for three variable models (Malinvaud, 1970:558), we know that OLS estimates of the coefficients of other variables will tend to be biased toward zero. Since we expect β_2, β_3, γ_2 and γ_3 to be positive, we expected their estimates to be downwardly biased.

Correction of OLS estimates for this problem requires at least four "waves" of observations. Our present data base does not furnish enough time periods of observation for us to make a correction. So the reader should keep the expected bias in mind in evaluating our results. The most important point is that there is no reason to suspect that the nature of the problem differs for the grower and decliner subsamples. Finally, given the tentative nature of the regression estimates, we will not calculate estimates of the parameters of the differential equation.

Examination of calculated residuals from OLS estimates of our models shows a fan-shaped pattern of dispersion with respect to the dependent variable. This suggests that the variance of the disturbances increases with the size of the organization. Organizational analysts ought not to find this surprising since yearly increments in, say, SUP in large organizations may exceed the size of SUP in small organizations. We ought to expect a multiplicative error structure.

We have applied a widely used version of the generalized least squares method known as *weighted least squares* to correct this problem. Given our guess as to the nature of the problem, the appropriate weighting is achieved by dividing through each equation by the relevant size variable (Johnston, 1972: 214–7). This transforms (5), for example, into

$$\frac{T_t}{E_{t-k}} = \beta_0 \frac{1}{E_{t-k}} + \beta_1 + \beta_2 \frac{T_{t-k}}{E_{t-k}} + \beta_3 \frac{\Delta E_t}{E_{t-k}} + \frac{u_t}{E_{t-k}} \tag{9}$$

Then OLS is applied to the transformed equations.[14] Examination of the residuals calculated from the weighted least squares estimation suggests that we have eliminated the heteroscedasticity problem. We use this method throughout.

Empirical Results

Our results can be stated very simply. We proceed by personnel categories, considering both two year and four year growth and decline. Means and variances are presented in Table 1.

A. The Direct Component

We expect no differences between growers and decliners in the effects of enrollments on the size of the teaching staff. The natural time dimension for this

TABLE 1 *Means and Variances*[a]

Variable	Full	Subsamples Defined by Changes in Direct Components from 1970 to 1972		Subsamples Defined by Changes in Enrollments from 1970 to 1972	
		Growers	Decliners	Growers	Decliners
Supportive Component SUP70[b]	.0285 (.0115)	.0289 (.0102)	.0285 (.0122)	.0307 (.0123)	.0266 (.0100)
Administrative Component A70[b]	.0032 (.0011)	.0033 (.0011)	.0032 (.0010)	.0032 (.0012)	.0031 (.0010)
Professional Staff PROF70[b]	.0028 (.002)	.0026 (.0016)	.0021 (.0013)	.0028 (.0018)	.0022 (.0015)
Nonprofessional Staff NPS70[b]	.0236 (.0104)	.0238 (.0094)	.0237 (.0112)	.0255 (.0112)	.0218 (.0088)
Direct Component (Teachers) T70[b]	.0430 (.0081)	.0433 (.0081)	.0443 (.0080)	.0450 (.0088)	.0416 (.0063)
"A/P RATIO" SUP70/E70	65.1 (20.5)	66.5 (19.8)	63.6 (20.4)	67.8 (21.3)	63.5 (19.7)
Student/Teacher Ratio E70/T70	23.7 (3.8)	23.6 (3.6)	23.3 (4.0)	22.9 (3.8)	24.6 (3.7)
Assessed Valuation Per Pupil	23.6 (26.1)	24.6 (27.4)	22.1 (34.3)	27.4 (31.3)	18.5 (16.1)
Enrollment E70[b]	5389.4 (24896.6)	4323.0 (6506.6)	11203.3 (64141.2)	3951.1 (6166.1)	6100.1 (10686.0)
n	805	250	106	255	248

[a] Because of space limitations, only 1970 statistics are presented. Variances are in parentheses.
[b] Variable divided by E70, as entered in weighted least squares regression analyses.

analysis would seem to be one or two year lags. The results for the two year samples, reported in Table 2, support our hypothesis. Neither the autoregression term nor the change term coefficient differ substantially between the two.

We attempted to replicate these findings with the sample of continuous four year growers or decliners, using a four year change score. This effort, reported in Table 2, produces some inconsistencies between the two samples. In particular, the autoregression term for growers is considerably greater than is the case for decliners. We are not sure what to make of this partially disconfirming evidence. We suspect that the long lag picks up trends unrelated to the enrollment-teacher relations and attributes them to the lagged dependent variables.[15]

B. The Supportive Component

The analysis of the entire supportive component discloses dramatic differences between growers and decliners. These differences appear when partitioning is based on enrollment changes (Table 3) and when it is based on changes in the

TABLE 2 *Effects of Growth and Decline in Enrollments on the Direct Component: Weighted Least Squares Estimates*

Subsample	Two-Year Samples		
Enrollment Growers	$T_{72} = .040 + .8990T_{70} + .0054E_{70} + .0402(E_{72} - E_{70})$ $\quad\quad\;\;(.035)\quad\;\;(.002)\quad\;\;(.003)$		$R^2 = .783$ $N = 255$
Enrollment Decliners	$T_{72} = .259 + .9284T_{70} + .0047E_{70} + .0412(E_{72} - E_{70})$ $\quad\quad\;\;(.036)\quad\;\;(.002)\quad\;\;(.005)$		$R^2 = .754$ $N = 248$
	Four-Year Samples		
Enrollment Growers	$T_{72} = .296 + 1.0958T_{68} + .0013E_{68} + .0394(E_{72} - E_{68})$ $\quad\quad\;\;(.089)\quad\quad\;(.004)\quad\;\;(.002)$		$R^2 = .736$ $N = 179$
Enrollment Decliners	$T_{72} = .392 + .7584T_{68} + .0143E_{68} + .0452(E_{72} - E_{68})$ $\quad\quad\;\;(.054)\quad\;\;(.002)\quad\;\;(.005)$		$R^2 = .661$ $N = 138$

Standard errors in parentheses.

direct component (Table 4). In each case, the differences occur for both the two year and four year samples.

Before considering the main hypotheses we raise a subsidiary issue. This concerns the role of demand, i.e., enrollments, in the determination of the size of the supportive component. Earlier we noted that there is reason to expect both "direct" effects and "indirect" effects (i.e., through size of the direct component). We find absolutely no evidence of any "direct" effects of enrollments on the size of the supportive component. That is, in the regressions reported in Tables 3, 4 and 5 the effects of enrollments are always insignificant (at the .05 level).

In three of the four comparisons in Tables 3 and 4 the autoregression term is very much greater for growers as hypothesized. In the fourth, for two year growers and decliners defined in terms of the size of the direct component, the two estimated autoregressions are within one standard error of each other. The results for γ_3, the coefficient of the change score, are fairly similar. In two cases, four year enrollment samples and two year direct component change samples, the estimate of $\hat{\gamma}_3$ is much larger for the growers. In the case of the four year direct component change samples, the estimates are close in value. However, the test of the null

TABLE 3 *Effects of Growth and Decline in Direct Component on the Supportive Component: Weighted Least Squares Estimates*

Subsample	Two-Year Samples			
Enrollment Growers	$SUP_{72} = .178 + .9369SUP_{70} - .0030E_{70} + .1802T_{70} + .4477(T_{72} - T_{70})$ $\quad\quad\quad\;\;(.057)\quad\quad\;\;(.003)\quad\;\;(.079)\quad\;\;(.086)$			$R^2 = .687$ $N = 255$
Enrollment Decliners	$SUP_{72} = .215 + .7618SUP_{70} + .0007E_{70} + .1834T_{70} + .4503(T_{72} - T_{70})$ $\quad\quad\quad\;\;(.042)\quad\quad\;\;(.002)\quad\;\;(.068)\quad\;\;(.092)$			$R^2 = .686$ $N = 248$
	Four-Year Samples			
Enrollment Growers	$SUP_{72} = .216 + .7138SUP_{68} - .0014E_{68} + .2654T_{68} + .6094(T_{72} - T_{68})$ $\quad\quad\quad\;\;(.086)\quad\quad\;\;(.005)\quad\;\;(.158)\quad\;\;(.059)$			$R^2 = .591$ $N = 179$
Enrollment Decliners	$SUP_{72} = .028 + .5698SUP_{68} + .0013E_{68} + .2942T_{68} + .3768(T_{72} - T_{68})$ $\quad\quad\quad\;\;(.071)\quad\quad\;\;(.004)\quad\;\;(.111)\quad\;\;(.118)$			$R^2 = .444$ $N = 138$

Standard errors in parentheses.

TABLE 4 *Effects of Growth and Decline in Direct Component on the Supportive Component: Weighted Least Squares Estimates*

Subsample	Two-Year Samples					
Dir. Comp. Growers	$SUP_{72} = $	$.071 +$	$.8823SUP_{70} +$	$.0019E_{70} +$	$.0713T_{70} +$	$.5722(T_{72} - T_{70})$ $R^2 = .744$
			$(.049)$	$(.002)$	$(.059)$	$(.070)$ $N = 250$
Dir. Comp. Decliners	$SUP_{72} = $	$-.307 +$	$.8101SUP_{70} -$	$.0040E_{70} +$	$.2799T_{70} +$	$.1269(T_{72} - T_{70})$ $R^2 = .761$
			$(.069)$	$(.004)$	$(.099)$	$(.131)$ $N = 106$
	Four-Year Samples					
Dir. Comp. Growers	$SUP_{72} = $	$-.431 +$	$.7385SUP_{68} +$	$.0058E_{68} +$	$.0473T_{68} +$	$.6344(T_{72} - T_{68})$ $R^2 = .638$
			$(.070)$	$(.004)$	$(.110)$	$(.046)$ $N = 199$
Dir. Comp. Decliners	$SUP_{72} = $	$.859 +$	$.5292SUP_{68} -$	$.0026E_{68} +$	$.4684T_{68} +$	$.6099(T_{72} - T_{68})$ $R^2 = .805$
			$(.137)$	$(.008)$	$(.241)$	$(.389)$ $N = 25$

Standard errors in parentheses.

hypothesis that $\gamma_3 = 0$ is strongly rejected for growers but cannot be rejected for decliners. So for the aggregated supportive component, both more specific hypotheses tend to be supported by the data.

C. Elements of the Supportive Component

Disaggregated data on categories of the supportive component are available only for the 1970–1972 period. This limits our analysis to that of two year growers and decliners. On substantive grounds outlined earlier we expect variations in administrative staff (A) and non-professional staff (NPS) to be causally related to changes in the size of the direct component. But variations in the size of the professional staff (PROF) who provide services directly to pupils, should be related to changes in enrollments. The regressions reported in Table 5 take these assumptions into account.

i. Administrative Staff. The hypothesis of divergence of growers and decliners is supported with respect to the change term but not the autoregression. In fact, for decliners, changes in number of teachers have no effect on administrators over the two year period.

ii. Non-Professional Staff. The situation for NPS is identical to that for administrative staff. Again the hypothesis of divergence of growers and decliners is supported.

iii. Professional Staff. Finally, for the professional (or "pupil services") staff the "featherbedding" hypothesis is supported on both counts. Both $\hat{\gamma}_1$ and $\hat{\gamma}_3$ are larger than the corresponding estimates for decliners.[16] PROF responds to growth and decline in ways more like the other parts of the supportive component than like teachers. If the reverse were true, we would be tempted to consider PROF part of the direct component.

As we noted above, we expected to find that correlations between the supportive and direct components are partly spurious due to the effects of enrollment on both of them (for all dependent variables but PROF). Our results indicate that

TABLE 5 *Effects of Growth and Decline in Direct Component and in Enrollments on Elements of the Supportive Component: Weighted Least Squares Estimates*

Subsample		
Dir. Comp. Growers	$A_{72} = .096 + .4600A_{70} - .00003E_{70} + .0362T_{70} + .0335(T_{72} - T_{70})$ $(.055) \quad (.0003) \quad\quad (.007) \quad\quad (.009)$	$R^2 = .499$ $N = 250$
Dir. Comp. Decliners	$A_{72} = -.002 + .4461A_{70} + .0003E_{70} + .0429T_{70} + .0081(T_{72} - T_{70})$ $(.070) \quad (.0003) \quad\quad (.0092) \quad\quad (.011)$	$R^2 = .656$ $N = 105$
Dir. Comp. Growers	$NPS_{72} = -.013 + .9154NPS_{70} + .0026E_{70} + .0262T_{70} + .4750(T_{72} - T_{70})$ $(.050) \quad\quad (.002) \quad\quad (.054) \quad\quad (.067)$	$R^2 = .724$ $N = 250$
Dir. Comp. Decliners	$NPS_{72} = -.045 + .8468NPS_{70} - .0041E_{70} + .2332T_{70} + .1036(T_{72} - T_{70})$ $(.063) \quad\quad (.003) \quad\quad (.091) \quad\quad (.125)$	$R^2 = .754$ $N = 106$
Enrollment Growers	$PROF_{72} = -.247 + .8925PROF_{70} - .0004E_{70} + .0155T_{70} + .0052(E_{72} - E_{70})$ $(.063) \quad\quad (.0005) \quad\quad (.014) \quad\quad (.001)$	$R^2 = .710$ $N = 175$
Enrollment Decliners	$PROF_{72} = -.019 + .7138PROF_{70} + .0001E_{70} + .0204T_{70} + .0042(E_{72} - E_{70})$ $(.040) \quad\quad (.0004) \quad\quad (.010) \quad\quad (.001)$	$R^2 = .740$ $N = 178$

Standard errors in parentheses.

enrollment (E) has no appreciable effect when teachers (T) is controlled, suggesting that the effects of E are channeled through T.

Discussion and Conclusions

The very large empirical literature on the relationship of size and administrative intensity is almost wholly cross-sectional. As a result this research tradition has depended heavily on the assumption that the relations are symmetric in growth and decline. We have advanced a number of arguments to the contrary and have conducted empirical tests of the counter-assertions. Our argument leads to a broad hypothesis that growers and decliners will be alike in the relations of size of direct (or production) component to demand for organizational products or services, but that the two will differ in the relation of sizes of supportive component size to the direct component size and to demand. This hypothesis is strongly supported in our analysis.

We developed more specific hypotheses concerning two parameters that describe adjustment of the supportive component to changes in the direct component. We expected direct component changes to have smaller effects in decline. And we hypothesized that this difference would be reinforced by a stronger dampening tendency in decline. The evidence is consistent with our hypotheses, and in a large number of comparisons we find dramatic differences in the predicted directions between growers and decliners.

These results have a number of implications. Returning to issues raised at the outset, our analysis suggests that A/P ratios are too complex to be useful in many analyses and that cross-sectional analysis of organizational demography may be quite misleading. The ratios are complex because the relations of the denominator, size of the direct (or production) component, behaves similarly in growth and decline while the numerator, size of the supportive component, does not. So the ratios are not unitary from a substantive point of view. The second point, concerning cross-sectional analysis, is obvious. One's inferences concerning the relationship of supportive component size to direct component size should change systematically with the growth/decline composition of the study sample. In other words, cross-sectional results will not be dependable.

Our research also suggests two complications for the study of organizational structure. First, growth and decline are likely to bring about different effects on such structural variables as degree of differentiation (both horizontal and vertical), centralization and formalization. For example, growth in manufacturing firms from 300 to 1000 personnel may lead to an increased use of written procedural rules, but a subsequent decline of the same magnitude would probably not have a comparable effect.

Second, in the model we have developed, variations in the demand environment drive the system. The process we formulated works something like a bumper-jack. When demand is increasing, the size of the direct component increases as does the supportive component. But when demand declines, the loss in direct component is not matched by loss in the supportive component. That is, the supportive component tends to increase on the upswings but decreases less on the downswings. Consequently, a turbulent environment producing oscillations in demand for the organization's products or services may produce an increase in administrative intensity even if there is no upward trend in the oscillations.

Notes

1. It is also decelerating for reasons Blau explains but which need not concern us here.
2. Their data spanned two periods in time, 1949–50 and 1955–56. The rate of growth was measured by the difference in enrollment.
3. We return to this issue after analyzing the separate subcategories of the supportive component.
4. Over short periods of time (one to four years), we expect these standards to change only slightly. California school districts have shown a tendency toward higher student/teacher ratios for several years. However, average class size has not changed substantially. This may be due, in part, to increased use of substitute teachers.
5. Very small districts are omitted from this study. We have no one-room school houses.
6. The California State Education Code places maximum limits on the ratio of administrators to teachers (A/T) which vary by district type: elementary, unified and high school. Controls for district type produced no substantial differences so far as growth and decline are concerned.
7. Dr. Mel Gype of the California State Department of Education and Professor Jane R. Mercer provided valuable help in the acquisition, preparation and analysis of these data.
8. From California State Department of Education (1973:v): "'Teacher' means an employee of a school district, employed in a position requiring certification qualifications and whose duties require him to provide direct instruction to the pupils in the schools of that district for the full time for which he is employed. 'Teacher' shall include, but not be limited to, teachers of special classes, teachers of exceptional children, teachers of physically handicapped minors, teachers of mentally retarded minors, substitute teachers, instructional television teachers, specialist mathematics teachers, specialist reading teachers, home and hospital teachers, and learning disability group teachers."
9. Data for the 1969 period are not available. Growth and decline are defined for the 1968–70 period where relevant.
10. In most analyses, assessed evaluation and expenditures per pupil had insignificant effects. Subsequent research efforts will concentrate on economic and demographic characteristics of the district's environment.
11. The translation from (2) to (1) requires that X change linearly over the interval. This restriction is unlikely to be met in our data since changes are presumably lumped together in time for changes in personnel categories. But, relaxing the restriction at this point would lead to undue complication with presumably low return.
12. This procedure involves statistical complications. The estimators in (4a)–(4d) use non-linear transformation (e.g., division) of ordinary least squares estimators of (1). But the desirable properties of ordinary least squares are not preserved under such transformations. In such situations one must employ maximum likelihood methods.

    We have not yet constructed a maximum likelihood estimator for this problem. In the meanwhile, we report weighted least squares estimates of (1) and state qualitative conclusions regarding (2). In particular, we do not present estimates of q, r and s nor do we report the test proposed by Coleman (1968:443).
13. An analogue to expression (3c), written in terms of (8), shows that s depends on γ_1, γ_2 and γ_3. It is clear that differences between growers and decliners in any of the three will also produce qualitative differences between growth and decline. We consider γ_1 below. The point here is to justify the emphasis on γ_3 when γ_2 also enters (3c). But as long as $0 \leq \gamma_1 \leq 1$, the coefficients of both γ_2 and γ_3 in (3c) will be positive. This means that f responds in essentially the same way to differences in γ_2 and γ_3. We focus our attention on γ_3 because the change term is more relevant to our causal reasoning.
14. Note that when we apply OLS to (9), the "constant" in the regression is actually the coefficient of E while the "slope" estimate for 1/E is actually the constant. The inclusion of 1/E in the regression and the alteration of the disturbance from u_t to u_t/E_{t-k} distinguishes this method from the more usual regression with ratio variables (cf. Freeman and Kronenfeld, 1973; Fugitt and Lieberson, 1974; Schuessler, 1973). Moreover, in this

procedure the estimated regression model is not a "structural model" but is a device to yield estimates for a different structural model, namely (5) and (6).

15. Average class size increases with enrollment. This may account in part for the fact that the autoregressions for T are not equal to 1.0 as expected. Unfortunately, we do not have average class size for each district and cannot determine whether growing districts differ from declining districts on this dimension.

16. Districts with no PROF members in either 1970 or 1972 were excluded from the analysis.

References

Blau, Peter, 1970, "A formal theory of differentiation in organizations." *American Sociological Review* 35:201–18.

———— 1972, "Interdependence and hierarchy in organizations." *Social Science Research* 1:1–24

———— 1973, *The Organization of Academic Work*. New York: Wiley.

Blau, Peter and Richard A. Schoenherr, 1971, *The Structure of Organizations*. New York: Basic Books. California State Department of Education, Bureau of Administrative Research and District Organization.

———— 1973, "Ratios of California public school nonteaching employees to classroom teachers; as of November 1, 1970, 1971 and 1972." Sacramento.

Coleman, James, 1968, "The mathematical study of change." Pp. 428–78 in Hubert Blalock, Jr. and Ann B. Blalock (eds.), *Methodology in Social Research*. New York: McGraw-Hill.

Freeman, John Henry and Jerrold E. Kronenfeld, 1973, "Problems of definitional dependency: the case of administrative intensity." *Social Forces* 52:108–21.

Fuguitt, Glenn V. and Stanley Lieberson, 1974, "Correlation of ratios or difference scores having common terms." in Herbert L. Costner (ed.), *Sociological Methodology: 1973–1974*:128–44.

Haas, Eugene, Richard H. Hall and Norman Johnson, 1963, "The size of the supportive component in organizations: a multi-organizational analysis." *Social Forces* 43:9–17.

Haire, Mason, 1959, "Biological models and empirical histories of the growth of organizations." Pp. 272–306 in Mason Haire (ed.), *Modern Organization Theory*. New York: Wiley.

Hannan, Michael T. and Alice A. Young, 1974, "Estimation in panel models: results on pooling cross-sections and time series." Technical report, Laboratory for Social Research, Stanford University.

Hendershot, Gerry E. and Thomas F. James, 1972, "Size and growth as determinants of administration-production ratios in organizations." *American Sociological Review* 37:149–53.

Johnston, J., 1972, *Econometric Methods*. (2nd edition), New York: McGraw Hill.

Malinvaud, E., 1970, *Statistical Methods of Econometrics*. (2nd edition), New York: American Elsevier.

Melman, Seymour, 1951, "The rise of administrative overhead in the manufacturing industries of the United States 1889–1947." *Oxford Economic Papers* 3:62–112.

Meyer, Marshall, 1972, "Size and the structure of organizations: a causal analysis." *American Sociological Review* 37:434–40.

Rushing, William, 1967, "The effects of industry size and division of labor on administration." *Administrative Science Quarterly* 12:273–95.

Schuessler, Karl, 1973, "Ratio variables and path models." in Arthur Goldberger and Otis Dudley Duncan (eds.), *Structural Equation Models in Social Science*. New York: Seminar Press.

Starbuck, William, 1965, "Organizational growth and development." Pp. 451–533 in J. G. March (ed.), *Handbook of Organizations*. Chicago: Rand McNally.

Terrien, Frederick W. and Donald L. Mills, 1955, "The effect of changing size upon the internal structure of organizations." *American Sociological Review* 20:11–3.

Tsouderos, John E., 1955, "Organizational change in terms of a series of selected variables." *American Sociological Review* 20:206–10.

The Process of Bureaucratization[1]

Marshall W. Meyer and M. Craig Brown

Max Weber's classic essay "Bureaucracy" (1947) delineates some of the characteristics of modern organizations which distinguish them from traditional forms of administration. These characteristics include division of labor, hierarchy of authority, written rules and regulations, and the like. The surface attributes of bureaucracy identified by Weber are not to be confused with its causes, however. In comparing traditional with bureaucratic means of administration, the latter based on belief in rational-legal authority, Weber was clearly suggesting that bureaucratization is but one aspect of the historical trend toward rationalization in the development of all institutional forms in modern societies. The substitution of authority based on rules for authority based arbitrarily on persons is central to the development of bureaucracy. Weber identifies other preconditions of bureaucratization, including a money economy which allows calculability of results and widespread literacy. To this list one might add such possible causes of bureaucratization as urbanization, mobility of resources, and religious beliefs permitting trust among strangers (see Stinchcombe 1965). The relative importance of these causes of bureaucratization is perhaps of less significance than the fact that they are external to organizations and arise largely as a result of historical processes. Rational-legal authority, cash economies, widespread literacy, and other conditions contributing to the development of bureaucratic forms are characteristics of whole societies which may change over time but need not vary from organization to organization in a society at any one point.

Contemporary research on organizations has apparently overlooked this fact in seeking to explain characteristics of bureaucracies in terms of internal characteristics while ignoring the changes in the larger social and political environments that Weber thought central to the growth of modern organizations. The reasons for concentrating on internal organizational characteristics as opposed to external ones are not difficult to identify. Quantitative research studies can take into account tangible aspects of organizational structures—size, job titles, levels of supervision, spans of control, and the like—much more easily than the less quantifiable elements of the environment which, while amorphous, may be exceedingly important. The work of Blau (1970) and his colleagues (see also Meyer 1972b) exemplifies the tendency to overlook qualitative elements of organizations in focusing almost exclusively on the implications of organizational size for structural differentiation and of differentiation for administrative overhead. What is disputed is not the accuracy of the results but their importance for understanding the development of bureaucratization. A theory which explains bureaucratic structures solely in terms of size runs afoul of the fact that large organizations existed well before bureaucratization became widespread (see, e.g., Dibble 1965). A second factor limiting the usefulness of most such studies is that they present data from one point only and thus overlook the possible effects of history. Current trends in research have

Reprinted in part from the *American Journal of Sociology*, vol. 83 (September 1977), pp. 364–384, by permission of the authors and the publisher. © 1977 by The University of Chicago Press.

precluded the possibility that the greatest variations occur over time and are due to environmental shifts affecting organizations of a given type almost uniformly. Given this inattention to qualitative historical aspects of organizational environments, it is not surprising that empirical research has not addressed the question Weber raised in his classic essay: How does one explain the development of large-scale, hierarchical, and rule-bound bureaucracies?

Only a partial answer can be attempted here. Our study is limited to a single set of organizations—city, county, and state finance agencies—and to a time span of six years. It concerns only causes and consequences of formalized personnel procedures, because the origins of these rules can be identified easily and because rules vary somewhat across the agencies studied. The results of this limited study are quite suggestive, however. They indicate that the extensiveness of formal procedures in bureaucracies is due in part to the historical era in which they were founded and in part to the subsequent effects of the environment. Formalization in turn gives rise to hierarchical differentiation and differentiation to delegation of decision-making authority. The effects of origins are shown to be results of openness to environment at the time of formation. In short, the process of bureaucratization begins with environmental pressures—in this case, the civil service movement—and proceeds by developing rules to accommodate these pressures, elaborating organizational structures consistent with the rules and delegating authority as necessitated by structure. The primacy of the environment as a determining factor of bureaucratization and the dependence of organizational structure on rules embodying external demands are emphasized here.

Though centrally concerned with the process of bureaucratization, this article touches on several other topics. Its method is necessarily intertwined with its substance. A key question to be considered is how history can be incorporated in organizational analysis. An understanding of history requires separating the effects of time of origin from the effects of changes in organizational environments which occurred in the past and could not be observed. Origins and environments are likely to have had opposite effects and to obscure each other, but estimates of the magnitude of the impact of each are important to understanding how bureaucratization or any other organizational process takes place over a lengthy period. The substantive findings developed in this article are also linked closely to the types of organizations studied, which are city, county, and state departments of finance, comptrollers' offices, and departments of administration, all of which are administrative units of local governments. Because they are government organizations, finance departments are bound by certain federal statutes which do not affect the private sector so directly. These statutes are crucial environmental elements, and it is unlikely that they have affected private organizations similarly. Whether the process of bureaucratization is similar for public- and private-sector organizations cannot be determined until there is comparable research on the latter. In all likelihood, similar patterns of behavior hold for both public and private organizations, but their histories and relevant environments may be so different that they do not behave in the same way at any given point.

We shall proceed by first outlining the broad hypotheses to be tested in this study and the nature of the research undertaken. The discussion will then be turned to some federal and local regulations affecting personnel matters. A complete history of civil service legislation is not possible, but important developments in it can be noted. The next section develops a model showing why effects of origins and of the environments are often confounded in organizational research, and it suggests a procedure for distinguishing between them. This procedure is then applied to data on the formalization of personnel procedures in finance agencies. In the following section, we examine the relationship among formal personnel procedures, multitier hierarchies, and decision making. The last substantive section returns to the question of the effects of origins on organizations by examining the formalization of personnel practices in a small number of agencies which reorganized completely during the interval between the two surveys reported here. The implications of the empirical results are discussed in the concluding section.

The data in this article are drawn from two surveys of city, county, and state finance agencies in the United States conducted in 1966 and 1972. The nature of the surveys is reported fully in two earlier articles (Meyer 1975a, 1975b), and little elaboration of the study design seems necessary here. The present article reports data on some 215 agencies which existed continuously from 1966 to 1972 and on 14 others which changed their names and reorganized between the two surveys. A point made in the earlier articles bears repeating: the data analyzed here are drawn from these two points only. A third survey of finance agencies now under way will provide additional data that can be used to replicate the results reported here.

Civil Service and Formalization of the Personnel Process

The history of the civil service movement in the United States is complex. . . . But one pattern is unmistakable: there has been increasing federal intervention in local-government personnel practices. Of the three most significant federal acts establishing merit procedures for appointment to public office in place of the spoils system, the first, the Pendleton Act of 1882, which created the U.S. Civil Service Commission, did not mention state or local government at all. State governments fell under the purview of the 1939 amendments to the Social Security Act, and both state and local governments were subject to provisions of the Intergovernmental Personnel Act of 1970. Each of these laws was aimed at removing politics from administration by requiring impersonal procedures for the selection and the advancement of employees. . . .

Several broad conclusions can be drawn from [a] brief review of civil service legislation in the United States. First, most state and local governments have adopted merit personnel policies in place of either patronage appointments or the spoils system. The only exceptions to this pattern are the more frequent use of temporary employees and the removal of policymaking officials from civil service protection. The historical trend toward the imposition of merit personnel standards constitutes an important alteration in the political environments of local government agencies. Second, effective merit standards usually entail substitution of impersonal procedures such as written job descriptions and fixed probationary periods for personal and political criteria for appointment. In other words, merit standards promote the formalization of the personnel process. Third, despite the ascendancy of merit principles, their application has been somewhat uneven. For this reason, an exact correspondence between federal legislation and the actions of state and local governments cannot be expected. Instead, considerable variation remains, and the actual procedures adopted by local agencies in conformity with requirements for merit personnel administration are themselves of interest. An important question is whether local government units have responded uniformly and fully to the demand for personnel standards consistent with merit principles or whether their personnel procedures have remained essentially unchanged over time. If the former, one would conclude that local government units are vulnerable to certain environmental pressures; if the latter, one would think them resistant to environments and hence bound by their origins. A fundamental sociological question is whether origins or environments dominate organizations. Only an approximate answer can be developed here. The research on finance agencies suggests, however, that both have substantial effects, even though environmental shifts may in the long run have greater impact than origins.

Origins, the Environment, and Formalization of the Personnel Process

A Model of Effects of Origins and the Environment

A fundamental problem in assessing effects of origins and environment is the lack of complete data tracing organizations from their beginnings to the present. Usually data from only one point are available, and inferences about the effects of history or age are made on the basis of contemporary differences between organizations with diverse origins. Exactly this procedure is followed by Stinchcombe (1965) in his analysis of stability of organizational types over time. Stinchcombe found small but consistent effects of era of origin on some characteristics of the labor force in several industries. The correlation between age and labor force (or organizational) structure, he surmises, can be accounted for by "the postulate that economic and technical conditions determine the appropriate organizational form for a given organizational purpose and the postulate that certain kinds of organizations . . . could not be invented before the social structure was appropriate to them" (p. 160).

This approach to the effects of age on organizations has several limitations, and we shall seek to overcome them here. One problem is that organizations are portrayed as essentially unchanging. The possibility that substantial differences due to origins are reduced over time by the environment is not considered. The source of this difficulty can be seen quite easily in figure 1, which displays values of a hypothetical index of bureaucratization (b) for three organizations at three points. Organization 1, which was founded in era 1, has index values of b_{11}, b_{12}, b_{13} at times 1, 2, and 3, respectively; for organization 3, only b_{33} is displayed, because it did not exist in eras 1 and 2. Ignoring organization 2 for the present, figure 1 shows the effects of origins on the index to be $b_{33} - b_{11}$. The effect of time, which is in fact a

		Era		
		1	2	3
	1	b_{11}	b_{12}	b_{13}
Organization	2	—	b_{22}	b_{23}
	3	—	—	b_{33}

Effects of origins $= b_{33} - b_{11}$
Effects of environment $= b_{13} - b_{11}$
Difference $= b_{33} - b_{13}$

Figure 1   Hypothetical Values of Bureaucratization (b) *for Three Organizations Formed in Different Eras*

surrogate for the environment, is $b_{13} - b_{11}$ for organization 1. There is no effect of time for organization 3, because it was only recently founded. Cross-sectional data do not permit separate estimates of effects of origins and of the environment as suggested by figure 1. Instead, only the difference, $b_{33} - b_{13}$, can be estimated. But this difference corresponds exactly to the difference between effects of origins and of the environment, $(b_{33} - b_{11}) - (b_{13} - b_{11})$, thereby confounding the two hopelessly. Since environmental effects often diminish differences due to orgins,[2] Stinchcombe's data in all likelihood underestimate both the effects of origins on organizations and the amount of change occurring over time.

Another problem with Stinchcombe's approach to the effects of history on organizations is its inability to link specified historical changes to enduring properties of organizations. This derives from his use of census data which do not reveal organizational characteristics other than labor-force composition. The importance of history for organizations can be demonstrated best if certain organizational properties varying with time of origin can be linked to specific historical developments. Showing differences between old and new organizations does not limit possible explanations for observed effects of age, but both showing that old organizations differ from new ones in some respects but not others and specifying historical changes that correspond to these differences narrow the range of possible explanations considerably and hence give greater credence to the historical argument. Indeed it may be that age does not affect organizations much in comparison with the impact of identifiable historical events.[3]

The data available from the study of finance agencies allow us to begin to distinguish effects of origins from those of the environment, although they do not permit precise estimates. They are sufficiently detailed to allow separation of organizational properties which should have been affected by historical changes from properties for which no such effects are anticipated. For 215 departments of finance, comptrollers' offices, and the like, we have information on the year in which they were founded, formalization of personnel procedures, and organizational structure for both 1966 and 1972. These agencies existed continuously over the six-year interval between the two studies; hence changes during this time cannot be due to origins. (The 14 departments which reorganized between 1966 and 1972 will be discussed later.) The finance agencies were classified according to the era of formation—19th century, 1901–39, and 1940 and later—so that the breaks between periods correspond closely to the dates of two major federal acts affecting personnel matters and the movement to reform city administration. It should also be noted that the third important piece of legislation—the 1970 Intergovernmental Personnel Act—became law in the interval between the 1966 and 1972 studies.

The appropriateness of finance agencies for the research undertaken here should be discussed, if only briefly. Two considerations should be kept in mind. First, whereas entire local governments as wholes would seem to be the natural unit of analysis in a study of effects of federal legislation and the reform movement, this approach would pose some difficulties. In particular, identifying a single time of formation of administration agencies employing civil servants would be impossible, because these agencies are typically founded and reorganized one at a time. One could of course find times during which reorganization of offices of elected officials occurred, but these offices are usually not affected by civil service laws, and reorganization of them does not necessarily generate reorganization of administrative agencies. Second, finance agencies are not atypical of administrative bureaus of local governments, and results concerning them may be treated as representative of

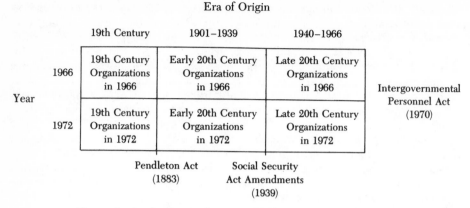

Figure 2 *Study Design for Research on Finance Departments*

local administrative agencies generally. Clearly it would be desirable to have information on other types of government bureaus for this study, but these data are not at hand.

The kinds of comparisons allowed by the study design are illustrated in figure 2. Differences appearing within the columns displayed here occurred between 1966 and 1972 and may be due to environmental shifts, although we must consider the possibility that they are due to other factors. The differences appearing across the rows are, as we have shown, due to differences between organizations at the time of their formation, less subsequent effects of the environment. If there were environmental effects between 1966 and 1972, then in all likelihood much greater effects of the environment occurred between the late 19th century and 1966, because the interval was longer and the impact of the federal legislation probably greater.

Origins and Formalization in Finance Agencies

The information collected from finance agencies included extensive data describing procedures for hiring and evaluating personnel. We have information about whether entry-level employees are usually placed through civil service or equivalent uniform personnel codes; whether written regulations govern the criteria used in promotion decisions; the length of the probationary period, if any, for new employees; whether the department head is appointed or elected; and the number of employees covered by civil service or similar merit systems. Civil service coverage for employees, written promotion regulations, and a meaningful probationary period suggest merit personnel administration of the sort envisioned by federal and state civil service statutes. Their absence and the presence of an elected department head are indicative of the old-fashioned patronage or spoils system. These items were included in both the 1966 and 1972 surveys. In table 1, they are cross tabulated by the era when a department was founded. The tabulations show effects of both era of formation and time of measurement, suggesting that the cross-sectional results in fact understate the true effects of origins. The tables should be reviewed in detail.

TABLE 1   *Measures of Formalization in 1966 and 1972 by Era When Departments Were Founded*

	Era		
	Pre-1900	1901–39	Post-1940
	A. % Departments Where Entry-Level Employees Are Placed through Civil Service or Equivalent Uniform Personnel Code (EMPLACE)		
1966	55	71	73
	(49)	(72)	(90)
1972	65	72	84
	(49)	(72)	(90)
	B. % Departments Where Written Regulations Govern Promotion Criteria (PROMO)		
1966	49	68	67
	(49)	(71)	(90)
1972	59	72	73
	(49)	(72)	(90)
	C. % Departments Where Probationary Period is Six Months or Longer (PROBAT)		
1966	65	72	88
	(49)	(69)	(89)
1972	69	75	89
	(49)	(71)	(90)
	D. % Departments Where Head is Elected (HEDEL)		
1966	74	24	7
	(49)	(71)	(90)
1972	69	22	6
	(49)	(72)	(90)
	E. Mean Proportion of Positions Covered by Civil Service (PSCE)		
1966	.607	.767	.746
	(47)	(70)	(88)
1972	.582	.691	.785
	(48)	(72)	(89)

Note: Figures in parentheses represent actual number of cases.

Section A of table 1 displays percentages of departments where entry-level employees are placed through civil service or an equivalent merit personnel code. As shown, in 1966 55% of 19th-century finance agencies, 71% of early 20th-century agencies, and 73% of those founded after 1940 hired newcomers through civil service. By 1972 these percentages had increased to 65, 72, and 84, respectively. Overall, the proportion of finance agencies placing entry-level employees through civil service increased by about 6% between 1966 and 1972. And in both 1966 and 1972, approximately 18% more of post-1940 than of 19th-century agencies had such civil service arrangements. The same pattern obtains for the use of written regulations governing promotion criteria. There is about a 6% increase between 1966 and 1972 and a nearly 16% spread between 19th-century and post-1940 agencies. Differences due to time of measurement are somewhat smaller in sections C and D of table 1, where data on the length of the probationary period for new employees and the method of selection of department heads are presented. Between 1966 and 1972, there was but a 3% increase in the proportion of departments with lengthy probationary periods and a 2% decrease in elected agency heads. The differences associated with era of origin are more prominent in section D, however. Indeed practically all of the variance in whether or not a department head is elected—though not, if he is appointed, in whether such appointment is at the discretion of the head of government or through civil service—can be explained by era of origin. [4] Finally, section E of table 1 displays mean proportions of positions in finance agencies covered by civil service in both 1966 and 1972. Whereas time of formation is positively associated with civil service coverage—newer agencies have more employees under merit systems—somewhat fewer positions were covered in 1972 than in 1966. The reasons for this contraction of civil service have already been noted and need not be pursued further.

Because the first four items describing finance agencies' hiring and evaluation procedures are dichotomies, they were combined in an index of formalization of the personnel process. Section E of table 1 was not included in either of the two indexes, because it declined between 1966 and 1972. Correlations among the four items between 1966 and 1972 and their autocorrelations over time are displayed in table 2. Generally the correlations are modest and in the expected direction, but there are some exceptions. For example, the correlation of placement of new employees through civil service with written promotion criteria is .6136 in 1966 but plummets to .3989 in 1972. And the correlations of whether department heads are elected with length of the probationary period are not very different from zero, −.1217 in 1966 and −.0319 in 1972. The autocorrelations are also of interest. For the first three items, they range from .4348 to .6321, but for election of department heads the autocorrelation is .8489. The index of formalization ranges from zero to one; its value is the proportion of the four elements of an agency's personnel procedures consistent with merit principles—entry-level placement through civil service, written regulations governing promotions, a probationary period of six months or longer, and an appointed department head. The index had mean values of .697 in 1966 and .745 in 1972.

In order to estimate effects of era of origin and year of measurement more precisely than the cross tabulations in table 1 allow, the index of formalization was regressed on era of origin. Six cross-sectional regressions are displayed in table 3, three each for 1966 and 1972. In these regressions, the 1966 and 1972 indexes of formalization are regressed separately on era of origin. In the first two regressions,

TABLE 2 *Correlations of Items in Index of Formalization (1966/1972 Correlations)*

	EMPLACE	PROMO	PROBAT	HEDEL
EMPLACE	.6321	.6136/.3989	.2568/.2884	−.2376/−.2015
PROMO	—	.4348	.2683/.1828	−.1628/−.2093
PROBAT	—	—	.5278	−.1217/−.0319
HEDEL	—	—	—	.8489

Note: Autocorrelations on major diagonal.

TABLE 3 *Regressions of Indexes of Formalization on Era of Origin and Other Environmental Variables*

Cross-sectional Regressions

1966 formalization = .3712 + .1484 · era
(.0255)

1972 formalization = .4334 + .1422 · era
(.0225)

1966 formalization = .3057 + .1539 · era − .0226 · state
(.0238) (.0557)

1972 formalization = .4095 + .1286 · era + .0399 · state
(.0231) (.0540)

1966 formalization = .3021 + .1542 · era + .0003 · nonsouthern
(.0241) (.0431)

1972 formalization = .4135 + .1281 · era + .0030 · nonsouthern
(.0234) (.0418)

Pooled Regression

Formalization = .3625 + .1328 · era + .0485 · year
(.0160) (.0277)

Note: Errors in parentheses.

no additional variables are controlled. Each increment of era—there are two increments, since we have three eras—adds .148 to the index in 1966 and .142 in 1972. The difference between the constants in the first pair of equations, .0622, is a rough estimate of the effects of year of measurement on the index of formalization. In the third and fourth equations in table 3, a dummy variable coded one for state finance agencies covered in the surveys and zero for others is added; in the fifth and sixth equations, a dummy variable coded one for nonsouthern states and zero otherwise is included. Neither of the added variables significantly predicts formalization of personnel practices, whereas the effects of era of origin remain. The time at which an agency was founded and subsequent environmental shifts account for formalization much better than either the level of government or geographic location.

In the last entry of table 3, the 1966 and 1972 data are pooled, and year of measurement is added to the model as a dummy variable coded zero for 1966 and one for 1972. The pooled regression allows estimates of the statistical significance of year of measurement and comparisons of effects of era and year on formalization. As can be seen from the error terms, the effects of era are far greater than might have occurred by chance, but the significance of year of measurement is uncertain in the pooled regression—the coefficient of year is 1.75 times its error. But the coefficient is in the expected direction, and more important, since the six-year interval between measurements is considerably shorter than the intervals between eras, which are 27 and 39 years, one would expect time of measurement to have considerably less impact than era of origin. Had the measurement interval been longer, the effects of year in all likelihood would have attained significance. While one cannot legitimately project recent trends backward to the 19th century, it may be reasonable to assume that the rate at which personnel procedures in local government agencies have been formalized since the turn of the century is such that changes in these procedures over time have been greater than differences occurring across organizations at any point due to persistent effects of origins. To speak of stability of personnel procedures in finance agencies would be accurate for short intervals only. The long-range effects of environmental shifts are in all likelihood far greater than differences due to origins.

Origins and Organizational Structure

Although era of origin shapes the personnel procedures used by local government finance agencies, it does not affect their organizational structures significantly. Table 4 displays mean size and number of divisions, sections (i.e., subunits of divisions), and levels of supervision for the 254 departments studied in 1966 and 1972. The largest agencies are the oldest ones, but early 20th-century departments are the smallest; even this difference is not statistically significant because of the large variance in size. Differences in numbers of operating divisions and sections are entirely artifacts of size, and the greatest level of numbers occurred, in 1966, among the early 20th-century agencies which are on the average the smallest. Overall, then, the organizational structure of finance agencies bears no direct relationship to the era in which they were founded. This is not surprising, given that there is no reason to anticipate such a relationship. Organizational structures, unlike personnel procedures, have not been the subject of federal legislation, and they are not directly linked to cultural and political preferences of different historical periods.

TABLE 4   *Measures of Organizational Structure in 1966 and 1972 by Era When Departments Were Founded*

	Era		
	Pre-1900	1900–1939	Post-1940
Mean size:			
1966	136.96	89.31	95.16
	(49)	(72)	(90)
1972	163.35	106.78	123.28
	(49)	(72)	(90)
Mean N operating divisions:			
1966	6.20	5.33	5.52
	(49)	(72)	(90)
1972	6.04	5.40	5.52
	(49)	(72)	(90)
Mean N sections:			
1966	12.90	10.14	11.40
	(49)	(72)	(90)
1972	12.48	11.37	13.17
	(48)	(71)	(90)
Mean N levels of supervision:			
1966	3.84	4.02	3.93
	(45)	(71)	(90)
1972	4.03	4.08	4.13
	(49)	(71)	(90)

Note: Figures in parentheses represent actual numbers.

Formalization, Hierarchy, and Delegation of Authority

If origins and subsequent effects of political and social environments account for the extent of formal personnel processes but not for administrative structure in local agencies, one would expect variables describing organizational structure to have little or no effect on formalization. This expectation, however, runs counter to inferences drawn from the results of several research studies, including some publications from the 1966 survey of finance agencies. Correlations between the extensiveness of hierarchy and delegation have been observed in several studies (see Blau 1968; Meyer 1968; Pugh, Hickson, Hinnings, and Turner 1968; Blau and Schoenherr 1971; Meyer 1972a), and they are replicated here. Table 5 displays the zero-order correlations of the index of formalization, the number of hierarchical levels in finance agencies, and two indicators of delegation of authority in personnel matters. The indicators of decentralization are (1) whether the department head or someone below him, such as a division head, formally recommends promotions and dismissals and (2) the relative influence of division heads in promotion decisions.[5] The 1966 and 1972 correlations are displayed to the left and right of the solidi, respectively. There are modest but positive associations of levels of supervision with decentralization in both 1966 and 1972. The correlations of levels with delegation of formal authority to recommend promotion and dismissal are .1814 in 1966 and .2326 in 1972; the correlations of levels with division heads' influence are .2645 and .3107, respectively. In contrast, the associations of formalization with delegation of authority in 1966 and 1972 are virtually zero. Of the four correlations of formalization with delegation in table 5, only one is significantly larger than zero, and, as can readily be seen from the table, this zero-order correlation drops to nonsignificance when the number of levels is controlled.

The minuscule correlations of formalization with decentralization and the small though significant links between era and formalization and between formalization and levels of supervision suggest that formalization precedes proliferation of hierarchical levels rather than the other way around. Cross-lagged path analysis shows that neither size nor levels affect formalization over time, whereas the 1966 measure of formalization affects 1972 levels net of 1966 levels, albeit slightly. The regressions are displayed in table 6. Unfortunately the link between levels and delegation of decision-making authority cannot be confirmed in the longitudinal analysis. Lagged regressions show no significant links between the extensiveness of hierarchy and decentralization. Decision-making practices can change rapidly, and the six-year interval between measurements may be far too long for meaningful results to appear. In sum, the cross-sectional analysis suggests links between formalization and hierarchy and between hierarchy and delegation; no direct relationship between formalization and decentralization was shown. The longitudinal analysis indicates that causality runs from formalization to hierarchy, not the reverse. While these results are not wholly conclusive, they are consistent with our

TABLE 5 *Correlations of Index of Formalization, Levels of Supervision, and Delegation of Decision-making Authority (1966/1972 Correlations)*

	Levels	Delegation 1	Delegation 2
Formalization	.2338/.2338	.0716/.1405	.0600/.0563
Levels	—	.1814/.2326	.2645/.3107

TABLE 6 *Lagged Regressions of Formalization, Size, and Levels*

	Regressions of 1972 Formalization on 1966 Formalization, 1966 Size, and 1966 Levels of Supervision	
	Zero Order	B*
1966 formalization	.7802	.7820
1966 size	.0603	(−.0182)
1966 formalization	.7802	.7651
1966 levels	.2433	(.0644)
	Regressions of 1972 Size and Levels of Supervision on 1966 Formalization and 1966 Size and Levels	
	Zero Order	B*
Regressions of 1972 size:		
1966 size	.9497	.9492
1966 formalization	.1005	(.0052)
Regressions of 1972 levels:		
1966 levels	.5700	.5432
1966 formalization	.2419	.1149

* Coefficients in parentheses are not statistically significant.

expectations: hierarchy follows from extensive personnel procedures and decentralized decision making from hierarchical differentiation.

Openness to the Environment at the Time of Formation

One final question remains: How does one account for the persistent though modest effects of era of formation on personnel procedures in finance agencies? Effects of origins, though diminished by environmental forces, do not disappear altogether; and it is not clear from the data describing modifications in ongoing organizations why this should be so. Put somewhat differently, the problem is to identify what takes place at the time an organization is formed that continues to influence it throughout its existence.

A partial solution is suggested by data describing a small number of finance agencies which reorganized totally between 1966 and 1972. These 14 departments were described in an earlier article (see Meyer 1975a). All changed their names and altered administrative arrangements so fully that the autocorrelations of variables describing organizational structure between 1966 and 1972 were zero. One other interesting property of these 14 agencies was noted in the earlier article: the correlations of size with environmental demands for their services were zero in 1966 and much higher in 1972 (Meyer 1975a, p. 614). Not examined in that article were changes in formalization of personnel procedures. A reasonable expectation is that, just as their size moved from inconsistency to consistency with environmental demands as a result of reorganization, so did their personnel procedures. The amount of this change is critical, however. As will be remembered from table 3, there was only a slight increase in formalization, .0622 on a 1.0 point scale, for the 215 ongoing organizations between 1966 and 1972. For agencies which reorganized totally, a somewhat greater increase in formalization was anticipated, if only because of the extent of other changes. We had not expected, however, to find that the environment had 10 times as much impact on this small group of agencies as it had on ongoing organizations in the six-year interval.

Following is the pooled regression of the two indexes of formalization on era of origin and year for the 14 reorganized finance agencies. Errors are in parentheses.

$$\text{Formalization} = .2977 + \underset{(.0512)}{.0320 \cdot \text{era}} + \underset{\cdot (.0936)}{.5411 \cdot \text{year}}$$

The regression model is the same as that at the bottom of table 3; only the results differ. Casual inspection of these pooled regressions reveals, first, that the constant terms are somewhat lower for the reorganized cases than for the others, indicating that formalized personnel procedures were nearly absent from the former in 1966. Era of origin has minuscule and nonsignificant effects for the reorganized cases, but this was expected because era describes the period during which the old organizations—those obliterated between 1966 and 1972—were formed. In contrast, year of measurement, which for the reorganized cases indicates whether they were formed before or after 1966, has very large effects on formalization; the metric coefficient of year is .5411. The coefficient of year is almost an order of magnitude larger for the 14 reorganized departments than for the 215 ongoing finance agencies. This suggests that the environment is much more intrusive when reorganization takes place than otherwise. And it helps explain why effects of era of origin appear and persist over time despite environmental forces which affect all organizations.

In brief, we would argue that the effects of origins (or what Stinchcombe [1965] calls the correlation of age with structure) are but artifacts of the discontinuous nature of change in organizations. Organizational change involves two types of effects of the environment: gradual alterations in the internal structure of ongoing organizations and replacement of organizations which were inconsistent with external demands by new ones highly consistent with the environment. The model in figure 3 depicts this process graphically. A hypothetical measure of bureaucratization is plotted as a function of time for a set of organizations, most of which continue but some of which are replaced at each time point. A secular trend toward bureaucratization is assumed due to environmental forces, and some of the organizations which are least bureaucratic, hence least consistent with the environment, reorganize at a level of bureaucratization higher than the others. The implications of this pattern are easily described. First, the association between age and structure can be explained entirely as the replacement of existing organizations with new ones. Second, the effects of era of origin on organizational properties increase over time and are limited only by whatever upper bound may exist for organizational age. The second implication follows directly from the first and can be easily shown by combining data from the 215 continuing finance agencies with data from the 14 reorganized cases and treating the post-1966 years as a fourth era of origin. For the 229 cases in 1966, the correlation of era with formalization of personnel procedures was .3487. In 1972—it should be noted again that the post-1966 agencies are treated as founded in a fourth era—the correlation was .4264.

The ultimate explanation for the discontinuous pattern of change in organizations lies in the nature of organization itself. At the time of formation, the elements

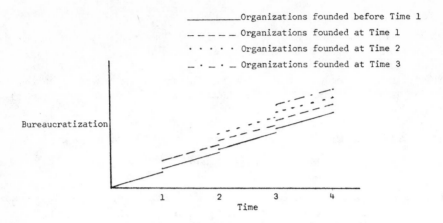

Figure 3   Discontinuous Change in Organizations

of organizations are not separable from the larger social structures in which they are embedded and thus are wholly dependent on their environments. Once organizations are founded, however, they must remain essentially stable, if only to satisfy the expectations of members and clients. These expectations may change gradually over time, but they are revised substantially when reorganization occurs and the environment intrudes. What has not been explained is why some anachronistic organizations manage to survive while others do not. Myriad hypotheses could be put forward, but this is not the place either to propound or to explore them.

Conclusions

A number of ideas about organizations have been developed in this article. We began by pointing out that Weber's theory of bureaucracy emphasizes the primacy of historical forces and in particular the influence of rational-legal authority as causes of bureaucratization. Most researchers acknowledge this but have been unable to grapple with the problem empirically. We took the civil service movement in the United States as an illustration of historical change and the ascendance of rational-legal over traditional standards of authority. The history of federal civil service legislation was reviewed briefly in terms of its effects on state and local governments, and it was hypothesized that the extent of formal personnel procedures in local government finance agencies would reflect both the historical period in which they were founded and the subsequent effects of the environment. Older agencies were less formalized than the newer ones, but over time all adopted procedures more in keeping with the idea of merit personnel administration and less conducive to the political spoils system. An increase in formalization, it was shown, gives rise to multitier hierarchies, and hierarchical differentiation in turn gives rise to the delegation of personnel decisions to lower levels. A causal chain from origins and the environment to formalization to hierarchy to decentralization was thus posited.

A small number of agencies which changed their names and reorganized totally between the two surveys of finance agencies was examined to determine whether the effects of origins could be due to extreme susceptibility to environmental pressures at the time of formation. Environmental effects on personnel procedures are almost an order of magnitude greater in the reorganized agencies than in the ongoing ones. The discontinuous pattern of change explains the observed correlation between age and certain organizational properties, and we predicted that this correlation would increase over time. Our prediction was substantiated by the 1966 and 1972 data describing finance agencies.

Several implications arise from these results. First, the patterns described here need not be peculiar to finance agencies or to the history of the civil service movement in the United States. Effects of origins and the environment and the discontinuous pattern of change should be evident for diverse institutional sectors. Second, if some of the key questions in organization theory concern the effects of societal forces on organizations over time, organizational research ought to be directed toward answering these questions. Historical and longitudinal studies are required, and they must take explicit account of qualitative as well as quantitative elements of environments which have heretofore been neglected. In all likelihood, research will have to be larger in scope and longer in duration than has been usual until now. Third, the results presented here, together with those in earlier articles, suggest means for stimulating change in organizations. Meyer's earlier article, "Leadership and Organizational Structure" (1975b) suggested that change in leadership and dependence of leaders on higher authority opens organizations to environmental influences. Here it has been shown that total reorganization speeds the process of accommodation to environmental pressures. These results are not surprising, but they do call into question the efficacy of attempting incremental change, the results of which are at best uncertain, compared with that of changing leaders or the total reorganization of agencies. Our results do not speak to the desirability of reorganization. For some organizations, particularly those performing mediating functions, continuity is essential. But our research suggests that, when shifts in administrative patterns are sought, they are obtained most efficiently through changes in leadership and fundamental alterations in organizational structures.

Notes

1. This research was supported by National Science Foundation grants GS-33509 and SOC 73-05688 (formerly GS-39637), which are gratefully acknowledged. Also acknowledged are the assistance of Phillip Robinette and the aid of Judith P. Meyer in retrieving various state civil service statutes. Comments on earlier drafts of this article by Edna M. Bonacich, John H. Freeman, Michael T. Hannan, John W. Meyer, Jeffrey Pfeffer, Arthur L. Stinchcombe, and Jonathan H. Turner are also gratefully acknowledged.
2. Charles Bidwell has suggested that organizations in shared environments may diverge over time. He cites in private correspondence the example of midwestern colleges founded in the late 19th and 20th centuries which were initially similar but became differentiated due to demands of controlling bodies, local constituencies, and the like. Divergence unrelated to time of formation, of course, cannot be captured in the model in fig. 1. It may well be that local conditions have caused some divergences in finance agencies over time, but our lack of information about these conditions renders it difficult to gauge their effects.
3. Only Starbuck (1965) has argued that age affects the degree of formalization in organizations, but there has been no empirical confirmation of this claim. While it is possible that organizational age influences bureaucratization apart from time of origin (i.e., cohort) or effects of the environment (i.e., period), neither the data nor justification for the strong

assumptions needed to separate the effects of cohort, period, and age exists. For a discussion of the problem of cohort, year, and age, see Mason et al. (1973). The literature also suggests that time of origin is more important than age. Aiken and Hage (1968, pp. 931–32) found no correlates of age in their study of 16 health and welfare agencies; Pugh et al. (1969), p. 94) found a negative but nonsignificant relationship of age with impersonality of origins of 54 diverse organizations in the Birmingham, England, area. Only Kimberly's recent (1975) study of sheltered workshops has corroborated Stinchcombe's results. Kimberly found post-World War II workshops to be more oriented toward rehabilitation than pre-World War II agencies. This in all likelihood reflects changing beliefs about the appropriate functions for sheltered workshops rather than effects of age per se.

4. Procedures for selecting department heads have been least affected by civil service laws. Environmental forces have not had much impact, and a strong effect of era of origin occurs in section D of table 1. It could be argued, though not proved, that the differences between the correlations of era of origin with whether the department head is elected and the correlation of era with the other items in table 1 are indicative of the magnitude of environmental effects of the other items from the time of origin to the present.

5. The first measure of delegation is coded zero if the department head officially recommends promotions and dismissals and one if someone below him does; the second measure is coded zero if their division heads' influence in promotion decisions is less than 80% and one if their influence, as reported by the department head, is greater than 80%.

References

Aiken, Michael, and Jerald Hage. 1968. "Organizational Interdependence and Intraorganizational Structure." *American Sociological Review* 33 (December): 912–32.

Blau, Peter M. 1968. "The Hierarchy of Authority in Organizations." *American Journal of Sociology* 73 (January): 453–67.

———. 1970. "A Formal Theory of Differentiation in Organizations." *American Sociological Review* 35 (April): 201–18.

Blau, Peter M., and Richard A. Schoenherr. 1971. *The Structure of Organizations.* New York: Basic.

Dibble, Vernon K. 1965. "The Organization of Traditional Authority: English County Government, 1558 to 1640." Pp. 879–909 in *Handbook of Organizations*, ed. James G. March. Chicago: Rand McNally.

Kimberly, John R. 1975. "Environmental Constraints and Organizational Structure: A Comparative Analysis of Rehabilitation Organizations." *Administrative Science Quarterly* 20 (March): 1–9.

Mason, Karen Oppenheim, William M. Mason, H. H. Winsborough, and W. Kenneth Poole. 1973. "Some Methodological Issues in Cohort Analysis or Archival Data." *American Sociological Review* 38 (April): 242–58.

Meyer, Marshall W. 1968. "The Two Authority Structure of Bureaucratic Organizations." *Administrative Science Quarterly* 13 (October): 211–18.

———. 1972a. *Bureaucratic Structure and Authority.* New York: Harper & Row.

———. 1972b. "Size and the Structure of Organizations: A Causal Analysis." *American Sociological Review* 37 (August): 434–40.

———. 1975a. "Organizational Domains." *American Sociological Review* 40 (October): 599–615.

———. 1975b. "Leadership and Organizational Structure." *American Journal of Sociology* 81 (November): 514–42.

Pugh, D. S., D. J. Hickson, C. R. Hinnings, and C. Turner. 1968. "Dimensions of Organization Structure." *Administrative Science Quarterly* 13 (March): 65–106.

———. 1969. "The Context of Organization Structures." *Administrative Science Quarterly* 14 (March): 91–114.

Starbuck, William. 1965. "Organizational Growth and Development." Pp. 451–533 in *Handbook of Organizations*, ed. James G. March. Chicago: Rand McNally.

Stinchcombe, Arthur L. 1965. "Social Structure and Organizations." Pp. 142–93 in *Handbook of Organizations*, ed. James G. March. Chicago: Rand McNally.

Weber, Max. 1947. "Bureaucracy." Pp. 196–244 in *From Max Weber: Essays in Sociology*, ed. H. Gerth and C. W. Mills. New York: Oxford University Press.

SECTION SIX
Problems of the Organizational Society

Organizations permeate virtually every aspect of modern life. Our lives and our hopes are molded within complex organizations. Yet the machinelike character of an organization often grinds down both its participants and the persons it allegedly helps because complex organizations and their imperatives have become the center of attention. People feel abandoned, misused, alienated. They grumble that "the system" really does not work. Yet a "better system" requires more, not less, attention to organizations. Sloughing off organizational society (assuming, for a moment, that this is a possibility) would not lead to utopia. Rather we would slip back to forms of localism, particularism, and tribalism that value individual diversity and accomplishments far less than they are valued today. The only practical alternative to organizational pathologies are less pathological organizations. The five selections in this section focus on key organizational problems of advanced societies.

Kanter studies the effects of sexism in complex organizations. She focuses especially on the responses to "token women." Different types of perceptions of tokens generate different responses to them: visibility creates performance pressures; polarization between tokens and the dominants leads the latter to tighten their boundaries; and assimilation fosters role entrapment for the tokens.

Lindblom considers the consequences of the two main ways that economic life in advanced societies can be organized: capitalism and socialism. He inquires about the ability of each to balance the need of economic growth, more equality, and the furtherance of democracy and liberty. He finds that significant, although different, organizational constraints operate in each type of system.

The pathologies of the workplace are a frequent target for critics in advanced society. The dehumanizing character of work and the lack of worker participation in decision-making are most often singled out for criticism. Two selections in this section treat these topics. Tichy examines the implications of the restructuring of work at the Volvo and General Motors plants. Since worker participation is usually touted highly in the sociological literature we present a dissenting view here.[1] Herbert R. Northrup analyzes worker participation in Europe, and cautions against its adoption in the United States.

Goffman's theory of total organization has been a contributing force in the so-called deinstitutionalization movement. Violent debates are raging over whether and how mental hospitals and other total organizations should be closed down. Butler and Windle attempt to bring a balanced perspective to this heated issue. They offer recommendations on how to plan for and evaluate programs of deinstitutionalization.

Notes

1. For positive analyses of worker participation see: Bengt Abrahamsson, *Bureaucracy or Participation: The Logic of Organization* (Beverly Hills: Sage Publications, 1977); Paul Blumberg, *Industrial Democracy: The Sociology of Participation* (New York: Schocken Books, 1969); and Michael Poole, *Workers' Participation in Industry* (London: Routledge and Kegan Paul, 1975). For a less positive overview, see: George Strauss and Eliezer Rosenstein, "Workers Participation: A Critical View," *Industrial Relations* 9 (February 1970): 197–214.

Women and Tokenism in Organizations: Some Effects of Proportions on Group Life

Rosabeth Moss Kanter

In his classic analysis of the significance of numbers in social life, Georg Simmel (1950) argued persuasively that numerical modifications effect qualitative transformations in group interaction. Simmel dealt almost exclusively with the impact of absolute numbers, however, with group size as a determinant of form and process. The matter of relative numbers, of proportion of interacting social types, was left unexamined. But this feature of collectivities has an impact on behavior. Its neglect has sometimes led to inappropriate or misleading conclusions.

This paper defines the issues that need to be explored. It addresses itself to proportion as a significant aspect of social life, particularly important for understanding interactions in groups composed of people of different cultural categories or statuses. It argues that groups with varying proportions of people of different social types differ qualitatively in dynamics and process. This difference is not merely a function of cultural diversity or "status incongruence" (Zaleznick, Christensen, and Roethlisberger 1958, pp. 56–68); it reflects the effects of contact across categories as a function of their proportional representation in the system.

Four group types can be identified on the basis of various proportional representations of kinds of people. *Uniform* groups have only one kind of person, one significant social type. The group may develop its own differentiations, of course, but groups considered uniform are homogeneous with respect to salient external master statuses such as sex, race, or ethnicity. Uniform groups have a "typological ratio" of 100:0. *Skewed* groups are those in which there is a large preponderance of one type over another, up to a ratio of perhaps 85:15. The numerically dominant types also control the group and its culture in enough ways to be labeled "dominants." The few of another type in a skewed group can appropriately be called "tokens," because they are often treated as representatives of their category, as symbols rather than individuals. If the absolute size of the skewed group is small, tokens can also be solitary individuals or "solos," the only one of their kind present. But even if there are two tokens in a skewed group, it is difficult for them to generate an alliance that can become powerful in the group. Next, *tilted* groups begin to move toward less extreme distributions and less exaggerated effects. In this situation, with a ratio of perhaps 65:35, dominants are just a majority and tokens a minority. Minority members are potentially allies, can form coalitions, and can affect the culture of the group. They begin to become individuals differentiated from each other as well as a type differentiated from the majority. Finally, at a typological ratio of about 60:40 down to 50:50, the group becomes *balanced*. Culture and interaction reflect this balance. Majority and minority turn into potential subgroups which may or may not generate actual type-based identifications. Outcomes for individuals in such a balanced peer group, regardless of type, will

Reprinted in part from "Some Effects of Proportions on Group Life: Skewed Sex Ratios and Responses to Token Women," *American Journal of Sociology*, vol. 82 (March 1977), pp. 965–990, by permission of the author and the publisher. © 1977 by The University of Chicago Press.

depend on other structural and personal factors, including formation of subgroups or differentiated roles and abilities. . . .

The characteristics of the second type, the skewed group, provide a relevant starting point for this examination of the effects of proportion, for although this group represents an extreme instance of the phenomenon, it is one encountered by large numbers of women in groups and organizations in which numerical distributions have traditionally favored men.

At the same time, this paper is oriented toward enlarging our understanding of male-female interaction and the situations facing women in organizations by introducing structural and contextual effects. Most analyses to date locate male-female interaction issues either in broad cultural traditions and the sexual division of labor in society or in the psychology of men and women whether based on biology or socialization (Kanter 1976c). In both macroscopic and microscopic analysis, sex and gender components are sometimes confounded by situational and structural effects. For example, successful women executives are almost always numerically rare in their organizations, whereas working women are disproportionately concentrated in low-opportunity occupations. Conclusions about "women's behavior" or "male attitudes" drawn from such situations may sometimes confuse the effect of situation with the effect of sex roles; indeed such variables as position in opportunity and power structures account for a large number of phenomena related to work behavior that have been labeled "sex differences" (Kanter 1975, 1976a, 1976d, and in press). Therefore this paper focuses on an intermediate-level analysis: how group structures shape interaction contexts and influence particular patterns of male-female interaction. One advantage of such an approach is that it is then possible to generalize beyond male-female relations to persons-of-one-kind and person-of-another-kind interaction in various contexts, also making possible the untangling of what exactly *is* unique about the male-female case.

The study of particular proportions of women in predominantly male groups is thus relevant to a concern with social organization and group process as well as with male-female interaction. The analysis presented here deals with interaction in face-to-face groups with highly skewed sex ratios. More specifically, the focus is upon what happens to women who occupy token statuses and are alone or nearly alone in a peer group of men. This situation is commonly faced by women in management and the professions, and it is increasingly faced by women entering formerly all-male fields at every level of organizations. But proportional scarcity is not unique to women. Men can also find themselves alone among women, blacks among whites, very old people among the young, straight people among gays, the blind among the sighted. The dynamics of interaction (the process) is likely to be very similar in all such cases, even though the content of interaction may reflect the special culture and traditional roles of both token and members of the numerically dominant category.

Use of the term "token" for the minority member rather than "solo," "solitary," or "lone" highlights some special characteristics associated with that position. Tokens are not merely deviants or people who differ from other group members along any one dimension. They are people identified by ascribed characteristics (master statuses such as sex, race, religion, ethnic group, age, etc.) or other characteristics that carry with them a set of assumptions about culture, status, and behavior highly salient for majority category members. They bring these "auxiliary traits," in Hughes's (1944) term, into situations in which they differ from other people not in ability to do a task or in acceptance of work norms but only in terms of these secondary and informal assumptions. The importance of these auxiliary traits is heightened if members of the majority group have a history of interacting with the token's category in ways that are quite different from the demands of task accomplishment in the present situation—as is true of men with women. Furthermore, because tokens are by definition alone or virtually alone, they are in the position of representing their ascribed category to the group, whether they choose to do so or not. They can never be just another member while their category is so rare; they will always be a hyphenated member, as in "woman-engineer" or "male-nurse" or "black-physican."

People can thus be in the token position even if they have not been placed there deliberately for display by officials of an organization. It is sufficient to be in a place where others of that category are not usually found, to be the first of one's kind to enter a new group, or to represent a very different culture and set of interactional capacities to members of the numerically dominant category. The term "token" reflects one's status as a symbol of one's kind. However, lone people of one type among members of another are not necessarily tokens if their presence is taken for granted in the group or organization and incorporated into the dominant culture, so that their loneness is merely the accidental result of random distributions rather than a reflection of the rarity of their type in that system.

While the dynamics of tokenism are likely to operate in some form whenever proportional representation in a collectivity is highly skewed, even if the dominant group does not intend to put the token at a disadvantage, two conditions can heighten and dramatize the effects, making them more visible to the analyst: (1) the token's social category (master status) is physically obvious, as in the case of sex, and (2) the token's social type is not only rare but also new to the setting of the dominants. The latter situation may or may not be conceptually distinct from rarity, although it allows us to see the development of patterns of adjustment as well as the perception of and response to tokens. Subsequent tokens have less surprise value and may be thrust into token roles with less disruption to the system . . .

Research has generally failed to take into account the effects of relative numbers on interaction. Yet such effects could critically change the interpretation of familiar findings. The research of Strodtbeck and his colleagues (Strodtbeck and Mann 1956; Strodtbeck, James, and Hawkins 1957) on mock jury deliberations is often cited as evidence that men tend to play initiating, task-oriented roles in small groups, whereas women tend to play reactive, socioemotional roles. Yet a reexamination of these investigations indicates that men far outnumbered women as research subjects. There were more than twice as many men as women (86 to 41) in the 12 small groups in which women were found to play stereotypical expressive roles.[2] The actual sex composition of each of the small groups is not reported, although it could have important implications for the results. Perhaps it was women's scarcity in skewed groups that pushed them into classical positions and men's numerical superiority that gave them an edge in task performance. Similarly, in the early kibbutzim, collective villages in Israel that theoretically espoused equality of the sexes but were unable fully to implement it, women could be pushed into traditional service positions (see Tiger and Shepher 1975) because there were often *more than twice as many men as women* in a kibbutz. Again, relative numbers interfered with a fair test of what men or women can "naturally" do (Kanter 1976*b*).

Thus systematic analysis of the dynamics of systems with skewed distributions of social types—tokens in the midst of numerical dominants—is overdue. This paper begins to define a framework for understanding the dynamics of tokenism, illustrated by field observations of female tokens among male dominants.

The Field Study

The forms of interaction in the presence of token women were identified in a field study of a large industrial corporation, one of the *Fortune 500* firms (see Kanter [in press] for a description of the setting). The sales force of one division was investigated in detail because women were entering it for the first time. The first saleswoman was hired in 1972; by the end of 1974, there had been about 20 in training or on assignment (several had left the company) out of a sales force of over 300 men. The geographically decentralized nature of sales meant, however, that in training programs or in field offices women were likely to be one of 10 or 12 sales workers; in a few cases, two women were together in a group of a dozen sales personnel. Studying women who were selling industrial goods had particular advantages: (1) sales is a field with strong cultural traditions and folklore and one in which interpersonal skills rather than expertise count heavily, thus making informal and cultural aspects of group interaction salient and visible even for members themselves; and (2) sales workers have to manage relations not only with work peers but with customers as well, thus giving the women two sets of majority groups with which to interact. Sixteen women in sales and distribution were interviewed in depth. Over 40 male peers and managers were also interviewed. Sales-training groups were observed both in session and at informal social gatherings for approximately 100 hours. Additional units of the organization were studied for other research purposes.

Theoretical Framework

The framework set forth here proceeds from the Simmelian assumption that form determines process, narrowing the universe of interaction possibilities. The form of a group with a skewed distribution of social types generates certain perceptions of the tokens by the dominants. These perceptions determine the interaction dynamics between tokens and dominants and create the pressures dominants impose on tokens. In turn, there are typical token responses to these pressures.

   The proportional rarity of tokens is associated with three perceptual phenomena: visibility, polarization, and assimilation. First, tokens, one by one, have higher visibility than dominants looked at alone: they capture a larger awareness share. A group member's awareness share, averaged over shares of other individuals of the same social type, declines as the proportion of total membership occupied by the category increases, because each individual becomes less and less surprising, unique, or noteworthy; in Gestalt terms, they more easily become "ground" rather than "figure." But for tokens there is a "law of increasing returns": as individuals of their type come to represent a *smaller* numerical proportion of the group, they potentially capture a *larger* share of the group members' awareness.

   Polarization or exaggeration of differences is the second perceptual tendency. The presence of a person bearing a different set of social characteristics makes members of a numerically dominant group more aware both of their commonalities with and their differences from the token. There is a tendency to exaggerate the extent of the differences, especially because tokens are by definition too few in number to prevent the application of familiar generalizations or stereotypes. It is thus easier for the commonalities of dominants to be defined in contrast to the token than it would be in a more numerically equal situation. One person can also be perceptually isolated and seen as cut off from the group more easily than many, who begin to represent a significant proportion of the group itself.

Assimilation, the third perceptual tendency, involves the use of stereotypes or familiar generalizations about a person's social type. The characteristics of a token tend to be distorted to fit the generalization. If there are enough people of the token's type to let discrepant examples occur, it is possible that the generalization will change to accommodate the accumulated cases. But if individuals of that type are only a small proportion of the group, it is easier to retain the generalization and distort the perception of the token.

Taylor and Fiske's (1976; Taylor 1975) laboratory experiments provide supportive evidence for these propositions. They played a tape of a group discussion to subjects while showing them pictures of the group and then asked them for their impressions of group members on a number of dimensions. The tape was the same for all subjects, but the purported composition of the group varied. The pictures illustrated either an otherwise all-white male group with one black man (the token condition) or a mixed black-white male group. In the token condition, the subjects paid disproportionate attention to the token, overemphasized his prominence in the group, and exaggerated his attributes. Similarly, the token was perceived as playing special roles in the group, often highly stereotypical ones. By contrast, in the integrated condition, subjects recalled no more about blacks than whites and evaluated their attributes in about the same way.

Visibility, polarization, and assimilation are each associated with particular interaction dynamics that in turn generate typical token responses. These dynamics are similar regardless of the category from which the token comes, although the token's social type and history of relationships with dominants shape the content of specific interactions. Visibility creates performance pressures on the token. Polarization leads to group boundary heightening and isolation of the token. And assimilation results in the token's role entrapment.

Performance Pressures

The women in the sales force I studied were highly visible, much more so than their male peers. Managers commonly reported that they were the subject of conversation, questioning, gossip, and careful scrutiny. Their placements were known and observed throughout the sales unit, while those of men typically were not. Such visibility created a set of performance pressures: characteristics and standards true for tokens alone. Tokens typically perform under conditions different from those of dominants.

1. Public Performance

It was difficult for the women to do anything in training programs or in the field that did not attract public notice. The women found that they did not have to go out of their way to be noticed or to get the attention of management at sales meetings. One woman reported, "I've been at sales meetings where all the trainees were going up to the managers—'Hi, Mr. So-and-So'—trying to make that impression, wearing a strawberry tie, whatever, something that they could be remembered by. Whereas there were three of us [women] in a group of 50, and all we had to do was walk in, and everyone recognized us."

Automatic notice meant that women could not remain anonymous or hide in the crowd; all their actions were public. Their mistakes and their relationships were known as readily as any other information. It was impossible for them to have any privacy within the company. The women were always viewed by an audience, leading several to complain of "overobservation."

2. Extension of Consequences

The women were visible as category members, and as such their acts tended to have added symbolic consequences. Some women were told that their performance could affect the prospects for other women in the company. They were thus not acting for themselves alone but carrying the burden of representing their category. In informal conversations, they were often measured by two yardsticks: how *as women* they carried out the sales role and how *as salesworkers* they lived up to images of womanhood. In short, every act tended to be evaluated beyond its meaning for the organization and taken as a sign of "how women do in sales." The women were aware of the extra symbolic consequences attached to their acts.

3. Attention to a Token's Discrepant Characteristics

A token's visibility stems from characteristics—attributes of a master status— that threaten to blot out other aspects of the token's performance. While the token captures attention, it is often for discrepant characteristics, for the auxiliary traits that provide token status. No token in the study had to work hard to have her presence noticed, but she did have to work hard to have her achievements noticed. In the sales force, the women found that their technical abilities were likely to be eclipsed by their physical appearance, and thus an additional performance pressure was created. The women had to put in extra effort to make their technical skills known, to work twice as hard to prove their competence. Both male peers and customers would tend to forget information women provided about their experiences and credentials, while noticing and remembering such secondary attributes as style of dress.

4. Fear of Retaliation

The women were also aware of another performance pressure: to avoid making the dominants look bad. Tokenism sets up a dynamic that makes tokens afraid of outstanding performance in group events and tasks. When a token does well enough to show up a dominant, it cannot be kept a secret, because all eyes are on the token. Therefore it is difficult in such a situation to avoid the public humiliation of a dominant. Thus, paradoxically, while the token women felt they had to do better than anyone else in order to be seen as competent and allowed to continue, they also felt in some cases that their successes would not be rewarded and should be kept secret. One woman had trouble understanding this and complained of her treatment by managers. They had fired another woman for not being aggressive enough, she reported; yet she, who succeeded in doing all they asked and had brought in the largest amount of new business during the past year, was criticized for being too aggressive, too much of a hustler.

Responses of Tokens to Performance Pressures

There are two typical ways tokens respond to these performance pressures. The first involves overachievement. Aware of the performance pressures, several of the saleswomen put in extra effort, promoted themselves and their work at every opportunity, and let those around them know how well they were doing. These women evoked threats of retaliation. On the gossip circuit, they were known to be doing well but aspiring too high too fast; a common prediction was that they would be cut down to size soon.

The second response is more common and is typical of findings of other investigators. It involves attempts to limit visibility, to become socially invisible. This strategy characterizes women who try to minimize their sexual attributes so as to blend unnoticeably into the predominant male culture, perhaps by adopting "mannish dress" (Hennig 1970, chap. 6). Or it can include avoidance of public events and occasions for performance—staying away from meetings, working at home rather than in the office, keeping silent at meetings. Several of the saleswomen deliberately kept such a low profile, unlike male peers who tended to seize every opportunity to make themselves noticed. They avoided conflict, risks, and controversial situations. Those women preferring social invisibility also made little attempt to make their achievements publicly known or to get credit for their own contributions to problem solving or other organizational tasks. They are like other women in the research literature who have let others assume visible leadership (Megaree 1969) or take credit for their accomplishments (Lynch 1973; Cussler 1958). These women did blend into the background, but they also limited recognition of their competence.

This analysis suggests a reexamination of the "fear of success in women" hypothesis. Perhaps what has been called fear of success is really the token woman's fear of visibility. The original research identifying this concept created a hypothetical situation in which a woman was at the top of her class in medical school—a token woman in a male peer group. Such a situation puts pressure on a woman to make herself and her achievements invisible, to deny success. Attempts to replicate the initial findings using settings in which women were not so clearly tokens produced very different results. And in other studies (e.g., Levine and Crumrine 1975), the hypothesis that fear of success is a female-linked trait has not been confirmed. (See Sarason [1973] for a discussion of fear of visibility among minorities.)

Boundary Heightening

Polarization or exaggeration of the token's attributes in contrast to those of the dominants sets a second set of dynamics in motion. The presence of a token makes dominants more aware of what they have in common at the same time that it threatens that commonality. Indeed it is often at those moments when a collectivity is threatened with change that its culture and bonds become evident to it; only when an obvious outsider appears do group members suddenly realize their common bond as insiders. Dominants thus tend to exaggerate both their commonality and the token's difference, moving to heighten boundaries of which previously they might not even have been aware.[3]

1. Exaggeration of Dominants' Culture

Majority members assert or reclaim group solidarity and reaffirm shared in-group understandings by emphasizing and exaggerating those cultural elements which they share in contrast to the token. The token becomes both occasion and audience for the highlighting and dramatization of those themes that differentiate the token as outsider from the insider. Ironically, tokens (unlike people of their type represented in greater proportion) are thus instruments for under*lining* rather than under*mining* majority culture. In the sales-force case, this phenomenon was most clearly in operation in training programs and at dinner and cocktail parties during meetings. Here the camaraderie of men, as in other work and social settings (Tiger 1969), was based in part on tales of sexual adventures, ability with respect to "hunting" and capturing women, and off-color jokes. Secondary themes involved work prowess and sports. The capacity for and enjoyment of drinking provided the context for displays of these themes. According to male informants' reports, they were dramatized more fervently in the presence of token women than when only men were present. When the men introduced these themes in much milder form and were just as likely to share company gossip or talk of domestic matters (such as a house being built), as to discuss any of the themes mentioned above, this was also in contrast to the situation in more equally mixed male-female groups, in which there were a sufficient number of women to influence and change group culture in such a way that a new hybrid based on shared male-female concerns was introduced. (See Aries [1973] for supportive laboratory evidence.)

In the presence of token women, then, men exaggerated displays of aggression and potency: instances of sexual innuendo, aggressive sexual teasing, and prowess-oriented "war stories." When one or two women were present, the men's behavior involved showing off, telling stories in which masculine prowess accounted for personal, sexual, or business success. The men highlighted what they could do, as men, in contrast to women. In a set of training situations, these themes were even acted out overtly in role plays in which participants were asked to prepare and perform demonstrations of sales situations. In every case involving a woman, men played the primary, effective roles, and women were objects of sexual attention. In one, a woman was introduced as president of a company selling robots; she turned out to be one of the female robots, run by the male company sales manager.

The women themselves reported other examples of testing to see how they would respond to the "male" culture. They said that many sexual innuendos or displays of locker-room humor were put on for their benefit, especially by the younger men. (The older men tended to parade their business successes.) One woman was a team leader and the only woman at a workshop when her team, looking at her for a reaction, decided to use as its slogan "The [obscenity] of the week." By raising the issue and forcing the woman to choose not to participate in the workshop, the men in the group created an occasion for uniting against the outsider and asserting dominant-group solidarity.

2. Interruptions as Reminders of "Difference"

Members of the numerically dominant category underscore and reinforce differences between tokens and themselves, insuring that the former recognize their outsider status by making the token the occasion for interruptions in the flow of group events. Dominants preface acts with apologies or questions about appropriateness directed at the token; they then invariably go ahead with the act, having placed the token in the position of interrupter or interloper. This happened often in the presence of the saleswomen. Men's questions or apologies were a way of asking whether the old or expected cultural rules were still operative—the words and expressions permitted, the pleasures and forms of release indulged in. (Can we still swear? Toss a football? Use technical jargon? Go drinking? Tell in jokes? See Greenbaum [1971, p. 65] for other examples.) By posing these questions overtly, dominants make their culture clear to tokens and state the terms under which tokens interact with the group.

The answers almost invariably affirm the understandings of the dominants, first because of the power of sheer numbers. An individual rarely feels comfortable preventing a larger number of peers from engaging in an activity they consider normal. Second, the tokens have been put on notice that interaction will not be "natural," that dominants will be holding back unless the tokens agree to acknowledge, permit, and even encourage majority cultural expressions in their presence. (It is important that this be stated, of course, for one never knows that another is holding back unless the other lets a piece of the suppressed material slip out.) At the same time, tokens have also been given the implicit message that majority members do *not* expect those forms of expression to be natural to the tokens' home culture; otherwise majority members would not need to raise the question. (This is a function of what Laws [1975] calls the "double deviance" of tokens: deviant first because they are women in a man's world and second because they aspire inappropriately to the privileges of the dominants.) Thus the saleswomen were often in the odd position of reassuring peers and customers that they could go ahead and do something in the women's presence, such as swearing, that they themselves would not be permitted to do. They listened to dirty jokes, for example, but reported that they would not dare tell one themselves. Via difference-reminding interruptions, then, dominants both affirm their own shared understandings and draw the cultural boundary between themselves and tokens. The tokens learned that they caused interruptions in "normal" communication and that their appropriate position was more like that of audience than full participant.

3. Overt Inhibition: Informal Isolation

In some cases, dominants do not wish to carry out certain activities in the presence of a token; they have secrets to preserve. They thus move the locus of some activities and expressions away from public settings to which tokens have access to more private settings from which they can be excluded. When information potentially embarrassing or damaging to dominants is being exchanged, an outsider audience is not desirable because dominants do not know how far they can trust tokens. As Hughes (1944, 1958) pointed out, colleagues who rely on unspoken understandings may feel uncomfortable in the presence of "odd kinds of fellows" who cannot be trusted to interpret information in just the same way or to engage in the same relationships of trust and reciprocity (see also Lorber 1975). The result is often quarantine—keeping tokens away from some occasions. Thus some topics of discussion were never raised by men in the presence of many of the saleswomen, even though they discussed these topics among themselves: admissions of low commitment to the company or concerns about job performance, ways of getting around formal rules, political plotting for mutual advantage, strategies for impressing certain corporate executives. As researchers have also found in other settings, women did not tend to be included in the networks by which informal socialization occurred and politics behind the formal system were exposed (Wolman and Frank 1975; O'Farrell 1973; Hennig 1970; Epstein 1970). In a few cases, managers even avoided giving women information about their performance as trainees, so that they did not know they were the subject of criticism in the company until they were told to find jobs outside the sales force; those women were simply not part of the informal occasions on which the men discussed their performances with each other. (Several male managers also reported their "fear" of criticizing a woman because of uncertainty about how she would receive it.)

4. Loyalty Tests

At the same time that tokens are often kept on the periphery of colleague interaction, they may also be expected to demonstrate loyalty to the dominant group. Failure to do so results in further isolation; signs of loyalty permit the token to come closer and be included in more activities. Through loyalty tests, the group seeks reassurance that tokens will not turn against them or use any of the information gained through their viewing of the dominants' world to do harm to the group. They get this assurance by asking a token to join or identify with the majority against those others who represent competing membership or reference groups; in short, dominants pressure tokens to turn against members of the latter's own category. If tokens collude, they make themselves psychological hostages of the majority group. For token women, the price of being "one of the boys" is a willingness to turn occasionally against "the girls."

There are two ways by which tokens can demonstrate loyalty and qualify for closer relationships with dominants. First, they can let slide or even participate in statements prejudicial to other members of their category. They can allow themselves to be viewed as exceptions to the general rule that others of their category have a variety of undesirable or unsuitable characteristics. Hughes (1944) recognized this as one of the deals token blacks might make for membership in white groups. Saleswomen who did well were told they were exceptions and were not typical women. At meetings and training sessions, women were often the subjects of ridicule or joking remarks about their incompetence. Some women who were insulted by such innuendos found it easier to appear to agree than to start an argument. A few accepted the dominant view fully. One of the first saleswomen denied in interviews having any special problems because she was a woman, calling herself skilled at coping with a man's world, and said the company was right not to hire more women. Women, she said, were unreliable and likely to quit; furthermore, young women might marry men who would not allow them to work. In this case, a token woman was taking over "gate-keeping" functions for dominants (Laws 1975), letting them preserve their illusion of lack of prejudice while she acted to exclude other women.

Tokens can also demonstrate loyalty by allowing themselves and their category to provide a source of humor for the group. Laughing with others, as Coser (1960) indicated, is a sign of a common definition of the situation; to allow oneself or one's kind to be the object of laughter signals a further willingness to accept others' culture on their terms. Just as Hughes (1946, p. 115) found that the initiation of blacks into white groups might involve accepting the role of comic inferior, the saleswomen faced constant pressures to allow jokes at women's expense, to accept kidding from the men around them. When a woman objected, men denied any hostility or unfriendly intention, instead accusing the woman by inference of lacking a sense of humor. In order to cope, one woman reported, "you learn to laugh when they try to insult you with jokes, to let it roll off your back." Tokens thus find themselves colluding with dominants through shared laughter.

Responses of Tokens to Boundary Heightening

Numerical skewing and polarized perceptions leave tokens with little choice about whether to accept the culture of dominants. There are too few other people of the token's kind to generate a counterculture or to develop a shared intergroup culture. Tokens have two general response possibilities. They can accept isolation, remaining an audience for certain expressive acts of dominants, in which case they risk exclusion from occasions on which informal socialization and political activity take place. Or they can try to become insiders, proving their loyalty by defining themselves as exceptions and turning against their own social category.

The occurrence of the second response on the part of tokens suggests a reexamination of the popularized "women-prejudiced-against-women" hypothesis or the "queen bee syndrome" for possible structural (numerical) rather than sexual origins. Not only has this hypothesis not been confirmed in a variety of settings (e.g., Ferber and Huber 1975); but the analysis offered here of the social psychological pressures on tokens to side with the majority also provides a compelling explanation for the kinds of situations most likely to produce this effect, when it does occur.

Role Entrapment

The third set of interaction dynamics centering around tokens stems from the perceptual tendency toward assimilation: the distortion of the characteristics of tokens to fit preexisting generalizations about their category. Stereotypical assumptions and mistaken attributions made about tokens tend to force them into playing limited and caricatured roles in the system.

1. Status Leveling

Tokens are often misperceived initially as a result of their statistical rarity: "statistical discrimination" (U.S. Council of Economic Advisers 1973, p. 106) as distinguished from prejudice. That is, an unusual woman may be treated as though she resembles women on the average. People make judgments about the role played by others on the basis of probabilistic reasoning about the likelihood of what a particular kind of person does. Thus the saleswomen like other tokens encountered many instances of mistaken identity. In the office, they were often taken for secretaries; on the road, especially when they traveled with male colleagues, they were often taken for wives or mistresses; with customers, they were usually assumed to be substituting for men or, when with a male peer, to be assistants; when entertaining customers, they were assumed to be wives or dates.

Such mistaken first impressions can be corrected. They require tokens to spend time untangling awkward exchanges and establishing accurate and appropriate role relations, but they do permit status leveling to occur. Status leveling involves making adjustments in perception of the token's professional role to fit the expected position of the token's category—that is, bringing situational status in line with master status, the token's social type. Even when others knew that the token saleswomen were not secretaries, for example, there was still a tendency to treat them like secretaries or to make demands of them appropriate to secretaries. In the most blatant case, a woman was a sales trainee along with three men; all four were to be given positions as summer replacements. The men were all assigned to replace salesmen; the woman was asked to replace a secretary—and only after a long, heated discussion with the manager was she given a more professional assignment. Similarly, when having professional contacts with customers and managers, the women felt themselves to be treated in more wifelike or datelike ways than a man would be treated by another man, even though the situation was clearly professional. It was easier for others to make their perception of the token women fit their preexisting generalizations about women than to change the category; numerical rarity provided too few examples to contradict the generalization. Instances of status leveling have also been noted with regard to other kinds of tokens such as male nurses (Segal 1962); in the case of tokens whose master status is higher than their situational status, leveling can work to their advantage, as when male nurses are called "Dr."

2. Stereotyped Role Induction

The dominant group can incorporate tokens and still preserve their generalizations about the tokens' kind by inducting them into stereotypical roles; these roles preserve the familiar form of interaction between the kinds of people represented by the token and the dominants. In the case of token women in the sales force, four role traps were observed, all of which encapsulated the women in a category the men could respond to and understand. Each centered on one behavioral tendency of the token, building upon this tendency an image of her place in the group and forcing her to continue to live up to the image; each defined for dominants a single response to her sexuality. Two of the roles are classics in Freudian theory: the mother and the seductress. Freud wrote of the need of men to handle women's sexuality by envisioning them as either madonnas or whores—as either asexual mothers or overly sexual, debased seductresses. (This was perhaps a function of Victorian family patterns, which encouraged separation of idealistic adoration of the mother and animalistic eroticism [Rieff 1963; Strong 1973].) The other roles, termed the pet and the iron maiden, also have family counterparts in the kid sister and the virgin aunt.

A. Mother. A token woman sometimes finds that she has become a mother to a group of men. They bring her their troubles, and she comforts them. The assumption that women are sympathetic, good listeners, and can be talked to about one's problems is common in male-dominated organizations. One saleswoman was constantly approached by her all-male peers to listen to their domestic problems. In a variety of residential-sales-training groups, token women were observed acting out other parts of the traditional nurturant-maternal role: cooking for men, doing their laundry, sewing on buttons.

The mother role is a comparatively safe one. She is not necessarily vulnerable to sexual pursuit (for Freud it was the very idealization of the madonna that was in part responsible for men's ambivalence toward women), nor do men need to compete for her favors, because these are available to everyone. However, the typecasting of women as nurturers has three negative consequences for a woman's task performance: (1) the mother is rewarded by her male colleagues primarily for service to them and not for independent action. (2) The mother is expected to keep her place as a noncritical, accepting, good mother or lose her rewards because the dominant, powerful aspects of the maternal image may be feared by men. Since the ability to differentiate and be critical is often an indicator of competence in work groups, the mother is prohibited from exhibiting this skill. (3) The mother becomes an emotional specialist. This provides her with a place in the life of the group and its members. Yet at the same time, one of the traditionally feminine characteristics men in positions of authority in industry most often criticize in women (see Lynch 1973) is excess emotionality. Although the mother herself might not ever indulge in emotional outbursts in the group, she remains identified with emotional matters. As long as she is in the minority, it is unlikely that nurturance, support, and expressivity will be valued or that a mother can demonstrate and be rewarded for critical, independent, task-oriented behaviors.

B. Seductress. The role of seductress or sexual object is fraught with more tension than the maternal role, for it introduces an element of sexual competition and jealousy. The mother can have many sons; it is more difficult for a sex object to have many lovers. Should a woman be cast as sex object, that is, seen as sexually desirable and potentially available ("seductress" is a perception, and the woman herself may not be consciously behaving seductively), share her attention widely, she risks the debasement of the whore. Yet should she form a close alliance with any man in particular, she arouses resentment, particularly because she represents a scarce resource; there are just not enough women to go around.

In several situations observed, a high-status male allied himself with a seductress and acted as her "protector," not only because of his promise to rescue her from the sex-charged overtures of the rest of the men but also because of his high status per se. The powerful male (staff member, manager, sponsor, etc.) can easily become the protector of the still "virgin" seductress, gaining through masking his own sexual interest what other men could not gain by declaring theirs. However, the removal of the seductress from the sexual marketplace contains its own problems. Other men may resent a high-status male for winning the prize and resent the woman for her ability to get an in with the high-status male that they themselves could not obtain as men. While the seductress is rewarded for her femaleness and insured attention from the group, then, she is also the source of considerable tension; and needless to say, her perceived sexuality blots out all other characteristics.

Men may adopt the role of protector toward an attractive woman, regardless of her collusion, and by implication cast her as a sex object, reminding her and the rest of the group of her sexual status. In the guise of helping her, protectors may actually put up further barriers to a solitary woman's full acceptance by inserting themselves, figuratively speaking, between the woman and the rest of a group. A male sales trainer typically offered token women in training groups extra help and sympathetically attended to the problems their male peers might cause, taking them out alone for drinks at the end of daily sessions.

C. Pet. The pet is adopted by the male group as a cute, amusing little thing and taken along on group events as symbolic mascot—a cheerleader for the shows of male prowess that follow. Humor is often a characteristic of the pet. She is expected to admire the male displays but not to enter into them; she cheers from the sidelines. Shows of competence on her part are treated as extraordinary and complimented just because they are unexpected (and the compliments themselves can be seen as reminders of the expected rarity of such behavior). One woman reported that, when she was alone in a group of men and spoke at length on an issue, comments to her by men after the meeting often referred to her speech-making ability rather than to what she said (e.g., "You talk so fluently"), whereas comments the men made to one another were almost invariably content or issue oriented. Competent acts that were taken for granted when performed by males were often unduly fussed over when performed by saleswomen, who were considered precocious or precious at such times. Such attitudes on the part of men in a group encourage self-effacing, girlish responses on the part of solitary women (who after all may be genuinely relieved to be included) and prevent them from realizing or demonstrating their own power and competence.

D. Iron maiden.   The iron maiden is a contemporary variation of the stereotypical roles into which strong women are placed. Women who fail to fall into any of the first three roles and in fact resist overtures that would trap them in such roles (like flirtation) might consequently be responded to as though tough or dangerous. (One saleswoman developed just such a reputation in company branches throughout the country.) If a token insisted on full rights in the group, if she displayed competence in a forthright manner, or if she cut off sexual innuendos, she was typically asked, "You're not one of those women's libbers, are you?" Regardless of the answer, she was henceforth viewed with suspicion, treated with undue and exaggerated politeness (by references to women inserted into conversations, by elaborate rituals of *not* opening doors), and kept at a distance; for she was demanding treatment as an equal in a setting in which no person of her kind had previously been an equal. Women inducted into the iron maiden role are stereotyped as tougher than they are (hence the name) and trapped in a more militant stance than they might otherwise take.

Responses of Tokens to Role Entrapment

The dynamics of role entrapment tend to lead to a variety of conservative and low-risk responses on the part of tokens. The time and awkwardness involved in correcting mistaken impressions often lead them to a preference for already-established relationships, for minimizing change and stranger contact in the work situation. It is also often easier to accept stereotyped roles than to fight them, even if their acceptance means limiting a token's range of expressions or demonstrations of task competence, because acceptance offers a comfortable and certain position. The personal consequence for tokens, of course, is a certain degree of self-distortion. Athanassiades (1974), though not taking into account the effects of numerical representation, found that women, especially those with low risk-taking propensity, tended to distort upward communication more than men and argued that many observed work behaviors of women may be the result of such distortion and acceptance of organizational images. Submissiveness, frivolity, or other attributes may be feigned by people who feel these are prescribed for them by the dominant organizational culture. This suggests that accurate conclusions about work attitudes and behavior cannot be reached by studying people in the token position, since there may always be an element of compensation or distortion involved. Thus many studies of professional and managerial women should be reexamined in order to remove the effects of numbers from the effects of sex roles.

Notes

1. Thanks are due to the staff of "Industrial Supply Corporation," the pseudonymous corporation which invited and provided support for this research along with permission for use of the data in this paper. The research was part of a larger project on social structural factors in organizational behavior reported in Kanter (in press). An early version of this article was prepared for the Center for Research on Women in Higher Education and the Professions, Wellesley College, which provided some additional financial support. Barry Stein's colleagueship was especially valuable. This article was completed while the author held a Guggenheim fellowship.
2. The 17 least active subjects (out of a total of 144) were dropped from the analysis; their sex is not mentioned in published reports. Those 17 might have skewed the sex distribution even further.
3. This awareness often seemed to be resented by the men interviewed in this study, who expressed a preference for less self-consciousness and less attention to taken-for-granted operating assumptions. They wanted to "get on with business," and questioning definitions of what is "normal" and "appropriate" was seen as a deflection from the task at hand. The culture in the managerial/technical ranks of this large corporation, like that in many others, devalued introspection and emphasized rapid communication and ease of interaction. Thus, although group solidarity is often based on the development of strong in-group boundaries (Kanter 1972), the stranger or outsider who makes it necessary for the group to pay attention to its boundaries may be resented not only for being different but also for giving the group extra work.

References

Aries, Elizabeth. 1973. "Interaction Patterns and Themes of Male, Female, and Mixed Groups." Ph.D. dissertation, Harvard University.

Athanassiades, John C. 1974. "An Investigation of Some Communication Patterns of Female Subordinates in Hierarchical Organizations." *Human Relations* 27 (March): 195–209.

Coser, Rose Laub. 1960. "Laughter among Colleagues: A Study of the Social Functions of Humor among the Staff of a Mental Hospital." *Psychiatry* 23 (February): 81–95.

Cussler, Margaret. 1958. *The Woman Executive*. New York: Harcourt Brace.

Epstein, Cynthia Fuchs. 1970. *Woman's Place: Options and Limits on Professional Careers*. Berkeley: University of California Press.

Ferber, Marianne Abeles, and Joan Althaus Huber. 1975. "Sex of Student and Instructor: A Study of Student Bias." *American Journal of Sociology* 80 (January): 949–63.

Greenbaum, Marcia. 1971. "Adding 'Kenntnis' to 'Kirche, Kuche, und Kinder.'" *Issues in Industrial Society* 2(2):61–68.

Hennig, Margaret. 1970. "Career Development for Women Executives." Ph.D. dissertation, Harvard University.

Hughes, Everett C. 1944. "Dilemmas and Contradictions of Status." *American Journal of Sociology* 50 (March): 353–59.

———. 1946. "Race Relations in Industry." Pp. 107–22 in *Industry and Society*, edited by W. F. Whyte. New York: McGraw-Hill.

———. 1958. *Men and Their Work*. Glencoe, Ill.: Free Press.

Kanter, Rosabeth Moss. 1972. *Commitment and Community*. Cambridge, Mass.: Harvard University Press.

———. 1975. "Women and the Structure of Organizations: Explorations in Theory and Behavior." Pp. 34–74 in *Another Voice: Feminist Perspectives on Social Life and Social Science*, edited by M. Millman and R. M. Kanter. New York: Doubleday Anchor.

———. 1976a. "The Impact of Hierarchical Structures on the Work Behavior of Women and Men." *Social Problems* 23 (April): 415–30.

————. 1976b. "Interpreting the Results of a Social Experiment." *Science* 192 (May 14): 662–63.

————. 1976c. "The Policy Issues: Presentation VI." *Signs: Journal of Women in Culture and Society* 1 (Spring, part 2): 282–91.

————. 1976d. "Women and Organizations: Sex Roles, Group Dynamics, and Change Strategies." In *Beyond Sex Roles*, edited by A. Sargent. St. Paul: West.

————. In press. *Men and Women of the Corporation*. New York: Basic.

Laws, Judith Long. 1975. "The Psychology of Tokenism: An Analysis." *Sex Roles* 1 (March): 51–67.

Levine, Adeline, and Janice Crumrine. 1975. "Women and the Fear of Success: A Problem in Replication." *American Journal of Sociology* 80 (January): 964–74.

Lorber, Judith. 1975. "Trust, Loyalty, and the Place of Women in the Informal Organization of Work." Paper presented at the annual meeting of the American Sociological Association, San Francisco.

Lynch, Edith M. 1973. *The Executive Suite: Feminine Style*. New York: AMACOM.

Megaree, Edwin I. 1969. "Influence of Sex Roles on the Manifestation of Leadership." *Journal of Applied Psychology* 53 (October): 377–82.

O'Farrell, Brigid. 1973. "Affirmative Action and Skilled Craft Work." Xeroxed. Center for Research on Women, Wellesley College.

Rieff, Philip, ed. 1963. *Freud: Sexuality and the Psychology of Love*. New York: Collier.

Sarason, Seymour B. 1973. "Jewishness, Blackness, and the Nature-Nurture Controversy." *American Psychologist* 28 (November): 961–71.

Segal, Bernard E. 1962. "Male Nurses: A Case Study in Status Contradiction and Prestige Loss." *Social Forces* 41 (October): 31–38.

Simmel, Georg. 1950. *The Sociology of Georg Simmel*. Translated by Kurt H. Wolff. Glencoe, Ill.: Free Press.

Strodtbeck, Fred L., Rita M. James, and Charles Hawkins. 1957. "Social Status in Jury Deliberations." *American Sociological Review* 22 (December): 713–19.

Strodtbeck, Fred L., and Richard D. Mann. 1956. "Sex Role Differentiation in Jury Deliberations." *Sociometry* 19 (arch): 3–11.

Strong, Bryan. 1973. "Toward a History of the Experiential Family: Sex and Incest in the Nineteenth Century Family." *Journal of Marriage and the Family* 35 (August): 457–66.

Taylor, Shelley E. 1975. "The Token in a Small Group." Xeroxed. Harvard University Department of Psychology.

Taylor, Shelley E., and Susan T. Fiske. 1976. "The Token in the Small Group: Research Findings and Theoretical Implications." In *Psychology and Politics: Collected Papers*, edited by J. Sweeney. New Haven, Conn.: Yale University Press.

Tiger, Lionel. 1969. *Men in Groups*. New York: Random House.

Tiger, Lionel, and Joseph Shepher. 1975. *Women in the Kibbutz*. New York: Harcourt Brace Jovanovich.

U.S. Council of Economic Advisers. 1973. *Annual Report of the Council of Economic Advisers*. Washington, D.C.: Government Printing Office.

Wolman, Carol, and Hal Frank. 1975. "The Solo Woman in a Professional Peer Group." *American Journal of Orthopsychiatry* 45 (January): 164–71.

Zaleznick, Abraham, C. R. Christensen, and F. J. Roethlisberger. 1958. *The Motivation, Productivity, and Satisfaction of Workers: A Prediction Study*. Boston: Harvard Business School Division of Research.

Capitalism, Socialism, and Democracy
Charles E. Lindblom

Liberty is a—perhaps the—big issue in the relation of capitalism to democracy. But just what is the connection?

Two people cannot both be free to build their houses on the same single building lot or to hold precisely the same job unless there exists some constraining or coordinating mechanism so that in fact only one actually wins the lot or the job. If the coordinator is a governmental authority, then—as most people use the term "free"—we say that neither person is free, for choice has passed from the two to government. So the coordinating mechanism must be something other than government.

For a large category of liberties, the market system provides the necessary constraint or coordination. No broad mechanism other than the market has yet been discovered for the purpose. You and I can both be free to live where we wish only because a landlord will decide, in the event that we both want the same apartment, which of us will get it. And only because, if both of us want the same job, an employer will decide which of us will get it. Similarly, we are free to use buses and airplanes only on condition that we have the consent of those who provide them in the market. We are free to choose between work or play only because in the market we are constrained to work in order to get the money with which to induce the landlord, grocer, and bus company to let us do what we choose to do. People can be free only if many of the things they want are not free.

Not all freedoms or liberties, however, require a system of constraint or coordination. Thinking and speaking as one pleases presumably do not. Yet effective and legal freedom to reach very large audiences cannot be established unless people are constrained, since newspaper space and broadcast time cannot be made available to all who wish it. For these larger civil liberties, consequently, the market is again indispensable.

At this point, however, the line of argument takes a sharp turn. Familiar market systems are made up of three sets of markets: markets in which consumers buy goods and services, markets in which people sell their labor, and the vast network of markets in which businesses buy from and sell to each other. But the markets that are required for liberty are only the first two of the three. It is consumer markets through which our options for food, clothing, housing, and transportation are constrained (by the prices we must pay) so that we can be "free" to choose them. It is labor markets that draw us into jobs in such a way that, although the labor force is allocated to the work that needs to be done, we are "free" to choose our jobs.

Two sets of markets do not mean capitalism. The Soviet Union and other non-capitalist nations operate the two (though not, as in capitalism, also the third). Although I do not mean to say that the Soviet Union is a free society (since it lacks other freedoms available only in the liberal democracies), for the freedoms just outlined, Soviet-style markets will do just as well. And so the conclusion at this juncture is that, although markets are necessary to these liberties, capitalism is not necessary—at least by this argument. If there is any surprise in that conclusion, it is only because of a long-established bad habit of equating capitalism with market systems in our minds.

But democracy is more than these liberties. Let us probe along a different line. Historically, the energies first thrown into the drive against absolutism were for the most part indistinguishable from the energies thrown into the drive to liberate trade from royal monopoly and to open up profit opportunities. Out of that combination of political zeal and avarice, constitutionalism first developed, to be followed by political democracy. Somehow only in capitalist systems have national democratic systems arisen. That is one of the great still valid generalizations about the world's political and economic systems. Historical origins aside, must that close relationship continue indefinitely into the future?

One answer is that capitalism is now a barrier to a more fully developed democracy because it is a system of inequality in the distribution of power. A distinguishing characteristic of capitalism is that many of the most important functions to be performed in the society—feeding and housing the population and providing it with power for its machines, among others—are assigned not to government officials but to a category of major functionaries called businessmen. If they do not perform well, unemployment or other economic instability can bring down a government. But by the rules of capitalism, government cannot command businessmen to perform their assigned functions. Instead, businessmen must be induced to do so. How? By granting them a privileged position—by granting them whatever benefits are necessary to elicit the required performance. The benefits include protected markets, tax advantages, the provision of many government services to business, easier consultation with government officials than is granted to others, and even some assignment of governmental authority to businessmen such as is not granted to others. At peril to their own positions, political officials know that they must do everything in their power to meet whatever level of business demands will produce economic stability and growth. The conclusion is that a high level of democracy can hardly be attained when government officials are subjected to so disproportionate an influence from business.

Capitalism shows another antagonism to further growth of democracy. The fabled "competition of ideas" long held necessary to democracy is a grossly lopsided competition when the media are largely controlled by corporate business. Although dissident voices make themselves heard, the flow of messages is overwhelmingly of much the same voice. To be sure, the media take pride in offering a conventional "two sides to every question." But two is hardly enough for a rigorous competition of ideas, and all the less satisfactory when the two are no further apart than, say, the positions of the two American political parties.

But might capitalism be necessary in order to maintain such democracy as we have already achieved, even if it is an obstacle to further democratization?

One possibility is that new demands for further democratization such as are represented, for example, in agitation for democratization of the workplace and in a rising skepticism about the genuineness of existing democracy mean that existing democracy is not stable. Democracy has to go either forward or backward. That is, either it must advance into further democratization; or frustration, divisiveness, and consequent repression will undercut it. But we have just argued that capitalism is a barrier to further democratization. The conclusion, then, is that capitalism will compel us to go backward.

Leave that complex possibility aside. Assume that it is possible to stabilize democracy at the level it has reached in Western Europe and North America. Is capitalism then necessary to its stabilization at that level?

Capitalism appears on certain counts to be a great bulwark of such democracy as we have achieved. It disperses power, compared to the distribution of power in a socialist state. It removes many divisive big issues of economic policy from the agenda of government, leaving them to be settled in the market. It provides a foundation for an ideology that, teaching that inequality is fair, persuades the public to moderate its demands on government. And it highly motivates at least one powerful group of citizens, businessmen, to resist governmental encroachments on liberty—specifically on their liberties—simply because their liberties are so profitable to them in capitalism.

Yet there are two ways in which a government might maintain democracy in the absence of capitalism. They constitute two forms of socialism.

One is through a heavy use of the market system, though not private enterprise—in short, a socialist market system. A full panoply of government-owned and -operated corporations, each given a high degree of autonomy subject to conventional market controls rather than detailed political control, might provide a sufficiently pluralistic dispersion of power, if in fact such a dispersion is necessary. A socialist market system could also keep many big issues of economic policy off the central government's agenda, leaving much of the critical decision-making on resource allocation, growth, and income distribution to be settled, as in a capitalist system, in the market.

Suppose, however, that the demands on a government drive it toward more centralized authority and away from reliance on the market—thus toward a non-market socialism. If so, a second way to maintain democracy is a possibility. The second is that society *learns*—learns both to control more centralized authority and to moderate its potentially divisive demands on government.

Societies do indeed learn. And governments learn. The most impressive evidence is democracy itself. Societies have learned—and it is a phenomenal accomplishment—to create large and enormously powerful multipurpose national governments whose rulers are chosen and removed by a process as peaceful as a casting of ballots. If 18th- and 19th-century man could learn to do this, it is not out of the question that 21st-century man can learn some equivalently remarkable additional lessons in the control of authority.

Among the obstacles to learning is capitalism itself, with its imperfect competition of ideas.

Restructuring Work

Noel M. Tichy

with the collaboration of Jay N. Nisberg

Every few years since Frederick Winslow Taylor introduced scientific management, new organizational "panaceas" have emerged. The list includes leadership training courses, human relations programs, operations research, T-groups, management by objectives, and organization development. More recent remedies include job enrichment, work restructuring, and quality of working life (QWL) innovations. The current fashion, QWL has taken on international significance; in the United States, it led to a national commission that resulted in the widely distributed and highly controversial study, *Work in America*. One unfortunate aspect of the waxing and waning of organizational improvement remedies is the limited understanding that exists on what works and what does not and under what conditions. Once a particular panacea is adopted by the "right" company, other companies either try it or dismiss it on the basis of hearsay. I've heard managers say, "General Motors tried it and it didn't work—so we aren't going to try it. . . ." Of course, what "it" consists of is never fully discussed or understood.

Understandable pressures have created this state of affairs and will continue to exert themselves on managers, consultants, and academicians. The pressure is on the manager to find ways of dealing with organizational problems, here and now, with minimal risk and investment. This makes the manager susceptible to quick-acting, cure-all sales pitches from consultants. (A consultant obviously has a vested interest in selling his services.) In earlier research we found that even when consultants carry out a general organizational diagnosis, they tend to conclude that what ails the organization is something that is treatable with their particular set of skills. Thus an operations research consultant finds production design problems that are solvable by linear programming; a psychologist consultant finds psychological problems that are solvable by sensitivity training. The academic researcher is not immune to these pressures, either. Research money tends to go where the action is; thus when a panacea becomes popular, so does research on that panacea. Currently there is a tremendous amount of research in progress on QWL programs.

The purpose of this article is to help us stand back and ask some penetrating questions about various organizational improvement programs so that we don't dismiss the good with the bad and buy the bad along with the good. We can also learn by systematically asking the right questions and examining the right issues in relation to organizational improvement programs that have been tried or are under way. Ideally, we would like to have solid scientific research to guide us. But given the current state of work in organization development, this is unrealistic; therefore we need a pragmatic yet conceptually sound framework to guide our analysis. We employ such a framework (presented below) in this article to compare two QWL programs—one at Volvo Skovdeverken in Sweden, the other at General Motors Coach. The former is reportedly a success, while the latter is admittedly a failure.

The framework can also be used to evaluate a variety of organizational improvement programs such as, for example, management by objectives and organization development.

We selected two QWL projects for consideration because QWL is the current best seller in the area of organizational improvement. The first half of the 1970s has produced numerous experimental programs in a variety of countries. Richard Walton of the Harvard Business School in the Winter 1975 issue of *Organizational Dynamics* presented a penetrating analysis of eight such projects and why they have not been more widely imitated.

Most of these QWL projects result from a variety of forces in Western industrialized countries. Worker alienation, blue-collar blues, discontent, alienation, and withdrawal typically are attributed to such factors as rising educational levels, rising levels of wealth and security, decreased emphasis on obedience to authority, a decline in achievement motivation, and a shift in emphasis from individual to social commitment. There are plenty of unanswered questions about how pervasive these trends are—or even whether some of them really exist. Nevertheless, they form the rationale for initiating QWL programs.

Framework for Evaluating Organizational Improvement Programs

The framework presented in Figure 1 identifies some key factors that influence the effectiveness of organizational improvement programs. The formulation envisions three major sets of variables as important to assess in evaluating improvement programs: (1) the environmental context, (2) the actual program, and (3) the outcomes.

The first set includes two kinds of contextual factors: (1) those external to the organization, and (2) the characteristics of the organization. Support for focusing on external factors is found in the works of Tom Burns and G. M. Stalker, Joan Woodward, Fred Emery and Eric Trist, and Paul Lawrence and Jay Lorsch—all of whom identify important linkages between external environment and internal organizational structure and functioning. In addition, the external political and social forces affect the way workers respond to various kinds of improvement programs. Last, the economy in general as well as the economic conditions of the particular industry affect the success of any improvement program.

The internal organizational factors most relevant to an improvement program are product and technology, structure, size, and organizational climate. The technology that organizations use to transform their inputs into outputs vary in terms of complexity, routinization, and stability. The nature of this technology shapes some limits and constraints on the way in which the organization gets structured.

Of special importance, according to Charles Perrow, is whether the technology entails many or few exceptions (*many* represented by custom-made products or services and *few* by mass-produced products) and whether the exceptions entailed are analyzable by search procedures. (An analyzable exception, for example, would occur in manufacturing a standard product, where the worker could refer for the answer either to a manual or to his own past experience—whereas an unanalyzable exception would occur in the production of nuclear fuel systems for which there is no relevant previous experience to analyze.) Each of these technologies exerts different social influences on the organization and the workers.

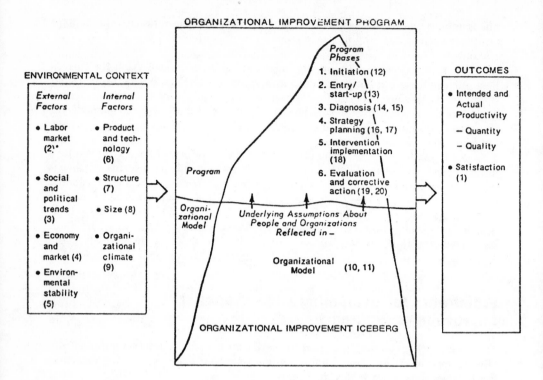

Figure 1   Framework for Evaluating Organizational Improvements
* Numbers in parentheses correspond to specific evaluation questions related to each of the above factors. The questions are presented in Figure 2.

Organizational structure, too, can vary. Some important variations are the complexity of task structure, the degree of vertical and horizontal differentiation, the degree of formalization of roles, and the degree of employee participation in decision making.

An organization's climate or culture reflects the norms held by its members. Norms regarding change and improving the organization are of particular concern in evaluating an improvement program. Many programs fail because of resistance to change—not because the program is intrinsically unsound.

The second set of factors in evaluating an organizational improvement effort is the program itself. As Figure 1 indicates, the program is envisioned as an iceberg with a set of concrete steps listed above the waterline and with the underlying assumptions about people and organizations reflected in an organizational model below the waterline. The iceberg analogy stresses a crucial point often overlooked in assessing a program. Events and activities depicted in the steps above the waterline grow out of people's assumptions and theories about human nature and organizations. These assumptions are usually implicit and therefore below the waterline, or below the threshold of awareness. Managers and consultants working to implement organizational improvement programs should be aware of and explicit about their underlying assumptions and theories or models. For those of us who try to evaluate a program, it is absolutely necessary to ferret out, even if by inference, the assumptions and models that guide the program. Doing so enables us to understand the causes of success or failure and helps us in transferring an approach to other settings.

Last, Figure 1 focuses our attention on the outcomes of an improvement program. Descriptions of improvement efforts are often presented with little hard data on outcomes, either in terms of productivity or in terms of other dimensions such as worker satisfaction and contribution to organizational health.

The framework presented in Figure 1 guided the development of 20 questions to ask as a guide to evaluating the effectiveness of an organizational improvement program. These questions and the issues to consider in evaluating the answers are presented in Figure 2 and discussed below before examining the Volvo and GM cases.

Twenty Questions for Evaluating Organizational Improvement Efforts

A rationale accompanies each of the 20 questions in Figure 2, which were developed to provide a systematic means of examining the complex array of factors affecting the success or failure of an organizational improvement effort. The remainder of this section discusses some of the issues involved in evaluating program success within the framework presented in Figure 1 and Figure 2.

Outcomes. The first question establishes the criteria for evaluating all the other questions: What were the intended outcomes of the program and how close did the program come to achieving them?

Environmental context. The success or failure of an organizational innovation is a function of the innovation or program itself and the environmental context within which it occurs. The context has been divided into two sectors in Figure 1, the external and internal. Figure 2 presents questions 2 through 9 for use in evaluating the environmental context as it relates to organizational innovations.

The external factors are important because of the issues of transferability and diffusion of organizational improvement innovations. In Sweden, for example, the labor market is very different than in the United States—as is the government's role in legislating worker participation and other factors relevant to QWL innovations. The Swedish labor market was operating under conditions of full employment at the start of Volvo Skovde's QWL innovation, so Swedish industry had to rely on a great deal of foreign labor, primarily Finns and Yugoslavs. By contrast, unemployment in the U.S. labor market has never been below 5 percent. Furthermore, the Swedish government has encouraged worker participation and industrial democracy through legislation.

The internal environmental factors, or the characteristics of the organization, are extremely important factors in evaluating any program. The recent popularity of contingency theories of organization and management reflects a growing realization that organizational effectiveness is largely a function of matching organizational structure, leadership style, planning, and control systems to demands of the organization's environment and the task or technology involved. This is why we emphasize technology and structure in our framework.

As technology varies in terms of the exceptions entailed and kind of search required to deal with them, so does the kind of people best able to perform successfully and so does the kind of structure most supportive of the work. Organi-

Figure 2   *Twenty Questions for Evaluating Organizational Improvement Efforts*

Factor	Question
OUTCOMES	
Objectives	1. *What were the intended outcomes of the program and what were the actual outcomes?* It is necessary to determine why the program was initiated and its impact on "bottom line" outcomes such as productivity, turnover, absenteeism and satisfaction.
ENVIRONMENTAL CONTEXT	
External Factors	
Labor market and characteristics of workforce	2. *How tight was the labor market and what were the characteristics of the available labor pool?* Ascertain unemployment level and characteristics of workforce when evaluating an organizational improvement program.
Social and political trends	3. *Were there changes occurring in society affecting workers and the organization?* The success of a program may be affected by how consistent it is with certain societal trends.
Economy and market	4. *What was the general state of the economy at the time of the improvement program?* Certain programs may work only in favorable economic conditions.
Environmental stability	5. *How much is the organization's immediate environment changing—and is the organizational structure appropriately matched?* A program may be greatly affected by the degree of congruence between an organization's structure and degree of environmental uncertainty that exists for the organization.
Internal Factors	
Product technology	6. *What is the product of the organization and the primary technology used to transform inputs into outputs?* Ascertain the match between technology, structure, and kind of people involved and whether the program is congruent with them or tries to make them congruent with the program.
Structure	7. *Where on the mechanistic-to-organic structure continuum is the organization?* The program should be consistent with the organization's structure or explicitly attend to changing that structure.
Size	8. *How large is the organization and the plant or division within which the program is taking place?* Size affects complexity of programs and the organizational resources available.
Organizational climate	9. *What are the prevailing norms and values in the organization regarding involvement in organizational improvement efforts?* Programs require changed behavior, thus changed climate—which requires program attention to resistance.
Guiding Assumptions and Models	10. *How explicit were the assumptions about organizations and change that guided the organizational improvement program?* Being explicit about assumptions increases the chance that all involved understand the program and that the assumptions are more carefully examined and tested.
	11. *How comprehensive and consistent with current organizational theory were the guiding assumptions and models?* The success of a program can be influenced both by internal logic and by failure to incorporate what we know about organizations and improvement.

Figure 2 *(Continued)*

Factor	Question
Program phases	
Initiation phase	12. *What was the reason for starting the program and who was initially involved?* Programs generally require a broadly shared "felt need" and involvement of affected people to succeed.
Entry and startup phase	13. *What were the initial activities at the start of the program and who was involved?* The pitfall to avoid is premature implementation; moving into a program without adequate diagnosis increases resistance stemming from lack of understanding and support. Prescription without diagnosis leads to malpractice.
Diagnostic phase	14. *What were the explicit diagnostic activities?*
	15. *What aspects of the organization were diagnosed and how?* Pitfalls include the "elephant problem" (sending eight blind men out to touch the organization and try to put the separate "felt" pieces together) and the "expert" problem, caused by outsiders who do a fancy diagnosis that no one understands.
Strategy planning phase	16. *How was the actual program planned and by whom?* The two dimensions to assess are (1) how available resources (internal and external consultants) were used, and (2) how the diagnostic model and data were used.
	17. *How explicit and detailed were the plans?* Lack of planning leads to seat-of-the-pants implementation of a program.
Implementation phase	18. *What was actually done, how, when, and by whom?* Two pitfalls are incomplete, patchwork implementation and *intervention interruptus*, or failing to carry the program through to completion.
Evaluation and corrective action phase	19. *Was there explicit evaluation and monitoring of the program and, if so, what was measured and how?* Political pressure resulting from overadvocacy of programs sets up forces against evaluation. Evaluative measures should be directly related to intended program outcomes.
	20. *What was done with the evaluation—did it result in corrective action or modification of the program?* Corrective action may fail because of lack of top-level organizational commitment and/or postimplementation letdown and regression when the novelty wears off.

zational improvement programs can succeed or fail depending on their degree of congruence with the organization's technology, structure, and staff.

Organizational improvement program. The iceberg analogy in Figure 1 stresses the importance of the underlying assumptions and models, typically implicit, that guide program formulation and implementation. The success of an organizational improvement program can be greatly affected by how explicit and aware key actors in the process are of these guiding assumptions. Being explicit increases the likelihood that all involved will understand the program and that the assumptions will be carefully examined and tested. Those of us who try to evaluate the program need to explicate the model whether the organization's members did or not.

In addition to explication, there is the issue of whether the guiding model reflects the current state of knowledge and practice in the field of organizational behavior and management.

Regarding the actual phases of the program as presented in Figures 1 and 2, several points are worth noting. First, the phases in reality are often not distinct but overlapping. Also, some phases may never occur. For purposes of analysis and evaluation, however, it is important to make the distinctions in order to identify and isolate specific factors relating to program success.

In considering the effectiveness of programs, it is useful to keep in mind that successful organizational improvement programs tend to have certain common characteristics:

1. *They are purposeful and goal directed*—there are relatively explicit goals and directions toward which the program is aimed.
2. *Form follows function*—the program is organized and resources are allocated on the basis of tasks to be performed, not on formal authority or power requirements.
3. *Decisions are based on the location of information*—relevant information, not roles in the hierarchy, determine where decisions are made. Expert resources are brought together to solve problems.
4. *The designers of the programs pay explicit attention to organizational context*—thus innovation is consistent with the contingency theory of organizational design and management.

The framework and twenty questions will be used to evaluate the GM and Volvo programs after a summary description of each program.

Work Restructuring at Volvo Skovde

Volvo Skovdeverken, which manufactures gasoline and diesel engines, has about 5,500 employees—of whom, 4,800 are hourly workers. About a third of the hourly employees come from Finland. The workforce has almost doubled during a five-year period. The people recruited are generally young people, with an increasing proportion of females to males.

Work with QWL started in 1969. The following year, a special study group was formed with representatives from the company and the unions. The decision to form it was made by the works council which includes management and union representatives. Impetus for the QWL programs stemmed from the combination of high personnel turnover and absenteeism, a few wildcat strikes, and an unstable workforce. In response to these factors, interest focused on the human problems created by short time-cycles and repetitive work.

In a parallel development, Norwegian experiments with work restructuring were attracting attention and interest in Sweden—and they provided a starting point for the newly formed study group. Members of the study group read and discussed the work of Fred Emery and Einar Thorsrud in Norway and made study visits to Norway to see the work experiments in action.

Out of their readings and visits emerged a proposal for two experiments, both of which involved job enrichment with extended work roles and job rotation. Carried out in 1971–1972, the experiments were implemented by management with union support but without actively involving supervisors and workers affected by the design process. This lack of involvement along with other factors contributed to the limited success of the experiments. The hoped-for impact on absenteeism and turnover did not materialize; furthermore, participants were divided in their reactions. These disappointing results can be attributed to a number of factors: (1) design of the experiments, which was based on limited notions of job rotation and enrich-ment and involved little teamwork and team responsibility for work; (2) resistance by first-line supervisors, whose authority was threatened; (3) a naïve assumption that all workers wanted to enrich their jobs (some prefer the old type of work); and (4) a fairly noncollaborative implementation process in which the "experts" told the units how they should restructure their work.

Still, the experiments generated enough interest and excitement over the potential of work restructuring that once the reference group and others analyzed the problems involved, a decision was made to begin new programs with the intention of profiting from the early mistakes. A related factor was the greater commitment at a corporate level being made throughout Volvo in support of QWL programs—a commitment initiated and strongly supported by Volvo's new presi-dent, Pehr Gyllenhammar. In this same period, planning was underway at Skovde for expanding the engine-building capacity. A comprehensive planning effort sought to create a new type of engine factory, with a great deal of attention devoted to developing sociotechnical-administrative changes aimed at enhancing the quality of working life. Planning was the responsibility of a special project organization made up of managers, staff specialists, and employee representatives.

The result was a new type of factory shaped like an "E"—with four legs instead of three, and with the legs connected to each other at both ends. The legs house the various machine departments, while the main body houses the assembly operation. Between the legs are areas of greenery. Physically, the factory is broken down into smaller components. Employees in one component cannot hear or see the other components. Each component operates as a semi-autonomous plant with all the resources necessary to do its own work. Although the overall factory design was innovative and supported new forms of work organization, actual social organization was not fully designed in advance. With the actual organization of work within the new E-factory, a shift in emphasis occurred.

In 1973 it was decided that a project team—made up of two production engineers, a sociologist, a psychologist, and both management and employees in the E-factory—would develop new forms of work organization. A new orientation toward QWL innovations began to emerge in the E-factory. Instead of innovation by decree from the experts, there was real participation by members of the different departments in working out their own solutions to their problems.

Another key point: Unlike the earlier approach, the new, more comprehen-sive one involved the entire E-factory, not just isolated departments. Beginning in 1974, almost every production department actively participated in a joint effort to discover new ways of handling problems and organizing work. The project team collaborated with other key organizational groups such as production management, production engineers, and union people.

Departments in the E-factory include several machining departments and a new engine-assembly department. Because the engine-assembly department is very similar to the Kalmar car-assembly plant using self-propelled assembly carts, buffer zones, and assembly teams, we will not describe it in detail. Instead, we will discuss a machining department that contains a larger proportion of the workforce at Skovde.

The engine-block line in the E-factory represents the most advanced level of automated machining in the plant. . . . The machining is done primarily in eight transfer machines. . . . Each cylinder block is machined by 475 cutting tools. The mechanized transport of the blocks is interrupted only at one place, where the bearing cap is put on the engine block. At the end of the line . . . finishing touches are put on the blocks. . . .

Technologically, the department represents something qualitatively different—in comparison both with the old engine-block line and with conventional line technology. In the conventional, highly mechanized line, jobs typically are highly repetitive. The machine determines work pace and the worker himself has little freedom of movement.

In the new engine-block line, repetitive short-cycle work has been replaced, to a great extent, by tasks of overseeing and inspecting machinery, tools, and the product. The exchange and adjustment of tools form an essential part of the total job. There is no longer the close dependency on machine pacing.' . . . Maximum utilization of manpower is less important than keeping the machinery going. Furthermore, traditional work measurements aren't appropriate because an important part of the job is not predictable—namely, trouble-shooting occurrences.

Traditionally, each job is evaluated separately in determining compensation. But this method posed problems because of the reorganization of work and the interchangeability of jobs within an area. The solution was to give all jobs within an area the same evaluation and pay level. This has not as yet created problems for the internal task group, but it has created problems when workers are transferred in or out of units—and these problems are as yet unresolved.

Last, the role of the supervisor in this section has shifted from that of a traditional, fairly directive first-line supervisor who focuses primarily on careful monitoring of workers to that of a more participative supervisor who focuses on providing resources for the workers and helping them facilitate innovations. Even though the department is organized into groups with responsibility for keeping the machinery going and for maintaining quality control, the supervisor encourages workers to trade across groups in order to learn more jobs. In addition, the supervisor has set up regular meetings both within work teams and between work teams to exchange experiences and to evaluate and plan new ways of working. Accordingly, the supervisor has been extremely supportive in helping make both technical and social changes desired by the workers.

The productivity and morale data from this department and from the E-factory as a whole indicate substantial positive gains over similar kinds of operations within Volvo. Turnover has dropped from 25 percent to below 20 percent, and absenteeism is down slightly—from over 11 percent to below 10 percent.

A report on Volvo by the Swedish Employers' Confederation concludes that the changes in the engine-block department—which made use of new work organization, new machines, and a high level of mechanization—resulted in an approach that not only provides more interesting work, but also competes favorably on an economic basis with previous arrangements.

They conclude that "Modern industrial engineering and work organization has thus made possible a production system that is both profitable and attractive to workers."

Summary of the General Motors Coach Program

In January 1971, General Motors Coach began to formulate plans for the building of the new GMC mobile home product. Not only did this new product include innovative design concepts, but new and innovative approaches to the work organization were also contemplated. The different approach to the assembly process was intended to improve employee attitudes, increase job interest, and reduce absenteeism and turnover. The end result would be both a higher quality product and more efficient operation.

The plan that emerged revolved around a work-team concept. Such an approach to the assembly of new vehicles was decided on because of such factors as these:

- The expected production rate was sufficiently low to permit some flexibility of operation.
- Although complex in system and design, the product had only two wheel bases and relatively few production variations between units—factors that presumably would lend it to the team concept.
- Workers could readily identify with this new recreation vehicle.
- The size of the plant operation and its layout were conducive to team operation.
- Last, the new method would appeal to workers as an alternative to performing routine, repetitive tasks.

Upon analysis, it was decided that the body-upfit, the air-conditioning, and the chassis areas were best suited to the new plan. Ultimately, a total of eight six-member teams were to produce 32 vehicles per shift in the body-upfit area. The chassis-assembly operation would be composed of 14 three-member teams to build at the same rate, and the air-conditioning department would include four four-member teams. A total of 106 employees were involved in the work-team process.

Setting up the workforce began with the selection of a nucleus of 30 hourly employees handpicked from truck-and-coach and sheet-metal operations. It was intended that this group would build the pilot vehicles and later function as team leaders and trainers as the project expanded.

This phase of the plan was completed when the first five pilot models were built in December 1972. Immediately thereafter, the workforce was expanded through recruitment of workers with specialized skills—such as welders, metal finishers, electricians, and so on. Recruitment was carried out in the remaining operations, where interested employees submitted applications for the specialized jobs. These employees were needed to begin production at levels of one or two completed jobs per hour.

Problems arose almost as soon as the work-teams got started. First, the motor home vehicle was more complicated to assemble than anticipated. Second, scant attention had been paid to how the team would organize and coordinate its activities. This combination—unexpected complexity and the unfamiliarity of employees both with the product itself and with such matters as working for the first time with adhesives, a totally new suspension system, and a different frame construction—prevented meeting the production schedule and interfered with the training of these employees. Knowledge of work cycles involving up to 18 half-hour work cycles further complicated matters—a complication compounded as other problems began to interfere with job training. On heavy and/or complicated assemblies, variations in skills and physical qualifications within the team required adjustment. In many cases the end result was to standardize assembly procedures, with each team member performing one specialized activity.

Moreover, new and untested tools and processes along with engineering changes—all of which are normal in the start-up of a new product—further hampered the operation and the team concept in particular.

Efficiency, one key reason for adopting a team concept in the first place, never reached an acceptable level. In some cases it was adversely affected because one or two team members failed to perform their fair share of work and the team as a whole was unable to maintain internal discipline. Nor did quality fulfill expectations.

In addition, absenteeism and turnover levels steadily increased during the innovation. Increased turnover in the form of voluntary quits probably stemmed from the inability of certain team members to keep pace with the schedule because of inadequate training and poor work layout—resulting in lowered morale in the motor home operation.

As a cumulative result of these conditions, it was necessary to reduce the use of the team concept in building motor homes. Individual workers were given the option to continue; as of May 1973, 28 workers continued performing their operations within the team concept. At that time there were six three-man teams on the chassis line as well as five two-man teams on the engine build-up. This number has contined to drop, and today only a few people work in teams.

Employee reactions to the teamwork concept were mixed. Those for, those against, and those without opinions each constituted about one-third. One worker "for" still felt that there was one big problem: "The only problem I have is sometimes the foreman tells me to put on one part and the group leader tells me to put on another part." Less positive workers indicated that "not all of the members of a five-man team performed their fair share of the work."

Applying the Framework to Volvo and GM

Let's look at how the evaluation framework is applied to the organizational improvement programs at Volvo and General Motors.

Outcomes

The intended outcomes for both GM and Volvo were improved employee attitudes and job content, reduced absenteeism leading to a better quality product, and greater efficiency. The data indicate that the desired outcomes were forthcoming at Volvo but not at GM.

Environmental context

Figure 3 summarizes the key contextual factors relevant for each case. Important external conditions helped to explain the success of the Volvo program—specifically, pressure to innovate from a tighter labor market and a tradition of union agitation for increased worker participation in decision making. Also, the internal organizational context was more supportive at Volvo. QWL programs were being accepted as standard practice in many parts of Volvo, whereas at GM they constituted a real exception and were regarded with suspicion by most GM managers.

Regarding top-management support, it is interesting to note that even though Volvo's top executive, Pehr Gyllenhammar, must be given a great deal of credit for the strong top-level support for new work organizations, General Motors was not lacking in top-level supporters—namely, Edward N. Cole, then president of GM. The difference was that other top-level managers at General Motors had divided opinions, whereas the top group at Volvo was united on this issue. The key, therefore, is the depth and unanimity of top-level support for new organizational innovations.

Organizational models

In neither case was there a formal organizational model to guide the program. Volvo did, however, employ an explicit model. The iceberg was more above the water than below for Volvo; in consequence, a lot of attention was paid to examining the assumptions underlying the innovations. The groundwork for such examination was created when the study group read Thorsrud and Emery's work on the Norwegian work experiments and subsequently visited some of the experiments in person. The sociotechnical model of organizations as formulated by Eric Trist and Emery was familiar to managers, staff, and a fair number of workers. The reference group supported this model of organizations and was guided by the following assumptions about the design of desirable jobs:

1. The need for the content of a job to be reasonably demanding of the worker in terms other than sheer endurance—yet to provide a minimum of variety (not necessarily novelty).
2. The need to be able to learn on the job and to go on learning; again, a question of neither too much nor too little.
3. The need for some minimal area of decision making that the employee can call his own.
4. The need for some minimal degree of social support and recognition in the workplace.
5. The need for the employee to be able to relate what he does and what he produces to his social life.
6. The need to feel that the job leads to some sort of desirable future (though not necessarily a promotion).

At General Motors, the most there was in the way of a shared model was an understanding among some staff and some managers of Herzberg's concepts and a limited view of sociotechnical systems. GM's was primarily a pragmatic, let's-do-it orientation.

Organizational improvement program phases

Initiation phase. Volvo ends up with more pluses in this phase for several reasons. As noted in Figure 3, involvement was more broadly based. Not only was there management and staff involvement in initiating the program, as at GM, but there was union and employee involvement before the decision to start the project was even made. The reason for selecting a team restructuring approach also varied in the two settings. At GM it was mandated by management, whereas at Volvo it grew out of the explorations, study, and experiments of the reference group (with union and employee representation).

Entry/start-up phase. At GM, the entry and start-up phase entailed staff and management's learning about teams and work restructuring, whereas at Volvo it involved meetings of small groups of workers to discuss possible plans and the establishment of a more formalized representative system to help in planning and guiding the program. Again, Volvo's approach contributed to building a broader base of support along with greater integration of ideas.

Diagnostic phase. For both, the QWL program entailed a new operation, with no need to analyze an existing organization and propose solutions to existing problems. However, a kind of diagnostic activity evolved in each case. Both companies looked at turnover, absenteeism, and recruitment data from other areas

Figure 3 Evaluating the Quality of Working Life Programs at Volvo Skovde and General Motors Coach

Factor and Question	General Motors	Volvo
OUTCOMES(1)*		
Intended	Improved satisfaction, reduced absenteeism and turnover, increased effectiveness.	Improved satisfaction, reduced absenteeism and turnover, increased effectiveness.
Actual	Decreased satisfaction, increased absenteeism and turnover, decreased effectiveness.	Outcomes achieved.
ENVIRONMENTAL CONTEXT		
External Factors		
—Labor market (2) and characteristics of workforce	Available pool of unskilled workers.	Tight market—unable to attract Swedes; one-third of workforce is Finnish.
—Social and political trends (3)	Emerging new life styles, none relevant to QWL.	Emerging new life styles. Industrial democracy (socialist tradition) legislation directly related to QWL.
—Economy and market (4)	Affluence—still in growth economy, GM performing well.	Affluence—still in growth economy, Volvo performing well.
—Environmental stability (5)	Moderately stable (before energy crisis) with appropriate structural fit.	Moderately stable with appropriate structural fit.
Internal Factors		
—Product and technology (6)	Mobile homes, assembly line.	Car and truck engines, assembly line.
—Structure (7)	Mechanistic.	Mechanistic.
—Size (8)	Total firm—600,000. Plant—5,000.	Total firm—60,000. Plant—5,500.
—Organizational climate (9)	Authoritarian tradition, adversary union relationship, little receptiveness to change.	Tradition of paternalistic management, good union-management relationship, fair receptiveness to change.
ORGANIZATIONAL IMPROVEMENT PROGRAM		
Guiding Assumptions and Models		
—Explicitness of model (10)	Not explicit.	Fairly explicit, especially regarding the organization of work.
—Comprehensiveness of model and its relationship to current knowledge (11)	Simplistic, limited to Herzberg theory.	Quite comprehensive, sociotechnical view of autonomous work teams.

Figure 3 (Continued)

Factor and Question	General Motors	Volvo
Program Phases		
—Initiation phase (12)	Concern for reduced turnover and absenteeism, and improved efficiency.	Series of QWL experiments in other parts of Volvo to deal with absenteeism, turnover, and recruitment problems.
	New product planned for assembly.	New engine being planned for assembly.
	Management and staff initially involved.	Management, staff, union, and workers initially involved.
—Entry and start-up phase (13)	Staff and management explored alternative way of designing work.	Representative group established to study issues and propose plans.
—Diagnostic phase Explicit diagnosis (14) Aspects diagnosed and means used (15)	(In both cases the QWL program was introduced into a new operation so that diagnosis entailed examining similar kinds of operations in the firm as well as analytic work to design new work procedures.)	
—Strategy planning phase How done and by whom (16)	Staff specialist and managers developed plans using production engineer resources.	Representative system used to develop plan incorporated production engineer, psychologist, and sociologist resources.
Explicitness of plans (17)	Plan was moderately comprehensive, with little planning to deal with implementation problems.	Plan was comprehensive with contingency plans for dealing with implementation problems.
—Implementation phase (18)	Implemented quickly with limited worker training and limited attention to "bugs" in work design.	Implemented total plan with much staff support and supervisory support for learning and working "bugs" out of new system.
—Evaluation and corrective-action phase Explicitness of evaluation and factors measured (19)	Regular control data on turnover, absenteeism, and productivity used as well as informal interviews.	Regular control data on turnover, absenteeism, and productivity used as well as interviews and regular worker meetings with supervisors.
Corrective action taken (20)	Of a crisis-intervention nature—dealt with immediate short-run problems.	Ongoing feedback and modification of QWL program.

* Numbers correspond to evaluation questions presented in Figure 2.

of their operation to guide them in setting objectives for the new operations. Also, much diagnostic work was done in comparing alternative work layouts. The data at GM were shared only among staff and management. At Volvo, data were shared broadly and employed by the reference group as an aid in planning.

Strategy-planning phase.   As Figure 3 indicates, Volvo's scope of involvement continues to make a difference here. In addition, Volvo used a greater variety of resources. At Volvo, staff included production engineers, various other engineers, psychologists, and sociologists. The strategy that emerged at Volvo was more comprehensive—involving, as it did, altering the production system, the social grouping, training, the wage system, supervision, and so on.

Intervention implementation phase.   As Richard Walton has indicated, a factor that can contribute to program failure is "internal inconsistencies in the original design." These inconsistencies existed at both Volvo and GM. They were, however, much more prevalent at GM—as indicated by the fact that work restructuring actually led to more repetitive job cycles and hence less job enrichment. Another damaging inconsistency at GM lay in its failure to give the team sufficient autonomy to control its internal process of accountability.

In addition, GM was also adversely affected by surrounding support systems (the wage system, information and control systems) that were not altered, as they were at Volvo, to be congruent with the restructuring of work. At Volvo, the wage system was changed by reclassifying all jobs equally. The information and control systems were designed with worker input and involvement and continue to be altered by worker input to better fit the needs of the new work organization. At GM, traditional systems that in many cases failed to reinforce the new work organization were continued.

Evaluation and corrective-action phase.   At GM, the program's failure led to its evaluation and corrective action. The workers themselves took corrective action by reverting to more traditional forms of work when they realized that the system wasn't working. Other "corrective action" took the form of increased absenteeism and transfers. No formal procedure existed, however, for systematically reviewing the program and improving it.

Volvo, on the other hand, not only systematically reviews its control data but evaluates its program through the continued involvement of a staff team of managers and behavioral scientists and through regular review meetings among workers themselves. As a result, new suggestions and plans for improving work performance have been generated and implemented at the shop-floor level. Workers have, for example, helped implement a systematic training program to teach each other all the jobs in a given work area. The supervisor, for his part, keeps records of who has mastered what jobs. . . .

Selected Bibliography

The basis for many of the current contingency models of management and organizational design is found in Tom Burns and G. M. Stalker's *The Management of Innovation* (Tavistock Publications, 1961)—a highly readable and insightful study of several British industrial firms that led to the concepts of mechanistic and organic systems; the work of

Joan Woodward—based on a study of more than 100 British firms and presented in *Industrial Organization: Theory and Practice* (Oxford University Press, 1965)—provided further evidence for the important relations between technology and organization structure. In the United States the work of Paul Lawrence and Jay Lorsch, reported in *Organization and Environment* (Harvard University Press, 1967), paved the way for new thinking about the contingency design of organizations based on the type of organizational environment. Fred Emery and Eric Trist also contributed to such thinking; their article, "The Causal Texture of Organizational Environments" (Human Relations, Vol. 18, 1965), presents a useful framework for analyzing organizational environments.

An excellent summary of some key QWL programs initiated in a variety of countries is found in Richard Walton's "The Diffusion of New Work Structures: Explaining Why Success Didn't Take" (*Organizational Dynamics*, Winter 1975). The work of consultants, some of their built-in biases, and the way they approach the decision to use one improvement technique rather than another are presented in an article by Noel Tichy, "How Different Types of Change Agents Diagnose Organizations" (*Human Relations*, December 1975).

Codetermination: A Critique

Herbert R. Northrup

Employe participation in the determination of corporate decisions has taken many forms, but none has captured the imagination like the German system of "codetermination." The European Commission is now advocating West German-style codetermination for all nine member countries, and similar proposals have been made in Japan, Canada and even in the United States. Unfortunately, such proposals ignore both the unique German heritage and the characteristics of its system.

Under the West German system, companies essentially have two boards—a supervisory board, whose main tasks are to select management and approve major expenditures, and a managing board, made up primarily of the officers who actually run the company. One-third of the members of the supervisory boards are selected from plant employes by the workers (all workers, not just union members).

The German system is an outgrowth of a number of factors peculiar to Germany (and to a lesser extent, Europe). For one thing, local unions don't exist. Contracts are regionally or nationally negotiated; local issues, such as overtime, plant expansion and closure, must be worked out with works councils, which traditionally have been distinct from unions though they may include union members.

Also, Germany's history of inflation has induced its workers to use restraint in their demands; and because of Germany's history of war, worker representation on the supervisory board was seen as a means of checking any resurgence of right-wing extremism. The two-tier board system kept most worker board members conveniently out of most management decision-making.

But things are changing. A new generation of leaders in the unions, including many radical intellectuals out of universities but without much plant work experience, are using the codetermination system to entrench their power. New legislation which takes effect July 1 will greatly enhance their influence on the supervisory board and could drastically alter the workings of the system.

The new law gives workers less than 50% representation on the board, but it provides for some union designation, rather than worker election, of employe board representatives, and for near shareholder-employe board parity. Where union designated board members are able to dominate other worker directors—and it is reasonable to expect that over time this will be increasingly the situation—the unions may force management to make many concessions in order to be able to operate the business.

Equal board participation means that key corporate decisions may be made on a political rather than an economic basis. Recently, the worker representatives at one major company, Stahlwerke Roechling-Burbach G.m.b.H. (SRB), persuaded the neutral chairman to vote with them to override management's decision not to make a DM 400 million investment in a new plant in Saar. The union wanted it because of unemployment among its members.

Volkswagen is 40% government owned. On its supervisory board sit representatives of government bodies, the president of IG Metall (Germany's largest union), a representative of a union-controlled bank which owns Volkswagen stock, plus employe directors. Private shareholders have only a minority representation. A review of Volkswagen's supervisory board decisions, including the long fight over a U.S. plant, show a potentially costly political tug-of-war as economic decisions were vetoed or modified by union-political control.

Under the new law, union control of Volkswagen's supervisory board has been enhanced and a union man recently was named labor relations director.

From a libertarian point of view, union control of industry must be regarded most gravely. In effect, it makes the social partners a single institution, thus negating checks and countervailing power. The idea that workers will be in a superior position because their union leaders are also their bosses is extraordinary on its face.

Fortunately, German-style codetermination is not a near prospect on the American scene. American workers participate in more decisions affecting their destiny—ranging from wages to layoff and rehiring procedures—than do their counterparts anywhere else in the world. Participation on the shop floor affords them protection against arbitrary action of their supervisors and assures that matters of grave importance to their present and future are codetermined. There is where the action is, and this is why German-style codetermination has little appeal here.

Despite a tongue-in-cheek suggestion at Chrysler, the United Automobile Workers aimed directly at the pocketbook rather than detouring toward the board of directors in the last labor negotiations. If the UAW officials had exchanged some cents per hour for a place on Chrysler's board, I suspect that they would soon be among the unemployed.

Meanwhile, George Meany was electing a President of the United States, has been telling Congress what to write in labor laws, and not worrying about representation on anything as insignificant as a company board of directors.

His executive assistant, Thomas R. Donahue, previously summed it all up by declaring that moves of unions to join a board of directors "offer little to American unions" on the job. "We do not want to blur in any way the distinctions between the respective roles of management and labor in the plant," he said. If unions were to become a "partner in management," he suggested that they would "be, most likely, the junior partner in success and the senior partner in failure." Unions, he noted, "currently bargain on more issues than the number we might have any impact on as members of a board of directors."

Planning and Evaluating Deinstitutionalization

Herbert J. Butler and Charles Windle

Over the past two decades mental health services have shifted radically from what has been called "total institution" custody toward community-located, outpatient-oriented services.[1] This massive relocation to the community of the mentally ill and mentally retarded has been termed "deinstitutionalization." Although the term connotes the harmful effects of custodial institutions, it ignores the potential value of community-located care, and by a semantic ambiguity implies that we will no longer need to "institutionalize," that is, maintain some systems for treating the chronically ill.

When the Kennedy Administration inaugurated the Community Mental Health Centers (CMHC) program in 1963, it set two goals. to reduce the state hospital resident population by 50 percent in a decade *and* to establish a comprehensive community-oriented care system.[2] Additionally, recently implemented CMHC legislation (PL 94-63) makes explicit the need to relate the deinstitutionalization process to CMHC services; minimally, it requires aftercare and the establishment of halfway house services within the CMHC, or at least the recognition that ex-hospital patients are entitled to equal services in CMHC programs.

Nevertheless, there is growing evidence that there have been new patterns of exclusion, neglect, and abuse in the community. For example, a comprehensive study of the current status of deinstitutionalization, reported to Congress this year by the Comptroller General of the General Accounting Office (GAO) under the descriptive title, *Returning the Mentally Disabled to the Community: Government Needs to Do More*, found the following:

> Many mentally disabled persons have been released from institutions and placed into decent housing in clean, safe neighborhoods with such structured in-house activities and outside programs as work, education, day activity centers, and recreational programs. In this environment, many mentally disabled persons have become less dependent on either public support or other people for financial and daily living needs and have learned to live normal or nearly normal lives.
>
> However, many other mentally disabled persons enter, reenter, or remain in public institutions when they could be treated in the community. Others have been placed into substandard and crowded facilities in unsafe neighborhoods, or facilities that could not or did not provide needed services or assurance that they would receive needed services.

This report makes clear the critical shortage of adequate and appropriate community facilities and services for people with mental disabilities. Zoning and other regulatory requirements of facilities for the mentally ill and mentally retarded

The authors wish to acknowledge the assistance of Judith E. Turner, Chief, Community Support Program, National Institute of Mental Health, in preparing the material in this article relating to community support systems.

serve to limit further the number of such facilities in operation rather than to provide special incentives for their development. Additionally, financial abuses have accompanied the shifting of funds to community locations, such as is documented for nursing homes by Mendelson (1974).

Therefore, the current Public Health Service view toward deinstitutionalization[3] is to recognize that a shift in treatment locations is occurring, but that complete deinstitutionalization is not in all circumstances an appropriate goal. On a more positive note, the Comptroller General's report strongly recommends that the Director of the Office of Management and Budget "direct federal agencies to develop and implement an interdepartmental objective for accomplishing deinstitutionalization," since there are at least 135 federal programs administered by 11 major departments and agencies that impact on the mentally ill or mentally retarded.

Success in the development of community alternatives to institutionalization will depend on several factors: knowledge development through research, policy-setting and program planning based on conceptual clarity, and unusually comprehensive forms of program evaluation. At present, the National Institute of Mental Health is actively involved in bringing together the results of deinstitutionalization experiments and studies, initiating a major community support program, and laying the groundwork for evaluation of program initiatives in this area.

Research Findings

Among the studies that NIMH staff are examining are two studies, *Halfway Houses for the Mentally Ill* and *Rehabilitating the Mentally Ill in the Community*, which NIMH supported the Joint Information Service in conducting. In these studies, clients who seemed highly promising in terms of test scores, general intelligence, affect, insight, and motivation often failed miserably in their rehabilitation efforts, whereas others who had been hospitalized for many years and seemed to have little rehabilitation potential often did well. Authors Glasscote *et al.* (1971) concluded in the second volume:

> What one would hope for from more intensive and extensive research efforts would be data that would allow one, first of all, to predict rehabilitation potential, so that he could with some justification divide prospects according to level of potentiality. Beyond this, one would hope for evaluative techniques that would enable him to differentiate particular programs for candidates with particular characteristics and aptitudes.

An NIMH-supported study by Kirk (1977), of the University of Kentucky Research Foundation, attempted to determine which discharged patients from state hospitals received services from comprehensive care centers and to determine the influence of community treatment on rehospitalization rates. What he found was that at least 55 percent of the 579 patients whose records were studied received some form of service from local community mental health programs during the three-year follow-up period, or until readmission; the patients most at risk of rehospitalization were those with more chronic histories, who were served frequently but only for a few visits; while aftercare extended some patients' community stay, the effects of chronicity were only partially alleviated.

An analytic review of deinstitutionalization by Bachrach (1976) points out that "just as pre-admission screening may serve to minimize dehumanization, so should an effort be made to enhance the role of pre-release planning at mental hospitals." Along with the importance of pre-release planning, she emphasizes the necessity to provide liaison personnel who work between hospital and community-based facilities. She also recommends that the territoriality exhibited by competing community-based treatment and service agencies be neutralized by cooperative effort. Regarding evaluation, Bachrach indicates that "the only way to assure that specific programs connected with deinstitutionalization efforts do not autonomously take on questionable latent functions is by effective monitoring and continuing assessment of their relevance through process and outcome evaluation."

In a comprehensive study of 212 severely disturbed mental patients reported by Coates et al. (1976), subjects were subdivided into five groups according to the cost of hospitalization and home care expenditures in order to evaluate the relative effectiveness of these two treatment methods. Their conclusions indicate that the outcome of treatment is viewed differently by a patient, relatives, program administrators, or clinicians; minimal home care expenditure coupled with a low hospital expenditure provided the most effective and most efficient rehabilitation of this population; and from the patients' and relatives' viewpoint, the combination of brief hospitalization with high home care expenditures produced a measurable incremental benefit with a minimal additional expenditure, and thus was most acceptable.

Much of our experience with deinstitutionalization has come from California, which enacted laws to shift care from state hospitals to county facilities. There, the counties were expected to pick up the responsibility for caring for patients, but did not receive dollar amounts equal to what the state hospital had received for caring for the same patient; additionally, a funding lag required counties to put up start-up and development money before they received reimbursement. Marlowe's (1972) study of the inhabitants of Modesto State Hospital, which was the first state hospital in California to be closed, showed that, although the intent was to return patients to the community, only one patient of the 429 studied remained out of an institution for the entire year of the study. Of this study population, which was unique in that approximately 40 percent were 65 years of age or older (as compared to 20 percent in the California mental hospital system as a whole), 18 percent were dead at the end of one year, 28 percent had deteriorated in mental and physical condition, 29 percent had remained unchanged, and only 25 percent had improved following relocation.

Community Support Programs

A first step in developing effective community support programs is the formulation of goals and objectives for services that individually and in combination will provide humane and effective care. One such goal would be to create maximum opportunity for the mentally ill, especially when consideration is being given to new legislative initiatives such as National Health Insurance. Another goal would be for hospitals, community-based mental health programs, and related human service agencies to began working together more effectively to develop comprehensive support systems. Another significant goal would be to improve the quality of care, whether this occurs in an institution or in community-based services; this need to stress the quality of care is particularly appropriate for the nursing and boarding homes that are emerging as the principal publicly-supported alternative to state hospital care.

NIMH's Community Support Program

In light of these goals, NIMH is in the process of initiating a new pilot program, the Community Support Program (CSP), through a change in the focus of the Hospital Improvement and Hospital Staff Development Programs. The purpose of CSP is to stimulate states in developing "comprehensive community support systems" for adults with severe or persistent mental health problems, and to develop better methods for organizing, funding, and monitoring such systems. As conceptualized by NIMH, a comprehensive community support system "must be designed to guarantee that appropriate forms of help are available to meet the needs and develop the potential" of the population. The ten basic components of such a system include: 1) identification of the population-at-risk, whether in hospital or in the community; 2) assistance in applying for entitlements; 3) crisis stabilization services in the least restrictive setting possible; 4) psychosocial rehabilitation services, including special living arrangements and vocational rehabilitation, where needed; 5) supportive living arrangements, employment opportunities, and other support services of indefinite duration; 6) medical and mental health care; 7) back-up support to families, friends, and community members; 8) involvement of concerned community members; 9) protection of client rights; 10) case-management. . . .

The conceptualization of a "comprehensive community support system" for the chronically disabled population crystallized through a series of working conferences held by NIMH during the period from August, 1975, to June, 1977; participants included leaders representing federal, state, and local mental health and human service agencies, consumer, citizen, and legal advocates, clinicians, researchers, hospital employees, researchers, and providers of innovative services for the chronically disabled. . . .[4]

Through the conferences, it has become clear that community support systems cannot be brought about by the mental health system's working in isolation. Nor can the mental health system fund the entire range of opportunities and services required. Many other agencies must be involved. Particularly important are the "mainstream" services, such as public health, medical assistance, social services, income maintenance, transportation, employment, housing, and vocational rehabilitation.

A major problem in community care at present occurs because no single agency is clearly responsible for assisting the mentally disabled in the community. In the recent conference series, representatives of key interest groups generally agreed that during the transition to community-based care, it is incumbent on the mental health system to provide programmatic leadership and advocacy at federal, state, and local levels to create more workable programs for the severely and chronically disabled population.

It is the philosophy of CSP that both hospitals and CMHCs can play vital roles at the local level. Where CMHCs have been established and no other agency has assumed a commitment to the comprehensive needs of the severely disabled, CMHCs are expected to assume the role of convener and catalyst, providing the currently mandated services and collaborating with hospitals and other human services agencies to fill in gaps. Where community support programs are well established under other auspices, the CMHC may play a less central role. Where there are no CMHCs, other solutions will be sought until CMHCs can be initiated. . . .

NIMH plans to establish a "learning community" and communications network among CSP leaders and persons associated with the program. This will be accomplished through several working conferences designed to exchange information, to identify policy implications of the projects, and to consider and plan for a national technical assistance and training strategy to facilitate CSP goals. In addition, a national evaluation of the program is being planned to document and synthesize the implications for policy and practice.

As problems are identified in state and local projects that relate back to federal policy, efforts will be made to channel the information to appropriate decision-makers within the Department of Health, Education, and Welfare (HEW). In particular, it is expected that information from the pilot projects will be fed into a HEW task force working to respond to the GAO study on deinstitutionalization. It is also expected that the President's Commission on Mental Health will make substantive policy recommendations that will affect the future evolution of community support systems. . . .

Program Evaluation Approaches

Federally-funded community mental health centers are required to do three types of program evaluation activities: 1) self-evaluation, focusing on a number of specified topics that include both various service processes, such as accessibility and availability of services, and outcome or, in the words of the law: "the impact of its services upon the mental health of the residents of its catchment area"; 2) disclosure to the general public and involvement of catchment area residents in reviewing the center's evaluative statistics; and 3) quality assurance procedures that involve clinical staff in peer and utilization review. Each of these three approaches should be applied to efforts at evaluating deinstitutionalization. These can be applied both by individual facilities that aim to deinstitutionalize and for entire regions where this is a goal. The CMHC Amendments of 1975 strengthen the requirements for CMHCs to serve persons who might otherwise go to or remain in state mental hospitals. Accordingly, the requirements for centers' self-evaluation include among the topics "that centers should address their impact on inappropriate institutionalization." A model study of the impact of a center on state hospital use, done by Wolford *et al.* (1972), compared changes in utilization rates over time in census tracts from the center's catchment area with similar tracts outside the catchment area.

The most important focus for studies of deinstitutionalization will be to go beyond studies of individual agencies to studies of system linkage. Because changing the locus of care from institutions to communities requires cooperation between facilities or coordination among facilities by a third party, studying single agencies is likely to miss essential aspects of care of the chronically ill, namely the chance that they will fail to be served by any agency. Procedures for studying networks of services have been developed (see Bass and Windle, 1972, and Burgess, Nelson, and Wallhaus, 1974) and should be applied.

In such studies, it will be important to keep in mind Davis' A VICTORY model (1973), the strength of which is its consideration of the major decision factors in evaluation. Of particular significance among these is the resistance factor. If one expects change in behavior as a result of evaluation there may be resistance, whether or not it is expressed openly. To counteract this resistance factor Davis emphasizes the yield that can be seen as a reward or benefit by the agencies being

evaluated; reward for excellence or better-than-average performance reduces the
resistance, and makes for a better change.

Notes

1. In 1955, 77 percent of all patient care episodes in mental health facilities were for inpatient care, usually in state mental hospitals. In 1975, only 27 percent were for inpatient care.
2. Although both goals are being achieved, the linkage between the two has been quite loose. Most centers were begun separately from the state hospital system, and generally serve quite different populations. Baker, Isaacs, and Schulberg (1972) found minimal interactions between centers and public mental hospitals. Additionally, Scully and Windle (1976) examined state hospital resident and admission rates longitudinally in 16 states and found no greater decreases in state hospital resident rates where federally-funded centers were located than in areas without centers; they did find a consistent difference in changes in state hospital admission rates, however, suggesting that centers were retarding the flow of clients to state hospitals, even if not reducing the number in residence at any one time.

   In terms of sheer numbers, the CMHC program was originally envisioned as needing 3,000 CMHCs, covering the country, to attain its goals. That figure has since been reduced to 1,500, which more closely approximates the number of catchment areas in the United States. As of May, 1977, there were 570 operational federally-funded CMHCs.
3. See the Public Health Service Comments on the General Accounting Office Draft Report entitled *Improvements Needed in Efforts to Help the Mentally Disabled Return to and Remain in Communities*, October 31, 1976.
4. For a summary of two conferences that helped formulate the Community Support Program, see "Community Living Arrangements for the Mentally Ill and Disabled: Issues and Options for Public Policy." Proceedings of an NIMH Conference held September 22–24, 1976, available through the NIMH Public Information Office, 5600 Fishers Lane, Rockville, MD. 20857.

References

Bachrach, L. *Deinstitutionalization: An Analytical Review and Sociological Perspective*. National Institute of Mental Health, L. L. DHEW Publication No. (ADM) 76-351. Washington, D.C.: U.S. Government Printing Office, 1976.

Baker, F., C. D. Isaacs, and H. C. Schulberg. *Study of the Relationships Between Community Mental Health Centers and State Mental Hospitals*. Contract report to the National Institute of Mental Health, Accession Number PB249-485. Springfield, Virginia: National Technical Information Service, August, 1972.

Bass, R. D., and C. Windle. "Continuity of Care: An Approach to Measurement," *American Journal of Psychiatry* (129, 1972), 196–201.

Burgess, J., R. H. Nelson, and R. Wallhaus. "Network Analysis as a Method for the Evaluation of Service Delivery Systems," *Community Mental Health Journal* (10:3, 1974), 337–344.

Coates, D. B., L. M. Kendall, E. A. Macurdy, and R. H. Goodacre. "Evaluating Hospital and Home Treatment for Psychiatric Patients," *Canada's Mental Health* (24:1, 1976), 28–33.

Davis, H. R. "Four Ways to Goal Attainment," *Evaluation* (1:2, 1973), 43–48.

Glasscote, R. M., E. Cumming, I. D. Rutman, J. N. Sussex, and S. M. Glassman. *Rehabilitating the Mentally Ill in the Community*. Washington, D.C.: Joint Information Service, 1971.

Glasscote, R. M., J. E. Gudeman, and J. R. Elpers. *Halfway Houses for the Mentally Ill*. Washington, D.C.: Joint Information Service, 1971.

Kirk, S. A. "Who Gets Aftercare? A Study of Patients Discharged from State Hospitals in Kentucky," *Hospital and Community Psychiatry* (28:2, 1977), 109–114.

Marlowe, R. A. In *Where Is My Home?*. Proceedings of a Conference on Closing of State Mental Hospitals, Grant Number MH 19222, Stanford Research Institute, 1972.

Mendelson, M. A. *Tender Loving Greed*. New York: Alfred A. Knopf, 1974.

Scully, D., and C. Windle. "Community Mental Health Centers and the Decreasing Use of State Mental Hospitals," *Community Mental Health Journal* (12, 1976), 239–243.

Turner, J. C. "Comprehensive Community Support Systems for Adults with Chronically Disabling Mental Health Problems," *Psychosocial Rehabilitation Journal* (1:3, 1977), 39–47.

U.S. Comptroller General Report to the Congress. *Returning the Mentally Disabled to the Community: Government Needs to Do More*. Washington, D.C.: U.S. Government Printing Office, 1977.

Wolford, J. A., J. Hitchcock, D. L. Ellison, A. C. Sonis, and F. Smith. "The Effect on State Hospitalization of a Community Mental Health/Mental Retardation Center," *American Journal of Psychiatry* (129, 1972), 202–206.

SECTION SEVEN
Methods for the Study
of Organization

Many areas of organizational analysis compete for the titles of relatively neglected, quite neglected, and most neglected. The study of methods, on the other hand, seems to be a field in which much work is conducted and progress constantly reported. The issues are basically these: to learn to apply to the study of organizations methods that have produced fruitful results in the exploration of other fields; to adapt techniques specifically developed for the study of other subjects as, for instance, small groups analysis; and to establish research methods that will answer the special needs of the field—needs generated by the "emergent properties" of this type of social unit.

The major difficulty rests in the fact that until about a decade ago the social sciences have applied mainly qualitative research techniques, particularly the case-study method, to the study of large social units, and quantitative techniques, such as surveys, to the study of individuals. The problem has been to bridge this gap by applying *quantitative techniques to the study of organizations*. To do so requires methods of data collection that make possible the gathering of quantitative materials on organizational variables, and methods of data processing that allow us to draw conclusions concerning the state of organizational variables from information collected from or about individual respondents. When this does not occur, quantitative analyses lapse into being predominantly studies of individuals in organizations rather than studies of organizations. The selection from Freeman and Hannan (in Section V) is a recent major contribution to bridging the gap that could be placed easily in this section. Here we present four additional contributions.

Lazarsfeld and Menzel analyze the logical and methodological differences between the properties of individuals and those of social units. Coleman reviews applications of this kind of logic to various research and sample designs and also its applicability to the analytical methods of actual research. A major innovation is the application of the sociometric approach to the study of large social units.

Lazarsfeld and Menzel are concerned with the methodological characteristics of various statements on "collectives" and "members." These distinctions can be applied to any unit and its participants, or to any unit and its subunits. For the purpose of organizational analysis, the major interpretation would be that of seeing the organization as a "collective" and its participants or groups of participants as "members."

Analytic properties of collectives are induced from information collected from or about members themselves; *structural* properties are based on information concerning their relations; and *global* properties are based on information, not on properties of members, but on collectives as such. Members' properties are *absolute* (concerning the individual alone); *relational* (his relations to others); or *comparative* (depending on the member's place in a distribution of the members); or *contextual* (following from a property of the collective). These and other conceptual distinctions differentiate and determine the nature of the various types of propositions dealt with in organizational analysis. The discussion therefore supplies a methodological paradigm for organizational analysis which may serve as a check list for the types of variables to be covered and for the classification of propositions. It gives a clear meaning to concepts, such as emergent properties, group climate, and organizational character, which are often used in a vague way. The paper also discusses the kinds of measurements that may be used to determine the values of various organizational variables.

Coleman reviews the methodological innovations in statistical analysis which the study of organizations and their relationships require. New *sampling* methods have been developed which make it possible to sample individuals as parts of a context, and which take into account their relations to, and place in, the organizational structure. Coleman concludes by discussing new *analytic* methods which have been devised to establish the effect of the context, the patterns of interaction, and the heterogeneity of the unit on the single actor or for characterization of the unit as such.

Frequently, students of organizational analysis try to explain the behavior of individuals by their membership in a certain organization or organizational unit. Such an approach assumes that the member is somehow affected by the unit. The channels through which the properties of the unit affect the properties of individuals are many (although they are rarely specified). A member may perceive the unit realistically and thus be affected. He may be *recruited* in ways that will ensure that his properties are in line with those of the unit, or he may be *socialized* to "fit" the unit after recruitment. Often it is implicitly assumed that he is *influenced by other members* of the unit. This belief implies that the member interacts with other members and that he is emotionally attached to them and/or respects their opinions. Until recently, this was more often assumed in organizational studies than demonstrated. One of the major reasons for this tendency is that standard methods for determining patterns of interaction and interindividual attachments were developed for the study of small groups and could not be applied to large-scale organizations. Sociograms are a typical example. However, methods have now been developed which attempt to overcome this limitation.

Zelditch points out that the essential nature of theorizing and experimentation is to understand the relations between variables rather than to establish their distribution in the population. Once this is understood we may state that, while we do not seek to put an army (or any other large-scale organization) into a laboratory, it is possible under experimental conditions to study the relationships between organizational variables which analytically characterize an army, such as the number of ranks, formalization of integration, and so forth.

Fieldwork and survey research are the most frequent methods applied to organizations, although they are also equally common in the study of other kinds of social units. However, antagonism persists between the proponents of each method. Sieber argues that benefits can be gained by using both in the same study. Each method, he feels, is strengthened by appealing to the special features of the other. Sieber examines several cases in which the two methods have been integrated in order to illuminate the benefits for design, data collection, and analysis of result. He concludes that genuine integration will require adjustments in traditional procedures, thus yielding a new style of social research.

On the Relation Between Individual and Collective Properties

Paul F. Lazarsfeld and Herbert Menzel

Introductory Considerations

1. Purpose

Social scientists often make use of variables to describe not only individual persons but also groups, communities, organizations, or other "collectives."[1] Thus one reads, for example, of "racially mixed census tracts," of "highly bureaucratized voluntary organizations," or of a "centrally located rooming-house district." At other times the variables, although describing individuals, are based on data about certain collectives, as in a comparison of "graduates of top-ranking medical schools" with "graduates of other medical schools." This paper attempts to clarify some of the operations involved in the construction and use of such variables in empirical research, and provides a nomenclature for the different ways in which information about individuals and about collectives may be interwoven in these properties. The properties will be classified according to the measurement operations involved in their construction.

2. Some Features of Generalizing Propositions

The intended meaning of the variables often remains ambiguous if they are not examined in the context of the propositions in which they are used. It is therefore necessary at the outset to highlight certain features which are common to all generalizing propositions, whether or not they involve collectives. (As an illustration, reference is made to the proposition "Children of rich parents go to college in greater proportion than do children of poor parents.")

a. Generalizing propositions assert something about a set of *elements* (children).
b. For the research purposes at hand, these elements are considered *comparable*. In other words, the same set of *properties* (wealth of parents; going to college) is used to describe each element.
c. Each element has a certain *value* on each property. The values (rich parents, poor parents; going to college, not going to college) may be quantitative or qualitative.
d. The propositions assert interrelationships between the properties of the elements.

3. Present Concern

The propositions with which the present discussion is concerned have the additional characteristic that their elements are dealt with either as collectives or as members of collectives. An example of the first kind is "There is a negative

This article is one of a series sponsored by the Documentation Project for Advanced Training in Social Research, Columbia University. It may be cited as Publication A-322 of the Bureau of Applied Social Research, Columbia University.

correlation between the rate of juvenile delinquency of American cities and the proportion of their budget given over to education." An example of the second kind is "Those recognized as leaders do not deviate very far from the norms of their group."

4. Special Meaning of "Collective" and "Member"

The terms "collective" and "member" are used here in a specific sense which needs clarification. A collective may be an element of a proposition; that is, it is one of a set of units which are regarded as *comparable* in the sense specified above: the same set of properties is used to describe all the elements. These elements are *collectives* if each is considered to be composed of constituent parts, called *members*, which are regarded as comparable in their turn. "Comparable" is used in the same sense as before: all members are described by a single set of properties. (This is usually not the same set as that used to describe the collectives.)

In other instances members are the elements of the propositions. Elements will be called "members" if they are considered to be constituent parts of larger units, called "collectives," which are regarded as comparable in the same sense as before.

Thus one set of properties is always used to describe or classify all the members, and another single set of properties is used to characterize all the collectives. It is clear that under these definitions one can speak of "collectives" only when their "members" are also being referred to, and of "members" only when their "collectives" are also involved. Furthermore, there must be a multiplicity of members if the term "collective" is to be meaningful. It is perhaps less obvious but will be seen later that there must also be a multiplicity of collectives—i.e., the members of more than one collective must be referred to—if the distinctions between properties to be described below are to be relevant.

By contrast, the notion of "element" is needed to characterize any generalizing proposition whatsoever. It is applicable even in situations where the notions of "member" and "collective" are not involved at all.

5. Distinction between "Individuals" and "Members"

In the examples that come to mind most easily, the members of collectives are individual persons. Thus, for example, cities are the collectives and people are the members in the following two propositions:

(1) "The oldest settlers of cities are most likely to hold political office," or (2) "The more industry there is in a city, the higher the proportion of Democratic voters." The first proposition has members and the second has collectives as elements. In the same sense, a precinct can be treated as a collective, with the inhabitants as members. However, the members of a collective are not necessarily individual persons. A city, for example, can be described as a collective with the voting precincts as members. It follows that what appears as a collective in one context (e.g., precincts), can appear as a member in another. In any analysis of a piece of writing in which some of the elements are collectives, it is always necessary to specify clearly of what members the collectives are composed (for the purposes at hand).[2]

The graph below will help to keep this terminology in mind. The circles symbolize the collectives, the crosses within it their members. The dots indicate

that we are dealing with collectives as elements of a proposition. This is the situation with which we deal in the first part of this paper. In Sections 10 and 11 we discuss research where members are the focus of attention. They are then the elements of propositions, but their membership in one of a series of collectives is one of their characteristics.

6. Possibility of "Three-Level" Propositions

In some studies, more than two levels appear: for example, inhabitants, precincts, and cities may all be elements of the same study. This whole matter could, therefore, be elaborated by pointing out the various relationships which can exist between inhabitants, precincts, and cities. The next few pages are restricted to collectives which have only one kind of member; the members in most illustrations will be individual persons, but we will also present some examples in which the members themselves are larger units. Only much later (in Section 16) will examples of "three-level" propositions be taken up, in which units, e.g., "union shops," are simultaneously considered to be both members of their locals *and* collectives of individual workers.

7. Propositions about Collectives as Substitutes and in Their Own Right

Propositions about collectives are sometimes made as substitutes for propositions about individual persons, simply because the necessary data about individual persons are not available. For example, a high Republican vote in "silk-stocking" districts is sometimes accepted to show that wealthy people are likely to vote Republican, when no records about individual votes and individual incomes are available.[3] For this reason it is often not realized that a large number of sociologically meaningful empirical propositions can be made of which only collectives are intended to be the elements. Thus, for example, an anthropologist may show that the political independence of communities is correlated with their pattern of settlement. A student of social disorganization may ask whether city zones with a high incidence of juvenile delinquency also show a high incidence of commitments for senile dementia. A small-group experimenter may hypothesize that "the probability of effective utilization of the insights that occur is greater in certain communication patterns than in others."[4] Much discursive writing also consists, in a hidden way, of such propositions.

A Typology of Properties Describing "Collectives" and "Members"

8. Properties of Collectives

It is often useful to distinguish three types of properties which describe collectives: analytical properties based on data about each member; structural properties based on data about the relations among members; and global properties, not based on information about the properties of individual members.[5] The following examples may clarify these distinctions:

A. Analytical.   These are properties of collectives which are obtained by performing some mathematical operation upon some property of each single member.[6]

> The average rental paid in a precinct and the proportion of its inhabitants who have "Old Immigrant" (English, German, Scottish, Scandinavian) names are analytical properties of a collective (precinct) composed of individuals.[7] The proportion of the communities of a given state that have their own high school is an analytical property of a collective (state) the members of which are communities. The diffusion of a message in a city, defined as the per cent of the target population knowing the message, is an analytical property of the city.[8]
>
> The standard deviation of incomes in a nation appears as an analytical property in the following example. The effect of postwar legislation in Great Britain was to make the income distribution much narrower. Economists have predicted that under these conditions people will save more, because they will spend less money on display consumption which might help them be socially acceptable in the higher strata.
>
> Correlations are sometimes used to characterize collectives and then also constitute analytical properties. The correlation of age and prestige in a given community, for example, has been used as a measure of its norms regarding old age. Sometimes more indirect inferences are involved. MacRae shows that in urban areas voting is highly correlated with occupation, while this is not the case in rural districts. He concludes from this vote that in rural districts there is a stronger spirit of community and cohesion.[9]

B. Structural.   These are properties of collectives which are obtained by performing some operation on data about the relations of each member to some or all of the others.

> Assume, for example, that a sociometrist has recorded the "best-liked classmate" of each student in a number of classes. He can then describe the classes by the degree to which all choices are concentrated upon a few "stars." Or he might, alternately, classify them according to their cliquishness, the latter being defined as the number of subgroups into which a class can be divided so that no choices cut across subgroup lines. In these examples the collective is the school class, and the members are the individual students; "concentration of choices" and "cliquishness" are structural properties of the classes.
>
> For an example in which the members are larger units, consider a map of the precincts of a city, which indicates the number of Negroes residing in each. Let a "Negro enclave" be defined as a precinct in which some Negroes live, but which is completely surrounded by precincts without Negroes. The proportion of the precincts of a city which are Negro enclaves would then be a structural property of the city.

C. Global.   Often collectives are characterized by properties which are not based on information about the properties of individual members.

> American Indian tribes have been characterized by the frequency with which themes of "achievement motive" make their appearance in their folk tales.[10] Societies have been classified as to the presence of money as a medium of exchange, of a written language, etc.[11] Nations may be characterized by the ratio of the national budget allotted to education and to armaments. Army companies may be characterized by the cleanliness of their mess equipment.

Voting precincts have been classified according to the activities and attitudes of their Republican and Democratic captains, including hours spent on party duties, number of persons known to the captain personally, and his expressed commitment to the party.[12] In experiments in message diffusion by leaflets dropped from airplanes, cities have been treated to different degrees of "stimulus intensity," defined as the per capita ratio of leaflets dropped.[13] All these are global properties.

The density of settlement is a global property of a district. Having a city manager form of government is a global property of a city. The insistence on specified initiation rites as a prerequisite to membership is a global property of a religious cult or of a college fraternity. Accessibility from the nearest big city is a global property of a village. A scale score assigned to each state according to the combination of duties assigned to the state board of education (rather than left to local authorities) is a global property of each state.[14]

"Emergent," "integral," "syntalic" and other terms have been used in meanings very similar to that of our term "global." It is not at all certain which term is most useful.[15]

Notice that all three of the above types of properties—analytical, structural, and global—describe collectives.

9. A Subsidiary Distinction among Analytical Properties of Collectives

An interesting distinction may be made among the analytical properties. The first two examples given above were the average income of a city, and the proportion of the communities of a given state that have their own high school. These properties of collectives have what one might call a similarity of meaning to the properties of members on which they are based. The wealth of a city seems to be the same sort of thing as the wealth of an inhabitant. The endowment of a community with a high school and the rate of high-school endowed communities in a state have a parallel meaning. This is not true for the remaining examples of analytical properties given above—the standard deviation of incomes in a nation, or correlations like that between age and prestige in a given community. Correlations and standard deviations can apply only to collectives and have no parallel on the level of members. The standard deviation of incomes in a city, for example, denotes something quite different—lack of homogeneity, perhaps—from individual income, the datum from which it is computed.

Another variable of this sort is "degree of consensus." When a Democrat and a Republican are competing for the mayoralty, the degree of political consensus in a particular club might be measured by the extent of the club's deviation from a fifty-fifty split. In this instance the analytic property is measured by a proportion, but it is not the simple proportion of adherents of either party; clubs which are 80 per cent Democratic and those which are 20 per cent Democratic are regarded as equal in consensus.

Whereas correlations, standard deviations, and similar measures always have a meaning peculiar to the group level, averages and proportions may or may not have a parallel meaning on the individual and collective levels.[16] Lack of parallel meaning is perhaps most clearly illustrated in the concept of a "hung jury," that is, a jury rendered indecisive by its inability to reach the required unanimity. Such a state of affairs is most likely when the individual jurors are most decisive and unyielding in their convictions.

10. Properties of Members

Another set of distinctions can be made between properties describing members in contexts where collectives have also been defined.

    a. *Absolute* properties are characteristics of members which are obtained without making any use either of information about the characteristics of the collective, or of information about the relationships of the member being described to other members. They thus include most of the characteristics commonly used to describe individuals.

        In the proposition, "Graduates of large law schools are more likely to earn high incomes at age 40 than graduates of small law schools," income is an absolute property of the members (the individual students).

    b. *Relational* properties of members are computed[17] from information about the substantive relationships between the member described and other members.

        Sociometric popularity-isolation (number of choices received) is a relational property. Many other sociometric indices fall into this category. For example, if each member of a small group has rated each other member on a 5-point scale of acceptance-rejection, each member can be characterized by the total score he received (popularity), by the total score he expressed (active sociability), by the average deviation of the scores he accorded the others (discrimination in his acceptance of other members), etc.[18] In a study of the diffusion of the use of a new drug through a community of doctors, the physicians were classified according to whether or not they had a friend who had already used the new drug on a certain date.[19]

Some investigators have clarified the structure of relational properties by the use of matrices.[20] This new device can be fruitfully applied to some older papers.[21]

    The distinction between relational properties of individuals and structural properties of collectives deserves emphasis. The former characterize members of collectives in their relations to one another. The latter characterize collectives and are aggregates over the relational properties of their members.

    c. *Comparative* properties characterize a member by a comparison between his value on some (absolute or relational) property and the distribution of this property over the entire collective of which he is a member.

        Sibling order is a comparative property of individuals in the proposition, "First-born children are more often maladjusted than intermediate and last-born children." Note that each individual is characterized by comparison with the age of the other individuals in his family; in the resulting classification, many of the "last-born" will be older in years than many of the "first-born." Being a "deviate" from the majority opinion in one's housing project unit is a comparative property.[22]

        Another example is contained in the following proposition: "Students who had the highest I.Q. in their respective high school classes have greater difficulty in adjusting in college than students who are not quite at the top in high school, even when their actual I.Q. score is equally high." Here the comparative property (being at the top in high school or not) is established in terms of the I.Q. distribution in each student's respective high school; the proposition pertains to a set of college students which includes boys from several high schools (collectives).

    d. *Contextual* properties describe a member by a property of his collective.

        Consider an example cited previously: "Graduates of large law schools are more likely to earn high incomes at age 40 than graduates of small law schools." In this proposition, "being a member of a large law school" is a contextual property of individuals.

        Contextual properties are also used in the following propositions: "Union members in closed shops are less militant than union members in open shops."

"Residents of racially mixed districts show more racial prejudice than those of racially homogeneous districts." "The less the promotion opportunity afforded by a branch (of the army), the more favorable the opinion (of soldiers) tends to be toward promotion opportunity."[23] In these propositions, being a member of a closed shop, residing in a mixed district, or being a soldier in a branch with frequent promotions are all examples of contextual properties.

Contextual properties are really characteristics of collectives applied to their members. Thus the classification of "collective properties" developed above could be repeated here as a subdivision of contextual "individual properties."[24] Note also that a contextual property, unlike a comparative property, has the same value for all members of a given collective.

11. Contextual and Comparative Properties Meaningful Only Where More Than One Collective Is Involved

It is not meaningful to speak of contextual or comparative properties when the elements under study are all members of the same collective—for instance, when only graduates of one law school are being studied—for the following reasons. Any *contextual* property would, in that case, have the same value for all the elements; hence nothing could be said about the interrelationship of this property and any other property. Any *comparative* property would, under these circumstances, classify the elements in exactly the same way as the absolute property from which it was derived, except that the calibration may be grosser. (If only children of one family are considered, the classification into "first-born," "intermediate," and "last-born" differs from that by age only in the grosser calibration. Similarly, if I.Q. scores of graduates of one law school are replaced by classification into lowest, second, third, and highest I.Q. quartile within their school, nothing will change except that the number of categories is reduced.)

12. Special Case Where the Typology Can Be Applied in Two Alternate Ways

A difficulty comes about when all the members of a set of collectives (or a representative sample of the members of each) constitute the elements of a proposition which includes a contextual property. Suppose, for instance, that the income ten years after graduation is recorded for all who graduate from fifty law schools in a certain year. A possible finding might be, "The income of law school graduates is correlated with the size of the school they graduated from." This is a proposition about students, relating their income (an absolute property) to the size of their law school (a contextual property). The same proposition could be interpreted also as one where the elements are the law schools; the average income of the students would then be an analytical property of each law school; its size would be a global property of these collectives.

13. The Present Classification Is Formal Rather Than Substantive

As stated at the outset, the scheme suggested above is intended for the classification of properties according to the operations involved in their measurement. Although a classification by the underlying concepts or forces that the properties may be intended to represent might have numerous parallels to the present classification, it would not be the same.[25] In the present methodological context, for example, "number of libraries in a community" and "occurrence of aggressiveness themes in folk tales current in a tribe" are classified as global properties because they are not based on information about the properties of individual members. Yet it would be convincing to argue that these properties are relevant to the behavioral sciences only because properties of individuals, of the relations among individuals, or of the resulting social structures are inferred from them. Similarly, the title of office held by a person in a hierarchy would here be classified as an "absolute" property, even when the researcher is actually interested in the incumbent's power over subordinates which the title implies.

At some points arbitrary decisions have to be made. On an intuitive basis we decided to consider the number of members in a collective (e.g., population size) as a global property, although one might argue that it is analytical, obtained by counting the "existence" of each member. Even more ambiguous is the classification of rates, based on the behavior of ex-members—e.g., suicide rates. No definitive practice is proposed for such borderline cases.

Combinations of Types of Properties

The types of properties which have been defined can appear in various forms of combinations.

14. Several Types in the Same Proposition

Very commonly, as many of the above examples have shown, one proposition will make use of properties of several types. An additional illustration of this can be drawn from a study of political processes within the International Typographical Union, which has been operating under an internal two-party system for many decades. The shops of this union were classified according to their degree of "political consensus"; shops in which 67 per cent or more of the members favored the same party were regarded as high in consensus, the remainder as low. Individual members were graded according to the amount of union political activity they engaged in. It was expected that men in shops where political consensus was high would be more active in politics than those in shops where consensus was low. The hypothesis, however, was borne out only in small shops (i.e., those with thirty men or less). The finding could therefore be expressed in the following proposition: "For workers in small shops, there is a correlation between consensus of the shop and degree of political activity of the men; for workers in large shops, there is no such correlation." In this proposition there appear two contextual properties (size and consensus of each man's shop) and an absolute property (political activity).[26]

The following hypothetical example again shows the use of several types of variables in one proposition—in fact, in each of several propositions. Ten preliterate tribes living in a certain country are classified according to the number of wars they have fought during the last hundred years. This characteristic, in the present terminology, is a global property of each tribe. A representative sample of one hundred men from each tribe is given a test of "aggressiveness"—an absolute property, from which a summary score for each tribe is computed, as an analytical property. At this point, the correlation between average aggressiveness and the number of wars can be computed. One may regard this computation as either a correlation between an analytical and a global property of ten collectives, or a correlation between an absolute and a contextual property of one thousand individual persons.

Now a factory is opened in the district, and some men from each of the ten tribes find employment there as laborers. Each is given the test of "aggressiveness"; each is also observed for a period of one month, and the number of fights he starts with other employees is recorded. Then the following two correlations can be computed:

a. The correlation between the score on the aggressiveness test and the number of fights. This is a proposition the elements of which are people and the properties of which are conventional psychological characteristics—absolute properties, in the present terminology.
b. The correlation between the number of fights and the number of wars reported for the tribe from which each individual came. This is again a proposition the elements of which are people. But one of the variables (number of wars) now is a contextual property.

The comparison between these two propositions is interesting. In proposition (a) actual fighting is related to the psychological trait of aggressiveness. In proposition (b) actual fighting is related to something that one might call the normative background of each person.

15. Properties of One Type Constructed from Properties of Another Type

The types of properties outlined can also be compounded in that a property of one type may be constructed from properties of another type. Contextual properties, for example, have been defined as properties describing a member by a property of his collective. But what property of his collective is to be used? In most of the examples given, contextual properties of members were based on global properties of their collectives, as in the phrase "men from tribes that have engaged in many wars." But contextual properties can equally well be based on any other kind of property of a collective—for example, on a structural property, as when doctors are classified according to whether or not they ever practiced in cities ridden by medical cliques. One might test whether those who formerly practiced in cliqueless cities have less tendency to form cliques in their new location.

This compounding is also illustrated by examples, cited earlier in another connection: "being a worker in a big shop" and "being a worker in a shop with high consensus." The first of these is a contextual property constructed from a global property; the second is a contextual property constructed from an analytical property.

16. Several Types from the Same Data

In some instances one body of research will construct properties of several different types from the same data, as in the following excerpts from a report on the adoption of modern farming practices by Kentucky farmers.

393 farm operators . . . in thirteen neighborhoods were interviewed. . . . Information was obtained on the extent to which each of the operators had tried and was following 21 farm practices recommended by the agricultural agencies. For each respondent, an adoption score was calculated. This score is the percentage of applicable practices which the operator had adopted. For example, if 18 of the practices applied to the farm operations being carried on and the operator had adopted 9, his

score was 50. Neighborhoods varied widely in the mean adoption scores of residents, which range from a low of 25 in one neighborhood to a high of 57 in another. . . . The neighborhoods were combined . . . into three types of neighborhoods: "low adoption areas," "medium adoption areas," and "high adoption areas." . . .

> The following operational hypothesis . . . is suggested: In areas of high adoption, those from whom other farmers obtain farming information have higher adoption rates than farmers in general; but, in areas of low adoption, the adoption rates of leaders are similar to adoption rates of farmers in general . . . the hypothesis is supported by data. In the "low adoption areas" the mean score of all farmers was 32 and that of the leaders 37, while in the "high adoption areas" the mean score of all farmers was 48 and that of the leaders 66.[27]

Here the farm operator's "adoption score" is used as an absolute property of information leaders and of farmers in general. It is also used as the datum from which the classification of neighborhoods into "high adoption areas" and "low adoption areas" is computed. This classification is an analytical property of the neighborhoods; when used, as in the proposition quoted, to characterize the farmers resident in the neighborhoods, it becomes a contextual property of the farmers.

17. Simultaneous Characterization of the Same Elements as Collectives and as Members

Complexity of another sort arises when one set of elements appears both as members and as collectives in the same proposition. Up to this point examples of such "three-level propositions" have deliberately been excluded. It is now appropriate to introduce such examples. Consider, for instance, the following assertion: "Women's clubs which are internally divided into cliques have less easy-going relationships with other women's clubs than have clubs which are not so divided." Here the elements (women's clubs) are first categorized according to a structural variable (internal division into cliques), and then an assertion is made about a relational property (relationship with other clubs) of the elements in each structural category.

In the study of political processes within the International Typographical Union, which was cited earlier, each printer's vote in a union election was recorded. A liberal and a conservative candidate competed for union office. Each printer's vote was compared with his own conservative-liberal predisposition, determined by an attitude scale. The individuals could thus be classified as voting according to or contrary to their own predisposition. Up to this point, no collective is involved; there is merely a combination of two absolute properties into one. This combined absolute property of each printer was then compared with two contextual properties: the majority vote in his shop, and the majority vote in the local to which his shop belonged. The question was whether the climate of opinion in a man's shop or that in his entire local is more important in affecting his decisions. The answer could be determined only by examining cases where the shop and the local were in conflict. It was found that more people voted contrary to their own predisposition when it was in conflict with the majority of their shop (but not of their local) than when it was in conflict with the majority of their local (but not of their shop). In this instance each person is first characterized as voting according to or contrary to his predisposition. This absolute variable is then correlated with two contextual variables, both describing the same members (persons), but each having reference to a different level of collectives (shops or locals).[28]

18. Outlook

The preceding analysis can be extended in many directions; three of them shall be briefly sketched. For one we can introduce status differences among the members of the collectives. Colleges have professors and administrators, factory teams have workers and foremen, platoons have soldiers and noncoms. This may call for extending the notion of structural properties if, e.g., we distinguish various types of supervision; or analytical properties may be generalized if we classify colleges according to the degree to which the administration and the faculty share the same values. Stouffer has made ingenious use of such status differences by developing what one could call partitioned analytical properties. He wanted to know whether the food provided for army units had an effect on soldiers' morale. If he had asked the soldiers to rate the food he would not have known whether their morale did not affect their rating of the food. So he asked the non-commissioned officers to judge the food and correlated their average rating with the average morale score of the soldiers; the elements of the correlation were of course the army units studied.[29]

A second line of analysis opens up if the elements of a proposition are pairs of individuals: people who are friends tend to vote the same way; egalitarian relationships are more enduring than those which are hierarchic. It would be artificial to call such notions "propositions about collectives." Obviously dyads can be characterized in an even more complex way: pairs of doctors who commonly discuss cases with each other as equals are more likely to use the same type of drug than are pairs of doctors who stand in an advisor-advisee relationship to each other.[30] A scrutiny of recent sociometric literature is likely to provide distinctions going beyond those offered in this paper.

Finally, the utility of the present approach deserves argument. Obviously no one wants to make methodological classifications for their own sake. They are, however, useful in reminding us of the variety of research operations that are possible, and in clearing up misunderstandings. It can, for example, be shown that many arguments about atomism versus "holistic" approaches in current sociological literature can be clarified by an explication of the formal types of properties which enter into speculative or empirical propositions. In another publication, the senior author has summarized passages from several recent works of social research which relate, often in quite complex ways, the characteristics and attitudes of individuals, their propensity to choose friends inside and outside of variously overlapping collectives, the composition of these collectives in terms of members' background and perceptions, and the recent occurrence of certain events in the history of the collectives. He attempted to show that such "contextual propositions" go a long way toward satisfying the frequently heard demand that social research should "consider structures" or "take the total situation into account."[31]

Notes

1. Individuals and collectives made up of individuals do not, of course, exhaust the matters which social scientists describe. Social-science propositions may, instead, have various

other units for their subjects. Not infrequently the subjects are acts, behavior patterns, customs, norms, "items of culture," and the like, as in the assertion that "items of culture that are . . . not much woven into a pattern . . . are least likely to encounter resistance to their diffusion." Ralph Linton, *The Study of Man* (New York: Appleton, 1936), 341–342. "Beliefs and practices have been sorted into four classes according to the pattern of their differential distribution among mobile and nonmobile holders of high and low positions in a stratification system."—Peter M. Blau, "Social Mobility and Interpersonal Relations," *American Sociological Review*, 21 (1956), 290–295.

2. It is, of course, also possible to make propositions about cities without reference to any members at all, just as it is possible to make propositions about individuals without reference to any collectives. Thus one may, e.g., correlate city size with number of churches, or location with building materials used, just as one can correlate individual income and education. In neither case are the distinctions made in the present paper relevant, because the individuals are not treated as "members" and the cities are not treated as "collectives" as here defined (i.e., as composed of "members"—constituent units described by their values on some one set of properties). It is thus clear that the typology of properties here presented is not always pertinent.

3. This procedure can lead to very misleading statistics, as pointed out by W. S. Robinson in "Ecological Correlations and the Behavior of Individuals," *American Sociological Review*, 15 (1950), 351–357. Sounder methods for inferring individual correlations from ecological data are proposed by Leo A. Goodman, "Ecological Regressions and Behavior of Individuals," *American Sociological Review*, 18 (1953), 663–664, and by Otis Dudley Duncan and Beverly Davis, "An Alternate to Ecological Correlation," *ibid.*, pp. 665–666.

4. For details on these and additional examples, see Paul F. Lazarsfeld and Morris Rosenberg (eds.), *The Language of Social Research* (New York: Free Press, 1955), pp. 302–322. Compare also Herbert Menzel, "Comment," *American Sociological Review*, 15 (1950), 674.

5. This classification of properties of collectives corresponds closely to the classifications presented earlier by Cattell and by Kendall and Lazarsfeld and reprinted in Lazarsfeld and Rosenberg (eds.), *op. cit.*, pp. 291–301. Analytical properties are Cattell's population variables and Kendall and Lazarfeld's Types I, II, and III. Structural properties are Cattell's structural variables and Kendall and Lazarsfeld's Type IV. Our global properties are Cattell's syntality variables and Kendall and Lazarsfeld's Type V. See also n. 25.

6. It should be understood that the distinctions here proposed do not depend on who performs the operations involved. For example, "average income of a city" would be classified as an analytical property regardless of whether the investigator (a) obtains individual income data from all inhabitants directly and then computes the average, (b) obtains individual income data from the files of the tax collector and then computes the average, or (c) looks up the average income in the published census reports. Compare also n. 17.

7. Phillips Cutright and Peter H. Rossi, "Grass Roots Politicians and the Vote," *American Sociological Review*, 23 (1958), 171–179.

8. Melvin L. DeFleur and Otto N. Larsen, *The Flow of Information* (New York: Harper & Row, 1958).

9. Duncan MacRae, Jr., "Occupations and the Congressional Vote, 1940–1950," *American Sociological Review*, 20 (1955), 332–340. For another example, see the evidence used to demonstrate differences in the norms of two housing projects in Leon Festinger, Stanley Schachter, and Kurt Back, "The Operation of Group Standards," in Lazarsfeld and Rosenberg, *op. cit.*, pp. 373–377.

10. See David C. McClelland and G. A. Friedman, "A Cross-cultural Study of the Relationship between Child Training Practices and Achievement Motivation Appearing in Folk Tales," in Guy E. Swanson, Theodore M. Newcomb, and Eugene L. Hartley (eds.), *Readings in Social Psychology* (New York: Holt, Rinehart and Winston, Inc., 1952), pp. 243–249.

11. See, e.g., Linton C. Freeman and Robert F. Winch, "Societal Complexity: An Empirical Test of a Typology of Societies," *American Journal of Sociology*, 62 (1957), 461–466.
12. Cutright and Rossi, *loc. cit.*
13. DeFleur and Larsen, *op. cit.*
14. Robert Redfield, *The Folk Culture of Yucatan* (Chicago: University of Chicago Press, 1941); and Margaret J. Hagood, and Daniel O. Price, *Statistics for Sociologists* (rev. ed.) (New York: Holt, Rinehart and Winston, Inc., 1952), pp. 144–152.
15. Although global properties of collectives are not based on information about members, the above examples are, of course, listed here on the assumption that assertions about the members are made somewhere in the same proposition or at least in the same body of work; otherwise the distinction between "global" and "absolute" properties would become pointless (cf. n. 2). It may also bear repeating here that any discussion of a "collective" requires clear specification of what its members are considered to be. The proportion of the buildings of a city which are devoted to cultural activities was given as an example of a "global property" of a city on the assumption that the city is treated as a collective of inhabitants; i.e., that statements involving the inhabitants are made in some connection with this measure of "cultural level." It is, of course, also possible to treat a city as a collective of buildings; then the proportion of buildings devoted to cultural activities would become an analytical property. Which of these two types of property it is can be judged only from the context. (See also Section 13.)
16. Compare the notion of "counterpart" in Edgar F. Borgatta, Leonard Cottrell, Jr., and Henry J. Meyer, "On the Dimensions of Group Behavior," *Sociometry*, 19 (1956), 233.
17. It may be worth repeating here that the distinctions proposed are independent of who performs the operations involved. Thus, e.g., "sociometric popularity" would be classified as a relational property when measured in any of the following three ways: (a) the investigator counts the number of choices accorded to a member by his colleagues in answer to a sociometric questionnaire; (b) the investigator observes the frequency of interactions between the member and his colleagues; (c) the member is asked, "How many visits did you receive from colleagues during the last week?" These distinctions are, of course, important in themselves but not relevant to the present typology (cf. n. 6).
18. Some sociometric indices are listed in Hans Zeisel, *Say It with Figures* (4th ed.; New York: Harper & Row, 1957), pp. 110–114, 148–153. The list includes indices not only of relational properties but of comparative and structural properties as well.
19. Herbert Menzel and Elihu Katz, "Social Relations and Innovation in the Medical Profession: The Epidemiology of a New Drug," *Public Opinion Quarterly*, 19 (1956), 337–352.
20. See Zeisel, *loc. cit.*, and Leon Festinger, Stanley Schachter, and Kurt Back, "Matrix Analysis of Group Structures," in Lazarsfeld and Rosenberg, *op. cit.*, pp. 358–367. In both instances matrices are also used to develop indices for structural properties of groups.
21. See, e.g., Robert R. Sears, "Experimental Studies of Projection," *Journal of Social Psychology*, 7 (1936), 151–163.
22. Festinger, Schachter, and Back, *loc. cit.*, pp. 367–382.
23. S. A. Stouffer, *et al.*, *The American Soldier* (Princeton, N.J.: Princeton, 1949), I, 256.
24. It is sometimes helpful to talk of "collective properties" instead of the cumbersome "properties of collectives"; the same holds for "individual properties." It is important, however, not to be misled by this linguistic condensation.
25. Cattell's classification of population, structural, and syntality variables (cf. n. 5 above), which is closely paralleled in form by our analytical-structural-global distinction, seems to be based on a mixture of measurement criteria and considerations of causality. The latter gain the upper hand in the critique of Cattell's scheme by Borgatta, Cottrell, and Meyer: e.g., "Aggregate measures, to the extent that they cannot be accounted for as population variables (in direct parallel measures), may be considered syntality variables. . . . Further, changes in population variables attributable to social interaction should be regarded as syntality variables."—Borgatta, Cottrell, and Meyer, *loc. cit.*, p. 234. Peter

M. Blau's "Formal Organization: Dimensions of Analysis," *American Journal of Sociology*, 63 (1957), 58–69, contains an analysis in terms of intended underlying concepts which parallels the present discussion of measurement operations in certain respects.

In addition, the literature contains, of course, classifications of group properties which are based on quite different criteria. See, e.g., John K. Hemphill and Charles M. Westie, "The Measurement of Group Dimensions," in Lazarsfeld and Rosenberg, *op. cit.*, pp. 323–324; and Robert K. Merton, "Provisional List of Group Properties," in his *Social Theory and Social Structure* (rev. ed.; New York: Free Press, 1957), pp. 310–326. The Hemphill-Westie categories are subjected to a factor analysis and compared with certain other schemes in Borgatta, Cottrell, and Meyer, *loc. cit.*, pp. 223–240.

26. See S. M. Lipset, Martin Trow, and James Coleman, *Union Democracy: The Inside-Politics of the International Typographical Union* (New York: Free Press, 1956).

27. C. Paul Marsh and A. Lee Coleman, "Group Influences and Agricultural Innovations: Some Tentative Findings and Hypotheses," *American Journal of Sociology*, 61 (1956), 588–594. Other varying examples of the use of properties describing or referring to collectives will be found in Lazarsfeld and Rosenberg, *op. cit.*, pp. 287–386.

28. Adapted from Lipset, Trow, and Coleman, *op. cit.*

29. Stouffer, *et al.*, *op. cit.*, I, 353–358.

30. James Coleman, Herbert Menzel, and Elihu Katz, "Social Processes in Physicians' Adoption of a New Drug," *Journal of Chronic Diseases*, 9 (1959), 18.

31. Paul F. Lazarsfeld, "Problems in Methodology," Robert K. Merton, Leonard Broom, and Leonard S. Cottrell, Jr. (eds.), *Sociology Today* (New York: Basic Books, 1959), pp. 69–73.

Relational Analysis: The Study of Social Organizations with Survey Methods

James S. Coleman

Survey research methods have often led to the neglect of social structure and of the relations among individuals. On the other hand, survey methods are highly efficient in bringing in a large volume of data—amenable to statistical treatment—at a relatively low cost in time and effort. Can the student of social structure enjoy the advantages of the survey without neglecting the relationships which make up that structure? In other words, can he use a method which ordinarily treats each individual as an isolated unit in order to study social structure?

The purpose of this paper is to describe some important developments in survey research which are giving us a new way of studying social organization.

It is useful to trace briefly the history of survey research, to indicate how it has grown from "polling" to the point where it can now study problems involving complex human organization. A look at this history indicates two definite stages. The first was a polling stage which was concerned with the *distribution* of responses on any one item: What proportion favored Roosevelt in 1936? What proportion was in favor of labor unions? This type of concern continues even today among pollsters, and to the lay public it is still the function of surveys to "find out what people think" or to see just how many feel thus and so.

Among sociologists, however, this purely descriptive use of survey research was soon supplanted by an *analytical* one. First there began to be a concern with how different sub-groups in the population felt or behaved. From this, the analysts moved on to further cross-tabulations. Finally, some survey analysts began, through cross-tabulations and correlations, to study complicated questions of why people behaved as they did. By relating one opinion item to another, attitude configurations and clusters of attitudes emerged; by relating background information to these attitudes, some insight was gained into the *determinants* of attitudes. It was in this analytical stage, then, beyond the simple description of a population, that survey research began to be of real use to social science.

But throughout all this one fact remained, a very disturbing one to the student of social organization. The *individual* remained the unit of analysis. No matter how complex the analysis, how numerous the correlations, the studies focused on individuals as separate and independent units. The very techniques mirrored this well: samples were random, never including (except by accident) two persons who were friends; interviews were with one individual, as an atomistic entity, and responses were coded onto separate IBM cards, one for each person. As a result, the kinds of substantive problems on which such research focused tended to be problems of "aggregate psychology," that is, *within*-individual problems, and never problems concerned with relations between people.

Now, very recently, this focus on the individual has shown signs of changing, with a shift to groups as the units of analysis, or to networks of relations among

Reproduced by permission of the Society for Applied Anthropology from *Human Organization* 17(4):28–36, 1958.

individuals. The shift is quite a difficult one to make, both conceptually and technically, and the specific methods used to date are only halting steps toward a full-fledged methodology. Nevertheless, some of these methods are outlined below, to indicate just how, taken together, they can even now provide us with an extremely fruitful research tool. This tool has sometimes been used for the study of formal organization but more often for the study of the informal organization which springs up within a formal structure. In both cases, it shows promise of opening to research, problems which have been heretofore the province of speculation.

Problems of Design and Sampling

The break from the atomistic concerns of ordinary survey analysis requires taking a different perspective toward the individual interview. In usual survey research and statistical analysis, this interview is regarded as *independent* of others, as an entity in itself. All cross-tabulations and analyses relate one item in that questionnaire to another item in the same questionnaire. But, in this different approach, an individual interview is seen as a *part* of some larger structure in which the respondent finds himself: his network of friends, the shop or office where he works, the bowling team he belongs to, and so on. Thus, as a part of a larger structure, the individual is *not* treated independently. The analysis must somehow tie together and interrelate the attributes of these different parts of the structure.

So much for the basic change in perspective—away from the atomistic treatment of the individual interview, and toward the treatment of each interview as a part of some larger whole. This basic perspective has several implications for the kind of data collected and for the sample design. Perhaps the most important innovation in the kind of data collected is sociometric-type data in the interview, that is, explicit questions about the respondent's relation to other specific individuals. Each person may be asked the names of his best friends, or the names of his subordinates in the shop upon whom he depends most, or any one of a multitude of *relational* questions. For example, in a study of two housing projects by Merton, West, and Jahoda,[1] one way to map out the informal social structure in the community was to ask people who their best friends were. Having obtained such data from all the families in the project, so that each family could be located in the network of social relations in the community, it was then possible to examine the relation between this social structure, on the one hand, and various values and statuses on the other. Specifically, this information allowed these authors to show that in one housing project social ties were based very largely on similarities in background and religion; in the other, social relations were more often built around common leisure interests and participation in community organizations.

More generally, the incorporation of sociometric-type data into survey research allows the investigator to *locate* each interviewed individual within the networks of voluntary relations which surround him. In some cases, these networks of voluntary relations will be superimposed on a highly articulated formal structure. In a department of a business, for example, there are numerous hierarchical levels and there are numerous work relations which are imposed by the job itself. In such cases, sociometric-type questions can be asked relative to these formal relations, e.g.: "Which supervisor do you turn to most often?" or, "Which of the men in your own workgroup do you see most often outside of work?" or, "When you want X type of job done in a hurry to whom do you go to get it done?" or, "When you need advice on such-and-such a problem, who do you usually turn to?"

Another kind of data is that which refers to some larger social unit. For example, in some research on high schools currently being carried out at the University of Chicago, it is necessary to find the paths to prestige within a school, so that the boys are asked: "What does it take to be important and looked up to by the other fellows here at school?" Then the responses to this question—aggregated over each school separately—can be used to characterize the *school* as well as the individual. Because of this, the question itself makes explicit reference to the school.

But apart from the kinds of data collected, there are also important *sampling* considerations. In this kind of research, it is no longer possible to pull each individual out of his social context and interview him as an independent entity. It is necessary to sample parts of that context as well or, to say it differently, to sample explicitly with reference to the social structure. There are numerous ways of doing this; only a few, which have been successfully tried, are mentioned below.

a. Snowball Sampling

One method of interviewing a man's immediate social environment is to use the sociometric questions in the interview for sampling purposes. For example, in a study of political attitudes in a New England community, Martin Trow has used this approach: first interviewing a small sample of persons, then asking these persons who their best friends are, interviewing these friends, then asking *them* their friends, interviewing these, and so on.[2] In this way, the sampling plan follows out the chains of sociometric relations in the community. In many respects, this sampling technique is like that of a good reporter who tracks down "leads" from one person to another. The difference, of course, is that snowball sampling in survey research is amenable to the same scientific sampling procedures as ordinary samples. Where the population in ordinary samples is a population of individuals, here it is two populations: one of individuals and one of *relations* among individuals.

b. Saturation Sampling

Perhaps a more obvious approach is to interview *everyone* within the relevant social structure. In a study of doctors in four communities, *all* the doctors in these communities were interviewed.[3] Sociometric-type questions were then used to lay out the professional and social relations existing among these doctors. This "saturation" method or complete census was feasible there, because the total number of doctors in these communities was small—less than three hundred. But in the study mentioned earlier which used snowball sampling, such an approach would have been practically impossible, for the community was about 15,000 in size. Thus this "saturation sampling" is only feasible under rather special circumstances. A borderline case is the study of high schools mentioned earlier. There are 9,000 students in the ten schools being studied. Only because these students are given self-administered questionnaires, rather than interviews, is it possible to use a saturation sample, and thereby characterize the complete social structure.

c. Dense Sampling

Another approach is to sample "densely." This is a compromise between the usual thinly dispersed random sample and the saturation sample. An illustration will indicate how this may be useful. In a study of pressure upon the academic freedom of college social science teachers, carried out by Paul Lazarsfeld, at least *half* of the social science faculty in every college in the sample was interviewed.[4] Thus, by sampling densely, enough men were interviewed in each college so that the climate of the college could be characterized, as well as the attitudes of the individual respondent.

d. Multi-stage Sampling

Any of the above approaches to sampling can be combined with an element found in many sample designs: the multi-stage sample. For example, in the academic freedom study referred to above, it would have been impossible to have a dense sample of social science teachers in *all* the colleges in the United States, so a two-stage sample was used: first sampling colleges, and then teachers within colleges. In doing this, of course, the crucial question is what balance to maintain between the sampling of colleges and the sampling of teachers within colleges. Enough colleges are needed to have representativity, yet few enough so that the sampling within each one can be dense. In a study of union politics, reported in *Union Democracy*,[5] we perhaps made a wrong decision: we interviewed in 90 printing shops, spreading the interviews so thinly that only one man out of three—at most—was interviewed within the shop. This meant that we had only a very few interviews in each shop, and could not use the interview material to characterize the climate or atmosphere of the shops, except in the very largest ones.

These sampling procedures are, of course, not the only possible ones. An infinite degree of variation is possible, depending upon the problem and upon the kind of social structure involved. The most important point is that the individual interview can no longer be treated as an independent entity, but must be considered as a part of some larger whole: in the sampling, in the questions asked, and in the subsequent analysis.

Analytical Methods

The real innovations in this new kind of research are in the techniques of analysis. I will mention several of these with which I am most familiar, to give an indication of the kinds of problems this research examines and the way it examines them.

a. Contextual Analysis

The first, and the one closest to usual survey research, might be termed contextual analysis. In essence, it consists of relating a characteristic of the respondent's social context—and the independent variable—to a characteristic of the individual himself.[6] A good example of this occurred in *The American Soldier*, where the attitudes of inexperienced men, in companies where most others were inexperienced, were compared to attitudes of similarly inexperienced men in companies where most others were veterans. It was found that inexperienced men in green companies felt very differently about themselves, and about combat, than their counterparts in veteran companies. That is, when men were characterized by both individual characteristics and by their social surroundings, the latter were found to have an important effect on their attitudes.

In the union politics study mentioned above, one of the major elements in the analysis was an examination of the effect of the shop context on the men within the shop. We had access to voting records in union political elections for these shops, and these made it possible to characterize the shop as politically radical or politically conservative and as high or low in political consensus. Then we could examine the different behavior or attitudes of men in different kinds of shops and compute a "shop effect." An example is given in Table 1. Each man is in a shop of high or low political consensus, depending on whether the men in the shop vote alike or are evenly split between the radical and conservative parties. And each man has a certain degree of political activity. In this table, the shop's political consensus and the man's political activity are related. The table indicates that in shops of high consensus, men are politically more active than in shops of low consensus. The inference might be that high consensus provides a kind of resonance of political beliefs which generates a greater interest in politics. In any case, the table exemplifies the use of an attribute of a *shop* related to an attribute of a *man* in the shop. This general kind of analysis, which bridges the gap between two levels of sociological units—the individual and his social context—seems to be a very basic one for this "structural" approach to survey research.

b. Boundaries of Homogeneity

A second kind of analysis attempts to answer the question: How homogeneous are various groups in some belief or attitude? In a medical school, for example, are a student's attitudes toward medicine more like those of his fraternity brothers or more like those of his laboratory partners? This question, incidentally, has been posed in a study of medical students presently being carried out at Columbia University.[7] The answer is, in the particular medical school being studied, that his attitudes are far more like those of his fraternity brothers. In other words, in this medical school, the "boundaries of homogeneity" of certain attitudes about medicine coincide very largely with fraternity boundaries.

The major problems is answering questions of group homogeneity are problems of index construction. Consider the above example: each student has twenty or thirty fraternity brothers, but only three laboratory partners in anatomy lab. How can the effects of variability between groups, due to small numbers in a group, be separated out from the actual tendency toward homogeneity of attitude? It can be done, and indices have been developed to do so. The indices, incidentally, are much like the formulas by which statisticians measure the effects of clustering in a random sample.

TABLE 1

		Shops of High Political Consensus	Shops of Low Political Consensus
Percent of men active in union politics		29%	7%
	N	(125)	(28)

An example of group homogeneity may indicate more concretely how this approach can be useful in research. In the study of doctors in four communities mentioned earlier, we were interested in the social processes affecting the physicians' introduction of a new drug into their practices. Through interviewing all doctors and asking sociometric questions in the interview, we were able to delineate seven "cliques" of doctors who were sociometrically linked together. (How to reconstruct such cliques is another problem, which will be considered shortly.) The question, then, became this: At each point in time after the drug was marketed, were cliques homogeneous or not in their members' use or non-use of the drug? If they were homogeneous, then this was evidence that some kind of social influence or diffusion was going on in relation to the measured sociometric ties. If not, this indicated that the cliques delineated on the basis of questions in the interview had little relevance to drug adoption. Table 2 shows, for several time periods, just how much homogeneity there was in the cliques, beyond that which would arise by chance. An index value of 1.0 means each clique is completely homogeneous in its use or non-use of the drug. An index value of 0 means there is no more homogeneity than would arise through chance variation between groups.

Table 2 shows that there was no homogeneity until around seven months after the drug was introduced, that is, until over 50 percent of the doctors had used the drug. The maximum homogeneity was reached at about eleven months, when three-fourths of the doctors had begun to use the drug. Then after that, the homogeneity receded to zero again.

This result helped to reinforce a conclusion derived from other findings in the study: that the social networks measured in the study were effective as paths of diffusion at certain times but not at others. However, apart from the substantive results of the study, this example indicates how such analysis of the boundaries of homogeneity may be useful for the study of the functioning of various social organizations.

c. Pair Analysis

Neither of the above kinds of analysis has required the use of sociometric-type data. An important kind of analysis which does use such direct data on relationships is the analysis of *pairs*. Here, the pair formed by A's choosing B becomes the unit of analysis. Speaking technically, "pair cards" may be constructed for each sociometric choice, and then these cards used for cross-tabulations. In other words, instead of cross-tabulating a man's attitude toward Russia with his attitude toward the United

TABLE 2

Months after Drug Was Marketed	Amount of Clique Homogeneity	Percent of Doctors Who Had Used the Drug
1 months	no homogeneity	14%
3	no homogeneity	32
5	no homogeneity	49
7	.07	66
9	.12	71
11	.18	76
13	.03	83
15	no homogeneity	86

TABLE 3

	Chosen			
	boy	girl		
boy	45	15	40	
girl	20	20	60	
			100	

Nations, we can cross-tabulate the man's attitude toward Russia with the attitude toward Russia of the man he eats lunch with at the cafeteria.

One of the most important problems which has been studied in this way is the similarity or difference in attitudes or backgrounds between the two members of a pair. That is, do people have friendship relations with those who are like them politically, with people of the same age, with persons in the same occupation?

This kind of problem can be illustrated by Table 3, which contains hypothetical data. This table, which looks very much like an ordinary contingency table, must be treated in a slightly different fashion. If allows us to raise the question: do boys tend to choose boys more than would be expected by chance? and, do girls tend to choose girls more than would be expected by chance? The answer, of course, depends upon what we take as chance. However, chance models have been worked out, so that one can assign measures of the tendency to choose others of one's own kind. One of these is outlined in Appendix B. For the above example, this measure (varying between 0 and 1) says that the tendency to in-choice for boys is .38 and that for girls is .17. By comparing such indices for numerous attributes, one could get a good glimpse into the informal social organization of the group. For example, in the medical study mentioned earlier which is being carried out at Columbia University, the values of in-choice tendency for friends shown in Table 4 were found:

TABLE 4

Sub-groups	Tendencies toward In-Choice
Class in school	.92
Fraternity	.52
Sex	.33
Marital status	.20
Attitudes toward national health insurance	.37

By looking at the relative sizes of these index values, we get an idea of just how the informal social relations—that is, the friendship choices—at this medical school mesh with the formal structure, and with the distribution of attitudes.

In the study mentioned above of drug introduction by doctors, these pair relations were used as the major aspect of the analysis: by examining how close in time a doctor's first use of a new drug was to the first use of the doctor he mentioned as a friend, it was possible to infer the functioning of friendship networks in the introduction of this drug.

These examples of pair analysis give only a crude picture of the kinds of problems which can be studied in this fashion. The important matter is to break away from the analysis of *individuals* as units to the study of *pairs* of individuals. To be sure, this involves technical IBM problems and problems of index construction along with conceptual problems, but the difficulties are not great.

d. Partitioning into Cliques

Another important kind of problem is the partitioning of a larger group into cliques by use of sociometric choices. This problem is a thorny one, for it involves not only the delineation of cliques, but, even prior to this, the *definition* of what is to constitute a clique. Are cliques to be mutually exclusive in membership, or can they have overlapping memberships? Are they to consist of people who all name one another, or of people who are tied together by more tenuous connections? Such questions must be answered before the group can be partitioned into cliques.

A good review of some of the methods by which cliques and subgroups can be treated is presented in Lindzey and Borgotta.[8] The two most feasible of these are the method of matrix multiplication[9] and the method of shifting rows and columns in the sociometric choice matrix until the choices are clustered around the diagonal.[10] This last technique is by far the more feasible of the two if the groups are more than about twenty in size. When the groups are on the order of a hundred, even this method becomes clumsy. An IBM technique was successfully used in the study of doctors and the study of medical students, both mentioned above, in which the groups were 200–400 in size. At the University of Chicago, a program has been developed for Univac, using a method of shifting rows and columns in a matrix, which can handle groups up to a thousand in size.[11] The necessity for some such method becomes great when, for example, one wants to map out systematically the informal organization of a high school of a thousand students.

Conclusion

These four kinds of analysis, contextual analysis, boundaries of homogeneity, pair analysis, and partitioning into cliques, are only four of many possibilities. Several other approaches have been used, but these four give some idea of the way in which survey analysis can come to treat problems which involve social structure. In the long run, these modes of analysis will probably represent only the initial halting steps in the development of a kind of structural research which will represent a truly sociological methodology. In any case, these developments spell an important milestone in social research, for they help open up for systematic research those problems which have heretofore been the province of the theorist or of purely qualitative methods.

There is one new development which should be mentioned, although the frontier is just opened, and not at all explored. This development is the construction of electronic computers with immediate-access storage capacities a hundred times the size of an 80-column IBM card. Such computers make it possible, for the first time, to lay out a complex social structure for direct and systematic examination. Instead of examining the similarity of attitudes between socially connected pairs, after laborious construction of "pair cards," it becomes possible to trace through a whole structural network, examining the points in the network where attitudes or actions begin to diverge. Methods for doing this have not yet been developed but, for the first time, the technical facilities exist, and it is just a matter of time until analytical methods are developed. IBM cards and counter-sorters were methodologically appropriate for the individualistic orientation which survey research has had in the past; electronic computers with large storage capacities are precisely appropriate for the statistical analysis of complex social organization.

Unfortunately, it has not been possible here to present any of the tools discussed above fully enough to show precisely how it is used. In giving a broad overview of a number of developments, my aim has been to point to an important new direction in social research, one which may aid significantly in the systematic study of social organization.

Notes

1. Robert K. Merton, Patricia S. West, and Marie Jahoda, *Patterns of Social Life: Explorations in the Sociology of Housing*, forthcoming.
2. Martin A. Trow, "Right Wing Radicalism and Political Intolerance: A Study of Support for McCarthy in a New England Town." Unpublished Ph.D. dissertation, Columbia University, 1957.
3. J. S. Coleman, E. Katz, and H. M. Menzel, "Diffusion of an Innovation among Physicians," *Sociometry*, XX (Dec. 1957).
4. P. F. Lazarsfeld and Wagner Thielens, *The Academic Man: Social Scientists in a Time of Crisis*, The Free Press, New York, 1956.
5. S. M. Lipset, M. A. Trow, and J. S. Coleman, *Union Democracy*, the Free Press, New York, 1956.
6. Peter Blau has emphasized the importance of such analysis in formal organizations for locating the "structural effects" of a situation upon the individuals in it. See his "Formal Organization: Dimensions of Analysis," *American Journal of Sociology*, LXIII (1957), 58–69.
7. Some of the work in this study (though not the work mentioned here) is reported in P. F. Kendall, R. K. Merton, and G. G. Reader (eds.), *The Student Physician*, Commonwealth Fund, New York, 1957.
8. G. Lindzey (ed.), *Handbook of Social Psychology*, Addison-Wesley, Cambridge, 1956, Chap. II.
9. See L. Festinger, "The Analysis of Sociograms Using Matrix Algebra," *Human Relations*, II, No. 2 (1949), 153–158, and R. D. Luce, "Connectivity and Generalized Cliques in Sociometric Group Structure," *Psychometrika*, XV (1950), 169–190.
10. C. O. Beum and E. G. Brundage, "A Method for Analyzing the Sociomatrix," *Sociometry*, XIII (1950), 141–145.
11. A description of this program, written by the author and Duncan McRae, is available upon request from the author and the program itself is available for copying, for those who have access to a Univac I or II.

Can You Really Study an Army in the Laboratory?

Morris Zelditch, Jr.

Introduction

No method has more influenced our conception of science than the experimental method; no method makes the contemporary sociologist more suspicious. The rapid and prolific development of the small groups field seems to argue a contrary thesis. But there is no sounder evidence of the way in which sociologists regard the experiment than the habit of calling them all "small groups" research. And because they think the laboratory group is a small group, many sociologists think that larger organizations cannot be studied in the laboratory.

If the idea is that the laboratory group resembles the smaller kinds of groups found in natural settings, then the idea is wrong. For the laboratory group, though usually small, is no more like small groups found in natural settings than it is like a formal organization. In fact, the laboratory group is not like *any* concrete setting in society. If the laboratory group were a small group, then we would be able to equate the following group with air force flight crews:

> Two air force staff sergeants are seated on either side of an opaque partition, each under the impression that the other is an air force captain. Projected on a screen in front of them is a consecutive series of 38 large rectangles, each composed of 100 smaller black and white rectangles in varying arrangements. Every rectangle contains almost the same number of black as white rectangles, but the sergeants are to decide, for each one, whether it is more black or more white. Each sergeant makes an initial decision, exchanges opinions with the other, and makes a final decision for each repetition of the stimulus. The exchange of opinions is controlled by the experimenter: in front of each sergeant there is a console of switches and lights, which permits one sergeant to operate a switch on his own console that flashes a light on the console of the other sergeant. The circuit passes through a master control panel, permitting the experimenter to arrange any desired pattern of agreement or disagreement between the two sergeants. If the two are made to disagree, each must either *change* his initial opinion or *repeat* his initial opinion in making his final decision.
>
> In the same setting, two air force sergeants may each be made to believe that the other is an airman third class. If this condition is compared with that described above, it is found that a "captain" more readily persuades a sergeant that his initial opinion was wrong than an "airman third class."[1]

But what is studied here is no more like an air force flight crew than it is like an air force wing, or any other more complex structure. An air force flight crew has a past, a future, a system of informal social controls, and some commitment to a common goal. The two staff sergeants in the laboratory group just described are an *ad hoc* group, transitory, with no informal social system that could bring social pressures to bear on the behavior of either subject, and not much committed to the goal.

Nor is the laboratory group more like an informal peer group. Such a group is typically a primary group; the laboratory group is typically not. Both laboratory and primary groups are typically small and face-to-face, but this does not make the laboratory group a primary group. Faris made the reason perfectly clear as long ago as 1932. He insisted that size and face-to-face interaction were not the criteria that defined a primary group, because a courtroom, or a housewife driving off a door-to-door salesman are both small and face-to-face, but certainly no one thinks they are primary groups. A primary group is a group having a certain system of norms,[2]—norms requiring affective, diffuse, particularistic role relations. But such norms are rarely found in laboratory groups.

The fact is that laboratory investigations are seldom efforts to study the small group *per se*, and even when they *are*, the groups studied are not often like small groups found in natural settings. But if the purpose of experiments is not to study the kinds of groups found in natural settings, just what *is* their purpose? The answer has a deceptive simplicity: *The purpose of the laboratory experiment is to create certain theoretically relevant aspects of social situations under controlled conditions*. Though the point looks simple, it has fairly profound implications for most of the issues that are most controversial about the experimental method in sociology. I will therefore first attempt to demonstrate that what I have just said is so; after which, I will point out some of its more important implications.

I will argue that the purpose of experiments is mainly to construct and test theories; that theories are necessarily abstract; and therefore experiments are also necessarily abstract. Consequently, the answer to the question which gives this paper its title is that one would not even *try* to study an army in the laboratory, if by that one means an army in the concrete sense of the term. One would try only to create those aspects of an army that were relevant to some theory. But from this it follows that, if there is any question about the possibility of studying organizations in the laboratory, the question can only be: Are there theoretically relevant aspects of organizations that cannot be created in a laboratory? To this question the answer is that nothing inherent in laboratory experiments bars us from creating many theoretically relevant aspects of organizations. But if the abstract organizations so created are not like those in natural settings, will one ever be able to generalize from the experimentally created aspect of an army to the concrete army in its natural setting? My answer is first, that the situation is no different for organizational experiments than for any other sort of analytic investigation; and second, that generalization, in the only sense meaningful in such a context, is the application of a theory supported by experiment rather than the direct extrapolation of the results of a single experiment. If the appropriate sense of "generalization" is really application of a theory in a particular setting, "application" is synonymous with the explanation or prediction of a particular event. Therefore, the widely accepted Hempel-Oppenheim paradigm of explanation can be used to study what application involves.[3] From this study there are two results: On the one hand, there is no reason why experimental results *must* be directly extrapolated for them to be applied, because it is *theories* that are applied to concrete settings. On the other hand, application always involves at least some knowledge that is not guaranteed by experiment; therefore, no amount of experimental support for a theory is itself sufficient to warrant its applicability in any particular setting.

The Abstract Character of Theory and Experiment

That experiments are mainly useful in constructing and testing theory is evident from the peculiar character of some of their advantages.[4] Among the aims of an experiment are: (1) To create states of affairs difficult to discover in natural settings, for example the continual open expression of disagreement between a status inferior and his superior in an organization. (2) To produce controls and contrasts that are difficult to find *ex post facto* in natural settings, for example a high and a low status source making an identical suggestion to similar individuals. (3) To replicate events that seldom recur under the same conditions in natural settings, such as the negotiation by several foreign offices of an international disarmament treaty. (4) To isolate a process from the effects of other processes that confuse our understanding of it, such as separating the effects of power from the effects of relative competence-expectations in the study of a status superior's influence in an organization. Such concerns are mostly dictated by the desire to build and test a theory, and the special advantages of the experiment are mostly advantages from the standpoint of theorists. Experiments would make much less sense if the purpose were to describe a particular concrete situation.

That theory is necessarily abstract derives from its desire to be general. It will contain universal statements, such as, "The greater the uncertainty of an individual about his status, the greater the social distance he will maintain from status inferiors," rather than singular statements such as "John Smith is uncertain about his status." While the objective is to explain more and more, the more of one *concrete entity* a theory explains, the less it explains of any other thing, because any concrete entity is unique.[5] If it explains everything about General Motors it will not even explain Ford Motor Company, much less an army. By a "concrete entity" I mean a particular object of the phenomenal world. To describe it, one lists its properties: Its color, mass, volume, velocity, age, gender, shape, price, status significance, purpose. . . . The list is always infinite, and the more complete it is the more it differs from any other description. By an "abstract" theory, I mean a system of properties that are thought to be related to each other dynamically. A system of abstract properties or variables will inevitably omit some of the properties of any concrete thing: it will omit precisely those properties thought to be independent of, or at least only minimally correlated with, those contained in the theoretical system. But omitting some properties, the system of abstract variables will never account for the whole of any concrete entity. It does not explain "General Motors," it explains only some property of General Motors. Economics explains General Motors' prices, sociology explains the stability of its status structure, and so on. Even the language of theory expresses this fact. Terms originally meant concretely, such as "bureaucracy," come to mean not the Pentagon or the Bureau of the Budget, but any social system that has a division of labor, a hierarchical structure, some separation from the kinship, power, and status structures of a community, and so on. Meant abstractly in this way, some things once thought to be bureaucracies come to seem less so, while others not thought of as bureaucracies at all from a phenomenal point of view come to be objects explained by the theory.[6] But often what is similar or different from the point of view of abstract theory cannot be formulated except in quite abstract terms: hence the use of expressions like "total institutions" or "utilitarian organizations" which do not even incidentally sound concrete. In no other way can the theory formulate notions that distinguish two armies, two hospitals, or two prisons from each other, while classifying *some* hospitals together with *some* armies and *some* prisons as one sort of thing.

Can You Really Study an Army in the Laboratory?

If no theory can be concrete, and experiments are for the purpose of constructing theory, there is no basis for the common argument that an experiment ought to be as close as possible to the concrete entity it most nearly represents. An experiment aims only to reproduce that part of a concrete entity that is made relevant by some particular system of abstract variables. Therefore, we do not even *try* to study armies in the laboratory, if by that is meant an army in the concrete sense of the word. We try only to create those aspects of armies relevant to some theory.

Therefore, if it is objected that one cannot study an army in the laboratory, the objection must be that the properties of some theory relevant to the army cannot be produced under laboratory conditions. Can this objection be sustained?

Size plays an interesting and ambiguous role in such arguments. Obviously one would not bring an entire army into a laboratory, but does this mean that an army cannot be studied in the laboratory? If size is not theoretically relevant there is no reason to reproduce it in the laboratory. Therefore, the argument must be that size is, or is correlated with, a property without which a laboratory group could not simulate what is theoretically relevant about organizations. To refute such an argument, one must show that size itself is *not* relevant; that what is relevant is something else, probably complexity; and finally, that adequate degrees of complexity can be produced independently of size.[7] The rebuttal may be made a little more complicated, for propositions about organizations include some in which complexity is a variable and some in which it is not. Where complexity is not relevant, there is no need to create it even if organizations are typically complex. Where complexity *is* relevant, we face two possible situations: We may be required to produce very great degrees of complexity, say fifty different kinds of subunits and five levels of authority. In this case, it is doubtful that a laboratory group will prove adequate to the requirement. Even if one could create such an organization—and probably one could—the cost would be great, and the loss of control over the organization would ensure that the cost exceeded the return. But if something less than such great complexity will do, say three or four kinds of subunits and two or three levels of authority, then nothing precludes constructing complex laboratory organizations, and constructing fairly large numbers of them.

A process that can be studied in quite small laboratory "organizations" is the way in which stability is built into the status hierarchy of an organization. Complex organizations typically consist of at least three status classes, such as officers, noncommissioned officers, and other enlisted men in the army; or executives, supervisors, and workers in a factory. Of each status class beliefs are held about their relative abilities to perform organizational tasks. Based on these beliefs, opportunities to actually perform, evaluations of performance, and rights to influence decisions are distributed. Because it accords with the status structure, the distribution of opportunities, evaluations, and rights to exercise influence also tends to perpetuate that structure.[8] Of particular importance to the stability of the status structure is the fact that expectations embodied in status are expansive; that is, confronting a new task or activity, one not previously associated in anyone's mind with statuses in the organization, members of the organization will often behave as if superiors in the status structure were superior at the new task—providing superiority in the new activity is something the organization positively values. To understand the stability of status hierarchies, it is important to discover under what conditions status conceptions have this expansive property.

It was to study the expansive properties of status that the experiment described in the second paragraph of this paper was designed. The experiment had some additional features that it now becomes important to understand:

> The two staff sergeants were told that the task and setting of the experiment were designed to simulate a new kind of decision-making situation being studied by the air force. They were told that the decisions were difficult, but there was a correct choice in every case; that the experimenter was interested not in testing their individual abilities, but in finding out how the correct decision was made, so that it was perfectly legitimate to use advice from their co-participant; and that the co-participant, who was identified by a fictitious name, was from a different unit than the sergeant himself. Great care was taken to make sure that the task ability, called "contrast sensitivity," was not already associated with status in the air force. That is, it was not already associated with the terms "captain," "sergeant," or "airman" in the way cooking might conventionally be associated more with "female" than with "male."[9]

Thus, the sergeants were in a situation where they typically wanted to do well, but the decisions were difficult; where they had help but did not know their partner well enough to know what ability he might have; and the only cues were status cues. Under such conditions, in spite of the irrelevance of status to the task ability, the sergeants yielded to the influence of the other participant more if he was a captain than if he was an airman.

This experiment accomplished three objectives: First, it artificially created one aspect of the organizational structure of the air force, its status structure— though only three of its status levels were used. Second, it artificially isolated one process through which status expands, separating expectations from other processes that might obscure them—such as the way in which resources, technical knowledge, or power are allocated to statuses. Third, it created those conditions, but *only* those conditions that are theoretically relevant to the way in which status-related expectations expand. It did not embody *all* the conditions that make a status structure stable, much less *all* the properties of an air force.

Bridging the Gap

If armies are not really brought into the laboratory, what can be said about an army as a result of a laboratory experiment? Or, to put the question as it has been put several times in the past, how does one bridge the gap between experiment and natural setting?[10]

Usually the problem is thought to be one of *generalizing* from the experiment, and by "generalizing" people often mean equating concrete features of the experiment with concrete features of the natural setting. In this view, to generalize from the status-expansion experiment one asks if the same thing will be found true of staff sergeants outside the laboratory room. But almost certainly it will not. Equating populations in this fashion will not be sufficient to guarantee the truth of the generalization, for often the result will be false of "real live" staff sergeants. On the other hand, it is not necessary either, for often the result will be true of generals, or even college professors.

If generalization meant equating concrete features of experiment and natural setting, no bridge between the two would ever be built. But it is not concrete similarities that form the basis of generalization. One generalizes from one situation to another when both situations are described by the same abstract properties and satisfy the same conditions. For example: Instead of using staff sergeants, imagine that the status expansion experiment was run in exactly the same way with junior college students as subjects. In the same interaction conditions, given the same task, subjects would be told that their partner is either a high-school student or a student at a four-year college. It happens that when this is done the same result is found as in the air force experiment: subjects are much less likely to be influenced if they are told their partner has the lower state than if told that he has the higher state of a status characteristic.[11] What allows us to generalize from one experiment to the other? The task and interaction conditions are the same; and the status characteristics, though concretely very different, have the same properties from an abstract point of view. Both embody value judgments and expectations of what a person is like and how he will behave.[12] What differences there are, are not differences that are part of the system of abstract variables forming the theory of status characteristics. They are therefore differences that make no difference.

It may seem to beg the question to show that the results of one experiment generalize to the results of another *experiment*, when the issue appears to be how to generalize to a natural setting. But in fact the problem is the same: *generalization from any one situation to any other relates, not concrete settings, but abstract variables*.

But even if focus is restricted to only those abstract variables that are part of a theoretical system, the results of an experiment are not directly extrapolated, because the results of experiments are always *conditional*. One does not generalize from an experiment any claim that the *initial conditions* established by the experiment are those typically found in natural settings. That air force sergeants typically believe officers are superior to enlisted men in ability is *not* a hypothesis tested or confirmed by the status-expansion experiment. Had a sergeant not believed in the status characteristic, he would not have been a suitable subject for experiment. That the sergeants used in the experiment did believe in the characteristic proves nothing about how many sergeants in the air force believe in its status structure. What is generalized from the experiment is not the descriptive hypothesis that its initial conditions are found outside the laboratory, but the conditional law that *if* a status characteristic is present, *then* influence is distributed so as to accord with its states. It is a gross fallacy of experimental logic to generalize only the *consequent* of a conditional—the "y" in "if x, then y." For what happens then is that the result of the experiment becomes subtly transformed into a description, such as: "In an organization like the air force, one finds y." But this is not the result of the experiment. The first part of the expression is not a set of abstract conditions that form the antecedent of a conditional; instead, substituted for such conditions, one finds a concrete entity masquerading as the antecedent. The effect is to transform "y" into a descriptive claim. How often does one hear that "Asch shows most people conform," or that "Sherif shows that all groups create norms"? What one means is that *under (abstract) conditions p, q, r . . .* , people conform or make norms.

It might be supposed that one could nevertheless generalize from a single experiment to any natural setting in which the same abstract, antecedent conditions are found. But even in this sense, a single experiment is almost never meant to be directly extrapolated. Rather, one thinks of an experiment as supporting a theory. It is the *theory* that is used to make predictions about natural settings. For the fact is that almost never is a single experiment decisively informative about a theory. Therefore, any single experiment is simply one part of a larger program, each part testing a different aspect of the theory. For example, the status-expansion experiment already described is actually only one of three run at the same time in the same setting, each of which focused on a different phase of the status-expansion process. To understand what takes place in some natural setting, therefore, one must understand it in terms of the theory, not of any one experiment designed to test some aspect of the theory. It is in this sense that theory is the bridge between experiment and natural setting, and for this reason that one seldom extrapolates an experiment directly.

If generalization from an experiment comes to mean the application of a theoretical formulation supported by that experiment, and by other experiments as well, then the difficulties in generalizing from experiments are really difficulties in applying theory. There are difficulties in generalizing from experiments, but these difficulties are not peculiar to generalization from experiments. They are difficulties that attend the application of *any* theories, whether supported by experiments, or by field studies, or by surveys, or indeed by any evidence whatsoever.

"Application" here does not mean social engineering, but simply the use of an abstract theory to reason about particular settings. For example, the theory of status characteristics might be applied to questions about the status order of schools in a city school system. In this sense "application" is essentially the same as "explanation" or "prediction" of particular events in the paradigm of Hempel and Oppenheim.[13] In this paradigm, explanation or prediction is a deductive argument in which what is to be explained or predicted is shown to be a valid conclusion from two kinds of premises: (1) One or more general laws; and (2) one or more statements describing conditions in the particular setting. For example, suppose that in city school system S considerable resources are to be invested to make racially imbalanced schools equal in objective quality. The purpose is to not only improve their quality, but also to make "Negro" schools more attractive to teachers, parents, and students by raising their status. The theory of status characteristics implies that equalizing the objective quality of teachers, programs, and even student performance in racially imbalanced schools will not succeed in making teachers, parents, and students attribute equal quality to a "Negro" and a "white" school.[14] In fact, the status order will remain unchanged. The argument is that a status characteristic differentiates the schools; and evaluations of school quality are a function of expectations determined by status independently of their objective quality. The first statement is a statement about the particular school system S. The second is a "general law" from the theory of status characteristics.

This application assumes, first, that the ordering of schools in city school systems is a status phenomenon of the kind formulated in the theory of status characteristics; second, that particular conditions in the school system have been correctly described; and third, that important other factors, not formulated by the theory, can be safely neglected in city school systems. Each of these assumptions can be disputed. While race may satisfy the definition of a status characteristic, it is still possible that school systems fall outside the scope of the theory. This would be the case if race were an individual but not a collective property in the system.[15] In that case, schools would not be thought of as "Negro" or "white" and the theory might have nothing to say about their relative ordering. Even if race were a collective property, and the theory was applicable to schools in city school systems, the descriptive knowledge used in the application might be wrong. The schools might actually differ in objective quality, or it might be wrong to suppose that the status of schools in the system depends on the "quality" attributed by people to the schools. Even if the descriptive knowledge is accurate, the effect of interscholastic athletics has been ignored, and might be sufficiently important to change any predictions made about status ordering from a knowledge of status characteristics alone.

What is important about such disputes is that they do not simply depend on the degree to which the theory that is applied has been confirmed. They are disputes about the theory's *applicability*, not about the evidence in its favor. Some disputes about applicability can be resolved by experimental means. For example, the effect of processes that were neglected in confirming a theory but become important in some application can sometimes be studied in the laboratory. On the other hand, some disputes about applicability cannot be resolved by such means. They depend on descriptive knowledge of the particular situation, and *no* amount of experimental investigation will provide such knowledge. *Therefore, no application can ever depend entirely on experimental investigation.*

Summary

I have argued that experiments are mainly for the purpose of building and testing theories; that theories are necessarily abstract; therefore, experiments too are abstract. Neither the organizational experiment, nor any other kind of experiment, attempts to recreate a completely "real" instance of any concrete organization in the laboratory. One would not even *want* to bring an army into the laboratory, much less defend the possibility of actually doing so.

If the laboratory organization creates only the aspects of an organization relevant to some theory, then only a theory can bridge the gap between experiment and natural setting. I have rejected the view that generalization requires direct extrapolation of the results of a single experiment. In place of it I have suggested that experiments are relevant to theory, and *theory* is applied to natural settings. Two interesting consequences follow: First, if an experiment is informative for a theory, and the theory applicable in a given setting, the findings of an experiment are "generalizable" even if they bear little resemblance to the typical findings in the natural setting. For if theory is thought of as a bridge, the main requirement of the bridge is that it span both settings, not that the two settings be identical. Put a little less metaphorically, if f_1 is found in an experiment and f_2 in some natural setting, it is sufficient for some theory to imply both f_1 and f_2 for that theory to bridge the gap. It is not required that $f_1 = f_2$. But second, if the Hempel-Oppenheim paradigm is accepted as applying to an application, then application uses not only laws from some theory, but also descriptive knowledge about some domain of application. Therefore experimental support for a theory is never sufficient warrant for its applicability. But the situation is no different for theories supported by survey or other sorts of field evidence; whatever the evidence for the theory, the problem of application remains. Hence the problems of application raise no special objections to experimental studies of organizations.

Notes

1. J. Berger, B. P. Cohen, and M. Zelditch, *Status Conceptions in Social Interaction*, Chap. 5, forthcoming.
2. E. Faris, "The Primary Group: Essence and Accident," *American Journal of Sociology*, 38 (1932), 41–50.
3. C. Hempel and P. Oppenheim, "Studies in the Logic of Explanation," *Philosophy of Science*, 15 (1948), 135–175.
4. See M. Zelditch and W. Evan, "Simulated Bureaucracies: A Methodological Analysis," in H. Guetzkow, *Simulation in Social Science: Readings* (Englewood Cliffs, N.J.: Prentice-Hall, 1962), 48–60, which expands this argument.
5. This point, as well as the whole of the present paper, owes a great deal to the argument made in B. P. Cohen, "On the Construction of Explanations," Technical Report #19, Laboratory for Social Research, Stanford University, 1966.
6. Cf. the argument in A. Etzioni, *A Comparative Analysis of Complex Organizations* (New York: Free Press, 1961), chap. 3.
7. This part of the argument is expanded in M. Zelditch and T. K. Hopkins, "Laboratory Experiments with Organizations," in A. Etzioni (ed.), *Complex Organizations: A Sociological Reader* (First ed.), (New York: Holt, Rinehart and Winston, Inc., 1961), 465–478. There it is argued that the character of formal organizations, for example their complexity, high degree of institutionalization, and scale, do not in most circumstances preclude experimentation.
8. For further theoretical background, see B. Anderson, J. Berger, B. P. Cohen, and M. Zelditch, "Status Classes in Organizations," *Administrative Science Quarterly*, 11 (1966), 264–283; and J. Berger, B. P. Cohen, ad M. Zelditch, "Status Characteristics and Expectation States," in J. Berger, M. Zelditch, and B. Anderson (eds.), *Sociological Theories in Progress*, vol. 1 (Boston: Houghton Mifflin, 1966), 47–73.
9. J. Berger, B. P. Cohen, and M. Zelditch, *Status Conception in Social Interaction*, chap. 5.
10. See B. Anderson, *The Use of Experimental Data in the Interpretation of Survey Results* (Technical Report, Bureau of Applied Social Research, Columbia University, 1961); H. Riecken, "Narrowing the Gap between Field Studies and Laboratory Experiments in Social Psychology," *Items*, 8 (1954), 37–42; and S. Verba, *Small Groups and Political Behavior* (Princeton, N.J.: Princeton University Press, 1961), 90–109.
11. J. Moore, *General Status Characteristics and Specific Performance Expectations*, unpublished Ph.D. dissertation, Stanford University, 1966.
12. See J. Berger, *et al., op. cit.,* pp. 29–46.
13. C. Hempel and P. Oppenheim, *op. cit.*
14. B. P. Cohen, "White Expectations and Negro Aspirations: One View of *De Facto* School Segregation" (Technical Report #18, Laboratory for Social Research, Stanford University, 1965).
15. See the paper by P. Lazarsfeld and H. Menzel, "On the Relation between Individual and Collective Properties," in this volume, pp. 499–516.

The Integration of Fieldwork and Survey Methods[1]

Sam D. Sieber

Prior to World War II, fieldwork[2] dominated social research. Such classics as the Hawthorne studies, the Middletown volumes, the Yankee City series, and the Chicago studies of deviant groups, not to mention the anthropological contributions, attest to the early preeminence of fieldwork. Following the war, the balance of work shifted markedly to surveys. This shift was largely a consequence of the development of public-opinion polling in the thirties. Mosteller, Cantril, Likert, Stouffer, and Lazarsfeld were perhaps the major developers of the newer techniques. In particular, Lazarsfeld's interest in the two major nonacademic sources of social surveys—market studies and public-opinion polling—and his adaptation of these traditions to substantive and methodological interests in sociology gave special impetus to the advancement of survey research in the universities.

With the rapid growth of this vigorous infant, there emerged a polemic between the advocates of the older field methods and the proponents of the newer survey techniques. In fact, two methodological subcultures seemed to be in the making—one professing the superiority of "deep, rich" observational data and the other the virtues of "hard, generalizable" survey data. That the fieldworkers were more vocal about the informational weaknesses of surveys than were survey researchers with respect to fieldwork suggests the felt security of the latter and the defensive stance of the former. An extreme point in the polemic was reached by the statement of Becker and Geer (1957): "The most complete form of the sociological datum, after all, is the form in which the participant observer gathers it; an observation of some social event, the events which precede and follow it, and explanations of its meaning by participants and spectators, before, during, and after its occurrence. Such a datum gives us more information about the event under study than data gathered by any other sociological method. Participant observation can thus provide us with a yardstick against which to measure the completeness of data gathered in other ways" (p. 28).

This position was strongly contested in a rebuttal by Trow (1957), who pointed out that no single technique could claim a monopoly on plausibility of inference; and, indeed, as he argued, many sociological observations can be made only on the basis of a large population. One technique is suitable for one type of information and another technique for another: "It is with this assertion, that a given method of collecting data—any method—has an inherent superiority over others by virtue of its special qualities and divorced from the nature of the problem studied, that I take sharp issue. . . . Different kinds of information about man and society are gathered most fully and economically in different ways. . . . The problem under investigation properly dictates the methods of investigation" (p. 33).

In his brief rebuttal, Trow did not seek to propose a scheme for determining the suitability of fieldwork or survey research for the collection of given types of

Reprinted from the *American Journal of Sociology*, vol. 78 (May 1973), pp. 1335–1359 by permission of the author and the publisher. © 1973 by The University of Chicago Press.

data. This task was undertaken a few years later by Zelditch (1962), who applied the criteria of "efficiency" and "informational adequacy" of surveys, participant observation, and informant interviewing in gathering three kinds of data: (1) frequency distributions, (2) incidents and histories, and (3) institutionalized norms and statuses. Thus, if the objective is to ascertain a frequency distribution, then the sample survey or census is the "prototypical and best form"; but not so with incidents and histories, which render the survey both "inefficient and inadequate," according to Zelditch. This contribution was a long step forward in mediating between the two historically antagonistic styles of research.

But even this formulation showed the traces of an assumption that undergirded the earlier polemic, namely, that one uses either survey or field methods. The fact of the matter is that these techniques are sometimes combined within a single study. If all three types of information noted by Zelditch are sought within the framework of a single investigation, then all three techniques are properly called into play. In such cases, the inefficiency of a survey in studying "institutionalized norms and statuses" falls by the wayside; if one is conducting a survey anyway (because of other information needs), then why not proceed to measure norms and statuses in the questionnaire? Likewise with the investigation of incidents and histories by means of a survey. If combined with other approaches, according to Zelditch, the survey becomes "adequate" for the collection of incidents and histories; so if one is already doing a survey, the question of efficiency once again becomes irrelevant. But there is a second implication of combining field and survey methods that is much more important to the progress of social research than the needed qualifications in Zelditch's scheme.

The integration of research techniques within a single project opens up enormous opportunities for mutual advantages in each of three major phases—design, data collection, and analysis. These mutual benefits are not merely quantitative (although obviously more information can be gathered by a combination of techniques) but qualitative as well—one could almost say that a new style of research is born of the marriage of survey and fieldwork methodologies. Later on, we shall argue that the respective techniques need to be modified for their special roles in a set of interlocking methods. It is this combination of adjustments which, in our opinion, produces a distinctly new style of investigation.

It is curious that so little attention has been paid to the intellectual and organizational problems and to the prospects of the integration of research methods. A few methodologists have sought to compare the results of different approaches, but these endeavors were conceived within the traditional framework of mutually exclusive techniques, inasmuch as the problem was to determine the consequences of using either one or another technique.

The authors of a recent compendium of "unobtrusive measures" have noted our doggedness in viewing social research as a single-method enterprise: "The usual procedural question asked is, which of the several data-collection methods will be best for my research problem? We suggest the alternative question: which *set* of methods will be best?" (Webb et al. 1966, pp. 174–75). These authors were prompted to raise this question on the assumption that every technique suffers from inherent weaknesses that can be corrected only by cross-checking with other techniques: "No research method is without bias. Interviews and questionnaires must be supplemented by methods testing the same social science variables but having different methodological weaknesses" (p. 1). In its own way, this assumption is as radical as that of Becker and Geer. To be sure, there are areas of informational overlap between methods, but there are also large areas of information which can be gained only by a particular technique. If each technique has an inherent weakness it also has an inherent strength unmatched by other techniques. The opinions held by a large population can be measured only by survey techniques; the unverbalized normative pattern of a small group might be measurable only by observation. Further, what if the results obtained from two or more different techniques do not agree? Are we to abandon our findings altogether, or should we reexamine the techniques to discern a special weakness in one of them that invalidates its results? If the latter strategy is chosen, then we are admitting the superiority of one of the techniques in gathering the desired information. An illustration from a class experiment at Columbia University will make the argument more concrete.

A Class Experiment[3]

In a seminar on research methods, nine graduate students were provided with the field notes of an observer-informant interviewer who had investigated the settings of Job Corps trainees in two city agencies. On the basis of these notes, the project director had selected one of the settings as "good" and the other as "bad" in terms of the trainees' morale, opportunities for training, and meaningful participation in the work of the agencies. (Although several agencies had been investigated, these two were selected as polar cases for the purpose of the class experiment.) The nine students were instructed to scrutinize the *field notes* very carefully and then to select those items from a *questionnaire* (later distributed to the trainees) which they believed would confirm the conclusions of the project director as to the value of the two settings (the *direction* of the predicted difference being obvious in most cases since the items were clearly evaluative of morale, participation, etc.). After the students had made their individual selections, the results of the questionnaire survey in each of the two agencies were tabulated and compared item by item. If at least half of the judges predicted that an item would discriminate, and it did in fact discriminate, it was classified in a category of "congruence" between fieldwork and survey results. If less than half of the judges predicted a difference on the item, but the item nevertheless discriminated, it was classified in a "noncongruent" category; and so on. Table 1 shows the percentage of 75 questionnaire items that fell into each of four logical classes.

Table 1 discloses that 45% of the survey items were predictable on the basis of the field notes (cells 1 and 4). Virtually all of the items in cell 1 referred to the match between the trainees' interests and qualifications and the job he was performing. (Of all the items, 21% fell into this cell.)

Another 24% of the items were accurately regarded by the judges as revealing no difference (cell 4). The items in this category focused mainly on the administration of the overall program, such as selection procedures, training, general administration, etc.; in other words, experiences that the trainees in the two agencies were known to have shared. As these experiences were not specific to a particular agency, the judges assumed correctly that the items bearing on them would not discriminate between the agencies.

Cells 2 and 3 clearly reveal incongruence between the field notes and the survey results. In cell 2 we find items that in fact discriminated but that the field notes did not provide grounds for such discrimination (36% of the items). This percentage may be taken as a rough measure of the unique contribution of the survey as perceived by the judges. The items falling into this cell were of three distinct kinds: (1) *statistical data* such as number of hours per week with little or nothing to do, income expected from Urban Corps, present pay rate; (2) *personal history* such as how income compares with what was previously expected, whether another job was turned down to work for Urban Corps, attitude toward job when applied; (3) *personal interests and values* such

TABLE 1 *Questionnaire Items Classified According to Their Congruence with Fieldwork Observations (% of 75 Items)*

Item Actually Discriminated Between Agencies[a]	Consensus among Judges[b]	
	Half or More (5–9)	Less than Half (0–4)
Yes	(1) Congruence (prediction of difference confirmed) 21%	(2) Noncongruence (failure to predict difference) 36%
No	(3) Noncongruence (inaccurate prediction of difference) 19%	(4) Congruence (prediction of no difference confirmed) 24%

[a] 10% difference between the agencies was regarded as determining whether an item "discriminated."
[b] No. of judges predicting a difference between survey responses of trainees in two city agencies on basis of field notes.

as kinds of summer jobs preferred, enjoyment of life in the city, occupational values, career plans, interest in hearing different types of speakers in Urban Corps Seminars.

Perhaps more lengthy exposure to the agencies and their trainees would have contributed more information on these points in the field notes. However, the survey was clearly a more economical means of disclosing such information. In addition, by being gathered in a standardized fashion the information could be dealt with statistically in examining the differential impact of the two agencies on different trainees. For example, it now became possible to see if trainees with lower occupational aspirations were less satisfied with the "bad" agency.

Finally, in cell 3 we find items that were expected to discriminate but which in fact did not discriminate between the two agencies (19% of the total items). Here it is plain that the field notes misled the judges into assuming that the trainees in the "bad" agency (1) were disliked by their superiors and other regular staff, and (2) blamed the agency itself for their unsatisfactory assignment. In short, an assumption of mutual animus was conveyed by the field notes. Here are some examples of items that were mistakenly thought to discriminate between the two agencies (in each case the trainees in the "bad" agency were expected to give the more negative response):

How do you think your supervisor would rate your performance?

If you have switched jobs, what were the reasons? (Agency or supervisor was dissatisfied.)

Have you complained to the Urban Corps staff about any aspect of your job?

When you first arrived in this agency, how much did the agency prepare you for what you would be doing?

Do you like your supervisor as a person?

Would you say your non-Urban Corps co-workers are friendly or unfriendly to you?

How would you characterize your agency? As: (*a*) open to new ideas, (*b*) bureaucratic, (*c*) sympathetic toward clients.

We encounter here a common pitfall of fieldwork that might properly be called the "holistic fallacy"—that is, a tendency to perceive all aspects of a social situation as congruent. In the present instance, because of the wholly unsatisfactory job assignments of the trainees in one of the agencies, it was assumed that they would be displeased with the agency and, in turn, would feel resented by the regular agency staff. The survey corrected this assumption.

While the above experiment confirms Webb et al., in the advisability of using several techniques to validate inferences, it also demonstrates that certain information can be gathered only by means of a single technique (see cells 2 and 3 above). However, by drawing upon its special strengths, one technique may contribute substantially to the utilization of the other technique. It is this principle that we wish to demonstrate in the remainder of this essay.

To recapitulate: the original polemic between advocates of field methods and of survey research was mediated by the assertion of Trow and Zelditch that the nature of the problem dictates the method to be applied. Later on, Webb et al. rejected a commitment to any single method in solving a particular problem because of an inherent bias in all techniques. Their argument in behalf of multitechniques is based on an assumption of interchangeability—otherwise it would be meaningless to plead for cross-validation. In contrast, we believe that survey and field research each possesses special qualities that render these methods noninterchangeable; nevertheless, each method can be greatly strengthened by appealing to the unique qualities of the other method.

Despite the plausibility of this claim, the advantages of the interplay between surveys and field methods are seldom recognized and rarely exploited. To the contrary, it seems that most sociological research either utilizes only a single method of investigation, or assigns an extremely weak role to a second. To show the value of fully integrating the respective techniques by drawing upon existing research for examples, we hope to focus serious attention on the enormous opportunities that lie at hand for improving our social research strategies.

We shall first deal with the contributions of fieldwork to surveys and then reverse ourselves and consider the contributions of surveys to fieldwork. In each case we shall give illustrations that bear on the phases of design, data collection, and analysis associated with each method.[4] Then, in a final section, we shall take up the question of time-order in which the methods are applied. Considerations of time-order are of major importance to the management of a research study that seeks to benefit from both techniques. This point will become clearer when we turn to the formulation of an optimal research schedule.

Contributions of Fieldwork to Surveys

Contributions to Survey Design

More and more, surveys are conducted among selected communities or organizations rather than among samples of isolated individuals. In these cases, a great deal of careful thought must be given to the selection of the collective. It is not unusual, therefore, to find survey researchers scouting among an array of potential collectives in order to select those that promise to maximize the advantages of comparative study. An account of one such scouting expedition is given by Wilder and Friedman (1968, appendix A) who had tentatively selected seven communities to be included in their investigation of school-community relations. (Parents, students, and teachers in these communities were eventually interviewed.) We quote:

> The Project Director and his assistant visited each of the communities to see whether they appeared to "fit" their census descriptions. Since we had found it necessary at several points to compromise with our *a priori* assumptions about what constituted criteria for the various types of communities, we had certain misgivings about some

parameters and cutting points and we felt it would be useful to verify qualitatively our sampling framework. In addition we were curious to *see* these communities with which we had become so familiar on the basis of census data.

In general, the tours served to confirm our expectations. Schools in settled towns were often pre-1900 vintage, while in growing communities they were either new or had new additions. Homes and people in middle-class communities "looked" middle-class and shops displayed quality merchandise. In the working-class towns homes were smaller, lawns were tiny or non-existent, Methodist churches were predominant. Boxy developments were mushrooming in the growing working-class suburb, while more expensive split-level developments abounded in the growing middle-class suburb. The trips served to convince us that the communities we had selected on the basis of the available published data did indeed "fit" their census descriptions.

The contribution of field observations to the study design of a survey need not be restricted to a confirmatory role, as in the above example, but can provide the sole rationale for the design. An illustration is provided by our own research on suburban schools.

While conducting exploratory interviews and observations in a single suburban school system located just beyond the crest of a migratory wave originating in a large city, our attention was drawn to the school system's vulnerability as its public composition gradually changed. In our interviews, we heard stories about a neighboring system that had already felt the full impact of migration. The informants were fearful that the same kinds of conflict between school and community would overtake their own system in the near future. After about two months of fieldwork in the less urbanized system, we decided to include the neighboring system in our study and to focus on the response of the schools to increasing vulnerability arising from suburbanization. Fieldwork was then pursued in both systems for several months before launching a questionnaire survey of all staff members in the two systems. Thus, the initial fieldwork sharpened the focus of the investigation on a specific educational problem by directing attention to the contrast between pre- and post-suburbanized systems, necessitating the inclusion of a second system. A survey was then conducted to gain fuller knowledge of the impact of suburbanization on the schools. Fieldwork, in sum, dictated the design of the survey investigation.

Broadly conceived, qualitative fieldwork includes any source of personal familiarity with a setting or group to be surveyed. This knowledge may be derived from nonprofessional sources, such as family members or previous work experience. These sources can provide insights and "privileged" information that can make a major contribution to the development of a meaningful survey design. A striking illustration of the benefits of nonprofessional familiarity with a social group prior to the conception of a survey is afforded by Lipset (1964) in his "biography" of the project that eventuated in the well-known monograph, "Union Democracy." Lipset's interest was in explaining the high level of participatory democracy in the printers union, a phenomenon that disconfirmed classical theories of the development of oligarchical control in socialist parties and trade unions. An innovation of the project was the sampling of collectives (union chapels), a design permitting elaborate analysis of contextual effects on individual political attitudes and behaviors. Referring to this unusual design, Lipset says: "The methodological innovations evidenced in our sample design did not stem from any special concern with creative methodology. . . . It was a sophisticated survey design precisely because years of prior investigation of the attributes of a complex system had preceded it" (p. 125). The history of that prior investigation began in Lipset's youth: "My first contact with the International Typographical Union came when I was quite young. My father was a lifelong member of the union. . . . While in elementary school and high school, I frequently overheard discussions of union matters, and occasionally my father would take me to the monthly meetings of the New York local at Stuyvesant High School—a set of experiences which was to play a role later in my conceiving of the 'occupational community' as an important part of the environment of the union" (p. 112). Lipset's survey design was developed expressly to study the effect of varying degrees of "occupational community" within the different chapels in promoting the members' political participation.

The contribution of field methods to survey design is by no means restricted to the study of collectives. Sometimes, for example, there are special categories of individuals whose existence is brought to light by exploratory fieldwork and which are then incorporated into the design of the survey.

> In preparing for an investigation of the organization of research in schools of education, in which deans and bureau directors were to be surveyed, Lazarsfeld and I (1966; Sieber 1972) interviewed expert informants. One informant noted the presence of "faculty research coordinators," an emerging status that had been overlooked in the study design. The informant himself filled this role in his institution. Therefore a special questionnaire was prepared for these persons. Further, since we realized that the data to be collected from these respondents would permit a comparison of organized and unorganized settings for research, the former represented by bureau directors and the latter by faculty coordinators, the existing questionnaires were modified by expanding the number of items on which comparisons would be fruitful. In effect, a new study design was adopted. These comparisons later afforded a perspective on bureau research that was not attainable in any other way.

Contributions to Survey Data Collection

The exploratory interviews and observations that often precede social surveys yield valuable information about the receptivity, frames of reference, and span of attention of respondents. Since a great part of the value of systematic pretesting resides in the gathering of such intelligence, it is justifiable to consider this aspect of pretesting under the rubric of qualitative fieldwork. Improvements in the questionnaire stemming from qualitative pretest information enhance rapport between interviewer and respondent, reduce nonreturns of mailed questionnaires or refusals to be interviewed, and generally ease the data-collection efforts of the research staff.

In addition, the instrument can be broadened or narrowed, depending upon the identification of topics that are salient to pretest respondents. That is, by identifying the respondents' level of interest and scope of concern, the instrument can be modified to avoid overtaxing each respondent, on the one hand, or underrepresenting his views, on the other. An example of expanding a questionnaire on the basis of this type of information is taken from a survey of college students on a single campus. A chronicle of the questionnaire's development (Langenwalter 1967) contains the following observation:

> The pre-test was administered to about thirty students, and the results were very heartening. Almost all of the interviewers reported that the respondents seemed to be interested in cooperating. This information caused an over-all change in the form of the questionnaire. In the pre-test, the emphasis had been on limiting the number of questions for fear of antagonizing the busy students. The interviewers' reports seemed

to indicate that the fear was ungrounded and the items that had been limited could be expanded.

The general direction of the expansion was the addition of *contingent sections* to existing questions. . . . The discovery of student interest *allowed* us to add more sections according to our own interests. [Pp. 5–6]

Pretesting is only one means of exploring issues that bear on the development of an instrument. Often a good deal of exploratory work precedes even the pretest questionnaire. As a rule, the more knowledgeable the questionnaire designer about his ultimate population, the more sophisticated the instrument and the smoother its administration.

Apart from the formulation of the questionnaire, fieldwork often provides a means of gaining legitimation for the survey. If the population has a central leadership, contacts with leaders will often smooth the way for contacts with followers. If there are factional fights, of course, the endorsement of only a single leader may set a large number of the followers in opposition to the survey. But information about political in-fighting should come to the attention of the sophisticated fieldworker in the normal course of informant interviewing, thereby prompting him to gain endorsements in a way that will appeal to all sectors of the constituency.

The importance of identifying and gaining support from the appropriate authority during the exploratory phase preceding a survey, and of grasping the political context in which approval is sought, are perhaps best demonstrated by a negative instance.

Voss (1966) describes the case of a school survey that was terminated by the superintendent on the grounds that it was "unauthorized by the school." Although in reality the superintendent was responding to pressures from a group of right-wing parents, the survey having been duly approved by lower level administrators, he was able to claim that he had not personally endorsed the survey and could therefore cancel it on legalistic grounds. Voss concludes from this experience: "Lack of familiarity with the structure of the organization may spell disaster. For some time sociologists have recognized that persons without portfolio may influence the decision of the titular head of the organization. The only means of avoiding such a problem is to obtain unequivocal support from the highest level possible."

Our investigation of two suburban districts, mentioned earlier, affords a case at the opposite end of the spectrum of cooperation.

After conducting fieldwork for several months—which included the privilege of walking unannounced into the superintendents' offices at any hour and attending closed strategy meetings of the teachers' association—there was never really any question of gaining endorsements for the survey. Every administrator in the district cooperated fully in urging teachers to respond and in collecting the completed questionnaires. And the many helpful, marginal comments of the teachers, some addressing the survey designer by name, suggested that the questionnaire was completed with uncommon seriousness. (The return rate was about 90% of the entire staff.)

The two projects are not exactly parallel since Voss surveyed students rather than staff members, thereby touching off community hostility; but the problems encountered by Voss are also faced in gaining access to school staff. The crucial point is that rapport which stems from fieldwork can smooth the way for the more elaborate, time-consuming, and often more threatening aspects of survey data collection. Apparently, the impersonality of a survey can be counteracted by the subjects' personal acquaintance with the investigator and the goals of his study.

Contributions to Survey Analysis

Information that is gathered in the course of fieldwork can assist in the analysis and interpretation of survey data in several ways. First, the *theoretical structure* that guides the analysis can be derived wholly or largely from qualitative fieldwork. Second, as emphasized by Webb et al. (1966), certain of the survey results can be *validated*, or at least given persuasive plausibility, by recourse to observations and informant interviews. (This contribution is limited to areas of informational overlap, as noted earlier.) Third, statistical relationships can be *interpreted* by reference to field observations. Fourth, the selection of survey items for the *construction of indices* can be based on field observations. Fifth, *external validation* of statistical constructs (indices) is afforded by comparison with observational scales. Sixth, *case studies* that illustrate statistical and historical types are supplied by field protocols. Seventh, provocative but puzzling replies to the questionnaire can be *clarified* by resort to field notes. Illustrations of each of these contributions to survey analysis follow.

1. The derivation of a theoretical structure from fieldwork is perhaps more common than appears from reports of survey work. Often, only passing acknowledgment is made of prior, personal familiarity with the situation, a familiarity that has produced rather definite ideas for research. A sociologist who conducts a survey of college faculty has made many observations of his own institutional context which contributed, no doubt, to his theoretical guidelines, but his monograph might omit any reference to this fact. And rare indeed is the report that systematically traces the intellectual history of a study to its qualitative antecedents.

Such an effort has been made by Lipset in his chronicle of the "Union Democracy" study (Lipset 1966). As a consequence of his personal familiarity with the International Typographers Union, Lipset says, "I had a fairly clear picture in mind of factors which had created ITU democracy and those which sustained it. . . . The main task of the survey was to convert hypotheses which had been developed earlier into questions for a schedule which could be administered to a sample of union members" (pp. 123–24).

In an investigation of high school rebellion, Stinchcombe (1964) asserts that the four hypotheses that guided his analysis "were developed during the course of about six months of anthropological observation and exploratory survey research in a California high school" (pp. 9–10). In the preface to his monograph, Stinchcombe candidly notes his debt to informant interviewing: "I became quite suspicious of any hypothesis that was never formulated, in one guise or another, by at least one of the teachers or administrators of the school, and many were suggested by them." It would appear that an optimal schedule for theoretical survey research would include a lengthy period of fieldwork prior to the survey. As a result of our perusing the literature for examples, however, our impression is that this practice is rarely followed.

2. The verification of survey findings by reference to fieldwork is especially useful when the finding is both surprising and strategic. A statistic of this kind was discovered in our study of educational research organizations (Sieber and Lazarsfeld 1966).

Tabulation of the questionnaire showed that extremely few doctoral recipients who had worked in research bureaus as assistants remained as staff members. On the average, only .7 students per unit had stayed on after the doctorate in the past three years. It occurred to us that this fact might explain the lack of continuity in research bureaus, the difficulty of recruitment and the strong influence of each succeeding director. Here was an explanatory factor that was wholly unanticipated. But since only about two-thirds of the respondents had answered this difficult statistical question, we felt uneasy about resting our case on the survey finding alone. When we later did informant interviewing, therefore, we asked the directors how they felt about retaining research assistants as professional staff members. With only one exception, the dozen or so directors whom we talked to believed that students should be encouraged to leave the bureau after getting their degrees. The reason given was that students would not become independent of their mentors unless they took positions elsewhere. Since this viewpoint was expressed with great conviction by the informants, the field interviews lent plausibility to the survey finding.

The invalidation of survey results by qualitative methods should also be counted as a contribution to survey analysis. For example:

In her study of working-class marriage, it was very important for Komarovsky (1962) to classify her subjects according to differing degrees of marital happiness in as reliable a manner as possible, for marital happiness was a crucial dependent variable. She therefore drew upon information gathered in a series of detailed and indirect probes. Comparing her distribution of cases with large, representative samples of the same social strata which employed more direct self-ratings, she found that her own population contained a larger proportion of unhappy marriages. In one nationwide survey only 5% of the grade school graduates were classified as "not too happy"; while in her study, 14% were judged to be "very unhappy." Komarovsky accounts for this discrepancy by reference to the more subtle techniques of qualitative case study, making it more difficult for the respondent to conceal the unpleasant aspects of marital relations. As she states: "Our detailed and indirect probing may have brought to light unfavorable facts which are not readily admitted in answer to direct questions used in surveys. . . . In our own interview, answers to the direct questions on dissatisfaction with communication were at variance with the admissions made elsewhere by the same people" (p. 348). Consequently, instead of being misled by the results of typical survey items, Komarovsky employed a more qualitative approach when classifying her subjects according to certain major variables in her study.

The testing of a survey's reliability may extend to the entire study as well as focusing on selected items or variables. Riesman visited a large number of the social science professors who had been interviewed in the study of threats to academic freedom during the McCarthy years (Lazarsfeld and Thielens 1958). He also interviewed the interviewers. As a result, he was able to arrive at the overall assessment of the survey's reliability. He states in Lazarsfeld and Thielens: "Deficiencies in the interviewing did not seriously impair the information gathered. Or, to put it another way, the interviewing was, in general, sufficiently skillful to carry the somewhat unusual demands of this particular survey" (p. 269).

3. Qualitative fieldwork is also useful for the interpretation of statistical relationships. The identification of a whole series of interpretative variables is illustrated by Kahl's study of "common man" boys (1953).[5] Kahl found that IQ and occupation contributed independently to students' plans to attend college. He then became interested in the chain of causality linking SES to college aspirations. Through intensive interviews with the parents of a small subsample of the students (i.e., those in the upper lower and lower middle brackets) who had completed questionnaires, he found that overt parental pressure largely accounted for the students' college plans. This variable had not been measured in the original survey. Kahl then proceeded even farther in his search for interpretive variables by discern-

ing those factors that impelled the parents to urge college upon their children. The following is my own synopsis of his findings on this point.

> Parents who propelled their children toward college had adopted the upper middle class as a normative reference group, frequently owing to the father's proximity to middle-class workers within his job setting. Because these better trained and higher paid employees had high visibility for the father, he had become dissatisfied with his own occupational role and therefore placed great emphasis on his children's getting ahead. Those who were content for their children to stay out of college seemed more oriented to peers rather than to individuals placed immediately above them in the work hierarchy. Moreover, these fathers were not socially acquainted with professionals or semiprofessionals. Consequently, they tended to exhibit "short-run hedonism," that is, a concern with present enjoyments rather than with delayed gratifications. Rather than "getting ahead," as Kahl puts it, they were interested in "getting by."

In summary, Kahl's interview materials permitted him to refine the original survey correlation between SES and college plans among high IQ "common man" boys whose chances of planning to attend college were about 50–50.

Direct observation of behavior may also aid in the interpretation of a statistical relationship. The following example is drawn from our own study of suburban schools.

> In the questionnaire, the teachers in the two suburban systems were asked if they had easier access to administrators than most other teachers. In the smaller, less bureaucratized system, teachers with easier access held more favorable attitudes toward the administration. This was not the case in the larger district, however, where access and attitudes were unrelated. I tried to recall any difference that was observed between the two districts in the nature of personal interaction between teachers and administrators. By reflecting on my observations of actual meetings, I noted a distinction which had escaped me before. In the larger district both teacher and administrator observed formal protocol in the course of interaction. For instance, appointments were made, the participants sat with rigid postures on opposite sides of the administrator's desk, and the discussion pursued a business-like course. In the smaller district, the situation was highly informal. The teacher walked unannounced into the administrator's office, the participants sat back comfortably at a large conference table and enjoyed a smoke together, and the conversation roamed over a variety of topics. In short, a considerable amount of social distance was maintained in teacher-administrator relations in the larger district, reflecting the widely shared bureaucratic norms in that district. Consequently, personal sentiments of liking or disliking did not arise from teacher-administrator contacts. In the smaller district, the distance between formal ranks was almost obliterated by personal friendships, making it possible for mutual trust to develop more readily out of frequent interaction.

4. The construction of indices for use in survey analysis may derive from systematic informant interviewing or from more casual observation. The value of informants is demonstrated by Carlin's study of the social factors affecting the ethical behavior of lawyers (1966).

> Before the analysis could precede, it was necessary to develop a scale to measure the ethical proclivities of the lawyers. Therefore, questionnaire items were assembled from information about the ethical conflicts that commonly arise in legal practice. Much of this information was gleaned from informal interviews with lawyers. Carlin gives the following account of his strategy: "Detailed interviews were conducted with a dozen lawyers. They were asked certain general questions relating to professional ethics; also, they were asked to identify borderline unethical practices. Among the

general questions were the following: In what ways do lawyers take advantage of other lawyers? In what ways do lawyers act unethically toward public officials? What kinds of activities do you consider unethical or improper? How do you distinguish more from less ethical lawyers? How important are such distinctions in your judgments of other lawyers?" Several hypothetical situations that presented opportunities for unethical conduct were eventually devised. Responses to these items in the questionnaire made it possible to score the lawyers according to their ethical tendencies.

A similar approach was employed in the development of an index of "apprehension" on the part of social science professors regarding threats to academic freedom (Lazarsfeld and Thielens 1958). The authors discuss the development of this index in great detail, but what interests us here is the preliminary phase of exploratory interviewing.

> The first step was to conduct a series of detailed interviews with a number of college professors who were prevailed upon to describe in detail any situation encountered in their capacity as teachers which had somehow made them feel uneasy. We asked them to remember as much as they could of both important and trivial experiences which create problems in a teacher's professional career, experiences they had already encountered or which might arise in the future. From these preliminary interviews we selected a list of about twenty relatively specific experiences. Questions were then worded so that the respondent simply had to say whether or not these things happened to him. . . . Twenty-one items were included in the questionnaire to gauge a professor's apprehension. But further screening was necessary to select the items most suitable for the classificatory task at hand. . . . As a result of this sifting, eleven items remained suitable for an index of apprehension. [Pp. 73–74]

5. The validation of a statistical index by reference to fieldwork is illustrated by our procedure in testing a measure of "formal authority" among the directors of research bureaus.

> The index was based on replies to such questions as whether the director participated in the decision to undertake a study, whether he determined the salaries and promotions of staff members, whether he was a member of the board of directors, etc. After each director had been scored on the index, a small subsample was visited to gain firsthand information about certain bureaus. In the course of the interviews with the directors, the interviewer sought to explore the amount of formal authority that the directors had. Finally, the directors were told that they ranked high, low, or medium on the index and asked if their score accurately reflected their position. In virtually all cases, the directors confirmed their position on the index. One director who scored very low on the index explained that he ran the bureau in a very informal manner but nevertheless had a great deal to say about what went on. Further probing revealed that the director in question was a highly esteemed scholar who was frequently sought out by the staff for advice and support. Thus, we were alerted to a weakness in the index that was later compensated for by using a measure of the directors' research productivity to reflect their informal status among colleagues.

6. The use of case studies to illustrate statistical and historical types that are derived from survey analysis is so common a practice that it only seems necessary to refer to it here. Some investigators who have employed this technique are Kahl (1953), Gordon (1957), Komarovsky (1962), and Sieber and Lazarsfeld (1966). In all these cases—and the reader can undoubtedly think of his own examples—fieldwork reports were used to exemplify certain types of individuals or situations that were disclosed in the analysis of survey data.

7. A final contribution of fieldwork to survey analysis entails the clarification of ambiguous but provocative responses to a questionnaire.

In our survey of the directors of educational research bureaus, we asked the following: "In general, how *fruitful* have interchanges been with the academic departments in the university; what *problems* have been encountered, if any; and what *directions* would you like future interchanges to take?" One director wrote the following reply: "Professors in the liberal arts seem not to be able to make advancements within their respective departments if they participate heavily in the activities of the Center." The response was curious, possibly significant, but far from clear. Later, in the course of fieldwork among selected bureaus, we asked the director to clarify his answer. He explained that academic personnel who became associated with his organization lost visibility in their departments. Their frequent absence from the department was interpreted as a lack of departmental commitment. His clarification illuminated the problem of integrating research bureaus into the universities, which became a dominant theme in our subsequent thinking.

Contributions of Surveys to Fieldwork

We now shift to the other end of the two-way street between fieldwork and survey methodologies. The contribution of surveys to fieldwork is probably less well appreciated than the reverse; but as we shall see, there are many ways in which fieldwork can take advantage of survey techniques. Indeed, on many occasions it would seem to be methodologically obligatory.

Contributions to the Design of Fieldwork

We noted earlier that fieldwork is useful for identifying the most suitable collectives or individuals to be surveyed. The same holds for the contribution of surveys to the design of fieldwork.

When selecting collectives or individuals for qualitative case study, it is common to rely upon a statistical profile of the population containing the units to be observed. For example, in selecting schools for intensive fieldwork, we might peruse the following kinds of information about a number of districts: racial and occupational composition, density, school size, teachers' salaries, etc. These data are often used because they are readily available. But there is frequently a need for other information which is more pertinent to the goals of a study. Thus, a field exploration of the school characteristics that promote innovative behavior would benefit from precise data showing the range of "innovativeness" among a number of schools. With this information in hand, it would be easy to select schools at different points on the continuum for qualitative study. Other kinds of information that are not generally available but might be collected in a preliminary survey include staff morale, educational goals of parents or school personnel, backgrounds of school board members, and proportion of graduates who attend college. For example, before visiting the research units for our fieldwork (in connection with the study of graduate schools of education), we stratified the units according to certain data already collected in a national survey. The degree of emphasis on research versus service, whether the unit mainly facilitated faculty research or staff research, and public or private sponsorship were the stratifying variables. The first two items of information were contributed by the survey.

The purpose of selecting the research bureaus according to a sampling frame was to provide cases that represented the main types of bureaus. Another use of survey data is to select unrepresentative cases for the analysis of subtypes.

As an example, Kahl (1953) used survey data to select a particular subsample of students and their parents for intensive interviewing. He examined the distribution of all cases according to IQ, fathers' occupations, and the students' expectations of college attendance. Those students whose plans were least predictable on the basis of IQ and fathers' occupation—that is, high IQ and low occupation—were selected for follow-up study.

Kahl selected subjects who conformed to his theoretical expectations but who were under the cross-pressures of relatively low occupational background and high IQ. Consequently, only about half planned to attend college. The purpose of his follow-up interviews was to find out what distinguished the college- from the non-college-going students in this group. He might have chosen, however, to study those students who went counter to his expectations, for instance, the boys of high IQ and high occupational background who did not intend to enroll in college (11% of his cases); or the boys of low IQ and occupational background who did intend to enroll in college (9%). If he had adopted this approach in refining his theory, he would have been engaged in what has come to be known as "deviant case analysis." As Kendall and Wolf (1949) point out, "Through careful analysis of the cases which do not exhibit the expected behavior, the researcher recognizes the oversimplification of his theoretical structure and becomes aware of the need for incorporating further variables into his predictive scheme" (pp. 153–54). But often the researcher does not have in hand the additional information necessary for measuring the further variables. Since it is extremely rare for a survey researcher to reenter the field for intensive interviewing after the completion of a survey, the needed information is almost never collected. This methodological embarrassment might account for the superficiality of a good many reports based on survey analysis.

Qualitative fieldworkers, of course, also search for relationships among variables. But since evidence that can be examined in tabular form is seldom collected, the identification of deviant cases is more difficult than in survey work and therefore more prone to escape attention. Here is where a preliminary survey can be most fruitful, for it constrains the fieldworker to notice departures from theoretical expectation and clearly identifies those cases that deviate. The fieldworker can then focus on these cases for intensive observation.

In sum, a survey can improve the design of fieldwork by identifying both representative and unrepresentative cases, the former serving the goal of generalizability and the latter the function of theory refinement.

Contributions to Fieldwork Data Collection

A common pitfall in qualitative data collection is an "elite bias" in the selection of informants and in the evaluation of statements. There are several reasons for gravitating to the elite of a social system in the course of fieldwork. First, initial contacts are often made with the "gatekeepers" of a group to insure access to subjects. Consequently, the fieldworker tends to feel gratitude toward the elite and is careful to keep on good terms with them, especially in the early period while establishing his credentials. These early constraints on the fieldworker's role might color his objectivity throughout the ensuing study. Second, if the upper-status persons are esteemed in society at large, the fieldworker might tend to value personal association with them to the detriment of other contacts. Such overvaluation might stem from the prestige conferred on the sociologist by familiarity with (and later specialization in) a certain elite strata. A third reason for the elite bias is that upper-status individuals are often more articulate and give the impression of being better informed about the group than any other member. Thus, they might seem to display greater knowledge and equanimity, enhancing their qualification as informants. Finally, it is often more interesting to study elites who have remained hitherto inaccessible to sociologists than to study lower-level participants, even though a goal of the study might be to observe all strata. Consequently, the fieldworker might spend more time collecting information from the elites, ultimately giving greater weight to their viewpoints than to those of lower-level participants.

With hindsight, all of these factors probably entered into our own fieldwork in a study that set out to examine the structure of two suburban school systems, but developed into a study of school boards, superintendents, and the leaders of the high school teachers. After conducting a survey, however, I was able to correct certain impressions that emerged from my elite bias. This can be shown quite simply. Prior to looking at the results of the survey, I predicted the proportion of teachers who would respond in particular ways to the survey questions. I then compared my predictions with the actual responses. It became obvious when observing these comparisons that I had unwittingly adopted the elites' version of reality. For example, I overestimated the extent to which teachers felt that the administration accepted criticism. Here are the relevant questions and the statistics: "Do you think that teachers who are interested in administrative openings jeopardize their opportunities in this district by voicing criticism of present school policies and practices?" (% responding "definitely" and "possibly"):

	Predicted	Observed
System A	40	60
System B	40	65

Similarly, I had assumed that the teachers were more satisfied with evaluative procedures than was in fact the case: "All in all, how well do you think the evaluation of teachers is done in your school?" (% responding "as well as possible" and "fairly well"):

	Predicted	Observed
System A:		
Elementary	80	65
Secondary	50	36
System B:		
Elementary	80	74
Secondary	75	56

Although to a lesser extent, I also overestimated the rank-and-file support for the leaders of the teachers association, with whom I had spent a good deal of time. In short, I had fallen prey to the elite bias, despite recent training in the dangers of giving greater weight to prestigious figures as informants.

The survey not only constrained me to see that my qualitative data-collection procedures had been faulty, but also provided the opportunity to learn about an entire stratum which I was aware of having glossed over in the fieldwork, namely, the elementary teachers. Apparently the elite bias had operated also in my preference for secondary teachers, who are the more esteemed both in the profession and the community.

If the survey results had been available to me in the midst of fieldwork, I would have been able to alter my data-collection procedures. This sort of concurrent scheduling of field- and survey work was utilized by Vidich and Shapiro (1955) in their study of a rural community.

The field observer, who had spent a year in the community, sought to rank a large sample of residents according to certain prestige groupings. A sociometric survey was then conducted among these individuals. In comparing the results, it was found that individuals who were not known to the observer contained a disproportionate number of those with low prestige. As the authors put it on page 31, "Thus, even though the observer had made deliberate efforts to establish contact with lower prestige groups, his knowledge of community members was biased in favor of individuals with higher prestige. . . . Without the survey data, the observer could only make reasonable guesses about his areas of ignorance in the effort to reduce bias. The survey data give him more exact information regarding the degree and kind of selectivity operating, and thereby allow him to make better compensatory allowances in planning his observational activities."

As in my own case, moreover, the field observers were now able to classify a large number of cases with whom they were unacquainted. In sum, here are two ways in which surveys contribute to data collection in fieldwork: (1) they correct for the elite bias in the interpretation of events, and (2) they provide information about the informants or subjects who were overlooked.

There are other contributions, too, providing that the survey is conducted prior to fieldwork. Replies to survey questions provide leads for later interviews and observations and eliminate the need to ask routine "background" questions. They thereby afford greater realism, enhance rapport, and offer guidelines for probes.

Before arriving for our appointments with the directors of research bureaus, we carefully studied the information they had given us in the questionnaires. Background data on the directors and routine organizational information gave us an imagery of the man and his setting. And it was especially helpful to be able to forgo asking tedious questions about the activities, structure, and purposes of the organization. As a result, the interviews were relaxed, focused on subtle points of research administration, and relatively brief. In certain instances, replies to the mailed questionnaire were followed up with probes.

Contributions to the Analysis of Qualitative Field Materials

We will discuss four contributions of surveys to the understanding of field observations: (1) correction of the holistic fallacy, (2) demonstration of the generality of a single observation, (3) verification of field interpretations, and (4) the casting of new light on field observations.

1. Correction of the holistic fallacy. In our earlier discussion of a class experiment in predicting survey results from fieldwork, we referred to the "holistic fallacy" as a tendency on the part of field observers to perceive all aspects of a social situation as congruent. This tendency is a common pitfall. The anthropological method was developed in response to the needs of studying a particular type of social setting—small, isolated, relatively homogeneous cultures. In transferring the method to industrial societies, certain intellectual assumptions underlying the technique were also transferred, that is, every social situation can be perceived in an ideal-typical fashion. When the search for congruence overrides important refinements or dictates assumptions that are unsupported by direct evidence, and especially when striking exceptions to one's theory are subtly discounted in behalf of a unified conception, one is indulging in the holistic fallacy.

It will be recalled that this tendency was demonstrated in the class experiment reported earlier: evidence that the trainees were poorly suited for their assignments was extended to their attitudes toward supervision, when in fact the survey showed that these trainees felt no more hostile toward supervisors than trainees in a more satisfactory work setting. Another example of the holistic fallacy corrected by survey results is drawn from our study of suburban schools.

> It was our impression that the smaller school district approximated the *Gemeinschaft* form of society, while the larger one was much more bureaucratized, impersonal, up-to-date, that is, a *Gesellschaft* setting. In pursuing the fieldwork, I became more and more convinced that this distinction applied to almost all aspects of the two systems and would be reflected in the attitudes of the participants.
>
> The survey seemed to confirm that there was greater social cohesion in the smaller district. When asked how many of the faculty were close personal friends, 21% in the smaller district stated six or more, while only 7% in the other district claimed as many personal friends. But other results upset my expectations. With respect to the perception of red tape ("an excessive number of rules and regulations which hamper the abilities of the staff of my school") there was no difference. And with respect to the perception of faculty morale and cohesion the attitudes of the staff in the larger district were clearly more favorable. Overall, there turned out to be many more similarities than differences between the two districts. Apparently, my observation of greater informality among the staff members in the smaller district had led me to assume that morale in general was higher, and that less strain was created by bureaucratic regulations because of the informal nature of the administration. Thus, the survey made it possible to refine the attitudinal climate so as to disconfirm those impressions that had arisen from the holistic fallacy.

2. Demonstration of the generality of a single observation.   Surveys also afford the means of demonstrating the generality of a single observation. When the observation plays an important role in the theoretical structure of fieldwork, survey data become essential for buttressing the argument. The following illustration is taken from a comparative study of school boards (Kerr 1964).

> The field observer was impressed by the superintendents' unwillingness to allow board trustees to discuss educational matters, including those that fell legally within the board's domain. The observation was critical for Kerr's thesis that superintendents sometimes convert the boards into "legitimating agencies" in order to preserve professional autonomy. Since only two superintendents were observed, Kerr was uncertain as to the generalizability of their attitudes. By referring to the results of a survey conducted among the staff, he was able to show that the resistance to legally constituted lay control was generally held by school administrators. We quote from pages 51–52: "The superintendents were not the only administrators in the districts who disapproved of the boards' intervention in professional matters which legally came under the boards' jurisdiction. For example, questionnaire survey in the districts included a question concerning the role that the school board should play in hiring teachers: 'To what extent do you think the following persons or groups *should* influence the selection of new teachers?'" Eight out of 13 administrators in one district and five out of eight in the other replied that the school board should be "not at all" involved in selecting teachers.
>
> Since legally all personnel appointments had to be approved by the board members, the survey finding confirmed the hostility of professional educators to the nominal authority of school trustees. Kerr then showed how this attitude led to manipulative measures in the interest of protecting professional autonomy.

3. Verification of field interpretations.   The verification of observations based on fieldwork is a third, major contribution that surveys make to the analysis of field materials. Here we return to the point made by Webb et al., that multiple techniques are often necessary for the validation of results.

> In the course of fieldwork among medical students, Becker et al. (1961) were impressed with what they called the "long-range perspective" of the freshmen students, a perspective characterized by a vague notion of the physician's role and an idealistic view of medicine. According to the researchers, the students conveyed this perspective mainly "by gesture and tone of voice" and "the innumerable other nuances of human interaction impossible to record or quantify." In addition to the field data, however, they had materials from interviews with a random sample. When asked to express their idea of a successful physician, the freshmen rarely mentioned money, and generally responded in ways that reflected an idealistic conception. Also, it was found that the students decided on a medical career at an early age, and learned about the profession from the same sources as the public at large, that is, from movies, books, and from being patients. As the researchers sum up: "With data from the interviews thus supporting the field work, we conclude that freshmen enter medical school full of enthusiasm, pride, and idealism about the medical profession" (p. 79).

4. The casting of new light on field observations.   Survey results can cast a new light on field observations, or more precisely, the serendipitous nature of some survey findings can illuminate a field observation that was hitherto inexplicable or misinterpreted. It is common to think of fieldwork as being more congenial to serendipity than survey work. Sometimes we hear that surveys should be actuated by specific problems or hypotheses, while fieldwork is uniquely qualified for exploratory investigations. But survey analysts make many observations that were unanticipated; and in another context, I argue that surveys are uniquely qualified for the measurement of unanticipated concepts (Schenkel and Sieber 1969).

The exploratory portion of survey analysis can be exploited for the better understanding of field observations. A simple illustration will suffice.

> In our study of two suburban districts, it was observed that a smaller proportion of teachers turned out to vote in the bond issue election in the larger district. When this observation was shared with informants, many explanations were offered. We tentatively attributed the poor turnout to the alienation of many teachers in the more bureaucratized system. (We have already seen that this holistic assumption was challenged by the survey data.) While perusing the distribution of responses to the survey, we noticed with surprise that 39% of the teachers in the larger district resided outside of the district, compared with only 18% in the smaller district. The teachers in the larger district were simply less often legally qualified to vote. The observations of poorer turnout was therefore reinterpreted. Moreover, we then began to explore the implications of living inside or outside the district for the teachers' involvement in the affairs of the system and in their relationships with parents.

Problems of Scheduling

Many of the examples that we have given depend upon a particular time-ordering of field observations and survey work. Thus, the contribution of fieldwork to the formulation of the theoretical structure underlying a survey study requires that the fieldwork be performed prior to designing the survey study. But if the purpose of the fieldwork is to clarify or extend a survey finding, then it must be conducted after the survey. Further, several of our examples depended upon concurrent scheduling of the methods—correction of the elite bias in fieldwork, repeated pretests of a questionnaire, and perhaps also correction of the holistic fallacy. Further, if the survey investigator is in the field during data collection, he might learn a great deal about the meaning of the survey questionnaire to respondents. To some extent, the "obtrusiveness" of a questionnaire can be assessed and taken into account in the analyst's interpretations. This latter information is sometimes conveyed to the survey worker by professional interviewers, but firsthand experience with the instrument during its administration is probably also needed. An optimal research schedule, therefore, would entail an interweaving of field observations and survey work over the duration of the project, regardless of the primary method of data collection. (If the techniques were assigned to different staff members having special competencies, the work load on the project director would be lightened.)

The problems of integrating survey and fieldwork are reduced when studying a small number of formally organized collectives, such as schools, since the respondents are clustered within settings having definite boundaries. But even the typical large-scale survey of individuals could be rearranged so as to profit from fieldwork. In the first place, respondents could be selected who are socially related to one another. These networks could then be treated in much the same fashion that a fieldworker deals with a more formal collective. If for some reason this type of survey design is not feasible, then every nth interviewer could be instructed to make certain observations or to extend the interview into an unstructured format. Such interviewers would have to receive special training in fieldwork, or they might be recruited from among individuals who have specialized in fieldwork in the past.

In other instances, the traditional design of fieldwork might need to be modified to take advantage of a survey. Certain clusters of actors might be identified; then, a large number of such clusters could be selected in order to enhance the usefulness of statistical study. Or networks of relationships could be sought in fieldwork in order to select individuals who will receive questionnaires.

The adjustments in traditional research designs called for by the integration of field and survey methods would seem to produce a new style of research. At present there are far too few examples of this style to adduce general principles to be followed in organizing future projects. The task of collecting specimens of projects that have sought to profit from the interplay of fieldwork and surveys, rather than instances bearing on a single aspect of projects, remains for the methodologist of the future—providing that the boundaries between the two traditions are dissolved and attention is turned to their intellectual integration in the interest of improving our strategies of social research.

Notes

1. We are especially indebted to John D. Ferguson for his stimulating ideas regarding the interplay of fieldwork and surveys.
2. That is, participant observation, informant interviewing, and use of available records to supplement these techniques in a particular setting.
3. Catherine Bodard Silver was most helpful in analyzing the results of the experiment. We also appreciate the cooperation of George Nash in making available his data.
4. All illustrations are indented and set in smaller type for easy reference.
5. The term "interpretive variable," as used here, denotes a variable that intervenes in time between two variables whose relationship is already established.

References

Becker, Howard S., and Blanche Geer. 1957. "Participant Observation and Interviewing." *Human Organization* 16 (Fall): 28–32.

Becker, Howard S., Blanche Geer, Everett C. Hughes, and Anselm L. Strauss. 1961. *Boys in White: Student Culture in Medical School*. Chicago: University of Chicago Press.

Carlin, Jerome E. 1966. *Lawyer's Ethics: A Survey of the New York City Bar*. New York: Russell Sage Foundation.

Gordon, C. Wayne. 1957. *The Social System of the High School*. Glencoe, Ill.: Free Press.

Kahl, Joseph A. 1953. "Educational and Occupational Aspirations of 'Common Man' Boys." *Harvard Educational Review* 23 (Summer): 186–203.

Kendall, Patricia L., and Katherine M. Wolf. 1949. "The Analysis of Deviant Cases in Communications Research." In *Communications Research, 1948–49*, edited by Paul F. Lazarsfeld and Frank W. Stanton. New York: Harper.

Kerr, Norman D. 1964. "The School Board as an Agency of Legitimation." *Sociology of Education* 38 (Fall): 34–59.

Komarovsky, Mirra. 1962. *Blue-Collar Marriage*. New York: Random House.

Langenwalter, Suzanne. 1967. "History of a Questionnaire." Mimeographed. New York: Bureau of Applied Social Research, Columbia University.

Lazarsfeld, Paul F., and Wagner Thielens, Jr. 1958. *The Academic Mind*. Glencoe, Ill.: Free Press.

Lipset, Seymour M. 1964. "The Biography of a Research Project: Union Democracy." In *Sociologists at Work*, edited by Phillip E. Hammond. New York: Basic.

Schenkel, Walter, and Sam D. Sieber. 1969. *The Design of Survey Questionnaires: A Case History Approach*. Mimeographed. New York: Bureau of Applied Social Research, Columbia University.

Sieber, Sam D., and Paul F. Lazarsfeld. 1966. *The Organization of Educational Research*. Cooperative Research Project No. 1974 (USOE). New York: Bureau of Applied Social Research, Columbia University. See also *Reforming the University: The Role of the Research Center*. New York: Praeger, 1972.

Stinchcombe, Arthur L. 1964. *Rebellion in a High School*. Chicago: Quadrangle.

Trow, Martin. 1957. "Comment on 'Participant Observation and Interviewing: A Comparison.'" *Human Organization* 16 (Fall): 33–35.

Vidich, Arthur J., and Gilbert Shapiro. 1955. "A Comparison of Participant Observation and Survey Data." *American Sociological Review* 20 (February): 28–33.

Voss, Harwin L. "Pitfalls in Social Research: A Case Study." *American Sociologist* 1 (May 1966): 136–40.

Webb, Eugene J., Donald T. Campbell, Richard D. Schwartz, and Lee Sechrest. 1966. *Unobtrusive Measures: Nonreactive Research in the Social Sciences*. Chicago: Rand McNally.

Wilder, David E., and Nathalie S. Friedman. 1968. "Selecting Ideal-Typical Communities and Gaining Access to Their Schools for Social Research Purposes." In *Actual and Perceived Consensus on Educational Goals between School and Community*, by David E. Wilder, Nathalie S. Friedman, Robert B. Hill, Eva E. Sandis, and Sam D. Sieber. New York: Bureau of Applied Social Research, Columbia University.

Zelditch, M., Jr. 1962. "Some Methodological Problems of Field Studies." *American Journal of Sociology* 67 (March): 566–76.